AND

CARMEN SAECVLARE

EDITED BY

RICHARD F. THOMAS

George Martin Lane Professor of Classics, Harvard University

CAMBRIDGE
UNIVERSITY PRESS

CAMBRIDGE
UNIVERSITY PRESS

University Printing House, Cambridge CB2 8BS, United Kingdom

Published in the United States of America by Cambridge University Press, New York

Cambridge University Press is part of the University of Cambridge.
It furthers the University's mission by disseminating knowledge in the pursuit of education, learning and research at the highest international levels of excellence.

www.cambridge.org
Information on this title: www.cambridge.org/9780521587662

First published 2011
3rd printing 2013

Printed in the United Kingdom by Clays, St Ives plc.

A catalogue record for this publication is available from the British Library

ISBN 978-0-521-58279-7 Hardback
ISBN 978-0-521-58766-2 Paperback

CONTENTS

PREFACE

This commentary has been some time in the making, in part thanks to recurring administrative duties. That has perhaps been for the good, in that my thinking about the poems included has evolved in what I hope will prove to be productive ways. The *Carmen saeculare* and book 4 of the *Odes* are not easy to situate in their political and aesthetic contexts. Fundamental issues of tone, purpose and meaning are still under debate, in spite of the fact that the Horace of the 30s and 20s BCE has seemed perhaps the most familiar of the Augustans. The poems of *C.* 4 have seemed at the same time, to many readers, to represent a falling away from the first collection. It has therefore been useful to spend some time, while engaged on other projects to which inclination or duty consigned me, to reflect about these poems, which have to me become more interesting as I kept their company.

It has been my fate now for the second time to be completing a commentary on the same text on which other commentaries were imminent or recently published. I received the Italian commentary of Paolo Fedeli and Irma Ciccarelli (*Q. Horatii Flacci Carmina: Liber IV*, Florence 2008), after I had finished a penultimate draft of my commentary. At the same time Philip Hills generously sent me an electronic copy of his impressive 2002 Cambridge Ph.D. dissertation on *Odes* 4.1, 2, 10, 11, 15. I have consulted both but ended up not really noticing either, in large part through a concern that the commentary was getting somewhat detailed for the present series, particularly since the size of the two commentaries in question was considerably greater than mine. Fedeli and Ciccarelli usefully give full references to secondary literature before the commentary on each poem, where I have been more selective. Hills sees in *Odes* 4 a much greater presence of Ennius than has previously been detected. As appears to be the case with my *Georgics* commentary (Cambridge 1988) and that of Sir Roger Mynors (Oxford 1990), it is my hope that the two commentaries on *Odes* 4 now available, and the third soon to be available, will be of use to students and scholars, who have been without modern commentaries for so long.

I acknowledge support from the Loeb Classical Library Foundation for financial help that enabled my first full year's leave in 2006–7, particularly since I was therefore able to take up a Visiting Fellowship, in Michaelmas, 2006, in the stimulating surroundings of All Souls College, Oxford, which housed, fed and entertained me in the hours I was not working exclusively on the commentary in the equally interesting setting of the Lower Reading Room of the Bodleian. I am particularly grateful to Dean of Visiting Fellows, Jim Adams, for help, encouragement and friendship towards a fellow antipodean. Over the years I have received generous help and suggestions from friends and colleagues too numerous to recall, but I mention a few who read and reacted to the commentary in a complete draft in 2008–9. For their the vigilance, intelligence and generosity I thank, again, Jim Adams, Stephen Harrison, Philip Hardie, John Henderson, Peter Knox, John D. Morgan and David Ross, who read the entire commentary. Nicholas Horsfall helped with comments on the *Carmen saeculare*. As a result of this assistance the commentary is changed from what each of them then received, here and there doubtless in ways of which any given one of them might not approve. Lizzie Mitchell, who read parts of a draft, also sent me her excellent Cambridge M. Phil. thesis (to which I refer sparingly ahead of publication plans), while Tom Zanker gave good comments on a draft of the *Carmen saeculare* commentary. David Kovacs commented on a draft of *C.* 4.8, on which he subsequently published an interesting article, included in my bibliography. At a workshop on commentaries held at Corpus Christi College Oxford, on 14 March, 2009, I was fortunate to receive helpful reactions to my commentary on *C.* 4.15 from Stephen Heyworth, Gregory Hutchinson, Bruce Gibson, Robert Maltby and others who spoke at that event. The book has been much improved by the expert, perceptive and thorough copy-editing of Andrew Dyck. Thanks are also due to Tom Keeline, whose proofreading led to a number of improvements. Finally, my deep gratitude to my wife, Joan Thomas, for reading the entire commentary, and for her support throughout its composition, as throughout all else.

17 May 2010 R. F. T.

ABBREVIATIONS

In abbreviating I generally follow the practice of the *OCD*. H.'s works are cited as *AP* (*Ars Poetica*), *C.* (*Odes*), *CS* (*Carmen saeculare*), *Epod.* (*Epodes*), *Epist.* (*Epistles*), *S.* (*Satires*). In citations of individual lines from *C.* 1–3, '*C.*' is generally omitted (e.g. 'cf. 2.3.14; 3.1.4'), while '*C.* 4' is omitted in citations from that book (e.g. 'cf. 5.6–7, 10.4'). '22' means 'see p. 22', and refers to the introduction of this volume, while 'see 5 intro.' means 'see the Introduction to *C.* 4.5'.

Adams	J. N. Adams, *The Latin sexual vocabulary* (London 1982).
AE	*L'Année epigraphique* (Paris 1888–).
Axelson	B. Axelson, *Unpoetische Wörter. Ein Beitrag zur Kenntnis der lateinischen Dichtersprache* (Skrifter utgivna av Vetenskaps-societeten i Lund 29, Lund 1945).
BA	*Barrington atlas of the Greek and Roman world*, ed. R. J. A. Talbert (Princeton and Oxford 2000).
Bentley	R. Bentley, *Q. Horatius Flaccus*, 3rd edn., 2 vols. (Berlin 1869).
BNP	M. Beard, J. North, S. Price, *Religions of Rome. Volume 1. A history* (Cambridge 1998).
Bo	D. Bo, *Lexicon Horatianum*, 2 vols. (Hildesheim 1965–66).
Brill's New Pauly	H. Cancik and H. Schneider, eds. *Brill's New Pauly: encyclopaedia of the ancient world* (Leiden 2002–2010).
Brink	C. O. Brink, *Horace on poetry*, 3 vols. (Cambridge 1963–82).
CAH	A. K. Bowman, E. Champlin, A. Lintott, eds. *Cambridge ancient history*, Volume X: The Augustan empire, 43 B.C. – A.D. 69, 2nd edn. (Cambridge 2008).
Chantraine	P. Chantraine, *Dictionnaire étymologique de la langue grecque*, 4 vols. in 5 (Paris 1968-80).
CIL	*Corpus inscriptionum Latinarum* (Berlin 1863–).
Clausen	W. V. Clausen, *Virgil, Eclogues* (Oxford 1994).
CLE	F. Bücheler and E. Lommatzsch, eds. *Carmina Latina epigraphica*, 3 vols. (Leipzig 1895–1926).
Courtney	E. Courtney, *The fragmentary Latin poets* (Oxford 1993).
EJ	V. Ehrenberg and A. H. M. Jones, *Documents illustrating the reigns of Augustus and Tiberius*, 2nd edn. (Oxford 1967).

EO	*Enciclopedia Oraziana* (Rome 1996–8).
EV	*Enciclopedia Vergiliana* (Rome 1984–91).
Ernout-Meillet	A. Ernout and A. Meillet, *Dictionnaire étymologique de la langue latine. Histoire des mots*, 4th ed. rev. J. André (Paris 1985).
Fraenkel	E. Fraenkel, *Horace* (Oxford 1957).
FGrH	F. Jacoby, *Die Fragmente der griechischen Historiker* (Leiden 1923–).
Gildersleeve and Lodge	B. Gildersleeve and G. Lodge, *Latin Grammar*, 3rd edn. (London 1971).
G–P	A. S. F. Gow and D. L. Page, *The Greek Anthology. Hellenistic epigrams*, 2 vols. (Cambridge 1965).
Hofmann	J. B. Hofmann, *La lingua d'uso latina*, expanded by L. Ricottilli, 3rd edn. (Bologna 2003).
Hollis	A. S. Hollis, *Fragments of Roman poetry c. 60 BC–AD 20* (Oxford 2007).
ILLRP	A. Degrassi, ed. *Inscriptiones Latinae liberae rei publicae* (Florence 1957–63).
ILS	H. Dessau, ed. *Inscriptiones Latinae selectae*, 3 vols. (Berlin 1892–1916).
Johnson	T. S. Johnson, *A symposion of praise. Horace returns to lyric in* Odes *IV* (Madison 2004).
Keller-Holder	O. Keller and A. Holder, eds. Q. Horati Flacci *Opera* (Leipzig 1899).
K–H	A. Kiessling and R. Heinze, *Q. Horatius Flaccus*, 7th edn. 3 vols. (Berlin 1930).
K–S	R. Kühner and C. Stegmann, *Ausführliche Grammatik der lateinischen Sprache*, 4th edn., rev. A. Thierfelder, 2 vols. (Hannover 1962).
L–H–S	M. Leumann, J. B. Hofmann and A. Szantyr, *Lateinische Grammatik II. Lateinische Syntax und Stilistik* (Munich 1965).
LIMC	*Lexicon iconographicum mythologiae classicae*, 18 vols. (Zurich 1981–99).
LGPN	P. M. Fraser and E. Matthews, eds. *Lexicon of Greek Personal Names* (Oxford 1987–). www.lgpn.ox.ac.uk/online/index.html
LTUR	E. M. Steinby, ed. *Lexicon topographicum urbis Romae*, 6 vols. (Rome 1993–9).
Löfstedt	E. Löfstedt, *Syntactica. Studien und Beiträge zur historischen Syntax des Lateins*, 2 vols. (Lund 1956).
Maltby	R. Maltby, *A lexicon of ancient Latin etymologies* (Leeds 1991).

Mankin	D. Mankin, *Horace Epodes* (Cambridge 1995).
McKeown	J. C. McKeown, *Ovid: Amores. Text, prolegomena and commentary in four volumes* (Liverpool and Leeds 1987–).
N–H	R. G. M. Nisbet and M. Hubbard, *A commentary on Horace: Odes Book I, II* (Oxford 1970, 1978).
N–R	R. G. M. Nisbet and N. Rudd, *A commentary on Horace: Odes Book III* (Oxford 2004).
N–W	F. Neue and C. Wagener, *Formenlehre der lateinischen Sprache*, 3rd edn., 4 vols., (Berlin 1892–1905).
Orelli	J. K. Orelli et al., eds., *Q. Horatius Flaccus*, 4th edn. (Hildesheim-New York 1975; orig. Berlin 1886–92).
Page	T. E. Page, *Q. Horatii Flacci Carminum Libri IV, Epodon Liber* (Glasgow 1895).
Pasquali	G. Pasquali, *Orazio lirico* (Florence 1920).
PHI	Packard Humanities Institute, CD ROM 5.3 *c.* 1991
Pighi	G. B. Pighi, *De ludis saecularibus populi Romani Quiritium libri sex* (Amsterdam 1965).
PIR	*Prosopographia imperii Romani*, 2nd edn. (Berlin and Leipzig 1933).
Porph.	*Pomponi Porfyrionis Commentum in Horatium Flaccum*, ed. A. Holder (Innsbruck 1894).
POxy.	*The Oxyrhynchus papyri* (London 1898–).
ps.-Acro	*Pseudacronis Scholia in Horatium vetustiora*, ed. O. Keller, 2 vols. (Leipzig 1902, 1904 (repr. Stuttgart 1952–4)).
Putnam	M. C. J. Putnam, *Artifices of eternity. Horace's fourth book of Odes* (Ithaca 1986).
Quinn	K. Quinn, *Horace: The Odes* (Basingstoke 1980).
Race	W. H. Race, ed. and trans. *Pindar*, 2 vols. (Cambridge, MA and London 1997).
RE	G. Wissowa, ed. *Paulys Realencyclopädie der classischen Altertumswissenschaft* (Stuttgart 1893–1980).
RIC	H. Mattingly and E. A. Sydenham, *Roman imperial coinage I*, 2nd edn. (London 1984).
Richardson	L. Richardson, Jr., *A new topographical dictionary of ancient Rome* (Baltimore and London 1992).
ROL	E. H. Warmington, ed. and trans. *Remains of Old Latin*, 4 vols. (London 1956–61).
Schnegg-Köhler	B. Schnegg-Köhler, *Die augusteischen Säkularspiele* (Archiv für Religionsgeschichte 4, Munich 2002).

Shackleton Bailey	D. R. Shackleton Bailey, ed. *Q. Horati Flacci opera* (Stuttgart 1985, 3rd edn., 1995).
Syndikus	H. P. Syndikus, *Die Lyrik des Horaz: eine Interpretation der Oden*, 2 vols. (Darmstadt 1972–73).
Thomas	R. F. Thomas, *Virgil, Georgics*, 2 vols. (Cambridge 1988).
TLL	*Thesaurus linguae Latinae* (Leipzig and Munich 1900–).
Tränkle	H. Tränkle, *Die Sprachkunst des Properz und die Tradition der lateinischen Dichtersprache* (Hermes Einzelschriften 10, Wiesbaden 1960).
VT	J. M. Ziolkowski and M. C. J. Putnam, eds. *The Virgilian tradition. The first fifteen hundred years* (New Haven 2008).
Walde-Hofman	A. Walde and J. B. Hofmann, *Lateinisches etymologisches Wörterbuch*, 2 vols., 4th edn. (Heidelberg 1982).
Watson	L. C. Watson, *A commentary on Horace Epodes* (Oxford 2003).
West	M. L. West, *Greek metre* (Oxford 1982).
Wickham	E. C. Wickham, *The works of Horace*, 2 vols. (Oxford 1891–6).
Wilkinson	L. P. Wilkinson, *Golden Latin artistry* (Cambridge 1963).
Wills	J. Wills, *Repetition in Latin poetry. Figures of allusion* (Oxford 1996).
Woodcock	E. C. Woodcock, *A new Latin syntax* (London 1959).

MAP

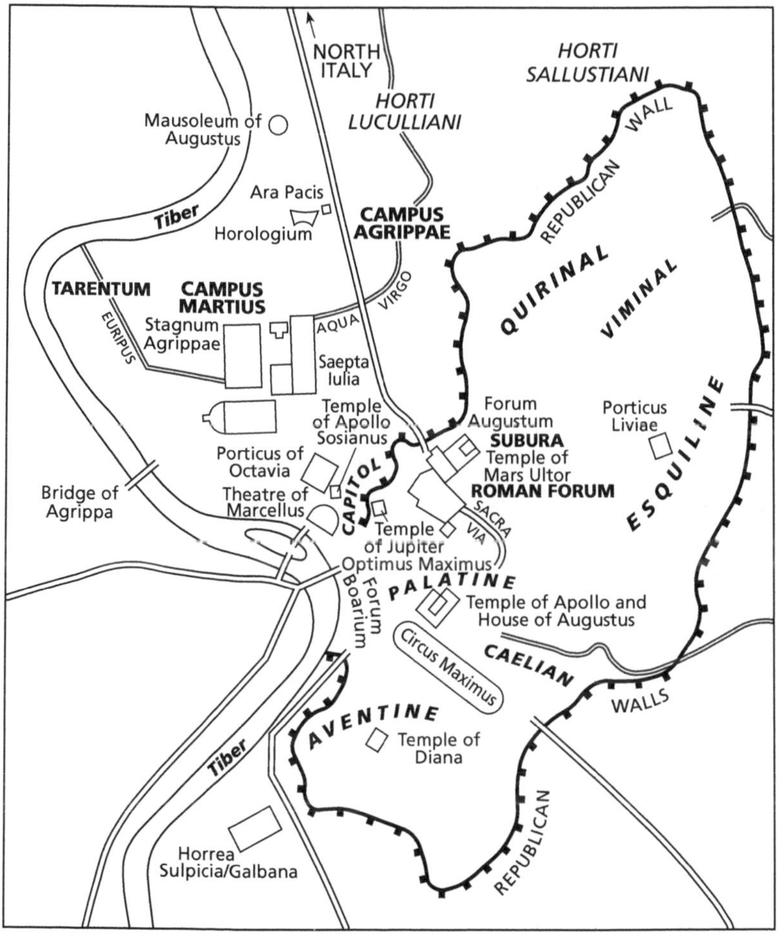

Horace's Rome

INTRODUCTION

1. HORACE'S LITERARY CAREER

By the year 23 BCE H. had published his first three books of *Odes*, probably as a single, finished collection – as it was clearly intended to stand, whatever the particulars of publication.[1] Three or four years later he put out the first book of *Epistles*, whose *sphragis* helpfully provides the age of H. – 44 years old in 21 BCE (*Epist.* 1.20.26–8) – if not the date of publication. That was a year or two later, as is clear from references to events of 20 (*Epist.* 1.3.1–2; 1.12.26–7, Tiberius in Armenia; *Epist.* 1.12.27–8, Parthian standards recovered) and 19 BCE (*Epist.* 1.12.26, Agrippa successful in Spain).

Around this time, it would seem, H. returned to lyric. For all we know he never stopped composing in lyric meters, though the hexameter form was reclaiming his immediate attention in the years following the appearance of *C.* 1–3. There is no substantial evidence for the view that *Odes* 1–3 had been poorly received. Fraenkel was a strong advocate of that view, referring to H's 'annoyance at the cool reception which the three books of his *carmina* met with after their publication in 23 B.C.', 'the anger which he vented in the nineteenth epistle' (1.19) and his resolve 'to accept the failure of his proud venture and never to write lyrics again', 'as solemnly announced . . . in the overture of his book of *Epistles* (1.1.10ff.)'.[2] All of this is to misjudge the programmatic aspects of the poems in question, and subsequent studies have provided a less biographically focused picture, one more in line with other Augustan poetic programmes and genre shifts.[3] Fraenkel's wording is telling (339): 'Horace vented his annoyance in a letter to Maecenas (i. 19).'

There are two components to the poetics of *Epist.* 1.19. Firstly, H. directs a vigorous response to servile and superficial imitators: 10–20, culminating in the outburst at 19–20 *o imitatores, seruum pecus, ut mihi saepe | bilem, saepe iocum uestri mouere tumultus!* And secondly, at 37–49, he pinpoints the real reason for the public carping of critics, as opposed to their private praise (35–6) – a combination which, even taken in a purely autobiographical way, is hardly evidence for the poor reception of the *Odes*. Why not the other way around? Their criticism, levelled even if H. is taken at his word *in spite of* the actual (i.e. private) admiration of critics (35–6 *cur . . . lector | laudet ametque domi*), is due to H.'s refusal to pursue the

[1] See Hutchinson 2002 for the possibility of *seriatim* publication between 27 and 23 BCE, with Nisbet 2007: 13–14 for scepticism.

[2] Fraenkel 365; also 339–50, with similar language: 339 'vented his annoyance'; 348 'vents without restraint his anger at . . .', 349 'mood of resentment', 350 'thoroughly bitter'. See also the introduction of K-H *ad Epist.* 1.19.

[3] See Kambylis 1965: 162; McGann 1969: 84–5; for more extended studies, focused on H.'s moralizing, cf. Macleod 1977; and on his poetics, Smith 1984.

votes of the fickle mob (37 *non ego uentosae plebis suffragia uenor*). What did H.'s critics criticize? Nothing, so far as this poem tells us, about the *Odes* themselves. Rather, the (putative) unpopularity of the poet comes from his refusal to involve himself with the public, to court popular votes at the price of meals and second-hand clothes (37–8). The electoral metaphor gives way to the literary (39–45), but the point is the same. The popular dislike is now tied to his refusal have his verse recited from the lecterns of the *grammatici*.

None of this has anything to do with actual criticism of Horatian lyric. The stance rather allows H. to engage the now familiar trope of rejecting the popular, a Callimachean motif that goes back, through *C.* 3.1 (*Odi profanum uulgus et arceo*) with its translation of Callim. *Epigr.* 28 Pf. (cf. 4 σικχαίνω πάντα τὰ δημόσια 'I hate all public things'), to the end of *Satires* 1.10 – parallel in placement to *Epist.* 1.19, given the fact that 1.20, the address to the book, is a separable envoi.[4] *S.* 1.10 is a response to those who had (?putatively) criticized *S.* 1.4, and specifically had criticized the earlier poem's finding fault with H.'s genre model Lucilius, guilty for H. of lack of Callimachean polish. The criticism of *S.* 1.4, whether or not it happened, allows H. to reiterate his grounds for faulting the earlier poet, who, H. assures his readers, would have composed very differently had he been active in H.'s day (67–70). Then, before ending *S.* 1.10 with a list of his ideal readers (81–90), juxtaposed to those about whom he cares nothing (76–80), H. makes his point: care of composition and artful writing may result in a small readership, but that is in fact preferable to striving for the admiration of the mob (73 *neque te ut miretur turba labores*) and having your poetry consigned to school curricula (73–5, 90–1).

This aversion is the context in which the central section of *Epistle* 1.19 (21–34) is to be understood. There, in addition to describing his relationship to his Greek models – that is, to explaining how non-servile imitation works – H. declares his primacy in bringing Archilochean iambic and the lyric of Alcaeus to Latin verse:

> libera per *uacuum* posui *uestigia* princeps,
> *non aliena* meo *pressi pede*. qui sibi fidet,
> dux reget examen. Parios ego primus iambos
>
> ostendi Latio . . . 21–4
> hunc [scil. Alcaeum] ego, *non alio* dictum prius ore, Latinus
> *uulgaui* fidicen. 32–3

In other words the centre of the epistle elaborates the claim made in the envoi of *Odes* 1–3: 3.30.10–14 *dicar . . . ex humili potens | princeps Aeolium carmen ad Italos | deduxisse modos*.[5] The end of the first book of the *Epistles* reiterates that earlier poem's pride in the achievement of Rome's lyre player. It does so, moreover, from

[4] See Macleod 1977: 373 for reference to *Epigr.* 28.
[5] For the connection see Kambylis 1965: 162.

an intensely Callimachean perspective that had always been the programmatic focus of H.'s verse, in particular adapting the famous injunction at *Aet.* 1 fr. 1.25–8 Pf.:

> πρὸς δέ σε] καὶ τόδ' ἄνωγα, τὰ μὴ πατέουσιν ἅμαξαι
> *τὰ στείβε*]*ιν, ἑτέρων ἴχνια μὴ καθ' ὁμά*
> δίφρον ἐλ]ᾶν μηδ' οἶμον ἀνὰ πλατύν, ἀλλὰ κελεύθους
> *ἀτρίπτο*]υς, εἰ καὶ στει⌊ι⌋νοτέρην ἐλάσεις.'

> 'this too I bid you, to *tread* where wagons do not go, and *not* to drive your chariot in the *common tracks of others*, nor along a wide road, but on *untrodden* ways even though you drive a narrower path'.

With *uulgaui* (*Epist.* 1.19.33) H. takes things a step further, as through his own achievement he has *created* the commonplace and put imitation of his own work on the side of the artless – as he would do again at *C.* 4.9.3–4 *non ante uulgatas per artis | uerba loquor socianda chordis* (see 9.3n.). At *G.* 3.3–4 Virgil, turning to the *Aeneid* as he put the finishing touches to the *Georgics*, noted the now commonplace status of the predominantly Hellenistic topics that might otherwise have diverted him: *cetera, quae uacuas tenuissent carmine mentes, | omnia iam* uulgata. Virgil's new and future topic, figured in the metaphor of a temple, would be the battles of Caesar and his line back to Tithonus (*G.* 3.46–8), and in this he claimed primacy, as H. would do a few years later:

> *primus* ego in patriam mecum, modo uita supersit,
> Aonio rediens deducam uertice Musas
> *primus* Idumaeas referam tibi, Mantua, palmas
> Virg. *G.* 3.10–12

As in H.'s opening to his third book (*C.* 3.1 *Odi profanum uulgus et arceo*), so in Virgil's *omnia iam uulgata*, it is natural to see an allusion to Callimachus' disdain for the commonplace, as found in *Epigr.* 28 (πάντα τὰ δημόσια, with *omnia* perhaps recalling the differently functioning πάντα) and in the *Aetia* preface (26 καθ' ὁμά).

That *Epist.* 1.19 comes across as full of annoyance, anger and resentment is also part of the game and cannot be used to create the sweeping conclusions found in Fraenkel and elsewhere. The emotions that H. conjures up in *Epist.* 1.19 are, then, elements of a literary trope, going back through *Epod.* 10 and poems like Catullus 16 to the prologues of Terence, and on the Greek side to the *Aetia* preface of Callimachus (*Aet.* 1, fr. 1.1–20 Pf.), along with his epigrams (*Epigr.* 28 Pf.) and iambics (*Ia.* 13). The voicing of strong hostility to poetic rivals and to critics is part of the poetics of *aemulatio* and in keeping with H.'s Callimachean affiliations. The same may be said of H.'s famous quote from Terence, *Andr.* 126, which comes immediately after his disavowal of the popular: *Epist.* 1.19.41 *hinc illae lacrimae*. Here Fraenkel discusses the metrical trick whereby the iambic hemiepes is in the right circumstances, as here, by accident indistinguishable from and therefore interchangeable with the dactylic hemiepes. By way of example he notes 'So Callimachus borrows half a line from the *Bacchae* of Euripides and makes it the beginning of a pentameter [*Epigr.* 48.6], 'ἱερὸς ὁ πλόκαμος', τοὐμὸν ὄνειαρ ἐμοί.'[6]

Like Fraenkel, H. noticed and emulated the Callimachean game of exploiting the shared prosody of his intertext. He did so, moreover, at the end of a book that had announced at its outset that the time for poetic play was no more:[7] *Epist.* 1.1.10–11 *nunc itaque et uersus et cetera* ludicra *pono:* | *quid uerum atque decens curo et rogo et omnis in hoc sum.* These lines come immediately after H., resisting Maecenas' purported attempt to have him continue with lyric (2–3 *quaeris,* | *Maecenas, iterum antiquo me includere* ludo), compares himself to a retiring gladiator, then to an old horse, ready to be released from service. Similarly, the Callimachean *ludus* of *Epist.* 1.19.41, concluding the Callimachean defence of *C.* 1–3, is followed by the metaphor of the gladiator not now retiring, but rather asking for an intermission: 47 diludia *posco.* Thus the frame reveals that games are still being played, and that the *Epistles* are an interlude, necessary, since games lead to contest, anger, hostility and war, as the poem, and effectively the book of *Epistles*, comes to an end: 48–9 ludus *enim genuit trepidum certamen et iram,* | *ira truces inimicitias et funebre bellum.* When the *ludus* of lyric is resumed, it will take the form of warfare, but not of the conventional kind: *C.* 4.1.1–2 *intermissa, Venus, diu* | *rursus bella moues?* So the beginning and the end of the first book of *Epistles* ostentatiously display their relationship to the Horatian lyric that surrounds that book. Again, and to reiterate, there is no reliable evidence within the corpus of H. or anywhere else to indicate that the earlier lyric collection was received with anything short of appreciation.

On the contrary. The success of *Odes* 1–3 must have induced Augustus to choose H. as the composer of the hymn that would be performed at the Secular Games of 17 BCE, the most important state festival in Augustan and later imperial propaganda. This choice, like the decision to stage the Games, was presumably made soon after publication of *Epistles* 1, at which time there is no reason to think H. was not at work on the fourth book of *Odes.* In that connection, this is a good place to deal with what looks like another fiction, a well-known passage from the Suetonian *Vita Horati*:[8]

> scripta quidem eius usque adeo probauit [sc. Augustus] mansuraque perpetuo opinatus est, ut non modo saeculare carmen componendum iniunxerit sed et Vindelicam victoriam Tiberii Drusique, privignorum suorum, eumque coegerit propter hoc tribus Carminum libris ex longo intervallo quartum addere. Suet. *Vit. Hor.* pp. 297.35–298.1 Roth

[6] Fraenkel 349, noting a similar practice at *S.* 2.3.264.
[7] As Mayor 269 notes, 'strictly speaking this is the last epistle of the collection, since the next poem [*Epist.* 1.20] abandons the epistolary fiction for direct address'.
[8] The details are disputed by Fraenkel 364.

The sentence is unobjectionable as far as *iniunxerit*; moreover it could have been composed by anyone, at any time, aware of the authorship and occasion of the *Carmen saeculare*: 'Augustus so approved of H.'s writings and thought they would last for ever [an extrapolation from H.'s own claims at *C.* 3.30, *exegi monumentum* etc.?], that he imposed on him not only the composition of the Secular Hymn . . . ' However the continuation is problematic: 'but also [imposed on him the compositions on] the victory over the Vindelici of his stepsons Tiberius and Drusus and for this reason compelled him after a long interval to add a fourth to the three books of *Odes*'. It is worth noting that the *Vita*, short as it is, is almost all made up of observations supported by direct quotes, mostly of H., Augustus or Maecenas. Peter White argues that Suetonius is here paraphrasing a letter of Augustus, but that is open to debate.[9] The verb *iniunxerit*, 'imposed as a duty' is appropriate to the *CS*, since a text was actually commissioned as part of a state festival, but that is not the case with 4.4 and 4.14, the poems on Drusus and Tiberius. White takes *Vindelicam uictoriam* as a title on the same level as *Carmen saeculare*, but since this is a matter of two separate poems, that seems difficult, as does the notion that Augustus imposed composition on H., a concept otherwise unparalleled except for the special case of the *CS*. If the same *Vita* is to be believed, H. was under no compulsion to write anything for Augustus, nor to agree to the princeps' request that he serve as his secretary. The Loeb translation finesses the difficulties by filling the gap before *Vindelicam uictoriam* with an implicit verbal idea 'but also bade him celebrate', but this only draws attention to the oddity of the text. Even more odd is the notion that H., finding himself with his two imposed poems on Drusus and Tiberius, was therefore (*propter hoc*) compelled by Augustus (*coegerit*) to come up with thirteen more poems so as to add his fourth book of *Odes*. Much more likely, this narrative was constructed, in the very changed circumstances that existed in the early second century CE, by the biographer of the Caesars, who will therefore have been interested to account for the composition of the *CS* but also that of the poems on the future emperor Tiberius and his brother.

2. THE DATE OF *ODES* 4

The last fifteen years of H.'s life (8 December 65 BCE–27 November 8 BCE), were less productive (108 Teubner pages) than the years which saw publication of the *Epodes*, two books of *Satires* and the first three books of *Odes* (222 pages). In the latter years there is also a sense of less concentrated production and generic clarity, with uncertainty about publication dates for *Epistles* 2 and the *Ars Poetica* and the fourth book of *Odes*. Once the poetic programmes of *Epist.* 1.1 and 1.19 are recognized for what they are – literary justification for the work of which the two poems provide a frame – and for what they are not – a general flight from lyric in the wake of hostile reception of *C.* 1–3 – the questions of when the

[9] White 1993: 114–15.

fourth book was composed and published become even more difficult to resolve. There is no particular reason to assume that H. stopped writing lyric in 23 BCE and started again around 19 or 18. Indeed if Suetonius' detail were correct, the poems on Drusus and Tiberius (4.4, 4.14) would represent the first resumption of lyric, which would mean that H. did nothing for two or three years after publication of *Epist.* 1. As Nisbet notes, 'just as in the earlier collection, some of the non-political odes may have been written early'.[10] *C.* 4.12, addressed to Virgil,[11] has intertextual resonances with the *Eclogues* and *Georgics*, but not the *Aeneid*, and was therefore probably composed before, possibly well before, the death of Virgil, possibly even before the famous *Aeneid* 6 reading to Augustus and Octavia (the first reading to anyone?), some time after 23 BCE. And *C.* 4.1 is written with a consciousness that it cancels the retirement from erotic play marked by *C.* 3.26. Its addressee, Paullus Maximus (b. *c.* 46 BCE), is clearly a bachelor around thirty years old, while H. was perhaps fifty (4.1.6–7).

Scholars are divided on the lower terminus and likely publication date. The last firmly datable reference in *C.* 4 is provided by 4.5, which anticipates the return of Augustus from Spain and Gaul in 13 BCE, for which see Syme 1986: 396. Even this date is, however, somewhat unstable, since the poem could presumably have been written as early as 14 BCE or so, given that it only looks forward to the return, which is vaguely off in the future. Williams 1972: 44–7 somewhat radically suggested publication as late as 9 or even 8 BCE, on the assumption that 4.1 celebrated the addressee's consulship of 11 BCE (or the year before), while 4.8 celebrates that of its addressee, (perhaps) Gaius Marcius Censorinus (8 BCE, or the year before). In support of this principle (44: 'the habit of honouring a man in his consulship') Williams cites N–H 1, p. xxxvi, to similar effect on the dating of 1.4: H. 'has adopted the conventional practice of honouring a consul during his term of office'. The evidence cited for this (Syme 1958: II 672) is negligible and insufficient basis on its own to support such a late publication date.

Nisbet is right to point to the 'cluster of datable allusions' to the mid-teens, though he also entertains the possibility that references at *C.* 4.15.6–9 to the return of the standards lost to the Parthians, and the closing of the doors of Janus Quirinus, may refer to events of 11 BCE – a closing voted in that year, though perhaps not enacted, until 8 or 7 BCE.[12] His suggestion that the closings of 29 and 25 BCE 'hardly deserve such prominence years later' (in that they were followed by reopenings) is not entirely persuasive. The language of the *Res gestae* suggests that the acts of closing are what matters, not a continued state of closure: *Ianum Quirinum . . . ter me principe senatus claudendum esse censuit.* All said, the

[10] Nisbet 2007: 16.
[11] See 12 intro., for the position that the *Vergilius* of that poem is Virgil.
[12] Nisbet 2007: 17.

year 13 BCE seems to be about the right date for publication,[13] with composition for the non-political odes stretching back as much as a decade.

3. STRUCTURAL PATTERNS

Various structural patterns have been detected, none of which need exclude the others, with the possible exception of Belmont 1980: 8–10, suggesting a bipartitite structure (1–6 and 8–15, arranged around the central 7 *Diffugere niues*). There is no reason, other than one's admiration of 4.7, to see it as central to the book, and the poem at the *actual* centre, 4.8, has the distinction of being the only ode sharing its metre (First Asclepiadean) with the framing poems of H.'s earlier lyric collection (1.1 and 3.30). Moreover it enacts, albeit in curious ways, through this metrical sharing as through its own content, the 'monumental preservation of fame',[14] particularly in its reference to the actual inscribing of encomium (8.13 *incisa notis marmora publicis*), in the centre of the *monumentum* that is *C.* 4's response to the *monumentum aere perennius* that was the earlier lyric collection according to 3.30.1. That 4.8 as we have it (and perhaps as H. wrote it, on which see 8 intro.), uniquely among the 103 odes H. produced, offends against 'Meineke's Law' could also mark it as distinct from all other odes. Indeed it is the only central ode H. produced, in that the parts and therefore the whole of *C.* 1–3 are even-numbered.

The book also shows pairings, sometimes with, sometimes without reference to larger patterns. This is true for 4.8 and 4.9, encomia with problematic aspects, and with echoes back and forth: 8.20–2 *si chartae sileant* ~ 9.33–4 and *liuidas obliuiones*; 8.25–7 ~ 9.26–8 *uates* saves from oblivion; 8.21–2 ~ 9.45 impersonal second person; 8.13–20 ~ 9.34–44 anacoluthon/zeugma. Likewise 4.1 and 4.10, the two very different poems featuring Ligurinus, are clearly connected, though not by placement in the book. In 4.11 and 4.12 the theme of invitation to parties (11.14 *gaudiis*; 12.21 *gaudia*) creates a bond, even though the addressees (Phyllis and Virgil, see 12 intro.) create poems with a very different feel. More prominently, it is hard not to perceive in the close parallelism between the pairings 4.4/5 (Drusus/Augustus) and 4.14/15 (Tiberius/Augustus) the traces of a pentadic system – which would then create an interesting relationship in the juxtaposition of 4.9/10 (Lollius/Ligurinus).

[13] So Putnam 23, Du Quesnay 1995: 133, n.17, with further bibliography. Du Quesnay 133 believes 4.4 and 4.15, along with their 'companion pieces' 4.5 and 4.15, 'were written with a view to being performed and published in the context of celebrations that would mark Augustus' quasi-triumphal return'. Suetonius might be expected to have mentioned any such performance, since he does mention the poems to Drusus and Tiberius.

[14] Currie 1996: 82.

For Dettmer, Book 4 is primarily arranged, as are 1–3, in a ring structure, with numeric patterns to match:[15]

Ring	Poem	Subject	Number of lines
	4.1	*Recusatio*	40
	4.2	*Recusatio*	60
	4.3	*Carmen Saeculare*	24
	4.4	Augustus: military achievements through Drusus	76
c e_1			
	4.5	Augustus: social and economic achievements	40
	4.6	*Carmen Saeculare*	44
	4.7	Total annihilation through death	24
a b f	4.8	Poetry confers immortality	
	4.9	Poetry represents the only means of survival	52
	4.10	Old age	8
	4.11	Invitation to a symposium	36
d e_2			
	4.12	Invitation to a symposium	28
	4.13	Old age	28
	4.14	Inverse of a *recusatio*	52
	4.15	*Recusatio*	32

Num. Pattern (difference): a = 8, b = 8, c = 20, d = 20,
e ([4.4 – 4.5] – [4.11 – 4.12]) = 28, and f = 28

The labelling of this scheme is somewhat tendentious (especially for 4.7 and 4.14, for instance), and in such analyses the numerical pattern can be made to 'work', particularly when every poem involved is in quatrains. And her pattern

15 Cf. Dettmer 1983: 484–523, 486 for the scheme here given. She has a further, different scheme on 488 ('Interlocking-ring structure').

only works if 4.7.17–20 are excised, unlikely in my view. In this regard, however, Dettmer's structure would likewise support those who believe the irregularity of 4.8 – its violation of Meineke's Law – is Horatian and not due to subtraction or accretion in its transmission (see 8 intro.).

Fraenkel, on the other hand, saw a division into three, again with the central position of 4.8 and its two surrounding praise poems serving to isolate the centre: Fraenkel 426 'within the plan of the whole book *Ne forte credas* is no less fundamental than *Donarem pateras*, to which *Diffugere niues* forms a significant prelude. This central triad, firmly linked together, is kept separate from the poems which precede it and from those that follow it.' Indeed, most scholars have seen a triadic structure as being the dominant one, including Putnam, who arranged separate chapters on each of the poems into triads, meant to reflect the structure of book, and gave titles to each of the groups: 1–3 'The Loving Muse', 4–6 'Doctus Apollo', 7–9 'Time and Redemption', 10–12 'Festivity's Musics', 13–15 'Sorcery and Song'. These titles themselves are somewhat vague, and so rather easily support an assertion of triadic structure, but they also for the most part reflect a structural reality.

4. THEMATIC PATTERNS

Suetonius' hypothesis about how the entirety of *C.* 4 came to be – 4.4 and 4.14 commissioned, with H. additionally compelled to come up with the remainder of the book – is but the recorded beginning of a long tradition of dissatisfaction with the book and its apparent lack of unity of themes, motif and design. Although *C.* 1–3 had included personal and political poems, the Roman *Odes* (3.1–6) at least were segregated, and there is nothing quite like 4.4 or 4.14 in the earlier collection, so that the sympotic and erotic poems of the fourth book can seem in sharp contrast to those addressed to the aristocratic *nobiles* currently in service to the Augustan régime. Similarly, the march of history, the more urgent concerns about succession along with a larger presence of the house of Augustus, the relative remoteness of the Republic, along with other realities, meant that a poem such as *C.* 2.7, the welcoming home of a comrade-in-arms from Philippi, belong to a different world.

There is a constructive tension between the two cultures of the fourth book, and it does no service to H. to try to flatten out the difference. Juxtapositions and contiguities create interesting questions about what it means to sustain a lyric voice in the context of praising – or failing to praise – the principate and its machine. At the same time the fourth book is not a random assemblage of dissonant poetic forms, and integration is to be found in part through a variety of important motifs that persist across the boundaries between the personal and the public or political. Porter 1975: 189 begins by identifying three themes or categories into which the poems of *C.* 4 may be grouped:

> One theme is that of time's relentless passing and the melancholy occasioned by that passing. Six poems focus on this theme: 1, 7, 10–13. A second, more joyful theme is that of poetry and poetry's power to immortalize. This theme is dominant in five poems: 2, 3, 6, 8, 9. A third theme is celebration of Augustus, his house, and his régime. This theme is central in four poems, 4, 5, 14, 15, and in addition plays an important role in two of the poems which focus on poetry, 2 and 9.

The contrast between the first and second themes – melancholic contemplation of the passing of time versus a sense of joy in the power of poetry to compensate for that passing – both unifies and also serves to separate these poems from the nationalistic ones of the third group, with their focus on the exploits of Drusus, Tiberius and their adoptive father. Porter proceeds to trace the way in which a number of motifs run across the boundaries of these thematically distinct groups and so contribute to continuities within the generally disparate nature of the book. The motifs identified are indeed integral to the entire book: rivers in various states of flood, birds and flying, Venus and love, wealth, commerce and giving, war, fire and light, trees and flowers, music and dancing. And yet the distinctions and contrasts remain, productively in tension with each other, leaving readers to choose between the public and the private, politics and play, ideology and aesthetics.

5. POETRY AND PROPAGANDA

The last decade of Horatian poetry, particularly that which, even in passing, touches on the régime of Augustus, is to be understood first and foremost in the context of the *Carmen saeculare*. The poem was commissioned precisely as every other aspect of the celebration was commissioned, and the function of the entire event was to celebrate the régime while sustaining the fiction that the ceremony was a traditional, republican event, predicted by the Sibylline prophecies. Its composition and performance were part of the organization of opinion and propaganda, helping to sustain the fiction of unbroken continuity with previous republican iterations.[16] Whatever the connection between H.'s hymn and the actual proceedings,[17] the purpose of the hymn was simple and unequivocal: it was to contribute to the celebration of a Roman citizen who had through a series of civil wars established himself as the ruler of Rome.

There has been heated discussion of the term 'propaganda' in recent years, with attempts to soften it with apparently less loaded and dramatic terminology ('influence', 'organization of opinion', 'Publizistik').[18] I use the term unabashedly,

[16] See *CS* intro. for details.

[17] On which see, with bibliography, Barchiesi 2002.

[18] See Eich 2000: 20–45 for discussion, with extensive bibliography for the Augustan context.

to indicate the careful and thorough projection by the Augustan régime, through figures such as Ateius Capito in the case of the *CS*, of the images that would best serve to legitimate the *princeps* and persuade that the world was better off with power residing in one man. As for the realities of the *CS* in this connection, Morgan 2002: 27, in a review of Putnam 2001, put the matter well:

> if anything jars in this tidy little book it is a complacency in its analysis of the *Carmen*'s politics. Over and above any stylistic issue, after all, the really unappealing aspect of the *Carmen saeculare* is its wholehearted endorsement of an autocrat's exercise in mass manipulation . . . The Augustan peace which the *Carmen* immortalized was achieved by bloodshed on a huge scale, and its monuments were explicit on this point. The Apollo who oversaw those fresh-faced choristers, lyre and libation-bowl in hand, was the very embodiment of the *Pax Augusta*. But he stood on a high platform decorated with the prows of captured warships, spoils of Augustus' successes over fellow-Romans: and he derived his title 'Actian' from the decisive naval victory over Antony and Cleopatra in 31 BC, 'the Actian sea dyed red with Roman blood', in Seneca's formulation. We can call Horace's glorification of such things 'art', if we choose, but is it so easily redeemed? If it were Leni Riefenstahl we were discussing rather than Quintus Horatius Flaccus, *Triumph of the Will* rather than the *Carmen saeculare*, and the Nuremberg rally of 1934 rather than the *Ludi saeculares* of 17 BC, would we entertain that defence for a second?

The examples are apt, and the judgment of H. as participant in the régime's propaganda will vary in large part depending on the reader's sympathy or lack of sympathy with the régime. What is admirable patriotism and loyalty for one person will be despicable propaganda and jingoism for another. However, what seems beyond reasonable doubt is the fact that by agreeing to compose the *Carmen saeculare* H. participated willingly in the Augustan program. However, by the same token, that fact need not imply that poems of H. without the official origins and public function of the *CS* are necessarily part of the régime's program, nor indeed that every word even of that poem was somehow vetted, or without slight ambiguities and even aesthetic or ideological discomfort about its public status. In fact, Lipka 2009: 159–66 has argued for a degree of independence on the part of H., who demonstrably 'translates' features of the *Acta* and the Sibylline oracle, in particular by Romanizing the original Greek features of the proceedings (see Appendix 1, p. 273, 2, pp. 274–6), by magnifying the role of Diana (*CS* 1–4n.), and in various other ways.

It will be the position of the commentaries that follow that the praise or even the presence of Augustus and the Augustan aristocrats who figure so centrally in *C.* 4 are on some level a response to the public encomium of the *CS*. I avoid here proposing any single or coherent encomiastic position and will rather address the individual poems, both the public ones that engage the issue and the private ones whose lack of engagement may be interpretable. If the *ludi saeculares* were an exercise in Augustan propaganda, as I believe they were, the collaboration of H. in that propaganda, both in the *CS* and in the poems that followed it, is clearly of interest.

It will be useful briefly to observe the poet and the prince in the years before and after the staging of the Secular Games.

Two of the most prominent scholars of the twentieth century, perhaps the two most prominent in Roman studies, left very little space between Augustus and H. Of Syme's *The Roman Revolution* Jasper Griffin has stated, 'That great book, among its other merits, gives an interpretation of Augustus and his poets which is hard-headed and highly political.'[19] 'Augustus and his poets' – the presumption is explicit and entrenched, as indeed it was for Syme, who put the matter in a way that many have found (and would still find) acceptable:

> Virgil, Horace and Livy are the enduring glories of the Principate; and all three men were on terms of personal friendship with Augustus. The class to which these men of letters belonged had everything to gain from the new order. Both Virgil and Horace had lost their paternal estates in the confiscations that followed Philippi or the disorders of the Perusine War: they subsequently regained their property, or at least compensation. (Syme 1939: 464)

Almost every sentence of this passage is problematic, when held up, as Syme was not interested in doing, to the nuances and evolutions of Augustan poetry. Syme despised Augustus, understandably, and threw out the babies with the bath water. Fraenkel's *Horace*, on the other hand, as great a work as it is in many ways, suffered from a different problem, as has been recognized. This scholar, who barely acknowledged *The Roman Revolution* in his footnotes, found a different way, rooted in admiration for Augustus and committed to belief in a strong bond between poet and ruler. Some of Fraenkel's favourite poems are those that most celebrate the *princeps*, who is in the eyes of the refugee from Hitler's Germany an ideologically neutral figure. Fraenkel's views were also doubtless connected to events of the 1930s, as they had been for the formation of Syme's Augustus, but in the case of the German critic those events meant parallels between contemporary and ancient dictators and princes could not be parallels at all, if H. was to be palatable.

In what ways is H. an 'Augustan poet'? There can be no doubt about the response to that question on a number of levels: he is arguably the most Augustan of all of them: closest in age to the *princeps*, who was two years his junior, closest in friendship to Maecenas, the *princeps*' friend and adviser, at least through the year 23 or 22 BCE, when Maecenas may (or may not) have fallen somewhat from favour, after warning his wife Terentia of the discovery of the conspiracy of her brother (probably A. Terentius Varro Murena: Suet. *Aug.* 66.3; see 9.35–6n.). H.

[19] Griffin 1994: 43.

was also closest, it seems, in his liking for Rome, which Virgil and Varius, as best we can tell, seem to have avoided in preference for the intellectual milieu of Naples; and indeed closest in friendship to Augustus himself, as the tone and content of the latter's comments about the poet, and the poet's response in *Epistle* 2.1, would seem to indicate.

6. RELUCTANT PRAISE

That H. was chosen to write for the Games is natural for these reasons, natural too since he had just shown his prowess in lyric, the appropriate genre. And the last poem of *C.* 4 seems to repay the laureate honour, effectively coining the phrase 'Age of Augustus' (4.14.4 *tua, Caesar, aetas*), as noted by Breed 2004. The apparent finality and even resignation of that poem needs to be set into the context of the rest of *C.* 4, and into the context of what went before, much of which seems to conjure up the republicanism of H.'s earlier days and a reluctance to participate in the propaganda that had been taking form since the death of Julius Caesar. It will be useful to divide Horatian political poetry into four periods, to the extent that time of composition can be distinguished from time of publication of the work itself.[20]

1) *Before Actium (43–31 BCE)*. There is no appearance of Octavian in a poem whose date of composition can be confidently set before the battle of Actium, and the first book of *Satires* is the only Horatian publication before that battle, a fact that is perhaps of some note. Even in the journey to Brundisium, the name of Octavian is never more than implicit, though Antony's name appears, along with that of his agent C. Fonteius Capito (*RE* 20; cos. suff. 33 BCE) and M. Cocceius Nerva (*RE* 13), erstwhile supporter of L. Antonius, pardoned by Octavian and destined to be involved as one of the *quindecimuiri* in the Secular Games:

> huc uenturus erat Maecenas optimus atque
> Cocceius, missi magnis de rebus uterque
> legati, auersos soliti componere amicos.
> hic oculis ego nigra meis collyria lippus
> illinere. interea Maecenas aduenit atque
> Cocceius Capitoque simul Fonteius, ad unguem
> factus homo, Antoni non ut magis alter amicus.
>
> *S.* 1.5.27–33

It may be notable that within the frame created by the names of these *auersi amici* H. places himself, eyes shut tight, at the most politically engaged point of the poem. The absence of Octavian's name finds a curious parallel in Virgil's *Eclogues*, where other contemporary Romans are mentioned but Octavian is only

[20] See Brink III 523–72 on the periodization of the Augustan principate and its relationship to Augustan poetry.

alluded to anonymously (*E.* 1.42 *iuuenis*; *E.* 8.5 *tu* – unless that is Pollio). The reasons for this failure to name may only be speculated on, but it does not carry with it a general avoidance of confrontation with the desperate state of affairs in these years. Two other pre-Actian poems, *Epod.* 7 (*Quo, quo scelesti ruitis?*) and 16 (*Altera iam teritur bellis ciuilibus aetas*), very precisely constitute harangues against Rome. No side is taken, but neither Octavian nor Antony could have read them without entertaining the possibility that he was being addressed. Likewise in the same period, neither could have avoided seeing in Meliboeus' cry of injustice (*E.* 1.70–1 *impius haec tam culta noualia miles habebit* | *barbarus has segetes*) a possible reference to the land confiscations in which both were involved in the late 40s BCE.

2) *Actium to the permanent tribunate (31–23 BCE).* Things changed after Actium, and what is in many ways the most encomiastic piece of Horatian propaganda before the *Carmen saeculare*, *Epod.* 9, comes from the period immediately following the victory. Nevertheless, along with the cries of '*io Triumphe!*' (21, 23), as Seager 1993: 25 notes, H. keeps his focus on the fact that the engagement was a civil war, with a Roman serving a woman and her eastern eunuchs:

Romanus eheu–posteri negabitis–
  emancipatus feminae
fert uallum et arma miles et spadonibus
  seruire rugosis potest
interque signa turpe militaria
  sol aspicit conopium.
Epod. 9.11–16

What is notable both here and in the other post-Actian *Epode*, the first of the collection, is the indirectness of any encomium. Both are addressed to Maecenas and refer to Caesar in the third person, within the framework of personal and intimate engagement with the poet's patron:

Ibis Liburnis inter alta nauium,
  amice, propugnacula,
paratus omne Caesaris periculum
  subire, Maecenas, tuo
Epod. 1.1–4

This is a pattern that is repeated in the poems of the following years. It is a notable fact that of the dozen appearances of Augustus in *C.* 1–3, that is, from Horatian poetry produced between Actium and around the time of the *princeps*' assumption of permanent *tribunicia potestas*, there is only a single case where the poet addresses him directly (*C.* 1.2.41–52). At least from the year 29 BCE, H. had ample precedent for direct address, and he seems to have deliberately avoided it. Virgil, *Ecl.* 8.6–13 (if indeed directed to Octavian) and *Georgics* 1.24–42 directly and intensely address Octavian, figured with Hellenistic excess as a future deity (*tuque adeo . . . Caesar*, 24–5): 40–2 *da facilem cursum atque audacibus annue coeptis, | ignarosque uiae mecum miseratus agrestes | ingredere et uotis iam nunc assuesce uocari.* Similarly at the end of *Georgics* 1.503–5 *iam pridem nobis caeli te regia, Caesar, | inuidet atque hominum queritur curare triumphos, | quippe ubi fas uersum atque nefas.* Likewise, in the same period, Propertius has the direct address *Auguste* at 2.10.15, although he too tends to refer to Caesar in the third person, usually contrasting the military activities of the *princeps* with his own elegiac preoccupations.

The single exception in *C.* 1–3 is itself notable. As Fraenkel 243–5 and others have seen, *C.* 1.2 begins with a clear reminiscence of the end of *Georgics* 1, as it seeks a solution and a saviour for a war-weary world: *C.* 1.2.1–2 *Iam satis terris niuis atque dirae | grandinis misit pater* etc.; *G.* 1.501–2 *satis iam pridem sanguine nostro | Laomedonteae luimus periuria Troiae.* In both cases the answer to Rome's problems is indeed Augustus, still Octavian in this early but post-Actian ode. As at the beginning of the poem, so at the end, H. is intensely Virgilian, as he prays that the saviour may pass to heaven only after curing the ills of Rome. And even the identification is oblique: the last line of the poem provides the identity (*te duce, Caesar*), but we get there in a roundabout way, for, notoriously, this metamorphosed 'Caesar' (at first an unnamed *iuuenis*, 41, like Tityrus' Octavian in *Ecl.* 1.42) emerges as *Caesaris ultor* (44) after starting out as Mercury (*C.* 1.2.41–4). Caesar, the avenger of Caesar, is therefore here addressed for the only time in the great lyric collection.

Putnam 1990 has studied the issue of encomiastic ambiguity in *C.* 1–3, particularly in 2.9, whose first four stanzas urge Valgius Rufus, a writer inter alia of elegy, to restrain his elegiac lament (9 *flebilibus modis*) over the loss of Mystes, dead or gone to a rival. To this point the poem resembles 1.33, where an Albius, probably Tibullus, is advised to drop his *miserabiles elegos* over Glycera and to follow H. in a less preoccupied way that suggests the superiority of lyric eclecticism over elegiac obsessiveness. But 2.9 offers no such lyric comfort, rather the following:

desine mollium
tandem querellarum et potius noua
cantemus Augusti tropaea
Caesaris et rigidum Niphaten,

Medumque flumen gentibus additum
uictis minores uoluere uertices
intraque praescriptum Gelonos
exiguis equitare campis.

C. 2.9.17–24

As a solution to erotic problems, H. suggests rather a song of Caesar Augustus (the names appear together in the odes only here), and Putnam 1990: 234 is surely right to see this as almost a parody of encomium and a 'depoeticizing' and 'despiritualizing' of the pathos of the first part of the poem. One might add that Valgius' and H.'s competence for singing of such matters is called into question in the final lines, with the use of adjectives redolent of elegiac reduction (*minores . . . exiguis*; cf. *AP* 77 *exiguos elegos*). I also note here in passing the juxtaposition of the political with the erotic and sympotic, with the potential of the latter to subvert, particularly when the political has a moralizing feel to it.

A different sort of deflection, to use Putnam's term, takes place in the *recusatio* of *C.* 1.6, where Agrippa rather than Augustus is directly addressed, while the military exploits of both are eschewed by H., here at his most Callimachean. *C.* 1.12, the most Pindaric of the collection, beginning with its quote of the opening of *Ol.* 2, is another curious case. The poem opens with a question: 1–3 *Quem uirum aut heroa lyra uel acri | tibia sumis celebrare, Clio? | quem deum?* Horace takes us through a priamel of possible candidates, beginning with gods, first Jupiter, other Olympians, then Hercules and Castor and Pollux, then mortals, all Romans, from Romulus down to the Marcelli, both the famous consul of 222 BCE (Claudius *RE* 220) and the nephew and new son-in-law of the *princeps* (Claudius *RE* 230), who will be dead by the end of 23 BCE. The priamel seems complete at the end of the fourth triad:

crescit occulto uelut arbor aeuo
fama Marcelli: micat inter omnes
Iulium sidus uelut inter ignes
  luna minores.

C. 1.12.45–8

Fraenkel and others insist that *Iulium sidus* refers exclusively to Augustus, otherwise as yet unnamed in the poem, but the marriage of his daughter Julia to the young M. Claudius Marcellus, son of his sister Octavia, provides a double connection to the *sidus Iulium*, and readers would be excused for seeing the growing (*crescit*) star as referring to the young Marcellus. Either way, as Fraenkel notes (296), 'now we might expect a eulogy of the Princeps to follow immediately. But H. has something greater in store. Surprisingly the poem returns to Jupiter.' Surprising indeed: Augustus is there, but he is there as surrogate, again deflected, and as second to another, albeit Jupiter, sandwiched in the middle stanza of the final triad, his mind on the Parthians:

gentis humanae pater atque custos,
orte Saturno, tibi cura magni
Caesaris fatis data: tu secundo
  Caesare regnes.

ille seu Parthos Latio imminentes
egerit iusto domitos triumpho
siue subiectos Orientis orae
  Seras et Indos,

te minor latum reget aequus orbem:
tu graui curru quaties Olympum,
tu parum castis inimica mittes
  fulmina lucis.

Other appearances in *C.* 1–3 focus on the need to pursue a vigorous foreign policy and so avoid internecine conflict. *C.* 1.21.13–16 is a prayer to Apollo, asking that he protect from famine and plague 'the people and Caesar', diverting such catastrophe onto Persians and Britons. Similarly *C.* 1.35.29–40 prays that Fortuna keep Augustus safe as he is about to move against the Britons, the fresh swarm of young men (*iuuenum recens | examen*) safe as they move on the East. Famously, *C.* 1.37, *Nunc est bibendum*, has Caesar pursuing Cleopatra (designated *non humilis mulier* by the end of the poem), as a hawk hunts down the soft doves or the huntsman tracks a hare. *C.* 2.12.11–16 is a *recusatio*: Maecenas is to write a historical account of the *proelia Caesaris*, in contrast to H.'s preoccupation, the Muse of mistress Licymnia.

The Roman Odes (*C.* 3.1–6) might be thought to provide something of an exception, but on the contrary, even they fail to address Augustus directly. There are three appearances of Augustus. At 3.3.9–20 it is predicted that the *princeps* will join Pollux and Hercules in drinking nectar on Olympus; at 3.4.37–40 the Camenae are said to be refreshing Caesar as he hides away his wearied troops, perhaps after returning from the East in 29; and at 3.5.2–4 H. assures that the *princeps* will become a god once he has dealt with the Parthians and Britons.

The last two appearances bring politics into confrontation with the sympotic. In *C.* 3.14 Caesar is set into the context of the Horatian drinking party, occasioned by the *princeps*' return from Spain in 24 BCE. Third-person references frame the first, encomiastic part of the poem (3 *Caesar repetit . . . penates*; 14–16 *ego nec tumultum | nec mori per uim metuam tenente | Caesare terras*). This homecoming in the second half becomes an excuse for a party as the poet tells his slave to fetch garlands, wine and a girl, if he can get her away from the door-keeper. If not, he won't mind, since he's not the way he was about such things in the year of Plancus' consulship, the year H. fought on the republican side at Philippi.[21]

As for the final appearances in the collection, as Putnam (216–17) has suggested, 'they demonstrate how highly qualified Horace's acceptance of Augustus into his lyric world still remains'. *C.* 3.24 is a moralizing sermon on the evils of wealth (how did Maecenas read this?), with an otherwise unnamed person, again not actually addressed, told that he must restore virtue if he is to seek to be called *pater urbium*. This is immediately followed by 3.25, with a Bacchanalian, ivy-wreathed H. first wondering in what caves he will be heard planning to introduce Caesar's glory to the stars and the council of Jupiter (3–6); then reverting

[21] See Putnam 1990: 215–16.

once more to *recusatio*, its ambiguous main verb expressing wish or intention: 7–8 *dicam insigne, recens, adhuc | indictum ore alio*. As far as Augustus and *C.* 1–3 are concerned, the *insigne indictum* remains unspoken.

3) *Postludic interlude (23–17* BCE*)*. Nothing very much changed in the Horatian outlook in the third of our periods, from 23 to 17 BCE, towards the end of which Augustus, now fully entrenched, began the various programmes that would put the stamp on his principate and truly secure the transition from Republic to empire. H. was engaged in the composition of the twenty poems of the first book of *Epistles*. Maecenas still has pride of place, as the hook on which the collection is hung (1.3) and addressee of one of the best of these poems (1.7); Tiberius is a recipient of 1.9, but none is addressed to Augustus. Given the genre, Augustus is therefore once more only to be found in the third person, and his appearances look pretty casual. Julius Florus, part of the *cohors* of Tiberius, is to tell H. who is taking up Augustus' exploits: 1.3.7 *quis sibi res gestas Augusti scribere sumit?* The question stands at the head of a catalogue of genres imagined for the *studiosa cohors*, and there is no real expectation of a response or interest in a response. At 1.5.9–10, politics is again the peg for sympotic focus: Caesar's birthday is the following day, and so the chance to sleep in is used to persuade Torquatus to accept a dinner-invitation the night before: *cras nato Caesare festus | dat ueniam somnumque dies*. As for 1.12.25–8, in an epigrammatic PS to Iccius, H. casually informs that Agrippa has had success in Spain, Claudius in Armenia, and Phraates the king of the Parthians has surrendered to Augustus, a somewhat generous interpretation of the realities, but still pretty casual, though fufilling the desires expressed in *C.* 1–3. The closing telegram has the feel of a cliché: 28–9 *aurea fruges | Italiae pleno defudit Copia cornu*. *Epist.* 1.13 is a playful letter to Vinnius, perhaps Vinnius Valens, who is advised not to behave like an ass – his father had the cognomen Asina – by dropping his pack to deliver poems to Augustus; nor in delivering them should he tell everyone he sweated in carrying them, since the eyes of Caesar will be reading them. Surrogacy and second-handedness again close out these references in 1.16.25–9, a poem with, as Seager 1993: 34 put it, an 'elliptically subversive air'. Of the actual lines he also concedes 'the lavish praise of Augustus may be sincere'. So it might be, but H. still keeps his distance, with an indefinite interlocutor (*si quis . . . dicat*) elaborating the praise, whose referent is identified by H.'s addressee (*agnoscere possis*):

> siquis bella tibi terra pugnata marique
> dicat et his uerbis uacuas permulceat aures:
> 'tene magis saluum populus uelit an populum tu,
> seruet in ambiguo qui consulit et tibi et urbi
> Iuppiter', Augusti laudes agnoscere possis.
>
> *Epist.* 1.16.25–9

H. himself is just the commentator, but that was all about to change.

4) *Carmen saeculare* to *C.* 4 *(17–13 BCE).* Peter White has shown throughout *Promised Verse* that there is no cogent evidence that any pressure was brought to bear on the poets active through the end of the first century BCE to produce encomiastic poetry. But two millennia of reception have created an expectation of encomium, and this expectation is retrojected to the end of the Republic. In what precedes it is clear that H. is at times playful, at times deflective, rarely or never simply encomiastic on the subject of Octavian. Imperial patronage would become something very different in the decades to come, and the poetry of Statius is closer to that of Dryden in this respect than it is to that of H. or Virgil. Two things seem clear: there was great freedom, perhaps because, at least down to 18 BCE, literary freedom could help to imply the existence of a larger *libertas*, and that larger *libertas* was clearly becoming a fiction.

Nevertheless, if Suetonius is to be believed, Augustus seems finally to have noticed and to have reacted. The reaction seems to have come soon after publication of *Epistles* 1:

> post sermones uero quosdam lectos nullam sui mentionem habitam ita sit questus: 'irasci me tibi scito, quod non in plerisque eius modi scriptis mecum potissimum loquaris; an uereris ne apud posteros infame tibi sit, quod uidearis familiaris nobis esse?' expressitque eclogam ad se, cuius initium est:
>
> Cum tot sustineas et tanta negotia solus,
> res Italas armis tuteris, moribus ornes,
> legibus emendes: in publica commoda peccem,
> si longo sermone morer tua tempora, Caesar.

We may be grateful to Augustus for writing in this vein, since the poem whose opening is quoted by Suetonius, *Epistle* 2.1, is a brilliant glimpse into the history of Roman literature and an impassioned argument for the legitimacy of modernism against literary conservatism. That it is addressed to Augustus is relevant, but much of its value is independent of that fact, and ultimately, the epistle provides H. with yet another opportunity for *recusatio* (245–59). In these lines, he labels Virgil and Varius as beloved by Augustus, as capable as sculptors in bringing to life the *mores animique* of the great and in no way disgraced by the gifts their praises of Augustus generated. Could H. do encomium, he would gladly do so, but his *paruum carmen* is not sufficient for the *maiestas* of Augustus and the poet's *pudor* keeps him from trying things beyond his strength.

But praise was forthcoming, in the poem whose commissioning Suetonius goes on to mention (*ut non modo saeculare carmen componendum iniunxerit*), in *C.* 4.4 and 4.14, to the Augustan surrogates Drusus and Tiberius, and in 4.5 and 4.15 to Augustus himself. Then there are the rest, Paullus Fabius Maximus (4.1), Iullus Antonius (4.2), not exactly praised, but prominent, along with Censorinus, father or son (4.8), and Lollius (4.9), praised insufficiently or undeservedly.

But the result of the exchange reported by Suetonius is to be found in *C.* 4, specifically poems 4 and 14 on the victories of Tiberius and Drusus, and by implication, 5 and 15 on Augustus himself, with direct address finally achieved and even embraced. As Williams puts it, 'The time for explicit acknowledgement of his supremacy and for celebration of his achievements had come.'[22] We will question in the commentary whether that conclusion can be so easy. For now, just two reactions. First, the question of quality arises. When the encomiastic mission becomes dominant, something happens to the lyric voice. Fraenkel 382 called the *Carmen saeculare* 'the greatest triumph of Horace's achievement as a lyric poet'. It is hard to take that seriously unless one is more interested in the *laudandus* than the aesthetic effect of the *laus*. Second, there is the lyric voice that is not involved in encomia but almost in its opposite, in *otium*, in drinking parties, in regret at the passing of youth and a sense of the finality of life. Along with the youthful new Caesars, Drusus and Tiberius, and along with Paullus Maximus, Iullus Antonius and Marcus Lollius, consulars or consuls-to-be, all destined for political disgrace and execution, we find a powerful juxtaposition with Cinara/Cinura (see 1.3–4n.), Phyllis and Lyce, metonymic for the youth and the youthful verse of H. There can be little doubt as to where H.'s heart is, I think. This too may have been noticed. Seager 1993: 39 perhaps overstates it, perhaps not: 'And when he became more disgruntled and subversive, he was clever enough to cover himself well. It is hard to see how Augustus could have found plausible grounds for suppressing any poem that survives, even had he wished to do so. But nobody asked Horace to write a fifth book of Odes.'

7. PINDAR, CALLIMACHUS AND AESTHETIC CONTESTATIONS

The first poem of *C.* 4 reluctantly resumes the lyric voice that had been silent for a decade, the retirement of *C.* 3.26 surprisingly cancelled as the Venus of that poem has H. back in her thrall, if only in his dreams. The second poem functions in some tension with this opening by introducing the Pindaric baseline that will characterize the book's encomia, particularly those to the Nero brothers (4, 14). While warning of the difficulty of Pindaric emulation, *C.* 4.2 opens with 24 lines that are intensely Pindaric, in the long flow of the sentence beginning in line 4, the use of striking metaphor at 5–8, and the highly lyrical sense throughout. Along the way H. lyricizes the table of contents of the 17-book Alexandrian edition of Pindar (see 2.10–24n.).

H. draws attention to the difficulty of Pindaric composition, even as he seems to be carrying it off, to be performing a version of it. But we eventually realize we are in the priamel's foil, that part which sets up the climax and the preferred mode. This climax comes with *ego*, introducing H. the Matine bee:

[22] Williams 1990: 267 n. 18.

ego apis Matinae
more modoque,

grata carpentis thyma per laborem
plurimum, circa nemus uuidique
Tiburis ripas operosa paruus
carmina fingo.

C. 4.2.27–32

Everything about these lines suggests a separation from the public voice, and the lines give the lie to H.'s prediction, never realized, that he will be one of the crowd, chanting (46–7) '*o sol | pulcher, o laudande*' with the mob as Augustus passes by. It is important to note that 4.2.1–24, in spite of their relative Pindaric competence, are ultimately a rejection of the Pindaric, even, implicitly, of his own Pindaric exercises, 4.4 and 4.14, which will similarly open with extended and effusive periods of 28 and 24 lines respectively, openings without parallel in Horatian lyric. In 4.8 and 4.9 encomium continues, again Pindaric in nature, particularly in the former, as Stephen Harrison in particular has noted (see 8 intro.). The oddities of these poems – 4.8 does not actually get around to praising Censorinus, and the details of the praise of Lollius serve to draw attention to his military failures (see 9 intro.) – call into question the whole enterprise of what it means to be Pindaric in the context of Rome and lyric poetry. Johnson has put it well (92):

> *C.* 8 and 9 test the limits of panegyric: a generic hyperbolic set piece that fails to distinguish the addressee in any meaningful or lasting sense versus a *laudatio* that so risks opposition to the popular character and deeds of the praised that it is directly challenged by later historians.

And finally, praise of Augustus himself is forthcoming (4.5, 15), but the encomiastic style, in marked contrast with the openings of the poems on Drusus and Tiberius (see 5.17–24, 15.4–16nn.), seems closer to that of an inscription, again suggesting a gap between the lyric poet and the *laudator*.[23]

The lyric beauty of the non-encomiastic poems of *C.* 4 works against the voice of the *laudator*, as against that of the *Carmen saeculare*, whether that voice is effusively Pindaric, prosaic, at odds with the merits of its addressee or stylistically inscriptional. Whether or not it is 'the most perfect poem in the Latin language' (Housman on 4.7, see intro.), the seventh poem takes the reader back to the Parade Odes and refutes claims about waning lyric genius. The same is true of the sympotic run of 4.10–13, sandwiched between the paired praise of Censorinus and Lollius and that of the Julio-Claudians that will bring down the curtain. The world now belongs to Augustus, but the lyric poet, perhaps even the ageing republican, still inhabits a part of that world, his constructed erotic lifestyle

[23] On this see Lyne 1995: 207–14 (Ch. 12. 'Signs of resentment in *Odes* 4: "Sapping"').

still visible even as he follows up his secular celebration of moral legislation that was perhaps as little appealing to him as it would be to Augustus' own daughter. Memories of Cinara/Cinura and the torch of Lyce fallen to ash close out the private lyric (13.17–28). The poem before that invites Virgil (see 12 intro.), imagined at a time before the existence of the *Aeneid* (the time of *Odes* 1–3?), to join the party and forget the pursuit of profit, imputed *iuuenum nobilium cliens* though he may be. Those young – and less young – nobles are pointedly absent from 4.10–13, the domain of Ligurinus (10), Phyllis and Telephus (11), Lyce and Cinara/Cinura (13). That goes for Maecenas, mentioned uniquely in the book in the third person at 11.19, but not necessarily invited to the party at which Phyllis, in H.'s dreams and hopes, is to be the star attraction (see 11 intro.).

In the second half of the book, then, these two worlds are kept apart, which only underscores their incompatibility. The first half of the opening poem, the re-entry to the lists he had abandoned in *C.* 3.26, finds H. resisting the return of Venus, but he ends the poem with the tears of memory shed for the fleeting Ligurinus, to whom he will return in 4.10. Between the plea to Venus and those closing tears comes the first of the new aristocrats of the book, Paullus Fabius Maximus, potent ambassador of the goddess. He's your lover now, the ageing poet tells Venus, though Ligurinus arrives at the end to set up the poems that will keep the flame burning. Paullus, 'the scion of the patrician Fabii [who] was singled out for high distinction',[24] is here the emblem of youthfulness, and his political status puts other potential politicians into play, and Augustus in particular. Oswyn Murray said of 4.15, 'in fact our poem is not the last, but the first in a new collection addressed to his new patron Augustus . . . Why Horace chose to discard the poem and replace it with the unsatisfactory "Intermissa Venus diu rursus bella moues" is another problem.'[25] While this is clearly fanciful, the recent commissioning of the *Carmen saeculare*, and the realities of much of *C.* 4, might have led to the expectation that the *princeps* would take the place of Maecenas from other openers (*S.* 1.1, *Epod.* 1, *Epist.* 1.1). Lizzie Mitchell has noted that the poet was not the only one around 50 (1.6 *circa lustra decem*, as he said of himself) at the time of publication of *C.* 4 – in 13 BCE: H. turned 52 on 8 December, Augustus, 50 on 23 September.[26] She implicates Augustus in the ageing and productively explores the possibility that much of the poem and of the book is about replacing the old with the new in the political (particularly in the figures of Drusus and Tiberius) as well as the erotic sphere.

Politics will win in the end, once the *aetas Augusta* arrives in 4.15, as the erotic Venus of the book's first line is transformed into the mother of Aeneas in the final line. In 4.13, again the finale of the erotic poems, H. had asked the aged Lyce, rhetorically, *quo fugit Venus* (17). To Rome and to Augustus, we will soon find out. *C.* 4.3, H.'s own retreat from politics to his old lyric identity, set up by the image of the Matine bee at 4.2.27–32, addresses Melpomene, begins with

[24] Syme 1986: 404. [25] Murray 1985: 41. [26] E. Mitchell 2009: 1.

Callimachean reference and closes with allusion to the lyric envoi of *C.* 3.30 (1–2, 16, 21–4nn). Athletic games, and by implication Pindaric praise, along with martial and political achievements are all subordinated to Aeolic music. That music is set in Tivoli (4.3.10), so providing a replay of the priamel of *C.* 1.7, where the same place of retirement functioned as that poem's climax.

Drusus and Augustus make their appearance in the following two poems, but *C.* 4.6, which ends, uniquely in the *Odes*, with the poet's name (44 *uatis Horati*), resumes the struggle between politics and poetics, now through the figure of Apollo, absent since the choristers sang the *Carmen saeculare* before his temple next to the house of Augustus. Apollo himself embodies the polarity, as did Venus. Will he be the archer god, the Actian Apollo of the shield of Aeneas, or rather the god of the *Aetia* prologue and *Eclogue* 6, sponsor of the *recusatio* and its rejection of encomium and epic? As in 4.2, there are two, contrasting, possibilities. The Apollo on whom *C.* 4.6 dwells for the first six stanzas is the terrifying figure whose powers were felt by Niobe, Tityos and Achilles, the archer who together with Venus persuades Jupiter to spare Troy from total annihilation and so allow Rome to come into existence. But the final five stanzas shift the focus. Phoebus the lyre teacher (25 *doctor*), who gave the poet his breath, his art and the name of poet, stands at the beginning of the second half, with Thalia and the Daunian Camena, H.'s home-town Muse, and the poem will end with the words of the girl chorister, now married and remembering the song she sang, remembering that H. in turn had taught it to her:

dices 'ego dis amicum,
saeculo festas referente luces,
reddidi carmen docilis modorum
uatis Horati.'

TEXT AND SIGLA

The text is a combination of the Teubner editions of Shackleton Bailey (3rd edn. 1995), and Klingner (5th edn. 1970). It is more often with Klingner except in matters of punctuation. More or less broad or unanimous MS support is indicated with '**M**', less good with '**m**', and '**P**' is used to indicate support from Porphyrio and/or ps.-Acro, who are, however, of differing value for the constitution of the text. There is sparing mention of conjectural readings. For the sake of providing a text that is readable, if at times problematic, the obelus is avoided.

Q. HORATI FLACCI
CARMEN SAECVLARE

Q. HORATI FLACCI
CARMEN SAECVLARE

Phoebe siluarumque potens Diana,
lucidum caeli decus, o colendi
semper et culti, date quae precamur
  tempore sacro,

quo Sibyllini monuere uersus
uirgines lectas puerosque castos
dis, quibus septem placuere colles,
  dicere carmen.

alme Sol, curru nitido diem qui
promis et celas aliusque et idem
nasceris, possis nihil urbe Roma
  uisere maius.

rite maturos aperire partus
lenis, Ilithyia, tuere matres,
siue tu Lucina probas uocari
  seu Genitalis:

diua, producas subolem patrumque
prosperes decreta super iugandis
feminis prolisque nouae feraci
  lege marita,

certus undenos deciens per annos
orbis ut cantus referatque ludos
ter die claro totiensque grata
  nocte frequentes.

uosque, ueraces cecinisse Parcae,
quod semel dictum est stabilisque rerum
terminus seruet, bona iam peractis
  iungite fata.

16 Genitalis **M P** : Genetyllis *Bentley*   26 dictum est stabilisque rerum **M P** : dictum stabilisque rerum **m** : dictum stabilis per aeuum *Bentley*

fertilis frugum pecorisque Tellus
spicea donet Cererem corona;
nutriant fetus et aquae salubres
   et Iouis aurae.

condito mitis placidusque telo
supplices audi pueros, Apollo;
siderum regina bicornis, audi,
   Luna, puellas.

Roma si uestrum est opus Iliaeque
litus Etruscum tenuere turmae,
iussa pars mutare Lares et urbem
   sospite cursu,

cui per ardentem sine fraude Troiam
castus Aeneas patriae superstes
liberum muniuit iter, daturus
   plura relictis,

di, probos mores docili iuuentae,
di, senectuti placidae quietem,
Romulae genti date remque prolemque
   et decus omne.

quaeque uos bobus ueneratur albis
clarus Anchisae Venerisque sanguis,
impetret, bellante prior, iacentem
   lenis in hostem.

iam mari terraque manus potentes
Medus Albanasque timet secures,
iam Scythae responsa petunt superbi
   nuper et Indi.

iam Fides et Pax et Honos Pudorque
priscus et neglecta redire Virtus
audet, apparetque beata pleno
   Copia cornu.

augur et fulgente decorus arcu
Phoebus acceptusque nouem Camenis,
qui salutari leuat arte fessos
corporis artus,

si Palatinas uidet aequus aras,
remque Romanam Latiumque felix
alterum in lustrum meliusque semper
prorogat aeuum,

quaeque Auentinum tenet Algidumque,
quindecim Diana preces uirorum
curat et uotis puerorum amicas
applicat aures.

haec Iouem sentire deosque cunctos
spem bonam certamque domum reporto,
doctus et Phoebi chorus et Dianae
dicere laudes.

65 aras **M P** : arces **M P**

Q. HORATI FLACCI
CARMINVM LIBER QVARTVS

Q. HORATI FLACCI
CARMINVM LIBER QVARTVS

I.

Intermissa, Venus, diu
rursus bella moues? parce precor, precor.
non sum qualis eram bonae
sub regno Cinarae. desine, dulcium

mater saeua Cupidinum,
circa lustra decem flectere mollibus
iam durum imperiis; abi,
quo blandae iuuenum te reuocant preces.

tempestiuius in domum
Paulli purpureis ales oloribus
comissabere Maximi,
si torrere iecur quaeris idoneum.

namque et nobilis et decens
et pro sollicitis non tacitus reis
et centum puer artium
late signa feret militiae tuae,

et quandoque potentior
largi muneribus riserit aemuli,
Albanos prope te lacus
ponet marmoream sub trabe citrea.

illic plurima naribus
duces tura lyraeque et Berecyntiae
delectabere tibiae
mixtis carminibus non sine fistula;

illic bis pueri die
numen cum teneris uirginibus tuum

22–3 lyrae . . . Berecyntiae . . . tibiae **M** : -a . . . -a . . . -a **m**

laudantes pede candido
in morem Salium ter quatient humum.

me nec femina nec puer
iam nec spes animi credula mutui
nec certare iuuat mero
nec uincire nouis tempora floribus.

sed cur heu, Ligurine, cur
manat rara meas lacrima per genas?
cur facunda parum decoro
inter uerba cadit lingua silentio?

nocturnis ego somniis
iam captum teneo, iam uolucrem sequor
te per gramina Martii
Campi, te per aquas, dure, uolubiles.

2.

Pindarum quisquis studet aemulari,
Iulle, ceratis ope Daedalea
nititur pinnis, uitreo daturus
nomina ponto.

monte decurrens uelut amnis, imbres
quem super notas aluere ripas,
feruet immensusque ruit profundo
Pindarus ore,

laurea donandus Apollinari,
seu per audaces noua dithyrambos
uerba deuoluit numerisque fertur
lege solutis,

seu deos regesue canit, deorum
sanguinem, per quos cecidere iusta

13 -ue **m** : -que **M**

morte Centauri, cecidit tremendae
flamma Chimaerae,

siue quos Elea domum reducit
palma caelestes pugilemue equumue
dicit et centum potiore signis
munere donat,

flebili sponsae iuuenemue raptum
plorat et uiris animumque moresque
aureos educit in astra nigroque
inuidet Orco.

multa Dircaeum leuat aura cycnum,
tendit, Antoni, quotiens in altos
nubium tractus: ego apis Matinae
more modoque,

grata carpentis thyma per laborem
plurimum, circa nemus uuidique
Tiburis ripas operosa paruus
carmina fingo.

concines maiore poeta plectro
Caesarem, quandoque trahet feroces
per sacrum cliuum merita decorus
fronde Sygambros,

quo nihil maius meliusue terris
fata donauere bonique diui
nec dabunt, quamuis redeant in aurum
tempora priscum;

concines laetosque dies et urbis
publicum ludum super impetrato
fortis Augusti reditu forumque
litibus orbum.

tum meae, si quid loquar audiendum,
uocis accedet bona pars et 'o sol
pulcher, o laudande!' canam recepto
Caesare felix.

tuque dum procedis, 'io Triumphe!'
non semel dicemus, 'io Triumphe!'
ciuitas omnis dabimusque diuis
tura benignis.

te decem tauri totidemque uaccae,
me tener soluet uitulus, relicta
matre qui largis iuuenescit herbis
in mea uota,

fronte curuatos imitatus ignes
tertium lunae referentis ortum,
qua notam duxit niueus uideri,
cetera fuluus.

3.

Quem tu, Melpomene, semel
nascentem placido lumine uideris,
illum non labor Isthmius
clarabit pugilem, non equus impiger

curru ducet Achaico
uictorem, neque res bellica Deliis
ornatum foliis ducem,
quod regum tumidas contuderit minas,

ostendet Capitolio:
sed quae Tibur aquae fertile praefluunt
et spissae nemorum comae
fingent Aeolio carmine nobilem.

45 loquar **M** : loquor **m** 49 tuque dum procedis **m** : teque dum procedis (-it **m**) **M P** : isque dum procedit *Bentley* : atque dum procedit *Meineke*

Romae, principis urbium,
dignatur suboles inter amabiles
uatum ponere me choros,
et iam dente minus mordeor inuido.

o testudinis aureae
dulcem quae strepitum, Pieri, temperas,
o mutis quoque piscibus
donatura cycni, si libeat, sonum,

totum muneris hoc tui est,
quod monstror digito praetereuntium
Romanae fidicen lyrae;
quod spiro et placeo, si placeo, tuum est.

4.

Qualem ministrum fulminis alitem,
cui rex deorum regnum in aues uagas
permisit expertus fidelem
Iuppiter in Ganymede flauo,

olim iuuentas et patrius uigor
nido laborum propulit inscium,
uernique iam nimbis remotis
insolitos docuere nisus

uenti pauentem, mox in ouilia
demisit hostem uiuidus impetus,
nunc in reluctantes dracones
egit amor dapis atque pugnae,

qualemue laetis caprea pascuis
intenta fuluae matris ab ubere
lactante depulsum leonem
dente nouo peritura uidit:

4.15 lactente *Dillenburger* : iam lacte **M** : iam iamque *Bentley*

uidere Raetis bella sub Alpibus
Drusum gerentem Vindelici; quibus
mos unde deductus per omne
tempus Amazonia securi

dextras obarmet, quaerere distuli,
nec scire fas est omnia; sed diu
lateque uictrices cateruae
consiliis iuuenis reuictae

sensere quid mens rite, quid indoles
nutrita faustis sub penetralibus
posset, quid Augusti paternus
in pueros animus Nerones.

fortes creantur fortibus et bonis;
est in iuuencis, est in equis patrum
uirtus neque imbellem feroces
progenerant aquilae columbam.

doctrina sed uim promouet insitam
rectique cultus pectora roborant;
utcumque defecere mores,
indecorant bene nata culpae.

quid debeas, o Roma, Neronibus,
testis Metaurum flumen et Hasdrubal
deuictus et pulcher fugatis
ille dies Latio tenebris

qui primus alma risit adorea,
dirus per urbes Afer ut Italas
ceu flamma per taedas uel Eurus
per Siculas equitauit undas.

post hoc secundis usque laboribus
Romana pubes creuit et impio

34 roborant **M** : roborat *Shackleton Bailey*

uastata Poenorum tumultu
fana deos habuere rectos,

dixitque tandem perfidus Hannibal:
'cerui, luporum praeda rapacium,
sectamur ultro quos opimus
fallere et effugere est triumphus.

gens, quae cremato fortis ab Ilio
iactata Tuscis aequoribus sacra
natosque maturosque patres
pertulit Ausonias ad urbes,

duris ut ilex tonsa bipennibus
nigrae feraci frondis in Algido,
per damna, per caedes ab ipso
ducit opes animumque ferro.

non Hydra secto corpore firmior
uinci dolentem creuit in Herculem
monstrumue summisere Colchi
maius Echioniaeue Thebae.

merses profundo, pulchrior euenit;
luctere, multa proruet integrum
cum laude uictorem geretque
proelia coniugibus loquenda.

Carthagini iam non ego nuntios
mittam superbos: occidit, occidit
spes omnis et fortuna nostri
nominis Hasdrubale interempto.'

nil Claudiae non perficient manus,
quas et benigno numine Iuppiter
defendit et curae sagaces
expediunt per acuta belli.

67–8 geretque ... loquenda **M P** : feretque | praemia *Campbell* 73–6 *ab Hannibale fortasse dicta* 73 perficient **M** : perficiunt **m**

5.

Diuis orte bonis, optime Romulae
custos gentis, abes iam nimium diu:
maturum reditum pollicitus patrum
  sancto concilio, redi.

lucem redde tuae, dux bone, patriae.
instar ueris enim uultus ubi tuus
affulsit populo, gratior it dies
  et soles melius nitent.

ut mater iuuenem, quem Notus inuido
flatu Carpathii trans maris aequora
cunctantem spatio longius annuo
  dulci distinet a domo,

uotis ominibusque et precibus uocat
curuo nec faciem litore dimouet,
sic desideriis icta fidelibus
  quaerit patria Caesarem.

tutus bos etenim rura perambulat,
nutrit rura Ceres almaque Faustitas,
pacatum uolitant per mare nauitae,
  culpari metuit fides,

nullis polluitur casta domus stupris,
mos et lex maculosum edomuit nefas,
laudantur simili prole puerperae,
  culpam Poena premit comes.

quis Parthum paueat, quis gelidum Scythen,
quis Germania quos horrida parturit
fetus incolumi Caesare? quis ferae
  bellum curet Hiberiae?

condit quisque diem collibus in suis
et uitem uiduas ducit ad arbores;

hinc ad uina redit laetus et alteris
te mensis adhibet deum.

te multa prece, te prosequitur mero
defuso pateris, et Laribus tuum
miscet numen, uti Graecia Castoris
et magni memor Herculis.

'longas o utinam, dux bone, ferias
praestes Hesperiae!' dicimus integro
sicci mane die, dicimus uuidi,
cum sol Oceano subest.

6.

Diue, quem proles Niobea magnae
uindicem linguae Tityosque raptor
sensit et Troiae prope uictor altae
Pthius Achilles,

ceteris maior, tibi miles impar,
filius quamuis Thetidis marinae
Dardanas turres quateret tremenda
cuspide pugnax –

ille, mordaci uelut icta ferro
pinus aut impulsa cupressus Euro,
procidit late posuitque collum in
puluere Teucro;

ille non inclusus equo Mineruae
sacra mentito male feriatos
Troas et laetam Priami choreis
falleret aulam,

sed palam captis grauis, heu nefas, heu
nescios fari pueros Achiuis

31 uina **M** : tecta *Shackleton Bailey*

ureret flammis, etiam latentem
   matris in aluo,

ni tuis flexus Venerisque gratae
uocibus diuum pater adnuisset
rebus Aeneae potiore ductos
   alite muros:

doctor argutae fidicen Thaliae,
Phoebe, qui Xantho lauis amne crines,
Dauniae defende decus Camenae,
   leuis Agyieu.

spiritum Phoebus mihi, Phoebus artem
carminis nomenque dedit poetae:
uirginum primae puerique claris
   patribus orti,

Deliae tutela deae, fugaces
lyncas et ceruos cohibentis arcu,
Lesbium seruate pedem meique
   pollicis ictum,

rite Latonae puerum canentes,
rite crescentem face Noctilucam,
prosperam frugum celeremque pronos
   uoluere menses.

nupta iam dices 'ego dis amicum,
saeculo festas referente luces,
reddidi carmen docilis modorum
   uatis Horati.'

7

Diffugere niues, redeunt iam gramina campis
      arboribusque comae;
mutat terra uices, et decrescentia ripas
      flumina praetereunt.

Gratia cum Nymphis geminisque sororibus audet
ducere nuda choros.
immortalia ne speres monet annus et almum
quae rapit hora diem.

frigora mitescunt Zephyris, uer proterit aestas
interitura, simul
pomifer autumnus fruges effuderit, et mox
bruma recurrit iners.

damna tamen celeres reparant caelestia lunae:
nos ubi decidimus
quo pius Aeneas, quo diues Tullus et Ancus,
puluis et umbra sumus.

quis scit an adiciant hodiernae crastina summae
tempora di superi?
cuncta manus auidas fugient heredis, amico
quae dederis animo.

cum semel occideris et de te splendida Minos
fecerit arbitria,
non, Torquate, genus, non te facundia, non te
restituet pietas.

infernis neque enim tenebris Diana pudicum
liberat Hippolytum
nec Lethaea ualet Theseus abrumpere caro
uincula Pirithoo.

8.

Donarem pateras grataque commodus,
Censorine, meis aera sodalibus,
donarem tripodas, praemia fortium
Graiorum, neque tu pessima munerum
ferres, diuite me scilicet artium
quas aut Parrhasius protulit aut Scopas,
hic saxo, liquidis ille coloribus
sollers nunc hominem ponere, nunc deum.

sed non haec mihi uis, nec tibi talium
res est aut animus deliciarum egens:
gaudes carminibus; carmina possumus
donare, et pretium dicere muneri.
non incisa notis marmora publicis,
per quae spiritus et uita redit bonis
post mortem ducibus, non celeres fugae
reiectaeque retrorsum Hannibalis minae,
non incendia Karthaginis impiae
eius qui domita nomen ab Africa
lucratus rediit clarius indicant
laudes quam Calabrae Pierides, neque
si chartae sileant quod bene feceris,
mercedem tuleris. quid foret Iliae
Mauortisque puer, si taciturnitas
obstaret meritis inuida Romuli?
ereptum Stygiis fluctibus Aeacum
uirtus et fauor et lingua potentium
uatum diuitibus consecrat insulis.
dignum laude uirum Musa uetat mori,
caelo Musa beat. sic Iouis interest
optatis epulis impiger Hercules,
clarum Tyndaridae sidus ab infimis
quassas eripiunt aequoribus ratis,
ornatus uiridi tempora pampino
Liber uota bonos ducit ad exitus.

9.

Ne forte credas interitura quae
longe sonantem natus ad Aufidum
non ante uulgatas per artes
uerba loquor socianda chordis,

non, si priores Maeonius tenet
sedes Homerus, Pindaricae latent
Ceaeque et Alcaei minaces
Stesichorique graues Camenae,

15–19 non . . . rediit, 28, 33 del. *alii* 17, 33 *del. alii* *post* 32 *lacunam statuendam coni. Kovacs*

nec siquid olim lusit Anacreon
deleuit aetas; spirat adhuc amor
uiuuntque commissi calores
Aeoliae fidibus puellae.

non sola comptos arsit adulteri
crines et aurum uestibus illitum
mirata regalesque cultus
et comites Helene Lacaena,

primusue Teucer tela Cydonio
direxit arcu, non semel Ilios
uexata, non pugnauit ingens
Idomeneus Sthenelusue solus

dicenda Musis proelia, non ferox
Hector uel acer Deiphobus graues
excepit ictus pro pudicis
coniugibus puerisque primus.

uixere fortes ante Agamemnona
multi; sed omnes illacrimabiles
urgentur ignotique longa
nocte, carent quia uate sacro.

paullum sepultae distat inertiae
celata uirtus. non ego te meis
chartis inornatum silebo
totue tuos patiar labores

impune, Lolli, carpere liuidas
obliuiones: est animus tibi
rerumque prudens et secundis
temporibus dubiisque rectus,

uindex auarae fraudis et abstinens
ducentis ad se cuncta pecuniae,
consulque non unius anni,
sed quotiens bonus atque fidus

iudex honestum praetulit utili,
reiecit alto dona nocentium
uoltu, per obstantes cateruas
explicuit sua uictor arma.

non possidentem multa uocaueris
recte beatum; rectius occupat
nomen beati, qui deorum
muneribus sapienter uti

duramque callet pauperiem pati
peiusque leto flagitium timet,
non ille pro caris amicis
aut patria timidus perire.

10.

O crudelis adhuc et Veneris muneribus potens,
insperata tuae cum ueniet pluma superbiae
et quae nunc umeris inuolitant deciderint comae,
nunc et qui color est puniceae flore prior rosae,

mutatus, Ligurine, in faciem uerterit hispidam,
dices 'heu', quotiens te speculo uideris alterum,
'quae mens est hodie, cur eadem non puero fuit,
uel cur his animis incolumes non redeunt genae?'

11.

Est mihi nonum superantis annum
plenus Albani cadus, est in horto,
Phylli, nectendis apium coronis,
est hederae uis

multa, qua crinis religata fulges;
ridet argento domus, ara castis
uincta uerbenis auet immolato
spargier agno.

10.2 pluma **M**: poena *Withof*: *alii alia* 5 Ligurine *Torrentius*: Ligurinum **M** faciem **M**: filicem *Nisbet*: fruticem *Thomas*

cuncta festinat manus, huc et illuc
cursitant mixtae pueris puellae,
sordidum flammae trepidant rotantes
uertice fumum.

ut tamen noris quibus aduoceris
gaudiis, Idus tibi sunt agendae,
qui dies mensem Veneris marinae
findit Aprilem,

iure sollemnis mihi sanctiorque
paene natali proprio, quod ex hac
luce Maecenas meus affluentes
ordinat annos.

Telephum, quem tu petis, occupauit
non tuae sortis iuuenem puella
diues et lasciua tenetque grata
compede uinctum.

terret ambustus Phaethon auaras
spes et exemplum graue praebet ales
Pegasus terrenum equitem grauatus
Bellerophontem,

semper ut te digna sequare et ultra
quam licet sperare nefas putando
disparem uites. age iam, meorum
finis amorum

(non enim posthac alia calebo
femina), condisce modos, amanda
uoce quos reddas: minuentur atrae
carmine curae.

12.

Iam ueris comites, quae mare temperant,
impellunt animae lintea Thraciae,
iam nec prata rigent nec fluuii strepunt
hiberna niue turgidi.

nidum ponit Ityn flebiliter gemens
infelix auis et Cecropiae domus
aeternum opprobrium, quod male barbaras
  regum est ulta libidines.

dicunt in tenero gramine pinguium
custodes ouium carmina fistula
delectantque deum cui pecus et nigri
  colles Arcadiae placent.

adduxere sitim tempora, Vergili;
sed pressum Calibus ducere Liberum
si gestis, iuuenum nobilium cliens,
  nardo uina merebere.

nardi paruus onyx eliciet cadum,
qui nunc Sulpiciis accubat horreis,
spes donare nouas largus amaraque
  curarum eluere efficax.

ad quae si properas gaudia, cum tua
uelox merce ueni: non ego te meis
immunem meditor tingere poculis,
  plena diues ut in domo.

uerum pone moras et studium lucri
nigrorumque memor, dum licet, ignium
misce stultitiam consiliis breuem:
  dulce est desipere in loco.

13.

Audiuere, Lyce, di mea uota, di
audiuere, Lyce: fis anus; et tamen
    uis formosa uideri
      ludisque et bibis impudens

6 et **M** : heu *Campbell*   25 uerum **M** : rerum *Campbell*

et cantu tremulo pota Cupidinem
lentum sollicitas. ille uirentis et
doctae psallere Chiae
pulchris excubat in genis.

importunus enim transuolat aridas
quercus et refugit te, quia luridi
dentes, te quia rugae
turpant et capitis niues.

nec Coae referunt iam tibi purpurae
nec cari lapides tempora, quae semel
notis condita fastis
inclusit uolucris dies.

quo fugit uenus, heu, quoue color, decens
quo motus? quid habes illius, illius,
quae spirabat amores,
quae me surpuerat mihi,

felix post Cinaram notaque et artium
gratarum facies? sed Cinarae breues
annos fata dederunt,
seruatura diu parem

cornicis uetulae temporibus Lycen,
possent ut iuuenes uisere feruidi
multo non sine risu
dilapsam in cineres facem.

14.

Quae cura patrum quaeue Quiritium
plenis honorum muneribus tuas,
Auguste, uirtutes in aeuum
per titulos memoresque fastos

4 fastos **m** : -tus **M**

aeternet, o, qua sol habitabiles
illustrat oras, maxime principum?
quem legis expertes Latinae
Vindelici didicere nuper,

quid Marte posses: milite nam tuo
Drusus Genaunos, implacidum genus,
Breunosque ueloces et arces
Alpibus impositas tremendis

deiecit acer plus uice simplici,
maior Neronum mox graue proelium
commisit immanesque Raetos
auspiciis pepulit secundis,

spectandus in certamine Martio
deuota morti pectora liberae
quantis fatigaret ruinis,
indomitas prope qualis undas

exercet Auster Pleiadum choro
scindente nubis, impiger hostium
uexare turmas et frementem
mittere equum medios per ignes.

sic tauriformis uoluitur Aufidus,
qui regna Dauni praefluit Apuli,
cum saeuit horrendamque cultis
diluuiem meditatur agris,

ut barbarorum Claudius agmina
ferrata uasto diruit impetu
primosque et extremos metendo
strauit humum sine clade uictor,

te copias, te consilium et tuos
praebente diuos. nam tibi quo die

20 indomitas **M** : -tus **m**

portus Alexandrea supplex
et uacuam patefecit aulam,

Fortuna lustro prospera tertio
belli secundos reddidit exitus,
laudemque et optatum peractis
imperiis decus arrogauit.

te Cantaber non ante domabilis
Medusque et Indus, te profugus Scythes
miratur, o tutela praesens
Italiae dominaeque Romae.

te fontium qui celat origines
Nilusque et Hister, te rapidus Tigris,
te beluosus qui remotis
obstrepit Oceanus Britannis,

te non pauentis funera Galliae
duraeque tellus audit Hiberiae,
te caede gaudentes Sygambri
compositis uenerantur armis.

15.

Phoebus uolentem proelia me loqui
uictas et urbes increpuit lyra,
ne parua Tyrrhenum per aequor
uela darem. tua, Caesar, aetas

fruges et agris rettulit uberes
et signa nostro restituit Ioui
derepta Parthorum superbis
postibus et uacuum duellis

Ianum Quirini clausit et ordinem
rectum euaganti frena licentiae
iniecit emouitque culpas
et ueteres reuocauit artes

per quas Latinum nomen et Italae
creuere uires famaque et imperi
porrecta maiestas ad ortus
solis ab Hesperio cubili.

custode rerum Caesare non furor
ciuilis aut uis exiget otium,
non ira, quae procudit enses
et miseras inimicat urbes.

non qui profundum Danuuium bibunt
edicta rumpent Iulia, non Getae,
non Seres infidique Persae,
non Tanain prope flumen orti;

nosque et profestis lucibus et sacris
inter iocosi munera Liberi
cum prole matronisque nostris
rite deos prius apprecati

uirtute functos more patrum duces
Lydis remixto carmine tibiis
Troiamque et Anchisen et almae
progeniem Veneris canemus.

COMMENTARY ON *CARMEN SAECVLARE*

METRE

Sapphic stanza (see 4.2). In the *CS* there is no clausal enjambment from quatrain to quatrain, a feature that is rarer for the Sapphic than the Alcaic stanza, whose fourth line has inherently less of a closural feel to it than does the adonic. The triadic structure of the quatrains doubtless contributes to the need for stanzaic closure. There are a few instances of such enjambment in Sapphic stanzas elsewhere in the *Odes* (1.2.49; 2.2.21; 2.10.17; 2.16.37; 3.14.9; 3.20.13; 3.27.41, 65; 4.2.31; 4.6.9; 4.11.5). The avoidance of enjambment in the *CS* would have facilitated memorization for the boys and girls, and allowed a pause in the singing at the end of each verse, an obvious aid to memorization and performance.

INTRODUCTION

The ludi Latini saeculares *of 17 BCE*

> On behalf of the College of Fifteen, being head of it and with M. Agrippa as my colleague, I put on secular games, in the consulship of C. Furnius and C. Silanus. Augustus, *Mon. Anc.* 4.36–7

The *Acta* for the games of 17 BCE are at *CIL* VI 32323 = *ILS* 5050 = Pighi 1965: 107–19 = Schnegg-Köhler 2002: 24–45, hereafter '*Acta*' (for relevant parts of the text see Appendix 2); documentation of subsequent Games will be referred to by specific designation, e.g. 'the Severan *Acta*'. The inscription was discovered close to the site of the Tarentum (or Terentum) by the *pons Aelius* on the left bank of the Tiber in 1890. Edited by Mommsen (and now in the Terme Museum in Rome), it gives a precise picture of how the *ludi* proceeded. Fraenkel 364–82 remains a riveting account of the achievement of Mommsen, of what the inscription revealed and of the contestation (Mommsen vs. Vahlen) that followed in the wake of publication. It is hard to overstate the importance of this discovery, which gives an invaluable glimpse into Roman ritual and its ideological manipulation. The celebrations took place over three successive nights and days, beginning on the night of 31 May, and it is possible to reconstruct the details of the formal rituals more or less in their entirety. Of the extensive dramatic performances nothing is known other than the location of the plays. Augustus (*Acta* 90, 103, 115–16, 134–5, 139) and Agrippa (104, 120, 139) are the only named active officiants, though members of the *XVuiri* are also named (166–8) and issue a decree (110). Augustus was one of the four chairs of the *XVuiri*, and so could be seen to have officiated legitimately, but republican fictions are exposed as such by the participation of Agrippa, a member but not a chair, who also officiated. His and Julia's sons, Gaius and Lucius, were adopted by Augustus in the same year, 17 BCE. Famously, H.

is named as having composed the *carmen* (149 *carmen composuit Q. Horatius Flaccus*) which the choir of 27 boys and 27 girls sang (148 *cecinerunt*).

On the three nights of 31 May, 1 June and 2 June, Augustus, on his own and according to the Greek ritual (91 *Achiuo ritu*; chiefly marked by not covering the head with the toga), performed sacrifices at the Tarentum (90 *in Campo ad Tiberim*): burnt offerings (91 *prodigiuas*, 'to be consumed') of nine female lambs and nine she-goats for the Moerae (92–3, 31 May); nine *liba*, nine *popana*, and nine *pthoes* (all kinds of sacrificial cakes) for the Ilithyiae (115–16, 1 June); and again a burnt offering of a pregnant sow to Terra Mater (134–5, 2 June).

The prayer (*Acta* 93–7, Pighi 114, Schnegg-Köhler 36; cf. 3, 29–32 nn., Appendix 2), repeated to the several deities, looked for increase in the *maiestas* and *imperium* of the Roman people, obedience from the Latin people, victory and good health for the Roman people, favour for the Roman people and – notably – its legions and well-being and increase for the state. In all cases the officiant (Augustus or Agrippa) ended with a request for favour 'to the Roman people, the *Quirites*, the college of the *XVuiri*, to me, to my house and to my household' (99; cf. 118, 122, 137 *cetera uti supra*). Following the first night's sacrifices games were produced on a stage without the addition of a theatre, and without construction of seating (100–1). Each night's activities ended with 110 *matronae* setting up *sellisternia* to Juno and Diana.

The first day's activities (1 June) included Augustus and then Agrippa each sacrificing a bull to Jupiter Optimus Maximus on the Capitoline, with both delivering prayers identical to those at all the sacrifices, and with five other members of the *XVuiri* present (*Acta* 103–7). This was followed by *ludi Latini* (i.e. 'in Latin') back at the Tarentum (*Acta* 107), these being an extension of the previous night's performances, which were continuous though the next day (2 June, *Acta* 133), and into the third day (3 June, *Acta* 153). The first day also witnessed the *matronae* repeating *sellisternia* (a ritual involving setting out chairs for deities), after which the *XVuiri* issued a decree suspending mourning by women, in accordance with correct custom during times of celebration to the gods (*Acta* 111–14). Schnegg-Köhler (*ad Acta* 119–20) supplements persuasively to show that during the day of 2 June Agrippa alone (not with Augustus, as previously thought) sacrificed a heifer to Juno Regina, also delivering the prayer. He then dictated the prayer to the 110 *matronae*, and they repeated it. The third day, 3 June, was distinguished by bloodless sacrifices now on the Palatine to Apollo and Diana, each receiving the same offering (nine *liba*, nine *popana* and nine *pthoes*) that the Ilithyiae received on the night of 1 June.

It was at this point, immediately following the sacrifice, that the 27 boys and 27 girls, all with living fathers and mothers, sang the hymn H. composed, first on the Palatine, then again on the Capitoline. In attendance, apart from Augustus and Agrippa, were some 17 named members of the college of *XVuiri* (*Acta* 150–2), a larger named group than at any other part of the ceremony (the list at 166–8 refers to the entire *ludi*). After the song and cessation of the dramatic performances, chariot races were organized at the Tarentum along with displays by circus riders (*Acta* 154 *desultores*), and the *XVuiri* concluded by declaring a further seven days of celebration (*Acta* 160–1), involving Latin plays, different types of Greek dancing shows (*thymelici*) and stage shows (*astici*). On 11 June another edict announced animal hunts, Trojan Games and more such activity for the next day, with Agrippa presenting a chariot race and more hunting (*Acta* 163–5).

The festival was the most notable ritual of the Augustan principate and is prominent in the *Res gestae*: *Mon. Anc.* 4.36–7 *[Pr]o conlegio XVuirorum magist[er conl]e[gi]i, colleg[a] M. Agrippa, lud[os s]aecl[are]s, C. Furnio C. [S]ilano cos., feci.* The Augustan event was to have none of the old, dark associations (see Appendix 1), as the Secular Games came to celebrate not the doubling of old and new, but, more straightforwardly and more triumphantly, the establishment of the New Order. Price (*CAH* X² 820–4) in a treatment of restoration and innovation in Augustan religion notes that the *princeps* is involved not simply with restoration, but rather with a restructuring of traditions, of which the innovation of the format provides a strong example. Henderson 1998: 132 n. 157 also notes, on the basis of Zosimus and the Severan *Acta*, that it was an important part of the procedure to emphasize the novelty of the *carmen.*

As BNP 201 note, 'this occasion is uniquely well documented in a variety of surviving sources: ranging from the Sibylline oracle ordaining the procedures to the inscribed record of the games, and the hymn of Horace sung at the festival'. The mint at Rome commemorated the Games, as did other mints both in the East and West of the empire. One coin, issued in 17 BCE by the moneyer M. Sanquinius (*RIC* I²,, p. 66, no. 339,), has on the reverse 'AVGVST(*us*) DIVI F(*ilius*) LVDOS SAE(*culares*)', with a 'herald in long robe and feathered helmet holding winged caduceus and round shield on which is a six-pointed star' (Sutherland 1987: 17–19; Zanker 1988: 168–9); these heralds are mentioned at Suet. *Claud.* 21.2, in connection with Claudius' secular celebrations. Similarly coins of Domitian were to show the event of 88 CE. Varro (*ap.* August. *De ciu. D.* 22.28.11–12 = *De gent. p. R.* fr. 4 Peter = fr. 2 Fraccaro) quotes 'certain astrologers' (*genethliaci quidam*) on the topic of *palingenesia*, recording their belief that the same soul returns to the same body after a period of 440 years. This was presumably the basis on which Ateius Capito and the *XVuiri* responsible for holding the Games (Zos. 2.4.2) reckoned a *saeculum* at 110 years, 'establishing' previous celebrations for 456, 346, 236, 126 – whose consular dates were duly recorded in the Capitoline *fasti* some time after the event of 17 BCE, to which they thereby lent conveniently contrived antiquarian authority (see 21–4n.). The Sibylline oracle's mention of the 110-year cycle, along with the quindecimviral invention of Games in 126 BCE (cf. *Acta* 24–5 [*XVuiri s(acris) f(aciundis) dic(unt): | . . . centesimo et [decimo anno* etc.), show that the whole set-up was an Augustan fabrication, on which cf. Davis 2001: 112–18. These dates too feature Valerian consuls (see Appendix 1) but have the crucial advantage of permitting celebration in the target year, 16, that is *sub regno Augusti.* It may seem odd in view of such carefully contrived fictions that it took place in 17 rather than 16 BCE. There seems, however, to have been room for slight imprecision (hence the celebrations of 249 and 146, rather than 139 BCE), perhaps because the *saeculum* itself is an imprecise phenomenon, presupposing only that nobody be alive who was alive at the previous celebration.

For discussions of the 110-year cycle, cf. Censorinus, *De die natali liber* 17.9 *item Titus Liuius libro CXXXVI: eodem anno ludos saeculares Caesar ingenti apparatu fecit, quos centesimo quoque anno – his enim terminari saeculum – fieri mos fuit. contra ut decimo centesimoque anno repetantur, tam commentarii XVuirorum quam Diui Augusti edicta testari uidentur, adeo ut Horatius Flaccus in carmine, quod saecularibus ludis cantatum est, id tempus hoc modo designauerit: 'certus . . . frequentes'*; Serv. *ad* Virg. *Ecl.* 4.5 *saeculum quidam centum annorum definiunt, quidam centum decem: Horatius 'certus . . . annos'*.

The procedure for the Games was based closely on Sibylline oracles (at the time of the *ludi* safely transferred from the Capitoline and stored in the temple of Apollo, connected to Augustus' house), recently organized, and probably produced, in the case of those that predicted the Augustan *Ludi*, under the supervision of Ateius Capito (*RE* 8), a distinguished jurist and flatterer of Augustus and Tiberius (Tac. *Ann.* 3.75; Suet. *Gram.* 22; Dio 57.17.2) – doubtless honoured to be of service. The oracle is preserved by Phlegon of Tralles (*Macr.* 4 = *FGrH* 257 F 37 (V) (4); also in Zos. 2.6.1; see Appendix 3). Following Diels (and against Mommsen), Nilsson (*RE* I A 1712, 1717) and others (Diels 1890: 14; Momigliano, *JRS* 31 1941: 165; Fraenkel 365, n. 4) are clearly right in arguing that the oracle owes its origin to the planning and institution of the Augustan Secular Games. As noted, there is no evidence that the earlier (Tarentine) games of 249 and 146 BCE (if the latter even happened) involved any deities other than Dis and Proserpina, who are in turn absent from the sacrifices of 17 BCE. Other details necessitate this conclusion: for instance, sacrifices on the Palatine to Apollo, who only took up residence there in 28 BCE. The oracle and the *Acta* are pure products of Augustan propaganda, precisely in line with legislation, building programmes and everything else that the *princeps* introduced over the years. Finally, there are the syntactically separable last two lines of the oracle (37–8) praying for Roman domination over the people of Italy and Latium and so pointing to conditions well before the Augustan period, even before the dissolution of the Latin League in 338 BCE. The couplet archaizes, like the phrasing it generates in the *Acta* (*utique semper Latinus obtemperassit*), and provides fake authenticity as the entire oracle can then be retrojected onto the equally fictitious celebrations of earlier centuries, 'recorded' by the *fasti* after Ateius Capito and the *XVuiri* had invented them.

The Sibylline compositions further try to communicate their authenticity by mentioning only one location, and even that only vaguely topographical: 5 'in the Campus by the abundant water of the Tiber'. But they also mention sacrifice to Jupiter and Juno (12, 15) and to Apollo (16), because the new secular agenda of Augustus was to include the now more important sacrifice to these deities on the Capitoline and the Palatine respectively. Some telling details of the oracle are absent from the *Acta*, e.g. a bull sacrifice to Apollo: 17–18 ἶσα δεδέχθω θύματα 'he should receive the same offerings' (as Jupiter and Juno; see 49n.); that sheep and goats sacrificed to the Moerae be 'dusky' (9 κυανέας), recalling the *furuae hostiae* of the Tarentine games; similarly the pregnant sow sacrificed to Terra Mater is to be black (11 πληθομένη χοίροις ὗς . . . μέλαινα), whereas in the *Acta* it is merely pregnant and for consumption (134 *suem plenam prodigiuam*). The *Acta* refer to the Sibylline texts, notably in the opening formula of the prayers spoken by Augustus and Agrippa to the Moerae (*Acta* 92), Jupiter (105), Ilithyia (117), Juno Regina (121), Terra Mater (136), Apollo (141) and Diana (146 *eisdem uerbis Dianam*): *uti uobis/tibi in illeis libris scriptum est . . . uobis/tibi IX agnis feminis et IX capris feminis propriis* [mutatis mutandis] *sacrum fiat.*

As for post-Augustan celebrations, Claudius implictly ignored the new Augustan chronology and celebrated the games in 47 CE, the 800th birthday of Rome, and after eight 100-year *saecula* of the city's existence (Pighi 131–6). This event was repeated in 148 and 248 CE, but more as celebrations of Rome's birthday than as Secular Games *per se*. Those, on the other hand, were repeated by Domitian in 88 CE (six years early), and, back on the Augustan track, 220 years after our event, by Septimius Severus in 204 CE (Pighi 137–94). The timing was a political expedient for Augustus; for his successors it became even more a matter of convenience and self-interest.

The Carmen saeculare

Following the sacrifice to Diana on the third day of the *ludi saeculares* of 17 BCE (see Appendix 1 for the games and their context), the *Acta* (Appendix 2) record the closing ceremonies: 147–9 *pueri XXVII quibus denuntiatum erat patrimi et matrimi et puellae totidem | carmen cecinerunt. eo[de]m modo in Capitolio. | carmen composuit Q. Horatius Flaccus.* This inscription is as much a part of the performance of the games as any other detail recorded in the *Acta*. H. is the only human other than Imp. Caesar Augustus, Agrippa and the consular and the other quindecimviral persons named, a sign of his importance in Rome and a mark of the interest of Augustus in the poets, but also evidence that the *carmen* was integral to the proceedings. His poem must first therefore be understood in its ritual setting – unlike other Horatian hymns, be they to gods, goddesses or wine-jars. As Barchiesi 2002: 108 puts it, 'the poem was *performed*, full stop'. And yet only H.'s words were part of the performance. Presumably the poet was somewhere present, and he tells us in 4.6.41–4 that he trained the choir, but his presence is not material to the performance of the song, and the mode of reference in the *Acta* (148 *carmen composuit*) distinguishes his act of composition from the performative acts of the officiants, Augustus and Agrippa (90–1 *immolauit . . . precatusque est*; 139 *sacrificium fecerunt* etc.), the *XVuiri* (150 *adfuerunt*), and the assembled *matronae* (138 *sellisternia . . . habuerunt*).

Although the poem lacks the order of the ceremony desiderated by Mommsen, it constantly exhibits its place in the ritual. While it is impossible to reconstruct the *Acta* from the *CS*, once we have both it is easily seen how fundamentally the two relate, for all their considerable differences. All the deities to whom sacrifice is offered appear in the poem: 25 *Parcae* (= *Moerae*), 45, 46 *di* (= Jupiter and Juno; see 48n.), 14 *Ilithyia*, 29 *Tellus* (= *Terra Mater*), *passim* Apollo and Diana. The prominence of the last two deities reflects the occasion of the hymn in the ritual, immediately following sacrifice to these two gods (147 *sacrificioque perfecto*) on the third day. The Sibylline oracle is positioned right after the address to Apollo and Diana (5). The selection of choristers is recorded (6 *lectas*), similarly other details: the interval of 110 years (21–2), the duration of the *ludi*, with mention of night and day (23–4), sacrifice of oxen to (unnamed) Jupiter and Juno, performed by a periphrastic Augustus – without mention of Agrippa (49–52) – the role of the Palatine (65), the Latin – not just Roman – nature of the *ludi* (66), the authority of the *XVuiri* (70). Fraenkel 378, with the preponderance of critics since Mommsen's editing of the *Acta*, rejects the notion that the poem was sung as a processional song. Nor is it likely that the boys and girls sang antiphonally, responsively or in any mode other than unison (see 71n.) – though the oracle stipulated that they dance. Difference was built into the choreography and other aspects of performance, particularly given the Apollo-Diana gender dynamics. In this connection *C.* 1.21, a prayer to Diana and Apollo, links girls to Diana (1 *Dianam tenerae dicite uirgines*), boys to Apollo (2 *intonsum, pueri, dicite Cynthium*), addresses the second stanza to the girls (5 *uos*), the third to the boys (9–10 *uos* . . . *mares*) and ends with the fourth stanza focusing on Apollo. Diana's prominence in the *CS* is H.'s innovation (see 1–4n.).

The refusal to name and the Latinizing of the Moerae and Ilithyia, to whom sacrifices were offered *Achiuo ritu*, further demonstrate the loose fit between poetic composition and ritual, as H.'s own status as *Romanae fidicen lyrae* asserts itself, continuing the process at 3.30.13–14 *Aeolium carmen ad Italos* | *deduxisse modos* (see 15–16, 25 nn.). After all the *CS* is, formally speaking, still an ode of H. Whether it be called a hymn, a paean or the *Carmen saeculare*, particularly once held up against the *Acta*, it insists on its identity as a poem of H., and to that extent it is an individual poeticizing of the ritual of which it is part, with artistic, ideological and political implications. Habinek 2005: 150–7 wants seamlessness between performance and poem, but the poem does not simply record or memorialize the event, and it generally avoids the language of the event – to which, for all we know, H. may not even have been privy at the time of composition.

The *Acta* edited and understood, Mommsen was bitterly disappointed with the poem and thought H. could have done a better job by producing something more in line with the event itself, with its lavish prayers to the gods and its focus on Augustus and the household of Agrippa and Julia, which was at this juncture intended to provide the imperial succession (see Fraenkel 368–72 on the post-*Acta* reception of *CS*). And so he could have – though fortunately he did not. For all the public nature of the *Acta* and the *ludi* themselves, the *CS* is a poem, with striking dissimilarity to the details of the event at which it was sung. Barchiesi 2002 explores the difficulty of thinking about the *CS* separately from the national and even nationalistic feelings connected with it in the decades following publication of the *Acta*. The brief study of White 1993: 124–7 well shows H. working with his own view of the importance of civic continuities, rather than simply with panegyric; cf. 127: 'Drawing his inspiration from the content of the exotic ritual, he tried to illuminate for his fellow citizens meanings not conveyed by the brittle formulas of official prayer.' The poem has at times seemed reluctant in inspiration, ideologically ambiguous and even badly written – aspects that will come into focus in the commentary.

This is a good place to address the relationship of the new *saeculum* heralded by the *CS*, and the *ludi* at which it was performed, to the return of the Hesiodic golden age. Zanker discusses the poem and the celebration in a section entitled 'The Golden Age is proclaimed', and it is easy enough to map the *saeculum* of 17 BCE onto the *aurea saecula* that Augustus was to 'found/store away' (see Thomas 2001: 1–7 for the ambiguity of *condet* at *Aen.* 6.792) or the *Saturnia regna* whose return is the foundation of *Ecl.* 4. But there is not a single word in the *CS* or in the extensive record of the *ludi saeculares* to suggest H. draws any connection between the two (see 53–60, 67–8nn., e.g.). Galinsky 1996: 102 is quite right to keep the two separate and to note that the hymn, 'like the oracle and the acts of the games, stops short of proclaiming a Golden Age, and especially a Golden Age of automatic bliss or felicity'. In the same year Barker 1996 makes it quite clear how meticulous H. is in keeping the two concepts separate, and he speculates as to the meaning of the separation. In part, H. may have wanted to avoid precisely the ambiguities of the Virgilian metaphors (where Augustus and Aeneas resemble Jupiter rather than Saturn after all). In part, there are some very hard-nosed realities behind the ceremony and therefore the hymn. The prosperity of the Roman people, the success of its legions, its mastery over the world: these are the real issues behind the three days of ceremony. No room here for corn spontaneously yellowing in the fields, wine running freely in channels, or sheep dyeing themselves on hillsides of Italy.

H. has seemed to be downplaying the role of the Capitoline gods. Feeney 1998: 34 sees contestation: 'The eclipse of the old Capitoline deities by the Palatine gods of the princeps is most remarkable, and it is exposed more nakedly in ten minutes of singing than it had been in three days of ritual action.' Habinek 2005: 151 disagrees, pointing to Plut. *Publicola* 21.1 (see also Coarelli 1993), which has Valerius Publicola under the direction of the Sibylline oracles renewing games 'recommended by Apollo' (πυθοχρήστους). As Feeney acknowledges, the song was sung on the Capitoline as well as the Palatine, and in that it was sung on the day devoted to Apollo and Diana, it is hardly surprising it was weighted towards them. If we had the *ludi Latini* that immediately followed the sacrifice to Jupiter and Juno on the preceding days (*Acta* 108, 133), the imbalance would surely be partly redressed. It also makes little sense that Augustus and Capito would have so carefully constructed oracles, *ludi* and *Acta* to set up a festival which *innovated* by devoting two of the three days to Jupiter and Juno if the aim was to eclipse those gods.

The number three, along with its multiples, seems particularly associated with the three-day festival: the opening sacrifice to the Moerae consists of nine lambs and nine goats (three of each for each of the three of them), while Ilithyia on the second night and Apollo and Diana each on the third day receive nine *popana*, nine cakes, and nine *pthoes*, a total of 27 sacrificial cakes in each case, that also being the tally of each of the groups of boys and girls who sang the *CS*. Once it became clear, with publication of the *Acta*, that *uestrum* at line 37 refers not to Apollo and Diana, but rather to Jupiter and Juno (see 36–72n.), it became possible to realize the precise and intricate triadic structure of the poem. Starting from the 1868 observation of Christ that the highly Pindaric 1.12 is organized into strophe, antistrophe and epode, Menozzi 1905 pointed to the precise triadic structure of the *CS*. Two equal parts of nine quatrains each (1–36, 37–72) are concluded by a single stanza (73–76), itself marked off as the choral envoi (74–5 *reporto . . . chorus*). What is notable is the lack of any particular correspondence between the triadic pattern of the *ludi* and that of the poem. Even here we find poetic reformulation of this particular ritual feature:

Carmen saeculare	*ludi saeculares*
1st triad: stanzas 1, 2, 3	
1. First invocation of Apollo and Diana	Day 3
2. Occasion of the hymn	
3. Wish for eternity of Rome	
2nd triad: stanzas 4, 5, 6	
4. Invocation of Ilithyia, goddess of childbirth	Night 2
5. Connected allusion to *Lex Iulia de maritandis ordinibus* of 18 BCE	
6. Wish that *saeculum* be renewed for 110 more years	
3rd triad: stanzas 7, 8, 9 μεσωιδός–invocation of other gods	
7. Parcae (= Moerae in *ludi*)	Night 1
8. Tellus (= Terra Mater in *ludi*)	Night 3
9. Second invocation of Apollo and Diana	Day 3
4th triad: 10, 11, 12 the greatness of Rome (Jupiter and Juno)	Day 1/2
10. Trojan origins of Rome	
11. Aeneas goes from Troy to Italy	
12. Wish for prosperity and peace	
5th triad: 13, 14, 15 the emperor	
13. *gens Iulia* from Aeneas	
14. Achievements of Augustus in war	
15. Achievements of Augustus in peace	

6th triad: 16, 17, 18

16. Third invocation of Apollo — Day 3
17. Wish for the salvation and prosperity of the empire
18. Third invocation of Diana, mention of *XVuiri*, choristers — Day 3

ἐπῳιδός–*envoi*

19. Confidence of chorus, speaking in its own voice, that its prayers are answered

1–12 FIRST TRIAD

1–4 Formal address to Diana and Apollo highlights the reciprocity inherent in prayer and sacrifice: just as they have been and always will be worshipped, so they are to grant our prayers, with the hinge at *culti, date*: one action causes the other (see 73–7n.).

Phoebe . . . Diana: a frame with 75 *Phoebi . . . Dianae*, recapitulated in the middle: 34–6 *Apollo . . . Luna*.

siluarumque potens: looks to Diana the huntress, but also to Diana Nemorensis, worshipped at Lake Nemi (see 69–72n.); cf. 1.21.5 *laetam fluuiis et nemorum coma*; 3.22.1 *Montium custos nemorumque* (also Diana Aventina); Cat. 34.9–10 *montium domina ut fores | siluarumque uirentium*; Virg. *Aen.* 11.557 (Metabus' prayer to Diana) '*alma . . . nemorum cultrix, Latonia uirgo*'; also 9.405 (below).

Diana, | lucidum: cf. the juxtaposition at 7.25 (and 7.25–6n.) *tenebris Diana*. The goddess's name < *dīuus* 'bright', perhaps from an intermediary **dīuius*, with the long first syllable preserved at 7.25 *Dīana*), is particularly appropriate next to *tenebris*; also at Enn. *Ann.* 240 Skutsch; Virg. *Aen.* 1.499; Ov. *Met.* 8.353 (*OLD* s.v. *Diana*). For awareness of the association cf. Cic. *Nat. D.* 2.69 *Diana dicta quia noctu quasi diem efficeret* (with Ernout-Meillet s.v. *Diana*). The poem acknowledges the nocturnal aspects of the *ludi*, part of the daytime celebrations of the two gods of light, and stresses brightness in those parts devoted to them: 9 *curru nitido*; 23 *die claro*; 61 *fulgente decorus arcu*.

Lipka 2009: 164 has pointed to the greatly expanded role of Diana in the *CS*, in that she is not mentioned in the Sibylline oracle and in the proceedings receives a sacrifice only as a parhedros of Apollo, before his temple. Moreover the *Acta* give her short treatment (*Acta* 146 *eisdem uerbis Dianam*). Lipka claims her prominence is 'due to the necessity for balance between the male and female elements within the hymn, in order to ensure offspring and well-being'. Her expanded role also reflects the gender balance of the choristers.

lucidum caeli decus: a true ambiguity: of Apollo (φοῖβος' adj. = 'bright') and Diana, or just the latter? The problem has to do with how closely Apollo is to be identified with the sun, which receives its own apostrophe a few lines later, where it seems distinct from Apollo (9 *alme Sol*; see 9–12n.). Virgil had adopted a similar style at *G.* 1.5–6 *uos, o clarissima mundi | lumina*, the beginning of the poem's prayer, also of Apollo and Diana as Sun and Moon, though neither is named (see 37–72n.); cf. also the insistent notice in Porph.: *lucidum caeli decus: hoc ad ambos refertur: ad Phoebum, quia idem sol est, et Dianam, quia eadem luna est.* This is the view of Fraenkel 372, who calls the alternative (= Diana alone) a 'desperate expedient', also of Feeney 1998: 32 and Putnam 2001: 52, though neither discusses the problem. To exclude Apollo, who is clearly included in what follows (*o colendi* . . .), indeed seems improbable. On the other hand, the singular *decus* and the fact that Diana's clearly exclusive title (*siluarumque potens*) creates a syntactical separation of Apollo from the phrase in question lead to an ambiguity of identity. K–H cite Virg. *Aen.* 9.405 (Nisus' prayer to Luna) *astrorum decus et nemorum Latonia custos* in support of taking the phrase with Diana alone. At Sen. *Oed.* 405 *lucidum caeli decus* is used of Bacchus.

H.'s *Phoebe* without epithet (cf. 45–6 *di* . . . *di*) is, as K–H also note, against the practice of Hellenistic hymnic style, to which Fraenkel 372, n. 2 adds: 'Never mind Hellenistic poetry, but what about the style of Horace?' But it would have resonated strongly with the prayers of the *ludi*, each of which likewise opened with unadorned vocatives (*Acta* 92 *Moerae*, 105 *Iuppiter Optime Maxime*, 117 *Ilithyiae*, 121, 125 *Iuno Regina*, 136 *Terra Mater*, 141, 143 *Apollo*).

colendi . . . culti: the variation of forms produces an artful figure.

3 semper: ἀπὸ κοινοῦ with *colendi* and *culti*.

date quae precamur: cf. 47 *date*, and *Acta* 93, 106, 118, 122, 137, 142 for the formula *uos/te quaeso precorque uti* . . . In view of the fact that the choir starts the *CS* immediately after the sacrifice to Apollo and Diana (see intro.), it is reasonable to refer *precamur* not just to the prayers of the *CS*, but also to those just uttered by Augustus and Agrippa, once to Apollo, once to Diana. All six sets of prayers throughout the *ludi* were the same, with variation only in the specification of sacrificial object and in the number and/or gender of the deity addressed and of the officiants (see Appendix 2).

4 tempore sacro: cf. *Acta* 112 (in the decree of the *XVuiri* suspending female lament) *tam sollemnium sacrorum ludorumque tempore*; K–H refer to Pind. *Pae.* 6.5 Maehler ἐν ζαθέωι . . . χρόνωι. The phrase, though not exactly unusual, is found only here, while *sacro tempore* is completely unattested.

5 Sibyllini . . . uersus: see intro. and Appendix 3 for the oracle produced to justify the *ludi*. These were consulted during times of crisis but were also used to justify political actions, e.g. by the Catilinarian conspirator P. Cornelius Lentulus Sura, who claimed he was meant as the third 'Cornelius' (after Cinna and Sulla) destined to rule Rome (Cic. *Cat.* 3.9); or in 57 BCE, when they were used to prevent Pompey's being commissioned to restore Ptolemy Auletes to the throne of Egypt, which was to occur 'without a throng', i.e. army (Dio 39.15.2 and Cic. *Fam* 1.7.4 *sine multitudine* . . . *quem ad modum homines religiosi Sibyllae placere dixerunt*). Cicero's contemptuous view of such subterfuge is apparent in the privacy of his letters: *Fam.* 1.1.1 *senatus religionis calumniam non religione sed maleuolentia et illius regiae largitionis inuidia comprobat.* H. goes along with the programme of the *princeps* who 'clearly wished to persuade all that this new celebration was actually traditional in character: he preferred to conceal change under a cloak of continuity' (Davis 2001: 116).

monuere: common with oracles, portents, and the like (*TLL* s.v. *moneo* 1409.71–1410.10; 1412.32–47): Varro *ap.* Serv. Dan. *ad Aen.* 3.366 *monstrum, quod monet.* Cf. *Or. Sib. FGrH* 257 F 37 (V) (4) 3 μεμνῆσθαι, Ῥωμαῖε . . . 'remember, Roman . . .' – possibly based on the just-published *Aen.* 6.851 *tu regere imperio populos, Romane, memento*, which Augustus and others had also heard delivered by Virgil some time after the death of Marcellus in 23 BCE (Suet. *Vit. Verg.* 32). Both texts may, on the other hand, be independently drawing from lost Sibylline oracles. In such contexts *moneo* can mean either 'warn that something is happening' (Virg. *G.* 1.464–5 *ille* [sc. *Sol*] *etiam caecos instare tumultus* | *saepe monet*) or 'warn/advise someone to do something' (Virg. *Ecl.* 9.14–15 *nisi me . . . nouas incidere lites* | *. . . monuisset . . . cornix*). Clearly the latter is meant: *Or. Sib. FGrH* 257 F 37 (V) (4) 18–20 καὶ ἀειδόμενοί τε Λατῖνοι | παιᾶνες κούροισι κόρῃσί τε νηὸν ἔχοιεν | ἀθανάτων 'let the sound of Latin paeans sung by boys and girls fill the temple of the immortals'.

6 uirgines lectas puerosque castos: mentioned again at 34–6 *audi pueros . . . audi . . . puellas*; 71 (both groups) *puerorum*; 75 *chorus*. There were 27 of each, with living fathers and mothers in each case, that detail perhaps having to do with secular continuity or with the subjects being 'intact', 'made whole', as is the case with sacrificial animals. There may be a connection to the *camilli*, the boy attendants of priests (cf. Fest. p. 43 M. *camillus proprie appellatur puer ingenuus*). To judge from its prominence, the detail was important, though it is not mentioned by H.: *Or. Sib. FGrH* 257 F 37 (V) (4) 21–2 ἀλλὰ γονήων | πάντες ζωόντων, οἷς ἀμφιθαλὴς ἔτι φύτλη; 'all with living parents, their stock yet flourishing'; *Acta* 147–8 *puer. [XX]VII quibus denuntiatum erat patrimi et matrimi et puellae totidem* | *carmen cecinerunt.* Zos. 2.5 has πάντες ἀμφιθαλεῖς 'all with both flourishing'. Cf. Porph. *ad loc. cum enim saeculares ludos Augustus celebraret, secundum ritum priscae religionis a uirginibus puerisque praetextatis in Capitolio cantatum est*; cf. Aug. *Epist.* 71.20–1 Malcovati *pueros uirginesque patrimos matrim[osque* | *ad carmen can]endum chorosque habendos frequentes u[t adsint.* Cf. Horsfall on Virg. *Aen.* 2.238 *pueri innuptaeque puellae.*

lectas: like *castos* goes with both groups. *praetextatis* in the *Acta* indicates only that the boys are freeborn and not yet of age, but at 4.6.31–2 H. implies, as would seem likely, that they had some social status beyond that: *uirginum primae puerique claris* | *patribus orti.*

castos: not prescribed in any of the documents, but perhaps implied by the separation of the choir (for obvious reasons), also perhaps reflecting the marriage legislation to which the *Acta* explicitly refer. Cf. *Or. Sib. FGrH* 257 F 37 (V) (4) 20–1 χωρὶς δὲ κόραι χορὸν αὐταὶ ἔχοιεν | καὶ χωρὶς παίδων ἄρσην στάχυς 'let the girls have a dancing place apart, and the male progeny of boys be apart too'. See 41–2n.; also Cic. *Har. resp.* 4, on Clodius (where ritual and morality also play a role), *illum . . . cognoui muliebri ornatu ex incesto stupro atque ex domo pontificis maximi emissum.*

7 dis . . . colles: the hills of Rome figure because the hymn was sung first on the Palatine, then on the Capitoline. Jupiter and Juno are not named (see 37–72n.); the passage also looks to Diana's temple on the Aventine (69) – visible to those witnessing the *CS* in front of the Palatine temple? – which balances the allusion to Nemi in 1 *siluarum* (see 1–4, 69–72 nn.). *colles* echoes 2–3 *colendi . . . culti*, as at Stat. *Silu.* 1.4.9–13 *colunt . . . colles*, in connection with the Domitianic *ludi* of 88 CE.

septem . . . colles: the seven hills come in the seventh line of a poem highly aware of numbers. K–H note the periphrasis is an oracular feature: *Or. Sib.* 1.112 Geffcken οἵτινες ἀνδρωθέντες ἐφ' ἑπτὰ λόφοισι κραταιοῖς 'those brought up on the seven mighty hills'; also 115. For Ῥώμη ἑπτάλοφος 'seven-hilled Rome', see *Or. Sib.* 4.2.18; 13.45; 14.108; and for phrasing in the Sibylline oracle cf. *FGrH* 257 F 37 (V) (4). However, as Holland 1953: 33 has shown, '[i]t was probably Vergil who established the seven hills as the eternal symbol of Rome', without actually being clear which hills were included, since the canonical seven were established later. Virgil is the first to make Rome's 'seven hills' representative of the city: *G.* 2.535 *septemque una sibi muro circumdedit arces*; repeated as a prophecy, with tense adjustment, by Anchises at *Aen.* 6.783 *septemque una sibi muro circumdabit arces*; thence Tib. 2.5.55, in a poem redolent of the *Aeneid*, *carpite nunc, tauri, de septem montibus herbas | dum licet: hic magnae iam locus urbis erit*, and thence to *CS* 7. This is, as Holland shows, very much an Augustan development, based on Varro's thinking (*Ling.* 5.41; 6.24; but cf. also Cic. *Att.* 6.5.2 [26 June 50 BCE] ἄστεως ἑπταλόφου). The festival 'Septimontium' (11 Dec.) was derived in folk etymology from *septem montes*, but probably derives from the defences (*saepti montes*) of the central settlements on and around the Palatine. See Maltby s.v. *Septimontium.*

8 dicere carmen: a frame with 76 *dicere laudes*; cf. *Acta* 148 *carmen cecinerunt. cano* is used only of the Fates' song in the *CS* (25 *ueraces cecinisse*), though cf. 22 *cantus* of the song in its performance; also 4.12.9–10n. Cf. 4.6.43, the girl chorister, grown-up, '*reddidi carmen*'.

9–12 'There follows one of the most glorious passages in ancient poetry' (Fraenkel 371). The lines appealed to Goethe:

> Hohe Sonne, du weilst, und du beschauest dein Rom!
> Größeres sahest du nichts und wirst nichts Größeres sehen,
> Wie es dein Priester Horaz in der Entzückung versprach.
>
> *Römische Elegien* 15.26–8

The stanza is perhaps appealing more in its simplicity than its splendour. Fraenkel 373, n. 1 quotes Alfred Noyes' 1947 archaizing translation: 'O kindly Sun, who in thy glorious chariot bringest forth the day, and hidest it away at evening, and art reborn, another and the same forever, O, mayest thou never see in all thy course aught nobler than the city of Rome.' Cf. 4.14.5–6 *o, qua sol habitabiles* | *illustrat oras*. As the first triad ends with the sun, so the second will end with night (23–4n.).

The address to the Sun continues the ambiguity of the poem. The oracle insisted on the close identity of Apollo and the Sun: *FGrH* 257 F 37 (V) (4) 16–17 καὶ Φοῖβος Ἀπόλλων | ὅστε καὶ Ἠέλιος κικλήσκεται, 'and Phoebus Apollo, who is also called Helios'. H.'s sun here however does not look much like the Apollo of the rest of the poem, in spite of the reference in *curru nitido* to Apollo as sun god in his chariot atop the Palatine temple (see 9, 10–11n.). For a similar effect with Diana/Luna see 35n. Addresses to the Sun are doubtless paeanic in origin, as at Pind. *Pae.* 9.1 ἀκτὶς ἀελίου, κτλ. 'beam of the Sun . . .'

9 alme Sol: the epithet, *ab alendo* (Paul. Fest. p. 7 M., Servius *ad G.* 1.7), used only here of the sun as god, never of Apollo, would have led the Roman audience away from a close identification of the two. It is used of numerous female deities (*TLL* s.v. *almus* 1703.39–79), particularly those connected with generation, feeding, nurturing: Venus, Tellus, Ceres, Diana etc.; therefore also of Priapus at *CLE* 1504.31. The masculine vocative of the adjective is confined to such instances, and the nominative is in essence found only twice with *ager*, essentially = *Terra* or *Tellus* (Virg. *G.* 2.330 *parturit almus ager*), taken over by Ovid *Met.* 15.204–5 (also in a celebration of spring) *almus* | *ludit ager*. At Val. Flacc. 5.550–1 *o Iouis alma* | *progenies* Castor, as one of the Dioscuri, is a man-helper and is still a mortal at this stage anyway, so this barely counts, and the *TLL* and *OLD* should have distinguished. August. *De ciu. D.* 7.11 is unique in claiming a cult name *Almus* for Jupiter, *quod aleret omnes*, but this would be consistent with Jupiter as sky god, who mingles with Tellus so as to generate life, and cf. Virg. *G.* 2.325–7 *tum pater omnipotens fecundis imbribus Aether* | *coniugis in gremium laetae descendit, et omnes* | *magnus alit magno commixtus corpore fetus*. In fact H.'s *alme* belongs more with the examples at *TLL* 1704.41–56, in the company of *lux*, *dies*, which thereby become personified, a context frequent in Virgil: *Aen.* 1.306 (morning after the storm) *ut primum lux alma data est*; 8.455; 11.182–3, and cf. also Ov. *Met.* 5.444 *ubi alma dies hebetarat sidera*. Cf. 33, also of Apollo, *mitis placidusque*.

curru nitido: points in the direction of Apollo-Helios in his chariot on the Palatine temple. But the proximity of *Phoebo* to *Solis* at Prop. 2.31.9–11, the evidence for the statue, also suggests a relationship rather than identity: *templum,* | *et patria Phoebo carius Ortygia:* | *in quo Solis erat supra fastigia currus*. For good discussion of the pairing see Hardie 1986: 356 n. 64.

qui: markedly postponed.

10 promis et celas: Fraenkel 445, n. 3 sees *celare* as a variant for *condere*, with the Sun acting as *condus promus* (for which cf. Plaut. *Pseud.* 608). The doubling to capture night and day is quite close to the oracle, though H. refers to the results (nighttime *and* daytime) effected by the contrasting acts of Sun, while the oracle, of which H. shows awareness, refers to the result (nighttime) effected by the contrasting actions of night *and* sun: *Or. Sib. FGrH* 257 F 37 (V) (4) 6–7 νὺξ ἡνίκα γαῖαν ἐπέλθηι, | ἠελίου κρύψαντος ἑὸν φάος, 'when night comes over the earth as the sun hides its light'.

10–11 aliusque et idem | nasceris: with primary reference to the relationship of the morning sun to the setting one of the night before, but also underscores the Apollo-Sun ambiguity already in play, since *alius* and *idem* apply as well to that relationship and identity.

11–12 nihil urbe Roma | . . . maius: reflects the first item in each of the prayers of the *ludi*: *Acta* 93–4 *uti imperium maiestatemque p. R. Quiritium duelli domique auxis/auxitis. maius* suggests size as well as greatness, and cf. Virg. *Ecl.* 1.23–5 (of Tityrus' discovery of the size of Rome) *sic paruis componere magna solebam. | uerum haec tantum alias inter caput extulit urbes | quantum lenta solent inter uiburna cupressi*; cf. *Aen.* 7.602–3 *maxima rerum | Roma.*

urbe Roma: the formal title (*urbs Roma*), the unmarked way of saying 'the city of Rome', is otherwise only found in the Roman Odes (3.5.12 *incolumi Ioue et urbe Roma*, where 'the phraseology alludes to an old religious formula': N–R *ad loc.* with further references), not elsewhere in Roman poetry it seems. Enn. *Ann.* 77 Skutsch comes close (*certabant urbem Romam Remoramne uocarent*), but *Romam* is predicative; similarly Virg. *Ecl.* 1.19 *urbem quam dicunt Romam.* The prosaic touch anticipates the earth-bound language of the second triad.

13–24 SECOND TRIAD

The lines deal with childbirth, marriage laws and their connection to the secular celebrations. All three stanzas, particularly the central one, are marked by woodenness of language and studied poverty of poetic expression. So Page: 'if, as in stanza 5, even Horace halts, we may well pity the genial bard, who finds himself compelled to invoke a poetical blessing on legislation which his taste must have led him to dislike, and his common sense must have despised as visionary'. Fraenkel 374, on the other hand: 'I, for one, am not ashamed to confess that I am moved when I picture these handsome children, who represent Rome's finest youth, singing to the goddess *diua, producas subolem patrumque prosperes decreta . . .*' He ends up (375, citing lines 20–4) pleading with the reader: 'Let us admit that this is a lovely climax and that, whatever *raison d' être* lay behind this part of the ceremonies (the sacrifices to the Ilithyiae), the whole triad is excellent poetry.' Page's reading seems on balance the more true to the realities of these lines.

13–20 Both stanzas are addressed to Ilithyia, to whom sacrifices of nine *liba*, *popana* and *pthoes* were offered on the second night of the *ludi* (*Acta* 117–18).

13–14 rite . . . lenis 'gentle at duly opening up childbirth when its time is come' – the wording seems coy. Cf. ps.-Acro *ad loc.* on *rite*: *solito tempore. rite* characterizes the *ludi* at 4.6.37–8 *rite Latonae puerum canentes, | rite crescentem face Noctilucam. aperire* is an epexegetical infinitive, for which cf. 1.24.17 *non lenis precibus fata recludere.*

14 Ilithyia: Greek goddess of childbirth and labor pains. It is hard to know how puzzled the audience would have been by the opening word uttered by Augustus (*Acta* 117 *Ilithyia!*), sacrificing *Achiuo ritu* (*Acta* 91), since the name is attested in Latin in the *Acta* and here for the first time and otherwise appears only twice in Ovid (*Am.* 2.13.21; *Met.* 9.283) and once in the elder Pliny (*HN* 25.73). But the goddess and the name are old, unsurprisingly in view of her function. Eileithyia is a Cretan deity mentioned in the Linear B tablets, and although an etymology that connects to forms of ἔρχομαι (ἤλυθον, ἐλήλυθα) is appealing (referring to the *onset* of labor or *coming* to help; see Hainsworth on *Il.* 11.270), the name is probably pre-Greek, in which case it may be related to the important Cretan town of Eleutherna (*c.* 25 miles from the cave of Eileithyia). At *Od.* 19.188 the cave of Eileithyia is clearly a famous site, and the archaeologists have found in it evidence 'for continuous cult use from the third millennium BCE to the fifth or sixth century AD' (Russo *et al. ad Od.* 19.188). Crete was defeated and became a Roman province in 69–67 BCE, and the cave and its ritual potential, famous from Homer and still in business, may have come to Octavian's attention in his travels of 31–29. There are also connections with Apollo: at *Hymn. Hom. Ap.* 89–125 Eilithyia, twice with the epithet μογοστόκος 'causing birth-pangs', attends the birth of the god on Delos. At Pind. *Ol.* 6.41–2 Apollo sends Eileithyia and the Moirai to attend Evadne at the birth of Iamus. Homer has the name, also μογοστόκος/οι, in the singular (*Il.* 16.187) and the plural (*Il.* 11. 270). The plural also appears in the oracle, here with a propitiating epithet, suggesting a connection and even response to the Homeric Εἰλείθυιαι: *FGrH* 257 F 37 (V) (4) 9–10 ἐπὶ ταῖς δ' Εἰλειθυίας ἀρέσασθαι | παιδοτόκους θυέεσσιν, ὅπηι θέμις 'and also to appease the childbirth-favouring Eileithyiai with sacrifices in the proper way'. Such alternation of singular and plural occurs with other minor deities, such as Eros/Cupid, Genitalis (cf. 15–16n.).

15–19 probas . . . producas . . . prosperes . . . prolis: a productive accumulation.

15–16 siue tu Lucina probas uocari | seu Genitalis: the inclusion of variant names, presumably to assure the attention of the deity addressed, is usually thought a feature of Roman prayer, though it is noteworthy that Augustus and the *XVuiri* felt no such need in the actual prayer of the *ludi*, so the phenomenon may be more literary than actual. The textual examples, with variants of H.'s *probas uocari*, and including 3.21.4–6 *pia testa . . . | quocumque lectum nomine Massicum | seruas*, are collected by Pulleyn 1994: 19–20: Cat. 34.21–2 *sis quocumque tibi placet | sancta nomine*; Apul. *Met.* 11.2 *regina caeli, siue tu Ceres alma . . . seu tu caelestis Venus . . . seu Phoebi soror . . . seu nocturnis ululatibus horrenda Proserpina*; also Serv. *ad Aen.* 2.351; Macrob. 3.9.10. It is notable that H. has Lat. *Genitalis*, as he has Lat. *Parcae* (see intro.; 25–8n. on *Parcae*).

Lucina: the ambiguous identity continues. Juno will never be named in the hymn (although the sacrifice of the second day is devoted to her, as Juno Regina, *Acta* 119–32), but Juno Lucina is the chief goddess of childbirth and owner of the epithet. From 375 BCE she had a temple in a grove (*lucus*) on the Cispian Hill, close to the Clivus Suburanus, where cult inscriptions have been found; see Richardson s.v. 'Iuno Lucina, Aedes'. Cf. Virg. *Ecl.* 4.10 *casta faue Lucina*, where the rest of the line suggests an identity with Diana: *tuus iam regnat Apollo*. In fact, as Lipka 2009: 165 notes, H.'s assimilation of Ilithyia to Juno and/or Diana blurs what is a clear and strong distinction in the *ludi*, where the former is one of the Greek deities receiving night-time sacrifice and prayer outside the *pomerium* (*Acta* 115–18), while Juno Regina (119–31) and Diana (139–46) are worshipped by day on the Capitoline and Palatine.

Genitalis: Bentley rejected the name, in the belief that the *di genitales* are the *di geniti*, as opposed to the *di adoptiui*, and conjectured *Genetyllis*, a 'woman's goddess' (Dover on Ar. *Nub.* 52), or 'goddess of one's birth-hour' (LSJ), accepted by Shackleton Bailey. But Skutsch (on Enn. *Ann.* 110) argues cogently against this distinction, and a Latin epithet seems desirable here. If *genitalis* can = 'of or connected with one's birth or birthday' (*OLD* s.v. 3), *Genitalis* easily fits the deity connected to that event.

17–20 'Goddess, may you bring forth progeny, and may you further the decrees of the senate concerning the coupling of women and the marriage law productive of new offspring.' Clearly a reference to the *Lex Iulia de maritandis ordinibus* of 18 BCE, with the title's *disiecta membra* easily found in *super iugandis feminis* and *lege marita*. Cf. the wording at Livy *Perioch.* 59.17 *exstat oratio eius, quam Augustus Caesar, <cum> de maritandis ordinibus ageret, uelut in haec tempora scriptam in senatu recitauit.*

prosperes: otherwise in prose after Lucilius, and used in formal prayers (though not in the *Acta*) as at Livy 8.9.6–7 *Iane, Iuppiter . . . uos precor . . . uti populo Romano Quiritium uim uictoriam prosperetis*; perhaps belongs to old religious language. For the furthering of specific legislation (as here) and the like, cf. Tac. *Hist.* 4.53.3 [*praetor*] *deos precatus, uti coepta prosperent*; *Ann.* 3.56.3 [*Tiberius*] *principio litterarum ueneratus deos, ut consilia sua rei publicae prosperarent*; *TLL* s.v. *prospero* 2210.46–70.

decreta: only here in H. and not surprisingly found generally in prose. Ovid has three instances, and Luc. 1.489 *decreta senatus* only proves the point.

super iugandis | feminis: close to the syntax of the law's title, *de maritandis ordinibus*, a severely prosaic construction (prep. + noun modified by gerundive) notably absent from H.'s corpus with three exceptions, none from the lyrics, and each less ponderous than the current example: *Epist.* 1: 2.29 *in cute curanda* (a poeticizing of standard *in corpore curando* etc.); 16.68 *semper in augenda festinat et obruitur re* (word order deflects the prosaic); 19.7–8 *numquam nisi potus ad arma | prosiluit dicenda* (likewise); the monosyllabic prepositions provide additional relief. *super* + ablative (= *de*) likewise has a formal and official tone (see 2.42–3n.), and instances with the gerundive are otherwise only in prose (Davis 2001: 127, n. 77). At the same time, *iugare* itself is a poeticism, with avoidance of the official language of the *Lex Iulia de maritandis ordinibus*, but there is a general tension between the words and the Sapphic stanza that contains them.

feminis: the girls will become the *feminae* of whom they sing, the *nupta[e]* of 6.41, and the *matronae* of 15.27.

feraci: cf. *Epod.* 5.21–2 *Hiberia* | . . . *uenenorum ferax*, the first occurrence of the normal (agricultural) sense + objective genitive; modifies an incorporeal noun (*lege*) with such a genitive only here and at Livy 9.16.19 *illa aetate, qua nulla uirtutum feracior fuit* (cf. *TLL* s.v. *ferax* 489.47–8).

21–4 'so that the cycle firmly fixed through every ten times eleven years may bring back singing and games crowded three times by bright day and as often by welcome night'. A not particularly lyrical quatrain, though one that is typical of Horatian lyric in its economical inclusion of ceremonial details, the 110-year cycle, games and choral performances, over the course of three days and three nights. Unusual numbers are poetically challenging, and H., here faced with no choice, like Housman's Manilius (II: xiii), shows 'an eminent aptitude for doing sums in verse'; cf. also 1.7; *Epist.* 1.20.27.

certus: the emphatic insistence in the initial position only draws attention to the fact that the timing was 'fixed' by Capito's recent calculation.

undenos: the distributive form is used in Latin 'with an exactness which is foreign to our idiom whenever repetition is involved' (Gildersleeve and Lodge 187).

undenos deciens: see intro. for the 110-year cycle, discussed in a number of texts.

orbis: recurring temporal sequence, as of the cleansing of souls in Virgil's Underworld: *Aen.* 6.745 *perfecto temporis orbe*; cf. *TLL* s.v. *orbis* 912.51–64; *OLD* 16b; a rather new sense, perhaps calqued on the Greek κύκλος, as in the oracle: *FGrH* 257 F 37 (V) (4) 2 εἰς ἐτέων ἑκατὸν δέκα κύκλον ὁδεύσας 'traversing its circuit for 110 years'. On *orbis* . . . *referat* cf. 4.6.42 saeculo festas referente luces.

cantus . . . ludos: the only singing specified in the *Acta* is of the *CS* itself (147–9; see intro.), though the dramatic presentations may have had a musical element, and indeed at the very beginning of the ceremony we find reference to trumpet music, to which *cantus* (*OLD* s.v. 5) could refer: *Acta* 88 *aenatores in funere canere* [*solitos*. The designation *ludi* may be taken in two senses, referring to the overall celebration (*Acta* 83 *ludos Latinos saeculares comm*[*ittemus*) or to the various theatrical *ludi* that took place on the first night (100) and the first and second days (108–9, 133).

die claro: has the feel of a cliché but is found not so frequently: once in Catullus (61.85–6 *clarum ab Oceano diem uenientem*), and similarly in Virg. *Aen.* 5.43 *clara dies*. The gender split in *claro* . . . *grata* suits that of the twins – though *dies* in H. is masc. more often than fem. anyway.

grata: helps avoid any suggestion of the original aim of the *ludi*, nocturnal rites of Dis pater and Proserpina. Also of night as the time of welcome sleep:

Epist. 1.17.6 *grata quies et... somnus,* and cf. Virg. *G.* 4.402 (Proteus and his seals retire for a nap) *cum... pecori iam gratior umbra est.*

frequentes: the *Acta* record the performance and prayers of the *ludi* in great detail but have little to say about the audience, beyond identifying it (*populi Romani Quirites*) as the beneficiaries of each of the prayers. It may be assumed crowds came from throughout Italy and beyond, since the oracle also enjoined an 'abundant gathering' (35 παμπληθὴς ἄγυρις) by day and night, the source of H.'s *frequentes*?

25–36 THIRD TRIAD (μεσῳδός)

Mention of night in 24 well leads into this section, with a stanza each for the Fates and for Tellus, recipients of sacrifice on the first (*Moerae*) and third (*Terra Mater*) nights. It would have reflected the order of the *ludi* had Ilithyia been included in this triad, but her important connection to marriage laws and childbirth gave her an earlier role in the hymn. So the final stanza of the triad (33–6) will consist of a second invocation to Apollo and Diana, completing the frame of the opening lines.

The three Fates, Lachesis (Allotter), Clotho (Spinner/Spinster) and Atropos (Unswerving), are established and first mentioned by name at Hes. *Theog.* 905–6, where they are said to grant mortals the possession of good and of evil. Μοῖραι in the plural appear just once in Homer, at *Il.* 24.49, while *Od.* 7.197 has the 'dread spinners' (κλῶθές τε βαρεῖαι) who wove Odysseus' fate for him at his birth. For treatment of Μοῖρα/Μοῖραι, see Fraenkel on Aesch. *Ag.* 1535f.

25–8 The text printed here is the one given in most editions and the majority of MSS, but it is open to grave doubts. Following Lambinus a number of others, including Peerlkamp, Kiessling and Vahlen, believed, in the words of Wickham: 'The relative clause seems rightly taken... with "bona iungite fata," in a similar construction to "quod felix faustumque sit," etc.' That is, to modify Page, 'You Fates, truthful in your prophetic song – as has been once appointed, and so may the abiding landmark of our fortunes preserve it – link happy destinies to a happy past.' *id* is thus understood with *quod,* and *stabilisque* is a compression of *quodque stabilis.* Fraenkel 172 n. 3 finds this 'wholly artificial' and seems right to follow Lenchantin *Rendic. Istituto Lombardo, Cl. di Lettere* 77 (1943–4) 363–4 in taking *quod semel... seruet* as the object of *cecinisse,* whereby *quod* is both subject of *dictum est* and object of *seruet,* with optative force: 'You, O Fates, true in prophesying what has been once and for all decreed and which the immovable boundary marker of destiny is to preserve'. Lenchantin gives examples for the syntax: Varro, *Ling.* 9.7 *quae possunt dici atque* [sc. *quae*] *illic praeterii*; *Rust.* 1.30 *quae fieri oportuerit et* [sc. *quae*] *non sunt absoluta*; Cic. *De or.* 2.43 *illud tertium, quod a Crasso tactum est et, ut audio, ipse Aristoteles... adiunxit.*

Mueller pronounced the homophony of *-st st-* in 26 to be 'unmöglich', which PHI shows not to be *quite* the case, but it comes close enough to be an important factor: this would be the only instance in H., it is absent from Virgil (*Aen.* 7.552–3 *abunde est:* | *stant*, with line-end and strong punctuation, the only such instance, is less offensive), Catullus has one example (78.5 *Gallus homo est stultus*, where the offense and the effect may be deliberate), as does Lucretius (5.1365), Propertius has two (2.34.53; 3.15.30), Tibullus, none. Ovid is fairly unconcerned, with eleven instances (*Her.* 15.1; 19.146; *Ars* 2.444; *Rem.* 207; *Met.* 3.186; 4.300; 6.55; 8.451 (across line-end); *Fast.* 5.448; *Trist.* 2.1.257; 5.12.62), Lucan has three (3.461; 6.378; 8.592), Statius, one (*Ach.* 1.600). It was also avoided by prose authors, Livy, for instance, having only ten examples, with intervening punctuation in all but three cases. There is therefore something to be said for Bentley's emendation of lines 26–7 *quod semel dictum stabilis per aeuum* | *terminus seruet*, accepted by Mueller and now by Shackleton Bailey, particularly since *est* is thereby dispensed with. On the other hand, the awkwardness may be part of the effect, so *est* might be desirable, as in the case at Cat. 78.5.

ueraces cecinisse 'truthful in your prophetic song', or 'truthful in singing what...', in either case epexegetical infinitive. Fraenkel 375, n. 2 sees the prophetic song of the Fates as originating at Cat. 64.303–81 (cf. 306 *ueridicos Parcae coeperunt edere cantus*), noting that their song (if they sing it) at Ar. *Au.* 1734–42 is a *hymenaeus*, rather than prophecy (as for Cat. and H.); and cf. Virg. *Ecl.* 4.46–52 for the song of the Fates, especially the language of 46–7 *'talia saecla' suis dixerunt 'currite' fusis* | *concordes stabili fatorum numine Parcae*. The Catullan lines are both epithalamium and prophecy (of the outcome of the marriage, namely Achilles), and the association is found in Plato, *Resp.* 617c where the three Fates sing (ὑμνεῖν), 'Lachesis of things past, Clotho of the present and Atropos of what is to come': Λάχεσιν μὲν τὰ γεγονότα, Κλωθὼ τὰ δὲ ὄντα, Ἄτροπον τὰ δὲ μέλλοντα. *ueraces cecinisse* perhaps (like *ueridicus*) aims to capture Gr. ἀληθόμαντις, for which see Aesch. *Ag.* 1241 (Cassandra, of herself).

Parcae: the Fates are given their Latin name, in contrast to Augustus' hellenizing *Moerae* (*Acta* 91–2 *Achiuo ritu*... *Moerae*; the word otherwise surviving in Latin only at Gell. 3.16.11); see intro., 14, 15–16nn.

Parcae... semel... terminus: in view of the importance of numbers, there seems to be some word play as the (three) Fates come into H.'s focus.

stabilisque... seruet: the *terminus rerum*, 'boundary-marker of destiny', refers to the limits set for Rome, which will safeguard that which has been predicted, as at Acc. *Hec.*, fr. 481 Ribb. *ueter fatorum terminus sic iusserat*. The concept is in the air in Augustan Rome: so Jupiter's prophecy at *Aen.* 1.278–9 *his* [sc. *Romanis*] *ego nec metas rerum nec tempora pono:* | *imperium sine fine dedi*; 286–7 *Caesar,* | *imperium Oceano, famam qui terminet* [cf. *seruet* for the same mood] *astris* – with *terminus* distinct in sense from the example in Accius; 4.614 (of Dido's curse and wish that Aeneas' success and happiness be truncated) *et sic fata Iouis poscunt, hic terminus haeret*.

27–8 Understand *fatis* with *peractis*: the Fates are to yoke good future fates with those past.

fata < *fari*, picks up on 25 *cecinisse*, 26 *dictum* and ultimately 8 *dicere carmen*, a reminder that this is a poem with a life outside and beyond the ritual it marks.

29–32 Again with name-change (Tellus), reflects the sacrifice of the third night, 2 June, a burnt offering of a pregnant sow by Augustus alone to Terra Mater, with details as at the other sacrifices – prayer that good fortune may attend the Roman people etc. (see Appendix 2). The oracle has a detail absent from the *Acta*: *Or. Sib. FGrH* 257 F 37 (V) (4) 10–11 αὖθι δὲ Γαίηι | πληθομένη χοίροις ὗς ἱρεύοιτο μέλαινα 'then let there be a sacrifice to Earth of a pregnant black sow'. H. elsewhere talks of pig sacrifice, including one to Tellus, though the context is archaic and rustic (*Epist.* 2.1.143 [*agricolae prisci*] *Tellurem porco, Siluanum lacte piabant*; also *C.* 3.17.15; *S.* 2.3.165; *Epist.* 1.16.58). Not here, however, and the lines are of a more poetic nature than those preceding: earth, supportive of crops and herd, is to deliver grain, while the waters and breezes of Jupiter, in his capacity as sky god, are to nourish them. The words conjure up the *hieros gamos*, the procreative union of sky (*Iouis*) and earth (*Tellus*), very different from the context of the *Lex Iulia de maritandis ordinibus*. For the fulfilment of this prayer see 8.17–18 *tutus bos etenim rura perambulat, | nutrit rura Ceres almaque Faustitas*; 15.4–5 *tua, Caesar, aetas | fruges et agris rettulit uberes*... The planners of this part of the ceremony and the designers of the Ara Pacis worked with similar images and metaphors.

fertilis frugum: cf. Sall. *Iug.* 17.5 (in the ethnographical sketch of Libya) *ager frugum fertilis, bonus pecori*; Livy 5.34.2 (Gaul) *frugum hominumque fertilis*; 38.15.9 (Sagalassus in Turkey) *agrum*... *uberem fertilemque omni genere frugum*. The alliteration has an archaic effect, appropriate in the oldest and most important human prayer, for success of crops and herd. With the following *pecorisque* the alliteration recalls Cato's lustration of the fields at *Agr.* 141.3, well analyzed by Watkins 1995: 199:

utique tu
fruges frumenta   uineta uirgultaque
  grandire   (du)eneque euenire siris
pastores *pecuaque*   salua seruassis
duisque (du)onam salutem   ualetudinemque
  mihi domo familiaeque nostrae

Less artfully ordered alliterative patterns, and even the language, survive into the prayer of the *Acta*: 94 *duelli domique*; 95 *uictoriam ualetudinem*; 96 *saluam seruetis*; and Cato's final formula resonates in the mouth of Augustus, *uilicus* and *magister* both: 99 *mihi domo familiae*, in the plural when Agrippa joins the officiating: 130 *nobis domibus familiis*.

30 spicea... corona 'Ceres of the wheat-spiked crown'; ablative of description, of the 'original', external type (Woodcock 64–5), an extension of an ablative of accompaniment or attendant circumstances, e.g. *Ceres corona spicea graditur*. The adjective appears first in Virg. *G.* 1.314 *spicea*... *messis*; first with reference to material, also with *corona*, at Tib. 1.1.15–16 *corona | spicea*; see Maltby *ad loc.* with further references, especially to F. Cairns in *Emerita* 67 (1999) 219–30 and to Gell. 7.7.8, with the valuable information that the insignia of the Arval Brothers, whose cult Augustus seems to have revived around 29/8 BCE, included such a crown: *spicea corona et albae infulae*.

32 Iouis: ἀπὸ κοινοῦ with *aquae* and *aurae*, both controlled by Jupiter as rain- and sky-god, who is to provide them in the right measure. So of stormy rain and wind at Virg. *G.* 1.418 *Iuppiter uuidus Austris*; also *G.* 2.419, of storm and hail, which damage the ripening vines: *et iam maturis metuendus Iuppiter uuis*. Cf. 3.4.7–8 for the pairing in an idealized setting: *lucos, amoenae | quos et aquae subeunt et aurae*.

33–6 The third triad closes with recapitulation of the addressees of the opening to the first triad and to the poem (1–4), as H. asks Apollo and Diana to listen to the voices of the boy and girl choristers respectively, the separate subjects of the second stanza of the poem (5–8). The combination here creates a pleasing gender-driven chiasmus (*pueros, Apollo . . . Luna, puellas*), which, however, does nothing to back up claims of separate vocal parts for the two groups, though the identity of both comes across in the lyrics of the *carmen*. They return in the frame at the end (75).

condito . . . telo: cf. *Epod* 7.1–2 *aut cur dexteris | aptantur enses conditi*. The line seeks emphatically to leave the Actian Apollo behind and to identify the non-violent Apollo, with the enclosed adjectives reinforcing the participial clause; similarly cf. the Apollo of 4.6.25–44 (but *not* the one of 4.6.1–24), and cf. 2.10.19–20 *neque semper arcum | tendit Apollo*; 3.4.60 *numquam umeris positurus arcum*.

audi pueros . . . audi . . . puellas: who speaks? The choristers, with an emphasis on their gender separation, sing the words, so the audience at the *ludi* would have mentally supplied *nos* – 'hear our prayer'. On the other hand, H. avoids the personal pronoun, since, following Greek practice, the chorus speaks as a singular at 74–5 *reporto, | . . . chorus*.

35 siderum regina bicornis: cf. 4.6.38 *crescentem face Noctilucam*. Highly poetic phrasing, as Porph. noted: *poeticum est lunam siderum reginam dicere, quod clarior inter astra uideatur*. Similarly the use of *bicornis* for Luna/Diana, not found before H. (nor much after), who will have taken it from the Greek, where it is also rare: Philodem. *Epigr.* 9.1 GP = *Anth. Pal.* 5.123.1 νυκτερινὴ δίκερως φιλοπάννυχε φαῖνε, Σελήνη, 'Shine Moon of the night, two-horned one, lover of parties'. There is abundant evidence of statues, coins, lamps, vases, cameos etc., mostly dating to the Hellenistic period or Republic/early empire, in which Artemis-Diana/Selene-Luna is crowned with a crescent moon with its horns up: *LIMC* s.v. 'Artemis' 906, 907, 909; 'Astra' 52, 53; 'Selene, Luna' 2, 5, 14, 15, 21 (between the Dioscuri, each of whom has a star on his forehead), 23. *regina* is possible, where *rex*, even of the Sun King, remains ideologically problematic.

37–72 As became clear with publication of the *Acta*, *uestrum* (37) must refer not to Apollo and Diana, but rather to the Capitoline gods, chiefly Jupiter and Juno, to whom Augustus and Agrippa each sacrificed a bull and a heifer respectively (*Acta* 106, 122, and cf. 49 *bobus . . . albis* and n.). Once the identity was established the structure of the poem became clear, with division coming here, and the first half addressed to the other gods, the second introducing the Capitoline deities and shifting the focus to Rome (37–48) and Augustus (49–60), before returning to Apollo and Diana (61–72). The poem's ending then returns to Jupiter and all the gods (73 *Iouem... deosque cunctos*), but it is true that the absence of his name keeps the reader, if not necessarily the audience on the day, thinking of Apollo and Diana. It is also notable that the Palatine (65) and Aventine (69) are named, while there is no mention of the Capitoline.

37–48 FOURTH TRIAD

Here the focus shifts to Rome and its Trojan beginnings, with mention of Aeneas and Romulus and a prayer for the success of the race. The triad is a single twelve-line sentence addressed to unnamed gods (45, 46 *di*), whose identity depends on a knowledge of the Sibylline oracles and of the prayers inscribed on the Augustan *Acta*, where as would be expected in a real prayer, every deity is meticulously named. The contrast with the *CS* is as sure a sign as could be that H.'s poem has a poetic function and poetic aims that go beyond simply characterizing or participating with liturgical precision in the celebrations.

The period is enjambed, convoluted and hypotactic throughout the protasis, which occupies the first two stanzas, then paratactic and end-stopped in the third, as is appropriate for an actual prayer, with the triadic stucture reflected in its double tricola: three indirect objects, each with a modifier, *iuuentae-senectuti-genti*; three direct objects (*mores-quietem-remque*), shifting to a second tricolon *abundans* (*remque-prolemque-et decus omne*).

37–44 Virgil's pro-Trojan Jupiter throughout the *Aeneid*, about to be the focus of H.'s poem (see 40–4n.), and the reconciled Juno at its end, are unnamed (*uestrum... di... di*) guarantors of the eternity of Rome. The fact that Rome's past and origins are Trojan is therefore sufficient in and of itself to create an expectation of support from the unnamed Jupiter and Juno. Hence the emphatic *Iliaeque* in 37 (at line-end mirroring *Troiam* four lines later): provided that the squadrons that occupied the Etruscan coast were Trojan, then the success of the prayer should follow automatically.

The presence of Virgil is strongly felt, particularly the words of Ilioneus, Trojan envoy to Latinus at *Aen.* 7.213–48. He underscores the Trojan connection to Jupiter: 219–20 *'ab Ioue principium generis, Ioue Dardana pubes | gaudet auo, rex ipse Iouis de gente suprema'*. Cf. H.'s *iussa pars* ~ 7.241 *iussisque ingentibus urget Apollo*; *per ardentem... Troiam* ~ *Aen.* 7.244 *Troia ex ardente* – phrasing otherwise only at Sen. *Herc.* 19; *Tro.* 56.

37–40 si 'so long as', 'as sure as' (as at 65, and cf. *OLD* s.v. 6a), provides the basis on which a prayer is offered up and a positive response expected, assuming but not presuming. Cf. 65–72 and n.; also 1.32.1–4 *si quid uacui sub umbra | lusimus tecum... age, dic Latinum, | barbite, carmen*; 3.18.1–5 *Faune,... | per meos finis et aprica* *rura* | *lenis incedas abeasque paruis* | *aequus alumnis,* | *si tener pleno cadit haedus anno* (see N–H and N–R respectively *ad locc.*); *Epod.* 5.5–13 *'per liberos te, si uocata partubus* | *Lucina ueris affuit,* | *per hoc inane purpurae decus precor . . . quid ut nouerca me intueris . . . ?'*; *S.* 2.6.6–13 *si neque maiorem feci ratione mala rem* | *nec . . . ,* | *si . . . si . . . , hac prece te oro: . . .* These are all straightforward or varied versions of the *da quia dedi* prayer, on which see Pulleyn 1997: 16–38; for examples in Greek, see Horsfall on Virg. *Aen.* 11.786.

uestrum . . . opus 'your handiwork'; cf. *TLL* s.v. *opus* 849.6–45 'tropice spectat ad creationem mundi mundanorumque tamquam artificio dei, numinum, naturae sim. factam', though this instance is not included. At Livy 1.12.4 Romulus acknowledges Jupiter's authority for the foundation of Rome: *'Iuppiter, tuis' inquit 'iussus auibus hic in Palatio prima urbi fundamenta ieci.'*

litus Etruscum: here and at *Epod.* 16.40 (*Etrusca . . . litora*) of the coastline, at 1.2.14 (*litore Etrusco*) of the right bank of the Tiber. With *Roma* and *Iliaeque*, *Etruscum* hints at the origins of the city; cf. *G.* 2.532–4 *Sabini . . . Etruria . . . Roma.*

pars: appositional predicate of *turmae*, 'squadrons, consisting of the fragment [Aeneas, his family, and followers] ordered [sc. 'by the gods', whence the expected granting of the prayer] to take a journey of salvation in exchange for homes and city'.

mutare . . . cursu: the Loeb, like most translations, takes *sospite cursu* as a locative ('in a journey that brought salvation'), but Horatian practice supports a construction whereby the ablative of price is used for the thing taken in exchange; cf. 1.16.25–6 *nunc ego mitibus* | *mutare quaero tristia*; 1.29.14–15 *libros . . . et domum* | *mutare loricis Hiberis*; Virg. *G.* 1.7–8 *tellus* | *. . . glandem mutauit arista*; and *TLL* s.v. *muto* 1726.60–68; *OLD* s.v. 3b. Ablative of means, 'change home by means of a journey', seems less likely.

lares for *domum* (*OLD* s.v. 2; *TLL* 966.7–967.25, incl. uses of the plural, e.g. Prop. 4.1.128 *in tenues cogeris ipse lares*), so lower-case *lares* (with Klingner) is to be preferred. Aeneas did take his Lares with him, though not in Virgil, who only specifies Penates (*Aen.* 2.717 + *sacra*; 747).

41 cui: antecedent is *pars.*

sine fraude: *non 'sine fraude ardentem', sed 'sine fraude iter muniuit'* (ps.-Acro), i.e. 'without harm' (the predominant sense of the phrase; *OLD* s.v. *fraus* 1). But the placement between *per ardentem . . . Troiam* creates a true ambiguity, as Porph. noted, taking it closely with *patriae superstes*, 'surviving the fall of Troy without deception'. For this sense see Prop. 4.7.63, of Andromeda and Hypermestra, *sine fraude maritae* 'undeceiving wives'; Ov. *Met.* 2.558 *commissa duae sine fraude tuentur*; 15.120 *animal sine fraude dolisque*; *TLL* s.v. *fraus* 1276.65–1277.2, where both senses are gathered. Porph. adds that 'some think Aeneas survived his country's fall because in the view of certain people Aeneas was convicted of the charge of betrayal'. Servius (*ad Aen.* 1.242) connected H.'s passage with the scene on Dido's temple relief, where Aeneas recognizes himself 'mixing in with' (in warfare or treachery?) Greek leaders: 1.488 *se quoque principibus permixtum agnouit Achiuis.* H.'s phrase may be seen as one of the early attempts to reimpose an Augustan point of view on the anti-Aeneas variant. See Thomas 2001: 71–3, 78–9.

castus Aeneas: although the primary meaning is 'pure', 'unstained' from a religious viewpoint (as at 6 *puerosque castos*, linking singers and their subject), given recent publication of the *Aeneid*, with the goings-on of its fourth book, readers might see this too as a correction of Virgil, who does not, could not, use *castus* of Aeneas, though at *Aen.* 6.563 the Sibyl, soon after the encounter with Dido's shade, comes close; see Davis 2001: 127, n. 78. With sexual meaning the adjective is mostly applied to women and virgin goddesses, but cf. 3.7.14–15 *nimis* | *casto Bellerophontae*; *Epist.* 2.1.132 *castis cum pueris*; *TLL* s.v. *castus* 569.7–17.

patriae: Bo identifies as genitive, but dative is more likely, as at *Epod.* 5.101 *parentes, heu, mihi superstites*. For examples of both (including Livy 42.50.8 *superstes regno suo*), see *OLD* s.v. *superstes* 2b, where the genitive is shown to be a somewhat later development.

43–4 liberum muniuit iter 'built a road to freedom'. *libertas* refers mainly to the enslaving of those Trojans who did not escape from Troy, e.g. Andromache at Virg. *Aen.* 3.325–7 *nos patria incensa diuersa per aequora uectae* | *stirpis Achilleae fastus iuuenemque superbum* | *seruitio enixae tulimus*, a fate avoided by Creusa: 2.785–6 *non ego . . . Graiis seruitum matribus ibo*, with Horsfall *ad locc.* This description also suggests the Republic, where the road would ultimately lead, as on Aeneas' shield at *Aen.* 8.648, after the expulsion of Tarquinius Superbus: *Aeneadae in ferrum pro libertate ruebant.* For the phrasing of actual road building, cf. Caes. *BG* 7.58 *Labienus . . . iter munire conabatur*; also Cato *Agr.* 2.4 *per ferias potuisse . . . uiam publicam muniri*, and frequently; *TLL* s.v. *munio* 1658.42–63.

daturus | **plura relictis** 'destined to give his people more than they left behind'; Rome will be greater than Troy – recapitulating the comparative at 11–12 *nihil urbe Roma* | *. . . maius*, hinting at the descendent of Aeneas. Cf. 4.6.23–4 *rebus Aeneae potiore ductos* | *alite muros.*

45–8 See 37–48n. on the syntax and double tricolon. *date* is repeated from 3, so standing in the same metrical position (the only place it fits) in the opening stanza of both halves. The prayer for good morals for the young, tranquillity for the elderly, prosperity and progeny for the race is very much in line with the repeated prayer of the *ludi* (see 3n.).

di . . . di: the bare vocatives parallel *Phoebe* at the poem's opening, and the opening of each of the prayers of the *Acta*; see intro.; for the anaphora, 1.21n. This repetition is otherwise found only at Virg. *Aen.* 3.265–6, the urgent prayer of Anchises after Celaeno's ominous prophecy, '*di prohibete minas, di talem auertite casum,* | *et placidi seruate pios*', with Horsfall *ad loc.*; in the nominative at *C.* 4.13.1 and Prop. 3.11.65.

probos mores docili iuuentae: applied specifically to the Nero boys at 4.4.29–36 (*doctrina . . . cultus . . . mores*). 4.6.43 *docilis modorum* is an echo perhaps.

mores: cf. *Epist.* 2.1.1–4, a miniature *Res gestae*, *Cum tot sustineas et tanta negotia solus,* | *res Italas armis tuteris, moribus ornes,* | *legibus emendes . . . Caesar. mores* are a concern for H. elsewhere, as at 3.5.7 *inuersique mores*; 3.24.35–6 *quid leges sine moribus | uanae proficiunt?*

Romulae genti: cf. Cat. 34.22–4 *Romulique | . . . bona | sospites ope gentem*, from the hymn to Diana, sung responsively by choruses of boys and girls and a key intertext for H.; see 1–4, 15–16, 33nn.

45–6 An appealing couplet compensates for the conventional sentiment, with the syntactically and contextually parallel *docili* and *placidae* in the same metrical position, and the other parallel phrases chiastically arranged:

> **di**, probos mores *docili* i u u e n t a e,
> **di**, s e n e c t u t i *placidae* quietem,

The effect is close to that in the opening of the prayer to Liber and Ceres at Virg. *G.* 1.7–9:

> Liber et alma Ceres, uestro si munere tellus
> Chaoniam pingui g l a n d e m *mutauit arista*,
> p o c u l a q u e inuentis Acheloia *miscuit uuis*.

47–8 The marked style of the preceding couplet is continued in the musical chant of 47 *gen- remque -lemque*. At the same time the hypermetric blurring across line-division helps this third member of the stanza's tricolon come across as a single unit (see 37–48n.), as H. builds a link from Aeneas to Romulus (whose hut, close to the house of Augustus, is not far from the singers on the Palatine) and in the following lines to the living 'blood of Anchises and Venus'.

49–60 FIFTH TRIAD

A somewhat abrupt transition to the sacrificial activities, qualities and *res gestae* of Augustus, whose name, like those of the gods who are to watch over him, is omitted – as are any contemporary names, though H. makes very precise reference to specific legislation (17–20) and to the *XVuiri* (70). Three end-stopped stanzas express a wish for the success of the *princeps*' prayer, the realization of success abroad and the restoration of general morality and abundance. The 'famous offspring of Anchises and Venus' shifts imperceptibly from Aeneas to Augustus, with audience/readers expected to pledge their commitment to and faith in the new order, the new future of Rome. This blending of the persons of Aeneas and Augustus is also a feature of the *Aeneid* and part of the régime's propaganda, though H. makes this connection more explicit. Stylistically this triad is very different from the one that precedes, paratactic and simple in its expression of the achievements of Augustus, not unlike the style of 4.15.4–16.

49 quaeque uos . . . ueneratur 'the favours he petitions from you'; for the double accusative, as with any verb of asking, cf. Caecina, *Fam.* 6.7.2 *qui* *multa deos uenerati sint contra eius salutem*; cf. also *S.* 2.6.8 *si ueneror stultus nihil horum: 'o si . . .'*

bobus . . . albis: cf. Virg. *G.* 2.146–8 (sacrificial animals of Italy) *hinc albi, Clitumne, greges et maxima taurus | uictima, saepe tuo perfusi flumine sacro | Romanos ad templa deum duxere triumphos.*

See *Or. Sib. FGrH* 257 F 37 (V) (4) 12 πάνλευκοι ταῦροι 'all-white bulls', number unspecified, for Jupiter, while Juno is to get one heifer: 15 δαμάλης τε βοὸς. In the ceremony Augustus and Agrippa each sacrificed a bull to Jupiter Optimus Maximus (*Acta* 103–6), Agrippa, a heifer to Juno Regina (119–22), colours unspecified; the oracle then recommends 'like offerings' (17–18 ἶσα θύματα) for Apollo, which need not imply the offering of an ox, though it is hard to square with the reality of Apollo's offerings, namely nine *liba*, nine *popana*, and nine *pthoes.* Feeney 1998: 33–4 notes that without the *Acta* it was assumed that oxen were sacrificed to Apollo and Diana, generally identified with the *di* of 45–6, before Mommsen saw that was not possible (see intro.). But there is no ambiguity either in performance, since no oxen were sacrificed on the third day, or for an ancient reader familiar with the event from the *Acta* or its subsequent iterations.

50 Anchisae Venerisque sanguis: cf. 4.15.31–2 *Anchisen et almae | progeniem Veneris canemus* of the future song that will never come. The high style invokes epic; cf. Anchises' apostrophe to Julius Caesar at Virg. *Aen.* 6.834–5 *tuque prior, tu parce, genus qui ducis Olympo, | proice tela manu, sanguis meus!*; also H. of himself: 2.20.5–6 *non ego pauperum | sanguis parentum.*

51–2 impetret: the last subjunctive of the poem, which turns now to stating the fulfillment of the prayer.

bellante prior, iacentem | lenis in hostem 'better than the warring enemy, gentle towards him when laid low'. A clear reference to Anchises' lines from Virg. *Aen.* 6.851–3 *tu . . . Romane, memento | . . . parcere subiectis et debellare superbos.* Famously Aeneas did not remember to do precisely that at the end of the poem, and H. seems to correct Virgil's 'shortcoming' by having the two qualities be part of the actual *character* of Aeneas' descendent, as well as tied to his future actions; see Putnam 2001: 80; Davis 2001: 122. This sole, oblique mention of Augustus in the *CS* shows H. far removed from his republican youth and is in step with Augustus' own propaganda in the *Res gestae*: *Mon. Anc.* 1.13–16 *bella terra et mari c[iuilia extern]aque toto in orbe terrarum s[aepe gessi] uictorque omnibus [ueniam petentib]us ciuibus peperci. externas gentes quibus tuto [ignosci pot]ui[t, co]nseruare quam excidere m[alui.* See 4.15.4–16n., also Thomas 2001: 69–71.

53–60 Anaphora of *iam* (53, 55, 57; see 1.21n.) along with the present tenses (54 *timet*, 55 *petunt*, 59 *audet, apparetque*) show, as the hymn nears its end, that things have shifted from prayers, hopes and wishes, to the realization of *pax Augusta*; see 65–72n. This realization follows immediately after the stanza on Augustus, who is therefore implicitly projected as having effected the realization.

53–4 Reflects Augustan propaganda surrounding the recovery of the standards Crassus lost to the Parthians in 53 BCE. N–H vol. 1, xxxii–xxxiii treat the topic, a near obsession for H. before the diplomatically arranged recovery. See 14.41–4n., and *Mon. Anc.* 5.40–2 *Parthos trium exercit[u]um Roman[o]rum spolia et signa re[ddere] mihi supplicesque amicitiam populi Romani petere coegi.*

mari terraque: cf. *Mon. Anc.* 1.24–6 *ob res a me aut per legatos meos auspiciis meis terra m[ariqu]e pr[o]spere gestas qu[inquagiens et quin]quiens decreuit senatus supplicandum esse dis immortalibus*; also *Epod.* 9.27 (Antony after Actium) *terra marique uictus hostis*; *Epist.* 1.16.25 *bella tibi terra pugnata marique.* The phrase indicates intensity and totality of military action; see Mankin on *Epod.* 9.27.

Medus: Media proper is situated south of the Caspian Sea, here used of the Parthians.

timet: fear realized, elsewhere hoped for: 1.35.30–2 (fresh soldiers Augustus will lead against the East) *iuuenum recens* | *examen Eois timendum* | *partibus Oceanoque rubro.*

Albanasque . . . secures: the axes as part of the *fasces*, carried before a magistrate with *imperium*. Alba Longa, mother city of Rome as a consequence of the Hellenistic historiography that embarrassingly placed Aeneas 400 years before the founding of Rome, was destroyed probably in the seventh century. Though the city was never rebuilt, the Mons Albanus remained the religious center of the Latin confederacy, which Alba was perceived as leading (see 69–72). The most ancient part of the oracle makes it clear that the *ludi* look to Latium as well as all of Italy and are directed at keeping 'all the land of Italy, and all that of the Latins', beneath the Roman yoke: *Or Sib. FGrH* 257 F 37 (V) (4) 37 πᾶσα χθὼν Ἰταλὴ καὶ πᾶσα Λατίνων.

55–6 At *Mon. Anc.* 5.51–3 Scythians are listed with a number of others who sought friendship with Augustus: *nostram am[icitiam appetiuerunt] per legat[os] B[a]starn[ae Scythae]que*, etc.; *Mon. Anc.* 5.52–3 singles out the sending of *legationes* by the Indians, an honour accorded to no Roman leader before Augustus. See N–H on 1.12.56, also on the likelihood that that the Chinese sent embassies. As often, the terms are geographically vague.

responsa petunt: the regular term for envoys or individuals consulting a leader or governing body (*OLD* s.v. *responsum* 1b), but also used of consulting an oracle (*OLD* 2a), as at Virg. *Aen.* 6.151 (Sibyl to Aeneas) *dum consulta petis*; 7.86, 92 of Latinus consulting about the betrothal of Lavinia; also of clients seeking legal advice from a *patronus*, implying an inferior status (*OLD* s.v. 2b). Cf. also Virg. *Ecl.* 1.44–5 (Tityrus petitioning the *iuuenis*, i.e. Octavian) *hic mihi responsum primus dedit ille petenti:* | *'pascite ut ante boues, pueri; summittite tauros'.*

superbi nuper et Indi 'and the Indians, arrogant till of late', taking *et* as postpositive; or, with *et* in its normal position, of the Scythians, which seems more likely given the campaigns of M. Licinius Crassus of 29–28 BCE against the Bastarnae and other tribes of the Lower Danube (*CAH* X174). He celebrated a triumph in 27 BCE, so *superbi nuper* would work well with *Scythae.*

57–60 All's right with the world, a close reflection of the Augustan programme and of the propaganda that promotes it. The stanza takes its cue from descriptions of the return of the golden age, which, however, is again markedly absent in terms of language. Cf. *Epist.* 1.12.28–9, where Copia, there also *aurea*, appears in the context of Roman conquest. Also Barker 1996: 443–4, for speculation about the absence of golden age imagery in *CS*.

Fides: sister of Iustitia at 1.24.6–7, where Pudor and Veritas are also found, as former qualities of the deceased Quintilius. Spes and Fides are associated with the goddess Fortuna at 1.35.21–2 *te Spes et albo rara Fides colit | uelata panno.*

Pax cf. *Mon. Anc.* 2.38–9 *aram [Pacis A]u[g]ust[ae senatus pro] redi[t]u meo co[nsacrandam censuit*; 2.42–5 *[Ianum] Quirin[um, quem cl]aussum ess[e maiores nostri uoluer]unt, [cum p]er totum i[mperium po]puli Roma[ni terra marique es]set parta uic[torii]s pax, cum priu[s qua]m nascerer a condita urbe bis omnino clausum [f]uisse prodatur m[emori]ae, ter me princi[pe senat]us claudendum esse censui[t].* 5.1 *mare pacaui a praedonibus*; 5.10–13 *Gallias et Hispanias proui[n]cias, [item Germaniam qua clau]dit Oceanus a Gadibus ad ostium Albis flumin[is pacaui. Alpes . . . pacaui.*

Honos . . . Virtus: *Mon. Anc.* 2.29–30 *[Aram Fortunae Reducis ante ae]des Honoris et Virtutis, ad portam [Capenam, pro reditu meo se]natus consacrauit.*

Pudorque 'Decency', particularly in sexual matters, with clear reference to the *leges Iuliae* of 18 BCE, *de adulteriis* and *de maritandis ordinibus*. At *Mon. Anc.* 1.39 (reconstructed from the Greek) it is stated that Augustus declined the offer in 11 BCE to be *curator legum et morum summa potestate*, which slightly contradicts Dio's claim (54.10.5) that he held such a position from 19 BCE, renewed for a further five years, but Dio 54.30.1 places the renewal seven years later, in 12 BCE. But as Brunt and Moore (*ad Res gestae* 6.1) note, Augustus may well have been *praefectus moribus*, a good republican office (Shackleton Bailey *ad* Cic. *Fam.* 9.15.5), carried out by the censors. He may well have declined the powers *summa potestate* – which he hardly needed this far into his principate. *auctoritas* rather than *imperium* was the best tool for sustaining republican fictions.

pleno Copia cornu: almost a description of the soon-to-be-sculpted 'Tellus panel' (depicting Pax, Ceres, Tellus, Italia or some other female deity – what about Copia?) on the southeast side of the Ara Pacis, also central to the régime's projection of its achievements, as at *Mon. Anc.* 1.32–5 *non sum deprecatus in summa frumenti p]enuri[a c]uratio[n]em an[nonae qu]am ita ad[ministraui, ut intra dies pauco]s metu et periclo p[raesen]ti ciuitatem uniu[ersam liberarem impensa et] cura mea*; Augustus accepted the *cura annonae* in 22 BCE, when disease and consequent famine led to violent demonstrations (Dio 54.1.1; *CAH* X 88). *Epist.* 1.12.28–9 reflects the relief that must have attended the resolution: *aurea fruges | Italiae pleno defudit Copia cornu.* For specific donations of grain or money, see *Mon. Anc.* 33.7–21, 40–3.

iam . . . redire Virtus audet, apparetque . . . Copia: extravagant language, with a hint at, but ultimately with studious avoidance of, the terminology of Virgil's returning golden age at *Ecl.* 4.6 *iam redit et Virgo, redeunt Saturnia regna*; what is missing from the *CS* is precisely any equivalent of *redeunt Saturnia regna*. *redire* is moreover a natural part of secular language, as at Stat. *Silu.* 1.4.15 *aeuo redeunte*, with DuQuesnay 1976: 40; also Henderson 1998: 48.

61–72 SIXTH TRIAD

The prayer ends with the focus back on Apollo (61–8) and Diana (69–72), the third invocation of each, and with the assertion that the prayers of the *ludi* have been answered (see 65–72n.). 'As (*si*) Phoebus – prophet, archer, dear to the Muses, healer of the sick – looks with favor on the Palatine altars, so he calls the power of Rome and abundance of Latium into the next lustrum and to better and better times; so does Diana, holder of Aventine and Algidus, as (*si*) she heeds the prayers of the *XVuiri* and lends favouring ears to the children's vows.' Translators and commentators (Rudd, Putnam) take *prorogat* on the one hand (Apollo) and *curat* and *applicat* on the other (Diana) as being on the same syntactical level: Apollo brings prosperity to Rome and Latium, while Diana heeds the prayers and vows. But Porph. seems right to understand *si* before *quindecim* in 70, and to have Diana *and* Apollo share in effecting the result (continued prosperity of Rome and Latium, 66–8) as a consequence of the events of the *ludi*, namely the Palatine sacrifice, the prayers of the *XVuiri* and the hymn of the boys and girls. Sight and sound figure in each of the protases, in Apollo's favourable response to the scene of sacrifice (65 *uidet aequus aras*) and Diana's friendly hearing of prayer and song (71–2 *amicas applicat auris*). Her cult places (68 Aventine, Algidus) correspond as identifiers to his cult functions (61–4 augur etc.), notably *not* to the Palatine, the site of sacrifice to both god and goddess (*Acta* 139 *A. d. III non. Iun. in Palatio [Apollini et Dianae] sacrificium fecerunt* etc.

61–4 The stanza, uniquely in H., captures the four chief aspects of Apollo, as god of prophecy (*augur*), archery (*arcu*), music (*acceptusque . . . Camenis*) and medicine (*salutari . . . arte*); cf. Virg. *Aen.* 12.392–4 on the healer Iapyx, *acri quondam cui captus amore* | *ipse suas artis, sua munera, laetus Apollo* | *augurium citharamque dabat celeresque sagittas.*

augur: cf. 1.2.32; Virg. *Aen.* 4.376 *augur Apollo.* Like Gk. μάντις, the word is used indifferently of gods and humans with divine powers.

fulgente decorus arcu: visual phrasing suggests statuary (cf. Virg. *Aen.* 10.171 *aurato fulgebat Apolline puppis*) and adornment rather than danger, a fulfilment of 2.10.19–20 *neque semper arcum* | *tendit Apollo.* Things will change: see 4.6.1–2n.; *fulgente* may, however, suggest aggression, since the participle is used frequently with weapons (*TLL* s.v. 1513.29–38).

nouem Camenis: although plural *Camenae* are as old as Naevius (fr. 64.2 Morel *flerent diuae Camenae Naeuium poetam*), the combination with *nouem* fully Hellenizes the Roman Muses; the singular in Liv. Andron. *Od.* fr. 1 is of course a translation of the singular of the Greek Μοῦσα.

salutari . . . arte: cf. 1.21.13–16 *hic miseram famem* | *pestemque a populo et principe Caesare . . . aget.* The expression also appears at Plin. *HN* 27.146 of the 'healthful medicines' (Loeb) implanted by Mother Nature in all living creatures; cf. *OLD* s.v. *salutaris* 2.

arte . . . artus: the homophony (picking up *salutari*), is notable; perhaps a wordplay or *figura etymologica.* The incantatory effect may underscore the prayer for healing and health that is intensified in this stanza. Music and healing are intertwined, as at 1.32.13–15 *o decus Phoebi et dapibus supremi | grata testudo Iouis, o laborum | dulce lenimen medicumque.*

fessos 'debilitated' (*OLD* s.v. 3a), as at 2.7.18 *fessum militia latus*, also implied at 3.4.37–8 *militia . . . | fessas cohortes*; cf. Virg. *G.* 4.190 *fessos . . . artus*; *Aen.* 3.511 *fessos sopor irrigat artus.*

corporis artus: pleonastic. H.'s contemporary Vitruvius also uses the phrase, which he may have picked up from H., of medical symptoms, *De arch.* 8.6.11 *uapor ex eo* [sc. *plumbo*] *insidens corporis artus et in diem exurens eripit ex membris eorum sanguinis uirtutes.* Other attestations, all after H., involve metamorphosis or transformation, so that *corporis* is more meaningful: Ov. *Met.* 7.317 *minuunt ea corporis artus*; App. Verg. *Cir.* 198 *humanos mutatae corporis artus.*

65–72 See 37–40n. Page, with hesitation, reads *proroget, curet, applicet*, supported by some MSS: 'The whole hymn has hitherto been a supplication, and the use of *si* in l. 65 seems to point to a continued appeal, cf. its use in l. 37. On the other hand it is urged that "the time for urgent prayer and expostulation is past: the chorus has now assumed the tone of confidence and promise," and that the assertion in the last stanza would be abrupt if the prayer be continued to l. 72.' The verbs should not be normalized in this way, and the indicatives clearly belong, but Page does draw attention to the oddness of the indicatives, unique in this type of prayer. The hymn states the fulfilment of its imprecations even in the course of its own performance. So H. tries to turn a prayer (*si* retains some of its conditionality, even with the present indicatives) to the gods into an assurance of the gods' favour, in an ending that looks as much like a public-relations exercise as a hymn. Here in its performative context at the end of the three-day festival, the prayers of Augustus, Agrippa and the régime are ruled to have been answered.

65 'as he/if he looks with favour on the altars of the Palatine'; for *si* in this sense cf. 37–40n. and cf. *OLD* s.v. 6a.

Palatinas . . . aras: Shackleton Bailey reads *arces* with some of the MSS, but *aras* is surely right since *aequus* looks to the reciprocity resulting from the sacrifice by Augustus and Agrippa that immediately preceded the performance of the *CS*: *Acta* 139–40 *A. d. III non. Iun. in Palatio [Apollini et Dianae] sacrificium fecerunt Imp. Caesar Augustus, M. A[grippa libeis VIIII]| popanis VIIII pthoibus VI[II. Palatinas*, of Apollo's temple, is in the same metrical *sedes* as *Aventinum*, of Diana's, at 69.

66 remque Romanam Latiumque felix: cf. Enn. *Ann.* 494–5 Skutsch *audire est pretium operae procedere recte | qui rem Romanam Latiumque augescere uoltis. Acta* 93–4 (wording repeated through all the prayers and sacrifices, though omitted from the inscription, but clearly repeated in performance, as is indicated by the phrase: *cetera uti supra* at 106, 118, 122, 137) *uos quaeso precorque uti imperium maiestatemque p. R.] Quiritium duelli domique au[xitis utique semper Latinus obtemperassit.*

felix: proleptic: 'keeps it going in fertility' (cf. 31 *fetus*).

67–8 'keeps it going on to yet another lustrum and forever into a better and better time'. A strong sense of continuity pervades the couplet, as it did the repeated prayer of the ceremony: *Acta* 93–7 (see Appendix 2).

alterum in lustrum: referring perhaps to the five-year extension, presumably voted in 18 BCE, of Augustus' original ten-year *imperium*; perhaps also more generally meant: 'yet another lustrum (and another after that)'. Cf. 1.6; 14.37 nn. At Stat. *Silu.* 4.1.37–8 Janus looks forward to Domitian's celebration of the next *ludi saeculares* (103 years off) *mecum altera saecula condes, | et tibi longaeui renouabitur ara Tarenti.* K–H equate *lustrum* with *saeculum.*

69 Auentinum . . . Algidumque: Diana Aventina and Nemorensis respectively (see 1–4n.). The Aventine temple was outside the *pomerium* and therefore not perhaps appropriate for this part of the *ludi* (see Appendix 1), in which it seems to have played no part at all (see Schnegg-Köhler 55–6). On the basis of the Marble Plan, Richardson 108 locates it just to the south of the Temple of Minerva, on the plateau of the hill, but Lisa Mignone shows that there is no certainty on this ('The Aventine Hill in the Roman Republic', diss., Columbia, 2010). It may have looked across the Circus Maximus and so in the general direction of Palatine Apollo. According to Suet. *Aug.* 29.5 it was rebuilt by L. Cornificius as part of Augustus' refurbishment of the city. Traditionally founded by Servius, it seems to have been modelled on the Artemision of Ephesus (Livy 1.45.2). Ogilvie (*ad loc.*) notes that the temple was founded around 540 BCE, as a response to the older temple of Diana Nemorensis between Aricia and Mons Algidus at the southern foot of Mons Albanus (BA 43), centre of the Concilium Latinorum, from which Etruscan Rome of the sixth century was excluded. In including both cult sites H. may be bringing out the importance of Latium in the original *ludi* (see intro.; 53–4n.). Diana, important to the Romans and the Latins separately, is to bring them prosperity in unity, her two cult places mapping onto 66 *remque Romanam Latiumque felix*. Cf. 4.57–8 for the holm oaks of Mons Algidus.

70 quindecim . . . preces uirorum: the tmesis makes the official term – metrically impossible anyway – slightly less prosaic. The college of *quindecimuiri sacris faciundis* was responsible for guarding the Sibylline oracles, traditionally from the time of Tarquinius Priscus, and for holding the *ludi*. Originally there were two of them (*duouiri*), then ten from 367 BCE (*decemuiri*), then fifteen under Sulla and sixteen under Julius Caesar. In February they delivered a *relatio* to the senate, which then passed a *SC de ludis faciendis*; on 29–31 May groups of two received offerings of grain while the whole board issued edicts; on 1 June they delivered the edict curtailing excessive female lamentation, *Acta* 111–14 (Appendix 2 – their only active role in the three-day ceremony). At *Acta* 150–2 nineteen of them are listed as being present, right after mention of H. and his *carmen*. Augustus had been a member of the college for 20 years, so by 17 BCE its function was to lend an air of republican plausibility to those gullible enough to believe the whole business. One of the four presidents of the board, Augustus installed Agrippa (who was not) in the place of the other three. The fiction is sustained in the *Res* *gestae*: *Mon. Anc.* 4.36 *pro conlegio XVuirorum magister conlegi, collega M. Agrippa, ludos saeculares, C. Furnio C. Silano cos., feci.*

preces: presumably refers to those of Augustus and Agrippa, representing the *XVuiri*, who do not offer prayers as a group: *Acta* 90–1 *Augustus . . . precatus est hoc modo*; 103–4 *Caesar Augustus, ibidem alterum M. Agrippa, p[re]cati autem sunt ita* etc.

71 puerorum: self-referential, for the choir as a whole, and bringing to pass 34–6 *audi pueros . . . audi . . . puellas* (and 33–6n.). There is no reason to imagine (as do K–H and others) that the boys alone sang the second half, since *pueri* = 'children' is standard (*OLD* s.v. 4a) and Horatian: *Epist.* 1.7.7 *dum pueris omnis pater et matercula pallet*; as such it clearly had legal status *Dig.* 50.16.163.1 *'pueri' appellatione etiam puella significatur.*

72 applicat aures: cf. in the same metrical position 3.11.8 *applicet aures*, a minor breach of the principle that 'Horace never repeats the same phraseology in the *Odes*, even when the thought is identical' (Highbarger 1935: 245), as are 1.19.1~4.1.5 (but there name+epithets) and 3.25.20~4.8.33 (which may not be genuine; see *ad loc.*). The verb is not otherwise found with *aures* (Varro, *Rust.* 2.7.5 *auribus applicatis* is of course another matter), though it is an easy extension of *animum/mentem applicare*, found in comedy (*OLD* s.v. *applico* 6b). For unsuccessful prayer cf. 1.2.27–8 *minus audientem | . . . Vestam.*

73–6 Apollo and Diana close out the hymn just as they opened it. The choristers sing their praises in recompense for prayers (3 *date quae precamur*) now fulfilled.

73–4 The chorus backs off from the confident assertions that precede (*prorogat*), now merely taking home (sure and good) hope that Apollo's and Diana's positive response is felt by Jupiter and the other gods. Somewhat tortuous word order, with the opening noun clause dependent on the verbal idea in *spem*, itself the object of *reporto*. The wording, both *sentire* and *spem certam*, seems to back off from some of the certainty communicated by the indicatives of 65–72.

Iouem . . . deosque cunctos: Jupiter, alluded to in 37 (*uestrum*), is named at the end of the hymn, but almost as an outsider to the proceedings.

domum: a nice touch, reminding that the twenty-seven boys and twenty-seven girls all had living fathers and mothers and complete households to which they would be bringing back their optimistic message (see 6n.).

74–5 reporto, | . . . chorus: the unambiguous identity of the speaker's voice is present only here at the end, where it functions as a *sphragis* or 'signature' (see 6.44). The choral singular is a much-discussed feature of Greek choral lyric.

75–6 doctus . . . | dicere: epexegetical infinitive. Cf. 6.43–4 (the imagined *puella* in years to come) *docilis modorum | uatis Horati.*

dicere laudes: cf. 8 *dicere carmen* and n.

COMMENTARY ON *ODES* IV

I

METRE

Second (Third, according to some text books) Asclepiadean: alternating glyconic (– – – ⏑⏑ – ⏑ ×) with 'lesser' Asclepiadean (glyconic with choriambic expansion: – – – ⏑⏑ – | – ⏑⏑ – | ⏑ ×), as in 1.3, 13, 19, 36; 3.9, 15, 19, 24, 25, 28; 4.3.

INTRODUCTION

Venus, spare me the battles of love, against which I'm hardened by age. Go off and answer the prayers of youthful lovers, in particular to the house of Paullus Maximus. He's a fine boy and will ably carry your standards. After defeating his rival he will dedicate a statue to you by the Alban lake, and celebrate with music and dancing in the company of the young. As for me, my days of women, boys and parties are over. But why these tears, Ligurinus, and why my unwonted silence? In my dreams I hold you and pursue you through fields and waters, hardhearted as you are.

The poet returns reluctantly to the subject of love, recalling with the opening theme of *militia amoris* his retirement from such activity towards the end of *C.* 1–3, in the last purely erotic poem of the earlier lyric collection:

Vixi puellis nuper idoneus,
et militaui non sine gloria:
  nunc arma defunctumque bello
  barbiton hic paries habebit
(3.26.1–4)

That poem had itself closed out the process begun in *C.* 1.6, the chief *recusatio* of *C.* 1–3, in which the battles of youthful lovers, not those of Agrippa and Caesar, were announced as fit lyric occupations: 1.6.17–19 *nos conuiuia, nos proelia virginum cantamus.*

Also engaged is the *recusatio*/priamel of *C.* 2.12, in which Maecenas (9 *tuque*) is to write a history of the *proelia Caesaris* (9–12), while H. (13 *me*) is bidden by his Muse to sing of Licymnia and the symposium (see 30, 31nn.).

In the opening poem of the new collection the reluctant lyricist reverses that movement, beginning with an insistence that the position of 3.26, appropriate for the 50-year-old singer, is his preferred stance and that Venus should rather seek out *iuuenes* such as Paullus Maximus. By the end of the poem H. is now back in the thrall of Venus, albeit now with a *puer* as his distraction. That stance is in line with Callimachus' sympotic amatory epigrams, which are consistently pederastic. The final two quatrains of the poem bring the reversal and punch line characteristic of the final couplet of Callimachean epigram (see Wilamowitz 1924: I 178, II 129), and lines 33–40 can themselves be seen as an embedded epigram. Otherwise a primary intertext may be found in Ibycus 287 *PMG*:

> Ἔρος αὖτέ με κυανέοισιν ὑπὸ
> βλεφάροις τακέρ' ὄμμασι δερκόμενος
> κηλήμασι παντοδαποῖς ἐς ἄπει-
> ρα δίκτυα Κύπριδος ἐσβάλλει·
> ἦ μαν τρομέω νιν ἐπερχόμενον,
> ὥστε φερέζυγος ἵππος ἀεθλοφόρος ποτὶ γῆραι
> ἀέκων σὺν ὄχεσφι θοοῖς ἐς ἅμιλλαν ἔβα.

'Again does Eros, giving me melting looks beneath dark eyelids with innumerable charms, hurl me into the inescapable nets of Venus. I fear him as he comes on, as a yoke-bearing prize-winning horse in old age goes unwillingly with swift chariot into the race.'

Ibycus' poem has particular potency for H., who also alludes to it on his retirement from love's game in *Epist.* 1.1.1–12, where the metaphor of a retiring gladiator is followed by that of the horse rightly put out to pasture; cf. 7–9 *est mihi purgatum crebro qui personet aurem: | 'solue senescentem mature sanus equum, ne | peccet ad extremum ridendus et ilia ducat'*. Ennius had already adapted the metaphor: *Ann.* 522–3 Skutsch *sicuti fortis equos spatio qui saepe supremo | uicit Olympia* (cf. ἀεθλοφόρος) *nunc senio confectus quiescit.* The poem is in keeping with the other beginnings of Horatian books in having the prioritizing aspect of a priamel: (foil) *Paullus Maximus* . . . (climax) *me nec femina nec puer* (see 29n.).

As K–H note (386), the opening is a reversal of the ὕμνος κλητικός ('hymn of invocation'), an ἀποπομπή ('valediction') (Fraenkel 410). Lefèvre 1968 takes issue with this characterization, seeing the poem more as a *recusatio*, which of course it is, but that does not remove the hymnic essence, which continues beyond the opening lines: at 7–8 (see n.) the poem goes through a reversal, shifting from dismissal (*abi*) to what may be seen as a vicarious (and now fully positive) ὕμνος κλητικός, but on behalf of the more suitable Paullus. In this generic aspect H. may be seen as specifically inverting the invitation to Aphrodite of Sappho 1 (Putnam 39–41; Nagy 1994: 417–21; Feeney 1998: 101–2; Barchiesi 2000: 172–3; Hunter 2007: 213–14). Barchiesi further notes the military language shared by H. and Sappho's invocation of Aphrodite as ally (128 σύμμαχος ἔσσο), while Hunter notes the Sapphic intertext here at the opening of *C.* 4, appropriate in that H. inverts the prayer 'with which the Alexandrian edition of Sappho all but certainly opened' (see further 10, 21–8, 35–6nn.).

Bradshaw 1970, following Kiessling, saw the poem as a disguised epithalamium and is followed in this by Syme 1986: 403–4, who thereby dated the marriage of Marcia, daughter of the younger Atia and L. Marcius Philippus (cos. suff. 38 BCE) and first cousin of Augustus; cf. also Habinek 1986, on ideal spousal qualities particularly in Isidore *Etym.* 9.7.28–9, which match those assigned to Maximus. On the other hand, neither Marcia nor Augustus would probably be impressed by an epithalamium that referred to Maximus' future cutting with a broad swath (16 *late signa feret militiae tuae*), and we would also be compelled to seek the identity of the generous rival for Marcia's hand (17–18 and n.), to be supplanted by Maximus only *after* the epithalamium. Still, the possibility cannot be absolutely ruled out and would be in line with *C.* 4's focus on Augustan aristocrats.

The poem is framed by two sets of eight lines (1–8, 33–40), with a central, more narrative section 9–32 (two sets of 12 lines each), whereby each of the three sections treats its own *dramatis personae*. Tarrant 1995: 43–6 argues for a close relationship between the frames. The opening, after addressing Venus, insists on the poet's post-erotic condition; now hardened to love's impulses (7 *durum*), he is not the man he was under the rule of the mysterious Cinara/Cinura (see 3–4n.). In the final phase, in spite of the opening remonstrances, and with the change occurring in mid-poem, he finds himself pursuing in his dreams the equally mysterious Ligurinus (see 33n.), that one now hard-hearted (40 *dure*) towards (the now sexually inclined) H. In the central panel the speaker presents the less mysterious and very real figure Paullus Fabius Maximus, a more suitable object of Venus' attention, who will set up a temple for the goddess, at which dancing will occur. And so H., after describing the attractions and sympotic activity of the 30-year old *puer* Maximus and having disavowed interest in woman or boy, finds himself, like the rival of Maximus (18), pursuing in his dreams a lover, the *puer* Ligurinus, who will not have him. There is a mysteriousness to the identities of the players and to the connections among them (see 15–16, 33–4nn.).

The context is a merging of general festivity and the *komos*, or symposium, one of whose literary illustrations is the sympotic epigram, of which this poem may be seen as an expansion. Indeed, the frames (1–8, 33–40) could function as self-standing epigrams of eight lines each, in which guise they find a sequel in 10, also to Ligurinus, also eight lines long, and as close as we come in Latin to a free translation of any number of poems from Strato's *Musa puerilis* (*Anth. Pal.* 12). The embedding is much like that of Prop. 1.1.1–4, which transforms Meleager, *Anth. Pal.* 12.70 (103.1–4 G–P) into its new, elegiac site. The two parts of the poem, a return to erotic poetry and the praise of a young Roman aristocrat, set the stage for the duality of the book as a whole; on this see Fraenkel 413–14 and pp. 21–3.

1–2 Intermissa . . . diu . . . bella: refers both to the putative cessation of the 50-year-old narrator's erotic activities and to the time elapsed since the writing of (erotic) lyric (*C.* 1–3 published 23 BCE). Previously *intermitto* is mostly attested in prose, in poetry (after Ter. *Ad.* 293) first here and at Prop. 4.4.80 (a prosaic context: *intermissa . . . tuba*).

The opening line of the book – which should be comprehensible on its own, as in *C.* 1–3 – entraps the reader in a momentary ambiguity: 'sexual activity long discontinued' (*intermissa Venus diu*); on arriving at *bella* one adjusts; cf. Virg. *Aen.* 4.19 '*huic uni forsan potui succumbere culpae*', where the final noun corrects the impulse to take Dido's *huic*... *succumbere* in an erotic sense. See Clausen 1987: 42, and Thomas 2001: 76–7 for Ovid's recognition of this ambiguity.

Venus: with the exception of *S.* 2.1 (dramatically a continuation of *S.* 1), the only opening poem not addressed to Maecenas, who has receded somewhat (see 11.19n.). Venus is addressed by name at *C.* 1.18.6 (with Bacchus); 1.30.1 (4–5n.). See Bradshaw 1970: 144–5 for other appearances of Venus in H. She frames the entire Book 4, appearing here in the middle of its first line, and in the middle of its last (15.32 *progeniem Veneris canemus*, with a shift from the purely erotic Venus at the book's beginning to the more ideologically Augustan mother of Aeneas at its end). Venus presides over generational change: Maximus and his generation are on their way in, H., left only with his dreams of Ligurinus (33–40), on his way out, on which see Mitchell 2009. In the process the Venus of Maximus already prefigures the dynastic, Augustan function she will have by book's end.

2 bella: picked up at 16, where Paullus Maximus, unlike H., will be up for Venus' fight (*militiae*).

parce, precor, precor: urgent repetition, as at *C.* 2.19.7–8 (also in the presence of the god) *Euhoe, parce, Liber, | parce graui metuende thyrso!* The adjacent gemination of *precor* occurs only here in Latin. Cf. 4.70 *occidit, occidit*; 2.17.10 *ibimus, ibimus*. Wills 102–6 demonstrates the rarity of such adjacent repetitions, with separation preferred by epic and standard in Virgil. The pairing *parce, precor* is common, though found before this only at Tib. 1.8.51, where, as often, it has an object: *parce, precor, tenero*. Ovid, who has twelve examples of the pairing, perhaps responds to the Horatian repetition at *Met.* 2.361–2: *'parce, precor, mater', quaecumque est saucia clamat. | 'parce, precor: nostrum laceratur in arbore corpus!'* Sappho fr. 1.2 L–P (λίσσομαί σε 'I beg you') is an impulse (see 10n.).

3–4 bonae | sub regno Cinarae: much is at stake here. Fraenkel 411 is representative of many readers: 'the simple words *non sum qualis eram bonae sub regno Cinarae*, where the epithet *bonae* is full of feeling, breath true regret. Cinara, whom Horace mentions only in poems of his later period when she had long been dead, is different from the many girls who swiftly pass through his songs; she seems to be more real than any of them.' Lee 1998: 260 states more tersely that she 'must be a real person', the preference also of Coletti 1996: 689–90, who sets out most of the competing options, though not Davis 1991 (below). But if she is/was real, why did he not speak of her when she was alive? Other occurrences of the name (13.21, 22; *Epist.* 1.7.28; 1.14.33) conspire with this to support the suggestion of K–H (*ad loc.*) that mention of Cinara/Cinura is symbolic of the poet's youth, or perhaps better, the generic erotic interest of *C.* 1–3. Given the quotation of *C.* 1.19.1 *mater saeua Cupidinum* (4–5, 21–2nn.), K–H also suggest that C. may refer us to Glycera. In 3.19 (like 1.19 also Second Asclepiadean), again recording his love for Glycera (28), we find the phrase *Berecyntia tibia* (18–19), otherwise only in this poem (22–3). Similarly Gallus' Lycoris and Cytheris refer to the same woman, while in 1.33 H. has Tibullus (whose admitted obsessions were Delia and Nemesis) singing elegies for a Glycera. K–H on 3 note that κινάρα = 'artichoke', the basis for the suggestion of Davis 1991: 69 of a sympotic nuance to the name (as for Ligurinus; see 33–4n.), since Alcaeus fr. 347 L-P urges sympotic activity when the 'artichoke is in bloom' (4 ἄνθει δὲ σκόλυμος). Columella's description of the artichoke at 10.235–41 sounds a little risqué.

John D. Morgan *per litteras* makes an intriguing and potentially revolutionary suggestion that may nullify the preceding. He points to a late republican/early Augustan inscription from H.'s home town of Venusia, marking the grave of a slave of L. Salvius (*AE* (1994) 472): *Cinura | L. Salui (serua) h(ic) | sita est. | Silo L. Sal(ui seruus) | posuit.* The MSS of H. show great variety in the orthography of Cinara's name: Cinar-/Cinayr-/Cinyr-/Cynar-/Cynir-/ (for which see the apparatus of Keller-Holder); similarly the MSS of Porphyrio, which suggests the variation may go back at least to the third century CE. The possibility that H. reflects on a real, short-lived (13.22–3 *sed Cinarae breues | annos fata dederunt*) Cinura/Cinyra of his youth is worth considering, though, as Morgan notes, if H.'s mistress/girlfriend was named Cinura/Cinyra, even more appropriate etymological possibilities open up. At Pind. *Pyth.* 2.15–17 Cinyras is closely connected to Apollo, and Cinura/Cinyra, whether based on a real person or not, would evoke, as Morgan notes, the Greek loan word from Hebrew for a stringed instrument, κινύρα, giving not 'Ms. Artichoke', but rather 'Ms. Lyre', a fitting retrospective metonym for the sympotic and lyric past of H.

bonae: the epithet *bonae* ('kindly') is indeed 'full of feeling' (Fraenkel), but here perhaps of a particular type (*Epist.* 1.14.33 *quem scis immunem Cinarae placuisse rapaci*): though she was by nature grasping, H. didn't have to pay. For *bonus* thus, see *OLD* s.v. *bonus* 4 'obliging, accommodating, kind(ly), gracious, good . . . (with reference to sexual behaviour)'; Cat. 89.1, 3; 110.1–2 (*Aufillena, bonae semper laudantur amicae: | accipiunt pretium, quae facere instituunt*); Prop. 2.21.16.

regno: cf. 3.9.9 *me nunc Thressa Chloe regit*; Ov. *Rem.* 15 *at si quis male fert indignae regna puellae.*

4–7 'Stop trying to steer with gentle commands one who around two score years and ten now is hardened to them.' Thus with K–H (*contra* Page) taking *mollibus . . . imperiis* as instrum. abl. with *flectere* ('steer with') but also, with 'hardened (to them)', allowing a slight amphibole whereby *imperiis* is taken as dative with *durum*, a construction hard but not impossible to parallel: Ov. *Met.* 14.704 *ne sibi dura foret*; Val. Flacc. 2.355 *iam non dura toris*. See *TLL* s.v. *durus*, 2311.62–5, 'c. dat. . . . inc.' For the phenomenon of amphibole, as 'the use of a single word in two different relations in the same clause or sentence' see (with examples) Bell 1923: 293–303. *circa lustra decem* functions as an adnominal complement, with *eum* understood; *durum*, as a predicate, with causal force. There is an aesthetically artful arrangement of contrasting epithets, distributed one per line: *dulcium* | . . . ***saeua*** . . . *mollibus* | . . . ***durum***.

4–5 dulcium | mater saeua Cupidinum: cf. Pind. *Enc.* fr. 122.4–6 ματέρ' Ἐρώτων | . . . Ἀφροδίταν 'Aphrodite, mother of the Erotes', and esp. Philodemus, *Anth. Pal* 10.21.2 (15.2 G–P) Κύπρι Πόθων μῆτηρ ἀελλοπόδων 'Cyprian mother of the storm-footed Pothoi' (ποθέω = *cupio*); also, inter al., Bacchylides 9.73 μ]ατ[έρ' ἀκ]νάμ[π]των Ἐρώτων 'mother of the unbending Erotes'; cf. N–H *ad* 1.19.1. The phrase (there in the nominative, here vocative) opens *C.* 1.19, a poem in which H. also returns reluctantly to love (4 *finitis animum reddere amoribus*). By the end of Book 4 Venus has become *alma* (15.31), which forms a ring with the contrasting *saeua* here; see Lowrie 1997: 349.

6 circa lustra decem: around fifty, which fits with publication in 13 BCE, when H. turned fifty-two. The line looks back to and invokes the end of the first book of *Epistles* (1.20.26–8), of his age in 21 BCE: *forte meum si quis te percontabitur aeuum, | me quater undenos sciat impleuisse Decembres, | collegam Lepidum quo duxit Lollius anno.* The *senescentem... equum* of that collection (*Epist.* 1.1.8) has even less reason now to be involved with (love) lyric. For the style, cf. *C.* 2.4.22–4, where H. with irony implies that forty is already too late an age for erotic interest, as he assures Xanthias that he is dispassionate in his praise of the *ancilla* in whom the latter is interested: *fuge suspicari | cuius octauum trepidauit aetas | claudere lustrum.* Cf. 14.37; *CS* 67nn. Mitchell 2009:1 suggests the phrase could well apply to Augustus, two years H.'s junior and fifty in 13 BCE.

6–7 flectere... iam durum imperiis: resumes the reference to *Epist.* 1.1, where H., the *senescentem... equum* (8) goes into retirement (from lyric), figured under the same metaphor; cf. ps.-Acro *ad loc. est metaphora a pecoribus, quibus cum iam aetate duris iugum ac frena adhibentur, peredomari non possunt.* There will be an ironic shift in the last line of the poem, where it is Ligurinus, not H., who becomes *durus*, and towards H.

7 abi: the opposite of the usual address to a god. (*S.* 2.6.15 *adsis*; *C.* 1.2.30 *uenias precamur*). Frequent in comedy, the word may be colloquial depending on context (Hofmann 151). Although the tone can be either annoyed, 'off with you' (Ter. *Eun.* 221 *abi, nil dicis*), or sympathetic and friendly, 'on your way' (Ter. *Ad.* 564 *abi, uirum te iudico*), *abi* is somewhat brusque as an address to a deity; cf. 3.14.24 *abito*; Philippus to his slave at *Epist.* 1.7.52–3 *'Demetri... abi, quaere et refer'*; *Epod.* 11.20 of H.'s own dismissal, *iussus abire* (and Mankin *ad loc.*); *Epist* 2.2.205 *non es auarus: abi* (Brink *ad loc.*). For the inversion of Sappho fr. 1.5 L-P (ἀλλὰ τυίδ' ἔλθ') see 10n.

8 reuocant: Venus has left the *iuuenes* to bring her assault to H. *abi quo... reuocant* may be seen as a cletic hymn by proxy (on behalf of Paullus Maximus), with 9–28 vicariously detailing the arguments in his favour.

blandae... preces: substantival counterpart to 2 *precor, precor*. The adjective is appropriate to the context, but cf. non-erotic *AP* 395 *prece blanda*; *Epist.* 2.1.135 *docta prece blandus*.

9–11 tempestiuius... comissabere 'you will more appropriately lead the κῶμος'. Cf. Varro, *Ling.* 7.89 κῶμος, *inde comissatio Latine dicta*, although in late sources and MSS (including those of H.) there is (naturally enough) confusion with *comedo* (see *TLL* s.v. *comissor* 1790.17–25), and the spelling *comessor, comessatio* abounds, perhaps by analogy with the noun *combibo*, συμπότης 'drinking companion' (Lucil. 665; Cic. *Fam.* 9.25.2). For a full account of the details surrounding the κῶμος, see Headlam on Herodas 2.34–7. Prop. 2.12.17–18, also an ἀποπομπή, addressed to Cupid, has a similar use of the comparative: *si pudor est, alio traice tela, puer! | intactos isto satius temptare ueneno.*

9 in domum: the preposition indicates actual passage into a specific house, the goal of the κῶμος being to gain entry to the house of the beloved. The phrase is common enough (some 100 occurrences), but apart from Ter. *Eun.* 382 and Acc. fr. 671 Ribb, this is the only instance in poetry, where metonymy is generally preferred (*sub tecta*, etc.). Those who believe the poem alludes to the wedding of Maximus and Marcia (see intro.) may see a veiled reference to the bride coming into the house of the groom.

10–11 Paulli . . . Maximi: on Paullus Fabius Maximus (*RE* VI 1780–9; *PIR*² F47), born *c.* 46 BCE, and destined to be consul in 11 BCE, see Syme 1986: 396–402, 403–20, and index. He has the unique distinction of being addressed by both H. and Ovid, who some thirty years after H.'s poem himself writes two poems (*Pont.* 1.2; 3.3), and possibly a third (3.8, if it is not to Cotta Maximus), entreating Maximus to intercede with Augustus. Tacitus (*Ann.* 1.5, with inconsistent variants in Pliny, Plutarch, Suetonius and Dio) reports a rumour to the effect that Augustus had confided in Maximus and taken him along on a secret visit to Agrippa Postumus on Planasia (Elba), where the latter was confined. He told his wife, Marcia, who in turn passed news of the visit on to Livia. She told Augustus, with the death of Maximus soon following, 'possibly by his own hand' (*dubium an quaesita morte*). It makes a dramatic story, but Charlesworth 1923 exposes it as highly improbable, and cf. Syme 1978: 149–52; 1986: 414–16, 'a fable'. His death, for which Ovid blames himself at *Pont.* 4.6.11–12, occurred by the summer of 14 CE, not long before that of Augustus, whose favour Maximus clearly enjoyed. The unflattering jest of Cassius Severus, perhaps an allusion to *C.* 4.1 (*ap.* Sen. *Contr.* 2.4.11–12 '*quasi disertus es, quasi formosus es, quasi diues es, unum tantum es non quasi, uappa*'), may indicate the continuing sympotic lifestyle of H.'s not so youthful addressee. Ovid refers to their enjoyment of *conuiuia* together: *Pont.* 1.2.129–30 *ille ego sum, qui te colui, quem festa solebat | inter conuiuas mensa uidere tuos.* This is the only use in the *Odes* of a praenomen and cognomen, perhaps an indication of the greater prominence and historicity of the Augustan aristocrats who are to populate *C.* 4 – though there may be play on the antonyms: *paullus . . . maximus.* The extreme separation of praenomen and cognomen is odd; cf. also 4.2n. on 2 *Iulle . . .* 26 *Antoni.*

10 purpureis ales oloribus 'winged with gleaming swans'. Cf. 3.28.14–15 *Paphum | iunctis uisit oloribus.* The notorious 'purple swans' may be less problematic than some (e.g. Schoonhoven 1978) think, although the adjective does behave oddly from the perspective of English usage. André 1949: 90–102 treats the range of meanings of the word. There is play with and inversion of Sappho 1, where the poet urges Aphrodite again to visit her, as before, in her sparrow-drawn chariot (see intro.). Fordyce notes on Cat. 45.12 that *purpureus* 'often expresses the idea of radiance or sheen without any reference to colour. Swans (Hor. *Od.* iv.1.10), snow (*Eleg. in Maec.* 1.62), salt (Val. Flacc. iii.422) are none of them red or anything like it, but all may be sparkling'. Moreover, Anacreon (12.3 Page) has πορφυρῇ τ' Ἀφροδίτῃ 'rosy Aphrodite', and Ovid, *purpureus . . . Amor* (*Am.* 2.1.38 and McKeown *ad loc.*); if Venus can be 'purple', so can her swans, since in H.'s expression (bare *ales*) the two are almost merged into a single object: is she riding the swans or in a chariot? Putnam 45 mentions Virg. *Aen.* 1.590–1 where Venus sheds the 'purple light of youth' (*lumenque iuuentae | purpureum*) on her son.

12 torrere iecur: ps.-Acro *ad loc. ideo iecur amori dedit pro hoc, quod iecore amari uolunt, felle irasci, corde dolere.* The liver was believed to be the seat of various emotions, for H. of anger, particularly when it was heated with bile (*S.* 1.9.66 *meum iecur urere bilis*; *C.* 1.13.3–4 *uae meum | feruens difficili bile tumet iecur*; see N–H *ad loc.*) and sexual lust, as here (also *C.* 1.25.13–15 *amor et libido . . . | saeuiet circa iecur ulcerosum*; *Epist.* 1.18.72 *non ancilla tuum iecur ulceret ulla puerue*). It is so used in Latin first by H. and otherwise not until Juv. 1.45 (anger) and Sen. *Herc. O.* 574 (lust). At Bib. 2.7 Courtney it is parallel to *cor* and seems to indicate intelligence (Courtney *ad loc.*).

The infinitive with *quaero* (for which cf. 1.37.22) is a poeticism, though taken on by Tacitus (*Germ.* 2.1 *mutare sedes quaerebant*); see *OLD* s.v. *quaero* 6b.

13–16 This quatrain is emblematic of the poem and of the whole book, alternating as it does between the sympotic/erotic and the political. Maximus has both civil (*pro . . . reis*) and military (*militiae*) skills, the latter of which turn out in the last word of the stanza (*tuae*) to be no military skill at all, but rather those same qualities that H. himself had *sub regno Cinarae.* The polysyndeton connecting the positive qualities of Maximus, and furthered by *et* in 17, which connects *feret* to *ponet*, will find precise responsion in negative portrayal of H. in 29–32, with *nec* appearing five times, in the last instance connecting the two subject infins. of *iuuat*, namely *certare* and *uincire*. The effect is strongly contrastive of Maximus and H.

13 et nobilis et decens 'both noble and handsome', and so an appropriate object for Venus' attention. The description of lineage and appearance, along with the *acta* in 14, are reminiscent of the Scipionic epitaph, *CIL* I² 7.1–3 *Cornelius Lucius Scipio Barbatus Gnaiuod patre prognatus, fortis uir sapiensque, quoius forma uirtutei parisuma fuit.* For Virgil's adaptation of this mode to his description of Turnus at *Aen.* 7.473–4 (*hunc decus egregium formae mouet atque iuuentae, | hunc ataui reges, hunc claris dextera factis*), see Thomas 1998a: 283–5. *decens*, like *non tacitus* (14n.), contrasts with *parum decoro . . . silentio* of H. at 35–6; see 13–16n.

14 pro sollicitis non tacitus reis: i.e. *disertus* (see 9–12n. on Paullus). Also invoked as an advocate, as the poet hopes, at Ov. *Pont.* 1.2.67–8 *suscipe, Romanae facundia, Maxime, linguae, | difficilis causae mite patrocinium*, 115–16 *uox, precor, Augustas pro me tua molliat aures, | auxilio trepidis quae solet esse reis.* Syme 1986: 409 finds no evidence that he ever in reality filled such a position. That the litotes *non tacitus* is appropriate to oratorical contexts is clear from its one Ciceronian appearance at *Fam.* 15.4.12 (Cicero's service to Cato) *ut praestantissimas tuas uirtutes non tacitus admirarer*. Cf. Prop. 1.4.17–18 (also of an adversarial context) *sciet hoc insana puella | et tibi non tacitis uocibus hostis erit*. Ovid has *Am.* 3.7.63 *non tacita . . . mente*; *Fast.* 1.356 *non tacito . . . dolore*; *Tr.* 1.3.22 *non taciti funeris*.

15–16 et centum puer artium | late signa feret militiae tuae: Maximus was around 30 at the time, which makes the application of *puer* to him surprising (John D. Morgan notes uses at Cic. *Att.* 1.16.10 and 6.6.3 referring to the immaturity of P. Clodius and C. Coelius Caldus, who had recently been elected to the quaestorship, for which the minimum age was 30; also Trebatius' address to H. at *S.* 2.1.60 *o puer*, looking more to the status and age of the speaker). At 25 *pueri* will dance and sing; at 29 H. will claim to be moved by neither woman nor boy (*puer*), but the poem will end with him pursuing the boy Ligurinus (10.7 *puero*) if only in his dreams. In this connection, in a poem addressed to Venus, and ending with an erotically afflicted H., the lines seem to suggest Cupid the eternal *puer*, the exponent of *militia amoris*. Cf. Prop. 2.8.39–40 *inferior multo cum sim uel matre uel armis, | mirum, si de me iure triumphat Amor?* Likewise Propertius 2.12 on the statue of Amor, both in the details of its iconography (1 *puerum . . . Amorem*; 13 *puerilis imago*), and in that god's actions (16 *assiduusque meo sanguine bella gerit*). Virgil's Iulus as Cupid provides a parallel. If Maximus is so disguised, we perhaps can understand the peripety at 34: H., the denier of erotic feeling, has it thrust upon him by contemplating the 'boy of a hundred arts'. Cf. Prop. 1.1.17 *in me tardus Amor nonnullas cogitat artes*; Virg. *Aen.* 1.657–9 *at Cytherea nouas artes, noua pectore uersat | consilia, ut faciem mutatus et ora Cupido | pro dulci Ascanio ueniat*, Ov. *Pont.* 1.4.41 *illum furtiuae iuuere Cupidinis artes*.

late: Jacobson 1996: 583, following the view of Bradshaw 1970 that the poem is a virtual epithalamium (see intro.), suggests *laete*; this is hardly right, but evidence that *late . . . feret* does not square with such an interpretation.

17–18 'and when getting the upper hand he comes to laugh at the gifts of his lavish rival'. The lines and the future tense work against the view that the poem is an epithalamium for Maximus and Marcia, already betrothed or even married, for which see intro.

17 quandoque 'at which time (whenever it may be)'; indefinite relative, even less definite than *quandocumque*; see *OLD* s.v. *quandoque* 1; L–H–S 608, and cf. 2.34–6. As a relative adverb the usage seems often to be legalistic: Cato *Fil.* 1 J; Cic. *Caec.* 54 *quandoque te in iure conspicio*; *Rep.* 6.24 (speech of Scipio Africanus); Livy 1.31.4 (official context); but it is favoured in H.'s later works: 2.34; *AP* 359. At Petr. *S.* 133.3.10 the Horatian flavour is pointed: *et quandoque mihi fortunae arriserit hora, | non sine honore tuum patiar decus*. At Tac. *Ann.* 4.38.3 (the closing prayer of Tiberius on imperial cult, which in other ways recalls Africanus' speech in Cicero; see Martin and Woodman 1989: *ad* 38.1, 3), the archaism (cf. *duint* in the same section) may reflect Tiberius' stylistic predilections: *precor . . . illos* [*sc.*

ciues] *ut, quandoque concessero, cum laude et bonis recordationibus facta atque famam nominis mei prosequantur.* Parallel formations: *quisque* = *quicumque*; *qualisque* = *qualiscumque*; *utique* = *uticumque*; *quotiensque* = *quotienscumque*.

potentior: cf. of Ligurinus, 10.1 *Veneris muneribus potens* (where *muneribus* is a causal ablative, while here the same form is ablative of comparison); used of erotic power or success, with (*TLL* s.v. *potens* 279.23–40), or without (ib. 280.78–281.5) *in* + ablative: cf. Cat. 100.8 *sis felix, Caeli, sis in amore potens*; Prop. 2.26a.21–2 *nunc admirentur quod tam mihi pulchra puella | seruiat et tota dicar in urbe potens!* Also of the woman's appeal: Prop. 2.5.28 *'Cynthia, forma potens: Cynthia, uerba leuis'*; 3.20.7 *est tibi forma potens*; of a wealthy rival at Plaut. *Epid.* 153–5 *est Euboicus miles locuples, multo auro potens, | qui . . . continuo orabit ut illam tramittas sibi.* For *potentia* in a more strongly sexual sense, see Casali 1995: 85–6.

18 largi muneribus . . . aemuli: for *aemulus* as the love rival, see *TLL* s.v. *aemulus* 979.58–81. See 11.21–4 and n. for Telephus, H.'s rival for the love of Phyllis. The figure, and the jealousy (ζῆλος/ζηλότυπος) connected with him, were central features of Greek New Comedy: Men. *Perik.* 987; Ter. *Eun.* 214–15 *munus nostrum ornato uerbis, quod poteris, et istum aemulum, | quod poteris, ab ea pellito.* He is a central character in Roman love poetry: Cat. 71.3 *aemulus iste tuus, qui uestrum exercet amorem*; Prop. 2.34.18–20 *riualem possum non ego ferre Iouem. | ipse meae solus, quod nil est, aemulor umbrae, | stultus*; Ov. *Rem.* 768 *aemulus est nostri maxima causa mali.* Cf. 3.16.13–15 of Alexander's use of *munera* against political rivals: *diffidit urbium | portas uir Macedo et subruit aemulos | reges muneribus.*

19 Albanos prope . . . lacus: presumably on the estate of the *domus* of 9, or at any rate on some property of Maximus around Castra Albana, off the Via Appia between Bovillae and Aricia, and in the neighbourhood of the future Villa Domitiani, on the southwest shore of the Albanus Lacus – although the plural could indicate proximity also to the Nemorensis Lacus, three km to the southeast; see *BA* 43.3C. On the other hand, Löfstedt I 31–2 treats the use of plural for singular with respect to location. On the villas of this area in the Republican and Augustan periods see Lugli 1914, with no mention, however, of *C.* 4.1.

te: the object of *ponet* is oddly positioned within the prepositional phrase.

19–20 te . . . | ponet marmoream 'he will make a marble statue of you'. The adjective indicates the expense of the statue, though in the shepherd's exchange at Virg. *Ecl.* 7.29–36, marble is only the middling medium: Corydon will give Diana a marble statue to replace the wooden effigy of a stag, while Thyrsis caps him by referring to the marble statue of Priapus (a god normally in wood; see Clausen *ad* 7.35) that he will replace, fantastically, with a gilt one: *nunc te marmoreum pro tempore fecimus; at tu | si fetura gregem suppleuerit, aureus esto* (35–6). Cf. also Virg. *G.* 3.13 *templum de marmore ponam.* In the real world, cf. Cic. *Verr.* 2.4.135 *quid arbitramini Reginos, qui iam ciues Romani sunt, merere uelle ut ab iis marmorea Venus illa auferatur?* Cf. also Ov. *Fast.* 4.135 on the washing of the statue of Venus: *aurea marmoreo redimicula demitte collo.* The wording, in which the addressee is equated to the material of the statue, 'set you up in (e.g.) marble', is found in late inscriptions in elegiac couplets from Aphrodisias: νῦν δέ σε μαρμάρεον | στῆσεν 'now he has set you up in marble'; R. Merkelbach and J. Stauber, *Steinepigramme aus dem griechischen Osten* (Leipzig 1998) I.238, 02/09/09.10–11; also I.230, 02/09/01.5–7 (gold); (from Smyrna) I.515 05/01/25.1–3 (bronze). It seems likely that the inscriptional formulae preceded the examples in Virgil and H., who here makes the vow on behalf of Maximus, continuing the reciprocity that is part of his vicarious cletic hymn (see 8n.).

20 sub trabe citrea: the beam of citrus wood (*Callitris quadriualuis Vent.*; Gr. θύον, i.e. burnt at sacrifices) stands for the statue's shrine or temple; Porph. *ad loc. id est: marmoreum signum tibi et templum decorum statuet.* Theophr. *Hist. pl.* 5.3.7 records that it was used in earlier days in Cyrene for roofs and that it was expensive: cf. Cic. *Verr.* 2.4.37 *tu maximam et pulcherrimam mensam citream . . . abstulisti*; at Luc. *BC* 9.426–30 Rome searches the wood out as material for banquet tables, while the primitivist African is content to sit under the tree's shade; with the same connotations at Petr. 119.27–8 *ecce Afris eruta terris | citrea mensa*; Stat. *Silu.* 4.2.39 *robora Maurorum.* For full treatment of its history and use as a wood for luxury furniture, see Meiggs 1982: 286–91. It has a pleasant odour and so sits well with the next quatrain.

21–8 The ingredients of a *conuiuium* with frankincense, music and dancing, and by implication wine and garlands (31–2). Some of the details are not strictly sympotic, rather festive in a general sense (e.g. 25–6). Hunter 2007: 214–16, with reference to Hills' 1999 dissertation, detects a number of Sapphic ingredients in these lines, particularly the shared spices involved at Sappho fr. 44.30 L-P.

21–4 'There you will inhale abundant frankincense and delight in the mingled strains of lyre and Berecynthian reed-pipe together with the pan-pipe.' Here *lyrae, Berecyntiae, tibiae* is read with Page, other editors and the majority of MSS; these are taken as genitives dependent on *carminibus*, against the Blandinianus, which has ablatives, the preference of Heinsius, Bentley, Shackleton Bailey and others. Bentley took these ablatives with *delectabere*: 'delight in the lyre and the reed-pipe, with songs mingled in, along with the pan-pipe'. Page has a point when he notes that this credits H. 'with lines which for their confusion of ablatives and poorness of sound would discredit a schoolboy'. Others take the presumed ablatives as dependent on *mixtis*, which expects much of the reader: (Putnam) 'you will be gladdened by songs blending with lyre, and Berecyntian flute, and pipe as well'. The confusion stems from *carminibus*, which in both ablatival readings is taken to mean 'songs'. But Page is right to see the stanza as implying only instrumental music: 21–4 there you will delight in music, 25–8 there the youthful will dance as they praise (in song) the gods. At 15.29–32 actual song is present, *duces | Lydis remixto carmine tibiis . . . canemus*, but the better parallel is *Epod.* 9.5, where the lyre and pipes similarly mingle their sound, *sonante mixtum tibiis carmen lyra*. The 'song' of the lyre, trumpet, cithara etc. is of course quite normal usage (*TLL* s.v.

carmen 468.61–469.11; OLD s.v. *carmen* 5). See 15.29–32n. on the musical modes involved with these instruments.

21 illic: in the house of Maximus, and repeated at quatrain opening at 25, a favoured means of emphasis for H., developed from hymnic use. Line-initial repetition in *C.* 1–4 behaves in particular ways in H.: for this type, anaphora (exact unless noted) **at the outset of consecutive quatrains** (A), cf. 1.10.5, 9; 17.17, 21; 21.5, 9; 22. 17, 21; 35. 5, 9 and 17, 21; 2.13.1 (*ille*), 5 (*illum*); 16.1, 5; 19.9, 13 and 17, 21; 20. 9, 13; 3.2.17, 21; 3.9, 13; 4.21 (*uester*), 25 (*uestris*) and 37, 41; 9.1, 5 and 9, 13; 21.13, 17; 29.17, 21; 4.2.13 (*seu*), 17 (*siue*), with preceding *seu* at 10; see n.; 6.9, 13; 8.13, 17; 14.41, 45, 49 (*ter*); *CS* 53, 57. Somewhat more common is repetition **at the initial position in the first and third lines of the quatrain** (B): 1.3.25, 27; 4.9, 11; 19.5, 7; 31.5, 7; 36.13, 15; 2.1.17, 19; 3.17, 19; 14.13, 15; 18.1, 3; 3.4.33, 35; 5.33, 35; 6.5 (*dis*), 7(*di*); 11.45, 47; 19.5, 7; 24.33, 35 and 45, 47; 4.3.17, 19; 8.1, 3; 12.1, 3; 14.45, 47; 49, 51 (a unique pattern; see 14.41–52n.); 15.21, 23; *CS* 45, 46; 53, 55. A third type involves anaphora **at the opening of the first and second lines** (C): 1.18.5, 6; 22.5, 6; 34.9, 10; 2.3.5, 6; 8.21, 22; 16.5, 6 (of *otium*, mirroring type (A) with the same word); 19.17, 18 (of *tu*, mirroring type (A) with the same word, with internal anaphora in 17, a particularly intense hymnic type); 3.1.5 (*regum*), 6 (*reges*); 3.4.65 (*uis*), 66 (*uim*); 11.37, 38; 19.9, 10 (with further internal anaphora in 10); 25.17, 18; 26.49, 50; 4.5.25, 26; 6.37, 38; 13.1, 2; 13, 14 and 17, 18.

The exceptions to these three classes are in some cases only apparent, and all involve anaphora of *non*, *nec*, *seu* or other monosyllables. In some, the first word is itself a repetition of a prior, non-line-initial item, and the anaphora continues: 1.36.11, 12 ((10 *ne* . . .)| *neu* . . . | *neu*, with 13–15 (B) continued by internal anaphora in 16); so too 3.10.14,15 ((13 *neque* . . . *nec* . . .) | *nec* . . . | *nec*, with further examples in 17, and 18); at 4.9.3, 5 (*non* . . . *non*) there is a syntax break; at 4.15.19, 21, 23, 24 there is a concatenation of *non*, beginning internally at 17. In the Roman Odes, the exceptions (3.3.2, 3 *non*; 37, 40 *dum*; 55, 56 *qua*; 4.3, 4 *seu*) may suggest lyric straying into epic in style as well as content (particularly the three instances in 3.3, whose ending suggests the body of the ode has shifted genres: 69–70 *non hoc iocosae conueniet lyrae; | quo, Musa, tendis?*). In other cases there are poetic reasons at work: cf. 3.21.2–4, where *seu* . . . *seu* . . . *seu* proceeds hymnically from the solemn address to the (as yet unidentified) *pia testa* (1 *O nata mecum consule Manlio*); 4.5.32, 33 is artful in that line-initial, quatrain-end *te* sets up the felt internal anaphora of 33 (*te multa prece, te prosequitur mero*); at 4.11.1, 4 the effect is combined with a strongly enjambing style in 9 (see 11.1–12n.); 2.6.6, 7 (*sit*) is a true exception, though transposition of 5 and 6 would remove it. Also exceptional is 4.12.16, 17, stanza end and beginning, for emphasis. For a treatment of anaphora in H., see Tosi 1997: 847–9; in general Wills *passim*.

21–2 plurima naribus | duces tura: cf. Lucr. 6.765–6 *naribus alipedes ut cerui saepe putantur | ducere*. On *tus* (frankincense, aromatic gum from the tree *Boswellia carterii*) see Coleman 1988: 228. Its abundance here (*plurima*) is an indication of the opulence of the *conuiuium*. Cf. (all in the context of sacrifice and feasting)

2.51–2 *dabimusque diuis | tura benignis*; 1.19.13–15 *hic | uerbenas, pueri, ponite turaque | bimi cum patera meri* (see 3.4, 4–5nn.); 1.36.1–3 *Et ture et fidibus iuuat | placare et uituli sanguine debito | custodes Numidae deos*; 3.8.2 *quid uelint flores et acerra turis*; 3.23.3 *si ture placaris*.

22–4 lyraeque et Berecyntiae . . . tibiae | non sine fistula: cf. in sympotic contexts 3.19.18–20 (all three instruments): *cur Berecyntiae | cessant flamina tibiae? | cur pendet tacita fistula cum lyra?*; 1.12.1–2 *Quem uirum aut heroa lyra uel acri | tibia sumis celebrare . . . ?*; *Epod.* 9.5 *sonante mixtum tibiis carmen lyra*. Elsewhere these instruments play solo. The lyre signifies both the *conuiuium* at which it is to be played, and the art of the poet of *C.* 1–4. H. has *lyra* sixteen times, *cithara* and *fides* each thirteen times; see *TLL* s.v. *lyra* 1948.79–1949.11. On the *tibia* (Gk. αὐλός = 'reed-pipe') see Brink *ad AP* 202, 203, and for the *fistula* (Gk. σῦριγξ = 'pan-pipe'), cf. 12.9–10, appropriately a Virgilian context, *dicunt in tenero gramine pinguium | custodes ouium carmina fistula* (and 12.10n.); also 15.29–32n.

delectabere: echoing 11 *comissabere* in the same relative metrical *sedes*. The form in *-bere* is otherwise found in H. only at *Epist.* 1.18.96 *percontabere*, with *-beris* at *C.* 3.13.3 *donaberis*; *Epist.* 1.18.37 *scrutaberis*; 2.2.8 *imitaberis*; *AP* 132 *moraberis*. Virgil has no forms in *-beris*, 18 in *-bere*, an imbalance which cannot be ascribed simply to metrical convenience, as H.'s hexameter instances of *-beris* show: *Ecl.* 2.31 *imitabere*; 3.35 *fatebere*; *G.* 1.459 *terrebere*; 1.155 *insectabere*; 1.159 *solabere*; 1.228 *aspernabere*; 2.274 *metabere*; 3.410 *uenabere*; 4.60, 197 *mirabere*; 4.240 *miserabere*; 4.547 *uenerabere*; *Aen.* 7.318 *dotabere*; 7.547 *uenerabere*; 8.76 *celebrabere*; 10. 740 *laetabere*; 10.826 *solabere*; 10.866 *dignabere*.

25 bis . . . die: cf. Tib. 1.3.31–2 (and Smith 1913 *ad loc.*) *bisque die . . . tibi dicere laudes* (to Isis).

25–6 pueri . . . cum teneris uirginibus: the pairing is almost formulaic in sacral and festive contexts: 1.21.1–2 *Dianam tenerae dicite uirgines, | intonsum pueri dicite Cynthium*; *CS* 6 (and n.) *uirgines lectas puerosque castos*. H. serves as *praeceptor* to this group at 6.31–6 *uirginum primae puerique claris | patribus orti . . . | Lesbium seruate pedem meique | pollicis ictum*; 3.1.3–4 *sacerdos | uirginibus puerisque canto*; also *Epist.* 2.1.132–3 *castis cum pueris ignara puella mariti | disceret unde preces, uatem ni Musa dedisset?* Also paired when there is sexual danger from enemies of the state: Sall. *Cat.* 51.9 *quae belli saeuitia esset, quae uictis acciderent, enumerauere: rapi uirgines, pueros*; Cic. *Phil.* 3.31 *matres familiae, uirgines, pueri ingenui abripiuntur, militibus traduntur*; Livy 26.13.15 (the Campanian view of Rome) *'nec dirui incendique patriam uidebo, nec rapi ad stuprum matres Campanas uirginesque et ingenuos pueros'*. This nuance will connect to the development in the next stanza (*me nec femina nec puer*). Ovid combines the sacral and the sexual in a justification of his amatory verse at *Trist.* 2.369–70 *fabula iucundi nulla est sine amore Menandri, | et solet hic pueris uirginibusque legi*.

27 laudantes: i.e. ὑμνοῦντες; ps.-Acro *ad loc. Ymnum canentes*.

27–8 pede . . . | ter quatient humum: cf. 1.4.6–7 (celebrating spring) *iunctaeque Nymphis Gratiae decentes | alterno terram quatiunt pede*; 1.37.1–2 (the death of Cleopatra) *nunc pede libero | pulsanda tellus*; 3.18.15–16 (when Faunus secures the farm) *gaudet inuisam pepulisse fossor | ter pede terram.* The triple time (*ter*) refers to dance ('waltz') time in general and here to the *tripudium* of the Salii (see below), for which cf. Livy 1.20.4 *per urbem ire canentes carmina cum tripudiis sollemnique saltatu iussit*; at *S.* 1.10.42–3 *Pollio regum | facta canit pede ter percusso* it refers to the tragic trimeter (*senarius*).

pede candido: a sign of beauty (ps.-Acro *ad loc. pulchro*); otherwise only (differently) of an ivory bed leg at Cat. 61.108 *candido pede lecti*; metonymically of Theseus' feet at Cat. 64.162 (Ariadne imagining) '*candida permulcens liquidis uestigia lymphis*'. For a similar aesthetic cf. Cat. 68. 70–2 *quo mea se molli candida diua | intulit et . . . fulgentem . . . plantam | . . . constituit.*

in morem Salium 'after the Salian fashion'; cf. 1.36.12 (with N–H *ad loc.*) *neu morem in Salium sit requies pedum.* For *in* + accusative 'in accordance with', 'after', see *TLL* s.v. *in* 757.30–758.4, for *in morem* specifically, 757.63–72. For the adjective (= *Saliarem*; better thus than genitive plural = *Saliorum*, which sits less well with the gender of H.'s dancers), cf. Cinc. *ap.* Fest. 329.18–20 (439 L.) *Salias uirgines: Cincius ait esse conducticias, quae ad Salios adhibebantur, cum apicibus paludatas.* The *Salii* were priests of Mars, instituted by Numa, and they took care of the *ancilia* (ritual shields), though there seems to be no association with Mars in H.'s references; see Livy 1.20.4 (and Ogilvie *ad loc.*); Dion. Hal. *Ant. Rom.* 2.70–1 for details. They were noted for their dancing, which is doubtless where their name comes from in reality, as in ancient perception: Varro, *Ling.* 5.85 *Salii ab salitando, quod facere in comitiis in sacris quotannis et solent et debent.* The lead dancer was the *praesul*, which supports the etymology against Polemon fr. 38 Preller *ap.* Fest. 329.1 *tamen Polemon ait Arcada quendam fuisse nomine Salium, quem Aeneas a Mantinea in Italiam deduxerit, qui iuuenes Italicos* ἐνόπλιον *saltationem docuerit.* See Ernout-Meillet s.v. *Salii.* Virgil associates them with Evander, Hercules and the cult of the Ara Maxima: *Aen.* 8.285–8 *tum Salii ad cantus . . . adsunt . . . qui carmine laudes | Herculeas et facta ferunt*, where the lack of specific reference to dancing (implied by 287 *chorus*) may be due to epic or Virgilian decorum, though cf. 8.663 *exsultantes Salios.*

29–32 See 13–16n. on the polysyndeton and the strong contrast it creates between Maximus and H. Exquisite miniature style with the first two lines forming a tricolon *abundans* with anaphora of *nec* and three subjects of *iuuat*, the last two lines a doublet with two subject infinitives (also with anaphora of *nec*) of *iuuat* in the 'same' metrical *sedes*. The quatrain, in response to what preceded, communicates a mood of anti-*conuiuium*: no woman or boy, no naive hope for reciprocated feelings, no pleasure in wine or garlands.

29 me: the final marker and climax of the priamel, here opposed to Paullus. So with similar preceding contrast: *ego* at 2.27; *me* at 2.54; 1.1.29, 30, 35; *meae* at 2.45; *nos* at *Epod.* 1.5; *ego* at *S.* 1.1.79 (where the bulk of the poem is the satirist's elaboration of the rejected options of the priamel); *pono* at *Epist.* 1.1.10; *praesenti tibi* (Augustus, in contrast to Romulus, Liber, Castor and Pollux) at *Epist.* 2.1.15. See Race 1982: 122–9 on some of the priamels in H. (129 'Next to Pindar's choral lyrics, H.'s *Odes* exhibit the most sophisticated use of priamels'), and for bibliography see Gianotti 1997: 726–7.

nec femina nec puer: a negation of 25–6 *pueri die | numen cum teneris uirginibus*, with the change to *femina* appropriate to a more openly erotic situation. Cf. *Epigr.* 25 Pf. (= *Anth. Pal.* 5.6.2 = 11 G–P), where Callimachus' Callignotus swears to Ionis that he will prefer neither male nor female to her: μήτε φίλον κρέσσονα μήτε φίλην. For *femina* paired with *puer* in this purely sexual sense, cf. Ovid *Met.* 4.379–80 (the metamorphosis of Hermaphroditus) *nec femina dici | nec puer ut possit*; 9.790–1 (similarly of Iphis) *nam quae | femina nuper eras, puer es!*; 9.794 DONA PUER SOLVIT QUAE FEMINA VOVERAT IPHIS. The pairing more normally indicates vulnerability, chiefly of non-combatants ('women and children'): Livy 25.36.9; 27.11.5; 28.19.13 etc.; Luc. 10.458.

puer: a surprise, setting up the final dénouement and pointing not so much to the lyric stance of *C.* 1–3, where H. shows less overtly erotic interest in boys – although he touches on that of others: 1.4; 2.5; 3.20; also *S.* 1.2.116, where he advises such sexually indiscriminate action; and *S.*2.3.325, where Damasippus levels at H. the charge '*mille puellarum, puerorum mille furores*'; and Thaliarchus (1.9) or Xanthias (2.4) come to mind. The flavour is rather that of *Epode* 11, where H.'s bisexuality is in a strong context of Greek iambic, comedy and (like *C.* 4.1) Hellenistic epigram. That does not mean pederastic activity was not socially and culturally possible for H. (as Shackleton Bailey 1982: 67–75 well shows), just that its presence in these two poems is a literary phenomenon. See 33–4n.

30 spes animi credula mutui 'naive hope of reciprocal feelings'; see 2.12.13–16, where H. had abundance of such reciprocity, *Musa . . . me uoluit dicere . . . bene mutuis | fidum pectus amoribus* (see intro. and 31n.). For the phrasing, cf. Cat. 45.20 *mutuis animis amant amantur*, and *C.* 1.5.5–11 (where H. had learned his lesson) *heu quotiens fidem | mutatosque deos flebit . . . | qui nunc te fruitur credulus aurea, | qui semper uacuam, semper amabilem | sperat.*

31 nec certare iuuat mero: cf. *Epist.* 1.19.10–11 *non cessauere poetae | nocturno certare uino, putere diurno*; also *C.* 2.12.18 (also in the context of prior action and *recusatio*; intro.n.) *nec certare ioco*. H. alludes to the competitive toasting that was integral to the symposium, in which draughts of unmixed wine (ἄκρατος = *merum*) were integrated into various ludic aspects of the party, often controlled by the symposiarch (see Cameron 1995: 80–1), or *magister bibendi*, determined by the throwing of dice, as at 1.4.18 *nec regna uini sortiere talis*, and 2.7.25–6 *quem Venus arbitrum | dicet bibendi?* The toasting and competition (*certare*) has to do with the *eromenos* in Callim. *Epigr.* 29 Pf. (= *Anth. Pal.* 12.51 = 5 G–P) 1–2 ἔγχει καὶ πάλιν εἰπὲ 'Διοκλέος'· οὐδ' Ἀχελῶιος | κείνου τῶν ἱερῶν αἰσθάνεται κυάθων 'pour away and repeat the toast "To Diocles", and Achelous has nothing to do with that one's sacred cups'; adapted by Meleager to a heterosexual context (*Anth. Pal.* 5.136 = 42 G–P) 1–2 ἔγχει καὶ πάλιν εἰπέ, πάλιν, πάλιν Ἡλιοδώρας'· | εἰπέ, σὺν δ' ἀκρήτωι τὸ γλυκὺ μίσγ' ὄνομα 'pour away and repeat the toast again and again "To Heliodora", and mix the sweet name with wine unmixed'. See 32n. for the combination of *merum* and garlands.

32 nec uincire nouis tempora floribus: cf. 1.4.9–10 *nunc decet aut uiridi nitidum caput impedire myrto | aut flore terrae quem ferunt solutae*; at 3.15.13–16 (of the wife of Ibycus, whose years, as with H. here, put her beyond the music, garlands and drinking contests of the symposium) *te . . . non citharae decent | nec flos purpureus rosae | nec poti uetulam faece tenus cadi*; 3.29.2–3 *uerso lene merum cado | cum flore . . . rosarum*; 3.8.2; 3.13.2; *Epist* 1.5.14; 2.1.144; also *C.* 1.38 on the simplicity of the garland. Again, a standard feature of the archaic and Hellenistic symposium (G–P 2.251) as of the κῶμος (G–P 2.124, 125, 535, 576).

33–40 The apparent peripety occurs as H.'s denial is refuted by the tears and speechlessness occasioned by his dream of Ligurinus, whom he pursues through the fields and waters of the Campus Martius. This surprise twist is profoundly imitative of the ending of the Callimachean epigram (see intro.). This does not, however, return him to the arena of Venus, but rather creates a poignancy that reinforces his reluctance to experience her epiphany, for, as Bradshaw 1970: 153 noted of the last stanza, it 'describes a dream in the present *about the past*, H. dreams of running after Ligurinus on the race-track and going after him in the Tiber, or better, perhaps, the Euripus (see 39–40n.) which clearly indicates a young, athletic man's passion for a younger one. The last four lines express, with a haunting sadness, H.'s longing for what he once possessed but could not now recapture except in dreams – not really Ligurinus, who never existed, but his own youth.' In the end he is still not the man he was under the rule of Cinara/Cinura, but that does not protect him from the memory of those days. This seems better than thinking of the fifty-year-old H., already *exigui corporis* and *praecanus* at the time of the *Epist.* 1.2.23, chasing a young man across the playing fields.

33–4 Ligurine: H. does not use provenance names ('the man from Liguria') except as nicknames, whence the real identity can sometimes be recovered (*S.* 1.10.36 *Alpinus* = ?Furius Bibaculus; *Epist.* 1.16.49 *Sabellus* = himself); so this name, attested in inscriptions and in literary texts, is either a real cognomen (highly unlikely in the context) or, like that of Cinara/Cinura (see 3–4n.), susceptible to symbolic or etymological interpretation. Putnam 43–7 suggests an impulse in Virg. *Aen.* 10.185–93, the aetiology of Cupavo the Ligurian, son of Cycnus, who turned into a swan on the death of his lover Phaethon (see also Nagy 1994: 424–5); he then identifies Ligurinus with the young(er) H., who in *C.* 2.20.9–12 turns into a swan. I incline rather towards the view of Davis 1991: 65–71, who sees a sympotic significance (as with Cinara the 'artichoke'). Ligurinus may be related to *ligurrio* and *liguritio* ('fondness for dainties'), as is appropriate to the *conuiuium*: so the name evokes '*gastronomic* preciosity, if not gourmandism'. But H. may have different 'licking' in mind for Ligurinus: a line from Atellan farce, applied to the proclivities of Tiberius (Suet. *Tib.* 45 '*hircum uetulum capreis naturam ligurire*') suggests the antiquity of the meaning, and may be supported by Cat. fr. 3 *de meo ligurrire* *libido est*; see *TLL* s.v. *ligurrio* 1396.79–81; Ausonius could write (128 tit. p. 344.1 P) *Eunus Syriscus, inguinum ligurritor*; cf. 3–4n. on Cinara/Cinura, 13.6–8n. on Chia. The difference in quantity between *Ligŭrinus* and *ligūrio* does not exclude such etymological play. Lyciscus in *Epod.* 11.23–4 (*nunc gloriantis quamlibet mulierculam | uincere mollitie amor Lycisci me tenet*), H.'s only other named *eromenos*, is patently symbolic; see Mankin *ad loc.* That 'Lyciscus' is a real name does not impede its associations as 'little wolf' with the sense 'prostitute'; cf. *lupa* at Plaut. *Epid.* 403; Cat. 99.10 et al. and *TLL* s.v. *lupa* 1859.25–71; at Juv. 6.123 Messalina as prostitute is 'Lycisca'. It is unclear whether the Licymnia of 2.12 is to be attached to H. or Maecenas (see N–H). If the former, there is a further similar wordplay at work: 13–14 *dulces . . . Licymniae | cantus* with *dulces . . . cantus* = γλυκύς/λιγύς + ὑμνεῖν = Licymnia (with λιγύς doubted by N–H *ad* 13).

sed cur heu . . . cur: the monosyllables (glossed by 36 *silentio*) communicate the shock and pain of the revelation.

cur | manat . . . lacrima: the tone of puzzlement and inner dialogue is particularly evocative of Hellenistic epigram; cf. (in pederastic contexts) Asclep. *Anth. Pal.* 12.50 (= 16 G-P) τί τὰ δάκρυα ταῦτα 'why these tears?' Mel. *Anth. Pal.* 12.92.5–6 (= 116.5–6 G-P) [ὀφθαλμοὶ] τί μοι νενοτισμένα χεῖτε | δάκρυα, πρὸς δ' Ἱκέτην αὐτομολεῖτε τάχος; 'eyes, why shed soaking tears, and go running off to Hiketas?'; 12.132b.3 (= 22.3 G–P) τί κλαίεις; 'why do you weep?'; Mel. *Anth. Pal.* 12.144.1 (= 106.1 G–P, to Eros, himself afflicted by Myiscus) τί κλαίεις, φρενολῃστά; 'why do you weep, stealer of wits?'; Posidipp. *Anth. Pal.* 5.211.1–2 (= 3 G–P) δάκρυα καὶ κῶμοι, τί μ' ἐγείρετε, πρὶν πόδας ἆραι | ἐκ πυρός, εἰς ἑτέρην Κύπριδος ἀνθρακιήν; 'tears and partying, why even before I've got my feet out of one fire do you arouse me to another of Venus' bonfires?' Also a feature of Roman erotic and elegiac distress, though not in self-address: 3.7.1 *Quid fles, Asterie . . . ?*; Prop. 2.20.1–2 *Quid fles abducta grauius Briseide? quid fles | anxia captiua tristius Andromacha?* and for generalized tears as a feature of erotic elegy, Pichon 1902: s.v. *lacrimae.*

rara: 'occasional', also perhaps 'unusual', picking up on *intermissa* from the opening line.

35–6 The paralysis and silence resonate with Sappho 31.7–9 L-P ὡς γὰρ ἔς σ' ἴδω βρόχε' ὥς με φώναι- | σ' οὐδ' ἒν ἔτ' εἴκει, | ἀλλ' ἄκαν μὲν γλῶσσα †ἔαγε ('when I look at you, I am no longer able to speak, and my tongue ?breaks'), and its adaptation at Cat. 51. 6–9 *nam simul te, | Lesbia, aspexi, nihil est mi* | <e.g. *uocis in ore*> | *lingua sed torpet.* See intro. For *cadit lingua* cf. of imminent death Stat. *Silu.* 2.1.149–50 *linguaque cadente | murmurat.* H.'s usage is striking, perhaps a variation on the Catullan metaphor, perhaps a development of the verb with other body parts (*manus, lacerti, oculi* etc.; cf. *OLD* s.v. *cado* 7a). It is distinct from Plaut. *Poen.* 259–60 (where perfect tense and compound create a different image) *nil respondes? | lingua huic excidit, ut ego opinor* ('he's lost his tongue'). Cf. Serv. *ad* Virg. *Aen.* 4.76 *incipit effari mediaque in uoce resistit: sic Horatius 'cur facunda parum decoro inter uerba cadit lingua silentio?'*

parum decoro | . . . silentio: in contrast to Maximus: 13–14 *decens* | *et . . . non tacitus.*

parum decor(o) | inter: iconically hypermetric: *decor(o)* itself becomes 'too little,' or, with Commager 1980 (cf. for all hypermetric lines of *C.* 4): 66: 'the sudden breaking off of the word reproduces the sudden silence to which, as an unregenerate lover, he now falls prey'.

37–40 An artful stanza, with all four lines treating the relation of pursuer (*ego*) to pursued (*te*), and each couplet given shape by a doublet with anaphora: 38 *iam . . . iam*; 39–40 *te per gramina . . . te per aquas.* This artistry brings home the speaker's alternating success (*captum teneo*) and failure (*uolucrem sequor*), where the adjective signifies both in the physical, and in a more psychological sense, 'fleeting'; cf. 3.28.6; 4.13.16 *uolucris dies*; see 40n. In spite of the difference in quantity *uolūbilis* picks up on the sound and sense of *uolŭcrem.*

37 nocturnis . . . somniis: The poignancy of the dream matches those of Virgil at *Aen.* 4.465–8 (Dido) and 12.908–12 (simile for the physical frustration of Turnus); cf. the less poignant erotic dream of *S.* 1.5.82–5 *hic ego mendacem stultissimus usque puellam | ad mediam noctem exspecto; somnus tamen aufert | intentum ueneri; tum immundo somnia uisu | nocturnam uestem maculant uentremque supinum.*

38 captum teneo . . . sequor: the hysteron-proteron construction brings out the elusive nature of Ligurinus.

39–40 per gramina Martii | Campi, . . . per aquas: athleticism in the Campus Martius and the Tiber is a frequent motif in H. (*S.* 1.1.91; 1.6.126; 2.6.49; 1.7.59; 1.11.4; *AP* 162; *C.* 3.7.26 *Martium gramen*); in some of these instances the Campus figures as an erotically charged setting, the equivalent in its connection with the young of the Hellenistic gymnasium (avoided by the lovelorn *C.* 1.8.4; rendezvous for young lovers *C.* 1.9.18); similarly for the Tiber: *C.* 1.8.8, 3.12.7, 7.28; *Epist.* 1.11.4; see Thomas 1996: 375–8. In fact, however, H. may be referring not to the Tiber, but rather to the newly constructed baths and Euripus. So Knox 2009: 664 'Commentators understand the *uolubilis aquas* as the "rolling waters" of the Tiber, and refer, for example, to *Carm.* 1.8.8 for the river as a place to swim, as indeed it was when H. was composing the first three books of *Odes* before 23 B.C.E. But after the completion of Agrippa's waterworks in the Campus Martius in 19 B.C.E. – the baths and the Euripus – that was the place to wash off after a workout, as it was for Ovid: *usus equi nunc est, leuibus nunc luditur armis, | nunc pila, nunc celeri uoluitur orbe trochus; | nunc ubi perfusa est oleo labente iuuentus, | defessos artus Virgine tingit aqua* (*Trist.* 3.12.19–22). Take *Martii Campi* ἀπὸ κοινοῦ with *aquas* to refer to the new bathing facilities of the Campus, more specifically to the rolling waters of the Euripus.'

40 aquas . . . uolubiles: cf. 37–40n. on *uolucrem*; here too there is a sense that the water snatches away both swimmer and image; cf. *Epist.* 1.2.42–3 *at ille* [*sc. amnis*] | *labitur et labetur in omne uolubilis aeuum.* Perhaps an echo of the loss expressed by Cat. 70.3–4 *sed mulier cupido quod dicit amanti, | in uento et rapida scribere oportet aqua.*

dure: cf. 6–7n.

2

METRE

Sapphic stanza, the second most common in H. (also in 6, 11, *CS*), consisting of three lines of sapphic hendecasyllable (–⏑–––⏑⏑–⏑–×), with an adonic (–⏑⏑–×) in the fourth. See *CS* intro.

INTRODUCTION

Taking on Pindaric emulation is risky business, Iullus, and can lead to downfall. Whatever of the genres he's engaged on, whether dithyrambs, hymns, epinicians, laments, he's like a river crashing down from a mountain. Antonius, a mighty breeze is needed to lift up the swan of Dirce: I on the other hand fashion my intricate song just like the Matine bee gathering thyme by the waters of Tivoli. You'll be better at singing of Caesar when he returns in triumph, and singing of the celebrations, while I just join the crowd in cheering him on to triumph. You can sacrifice ten bulls and ten cows, I'll just sacrifice a little calf, with markings like the moon at its third rising.

The first half of the poem treats the difficulty and danger of emulating Pindar, with the shift coming at 25–8, as the focus shifts from the addressee Iullus Antonius (26 *Antoni*) to the poet (27 *ego*), the swan to the bee, high Pindaric to small-scale Callimachean, Pindaric Thebes to Horatian Matinus. This sets up the contrasting sacrifices with which the poem ends (53–60n.).

The poem continues the programmatic and theoretical movement of *C.* 4.1. Where that poem had treated resistance to and acquiescence in the worlds of love and erotic lyric, 4.2 introduces and explores the theme of encomium and competence in encomium. Together the two poems prepare the reader for an alternation between these two themes throughout the book.

Davis 1991: 133–43, who well sets out the poem's play with laudation and *recusatio*, has a useful scheme, capturing the bifurcation of the second half:

(a) Disavowal of the grand style	(1–32)
(b) Double encomium of Augustus	(33–60)
(1) Grand-style specimen by addressee	(33–44)
(2) Plain-style specimen by speaker	(45–60)

The poem shares much with 1.6, 2.12 and Virg. *Ecl.* 6, in which, as here, the preferred mode is in attenuated contrast with that of another poet (Varus), who is to take on the task of encomium in a higher mode (see 25–32, 33–44nn.). Prop. 3.17, a hymn to Bacchus, had already explored the Pindaric as a high mode, even one opposed to the ideal, Callimachean alternative, particularly in the poem's envoi:

haec ego non humili referam memoranda coturno,
    qualis Pindarico spiritus ore tonat:
tu modo seruitio uacuum me siste superbo,
    atque hoc sollicitum uince sopore caput.

Bacchus is to free Propertius from the slavery of love (cf. 3 *insanae Veneris . . . flatus*); if so, Propertius will reverse his earlier, attenuated mode, when, like the Callimachus of *Aet.* 1, fr. 1.20 Pf. (βροντᾶν οὐκ ἐμόν, ἀλλὰ Διός 'it's Zeus's job to thunder, not mine'), he avoided the high style: 2.1.39–42: *neque . . . intonet . . . Callimachus* etc.

Pindar is the new epic, the foil of the *recusatio*, that which in the world of encomium is opposed to the Callimachean. The Propertian passage suggests that Pindaric encomium is *opposed* to the Callimachean, a proposition H. exploits in the second half of this poem and throughout the fourth book. Soon after publication of Prop. 3, H. had juxtaposed high Pindaric with Callimachean, complimenting Titius for his ability to excel in both: *Epist.* 1.3.9–11 *quid Titius, Romana breui uenturus in ora, | Pindarici fontis qui non expalluit haustus, | fastidire lacus et riuos ausus apertos?* See 13–14n. H. had of course emulated Pindar in his earlier lyric (notably 1.12 and 3.4), and he will do so again in his new collection. So 4.2 sets up the Pindaric poems that are to come (3, with 1–12n., 4, 14) and opens up the question of competence that will be set in play by compositional aspects of those poems. The retreat from the Pindaric to the Callimachean that occurs in the second half finds recapitulation in the poem to follow (3).

1–4 As John Henderson notes *per litteras*, there seems to be play with names and partial acrostics: the opening PINDARUM begins to generate an acrostic (P I N, of the type most famous at Arat. *Phaen.* 783–7 λεπτή | Λ Ε Π Τ Η), but instead creates incomplete P I N N–, an iconic image of what is going on in the lines, the crash of Icarus into the sea. *nititur pinnis* at the start of 3 descends in the next line to *nomina ponto*, with *nomina* drawing attention to the play. In this context *ope Daedaleo* may point to Virg. *Aen.* 6.28–33, where Daedalus' artwork participates in the narrative it creates (28–30 *regens . . . resoluit*) and where Icarus is denied participation in the Daedalian artwork (31 *opere in tanto*) as not he, but rather the hands of his father, fall, the ecphrasis ending in mid-line (33), as H.'s acrostic does in mid-word. Pindar himself does the falling, as a stream from a mountain, in the lines that follow. Cf. 53–60n. for metapoetics in the closing frame.

1 Pindarum: cf. 8 *Pindarus* and 9.5–12 and n.; otherwise in H. mentioned at *Epist.* 1.3. Cic. *Orat.* 4.9 has Pindar in the first rank of Greek poets, along with Homer, Archilochus and Sophocles, as representatives of the broad poetic genres; so too *Fin.* 2.115 (Homer, Archilochus and Pindar, contrasted with Phidias, Polyclitus, and Zeuxis). See 5–8n. on Quintilian's view, citing H.

quisquis: the referent is unclear (= *si quis*, as at 2.1.25: *OLD* s.v.; or = *ille qui*, as at 2.2.23: *OLD* s.v. 4, in which case, H. or Iullus?), setting up the general ambiguity about the status of H.'s and Iullus' poetry.

aemulari 'engage in competitive imitation of' (Gk. ζηλόω/ζήλωσις), a more combative term than *imitari* (Gk. μιμέομαι/μίμησις). It is otherwise absent from poetry of all periods after Terence and here functions as a technical term for intertextuality. Cf. Quint. 10.1.61 *nouem uero lyricorum longe Pindarus princeps spiritu, magnificentia, sententiis, figuris, beatissima rerum uerborumque copia et uelut quodam eloquentiae flumine: propter quae Horatius eum merito nemini credit imitabilem* (there is no

**aemulabilis*). Plin. *Epist.* 7.30.5 refers to a speech of Demosthenes, *quam sane, cum componerem illos, habui in manibus, non ut aemularer (improbum enim ac paene furiosum), sed tamen imitarer et sequerer*; 9.22.1 (of Passenus Paullus) *in litteris ueteres aemulatur exprimit reddit, Propertium in primis, a quo genus ducit.* The use of a prose word in the context of the difficulty of matching Pindaric poetry may be pointed. Cf. 57 *imitatus*.

2 Iulle: Iullus Antonius, so identified at 26 (*RE* I 2584–5; *PIR*[2] A800), son of Marcus Antonius and Fulvia. Coeval with Ovid (both born in 43 BCE), he was brought up by his stepmother Octavia and consequently enjoyed the support of Augustus, unlike his brother Antullus, who had joined his father in the East and was put to death after the capture of Alexandria. He was married in 21 BCE to Claudia Marcella maior, daughter of Octavia and C. Claudius Marcellus (cos. 50 BCE). He may have been aedile at the time of H.'s poem in 16 BCE, was *praetor urbanus* in 13 BCE, consul in 10 BCE. The fall of Iullus came in 2 BCE, after implication in the adultery of Julia, when he was killed or ordered to commit suicide (Dio 55.10.16); see Syme 1986: 62–3, 91, *passim*. That he was a poet, and of a higher style, may be assumed from the present context and is confirmed by ps.-Acro *ad* 2.33 *heroico metro Diomedias duodecim libros scripsit egregios*. Twelve books of post-Virgilian Latin epic in the years following the publication of the *Aeneid* (the work was presumably not a juvenile product) would have been something of a curiosity, and perhaps even more risky than Pindaric composition. H. will have had a view of the work.

The separation of names (2 *Iulle*; 26 *Antoni*) continues and greatly expands that of Paullus Maximus at 1.10–11 (see n.), and cf. 43 *Augusti reditu* . . . 47–8 *recepto* | *Caesare*.

2–3 ceratis ope Daedalea | nititur pinnis 'relies on wings worked with wax by the device of a Daedalus'. Artificiality is the chief danger from emulating Pindar. The person who attempts this ends up like Icarus, as a bird that will not fly – in contrast to the Pindaric swan of 25–7. In 2.20 H. himself turned into a swan in the context of his own poetic fame (see 3–4n.); things have become more ominous in the current context. There is a connection with 27–32, where H., a bee in contrast to the Dircaean swan (and implicitly a worker of wax), himself fashions *operosa* . . . *carmina*.

3–4 uitreo daturus | nomina ponto 'sure to give his name to a glassy sea'; as Icarus did to the Icarian Sea. At 2.20.13–14 (*iam Daedaleo notior Icaro* | *uisam gementis litora Bosphori*) H.'s fame is set into the context precisely of his similarity with (the still airborne) Icarus. Cf. Livy 1.3.8–9, also of death by water, *Tiberinus, qui in traiectu Albulae amnis summersus celebre ad posteros nomen flumini dedit*; Serv. *ad* Virg. *Aen.* 3.500 *Thybrim, qui in hunc cecidit fluuium et ei nomen dedit*; Serv. *ad* Virg. *Aen.* 3.202 (Palinurus) *qui Aenea de Sicilia ad Italiam ueniente praecipitatus in mare nomen in Lucania monti celebri dedit*; 6.659 (Eridanus) *Phaethon appellatus est, et pristinum nomen fluuio dedit*; also Virg. *Aen.* 10.199–200 *Mantus et Tusci filius amnis,* | *qui muros matrisque dedit tibi, Mantua, nomen.*

nomina: plural, as at 3.27.75–6 (with N–R *ad loc.*) *tua sectus orbis* | *nomina ducet.* The poetic plural, here with an abstract noun, is treated by K–S II 1.77–82; also

Löfstedt I 34–6. Cf. 12.13 *tempora*. As in H., such instances of *nomina* elsewhere often have to do with etymological aetiology or metamorphosis: Prop. 4.2.50 *unde hodie Vicus nomina Tuscus habet*; Ov. *Fast.* 2.449 *gratia Lucinae: dedit haec tibi nomina lucus*; *Met.* 14.396 *nec quicquam antiquum Pico nisi nomina restat*; 14.616; *Trist.* 1.1.90 (also of Icarus) *aequoreis nomina fecit aquis*; *Ib.* 370 *qui noua Myrtoae nomina fecit aquae*; 514, 522; Manil. 4.609 *Hadriaco mutatum nomina ponto* etc. The instance at Prop. 2.19.31 *quin ego in assidua metuam tua nomina lingua* may have to do with the ?rival's repeated use of Cynthia's name; here see, with further bibliography, Heyworth 2007: 192–3.

5–24 A sentence whose length and periodicity reflect the elaborate style of Pindaric verse. Cf. 4.1–28 and 14.1–24 and nn. for more elaborated instances of H.'s syntactical *aemulatio* of Pindar.

5–8 The stanza well reflects Pindar's own metaphorical audacity, as simile (*monte decurrens uelut amnis*) and metaphor (*feruet immensusque ruit... Pindarus*) come into close contact. See Gildersleeve 1899: xlii–xliii on Pindar's rich use of metaphor. There is a marked similarity and contrast with 27–32 (see n.), with *ripas* (6, 31) inviting comparison between the effusive style of Pindar and the attenuated, Callimachean mode of H. Quintilian picked up on the metaphor (In.) 10.1.61 *copia et uelut quodam eloquentiae flumine.*

amnis: twelve occurrences in H., who has 21 of *flumen*, five of *fluuius*. None of the twelve would permit the use of *flumen* for metrical reasons, while in one case H. could have written *amnis* where he has *flumen* (*S.* 1.7.27). For distribution among various authors, see *TLL* s.v. *amnis* 1943.5–22, with the comment 'uox ipsa imprimis poetici uel elatioris stili'; *TLL* s.v. *flumen* 957.51–84. *amnis* is absent from Caesar, Nepos and the geographical writers, with the (non-)exception of Vibius Sequester p. 14 Gelsomino, since he quotes Cornelius Gallus (fr. 1 Courtney; 144 Hollis), *Hypanis Scythiae, qui, ut ait Gallus, 'uno tellures diuidit amne duas', Asiam ab Europa separat.*

5–6 imbres | quem super notas aluere ripas 'which the rains have swollen above their usual banks'. *alo* first here in this sense, though cf. Virg. *Aen.* 9.30–1 (and Hardie *ad loc.*) *ceu septem surgens sedatis amnibus altus* | *per tacitum Ganges*, 'fed by its seven placid tributaries', as argued by Williams 1968: 148; *alo* itself is otherwise only at Mela 2.62; Tac. *Hist.* 5.6.2 *idem* [sc. *Libanus mons*] *amnem Iordanem alit funditque*; *TLL* s.v. *alo* 1709.59–62. At Plin. *HN* 3.131 the Italian lakes, fed by the rivers that flow into them, are in turn said to be *alumni* of the tributaries of the Po.

7 feruet: not necessarily a positive attribute from the Callimachean point of view; cf. Volcacius fr. 1.7 *dein Naeuius, qui feruet*, for which see *TLL* s.v. *ferueo* 592.1, while H.'s example is included at 593.15–16, uniquely in Latin of a person (Pindar), but at the same time in a context having to do with the movement of water and wind. Cf. also the *ingenium* of the unfortunate Cassius at *S.* 1.10.62 *rapido feruentius amni*; also 32n.

7–8 immensusque ruit profundo . . . ore: continues the metapoetics of 7 *feruet*; as in that case, so here, *TLL* s.v. *immensus* 453.29–30 seems to imply that the adjective is within the simile. Cf. *S.* 1.7.26–8 (of unbridled oratory) *ruebat* | *flumen ut hibernum fertur quo rara securis.* | . . . *salso multoque fluenti*. Cicero uses similar language to describe the irrationality of partisan politics: *Planc.* 15 *sin hoc persaepe accidit ut et factos aliquos et non factos esse miremur, si campus atque illae undae comitiorum, ut mare profundum et immensum, sic efferuescunt quodam quasi aestu ut ad alios accedant, ab aliis autem recedant, tamen nos in impetu studiorum et motu temeritatis modum aliquem et consilium et rationem requiremus?*

profundo . . . ore: *os* is often used with an epithet to indicate stylistic register; see *TLL* s.v. *os* 1081.55–1082.3; Thomas 1978. The phrase is quite striking, otherwise only at Stat. *Theb.* 9.420–1 (appropriate to the river god, Ismenos) *cornua concutiens sic turbidus ore profundo* | *incipit*; at Stat. *Theb.* 7.816–17 of the gaping earth: *ecce alte praeceps humus ore profundo* | *dissilit*. With *profundo . . . ore* comes the culmination of a series of indicators (*ponto* | *monte decurrens uelut amnis* | *super ripas* | *feruet immensusque ruit*) of the non-Callimachean nature of Pindaric composition (e.g. Callim. *Hymn* 2.105–9).

9 laurea . . . Apollinari: with ellipsis of *corona*, as regularly (sometimes of *arbor*); cf. *TLL* s.v. *laureus, -a, -um* 1058.13–83, *contra OLD* s.v. l*aurea* ~ *ae*, f. The laurel crown is associated with triumphal victors (e.g. Cic. fr. 12 Courtney *cedant arma togae, concedat laurea laudi*) and victors in the Pythian Games as well as poets, although instances of the latter before Ovid are confined to this passage and (with epinician or Pindaric overtones) 3.4.19, 3.30.15–16 (*mihi Delphica* | *lauro cinge uolens, Melpomene, comam*) and Prop. 4.6.19 (on the victory at Actium) *pura nouum uati laurea mollit iter*. Harrison 1995: 111–12 notes that Pindar's laurel points directly to an association with the Pythian Games and thereby to an identification with H.'s own lyric aspirations at 1.1.30.15–16 (*Delphica* | *lauro*). Triumphal and poetic are also combined at Prop. 3.1.9–10 *a me* | *nata coronatis Musa triumphat equis*. At 2.1.15–16 Pollio will return to the tragic stage adorned with triumphal laurel, perhaps also combining both types.

donandus 'to be presented with'; he will win the laurel whatever genre he tries (10–24 *seu . . . seu . . . siue*). Varieties of giving run through the poem, from 3 *daturus* to 9 *donandus* to 20 *donat* to 38 *donauere* to 39 *dabunt* to 51 *dabimus*. The idea of reciprocity is particularly felt in in 9 and 20: (*Pindarus*) *donandus . . . donat*.

10–24 An artful narrative catalogue of Pindaric genres, progressing through dithyramb (10–12 and n.), hymns, paeans and prosodia (13–16), epinicians (17–20) and threnoi (21–4). The movement descends from gods, to heroes, to athletic victors, to lament for human death, starting on the mountain top (5 *monte*) and ending in the Underworld (24 *Orco*). The generic movement mirrors the contextual (5 *decurrens*). In each of the four cases the specifying of genre is followed by brief exemplary elaboration, so the whole passage functions both as catalogue and attenuated description, almost like a miniature of the *Pinakes* of Callimachus.

This makes it probable that H. had access to the Alexandrian edition of Pindar, whose seventeen books are enumerated in the *Vita Ambrosiana* (Maehler 1): hymns, paeans, dithyrambs (2), prosodia (2), partheneia (2); poems separate from the partheneia, hyporchemata (2), encomia, threnoi, epinicians (4). A slightly different order, with dithyrambs heading the list, and threnoi closing it, as occurs in H.'s lines, may be found in *P Oxy.* 2438.35–9 (see Race, Pindar II 222). For H.'s ordering of the catalogue see Freis 1983, with a focus on its function as *recusatio.*

10–12 Dithyramb was from its earliest appearance associated with Dionysus, not just with Dionysiac festivals at Athens, as is already clear in Archilochus 120 West ὡς Διωνύσου ἄνακτος καλὸν ἐξάρξαι μέλος | οἶδα διθύραμβον οἴνωι συγκεραυνωθεὶς φρένας 'for I know how to lead off the fair song of Lord Dionysus, the dithyramb, my wits thunderstruck by wine'. On the folk etymology (*Et. Magn.* s.v. ὁ δὶς θύραζε βεβηκώς 'he who came twice to the doors [of birth]') see Dodds on Eur. *Bacch.* 526, which plays on the putative derivation. The name may have referred to a dance step, and its termination is perhaps related to that of θρίαμβος, ἴαμβος and *triumphus*, but its origins are obscure. In general see Pickard-Cambridge 1962: 1–59; for possible connections between the dithyramb and the triumph-song in Propertius and Tibullus, see Cairns 1972: 168, 187. The genre was practiced by Pindar, Bacchylides and a number of fifth- and fourth-century poets.

10 seu: with 13, and 17 (*siue*) an unusual anaphora, permitted with conjunctions; see 1.21n. Fraenkel 1932–3: 5 draws attention to Dioscorides *Anth. Pal.* 7.407 (= 18 G–P), with its enumeration of the various aspects of Sappho (ἢ . . . ἢ . . . ἢ), an essentially hymnic style.

audaces: boldness of expression, balancing metrical license (11–12n.), as at Quint. 10.1.96, who applies the adjective to H. himself: *Horatius . . . uerbis felicissime audax.*

10–11 noua . . . | uerba deuoluit: the verb, with *fertur* continuing the image of a boisterous river, is itself audacious (see 5–8n.) and is applied here for the first time as a metaphor for style; cf. *TLL* s.v. *deuoluo* 870.9–12. Otherwise only so, perhaps under the influence of H., at Quint. 12.10.61 (of the high style) *at ille qui saxa deuoluat et 'pontem indignetur'* [Virg. *Aen.* 8.728] *et ripas sibi faciat multus et torrens iudicem uel nitentem contra feret, cogetque ire qua rapiet.*

noua . . . uerba: in particular through compounds, following Aristot. *Rhet.* 3.1406b1-2, on later dithyramb: διὸ χρησιμωτάτη ἡ διπλῆ λέξις τοῖς διθυραμβοποιοῖς 'therefore compound words are frequently used by dithyrambic poets'.

11–12 numerisque . . . lege solutis: by no means true of Pindaric dithyramb, as far as can be told. H. may be imputing to metre a freedom appropriate to Dionysus, the addressee of the genre: cf. *Epod.* 9.37–8 *curam metumque Caesaris rerum iuuat | dulci Lyaeo soluere*, where *soluere* (λύειν) acts as a bilingual pun, as Lambinus noted (see Mankin *ad loc.*). The play is already found in Pindar, at fr. 248 Maehler τῶι Λυαίωι λύοντι | δυσφόρων σχοινίον μεριμνᾶν 'to Lyaeus who loosens the cord of difficult cares'. Cf. also *Epist.* 1.16.78 (alluding to Eur. *Bacch.*)

'*ipse deus, simul atque uolam, me soluet.*' H. was probably aware that the post-Pindaric dithyramb (e.g. of Melanippides) abandoned its earlier, antistrophic conventions, according to Aristotle (*Prob.* 19.15), in the interests of an enhanced mimesis, and in the context of the professionalization of the solo (vs. choral) performer. Cf. Fraenkel 1932–3: 3–4 (citing Maas) and Pickard-Cambridge 1962: 25, 38–41. Privitera (*EO* I 850) believes the reference is not to the freedom from strophic responsion, but to the generally freer nature of Pindaric metrics, not just in the dithyrambs, from the perspective of the Sapphic and Alcaic stanza – an attractive suggestion. See Freis 1983: 30–1, n. 7.

13, 17 seu . . . siue: see 1.21n.

13–16 Hymns to gods and encomia to kings, the former unspecified, though we may imagine a reference to paeans and *prosodia*, both Pindaric genres. In fact the details of the stanza include only the feats of heroes, namely the conquest of the Centaurs (by Heracles and Theseus) and of the Chimaera (by Bellerophon). Without the examples of 14–16, *reges* could refer also to epinicians, e.g. to Hieron, as ps.-Acro *ad loc.* took it. The stanza is artfully crafted, with repetition (*deos . . . deorum* | *cecidere . . . cecidit*) and variation figured (*cecidere . . . Centauri* | *cecidit . . . flamma*) in a fully enjambed set of lines. The lines traffic in boundaries, between gods and humans, and humans and animals.

13–14 deos regesue . . . deorum sanguinem: the words create a pivot in the descending progression from gods to kings/heroes to mortals (10–24n.). Perhaps a passing allusion to Callim. *Aet.* 1 fr. 1.3–5 Pf. ἢ βασιλ[η . . . ἢ . . .] . . . ἥρωας, the topics eschewed by that poet, just as the Pindaric will be in contrast to the Callimachean H. at the end of the priamel (27–32 *ego . . . operosa paruus* | *carmina fingo*). If so, there are further grounds to read, with Shackleton Bailey and a few MSS, *regesue* (that is, ἤ) in 13. Wills 254–61 treats the polyptoton with genitival subordination *deos . . . deorum*, common in hierarchical progressions, as here.

deorum sanguinem: so, also in a predicate syntactical relationship, at 2.20.5–6 *non ego pauperum* | *sanguis parentum*. The sense is as old as Ennius: *Ann.* 108 Skutsch *o pater, o genitor, o sanguen dis oriundum!*; cf. also Virg. *Aen.* 6.835 *proice tela manu, sanguis meus*. For the usage cf. *OLD* s.v. *sanguis* 10.

14–15 cecidere . . . Centauri, cecidit . . . flamma Chimaerae: for this type of repetition with shift of number, elsewhere in H. at 2.8.13–14 *ridet . . . rident*, see Wills 290–5. The present instance is unusual in that there is a slight shift in meanings of the repeated verbs, caused by the periphrasis of the second subject, the so-called 'βίη Ἡρακλῆος construction', 'the strength of Hercules' = 'the mighty Hercules'. The repetition of verb, along with the parallel final placement of the proper names, is rhetorically pointed, creating emphasis and continuing that of the preceding *deos . . . deorum* (and cf. 33, 41 *concines*). For differing views on repetition in H., see Housman 1926: xxxiii, and Helmbold 1960: 173–4; also 5.17–18n.

The fire-breathing Chimaera (Virg. *Aen.* 6.288 *flammisque armata Chimaera*; also 7.785–8, on Turnus' helmet), according to Hom. *Il.* 6.179–82 in the form of a lion, goat and snake, was killed by Bellerophon, whose other labors include fighting the Amazons; the incident is mentioned at Pind. *Ol.* 13.90, as noted by Harrison 1995: 113. Lucretius will have none of this; since even lions are burnt by fire, 5.904–6 *qui fieri potuit, triplici cum corpore ut una, | prima leo, postrema draco, media ipsa, Chimaera | ore foras acrem flaret de corpore flammam?*

cecidere . . . cecidit: use of the third-person plural in *-ēre* rather than *-ērunt/-ĕrunt* 'is distinctly archaic, and was normally avoided by (for example) Caesar and Cicero, but was used by dactylic poets and imitated from them by prose authors such as Tacitus to give poetic colouring' (Lapidge 2005: 325–6, with further bibliography). In H. there are 74 occurrences of forms in *-ēre*, with distribution across all the works (for the *Epodes* only at 17. 11 *unxere* (*luxere* Brink), 15 *exuere*, 44 *reddidere*), compared to only nineteen in *-ērunt* and three in *-ĕrunt* (*Epod.* 9.17 *uerterunt*; *S.* 1.10.45 *annuerunt*; *Epist.* 1.4.7 *dederunt*). The preference for *-ēre* is not simply one of metrical stricture, since 36 of the 74 instances are found in the *Odes*, which on the other hand show a distinct aversion to forms in *-erunt* (only 3.6.7, 4.13.23 *dedērunt*). At the same time, the final trochee in *-ērĕ* forms is convenient.

iusta | morte: the half-horse, half-man Centaurs are emblematic of the threat posed by the wild to the civilized (see *OCD* s.v. 'Centaurs'); Hercules' killing of the Centaur Nessus (for attempting to rape Deianira), and Theseus' of the Centaurs in general (for their drunken violence at the wedding feast of the Lapiths), are seen as supreme examples of the application of human justice.

17–20 'or if he sings of those whom the crown of Elis leads back home equal to the gods, whether boxer or charioteer, and endows them with a gift more precious than 100 statues'. Understand *eos* as antecedent of *quos*, with *pugilemue equumue* functioning as appositional predicates. The stanza treats epinician, through accident of survival the prime Pindaric genre, but for H. just one of a number, though as Rutherford 2001: vii states, 'the signs are that for Pindar the supreme inspiration was provided by the great athletic contests.'

17–18 Elea . . . | palma: the palm leaves of the Olympian victor; cf. 1.1.3–5; Virg. *G.* 1.59 *Eliadum palmas [mittit] Epiros equarum*; 3.49 *Olympiacae miratus praemia palmae*; Prop. 3.9.17 *est quibus Eleae concurrit palma quadrigae.*

quos . . . domum reducit palma caelestes: the expression also recalls the priamel of 1.1.3–6 *sunt quos . . . metaque . . . palmaque . . . euehit ad deos*, along with its closing frame at 29–30 *me doctarum hederae praemia frontium | dis miscent superis.* In all three cases the final word captures the result of the success: *caelestes | ad deos | superis.* The thought is Pindaric: *Isthm.* 2.28–9 ἵν' ἀθανάτοις Αἰνησιδάμου | παῖδες ἐν τιμαῖς ἔμιχθεν 'where the sons of Aenesidamus mingled with immortal honours'.

reducit . . . caelestes: varied at 23 *educit in astra.*

18 -ue . . . -ue: only in poetry; cf. L–H–S 521 C (c).

pugilemue equumue: for the metonymy *equum* = *equitem*, see Bell 1923: 179 (with Prop. 3.4.17 *tela fugacis equi*). The pairing looks formulaic; cf. *AP* 84 (also of epinician poetry) *pugilem uictorem et equum certamine primum*; Livy 1.35.9 *ludicrum fuit equi pugilesque.*

19–20 centum potiore signis | munere: statues are a regular consequence of epinician success, but they pale beside the gift of the victor's Pindaric song. H. touches on the comparison of the visual and poetic arts, a theme going back to Simonides, and forward to the present day. H. here holds the view that poetic (or at least Pindaric) art bestows the greater fame on its subject. At 8.1–12 H. tells Censorinus he would get an outstanding gift (4–5 *neque tu pessima munerum | ferres*) if H. had skill in painting or sculpture; what he can give is the prize of song (11–12 *carmina possumus | donare, et pretium dicere muneri*) – although praise is not really forthcoming in that poem. At 8.13–20 the superiority of poetry to statuary is used to praise Ennius, and the general theme is resumed at *Epist.* 2.1.248–50, as noted by Harrison 1995: 113–14; also 1990: 35. For the notorious passage beginning *ut pictura poesis* (*AP* 361–5) and the various misunderstandings it has fostered, see Brink *ad loc.* For *potior* with similar hyperbole, 2.14.26–8 *mero | tinguet pauimentum superbo, | pontificum potiore cenis*; *Epist.* 1.10.11 *pane egeo iam mellitis potiore placentis*; 39–40 *sic, qui pauperiem ueritus potiore metallis | libertate caret.*

donat: cf. 9n.

21–4 The catalogue closes with Pindaric *threnoi* (see 10–24n.), the title glanced at by *plorat.* H.'s miniature again catches the spirit of the genre. For the themes of early loss, the excellence of the lamented and power of the *threnos* to provide a form of immortality seem to have been essential to the genre, as emerges even from the very fragmentary Pindaric remains (frr. 128–39 Maehler).

21 flebili sponsae iuuenemue raptum 'the youth snatched in death from his weeping/lamentable fiancée' – the language of epitaph: cf. the embedded epigram for the death of Lamia's brother at *Epist.* 1.14.6–8 *Lamiae . . . fratrem maerentis, rapto de fratre dolentis | insolabiliter*; also *C.* 2.17.5–6 *te meae si partem animae rapit | maturior uis*; 2.13.19–20 *improuisa leti | uis rapuit rapietque gentes. Threni* III fr. 128c 7–8 Maehler refers to the genre lamenting Hymenaeus' death on his wedding night: ἁ δ' Ὑμέναιον, <ὃν> ἐν γάμοισι χροϊζόμενον |νυκτὶ σύμπρωτον λάβεν, ἔσχατος ὕμνων 'the one (i.e. the song) that sang of Hymenaios, whom the last of the hymns (i.e. a dirge) took when at night his skin was first touched in marriage' (trans. Race, Loeb).

flebili sponsae: dative of 'disadvantage', as in similar contexts at Cat. 101.5–6 *fortuna mihi tete abstulit ipsum . . . frater adempte mihi* (also 68.20, 92). *flebili* is a form of amphibole: it is taken as passive ('lamentable', 'lamented' as at 1.24.9 *bonis flebilis occidit*) by *TLL* s.v. 891.2, but active ('tearful', 'weeping') by *OLD* s.v. 4, this latter usage occurring of persons at *AP* 123 *flebilis Ino*; Tib. 2.4.22 *ne iaceam clausam flebilis ante domum*, for which cf. *TLL* 890.49–60. With the active meaning the wife weeps for the dead youth, the context in which the word is found in sepulchral inscriptions (*TLL* 891.24–8); with the passive, the word captures the empathy of the poet and reader.

22 plorat: i.e. θρηνεῖ 'delivers a lament', in a technical, generically determined sense. Axelson 28–9 treats the apparent paradox that the verb is perceived as a vulgarism by prose writers (not found in Caesar, Sallust, Tacitus, Suetonius) and is generally absent from epic and tragedy, but is common enough in lyric and elegiac poetry of a more or less high register (cf. 2.9.14; 3.3.68; 3.10.4; 3.27.38; also Tibullus, Propertius and Ovid). There seems to be a sharp distinction in tone between *OLD* s.v. 1 on the one hand, where sound is uppermost ('utter a cry of grief or pain . . . wail, whine'), and s.v. 2 on the other, which is more psychological ('grieve', 'mourn'). But the complete absence from, e.g., Virgil, who has plenty of contexts for the latter sense, is noteworthy.

22–4 'leads out to the stars his strength, spirit and character of gold, and begrudges them to black Orcus'. The singer's lament has the power to elevate the heroic and noble dead. Quite close to *Threni* fr. 133.2–6 Maehler, preserved by Plato (*Meno* 81b, perhaps where H. found it), which treats the elevation to heroic status of the pious dead, with support of Persephone: ἐς τὸν ὕπερθεν ἅλιον κείνων ἐνάτωι ἔτεϊ | ἀνδιδοῖ ψυχὰς πάλιν, ἐκ τᾶν βασιλῆες ἀγαυοί | καὶ σθένει κραιπνοὶ σοφίαι τε μέγιστοι | ἄνδρες αὔξοντ᾽· ἐς δὲ τὸν λοιπὸν χρόνον ἥρωες ἁ- | γνοὶ πρὸς ἀνθρώπων καλέονται 'in the ninth year she returns their souls to the upper sunlight; from them arise proud kings and men who are swift in strength and greatest in wisdom, and for the rest of time they are called sacred heroes by men' (trans. Race, Loeb).

educit in astra: cf. 17–18 *reducit . . . caelestis.*

22–3 uiris animumque moresque | aureos: a perfect tricolon *abundans* (2 + 4 + 6 syllables); cf. 3.1–12n. See West 2007: 117–19 for this Indo-European phenomenon of 'Behagel's Law', or, as West calls it, the 'Augmented Triad'.

aureos: modifying all three nouns. Gold, both as a metal and as an ethical concept, is extremely common in Pindar, with over 100 surviving instances of χρυσός and compounds in the epinicia and the fragments, including three at *Threni* frr. 12bc 1, 12; 129.5 Maehler.

moresque | . . . nigroque |: as Commager 1980: 66 notes, the successive hypermetra 'are perhaps the most ostentatious in the *Odes*', forming a closing frame that proves the opening claims about Pindaric license (11–12 *numerisque fertur | lege solutis*) and setting up a contrast with H.'s own practice (27–32 *ego apis Matinae | more modoque | . . . operosa paruus | carmina fingo*). The consecutive hypermetric lines also instantiate the image of the rivers overflowing their banks in 6 *quem super notas aluere ripas*, with which cf. 1.2.19–20.

24 inuidet Orco: *inuideo* here takes accusative of thing or person refused, dative of person to whom it is refused or denied (cf. 21 *flebili sponsae*). Poetry gives fame which overcomes death, a notion adapted by Callimachus, where *Inuidia* is also present (*Epigr.* 21.4 ὁ δ᾽ ἤεισεν κρέσσονα βασκανίης 'his song was superior to Envy') as it is in earlier Roman adaptations of Callimachean epinician: Virg. *G.* 3.37–8 *Inuidia infelix Furias amnemque seuerum | Cocyti metuet*; Prop. 3.1.21–2 *at mihi* *quod uiuo traxerit inuida turba* | *post obitum duplici faenore reddet Honos*; see Thomas 1983: 99, 101, 103.

25–32 The transitional hinge of the *recusatio*, which also serves as the culmination of the priamel (27 *ego*), as H. moves from the Pindaric topics he cannot treat, figured through the swan which needs a great breeze (*multa . . . aura*) to fly, to his own Callimachean status, reduced in size (*paruus*) and elaborated (*operosa*), like the work of the bee. Cf. Harrison 1995: 114–15 on the possibility of ambiguity here, in that H. elsewhere associates himself with the swan (2.20.9–12), while Pind. *Pyth.* 10.53–4 likens the work of the epinician poet to that of the bee.

25–7 'It takes a mighty breeze to lift up the Dircean swan, Iullus, as often as it heads for the high trailways of the clouds.' The sense of effort and difficulty recalls the opening, where Pindaric emulation can bring about the fate of Icarus.

multa . . . aura: hard to parallel, but presumably analogous to *multus amnis, multa aqua* etc. (where visible corporeality is more evident), for which cf. *TLL* s.v. *multus* 1607.72–1608.19 – which does not include the present instance. H. perhaps strains the language to set up a contrast with both 30 *plurimum* and 31 *paruus*.

Dircaeum . . . cycnum | . . . apis Matinae: the Pindaric swan is perfectly contrasted with the Horatian bee in a chiastic arrangement. Greek Dirce was the mythical wife of Lycus, king of Thebes, Pindar's native city, while Italian Matinus/a is perhaps a promontory or mountain in Apulia or Calabria, so in the vicinity of H.'s birthplace. Only the adjective occurs in H. (and the noun at Luc. 9.185 resolves nothing), and certain identification is not easy: it is hard to reconcile 1.28.3 *litus . . . Matinum* and *Epod.* 16.28 *Matina . . . cacumina*, where Mankin *ad loc.* suggests 'tree-tops', which still does not resolve the puzzle. See Russi 1996: 396–7.

Antoni: praenomen (2 *Iulle*) and *gentilicium* (two lines from the end of the Pindaric section) create a frame, with the addressee's name associated with the non-Horatian enterprise. He will reappear unnamed at 33 (*concines*).

tendit, Antoni, quotiens: decidedly odd word order, with *quotiens* postponed not only after its verb, but also the vocative address. Perhaps a demonstration of the Pindaric swan's over-reaching (*tendit*)? See Harrison 1991: 187, with further bibliography, for more normal instances.

27–32 The Horatian enterprise, expressed in a single sentence, holds a tenuous place in the midst of the rejected genres and modes. The simile recalls by contrast that at the opening of the Pindaric catalogue (and cf. *ripas* at 6, 31). In both moreover there is a sort of trespass (see 5–8n.), as tenor and vehicle come into close contact: at 30–1 *circa nemus uuidique* | *Tiburis ripas* at first seems to situate the work of the bee (which however is Apulian) but in fact locates the activity of H. around his house at Tivoli: bee and poet become one, as did torrent and poet at 5–8 (see 32n.).

There is a strong reminiscence of *Epist.* 1.3.20–2 *ipse quid audes?* | *quae circumuolitas agilis thyma? non tibi paruum* | *ingenium, non incultum est et turpiter hirtum*, on which see Davis 1991: 136–7.

27 ego: cf. 54 *me* and 1.29n.

28 more modoque: the register is perhaps colloquial. The exact phrase is found only here, and variations (*more ac modo* etc.) occur in prose authors (Cic. *Mur.* 72; *Cael.* 33; *Tim.* 1; Quint. 11.1.29), also at Plaut. *Amph.* 221–2 (where Oniga 1985: 156–7 suggests the rhythmical sound patterns and repetitions are iconic of the topic, the drawing up and arranging of an army) *nos nostras more nostro et modo instruximus* | *legiones* – from Sosia's battle narrative; see *TLL* s.v. *mos* 2526.16–53. Wölfflin 1881: 68 adds Plaut. *Trin.* 295 (a moralizing lecture from the old man Philto) *meo modo et moribus.*

29–30 grata carpentis thyma per laborem | plurimum: reminiscent of the bees of Virg. *G.* 4, whose focus, like that of many bees, is also on thyme (112, 169, 181, 241, 270, 304) and whose world is characterized by *labor* (6, 114, 156, 184).

plurimum: with *laborem*, as the punctuation implies. Harrison 1995: 114 follows Bentley I: 232–3 in taking the adjective with *nemus*, which then 'seems to match ἐπ' ἄλλοτ' ἄλλον 'from one to another' (from Pind. *Pyth.* 10.53–4, on the activity of the bee/poet); but Pindar presumably means from one *flower* to another, and having multiple groves seems without point. If with *nemus*, *plurimum* would be better taken as 'exceedingly large' (*OLD* s.v. 6), providing a counterpart to 31–2 *operosa . . . carmina.* Bentley was motivated by the fact that phrases such as *per dolum, per iram, per otium, per iocum, per necessitatem, per uim* never have an accompanying epithet. While this is true, and meaningful in the case of a technical expression such as *per uim*, for instance (with 177 unadorned instances in PHI), *per laborem* is more of an *ad hoc* contruction, otherwise occurring only in Cato (fr. 17.1 Malc.), Sallust (*Cat.* 7.4), and Seneca (*Ep.* 51.7). *per laborem* | *plurimum*, moreover, sits better with the product of the toil (31–2 *operosa . . .* | *carmina*), and is supported by the fact that *labor* is a prominent quality of the bees of Virg. *G.* 4 (156, 185 and generally 149–218).

30–1 circa nemus uuidique | Tiburis ripas: Tibur (Tivoli), which appears 14 times in the corpus, functions as the primary *locus amoenus* for H., and its waters and orchards are its chief features: 3.10–11 *quae Tibur aquae fertile praefluunt* | *et spissae nemorum comae*; 1.7.13–14 *Tiburni lucus et uda* | *mobilibus pomaria riuis*; 3.29.6 *udum Tibur.*

uuidique: from the waterfall of the Anio; a mild hypallage.

31 operosa paruus: in Callimachean terms the two adjectives justify and support each other; see 15.1–4n.

32 carmina fingo: cf. the inversion at 3.10–12 *Tibur[is] aquae [me] . . .* | *fingent Aeolio carmine nobilem*, on which see Lee 1970: 246–7. *carmen/-ina fingere* is particularly Horatian, and always refers to the 'right' sort of poetry: 3.12; *Epist.* 2.1.227; *AP* 331 (see *TLL* s.v. *fingo* 773.82–744.13 for the verb in similar contexts); next at Luc. 6.577 of a magic spell. At Virg. *G.* 2. 45 *carmine ficto* is a different matter, referring to false, deceiving song, but is similarly artful. Like *feruet* (7 and n.), *fingo* works with tenor and vehicle and is appropriate to the work of the bee, as at Virg. *G.* 4.57, 179 (on which see Lee 1970: 262, n.1).

33–44 H. delivers an indirect encomium situated in the future and deflected onto the voice of Iullus, the subject of *concines* (33, 41) – a feature of the Virgilian *recusatio* of *Ecl.* 6.6–7 (*namque super tibi erunt qui dicere laudes, | Vare, tuas cupiant et tristia condere bella*), as also of H.'s at 1.6.1–4 (*scriberis Vario fortis et hostium | uictor*) and 2.12.9–11 (*tuque pedestribus | dices historiis proelia Caesaris*). In both Horatian poems, as in the current case (*quandoque trahet... Sygambros*), H. suggests details of the deflected encomium: 1.6.3–4 *quam rem cumque ferox nauibus aut equis | miles te duce gesserit*; 2.12.11–12 *ductaque per uias | regum colla minacium.* Cf. also Prop. 3.1.15–16 *multi, Roma, tuas laudes annalibus addent, | qui finem imperii Bactra futura canent.*

33 maiore poeta plectro 'a poet of greater plectrum'; ablative of description, perhaps also instrumental, an instance of amphibole (see 1.4–7n.). A metaphor for high style, opposed to the Callimachean stance of H., so described at 2.1.40 *leuiore plectro* (cf. of generic definition 1.26.11 *Lesbio... plectro*). For both registers, see Ovid's Orpheus in transition from Gigantomachy to erotic subjects: *Met.* 10.150–3 *cecini plectro grauiore Gigantas... | nunc opus est leuiore lyra, puerosque canamus | dilectos superis...*; or Virgil in transition from pastoral to a higher mode at *Ecl.* 4.1–2 *paullo maiora canamus! | non omnes arbusta iuuant humilesque myricae.* Harrison 1995: 115–22 argues, on the basis of various metapoetic uses of *plectrum* in Roman poetry, 'that Horace presents Iullus Antonius here as an epic rather than a lyric poet, and that the themes imagined for Iullus' poem on Augustus' return are those of panegyrical epic' (122).

poeta: avoided in *C.* 1–3, and in 4 only here and at 6.30, where it likewise implies an elevation of register (see n.).

34–6 feroces... Sygambros: a dangerous German tribe northeast of the Rhine around Cologne. For their initial success against M. Lollius in 17 or 16 BCE, see 9 intro. Their pacification (16 BCE) becomes a reality at 14.51–2 (*te* [sc. *Augustum*] *caede gaudentes Sygambri | ... uenerantur*; see n.); though they in fact made terms, and while they were more decisively beaten by Drusus in 12 BCE and by Tiberius in 8 BCE, they continued to be resistant: cf. Tac. *Ann.* 2.26.3 (of Tiberius) *se nouies a diuo Augusto in Germaniam missum plura consilio quam ui perfecisse. sic Sygambros in deditionem acceptos....* See Schönfeld, *RE* IVA 659–62.

Caesarem: the first appearance in the book; as in 43 *Augusti* and 48 *Caesare*, avoiding direct address, since Iullus is to be the primary encomiast, while Horatian praise is limited (46–7n.).

quandoque 'at which time (whenever it may be)'; see 1.17n.

35 per sacrum cliuum: something of a conflation, avoiding the actual name, *cliuus Capitolinus*, at the top of the *Via Sacra*, the final stage of the triumphal route to the temple of Jupiter Optimus Maximus on the Capitoline. Porph. felt the need to clarify (*id est: per uiam Sacram*), perhaps because by his time the world had changed: for Martial (1.70.5; 4.78.7) *cliuus sacer* is the route to the imperial residence on the Palatine, parting from the Via Sacra.

35–6 merita decorus | fronde 'adorned with the laurel wreath he has deserved'; cf. the Pindaric laurel of 9 *laurea donandus Apollinari. merita* is somewhat defensive, insisting the victory, and therefore the triumph that follows it, will be the actual achievement of Augustus.

37–9 quo nihil maius meliusue: 'Sentences in which there is a universal negative (*nihil, nemo, nullus, nec quisquam, numquam*) show the ablative, where the comparative adjective agrees with the nominative that constitutes the first term of the comparison. Such sentences are always equivalent to an affirmative superlative.' So Neville 1901: 43, with abundant examples chiefly from Cicero, e.g. *Rab. post.* 48 *huic optimo uiro, quo nemo melior umquam fuit*; *Rep.* 2.21 *princeps ille, quo nemo in scribendo praestantior fuit*, 27 *Polybium nostrum, quo nemo fuit in exquirendis temporibus diligentior*; *Q. Rosc.* 52 *quo nihil captiosius nec indignius potest dici*; *Sen.* 84 *Catonem meum, quo nemo uir melior natus est.* The specific phrase *quo nihil* in this construction is not found in poetry before H. (though cf. Lucr. 6.972 *qua nihil amarius*), who uses it only here.

Cf. *Epist.* 2.1.17 (of Augustus) *nil oriturum alias, nil ortum tale fatentes*. Cf. Fraenkel 1932–3: 5–6 for other uses, in encomiastic contexts, of a negative with the comparative as a periphrasis for the superlative: *S.* 1.5.41–2 (of Tucca, Varius and Virgil) *animae quales neque candidiores | terra tulit neque quis me sit deuinctior alter*; *C.* 1.12.17 *unde nil maius generatur ipso*; *CS* 9–12 *alme Sol . . . possis nihil urbe Roma | uisere maius.* Cf. Pind. *Ol.* 1.5–7 μηκέτ' ἀελίου σκόπει | ἄλλο θαλπνότερον ἐν ἁμέραι φαεννὸν ἄστρον ἐρήμας δι' αἰθέρος, | μηδ' Ὀλυμπίας ἀγῶνα φέρτερον αὐδάσομεν 'search no further than the sun for another bright star shining more warmly by day through the empty sky, nor shall we sing of a contest better than Olympia'.

maius meliusue: for the wording cf. Cic. *Acad.* 1.7 (of philosophy) *nec ullum* [sc. *studium*] *arbitror, ut apud Platonem est, maius aut melius a dis datum munus homini*; *Nat. D.* 2.80 *nihil autem nec maius nec melius mundo*; *Diu.* 2.4 *quod enim munus rei publicae afferre maius meliusue possumus, quam si docemus atque erudimus iuuentutem?*

39–40 quamuis redeant in aurum | tempora priscum 'even though the times should revert to their good old golden state'. A unique form of the golden age hyperbole. Elsewhere Augustus' age is predicted as a new golden age, but here it will be superior even to any such return. The excessive and Pindaric song will however be sung not by H. but by Iullus.

41–4 laetosque dies . . . | publicum ludum . . . | . . . forumque | litibus orbum: the language is formal and redolent of forensic oratory; cf. Cic. *Phil.* 1.30 (to Dolabella) *quem potes recordari in uita illuxisse tibi diem laetiorem quam cum expiato foro, dissipato concursu impiorum, principibus sceleris poena affectis, urbe incendio et caedis metu liberata te domum recepisti?* 10.8 *quamquam qui umquam aut ludi aut dies laetiores fuerunt quam cum in singulis uersibus populus Romanus maximo clamore et plausu Bruti memoriam prosequebatur?*; *Amic.* 12; *Ad Brut.* 23.8; Livy 22.30.6.

-que . . . et . . . -que: for the pattern, see L–H–S 515 on *-que et*; a feature of old Latin and perhaps already archaizing there, it is avoided by classical prose writers (unless following asyndeton; for which *TLL* s.v. *et* 878.19–33) but is a mark particularly of higher style in the poets. For examples, with varying combinations following the initial *-que et*, see *TLL* s.v. *et* 887.36–888.19. Instances in *C.* 4 are in the context of encomium and exaggeration, sincere or feigned: 9.34–36; 14.45–52.

urbis | publicum ludum super 'the City's public games in celebration of'; the syntax is rather prosaic, as is the term *ludus publicus* (Cic. *Clu.* 27; *Leg.* 2.38), not otherwise found in poetry. See Adams 1972: 358–9 on *super* + ablative (= *de*); from the Augustan period on it is generally archaizing, and occurs in official or formal contexts, as here and elsewhere in H.: 3.8.17 and *CS* 18.

42–3 super impetrato . . . reditu: the noun came to have a formal status; cf. Gallus fr. 2.4 Courtney (and n.) *postque tuum reditum*, addressed either to Julius Caesar or Octavian, on which see Courtney 265; Hollis 243–4.

fortis Augusti: the adjective suggests the heroic and even epic status Augustus is to have in Iullus' encomium, as Trebatius wanted him to have in the version H. would never actually produce: *S.* 2.1.16 *[Caesarem] iustum poteras et scribere fortem.* But there *fortem* is a predicate, and *fortis Augusti* as a pure noun-epithet phrase is distinct and hard to parallel as such of a living person. At *Epist.* 2.1.241 H. has (in sculptural representations) *fortis Alexandri* which, along with the present instance, would be better placed at *TLL* s.v. *fortis* 1147.58–68 ('de heroibus') than at 1146.41–2; that is, the parallels are to be found in epic and in myth: e.g. Virg. *Aen.* 1.579 *fortis Achates*; 12.127 *fortis Asilas*; 1.222 *fortemque Cloanthum*; 5.808 *Pelidae . . . forti* etc. Like *merita* (35 and 35–6n.), the epithet implies actual fighting on the part of the *princeps*; cf. Prop. 3.12.2 *Augusti fortia signa.* Harrison 1995: 113 sees a possible connection to the Pindaric first half: '*fortis* can suggest the prowess of an athlete as well as military courage.'

reditu: see 7.1–2n.

impetrato: in H. only in such public contexts (*Epist.* 2.1.137; *CS* 51) and in general a prose word – not used by Cat., Lucr., Virg., Tib. or Ov.; cf. *TLL* s.v. *impetro* 599.8–9.

43–4 forumque | litibus orbum 'and the forum bereft of its lawsuits'. Legal business was suspended on such days; cf. Cic. *Cael.* 1 *si quis, iudices, forte nunc adsit ignarus legum iudiciorum consuetudinisque nostrae, miretur profecto quae sit tanta atrocitas huiusce causae, quod diebus festis ludisque publicis, omnibus forensibus negotiis intermissis, unum hoc iudicium exerceatur*; Ov. *Fast.* 4.187–8 (of the *Ludi Megalenses*) *scaena sonat, ludique uocant: spectate, Quirites, | et fora Marte suo litigiosa uacent.*

45–52 H. explores the part he will play in the triumphal celebration, one of the crowd, adding his voice to the *uersus quadratus* of the populace. Such un-Callimachean behaviour (50–1n.) is counter to the aesthetics of 27–32, and of the Horatian outlook in general, and it is hard to take these stanzas with complete seriousness (see intro., 46–7n.). At Prop. 3.4.11–22, to which H. may here be responding, the poet imagines himself in the embrace of his girlfriend, not sharing in the spoils of war but part of the crowd cheering a future triumph of Augustus; cf. 22 *mi sat erit Sacra plaudere posse Via.* The Roman Callimachus is no more plausible than the Matine bee in such a role. H. also anticipates the end of the next poem, where *he*, master of the Roman lyre, will be the object of public attention: 3.22–3 *quod monstror digito praetereuntium | Romanae fidicen lyrae.*

45 tum meae: as in a priamel, the initial wording, *tum meae* [. . . *uocis*], shifts the focus from Iullus (33, 41, in the same metrical *sedes, concines*) to H. see 1.29n.

si quid loquar audiendum 'if I have anything to say worth listening to'; in view of what he is about to sing, this raises scepticism about the merit of the upcoming utterance; the lyric H. is usually less modest (*C.* 2.20; 3.30); see 46–7n. Shackleton Bailey prints *loquor*, also in the Harleianus, citing 9.4, where however *quae . . . uerba loquor* refers to the corpus of lyric he has already produced, the past, not the future.

46 uocis . . . bona pars 'a considerable part of my voice'; cf. *S.* 1.1.61 *bona pars hominum*; *AP* 297 *bona pars* [sc. *poetarum*]; Cic. *De Or.* 2.14 *bonam partem sermonis*; Ov. *Am.* 2.5.16 *pars bona uocis*; *Fast.* 5.150 *pars bona montis ea est*; *Pont.* 1.8.74; 3.2.4. These contexts suggest an idiomatic and perhaps colloquial register, in which case H. would be seen to continue the stylistic deflation of his contribution.

46–7 'o sol | pulcher, o laudande!' 'o beautiful day! o worthy of praise!' Doubtless the equivalent of 'hip hip, hooray!' The Callimachean poet, who will not, because he cannot (31–2 *operosa paruus | carmina fingo*), celebrate Augustus in Pindaric song, goes to the other extreme and becomes one of the crowd. As Heinze noticed, the metre is the first half of a trochaic septenarius, the *uersus quadratus* sung by soldiers to their generals: Suet. *Cal.* 6.1 *salua Roma, salua patria, saluus est Germanicus*; also of a schetliastic type at *Iul.* 49.4; and, relevant to the occasion imagined by H., *Aug.* 57.2 *reuertentem ex prouincia non solum faustis ominibus sed et modulatis carminibus prosequebantur.* For Fraenkel (439–40) this was all sincere and serious: 'Just as devotion to Augustus was not the privilege of any individual, but was felt by thousands of ordinary citizens, so the language in which that devotion was voiced should be one that seemed to come from the heart of the common man. "O sol pulcher, o laudande", that is how the poet echoes the grateful rejoicing of the mass of the people.' The question left hanging, however, is one of sincerity, particularly coming right after the embrace of Callimachean principles at 27–32.

o laudande: this bare vocative is unique (the two other examples of *laudande* are modified: Sil. *Pun.* 5.561 *laudande laborum*; 8.461 *rastris laudande*), and there is no parallel for the unadorned acclamation '*o -nde*' (Stat. *Theb.* 5.246 *hac sequere, o miserande* and Ov. *Am.* 2.9a.1 *o numquam pro re satis improbande Cupido* come closest). Vocatives of the gerundive occur with limitations and only in poetry; they are not found before the Augustan period. The instances that took hold seem to be Virgilian coinages: *memorande* (*G.* 3.1; *Aen.* 10.825; thereafter in Ovid, Martial, Silius); *miserande* (*Aen.* 6.882; 10.327; 11.42; therefter in Ovid, Seneca, Statius, Valerius Flaccus, Silius); *uenerande* (*Aen.* 9.276; thereafter in Ovid, *Laus Pisonis*, *Culex*, Statius, Valerius Flaccus, Silius, Martial). *metuende* occurs only at

Aen. 10.557 and, with expansion, at *C.* 1.12.23–4 *metuende . . . sagitta*; 2.19.8 *metuende thyrso. celebrande* (Tib. 1.7.63) is unique, as is *uerende* [*Creon*] at Stat. *Theb.* 11.709. Other examples are *hapax* or *dis legomena* and involve more expansive phrasing: *Epist.* 1.1.1 *dicende*; Prop. 4.7.13 *nec cuiquam melior sperande puellae*; Ov. *Fast.* 3.344 *colloquio non abigende*; Ov. *Pont.* 2.4.2 *non dubitande*; [Sen.] *Oct. deflende nobis*; [Virg.] *Cul.* 133 *deflende puellis*; *Catal.* 13.9 *improbande Caesari*; Martial was partial to the form: 1.49.1 *uir . . . non tacende*; 4.86.9 *inuersa pueris arande charta*; 5.30.1 *Sophocleo non infitiande coturno*; 5.30.2 *in Calabra suspiciende lyra*; 7.45.6 *nullis, Ouidi, tacende lingua*; 9.65.1 *agnoscende Tonanti*. The gerundive force is not really felt in *nefande*, of which there are eight instances. For the anaphora of *o* see 3.17–20n.; for its various shades of meaning see Dickey 2002: 225–9. For *laudandus* and other 'terms of affection and esteem', including *memorande, uenerande, uerende* (add *celebrande*), see Dickey 2002: 131–3.

47–8 recepto | Caesare felix 'happy at the return of Caesar'; cf 2.7.27–8 *recepto | dulce mihi furere est amico*; Virg. *Aen.* 9.262 (Ascanius of the return of Aeneas) '*nihil illo triste recepto.*' An aureus of Claudius has the motto *imper*(*atore*) *recept*(*o*): *RIC* Claudius 5, pl. 31.4.

49 tuque dum procedis 'and while you [Iullus] process' we, the entire state, will say "io Triumphe"'. Or possibly 'while you [Iullus] carry on [with your song]'; for this sense cf. *TLL* s.v. *procedo* 1503.62–9 ('pertinet ad uerba continuata'). Elsewhere, though in more figurative or imaginative settings, the encomiast is part of, or even leads, the triumphal procession; cf. Virg. *G.* 3.17–18 *illi* [sc. *Caesari*] *uictor ego et Tyrio conspectus in ostro | centum quadriiugos agitabo ad flumina currus*; 22–3 *iam nunc sollemnes ducere pompas | ad delubra iuuat*; Prop. 3.1.9–14 (metaphorical).

The text is far from certain, and Shackleton Bailey may be right to obelize. The alternative is to read *teque, dum procedit/procedis*, with *te*, and likewise *procedis*, referring to the apostrophized Triumphus, while the subject of *procedit* would be Augustus. So Porph. (similarly ps.-Acro): *ad ipsum triumphum conuersus haec dicit.* Throughout the poem, the contrast is between the *ego* of H. and the *tu* of Iullus and the song he is to sing. Page is surely right to claim that 'the fatal objection to this rendering [reading *te*] is not the difficulty of extracting the vocative *Triumphe* from the cry *io Triumphe* in order to find something for *te* to refer to, but the impossibility of referring *te* to anyone but Antonius. Antonius has been addressed in the second person in line 2, again in line 26, again in lines 33 and 41: the *te* which is placed with such marked prominence at the beginning of this stanza is followed by *te* in an exactly parallel position at the commencement of the next stanza, and anyone has read H. to little purpose who has not observed that he is specially fond of making his meaning clear by placing important and guiding words, especially pronouns, in emphatic positions.' In short, if *te* in 53 were accompanied by a vocative bringing the identification back to Iullus (to whom it refers, as nobody contests), we might imagine *te* or *tu* at 49 with a different referent; in the absence of such identification, that, *pace* Fraenkel 1932–3, seems as close to impossible as may be.

49–50 'io Triumphe!' . . . 'io Triumphe!': cf. Varro, *Ling.* 6.68 'it was called "to triumph" because the soldiers shouted "io Triumphe" when returning with their general as he went through the City up to the Capitoline; possibly derived from Greek θρίαμβος as a Greek name for Liber'. Here T. is treated as an address to the god, as at *Epod.* 9.21, 23 (and see Mankin *ad* 21), where the address is also repeated, at line-beginnings, and cf. Wills 59, 422. In the *Epode* the cry has to do with victory over Antony, here, with a triumph to be sung by the son of Antony.

50–1 dicemus . . . ciuitas omnis dabimusque: cf. *Epod.* 16.36, where H. spoke in the persona of a magistrate: *eamus omnis exsecrata ciuitas*; in the present context, singing along with the crowd is in some tension with the Callimachean poet's normal practice: 3.1.1 *odi profanum uulgus et arceo*, drawn from Callim. *Epigr.* 28.4 σικχαίνω πάντα τὰ δημόσια, 'I hate everything having to do with the public.'

52 tura: see 1.21–2n.

benignis: proleptic, their beneficence is anticipated.

53–60 A brilliant conclusion to the poem, displaying the genius of the lyric poet and the justice of the attenuated style, shown by the contrasting sacrificial offerings. As if by accident, the background of the calf whose sacrifice is sufficient for H. (while Iullus needs ten bulls and ten cows, tersely mentioned in one line), is elaborated with loving and microscopic detail, as H. returns to the lyric world of the *fons Bandusiae* (3.13.3–8) with its sympathetic description of the life of the sacrificed kid that is not to be. Callimachus and Virgil called for fat sacrificial animals and flocks, but slender Muses (*Aet.* 1, fr. 1.23–4 Pf. 'ἀοιδέ, τὸ μὲν θύος ὅττι πάχιστον | θρέψαι τὴ]ν Μοῦσαν δ' ὠγαθὲ λεπταλέην' 'singer, rear your sacrificial victim to be as fat as possible, but your Muse, my good fellow, make slender'; *Ecl.* 6.4–5 '*pastorem, Tityre, pingues | pascere oportet oues, deductum dicere carmen*'). H., slender of Muse at 31–2 (*operosa paruus | carmina fingo*), crowns this tradition, doing Callimachus one better by appropriating to himself even a small θύος, a *tener* (*tenuis*?) *uitulus*. Harrison 1995: 125–7 treats the epic associations of the offering of Iullus, with parallels from Hellenistic and Roman poetry. Cf., also at poem's end, 2.17.31–2; 3.17.14–16; *Epist.* 1.3.36 *pascitur in uestrum reditum uotiua iuuenca*.

The metapoetics may run deeper, appropriately at the end of a poem that began in highly ludic ways. Probably after the writing of *C.* 4, Iullus wrote an epic in twelve books on Diomedes (ps.-Acro *ad* 2.33 *heroico metro Diomedias duodecim libros scripsit egregios*). The contrast between Iullus' twice-twenty bulls and cows on the one hand, and H.'s one calf on the other, is reminiscent of the juxtaposition at Cat. 95 of the single-book *Zmyrna* of Cinna with the turgid and lengthy works of Hortensius, Volusius and Antimachus. Moreover, as John Henderson suggests *per litteras*, the *uitulus* that is to be H.'s offering may stand for the single papyrus roll on which *C.* 4 is being written, in marked contrast to what Iullus will come up with. For the contrast between the yellow (*fuluus*) parchment cover of a white papyrus roll (*niueus*), cf. [Tib.] 3.1.6 *lutea sed niueum inuoluat membrana libellum*; at Pers. 3.10–11 the book cover is itself two-tone: *iam liber et positis bicolor membrana capillis | inque manus chartae*. H.'s wording at 59 (*qua notam duxit, niueus uideri*) is particularly suggestive: 'white to look at where it has traced the lettering'. For *nota* = 'lettering' see *OLD* s.v. 6b, and cf. 8.13 *notis* 'lettering' of an inscription. The 'third rising' that is indicated by the appearance of the calf(-skin) is the third poem, which begins immediately, and which is in a close relationship with 4.2.

53 decem tauri totidemque uaccae: cf. the sacrifice of Aristaeus at Virg. *G.* 4.538, 540 (also 550–1) '*quattuor eximios praestanti corpore tauros . . . et intacta totidem ceruice iuuencas*'; also *Aen.* 6.38–9; 8.207–8; with variation in *Aen.* 5.97 *totque sues, totidem nigrantes terga iuuencos*. This formula is sobering at *Aen.* 10.517–9 (Aeneas' victims for human sacrifice) *Sulmone creatos | quattuor hic iuuenes, totidem quos educat Vfens, | uiuentes rapit, inferias quos immolet umbris*.

53–4 te . . . me: like 26–7 *Antoni . . . ego*, the pivot of the priamel (see 1.29n.), recapitulating the juxtaposition and contrast that marks the entire poem.

54 tener . . . uitulus: cf. 3.1.5 *si tener pleno cadit haedus anno*, of the kid sacrificed to Faunus in return for the security of H.'s farm.

(me) soluet: the verb is used both, as here, where the offering or a third party (as at 1.27.21) discharges the debtor, and also where the debtor discharges a vow or promise (*OLD* s.v. *soluo* 20–22), as e.g. at Virg. *G.* 1.436 *uotaque seruati soluent in litore nautae*.

54–5 relicta | matre qui largis iuuenescit herbis: cf. Virg. *G.* 3.187 (of the weaned colt) *depulsus ab ubere matre*. In Varro *Rust.* 2.5.17, the weaning of calves begins after six months: *semestribus uitulis obiciunt furfures triticios et farinam hordeaceam et teneram herbam et ut bibant mane et uesperi curant*.

iuuenescit 'grows to maturity' (i.e. becomes a *iuuencus*).

57–8 '(a calf) whose brow looks like the crescent light of the moon as it brings back its third rising' (i.e. the third rising of the new moon). The horns of the young calf are still in a subcutaneous state, with the bulge on either side giving the appearance of a crescent whose two ends point upwards. Cf. the kid in 3.13.4–6 *cui frons turgida cornibus | primis et Venerem et proelia destinat, | frustra*, with similar pathos and empathy, here expressed through metapoetic affiliation (53–60n.).

imitatus: cf. *aemulari* in the opening line.

59 qua notam duxit 'where it has a marking' (acquired at birth, hence the perfect); *nota* is used both of naturally occurring markings, and of brands, as at Virg. *G.* 3.158 *notas et nomina gentis inurunt*.

59–60 niueus uideri, | cetera fuluus (a calf) 'of white appearance (in its crescent-shaped marking), otherwise tawny' (see 53–60n.). *uideri* is an epexegetical infinitive, explaining the context of the colouring ('to the eye'); *cetera* is (Greek) accusative of respect, found with adjectives (particularly *cetera*), but not a natural Latin usage and occurring for the most part not before Virgil and Ovid, and chiefly in them, in prose not before Tacitus; cf. L–H–S 37–8. H. avoids the so-called 'retained accusative' much favoured by Virgil, on which see 11.5n.

3

METRE

Second Asclepiadean (as for 1).

INTRODUCTION

The person on whom Melpomene smiles will not gain fame from athletic or military exploits. Rather, the waters and groves of Tivoli will bring me poetic fame. The youth of Rome esteems me, now beyond the biting tooth of envy. All is due to the support of the Muse; she is the reason people point me out as Rome's preeminent lyricist.

The poem follows well on 2, whose themes it recapitulates, positively asserting H.'s lyric genius where the previous poem had only implied it through Callimachean metaphor (2.31, 33nn.) and through implicit contrast with the higher mode of both Pindar and Iullus Antonius. Now the poet is not opposed to other stylists but to the very subject of encomiastic poetry, athletic and military alike (3–9), as he insists that the private world of lyric, closely associated with his dear Tibur (9–10n.), is what will bring fame. The full-blooded Pindaric encomium that will follow (*C.* 4.4) will therefore come as a surprise and function in some tension with the mode represented by 4.2 and particularly with the pure lyricism of this final poem of the book's opening triad (see 21–4n.).

recusatio and priamel again come together, but with inversion as the *illum* of the poem's beginning turns out to be the poet of the poem's end. There is a close connection with *C.* 1.1, as many readers have noted. There the multiple foils of the first part of the priamel, 1–28 (3 *quos*, 7 *hunc*, 9 *illum* etc.), are in contrast to the climax of the last (29 *me*). Here, however, the poet (implicitly *illum*), his Muse and his poetry are present throughout. Estévez 1982 examines the poem in relation to the rest of the *Odes*, particularly *C.* 1.1 (14–15n.) and 3.30. Putnam 75–7 treats the poem in the context of the opening triad, establishing the return to lyric in opposition to other genres, styles and occupations.

1–12 Quem . . . illum non . . . non . . . neque . . . : sed . . . nobilem: a highly Pindaric variation on the priamel style, where a series of negatives (foil) is followed by the positive (climax), with which the speaker associates himself. Cf. 2.18.1–11 *non [mea] . . . , non . . . , neque . . . , nec . . . . at . . . me*, close in style and content to Bacchyl. 21 (see N–H *ad loc.*; Race 1982: 127–8).

H. eschews the glory that comes from boxing, chariot-racing (see 5–6n.) and triumphs (3–9). As elsewhere (cf. 2.22–3n., with reference to 'Behagel's Law'), the tricolon *abundans* is artfully structured, with each member progressively occupying parts of two, three and four lines. Each has a noun and epithet as subject (*labor Isthmius* | *equus impiger* | *res bellica*), while the second adds a modal ablative (*curru . . . Achaico*), and the third is expanded by two subordinate clauses (*ornatum foliis*; *quod . . . minas*). The style continues at the priamel's climax, with *aquae* and *comae* responding positively to the rejected nominatives and *Aeolio carmine* to the rejected ablatives. The priamel also involves a movement from Greek proper names that will *not* bring fame (*Isthmius* . . . *Achaico* . . . *Deliis*) to the Italian name that *will* (*Tibur*). This is inverted as *Capitolio* belongs to the priamel's negated foil, *Aeolio* (*carmine*) to its affirmed climax (see 9–10n.).

1–2 The reference to Hes. *Theog.* 81–4 has long been noted: ὅντινα τιμήσουσι Διὸς κοῦραι μεγάλοιο | γεινόμενόν τε ἴδωσι διοτρεφέων βασιλήων, | τῶι μὲν ἐπὶ γλώσσηι γλυκερὴν χείουσιν ἐέρσην, | τοῦ δ' ἔπε' ἐκ στόματος ῥεῖ μείλιχα, 'whom among god-nourished kings the daughters of great Zeus honour and look upon as he comes to birth, on that one's tongue they pour sweet dew, and from his mouth words flow gently'. K–H point to Callim. *Aet.* 1, fr. 1.37–8 Pf., verses Pfeiffer thought were interpolated to *Epigr.* 21.5–6 (where they hardly belong): Μοῦσαι γὰρ ὅσους ἴδον ὄθματι παῖδας | μὴ λοξῶι, πολιοὺς οὐκ ἀπέθεντο φίλους, 'as many as the Muses have not looked askance at as children, they do not thrust from their friendship when greying'. That both Greek intertexts are present in H. is assured by his *nascentem* which looks to Hesiodic γεινόμενον (cf. Callim. παῖδας), and *placido lumine*, which catches Callimachean ὄθματι μὴ λοξῶι (Hes. has simply ἴδωσι), a motif elsewhere adapted at *Epist.* 1.14.37–8: *non istic obliquo oculo mea commoda quisquam* | *limat, non odio obscuro morsuque uenenat* (see 16 and n.). Also Callimachean are the negatives in H.'s main clause (cf. πολιοὺς οὐκ ἀπέθεντο φίλους), not paralleled in Hes. The conflation of these two Greek authors is in line with other such blendings: Virg. *G.* 1.95–6; 2.176, with Thomas *ad locc.*; Prop. 2.10.25–6; cf. Wimmel 1960: 235–8; Ross 1975: 119–20.

Melpomene: selected, as at 3.30.16 in H.'s envoi to *C.* 1–3, to represent the Muses in general (see also 12n.). Although at 1.24.2–3, she may seem to have associations with tragedy (as at Agathias *Anth. Pal.* 5.222.3–4), the hardening of the Muses' attribution to specific functions and genres develops only in late antiquity, and she is elsewhere associated merely with song and stringed instruments (Diod. 4.7.4; Anon. *Anth. Pal.* 9.504.4; Cornutus *Nat. D.* 16.6), which may be as relevant for all three appearances in H. (see Fraenkel 306, n. 2; N–H *ad* 1.24.3). She is otherwise found in Latin poetry only at Mart. 4.31.7, and rarely in Greek until the imperial period, with the notable exception of Hes. *Theog.* 77 (see 1–2n.).

semel 'at any time, ever', going with *uideris*.

2 placido lumine: a striking and unparalleled expression, responding to the Greek model (see 1–2n.); K–H also note Bacchyl. 11.15–17 ἵλεώι νιν ὁ Δα[λ]ογενὴς υἱ- | ὸς βαθυζώνο[ιο] Λατοῦς | δέκτ[ο] βλεφά[ρω]ι 'the Delos-born son of deep-girdled Leto welcomed him with gracious eye'. For similar expressions, cf. Virg. *Aen.* 4.440 *placidas* . . . *aures*; 7.194 *placido* . . . *ore*; 11.251; Ov. *Met.* 8.703; 11.202; 15.692 *placido* . . . *uultu*. Shackleton Bailey admits *numine* (which has some MS support) to his apparatus, but that sits less well with *uideris*; cf. Sen. *Med.* 985 *o placida tandem numina*.

uideris: best taken as future perfect, the protasis of a future more vivid conditional, as supported by Hesiodic τιμήσουσι (1–2n.). For a similar and real ambiguity, see 8 *contuderit* and n.

3–4 labor Isthmius | clarabit pugilem: more than half of Pindar's *Isthmian Odes* (4–8) celebrate victory in the *pankration* (mainly boxing and wrestling). The vocabulary is markedly Pindaric – πόνος (*labor*) and κλέος (*clarus*) are key words and concepts in the epinicians.

4–12 pugilem . . . uictorem . . . ducem . . . nobilem: all predicates with *illum*. 'not make him famous etc. as a boxer, victor, leader, but fashion as distinguished'. Each designation occupies the final position of its clause, reinforcing the priamel as list.

4 equus impiger: the adjective is normally of persons (and horse and rider work together here), though cf. Lucr. 5.883–4, where, however, it need not be taken ἀπὸ κοινοῦ with horse and human: *principio circum tribus actis impiger annis | floret equus, puer haudquaquam*. At Priap. 83.12 there is clearly humorous personification: *cum tibi | senexue coruus impigerue graculus | sacrum feriret ore corneo caput.*

5–6 curru ducet Achaico | uictorem: the adjective specifies Greek games, although *uictorem* provides a transition to the (Roman) military triumph that immediately follows. Nowhere else in Latin is a chariot designated as 'Greek', but the ethnic epithet mostly situates the games (*TLL* s.v. *currus* 1522.50–1523.72), though cf. Virg. *G*. 1.59 *Eliadum palmas . . . equarum*; Prop. 3.9.17 (see 2.17–18n.) *est quibus Eleae concurrit palma quadrigae.*

6–9 H. distances himself from the glory that comes from triumph, a step back from his participation in the triumph at 2.45–52.

res bellica: for the less common singular ('a military exploit') see also Cic. *Diu*. 2.76 *bellicam rem*. Livy uses it in the collective sense at 4.41.2 etc.; *TLL* s.v. *bellicus* 1811.28–41 (without distinction as to meaning). There is nothing to support the view of Quinn *ad loc*. that the singular is a Horatian coinage nor that it is possibly pejorative; *res bellicae* would be hard to handle metrically.

Deliis . . . ostendet: possibly a bilingual wordplay (δηλόω = *ostendo*).

Deliis . . . foliis: i.e. a laurel wreath (Apollo's tree), held by a slave over the head of the triumphing general; see *OCD* s.v. 'triumph'.

7–12 Image and sound are connected, from (*clarabit*) *ornatum foliis* to *nemorum comae* to *carmine nobilem*.

8 quod regum tumidas contuderit minas 'for having crushed the puffed-up threats of kings', the basis for the triumph. *regum* is vague and generic. *contuderit* is best seen as perfect subjunctive in virtual indirect speech. H., the primary narrator who wants no part in delivering or receiving such encomium, is noncommittal about whether the crushing was or was not a reality, remarkable in that the victories of contemporary Roman princes may have been for show as much as anything else (see 4 intro.). Page, for whom this reading 'seems harsh', prefers future perfect, with *quod* = *cum* (which H. avoided to prevent a rhyming effect with *ornatum* and *regum*): 'he will triumph because he will have crushed'. But this seems more forced, and scepticism about the very grounds of the triumph is a natural part of the priamel, as in 1.1, where various negative or qualified elements attend the rejected options: e.g. 7 *mobilium*; 15 *luctantem*; 25 *detestata*; 25 *sub Ioue frigido*.

tumidas . . . minas: perhaps hinting at an etymological connection, since *minae* (*OLD* compares *mons*, *emineo*, etc.) is used of animals which become menacing (*OLD* s.v. 1b), in some cases by growing in size or stature, for instance at Virg. *G.* 3.421 [*colubrum*] *tollentemque minas et sibila colla tumentem*.

contuderit: for the evocation of violence cf. Estévez 1982: 283–4.

9 ostendet Capitolio 'display him *to* the Capitol', dative, rather than locative 'on' (Lee); the Capitoline, the final goal of the triumph, is seen as reviewing the victor, the object of the spectacle.

9–10 Capitolio . . . Tibur: the juxtaposition of the two places underscores the difference between H. and the triumphing general, Tivoli and Rome. For the same contrast cf. *Epist.* 1.7.44–5 *paruum parua decent. mihi iam non regia Roma, | sed uacuum Tibur placet aut imbelle Tarentum*; 1.8.12 (*quia*) *Romae Tibur amem uentosus, Tibure Romam*; also, contrasting less specifically to Rome, *C.* 1.7.19–21 *seu te fulgentia signis | castra tenent seu densa tenebit | Tiburis umbra tui*. Cf. the *sphragis* of the *Georgics* (4.559–66), where mighty Caesar strikes like lightning at the deep Euphrates, while Virgil flourishes in ignoble *otium* on the Bay of Naples (see 12n.).

10–11 quae Tibur aquae . . . praefluunt | et . . . nemorum comae: again its waters and groves distinguish Tivoli (see 2.30n.).

praefluunt 'flow in front of, flow past'; cf. 14.25–6 *Aufidus | qui regna Dauni praefluit Apuli*.

nemorum comae: as at 1.21.5 *nemorum coma*; also 7.2 *arboribusque comae*; Virg. *G.* 2.368 *tum stringe comas*. The metaphor is old: *Inc. trag.* 221 Ribb. (*ap.* Varr. *Ling.* 7.24) *frondenti coma* 'with hair-like foliage'.

12 fingent Aeolio carmine nobilem: here the *locus amoenus* fashions H. as a lyric poet because he celebrates it in lyric song, as at 2.32 (see n.), *carmina fingo*, with a sense of cooperation and reciprocity between singer, song and place. *Aeolio carmine* is retrospective to *C.* 3.30.10–14 (and see 1n.), where H. also defined his lyric achievement of *C.* 1–3 with reference to Sappho and Alcaeus: *dicar . . . princeps Aeolium carmen ad Italos | deduxisse modos*. For *fingo* ('create', 'produce') with a predicate adjective/adjectival phrase (*nobilem*), cf. *S.* 1.4.17–18 *di bene fecerunt inopis me quodque pusilli | finxerunt animi*; Sall. *Cat.* 1.1 *pecora, quae natura prona atque uentri oboedientia finxit*; Virg. *Aen.* 2.79–80 *si miserum Fortuna Sinonem | finxit*, and see *OLD* s.v. *fingo* 2.

nobilem: at the end of the sentence and middle of the poem, H.'s self-identification via a predicate adjective (with *illum*; see 1–12n.) finally reveals the identity anticipated since the framing relative pronoun (*quem*) with which the poem – and the sentence – opened. The next poem opens in similar fashion (see 4.1–18n.). In a book engaged with Rome, its triumphs and its young nobles, H. appropriates to himself a *nobilitas* of a different and higher sort. Possibly also a response to and 'correction' of Virg. *G.* 4.564 (see 9–10n.), where poetry, as opposed to warfare, is 'ignoble leisure', *studiis florentem ignobilis oti.*

13–24 The second half of the poem reflects on H.'s reputation, for which he credits the Muse.

13 Rome, emphatically fronted, comes suddenly and unexpectedly, following the preference for Tibur and Aeolic song over exploits leading to the Capitol, the contrast underscored by the rhyme from *Capitolio* to *Aeolio.*

Romae, principis urbium: the designation *R., p. u.* seems to be unique, and the combination of Rome and *princeps* perhaps led Porph., with some reason (cf. 3.24.27 *pater urbium*), to identify *suboles* (14 and n.) as Drusus and Tiberius: *subolem principis urbium Nerone<s> uult intellegi, quos August<us> priuignos loco filiorum diligebat.* Cf. 14.44 *Italiae dominaeque Romae*; Virg. *G.* 2.534 *rerum* (*urbium* will not go into the hexameter)... *pulcherrima Roma.* Cf. Ogilvie 1965: 536 (on Livy 4.4.2 *in aeternum urbe condita*) on Rome's immortality as a feature of Augustan propaganda.

14 dignatur 'deigns'; so with the infinitive first at Cat. 64.407; Lucr. 2.1039. Otherwise in H. only at *Epist.* 1.19.39–40, also in a context of literary appreciation, though now with negative, excluding force: *non ego... grammaticas ambire tribus et pulpita dignor*; and cf. Virg. *Ecl.* 6.1 *prima Syracosio dignata est ludere uersu*; see *TLL* s.v. *dignor* 1140.84–1141.44.

suboles 'rising generation'. The word is characterized by Cicero (*De or.* 3.153) as *grandior atque antiquior oratio*, but in its non-agricultural senses it clearly became less marked in the Augustan and later periods. It is classified among *uerba prisca* by Lebek (1970: 310).

14–15 inter amabiles | uatum ponere me choros: cf. 1.1.35–6 *quod si me lyricis uatibus inseres | sublimi feriam sidera uertice.*

amabiles: the adjective occurs five times in the *Odes*, three in the *Epistles*, and is otherwise sparingly used by poets before Ovid; cf., in the context of poetic initiation, 3.4.5–7 *auditis? an me ludit amabilis | insania? audire et uideor pios | errare per lucos.*

uatum: see Fraenkel 408, n. 3 for arguments against Buecheler's *uatem* (anticipated by Anchensen), accepted by Heinze, but surely wrong. The parallel with 1.1.35 (see above), valid only with *uatum*, is compelling.

16 et iam dente minus mordeor inuido: cf. 2.20.4 *inuidiaque maior.* In both cases the thought (immunity to envy through poetic supremacy) is Callimachean: *Epigr.* 21.4 Pf. ὁ δ' ἤεισεν κρέσσονα βασκανίης 'his song outdid Envy'; *Hymn* 2.105–14; also Virg. *G.* 3.37–9 *inuidia infelix Furias amnemque seuerum | Cocyti metuet...* (and Thomas *ad loc.*). Cf. Porph. *ad loc. hoc intellegi uult de se, quod ait Sallustius* [*Iug.* 10.2.6, Micipsa to Jugurtha]: *'gloria inuidiam uicisti'.* For the tooth as a metaphorical instrument of envy or hatred, see *TLL* s.v. *dens* 542.35–58, including *Epod.* 6.15 (see Mankin *ad loc.*) *si quis atro dente me petiuerit*; *S.* 2.1.77–8 *Inuidia... fragili quaerens illidere dentem | offendet solido*; *Epist.* 2.1.150–1 (Fescennine invective rather than envy;

see Brink *ad loc.*) *doluere cruento | dente lacessiti*. Cicero well captures the nature of human envy at *Balb.* 57 *more hominum inuident, in conuiuiis rodunt, in circulis uellicant, non illo inimico, sed hoc malo dente carpunt*, a passage that matches the situation of *S.* 1.4.91–3 *ego, si risi quod ineptus | pastillos Rufillus olet, Gargonius hircum, | liuidus et mordax uideor tibi*. Cf. also *TLL* s.v. *mordeo* 1486.39–59, including Ter. *Eun.* 410–11 *inuidere omnes mihi, mordere clanculum*.

17–20 A very mannered and visually marked stanza (as is the next; see 21–4n.), combining anaphora of *o* (see 1.21n.; also at 2.46–7; 1.32.13–16, 3.5.38–40, 1.14.1–2; *S.* 1.2.92; 2.6.8–10, 60–5 (*ter*)), postponement of the name of the addressee (cf. 10.1–5; 1.7.1–5; 3.21.1–4; 3.26.9–12), postposition of the pronoun in the fronted relative clause and onset of the parentheses (|*Pieri*, | *si libeat*) in the same metrical position.

17–18 o, . . . , Pieri: the separation of *o* from its vocative seems to be unusual before Ovid; cf. Virg. *G.* 1.12–14 (where *tuque* mitigates) *tuque o, cui prima frementem | fudit equum magno tellus percussa tridenti, | Neptune*; Prop. 3.19.21 (depending on how *uenumdata* is taken) *tuque, o, Minoa uenumdata, Scylla, figura | tondes purpurea regna paterna coma*. Klingner has no comma after *o*, thereby taking it with *quae*, but Porph. is right to gloss '*o Pieri, quae dulcem strepitum testudinis temperas*'.

testudinis aureae: *testudo* (tortoise shell, used as sound board for the lyre) is applied by synecdoche to the lyre itself beginning with the Augustan poets (*OLD* s.v. 2). For a golden lyre, cf. (prominently) Pind. *Pyth.* 1.1–2 Χρυσέα φόρμιγξ, Ἀπόλλωνος καὶ ἰοπλοκάμων | σύνδικον Μοισᾶν κτέανον, 'Golden lyre, just possession of Apollo and the violet-locked Muses'; also (not just the lyre) Callim. *Hymn* 2.32–4 χρύσεα τὠπόλλωνι τό τ' ἐνδυτὸν ἥ τ' ἐπιπορπίς | ἥ τε λύρη τό τ' ἄεμμα τὸ Λύκιον ἥ τε φαρέτρη, | χρύσεα καὶ τὰ πέδιλα· πολύχρυσος γὰρ Ἀπόλλων 'Golden is the tunic of Apollo, and golden his cloak, as are his lyre, his Lycian bow, and his quiver, golden also his sandals; of much gold is Apollo'. For a golden plectrum cf. 2.13.26–7 *aureo . . . plectro*, of Alcaeus, and see N–H *ad loc.*, with references to *Hymn. Hom. Ap.* 185, Pind. *Nem.* 5.24; Eur. *Her.* 351.

strepitum: first in H. with the apparently neutral meaning of 'music' (before and in general the word implies 'noise' or 'din'), as also at *Epist.* 1.2.29–31, where, however, the moralizing voice allows an implication of 'din', *iuuentus, | cui pulchrum fuit in medios dormire dies et | ad strepitum citharae cessatum ducere somnum*; similarly *Epist.* 1.14.25–6 *meretrix tibicina, cuius | ad strepitum salias terrae grauis*. In view of these contexts *dulcem* could be taken proleptically: 'regulate into sweetness the noise of the lyre' – it only sounds sweet if the Muse takes control of it. This makes the achievement more miraculous, and thus harmonizes it with that of 19–20, giving fish, previously silent (*mutis*), the music of the swan.

Pieri: the singular for one of the Pierian Muses appears in Latin only here, in Greek in Pratinas of Phlius (*ap.* Athen. 14.617d = fr. 3.6 Snell), Eur. *Rhes.* 349; in the only other instance in Latin, *Pieris* at Ov. *Fast.* 4.222 refers to Cybele.

19–20 'able to endow even mute fishes with the voice of the swan, should it please her'; adaptation of an ἀδύνατον, making the feat all the more impressive. Although fish and land animals often exchange places in this figure, a singing fish is found only here; see Dutoit 1936: 85–91. At 2.20.9–12 H. famously turns into a swan.

21–4 'This fact, that I, the player of the Roman lyre, am pointed out by the finger of those who pass by, is completely of your doing; that I have breath and give pleasure, if I do give pleasure, is your doing.' The contrast with 2.45–52 could not be more stark: there H. was in the crowd improbably chanting 'io Triumphe' as Augustus processed by; here he is the lyric poet of Rome, himself the centre of attention for those passing by. *fidicen* is presumably a generic fiction, and there is no evidence that H. composed musically, *pace* Lyons 2007; see also 9.4n. *totum . . . hoc* is the subject of the sentence while *quod . . . praetereuntium* is its predicate noun clause, both in subject relationship to *est*, while *muneris tui* is a predicative genitive of *est* and *Romanae fidicen lyrae* is a predicate of *monstror*. The syntax and diction are chiastically repeated: *tui est,* | *quod monstror* || *quod spiro . . . tuum est,* with *tuum est* the closing frame of the stanza as of the poem; cf. 1 *tu*. The arrangement forces attention onto the centrepiece, the crux of the poem: *Romanae fidicen lyrae*. This designation, like the address to Melpomene (see 1n.), ties the poem to the close of 3.30.10–14 *dicar . . . princeps Aeolium carmen ad Italos* | *deduxisse modos*.

quod . . . quod: see K–S II 2. 269–71 for the use of the subordinating pronoun to introduce a noun clause ('the fact that').

muneris . . . tui 'this is completely your doing'; genitive of description used predicatively (lit. 'of your gift').

monstror digito praetereuntium: cf. Suet. *Vita Verg.* 11 on the bashful Virgil: *cetera sane uitae et ore et animo tam probum constat, ut Neapoli Parthenias uulgo appellatus sit, ac si quando Romae, quo rarissime commeabat, uiseretur in publico, sectantes demonstrantesque se subterfugeret in proximum tectum.* H.'s position has evolved since his stance in *S.* 1.10.72–6 *saepe stilum uertas, iterum quae digna legi sint* | *scripturus, neque te ut miretur turba labores,* | *contentus paucis lectoribus. an tua demens* | *uilibus in ludis dictari carmina malis?* | *non ego.* Pers. 1.28–30 seems to be in dialogue with both Horatian passages: *'at pulchrum est digito monstrari et dicier "hic est."* | *ten cirratorum centum dictata fuisse* | *pro nihilo pendes?' Epod.* 4.9–10 is a negative context, involving envy and lack of merit, *ut ora uertat huc et huc euntium* | *liberrima indignatio.* K–H note Lucian, *Harm.* 1, which defines true fame in the same terms: καὶ τὸ ἐπίσημον εἶναι ἐν πλήθεσι καὶ δείκνυσθαι τῶι δακτύλωι, 'being noticed in a crowd (cf. *praetereuntium*) and being pointed at'. And cf. the Greek compound δακτυλοδεικτέω/ος, implying admiration or envy, as at Aesch. *Ag.* 1332–3 δακτυλοδείκτων . . . μελάθρων 'houses people point their fingers at'.

monstror: cf. 9 *ostendet*.

24 si placeo: uncharacteristic – and possibly disingenuous – modesty, or doubt, compared to the confidence of 1.1, 2.20, 3.30, though there is conditionality also at 1.1.35 *quodsi me lyricis uatibus inseres*. For the repetition *placeo, si placeo*, see Wills 175, n. 2.

spiro . . . placeo: forms a frame with the opening *nascentem placido*.

4

METRE

Alcaic stanza (as for 9, 14, 15), two lines of penthemimer + dodrans = Alcaic hendecasyllable (×–⏑––||–⏑⏑–⏑×), followed by a line of iamb + penthemimer (×–⏑–––⏑–×) and an aristophanean with dactylic expansion (–⏕–⏕–⏑–×). In origin the third and fourth lines were a single unit, so the un-Aeolic-looking third line is simply part of the iambo-trochaic head to the Aeolic 'fourth' line (see West 33). The third line is particularly suitable for a greater degree of solemnity, and perhaps for this reason the stanza, the most frequently used in the *Odes*, predominates in poems of a political and public mode, as throughout *C.* 4.

INTRODUCTION

Like a young eagle attacking sheepfolds or snakes, like a young lion about to slaughter a roe, so did Drusus appear to the axe-wielding Vindelici, who came to learn what Augustus had in mind for the adoptive Nero boys. A father's strength is inherited by the son, but education and the right values add to that. The defeat of Hasdrubal at the Metaurus, and the piety that followed the Second Punic War showed what Rome owed to the Neros, as Hannibal said, 'As is true for deer hunted by wolves, it is victory just to escape the Romans. The race that survived the fall of Troy, like an oak that survives axe blows or the Hydra and other such monsters, keeps coming back. No messages to Carthage, all is gone with Hasdrubal's death.' There is nothing Claudian hands cannot achieve, protected by Jupiter, trained for war.

Page 409 knew what he thought of this : 'It is a perfect model of a Prize Ode, and has long served as such. It exhibits little real poetic power but great skill in composition, and is the work of invention rather than inspiration: the elaborate comparison in the first four stanzas must have given Horace considerable trouble, and very glad he must have been when he got through it.' Having in the preceding three poems demonstrated his unwillingness or incompetence to be Pindaric, and most immediately in 4.3 having demonstrated ideal lyric song in its essentials, H. now embarks on the first of his two full-throated Pindaric encomia (see Syndikus 303–13 for many of the Pindaricisms of the poem). *C.* 4.4 and 4.14, both in Alcaics, praise the princes Drusus and Tiberius, and each is followed by a poem directed to the *princeps* (5, 15). The princes receive the Pindaric treatment, the *princeps* more that of the *uersus quadrati* promised at 2.45–52 (cf. 5.17–24, 15.4–16nn.). Dettmer 1983: 508–12 has gathered the compelling parallels between 4.4 and 4.5:

4.4			4.5
2, 4	*rex deorum . . . Iuppiter*	1	*diuis orte bonis* (Augustus)
5	*patrius*	5	*patriae*
7–9	*uernique . . . uenti*	6	*instar ueris*
21	*quaerere*	16	*quaerit*
26	*nutrita faustis sub penetralibus*	18	*nutrit . . . Faustitas*
29	*fortes creantur fortibus et bonis*	23	*laudantur simili prole puerperae*
36	*indecorant bene nata culpae*	24	*culpam poena premit comes*
38–9	Hasdrubal, one of Rome's former enemies	25–8	Rome's current enemies
48	*deos habuere rectos*	32	Augustus = *deus*
61–2	Labour of Hercules	36	Hercules, a demigod
74	*Iuppiter*	37	*dux bone* = Augustus

Like 4.14, 4.4 celebrates the victories of the two sons of Livia and stepsons of Augustus in the year 15 BCE. In the course of the summer they carried out separate operations – Drusus north through Tridentum, Tiberius a little later and further to the west – and then a combined engagement on 1 August (see 14.34–6) in which they subdued the Raetians of the central (Swiss) Alps and the northern foothills south of the Danube (Woolf, *CAH* X 537–8). Dio 54.20.1–2 reports that P. Silius Nerva (cos. 20 BCE), proconsular governor of Illyria, had in 16 BCE subdued and conquered the 'Camunii' and 'Vennii' ('Alpine tribes') and also countered a combined Noric and Pannonian invasion of Istria. Van Berchem 1968 and Wells 1972: 66–7 plausibly argue that Silius' activities may have been much more extensive than Dio indicates, in particular taking him farther west, essentially to the areas in which Drusus and Tiberius would operate the following year, when there may not have been too much serious work to be done; see van Berchem 1968 on the matter of how complete the victory will have been, a parallel to the conquest of Spain in 26/25 BCE (see 14.41–4n.). The campaign mostly 'gave Tiberius and Drusus, the two stepsons of Augustus, the opportunity of winning military glory cheaply and easily' (Woolf, *CAH* X 537). See also Plin. *HN* 3.136–8 and *CIL* 5.7817 = *EJ* 40 for the Tropaeum Alpium with its list of *gentes Alpinae deuictae*; see Wells 1972: 59–79.

Depending on the speaker of the last four lines (cf. 73–6n.), the substance of the poem falls roughly or perfectly into two parts, a fact that should not be neglected in determining the assignation of those lines. Lines 1–36 treat the achievement of Drusus, while the following 36 lines treat that of his ancestor C. Claudius Nero (cos. 207 BCE), victor with his colleague M. Livius Salinator (*RE* XIII 891–9), an ancestor of Livia, at the battle of Metaurus. The latter received a triumph (cf. Enn. *Ann.* 299 Skutsch *Liuius inde redit magno mactatus triumpho*), while Claudius was given an *ouatio* at the same time. The coda (73–6) treats the Claudii in general. Fraenkel 426 observes that the Pindaric patterns are 'the most daring ones in

Horace' (see 18–22n.) and therefore finds it remarkable that H. did not attempt, 'as he had done in i.12 and in the *Carmen saeculare*, to reproduce in his own way the triadic arrangement characteristic of Pindar's major odes'.

Within the general and specific Pindaric atmosphere, H. chose rather to create a binary structure, allowing a focus on two sets of Roman and barbarian opponents, Drusus and the Vindelici on the one hand, and Drusus' ancestor C. Claudius Nero and the Carthaginians on the other. In its length (76 lines) and general stanzaic shape (9+9+1) it is close to the *Carmen saeculare*. The poem is not addressed to Drusus or anyone else (see Fraenkel 431 and n. 2), as 14 is addressed not to Tiberius, but rather Augustus, to whom the *auspicia* for the victory belonged.

For the circumstances supposedly surrounding composition of this poem, see pp. 4–5.

1–28 A long, Pindaric sentence, marked by a peculiar parenthesis and *praeteritio* (see 18–22n.). Fraenkel 427 puts it well: '*Monte decurrens uelut amnis*, the beginning of the ode rolls along in a mighty period of full 28 lines until at last it comes to a stop with the momentous name of *Nerones*.' For a similar opening cf. 14.1–24.

1–18 qualem . . . Drusum: see 3.12n. (on *quem . . . nobilem*), for these consecutive poems opening with the same syntactical construction.

1–16 The extended double similes that open the poem and occupy its first 16 lines are hard to parallel in Augustan poetry (*pace* Fraenkel 427, Virg. *G.* 3.89–94 and *Aen.* 4.469–73 are not on the same scale). A more apt set of *comparanda* is to be found in Cat. 68B, which has three sets of double similes: at 53–6 the poet's passion is compared first to Aetna, then to the hot springs of Thermopylae, while at 57–65 the help Allius provided is compared first to the refreshment provided to wayfarers by a mountain stream, then to a slackening breeze for those at sea; at 119–34 Catullus' love is compared to the late-born child who saves the old man from intestate death and to the love felt by doves.

1–15 qualem . . . alitem . . . qualemue . . . leonem: cf. 14.20 *qualis* (Tiberius' first simile). Fraenkel points to the opening of Prop. 1.3: 1–7 *qualis Thesea iacuit cedente carina | languida desertis Cnosia litoribus, | qualis et accubuit primo Cepheia somno| libera iam duris cotibus Andromede, | nec minus assiduis Edonis fessa choreis | qualis in herboso concidit Apidano: | talis uisa mihi*. He further notes that the form of both Latin passages may be traced back to the *Catalogue of Women* or Ἠοῖαι so named from the phrase used to introduce new sections: ἢ οἵη/οἵην etc. (= *uel qualis*). This latter claim is slightly misleading; while Propertius gives a catalogue of women with whom he compares the sleeping Cynthia, and is therefore at least superficially similar to Hesiod, his *qualis* introduces the simile's subject (Ariadne, Andromeda, Edonian Bacchant), with the outer subject, Cynthia, figured as *talis*. The Ἠοῖαι, on the other hand, have no such metaphorical status; rather, the correlative introduces the subject itself. H. adapts the Propertian style, with the narrative subject, *Drusum*, coming after 16 lines of simile (as with Propertius' *talis*).

The parallelism of eagle and lion (both accusative) is set within a context of strong syntactical difference: youthful and inherited vigour and a love of feast and battle send the eagle against sheepfold and snakes, while the doomed roe-deer looks at the young lion, weaned from its mother's teat and ready for its first kill. The change of focalization in the second simile, along with its closure (16 *peritura uidit*), brings an intensity and a shift of empathy familiar from Virgil; indeed, in this reversal H. may be alluding to the lion simile which brings Turnus and Pallas into eye-contact soon before the death of the latter. Turnus is the subject in the preceding narrative, Pallas (like the *caprea*) in what follows: *Aen.* 10.453–8 *desiluit Turnus . . . utque leo, specula cum uidit ab alta | stare procul campis meditantem in proelia taurum, | aduolat, haud alia est Turni uenientis imago. | hunc ubi . . . credidit . . . Pallas . . .* There is at least a superficial similarity to the fable of Aesch. *Ag.* 717–36, in which a young lion turns in its maturity against the house that has reared it (see 13–16n.); if so, more than superficial dynastic issues come into brief focus.

1–6 ministrum fulminis alitem 'winged attendant of the thunderbolt'; the periphrasis for the eagle sets a high stylistic note. Cf. Virg. *Aen.* 5.254–5 (ecphrastic Ganymede) *quem praepes ab Ida | sublimem pedibus rapuit Iouis armiger uncis*; 9.564 (seizing a swan and a hare) *pedibus Iouis armiger uncis. ministrum* (from *minus*; cf. *magister*) is appropriate for delegated power (cf. *permisit* below and n.).

regnum in aues uagas 'rule over wandering birds'. For this use of *in* cf. 3.1.5–6 *regum timendorum in proprios greges, | reges in ipsos imperium est Iouis*; N–R *ad loc.* cite Plaut. *Pers.* 343 *meum, opino, imperiumst in te*; Ter. *Eun.* 415 *eone es ferus quia habes imperium in beluas?* For further examples (with *dominatio*, *licentia*, *uis*, e.g.) cf. *TLL* s.v. *in* 748.57–70. *OLD* s.v. *uagus* 1 misses this instance, the first of *uagus* applied to birds; cf. Sen. *Ben.* 4.18.2 (*gallinae uagae*); Cic. *Diu.* 2.80 *uolucres huc et illuc passim uagantes.*

permisit: Jupiter, as overall *rex*, grants limited *regnum* to the eagle; cf. Livy 34.7.2–3 (also unusual, see Briscoe *ad loc.*) *magistratibus in coloniis municipiisque . . . togae praetextae habendae ius permittemus.* Given the close relationship between tenor (*Drusum*) and vehicle (*ministrum . . . alitem*), it is hard to avoid seeing in this handover of royal power an allusion to the status of Augustus and his stepson, leading his own *aquilae* in 15 BCE, as *legatus Augusti pro praetore*, four years after Augustus secured permission for him to begin the *cursus honorum* five years early (Dio 54.10.4); cf. Tac. *Ann.* 1.3.1 *Tiberium Neronem et Claudium Drusum priuignos imperatoriis nominibus auxit* – probably after publication of *C.* 4, however.

expertus . . . flauo 'having found him reliable in the matter of the blond Ganymede'; cf. 3.20.15–16 *qualis aut Nireus fuit aut aquosa | raptus ab Ida* (with N–R *ad loc.*). In Hom. *Il.* 20.231–5 (see Edwards *ad* 233–5) the gods take him up to be Zeus' cup-bearer, with the pederastic aspect therefore muted, but already in *Hymn. Hom. Aphr.* 202–17 the erotic aspect, and the central role of Zeus, is fully activated.

5–12 Four main clauses, with each verb taking *ministrum* as direct object, with a temporal marker in each clause (5 *olim* 'previously', 7 *iam* 'presently', 9 *mox* 'soon',

11 *nunc* 'now'), and with characterizing predication indicating the development of the young eagle: *laborum . . . inscium* | *pauentem* | *hostem.*

5 patrius uigor: introduces the issue of patrilineage, which will become problematic later in the poem; cf. 27–8 *Augusti paternus* | . . . *animus*, 30–1 *patrum* | *uirtus* and nn.

6 laborum . . . inscium: so the first stage of training the young horse, right after weaning at Virg. *G.* 3.189 *inualidus etiamque tremens, etiam inscius aeui*; cf. the young plant 2.372 *imprudensque laborum.* The learning of *labor* and *labores* also suggests another father-son situation, Aeneas' advice to Ascanius at *Aen.* 12.435 '*disce, puer, uirtutem ex me uerumque laborem*'. For some distinctions among *inscius*, *insciens* (not possible in dactylic verse), *ignarus* and *nescius* see *TLL* s.v. *insciens* 1839.39–60.

7–9 iam: with *docuere* (see 5–12n.), but also ἀπὸ κοινοῦ with *nimbis remotis*: the winds of spring remove the wintry clouds, then the flying lessons begin.

insolitos . . . nisus 'endeavours that are new to it'.

pauentem 'still frightened': the process is gradual. The assonance of *uenti pauentem* is noteworthy.

9–10 ouilia: vulnerable to predators, though not in the Isles of the Blest: *Epod.* 16.51 *nec uespertinus circumgemit ursus ouile*; or when plague comes: Virg. *G.* 3.537 *non lupus insidias explorat ouilia circum.*

uiuidus impetus 'a lively attack', with some irony given the effect on the victim.

11–12 Cf. Hainsworth on Hom. *Il.* 12.200–50, the omen of the eagle and the snake: 'Eagle and snake, the bird of Zeus and the symbol of chthonic power'. The Homeric passage, in which the snake bites the eagle, which then drops it, was parodied in oracular hexameters by Ar. *Eq.* 197–8; it was made into a simile at Virg. *Aen.* 11.751–6, where Tarchon seizes Venulus and carries him off the battlefield: *utque uolans alte raptum cum fulua draconem* | *fert aquila implicuitque pedes atque unguibus haesit* etc.; the final outcome is not described (though cf. 11.741 *moriturus*). Cicero translated the Homeric lines in his poem *Marius* (*ap.* Cic. *de diu.* 1.106 = *Marius* fr. 17 Courtney); see Pease *ad loc.* for Marius' claim that his seven consulships were predicted by his finding seven eaglets as a boy (App. *B.C.* 1.75; Plut. *Mar.* 36); also for references to the image on coinage and in art.

reluctantes dracones: *draco* only here in H., indicating a Virgilian intertext; cf. Virg. *Aen.* 11.749 (Venulus) *repugnans*, 751–66 *draconem . . . luctantem.*

amor dapis atque pugnae: strong language, and *amor dapis* is Homeric: *Il.* 1.469 (and frequently) πόσιος καὶ ἐδητύος . . . ἔρον 'desire of drink and of food'. The singular *daps* has an archaic feel to it (N–W 1 692), and the genitive singular *dapis* is found first in H. (*Epod.* 5.33, 17.66; *S.* 2.6.89; *Epist.* 1.17.51) and here for the first time of an animal's food; cf. *OLD* s.v. *daps* 2b. This new use may look to Homeric δαίς 'feast, banquet', at *Il.* 1.5; 24.43 (in a lion simile), but it is something of a travesty, given the origin of the word, 'sacrificial feast', as at 2.7.17 *ergo obligatam redde Ioui dapem* (and N–H *ad loc.*).

13–16 qualemue: see 1, 13nn. The stanza is replete with words for abundance and consumption: *laetis . . . pascuis*, *ubere*, ?*lacte*/*lactante*, *dente*, *peritura*.

laetis . . . pascuis: dative with *intenta*; cf. *S.* 1.5.83–4 *somnus tamen aufert* | [*me*] *intentum Veneri*. Cf. Livy's description of the *locus amoenus* outside Croton at the temple of Juno Lacinia: 24.3.4–5 *lucus ibi frequenti silua et proceris abietis arboribus saeptus laeta in medio pascua habuit*. For *laetus* of crops 'flourishing, luxuriant, lush', of fields 'rich, fertile' see *OLD* s.v. 1 and Virg. *G.* 1.1 *quid faciat laetas segetes*.

lactante: *iam lacte* is transmitted, but *lacte* is obelized by Shackleton Bailey, who suggests *iam iamque*; cf. Bentley ('mihi quidem semper uisum est illud *lacte* otiosum et superfluum'), noting that either *ubere* or *lacte* would be sufficient (cf. Virg. *G.* 3.187–8 *atque haec iam primo depulsus ab ubere matris* | *audeat*; Suet. *Tib.* 44 *infantes firmiores necdum tamen lacte depulsos*); Nauck's comma after *ubere* does not change things. Bentley suggests *mane* for *lacte*, but Stat. *Theb.* 7.670, of a grown lion's morning hunting habit, does not work as well with a morning weaning; or *sponte*, which seems cartoonish (so eager is the young lion for the real thing) and does not work well with *depulsum*. Quinn takes *ubere* as adjectival, which would be without point – indeed the opposite (*deficienti*, uel sim.) would make more sense. Nisbet 1986: 229 attractively suggests *lactante* (anon. *ap.* Dillenburger), which could easily have been reduced by haplography to *lacte*, generating the filler *iam* which Shackleton Bailey 1990: 227 rightly notes does not quite = *modo*; the parallels are few but of good pedigree: Lucil. 176 M. *lactanti in sumine*; Lucr. 5.885 *ubera mammarum in somnis lactantia quaerit*; Ov. *Met.* 6.342 *uberaque ebiberant auidi lactantia nati*; *TLL* s.v. *lactans* 849.4–8. Shackleton Bailey (*Philol.* 134 (1990) 227) responds that '*lactante* (Cornelissen) trails uselessly after *matris ab ubere*, which is much better off without it'; but the Ovidian example shows the participle adds something. There is a similar emphasis at Aesch. *Ag.* 718–19, where the young lion is taken off its mother's milk (ἀγάλακτον) though still partial to it (φιλόμαστον); see 1, 13n.

dente nouo: of the new tooth that follows the 'baby tooth' in humans at Cels. *Med.* 8.1.10 *exque eadem radice in pueris nouus dens subit*.

peritura uidit: the final moments of the *caprea*, no longer occupied (14 *intenta*) with grazing.

16–17 uidit: | uidere: for the repeated verb at the boundary between simile and narrative, see Wills 348–9.

uidere . . . Vindelici: a straightforward clause in the middle of a complex period; cf. 22–5 *cateruae . . . sensere*; 14.8 *Vindelici didicere* and 14.7–9n.

Raetis: so codd. det. and Bentley, who argues that *Raeti* of the better MSS (i.e. *Raeti . . . Vindelici*) gives a single people while historical reality (Vell. 2.39, 95, 104, 122; Suet. *Aug.* 21; *Tib.* 9; Plin. *HN* 3.133; Tac. *Ann.* 2.17.4), like H. himself elsewhere (14.8 *Vindelici*, 15 *Raetos*), separates the two. Conjectural possibilities include adjectives to modify Vindelici (e.g. *taetri*) or *Alpibus* (*taetris*); Shackleton Bailey obelizes but records the late MS reading *et Vindelici*, which would cut the knot; cf. *CS* 55–6 *Scythae . . . et Indi*.

Raetis . . . sub Alpibus: i.e. the foothills on the northern slopes; Tac. *Germ.* 1 locates the source of the Rhine in the Raetic Alps (*Raeticarum Alpium*), north of Lake Como.

Drusum 'Drusus the Elder', Nero Claudius Drusus (*RE* III 2703–19; *PIR*² C857), to whom the *agnomen* 'Germanicus' was given after his death in 9 BCE, was the younger brother of the future emperor Tiberius (*RE* X 478–536; *PIR*² C941). They were sons of Tiberius Claudius Nero (quaestor pro praetore 48 BCE, praetor 42 BCE), an adherent of Julius Caesar in the war against Pompey and of L. Antonius (cos. 41 BCE) in the Bellum Perusinum, by his wife Livia Drusilla (*PIR*² L301), whence the cognomen of their younger son. He was born either 14 Jan. or mid-April 38 BCE, three months after his mother was married to Octavian, according to Dio 48.44.2 and Suet. *Claud.* 1. Octavian sent him to his father so as to allay suspicion about paternity, having previously secured pontifical permission to marry a pregnant woman (Dio 48.44.2), well described at Tac. *Ann.* 1.10.5 *abducta Neroni uxor et consulti per ludibrium pontifices an concepto necdum edito partu rite nuberet.* This did not stop circulation of a witty verse: τοῖς εὐτυχοῦσι καὶ τρίμηνα παιδία ('to the lucky are born three-month children'). This contributes to the oddity of 29–32, which imply Augustan paternity of the Neros (see n.). Drusus served out the remainder of Tiberius' praetorship in 16 BCE. Shortly before 15 BCE Drusus married Antonia minor (*PIR*² A885), the younger daughter of the triumvir by Augustus' sister Octavia (*PIR*² O66). Their happy marriage produced many children, of whom there survived two sons and one daughter, Claudia Livilla (Suet. *Claud.* 1). The elder son was known as Germanicus Caesar (*PIR*² J221) after his adoption by Tiberius Caesar in 4 CE; the younger son, Ti. Claudius Nero Germanicus (*PIR*² C942), was made emperor after his nephew Caligula was assassinated in 41 CE. Drusus died on 14 Sept. 9 BCE, after further campaigning and construction of the *fossa Drusina*, a channel connecting the Rhine to the Ijssel, which flowed into the Lacus Flevo, now the Zuider Zee (see Hurley *ad* Suet. *Claud.* 1.2; Wells 1972: 101–16). According to Suet. *Tib.* 3, the Livii Drusi received their cognomen in the fourth century BCE after Livius, an ancestor of Livia, defeated the Celtic leader Drausus (O. Celt. *dru- 'oak', also 'strong'). The opposition *Drusum . . . Vindelici* perhaps revisits the conflict. See intro. for Drusus' connections to the victorious generals at the Metaurus.

Vindelici: related to Celtic *vindos* 'white', 'fair', 'fortunate' (Delamarre 2003 s.v. *vindos*), situated in Bavaria, between the Alps and the Danube (cf. *RE* IXA 1–17). Servius *ad Aen.* 1.243 connects them with Liburnia in Croatia: *Raeti Vindelici* (see above on *Raetis*) *ipsi sunt Liburni, saeuissimi admodum populi, contra quos missus est Drusus.*

18–22 'what is the derivation of the custom, going back through their whole history, that armed their right hands with Amazon-style axes, I have put off enquiring, and the fact is one is not permitted to have knowledge of everything'. A stylistic reworking, as Scaliger noted (see Fraenkel 426, n. 2), of Pind. *Nem.* 5, elsewhere an intertext for H. (8.9–12n.), 14–17 αἰδέομαι μέγα εἰπεῖν ἐν δίκαι τε μὴ κεκινδυνευμένον, | πῶς δὴ λίπον εὐκλέα νᾶσον, καὶ τίς ἄνδρας ἀλκίμους | δαίμων ἀπ' Οἰνώνας ἔλασεν. | στάσομαι· οὔ τοι ἅπασα κερδίων | φαίνοισα πρόσωπον ἀλάθει' ἀτρεκής, 'I shrink from telling a great deed not ventured justly, how they left the famous island and what god drove the brave men from Oenona. I will stop, for not every exact truth is better coming to light.' H. has caught the essence of the Pindaric *praeteritio*, although where Pindar doubles the main clause as the frame (αἰδέομαι . . . στάσομαι), with the substance in an indirect question in the center (πῶς), H. achieves a more digressive style by leaving both *praeteritio* markers (*quaerere distuli . . . nec scire fas est*) until the end, with the indirect question (*quibus . . . obarmet*) temporarily unanchored. Fraenkel 429, n. 3 quotes from a letter of Macaulay (Trevelyan 1978: I 400–1): 'The most obscure passage – at least the strangest passage – in all Horace may be explained by supposing that he was misled by Pindar's example: I mean that odd parenthesis in the "Qualem ministrum" *quibus mos unde deductus per omne* – . This passage, taken by itself, always struck me as the harshest, queerest, most preposterous digression in the world. But there are several things in Pindar very like it.'

per omne tempus goes closely with *unde deductus*, and is more than just a periphrasis for *semper*, but rather conveys a sense of the custom's travelling through all of time.

Amazonia securi | dextras obarmet: Amazons are variously armed in Greek and Roman art of all periods (sword, spear, bow and arrow e.g.), but axe and light shields (*peltae*) are particularly characteristic, and in line with Arrian 7.13.2 πελέκεις ἀντὶ δοράτων ἐφόρουν καὶ ἀντὶ ἀσπίδων πέλτας 'they carried axes instead of spears and peltai instead of shields'. For axe-wielding Amazons cf. *LIMC* s.v. *Amazones* 104 c and g, 111, 127, 133, 194b, 155, 233a, 296, 299, 306, 315, 316, 319, 329, 322, 327, 329, 369, 370 etc.

obarmet 'furnishes for combat [against]'; the compound seems to add a measure of aggression to those so armed, and is a Horatian coinage that appealed only to Apuleius (*Met.* 8.16.4 *pastores . . . manus obarmauerant*; 9.1.1 *carnifex contra me manus impias obarmabat*; 2.25.1 (figurative) *perfrictis oculis et obarmatis ad uigilias*) and once to Auson. *epigr.* 25.1 G.

21–2 Somewhat obscure. There should be a reason for the *praeteritio*, as in *Nem.* 5.14–18 (18–22n.), where Pindar passes over the murder of Phocus by his half-brothers Peleus and Telamon. There may be some anecdote about the connection between the Vindelici and the Amazons, e.g. taunts about effeminacy of the enemy, that would offend against the assumed Pindaric decorum; cf. Virg. *Aen.* 9.617 *o uere Phrygiae, neque enim Phryges*, developed from Thersites' taunt of the Greeks at Hom. *Il.* 2.235. H. implies both that he does not know (*quaerere distuli*), but also that it may be a taboo topic (*fas*). Porph. *ad loc.* looks like a guess: *hi Vindelici sedibus ab Amazonibus eiecti ex Thracia in exilium se contulisse Alpiumque loca insedisse dicuntur, et, quod potentissim<a> in se tela secures Amazonum expert<i> fuissent, ipsos quoque usum earum in bello accepisse.* Servius *ad Aen.* 1.243 is no help: *hi autem ab Amazonibus originem ducunt, ut etiam Horatius dicit: 'quibus mos . . . distuli'.* There may be something to the argument of Gesner and Haupt *Opusc.* III 332–3 to the effect H. was attacking from a Callimachean standpoint the turgid *Amazoniad* of Domitius Marsus, which from Mart. 4.28.7–8 looks to have been a likely target for one such as H.

quaerere distuli 'I have put off asking'; *TLL* s.v. *differo* 1074.65–1075.7 gives this as the first instance of *differo* + infinitive, though Livy 27.24.1 (*ne differret obsides ab Arretinis accipere*) may be earlier; also 42.2.2, Curt. 6.9.9, then not until Petronius.

22–3 diu | lateque uictrices: magnifying the danger and power of the enemy is standard practice in such a context, but in fact the previous year may well have seen much of the area considerably softened up (see intro).

24 consiliis: cf. 75 *curae sagaces*, and 73–6n.

iuuenis: Drusus was barely 23 at the beginning of the campaign. A reminiscence of the common appellation of Octavian in the thirties and early twenties BCE: 1.2.41; *S.* 2.5.62; Virg. *Ecl.* 1.42 (and Clausen *ad loc.*); *G.* 1.500; cf. 5.9n.

reuictae: Shackleton Bailey shared Bentley's dislike after *uictrices* (most MSS) and like him accepts *repressae* (lemma in Porph. without further entry, δ *uar.*). Nisbet 1986: 229 favours Campbell's *retusae* ('beaten blunt'), which works well with 20 *securi*, but the repetition has a point: they who had conquered long and widely were in turn conquered. See Wills 443–5, though he does not include this example. Cf. Shackleton Bailey's own arguments (1982: 137–8) for a similar repetition of *rura* at 5.17–18: the ox takes nourishment from the countryside, Ceres puts nutrients into the countryside. Lucr. 5.380–415 treats the struggle of elements, particularly heat, wind and moisture (380–1 *inter se cum maxima mundi | pugnent membra*). Fire can only be victorious (407 *superare*) when bodies of its substance rise up from infinite space; then it loses its strength and is in turn conquered: 409 *inde cadunt uires aliqua ratione reuictae*; likewise moisture (411–13 *superare . . . recessit*).

25 sensere 'they felt', through the pain of defeat; cf. 17 *uidere* in the same position two stanzas earlier.

25–8 A tricolon marked by anaphora (*quid*) and with intricate ellipsis: the first two units share the adverb *rite*, and the participial clause (*nutrita . . . penetralibus*) in which *rite* belongs, and *posset* is to be understood: what the mind and character, duly nourished beneath an auspicious household, what the paternal attitude of Augustus with respect to the Neros, was capable of. The slight zeugma of *posset* draws attention to the power of the surrogate father.

mens rite . . . indoles | nutrita: innate intelligence and character properly nurtured; sets up the *nomos/physis* polarity developed over the next two stanzas (see 29–36n.).

nutrita: the issue of paternity is handled delicately (though cf. 29–32n.): according to Dio 48.44.4–5, when Drusus was born, three months into Livia's marriage to Octavian, the latter acknowledged (ἀνείλετο) the child, but sent him back to his father, formalizing the act with a memorandum: 'Καῖσαρ τὸ γεννηθὲν Λιουίαι τῆι ἑαυτοῦ γυναικὶ παιδίον Νέρωνι τῶι πατρὶ ἀπέδωκε'

'Caesar returned the child born to his wife Livia to Nero, the boy's father' – no doubts about succession here. He and Tiberius were then brought up (*nutrita*) in the household of the *princeps*, when Claudius Drusus Nero died a few years later; for details see *PIR* 2.195–6.

faustis sub penetralibus: the imperial household. *penetralis*, and the noun formed from its neuter, with singular and plural used without distinction, appears first, 'usu peculiari' (*TLL* s.v. 1064.24–30), in Lucr. where it = *penetrans* (1.494, 535; 2.382); with its usual meaning, but unique quantity, at Cat. 68B.101–2 *fertur lecta undique pubes | Graeca penetrales deseruisse focos*. Ultimately connected with *penus, -us/-oris* 'food, provisions' (cf. *nutrita*), on which see de Vaan 2008: 458–9, and used with *Penates*, at Cic. *Nat. D.* 2.68, so it surely occurred before Catullus and Lucretius, *di Penates, siue a penu ducto nomine . . . siue ab eo quod penitus insident; ex quo etiam penetrales a poetis uocantur*; *TLL* 1061.20–27. Virg. *Aen.* 5.744 plays on the connection: *Pergameumque Larem et canae penetralia Vestae* (see also 9.258–9 *penatis | Assaracique Larem et canae penetralia Vestae*); in Virgil adjectival and substantive forms alike frequently connote a hiddenness or interiority, often in contexts of violation: *Aen.* 2.297, 484, 508, 665; 4.504; 7.59.

Augusti paternus | in pueros animus: *pueros* is non-familial, and *paternus animus* denotes a state of mind rather than actual relationship, as at 2.2.6 *notus in fratres animi paterni*, a handy intertext for the present context, although one of the *fratres* of that earlier poem was the alleged conspirator of 23–22 BCE Varro Murena (see 9.35–6n.), so the reminiscence is another of the poem's oddities.

pueros . . . Nerones: the Nero boys, and the name in particular, close out the oversized period. For the etymology, cf. Suet. *Tib.* 1.2 *inter cognomina autem et Neronis assumpsit, quo significatur lingua Sabina fortis ac strenuus* – with gloss following in H.: 29 *fortes . . . fortibus*.

29–36 H. continues to play with the matter of paternity, now engaging the issue of *nomos/cultura* (35 *mores*) and *physis/natura* (36 *nata*), a familiar opposition: Cic. *Flacc.* 71 *agros habent et natura perbonos et diligentia culturaque meliores*; *Sen.* 53 (on observation of the vine) *cultura et natura ipsa delectat*. Much of Virg. *G.* 2 treats this dichotomy; see Thomas on Virg. *G.* 2.9, 22–34, 32–4, 47–82, 51, 420–5, 458–540. H. begins with the pro-*physis* point of view at 29–32 (cf. 29 *creantur*, 32 *progenerant*). At 33, however, with *sed* (δέ) the transition has taken place (already anticipated with 26 *nutrita*), arguing for the place of of *nomos* (34 *cultus*; 35 *mores*). The first stanza is emphatically Pindaric, as commentators have noted: cf. *Nem.* 3.40 (treating the Aeacidae and in transition from Telamon and Peleus to Achilles): συγγενεῖ δέ τις εὐδοξίαι μέγα βρίθει, 'one is mighty in inborn greatness'. Cf. also *Pyth.* 8.44–5 φυᾶι τὸ γενναῖον ἐπίπρεπει | ἐκ πατέρων παισὶ λῆμα 'by nature the noble spirit from the fathers is conspicuous in sons'. K–H also cite Pl. *Menex.* 237a to the effect that 'they are good because they are born from the good' (ἀγαθοὶ δ' ἐγένοντο διὰ τὸ φῦναι ἐξ ἀγαθῶν). Plato does then have Socrates praise upbringing (τροφή) and learning (παιδεία), whereas for Pindar birth is everything, indeed there is disparagement for learning: *Nem.* 3.41 ὃς δὲ διδάκτ' ἔχει, ψεφεννὸς ἀνήρ ('schooling makes a man obscure'). So emphatically does H., *libertino patre natus*, disagree with and correct Pindar that he uses postpositive *sed* for the only time in the *Odes* (see 33n.), getting the operative word out at the first possible opportunity: *doctrina sed* (whereby *sed* behaves like δέ). The claim to *doctrina* is also an assertion of the Callimachean; cf. 1.1.29–30 *me doctarum hederae praemia frontium | dis miscent superis.*

29–32 fortes . . . fortibus et bonis: Bell 1923: 4, 279 gives this as an example of A [+B] ~ A + B ellipsis, 'the expression of a union really fourfold by three terms' (279). At the same time the ellipsis has an ideological effect of defining bravery as virtue. For polyptoton of common adjectives in Latin poetry (where 'repetition makes plain words pointed') see Wills 227.

est . . . est: cf. 11.1–5. See Wills 415–18 for repetition in parallel hemistichs.

iuuencis . . . equis: oxen and horses are the animals of ploughing and warfare respectively, also the animals whose selection and subsequent death from plague form the frame of Virg. *G.* 3 (49–88 ~ 498–531).

patrum uirtus: the steer and horse are humanized, even though *pater* is common enough with animals; although he humanizes these animals in *G.* 3, Virg. does not allocate them *uirtus*, a word he only uses in the *Aeneid* and in the stylistically distinct *Eclogue* 4.

31–2 . . . imbellem (a) feroces (b) . . . aquilae (B) columbam (A): an appealing chiasmus (fierce eagles do not produce unwarlike doves) forms a frame with the opening simile of Drusus as eagle (1 *ministrum fulminis*). Although the trope is in the form of an adynaton, the lines invoke Virgil's famous simile on the powerlessness of poetry in the face of war at *Ecl.* 9.11–13 '*sed carmina tantum | nostra ualent, Lycida, tela inter Martia quantum | Chaonias dicunt aquila ueniente columbas*'. That was a civil war, this a war against external enemies, but the intertext does resonate, as does that of the simile of the Cleopatra ode: 1.37.17–20 *accipiter uelut | molles columbas aut leporem citus | uenator in campis niualis | Haemoniae.*

33–4 For the need to temper *uis*, cf. 3.4.65–7 *uis consili expers mole ruit sua, | uim temperatam di quoque prouehunt | in maius.*

promouet: teaching causes implanted power to move forward. *promouet* well suits the military context and answers 32 *progenerant.*

insitam is somewhat ambiguous, since although *insero* clearly means 'inseminate', 'plant' (*TLL* s.v. 1878.15–84 = *OLD* 1.1), it is also the standard word for grafting a slip into the scion tree, as at *Epod.* 2.13–14 *inutilesque falce ramos amputans | feliciores inserit* (*TLL* s.v. 1876.35–1877.48 = *OLD* 1.2), the most interventionist instance of *cultura*, and *not* of *natura* in Virg. *G.* 2 (see Thomas *ad* 2.32–4). So the *uis Neronum* may come both from their *gens* and from the household into which they were early transplanted, another of the poem's many ambiguities.

doctrina sed: the only instance of *sed* in second position in the *Odes*, *Epodes* or *Satires*; cf. *Epist.* 2.1.89 *nostra sed* (with *nostra* equally emphatic and repeated later in the line); similarly emphatic at 2.2.46 (with Brink *ad loc.*) *dura sed.* Brink notes without giving examples, 'first attempted, though rarely, by Lucr. and Cat.' I find only Cat. 51.9 *lingua sed torpet* (outdoing Sappho's Greek, which has not δέ but line-initial ἀλλά); 61.102–3 *lenta sed uelut assitas | uitis implicat arbores* (in neither of which is the fronted word stressed). The confinement of the feature in H. to the post-Virgilian years may have something to do with Virgil's *Aeneid*, which has the emphatic fronting (A): with *sed enim* (= ἀλλὰ γάρ): 1.19 *progeniem sed enim Troiano a sanguine duci;* 2.164 *Tydides sed enim scelerumque inuentor Vlixes*; 6.28 *magnum reginae sed enim miseratus amorem* (otherwise only thus at Stat. *Theb.* 5.699; 9.583; *Silu.* 3.1.123; 3.3.76; 4.8.42; 5.2.30 and Sil. *Pun.* 12.627); (B) just *sed*: *Aen.* 1.353 *ipsa sed in somnis inhumati uenit imago*; 3.37; 11. 631 *tertia sed*; 3.586 *obscuro sed nubila caelo*; 5.320 *longo sed proximus interuallo*; 6.315 *nauita sed tristis nunc hos nunc accipit illos*; 7.704–5 *aëriam sed gurgite ab alto | urgeri uolucrum . . . nubem*; 7.736–7 *patriis sed non et filius aruis | contentus*; 11.63 *misero sed debita patri*; 11.816 *ossa sed inter*. The only Virgilian instance outside the *Aeneid* is the high-register *Ecl.* 4.43 *ipse sed in pratis aries*.

rectique cultus pectora roborant: 'correct training strengthens personality'. Shackleton Bailey follows Porph. in taking *recti* as genitive singular and goes one step further, taking *cultus* as nominative singular (rather than Porph.'s nominative plural) and so printing *roborat*, which has appeal. He compares *rectum* at *S.* 2.6.75 *quidue ad amicitias, usus rectumne trahat nos*, but the issue is slightly different here, the contrast between *natura* and *cultura*, and therefore nominative plural *recti cultus* as a gloss on ὀρθοὶ νόμοι (cf. e.g. Pl. *Leg.* 715b3) seems preferable in context.

35–6 'to the degree values are deficient, faults mar the glory of the well-born (*physis*)'; a final refutation of the Pindaric emphasis on inherited virtues (see 29–36n.); without *doctrina*, *recti cultus* and *mores*, good birth is nothing; *pectora* is the object of *roborant* and, with *bene nata*, of *indecorant*.

37–72 The second 36-line half of the poem (see 73–6n.) is focused on the Second Punic war and the victory of Drusus' and Tiberius' ancestor, C. Claudius Nero, who with M. Livius Salinator defeated Hasdrubal in 207 near the Metaurus River (see intro.). This passage corresponds to the aretalogy of Augustus at 14.34–52. The non-Julian ancestors represent both sides of the princes' family; the princes' own fraternal relationship stands in happier contrast with the death of the Carthaginian brother.

37–44 A formal and artfully periodic sentence consisting of one quatrain with fronted indirect question carrying the weight of the period ('what you owe to the Neros') followed by a tricolon *abundans* (*flumen | Hasdrubal | dies*), sharing the predicate *testis*, and a second quatrain with subordinate clauses marked by a double simile.

37–8 quid debeas . . . | testis Metaurum flumen: H. models the opening on Ennius' *Scipio*, which treated the final encounter at Zama in 203 in the same style (*Var.* 8 V.): *testes sunt campi magni*, also *Sat.* 10–11 V. *testes sunt | lati campi quos gerit Africa terra politos* – there may have been similar *sententiae* preserved on the Metaurus. Also of a river (river gods can witness local events) at Cat. 64.348–64: cf. 357 *testis erit magnis uirtutibus unda Scamandri*; and 362 (Polyxena sacrificed) *denique testis erit morti quoque reddita praeda*; Tib. 1.7.9–12 (and Maltby *ad loc.*) *Tarbella*

Pyrene | *testis . . . testis Arar . . .* The figure obviously lends itself to highly rhetorical contexts: e.g. Cic. *Verr.* 2.5.10 (with anaphora) *testes enim sunt qui in consilio fuerunt, testes publicae tabulae, testis splendidissima ciuitas Lilybitana, testis honestissimus maximusque conuentus ciuium Romanorum: fieri nihil potest, producendi sunt*; also *Leg. Man.* 30.

o Roma: another Ennian touch, also probably from the *Scipio*, *Var.* 6 V. (ap. Cic. *De or.* 3.167 and *Fin.* 2.106) *desine, Roma, tuos hostes* [sc. *timere*]; Tib. 2.5.57 *Roma, tuum nomen terris fatale regendis*; Luc. 8.835–6 *tu quoque, cum saeuo dederis iam templa tyranno,* | *nondum Pompei cineres, o Roma, petisti.*

Neronibus: generic, with echo of the specific examples at 28 (*Nerones*), though the words that follow return the focus to the Second Punic War.

Metaurum flumen: cf. Priscian *GL* 2.170 Keil *'Histrum' pro 'Hister', et 'Rhenum', 'Tanagrum', 'Metaurum', 'Iberum', 'Vulturnum', 'Oceanum' (hoc tamen, quotiens 'flumen' sequebatur, solebant facere)*. The proper name in such cases is adjectival, as at *AP* 18 *flumen Rhenum*; *TLL* s.v. *flumen* 958.69–959.9; additional to adjectival forms per se, as at *Epist.* 1.11.4 *Tiberino flumine*, H. also has an appositive noun (15.24 *Tanain prope flumen*) and a genitive (2.6.10–11 *Galaesi* | *flumen*; *Epod.* 13.14 *Scamandri flumina*), 'appositive' according to *TLL* 958.31–56, better 'subjective' (cf. Virg. *Aen.* 4.143 *Xanthique fluenta*, and *TLL* s.v. *fluo* 969.25–68: *Rhodanus fluit* etc.). Distinct are instances such as Virg. *Aen.* 7.714 (*flumen Himellae*), 'defining' according to Horsfall *ad loc.*, and *ad* 7.697 and related to original identification with deities.

38–9 Hasdrubal | **deuictus** 'the utter destruction of Hasdrubal' (cf. 72 *Hasdrubale interempto*). The '*ab urbe condita* construction', wherein 'a predicative participle, usually past, coalesces with its noun in such a way that the two together form a complex of substantival character, capable of standing as subject or object of a verb, or of being governed by a proposition' (Laughton 1964: 84). Its use in the nominative is a particular development in Cicero, in whom it is normally combined with another nominative noun or pronoun (as here with *flumen* and *dies*) so there is no doubt about the syntax (Laughton 1964: 90). Hasdrubal is juxtaposed to *Neronibus* here, to *Claudiae* at 72. The verb implies total conquest, appropriate since he was killed and decapitated (see 70–2 n.).

39–40 pulcher fugatis | **ille dies Latio tenebris**: economical style: dative of interest or advantage + causal ablative both dependent on *pulcher*. The routing of darkness (reminiscent of *CS* 9–10 *alme Sol, curru nitido diem qui* | *promis*) will be picked up by the flight of Hannibal in the simile of 52 *effugere*. Cf. 3.21.24 *dum rediens fugat astra Phoebus*; Virg. *Aen.* 3.521 *iamque rubescebat stellis Aurora fugatis*; and (after H.) Ov. *Met.* 2.144 *effulget tenebris Aurora fugatis*; *Culex* 44 *crinibus et roseis tenebras Aurora fugarat.*

pulcher: a Claudian (Clodian?) compliment (cf. 65n.).

40–1 ille dies . . . | **primus alma risit adorea** 'first smiled with nurturing ?glory', well captures the true sense of relief and joy that must have come with news of Hasdrubal's defeat and death and the dashing of Hannibal's hopes. Livy (27.50.7–51.10) has a vivid description of the gradual dawning of the news in Rome, as reports trickled in, and of the ultimate ecstasy of the Romans after more than a decade of being threatened with extinction: e.g. 51.1 *tunc enim uero omnis aetas currere obuii, primus quisque oculis auribusque haurire tantum gaudium cupientes*; 51.6 *postremo etiam clamore uniuersae contionis cum uix gaudium animis caperent*. The *primus dies* formula is a marker of turning points, for good or ill: Cic. *Pis.* 34; Virg. *Aen.* 4.169. For *alma* see 7.7–8n.

risit: cf. 11.6n.

adorea: (or *adoria*) 'sans étymologie' (Ernout-Meillet); effectively only here and at Plaut. *Amph.* 193 in archaic or classical Latin; *OLD* s.v. gives 'glory, distinction'; there are two competing explanations: 1) from *ador/adoreus*, Paul. Fest. 3.22 M. *laudem siue gloriam dicebant, quia gloriosum eum putabant esse, qui farris copia abundaret*; Plin. *HN* 18.14 *gloriam denique ipsam a farris honore adoriam appellabant*; 2) from *adoro*, Serv. Dan. *ad Aen.* 10.677 *ueteres, qui 'adorare' alloqui dicebant: nam ideo et adorea laus bellica, quod omnes eum cum gratulatione alloquebantur, qui in bello fortiter fecit*. Although 1) looks a little less like a guess, and is in line with the concrete example of the word at *Amph.* 193 (as Christenson points out *ad loc.*) *praeda atque agro adoriaque* (doled out by the victorious Amphitruo), as well as *alma* in H., Walde-Hoffman rules it out, and the etymology is best considered unknown. See further de Vann 2008 s.v.

42–4 per urbes . . . Italas . . . per taedas . . . per Siculas . . . undas: conveys the relentlessness of Hannibal's invasion.

dirus . . . Afer 'the dreaded African' (Rudd) which captures the ambiguity (Hannibal or collective singular), though 3.6.36 *Hannibalemque dirum* suggests the former, who will soon be named with traditional Carthaginian epithet (49).

ut: extreme postposition, = *ex quo*, 'from the time that', 'since', as at *Epod.* 7.19; *S.* 2.2.127–8; *OLD* s.v. *ut* 27.

Afer . . . Italas: a mild paradox; this should not happen.

ceu: only here in H., perhaps because he has just used *ut* in a different sense, but also as an archaism (Norden 1957: 439), like 41 *adorea*.

flamma per taedas 'fire through pine-trees', the speed of Hannibal's blitzkrieg is reflected in the brevity of simile and the choice of tree (resinous pitch-pine). *taeda* is of the actual tree here for the first time; it seems (rather than the torch, wood or resin that come from it), a natural enough extension since it is thought to be borrowed from the accusative of δαΐς, namely δαΐδα, 'pine-torch', 'brand'; *OLD* s.v. *picea* 3; Ernout-Meillet s.v. Plin. *HN* 16.44, who also uses it of the tree, has it giving less resin than the *picea*, but of a more liquid and pleasant kind and good for lighting fires and torches. *Pace* Mynors *ad loc. taedas* at *G.* 2.431 surely means the torches, not the tree. H. here presents a compression of more extended similes in Homer (*Il.* 11.155–7) and Virg. *Aen.* 10. 405–9; 12.521–5.

Eurus | per Siculas . . . undas: the phrasing in H. seems to apply to any sea in the general vicinity of Sicily or southern Italy; cf. 3.4.28 (of the war with Sextus Pompey; see N–R *ad loc.*) *Sicula . . . unda*; 2.12.2–3 (in the context of the Punic Wars) *Siculum mare | Poeno purpureum sanguine*; also Virg. *Aen.* 3.696 *Siculis . . . undis*. *Eurus* may be a comment on the Euripidean intertext (see n. below), where the Phoenician women speak of sailing from Tyre to Delphi with the help of the Zephyr – which they would use to get into the Corinthian Gulf once in the eastern Ionian Sea.

equitauit: unusually displaced into the simile but to be taken with the outer context, if Quinn is to be followed: 'the subject of *equitauit* is of course *Afer*'. But cf. Virg. *Aen.* 2.417–18 (a simile of the Greeks at Troy's fall) *laetus Eois | Eurus equis*. Things are made more complex by an apparent intertext at Eur. *Phoen.* 209–12 περιρρύτων | ὑπὲρ ἀκαρπίστων πεδίων | Σικελίας Ζεφύρου πνοαῖς | ἱππεύσαντος '(I sailed) as the west wind galloped across the barren seas which flow around Sicily'. On the basis of this, K–H reasonably take *equitauit* with *Eurus* (similarly *TLL* s.v. *equito* ('de uento') 729.62–4), as well as with *Afer*, assuming a resulting zeugma with the first simile, with which they understand *uoluitur*, e.g. (see 57–60n.).

45–9 A studiously prosaic sentence, whose parataxis (*creuit et ... habuere ... dixitque*) contributes to the slightly clichéd effect: Roman youth grew strong through hard work, previously devastated temples were fixed up and finally (*tandem*, after two clauses) Hannibal spoke. Quinn *ad loc.* notes 'sounds like grafting contemporary propaganda (cf. 3.6) on to past history'. The picture of Roman youth toiling away and re-establishing piety has some irony, given that the years following the Carthaginian wars are traditionally seen as the beginning and cause of Roman decline in precisely such areas: Sall. *Cat.* 10 (and Ramsay *ad loc.* for other instances) *sed ubi labore atque iustitia res publica creuit ... Carthago ... ab stirpe interiit ... saeuire fortuna ac miscere omnia coepit. qui labores, pericula, dubias atque asperas res facile tolerauerant, eis otium diuitiaeque, optanda alias, oneri miseriaeque fuere. igitur primo pecuniae, deinde imperi cupido creuit ... deos neglegere*. H. does not cover the decline, but it is inevitable and casts a pall over Hannibal's speech celebrating the greatness of Rome, destined to pass, as historiography after Hannibal will acknowledge.

post hoc: the phrase occurs first in H. (at Plaut. *Aul.* 576 *post* is adverbial), here in the *Odes* and four times altogether in the *S.* (2.2.123; 2.8.31) and *Epist.* (2.1.175; 2.2.28), in casual contexts (*sermo merus*). This seems to signal a shift in tone from the previous stanza with its archaisms and grand simile. All other poets until Martial and Statius (only in the *Silvae*, 4.9.4; 5.*praef.* 8) avoid the phrase, as do Cicero and the historians, Vell. 2.21.4 excepted (*postea* and subordinate clauses of various types do the job more formally), but from Columella and the elder Seneca a number of instances are attested, mostly in prose.

secundis usque laboribus 'through a series of successful toils' – also perhaps an amphibole: 'second (Punic War) toils'.

impio ... tumultu: rather vague, and another cliché, which, however, foreshadows the following criticism of the devastation of Italy's shrines.

fana ... rectos: shrines got to house gods who were standing upright: the Carthaginians had pushed them over, the Romans stood them up again.

perfidus Hannibal: the final cliché of the sentence; so Livy on this quality of Hannibal: Livy 21.4.9 *has tantas uiri uirtutes ingentia uitia aequabant, inhumana* *crudelitas, perfidia plus quam Punica, nihil ueri, nihil sancti, nullus deum metus*; for general Carthaginian treachery, cf. *TLL* s.v. *perfidia* 1385.70–75; *perfidus* 1390.45–47; *perfidiosus* 1391.10–12. Notably there is no treachery in his actual speech.

50–72 The speech of Hannibal is consistent with the high register of the poem and reminiscent of the speeches of Juno (3.3) and Regulus (3.5) from the Roman Odes. Such lengthy speech within lyric is essentially Pindaric, as for instance in *Pythian* 9 (cf. Syndikus II 306–7). For the moment captured by H., immediately after Hannibal saw the severed head of his brother, see 70–2n.

50–2 This passage recalls the metaphors of 1–16, 31–2, now from the prey's point of view and paradoxically: although we Carthaginians are like stags and the Roman wolves our predators, we actually (*ultro*) keep pursuing them. Fraenkel 2007: 28–30, 51–2 gathers together Plautine instances of the 'identification motif' (cf. H.'s *cerui . . . sectamur*), e.g. *Merc.* 361 *muscast meus pater: nihil potest clam illum haberi*, where there is (28) 'a complete identity (not just a parity or similarity)'.

cerui: poor choice on Hannibal's part, given the story in Livy 10.27.8–9: in 295 BCE the Roman battle line is drawn up against Gauls on the right wing and Samnites on the left when in come a hind and a wolf (*cerua ad Gallos, lupus ad Romanos cursum deflexit*). The Gauls kill the hind, sacred to Diana (so a bad omen for them), while the Romans allow safe conduct for the wolf, after which a Roman soldier interprets: '*hinc uictor Martius lupus, integer et intactus, gentis nos Martiae et conditoris nostri admonuit*'.

luporum praeda rapacium: *luporum* is subjective genitive, with *praeda* related to *pre-hendo*; also glossed with 'ἁρπαγή, rapacitas, rapina' (*TLL* s.v. *praeda* 522.60–5; cf. Serv. *ad Aen.* 11.78 *praeda est quae eripitur*), so *praeda rapacium* is a powerful combination, with the idea of snatching doubled and reinforced by assonance. Some time before 27 BCE, Octavian raised the *Legio XXI Rapax* (*CIL* 5.4858, 4892, 5033), which would be based in Raetia after it was subdued and was presumably used by Drusus in 15 BCE (Keppie 1998: 159, also 139, 211–12), as is implied by 14.9 *milite . . . tuo*. It would therefore be a nice touch for Hannibal to allude to this legion (though 'Rapax' of the legion would be a *bird* of prey) in his metaphor for the legions of Claudius Nero.

sectamur: frequentative and includes the whole Punic enterprise against Rome.

quos . . . triumphus 'tricking and getting away from whom constitutes a rich triumph'; the infinitives are subjects of *est*, while *triumphus* is a predicate noun.

opimus . . . triumphus: the real triumph will go to the Romans and Livius Salinator; although he did not personally kill Hasdrubal, the latter did die, so the phrasing conjures up the *spolia opima*, for examples of which cf. *OLD* s.v. *opimus* 1.

fallere et effugere: as Hannibal himself did before Metaurus in 207 BCE, first at Grumentum after losing 8,000 men in a clash with Claudius Nero (Livy 27.42.5 *inde pauor incussus et fuga passim fieri coepta est*), then at Venusia after a second encounter and loss of a further 2,000 (27.42.17 *numquam Nero uestigiis hostis abstiterat*);

see Lazenby 1978: 186–7. Hannibal's evasions were tactical, his aim being to unite his army with that of Hasdrubal, rather than to engage on his own.

53–60 'A neat summary of the theme of *Aen.* 2–3' (Quinn). Hannibal's narrative is stripped of its mythological details – with *fortis* (*gens*), *natos* and *patres* hinting at Aeneas, Ascanius and Anchises, *sacra* at the Lares and Penates and with no mention of the sojourn in Carthage or the Carthaginian queen whose avenger Hannibal was supposed to become (*Aen.* 4.625–7).

cremato . . . Ilio: cf. Virg. *Aen.* 7.295–6 (and Horsfall *ad* 295 for Hannibal's reworking of Juno's thoughts) '*num incensa cremauit* | *Troia uiros?*'; also *Aen.* 2.624–5 (and see 57–8n.) '*considere in ignes* | *Ilium*'.

iactata Tuscis aequoribus: cf. Virg. *Aen.* 1.29–30 (of the Trojans) *iactatos aequore toto* | *Troas*; 1.3 *terris iactatus et alto*; also of the Carthaginians 1.442 *iactati undis et turbine Poeni*; H. has the storm in the Tyrrhenian Sea, keeping the Trojans well away from Carthage, again perhaps as a strategy of denying to Aeneas a Carthaginian sojourn. How was *Aen.* 4 received in official circles of Augustan Rome? The purple-cloaked Aeneas of that book bears no resemblance to the images in the Forum of Augustus or on the Ara Pacis, on which see Zanker 1988: 201–10.

sacra | natosque maturosque patres 'sacred objects, sons and elderly fathers'. Cf. Virg. *Aen.* 2.747 *Ascanium Anchisenque patrem Teucrosque penates.* The subject is *gens* but the absence of wives and mothers suits the implicit subject, Aeneas, particularly since the *Aeneid* specifies no other father among the Trojan survivors. *maturus* 'advanced in age' is found first in H., here and at *AP* 115 *maturusne senex*, and not much afterwards; see *TLL* s.v. *maturus* 500.33–43; *OLD* s.v. 6 includes e.g. Virg. *Aen.* 5.73 *aeui maturus Acestes*, parallel to 5.301 *senioris Acestae.* Lucr. 3.1039 already has *matura uetustas.*

pertulit Ausonias ad urbes: oddly reminiscent of Virg. *Aen.* 7.102–5 *haec responsa . . . Fama per urbes* | *Ausonias tulerat.*

57–60 A brilliant but odd simile, with tenor and vehicle blending or 'trespassing' into each other (*ducit* effectively functioning ἀπὸ κοινοῦ), as the Virgilian erasure of boundary between human and plant (see Thomas on Virg. *G.* 2.362–70) is rewritten in this miniature rewriting of the Virgilian epic. At Virg. *Aen.* 2.626–7 Troy's fall is famously compared to that of a tree: *ac ueluti summis antiquam in montibus ornum* | *cum ferro accisam crebrisque bipennibus instant.* H. perhaps corrects Virgil's simile: the tree is not destroyed, just damaged; it is also situated by Hannibal near Rome (*in Algido*), where Virgil's Aeneas placed it simply *in montibus.* As Fraenkel first noted (430, n. 2), the simile is Pindaric, as is also appropriate for this poem: *Pyth.* 4.263–9 'For if someone with a sharp-cutting axe should lop off the branches of a great oak and spoil its admirable beauty, although it loses its fertility, it gives an accounting of itself if ever it ends up at a winter fire, or, supported by the upright columns of its master, it pursues burdensome toil within alien walls, having had to desert its own land.' But H.'s *ilex* is quite different, in that branches are not mentioned and the tree itself does not serve as firewood or as a building beam; rather it seems – impossibly – to become stronger from its loss, unless H. means the reader to think of pruning.

ut 'like', introducing a simile, whose verb is understood, from the outer context: *OLD* s.v. *ut* 7b ('cl. reduced to its subj., obj., etc.'), as at Cic. *Fin.* 5.61 *indicant pueri, in quibus ut in speculis natura cernitur*; Virg. *Aen.* 12.261–2 '*o miseri, quos improbus aduena bello | territat inualidas ut aues*'.

57–8 'like a holm oak, lopped by hard axes on Mt. Algidus which produces dark foliage'.

duris . . . bipennibus: cf. Virg. *Aen.* 2.627 (in the tree-felling simile as Troy burns) *crebris bipennibus instant*; also *G.* 4.331 '*ualidam in uites molire bipennem*'; *Aen.* 11.135–6 *ferro sonat alta bipenni | fraxinus.*

ilex: the ilex, or holm oak (*Quercus ilex*, also known as evergreen oak, holly oak) is an evergreen oak of the white oak side of the genus. It is not a particularly serviceable tree: at *G.* 2.453 it is said to be useful only when rotten, as providing a hive for bees, *corticibusque cauis uitiosaeque ilicis aluo*. Perhaps a *figura etymologica:* <u>*il*</u>*ex* is a good tree to stand for <u>*Il*</u>*ium*. The Pindaric simile (57–60n.) treated not specifically a holm oak (πρῖνος), but rather the generic oak δρῦς – cognate of the Celtic etymology of Drusus (16–17n.).

nigrae: the holm oak's leaves are dark green on their upper side. See André 1949: 55–6 on the relative meaning of *niger*, particularly with respect to vegetation, as at Virg. *Ecl.* 6.54 (in opposition to the grass below) *ilice sub nigra pallentes ruminat herbas*; cf. also 12.11–12 *nigri | colles Arcadiae placent*; 1.21.7–8 (contrasted with *uiridis*) *nigris aut Erymanthi | siluis aut uiridis Gragi*. André sees this use of the adjective as poetic and as a specifically Virgilian development.

tonsa: *tondeo* is used of lopping, trimming or pruning, the latter at Virg. *G.* 2.406–7 *curuo Saturni dente relictam | persequitur uitem attondens fingitque putando*; 2.368 *tum stringe comas, tum bracchia tonde*, with obvious human associations; (cf. 53–60n. on *cremato*). There is, however, no indication that H. refers to pruning, and there would be no point in pruning an *ilex* on Mt. Algidus, or anywhere else.

Algido: in the Alban Hills, a mountain yoke to the south and east of *mons Albanus* (Monte Cavo), also at *CS* 69 (location of Diana Nemorensis; cf. *CS* 69–72n.); cf. 1.21.6 (with pun on *algidus*, 'cold', N–H *ad loc.*) *gelido . . . Algido*; 3.23.9 (same) *niuali . . . Algido.*

59–60 per damna, per caedes: the simile has ended, but a slight amphibole is felt: the tree, like the Trojan *gens*, suffers loss and 'cutting' (*OLD* s.v. *caedes* 5; e.g. Gell. 19.12.7–8, on unskilled pruning, *cur tantam ligni atque frondium caedem faceret percontatus est*), just as the Trojans suffer loss and 'killing' (*OLD* s.v. *caedes* 1). For the dramatic asyndeton cf. Hom. *Il.* 10.298 ἄμ φόνον, ἂν νέκυας 'through the slaughter, through the corpses'.

ab ipso . . . ferro: *ferrum* likewise binds simile to context, going well with both the sword and the axe. *ipso* captures the seeming paradox that cutting helps growth; *OLD* s.v. *ipse* 9 'to emphasize something regarded as exceptional or extreme' – with the hyperbaton contributing to this effect.

opes animumque 'power and courage'.

61–4 Rome from the Carthaginian point of view. The Romans are likened to the Hydra, the earth-born warriors Jason fought and the Sparti, who likewise grow from the earth. The 'eastern' Hannibal corrects from his point of view the Virgilian picture of Italy as a place emphatically unassociated with such oriental θαύματα ('wonders') and their dangers: *G.* 2.140–2 *haec loca non tauri spirantes naribus ignem | inuertere satis immanis dentibus hydri, | nec galeis densisque uirum seges horruit hastis.*

non . . . -ue . . . -ue: for disjunctive particles with negative force following a negative clause see K–S II 2.103–4 (*aut*); L–H–S 499–500. The use of *-ue . . . -ue*, essentially a poeticism, is in such a construction hard to parallel.

Hydra: the many-headed monstrous water-snake of marshy Lerna, killed by Hercules as his second labour. K–H point to Plut. *Pyrrh.* 19.5, where Pyrrhus' ambassador Cineas (c. 350–277), after observing and admiring Rome's system of government and its customs in general, expressed the fear its people would prove to be a Lernaean Hydra to fight against, given the numbers of armies they could raise. This looks to have been a Greek and Carthaginian topos.

62 uinci dolentem 'averse to/annoyed at defeat', i.e. *inuictus. doleo* + (prolative) infinitive appears first here and is very rare, parallel to *odi* + infinitive (e.g. 2.16.25–6 *laetus in praesens animus quod ultra est | oderit curare*) – not with ellipsis of *se* (so *OLD* s.v. *doleo* 3), which would mean 'grieving that he is being beaten', the sense at the superficially parallel Stat. *Achil.* 1.16 (the poet's laurel has ceded to the victor's) *olim dolet altera uinci.* Cf. *TLL* s.v. *doleo* 1827.19–30. The cult site of Hercules Invictus was associated with the Ara Maxima in the Forum Boarium; cf. Virg. *Aen.* 8.293 '*inuicte*' in the song the Salii sing to Hercules; Prop. 4.9.3 *inuictos . . . montes* and Hutchinson *ad loc.*

63–4 'nor did the Colchians or Thebes, home of Echion, push up a greater monster'. Jason had to plough with fire-breathing bulls, sow dragons' teeth and fight the warriors that sprang up from them (Ap. Rhod. *Arg.* 3.1278–1407). Echion ('Snake') was one of the five Sparti, who similarly sprang up from the dragon's teeth sowed by Cadmus after he had killed it, and as part of the latter's foundation of Thebes, he married Agave, daughter of Cadmus, and was the father of Pentheus (see *Brill's New Pauly* s.v. 'Echion', 'Cadmus').

summisere 'thrust up' (from the ground) – the Colchians and Thebes stand in for their earth, normally the subject of this verb; cf. Lucr. 1.7–8 *tibi suauis daedala tellus | summittit flores*, 193 *laetificos nequeat fetus summittere tellus*; Prop. 1.2.9 *aspice quos summittat humus formosa colores.*

Echioniaeue: first at Virg. *Aen.* 12.514–15 *Oniten, | nomen Echionium*, where Serv. *ad* 514 notes *id est Thebana gloria, per periphrasin: nam Echionii sunt Thebani a rege Echione.* Much used by Stat. in *Theb.*

65 'plunge it in the deep, it comes out all the more splendid'. Cannae on the one hand (or Trasimene, in view of the metaphor), the Metaurus on the other.

pulchrior euenit: both words have been suspected. Peerlkamp wanted *exsiliet* (some minor MSS have *exiet*), but although Rutil. Nam. 1.129–30 *mergi . . . exsiliunt* is a similar metaphor and context, *euenit* seems quite acceptable. The slight oddity of *pulchrior* may prove its authenticity: Claudius Nero will be *pulchrior* than the Claudii Pulchri. Shackleton Bailey, like others, was unhappy with *pulchrior*, and suggested *fortior* or *firmior*. Nisbet 1986: 232, however, notes H. already has *firmior* in 61, and himself suggests *clarior*, which would suit *enitet* (Lehrs): 'there may be a suggestion of the sun (cf. Milton, Lycidas 168 "so sinks the day-star in the ocean bed").' But *pulchrior* works just as well; cf. 2.46–7 (on the return of Caesar) '*o sol* | *pulcher!*'; also Virg. *G.* 2.533–4 *sic fortis Etruria creuit* | *scilicet et rerum facta est pulcherrima Roma*; Sall. *Cat.* 52.20 '*multo pulcherrumam eam* [sc. *rem publicam*] *nos haberemus*'; *OLD* s.v. *pulcher* 2b. The sense of agricultural plenitude is apparent in Festus' notice at 274.28 M. *pulcher bos appellatur ad eximiam pinguitudinem perductus.*

65–6 merses . . . luctere: present subjunctives in virtual protases of future less vivid conditionals ('should you sink it', 'should you wrestle'), with the apodoses more emphatic present general (*euenit* 'out it comes') and future more vivid (*proruet* 'it will knock over').

66–7 'wrestle with it and to great acclaim unscathed it will knock over its once victorious opponent'; the language of athletic contest is present throughout.

67–8 geretque | proelia coniugibus loquenda 'will wage battles to be talked about to their wives' (by their husbands back home and unscathed), for which cf. Ov. *Her.* 1.30 *narrantis coniunx pendet ab ore uiri*; also Tib. 1.10.29–32. Alternatively 'battles to be talked about by their wives', supported by 9.21 *dicenda Musis proelia*. A fine *thauma*, suitable to the hyperbole of Hannibal's speech, and a reversal of the reality: *Epod.* 16.8 *parentibusque abominatus Hannibal* (see Watson *ad loc.* for the possible meaning 'cursed by our ancestors' who fought him, and for other, less likely, possibilities); cf. also (unambiguously) 1.1.24–5 (and N–H *ad loc.*) *bellaque matribus* | *detestata*. Stat. *Theb.* 3.374–7 clearly includes wives (*thalamo, domus*) in the group of those who detest the results of war. Shackleton Bailey obelizes from *geretque* to *loquenda*, allowing as possible only Campbell's *feretque* | *praemia*, which seems weak, since it involves no hyperbole, just a certain gender attitude (Virgil's Camilla attracted to Chloreus' glitter?). For *loquor* in the sense of 'talking about (celebrating)', cf. *TLL* s.v. 1666.23–1667.4. Delz (*Gnomon* 60 (1988) 499) opts for *carminibus* (Peerlkamp) or *Pieriis* (Hunt), pointing to 9.4 *uerba loquor socianda chordis* (also 15.1; 1.24.4; 3.4.1–4).

69–70 Carthagini: dative with both *nuntios* and *mittam.*

iam non: i.e., unlike after Cannae in 216 BCE, when Hannibal's brother Mago reported back to the Carthaginian senate: Livy 23.11.8 *res gestas in Italia a fratre exponit.*

nuntios . . . superbos: the message after Cannae as Livy describes it (23.11.8–12.5) certainly enumerates the Carthaginian successes, and Mago is said to have emptied onto the floor a bushel of gold rings taken from Roman knights, aiming to secure further supplies from the senate. Perhaps Hannibal, focalizing the Roman view, is made to agree with the characterization of the Carthaginians at Livy 25.18.2 *superbae suopte ingenio genti* (and see below).

superbos: occidit: a telling juxtaposition – Carthaginian superiority is fallen with Hasdrubal.

70–2 There is sepulchral pathos in Hannibal's words, whose finality lends support to those who see Hannibal's speech ending at 72 (see 73–6n.). Embedded sepulchral epigrams have such closural effect elsewhere in Augustan poetry: Prop. 2.1.78; Virg. *Aen.* 4.702–3; 5.870–1; 6.882–6; 9.446–9. Livy 27.51.11 reports that following the battle at Metaurus Claudius Nero hurriedly marched south to Apulia, where he had left Hannibal's army, perhaps at Canusium, and had the head of Hasdrubal (*seruatum cum cura*) thrown in front of the Carthaginian encampment. H. captures this moment: Livy 27.51.12 *Hannibal tanto simul publico familiarique ictus luctu, agnoscere se fortunam Carthaginis fertur dixisse.* In Sil. *Pun.* 15.813–20 Nero carries the head on his spear-point and delivers himself of an exultant speech, which Hannibal bears stoically (819–20 *compressit lacrimas Poenus minuitque ferendo | constanter mala*), promising sacrifice to the shade of his brother. Cf. also *De uiris illustribus* 48 *Nero regressus pari celeritate, qua uenerat, caput Hasdrubalis ante uallum Hannibalis proiecit. quo ille uiso uinci se fortuna Carthaginis confessus*; Porph. *ad loc. haec re uera frequenter dixisse dicitur Hannibal, cum caput fratris sui Hasdrubalis uidisset.* Reckford 1960–1 is right to see a darkness of vision here, with intimations that Carthage is not the only empire destined to pass.

occidit, occidit: common in funereal or melancholic contexts; 7.21; 1.24.9; 1.28.7; for the repetition, highly pathetic, cf. Virg. *Aen.* 12.828 *occidit, occideritque sinas cum nomine Troia*; Cat. 5.4–6 *soles occidere et redire possunt: | nobis, cum semel occidit breuis lux, | nox est perpetua una dormienda.* For the rarity of such adjacent gemination see Wills 102–6 (suggesting a connection to Virg. *Ecl.* 4.24–5 *occidet . . . | occidet*); cf. also 1.2 and n. *parce, precor, precor.*

spes omnis et fortuna nostri | nominis: Metaurus and the death of Hasdrubal are the turning point, as Hannibal is made to acknowledge in Roman accounts (see above). *fortuna* is traditional (Livy 27.51.12 was presumably written before publication of *C.* 4), but *spes omnis . . . nostri nominis* has a pathos that resembles Virgilian instances of contemplation of the extinction of the race or line: Virg. *Ecl.* 1.15 *spem gregis a! silice in nuda conixa reliquit*; *G.* 3.73 *spem . . . gentis*, 471–3 *morbi | . . . corripiunt . . . | spemque gregemque simul cunctamque ab origine gentem*; 4.162 *spem gentis* (Thomas *ad loc.*). Cf. also Cic. *Fam.* 14.4.6 (still in near suicidal state, signing off to Tullia as he goes into exile) *mea carissima filiola et spes reliqua nostra.* See *OLD* s.v. *spes* 5b.

Hasdrubale interempto 'now that Hasdrubal has been killed'; the final positioning of the ablative absolute highlights Hannibal's sorrow at his brother's death.

interempto: the verb, which occurs frequently in comedy and in Cicero, once in Accius' *Erigona* (fr. 51 Ribb. *hospitem depositam interimes*), is found at *S.* 2.3.131 (*cum laqueo uxorem interimis matremque ueneno*) and otherwise appears in Augustan poetry only once in Virgil: *Aen.* 10.427–8 *primus Abantem | oppositum interimit.* Ernout-Meillet s.v. '*in*: préverbe et préposition' 312–13 discuss the group of words *intereo*, *interficio*, *interimo* (and cf. *pereo*, *perimo*) denoting privation, destruction and death.

73–6 Editors differ on the speaker, Hannibal or the poet; the dispute is as old as Porph. and doubtless older: *haec iam poetae uerba sunt, non enim adhuc Hannibalis* (likewise ps.-Acro *iam hic poeta loquitur Drusum Neronem significans* and *ad* 75 *curae sagaces*: *optima Augusti consilia*). There seems to be no resolution to the issue, and this constitutes a true amphibole – though here, since a choice must be made, the end of the speech is marked at 72. Fraenkel 428, n. 1 rightly notes that in other instances where H. has the final quatrain following a speech (admittedly this amounts only to 3.3 and 3.5), there is no doubt about the change: 'If a change of speaker took place after 72, how was a reader to realize it at a time when there existed no quotation marks and the like?' This of course works both ways, and the words *Hasdrubale interempto*, on the lips of his brother, are certainly capable of indicating closure (see 70–2n. esp. Anchises' closing address to Marcellus at *Aen.* 6.883–6). With the exception of Borszák, recent editors have not been convinced by Vahlen's vigorous arguments (1907–8: II 516–25), invoked by Fraenkel, for assigning to Hannibal: K–H, Klingner, Quinn, Shackleton Bailey all end the speech at 72.

The consequences of the choice are chiefly ideological. With Hannibal speaking the last lines Rome's enemy fully embraces the greatness of the Claudii Nerones present and/or future depending on the reading at 73 (see n.) *perficiunt/perficient*. This delivers a more triumphant ode. Vahlen argued, with abundant citation from Livy 27.38–46, that *curae sagaces*, particularly with its specifying dependent phrase *per acuta belli*, points to the strategic brilliance in Claudius Nero's strategic manoeuvres before and during the Metaurus engagement. If the poet speaks the final lines, Hannibal ends at 72 on a note of resigned pathos but does not go so far as to praise the sagacity of the man who delivered his brother's decapitated head to him. In that case *Claudiae . . . manus* more easily includes Augustus' stepsons, and *curae sagaces* will refer chiefly to the good judgement of Augustus in choosing Drusus, himself however not without such capabilities if 24 *consiliis iuuenis* be taken seriously.

73 nil Claudiae non perficient manus 'Claudian hands will get every job done'; the Blandinianus (V) – which clearly preserves peculiar and valuable readings (Shackleton Bailey iv) – reads *perficiunt*, though caution against Pasquali's (1952: 382–3) 'optimistic list' is enjoined by Fraenkel 100–1. The confusion doubtless comes from the identity of *Claudiae* (past or contemporary Claudii?). Their ancestors got the job done at the Metaurus, now these two are being trained for the wars of Augustus.

76 acuta belli 'sharp crises of war' (Rudd), catches the application from violent and acute onset of pain or disease, as at *S.* 2.3.163 *renes morbo temptentur acuto*; *OLD* s.v. *acutus* 7 – with a hint of Hasdrubal's impaled head. The use of an adnominal genitive with the neuter of the adjective functioning as a noun is often felt as a Grecism and is a high-register construction: cf. 12.19–20, in a

Virgilian context, *amaraque | curarum*. The construction is first in Enn. *Ann.* 84, with Skutsch *ad loc.*, *infera noctis*; 264 *caeli uasta*; *scen.* 112 *caua caeli*. See Coleman 1975: 126–7; L–H–S 53; for further examples, see Austin on Virg. *Aen.* 1.422 *strata uiarum*.

5

METRE

Third Asclepiadean: three lesser Asclepiadeans (glyconic with choriambic expansion: – – – ⏑⏑ – | – ⏑⏑ – | ⏑ ×) followed by a glyconic (– – – ⏑⏑ – ⏑ ×), as in 12; also 1.6, 15, 24, 33; 2.12; 3.10, 16. Belmont 1980: 6–9 notes the importance of this metre throughout the *Odes*, not far removed from the primacy of the Alcaic and Sapphic stanzas.

INTRODUCTION

You have been away too long, so fulfil your promise and return to work with the senate, good leader. When your face shines for the people, things go better. Your country longs for you, like the mother watching on the shore for her son, off at sea more than a year. The countryside is safe and productive, the sea is pacified, morality, law and order are in place, marital fidelity is valued and punishment takes care of wrongdoing. Who cares about foreign enemies as long as Caesar is safe? At the close of his working day the rustic celebrates, pouring libations to you and calling on your godhead. 'May you provide lengthy holidays, good leader', this we say sober in the morning, drunk at the setting of the sun.

Augustus had been in Gaul from the summer of 16 BCE, following the defeat of Lollius by the Sygambri (see 4 intro.). Fraenkel 440 is enthusiastic: 'whereas some time ago he had declined to write a solemn triumphal song, he now, unasked and unprompted, endeavoured to express his own feelings and those of his fellow citizens and so produced one of his most perfect poems'. There is, however, something muted in this encomium, which takes the form of a wish that the worthy leader continue to provide long holidays for Hesperia, a refrain to be repeated by H. and his fellow citizens, sober in the morning, moist after nightfall. The celebration in fact occurs not on the occasion of any return, but as a symptom of Caesar's being safe (27 *incolumi*), which keeps Rome safe from foreign foes, with whom he is engaged. Thus the poem is about absence as much as desired presence.

H.'s only appearance on the scene is thus as a symposiast. The rest of the poem describes the yearning of the state, the *patria*, for Augustus' return (5–16). Although the *patria* does not speak, its representation through the simile of 9–16 as a mother on the shore constitutes a virtual prosopopoeia, the rhetorical figure in which a speaker is conjured up. As Cicero in the famous instance at *Cat.* 1.18 has the *patria* speak 'with the voice of the average senator and citizen' (see

Dyck 2008: 99), so here H. uses the *patria* as a vessel for the simple yearnings of the average citizen. The Pindaric swan and the Matine bee have both been grounded for the time being. The only other celebrant is an unnamed rustic in his native hills, who celebrates Augustus after a long day's agricultural work, by now something of a cliché, and hard to identify closely with the voice of the lyric poet (29–36).

Du Quesnay 1995 sees the poem as 'a perfectly conceived and perfectly executed *donum adventicium pro reditu Imperatoris Caesaris Divi filii Augusti*' (p. 187). He believes the ode was written to be performed on the return of Augustus on 4 July 13 BCE, as he believed 4 and 14 were written for performance, for which there is no real evidence. Du Quesnay also sees a justificatory updating of the bleak situation of Virg. *Ecl.* 9 (see 29–30n.): the world is now in better hands, and H. is happy to say as much and to join the celebration.

The poem has a close relationship with 15, as 4 does with 14 (see 4 intro.).

1–16 As Du Quesnay 1995: 162 notes, 'A sustained allusion to a famous passage of Ennius underlies the four opening stanzas.' Cic. *Rep.* 1.64 treats the longing of the people for the deceased Romulus, citing the poet (*Ann.* 105–9 Skutsch):

pectora . . . tenet *desiderium*: simul inter
sese sic memorant: 'o *Romule*, *Romule* die,
qualem te *patriae* custodem di genuerunt!
o *pater*, o genitor, o sanguen *dis oriundum*!
tu produxisti nos intra *luminis* oras.'

The intertext is unmistakable, and signalled strongly by H.: 1 *diuis orte*, *Romulae*; 5 *lucem*, *patriae*; 9 *mater iuuenem*; 15 *desideriis*; 16 *patria*. Just as Augustus immediately follows Romulus in Virgil's parade of future Romans (*Aen.* 6.777–807), so H. draws a parallel between the two founders and sets himself in an Ennian encomiastic tradition. See also Hardie 2002: 341–3 for a connection between Romulus and Ganymede (mentioned in the opening stanza of 4).

1–4 The style (from the genre *kletikon*, on which see Du Quesnay 1995: 150–1, 182) is in its immediacy and directness somewhat epistolary and the inverse of the opening of *Epist.* 1.7.1–2, where the speaker is the one who has failed to live up to his promise to return, *quinque dies tibi pollicitus me rure futurum* | *Sextilem totum mendax desideror*.

1–2 Diuis orte bonis 'sprung from worthy gods'; ablative of source as at 6.31–2 *claris* | *patribus orti*; 1.12.50, of Jupiter in the context of Augustan genealogy, *orte Saturno*; 3.6.33 *non his iuuentus orta parentibus*; *S.* 1.6.10 *nullis maioribus orti*. A preposition is more common outside the lyrics: *S.* 1.5.55 *ab his maioribus ortos*; 1.6.73 *pueri magnis e centurionibus orti*. These work against Page's 'born by the favour of heaven' (ablative absolute, as at *S.* 2.3.8 *iratis natus paries dis atque poetis*), though he is probably right to see ambiguity here: 'Augustus is at once proof of heaven's favour and himself of heavenly race.' For Virgilian ambiguity when Augustan ideology is in the offing see Thomas 2001: 1–14.

bonis, optime: a slightly curious juxtaposition, inviting reflection on the maxim at 3.6.5 (*dis te minorem quod geris, imperas*), although the superlative (of Augustus) need not imply a comparison to the detriment of Julius Caesar. Cf. Ovid's excess at *Met.* 15.850–1, of the deified Caesar's contemplation of Augustus, *natique uidens bene facta fatetur | esse suis maiora et uinci gaudet ab illo.*

Romulae | . . . gentis: cf. *CS* 47 *Romulae genti*; Virg. *Aen.* 6.876–7 *Romula . . . tellus*; Prop. 4.4.26 *Romula . . . hasta*; Ov. *Fast.* 2.412 *Romula ficus.* At Cat. 34.22–4 Fowler, reported approvingly by Lyne 2007: 287, reads *Romulamque . . . gentem* for MSS *Romulique . . . gentem.* H.'s *Romulae* may mean little more than 'Roman' (as at Prop. 3.11.52 *Romula uincla*), but also triggers the Ennian intertext (1–16n.). The adjectives *Romulus* and *Romuleus* (Virg. *Aen.* 8.654, then in Ovid, Statius, Juvenal, Martial, Silius, who also has *Romula facta* at *Pun.* 13.793, *Romula uirtus* at 16.254) appear first in Augustan poetry, perhaps because the genitive of the noun (8.24; 2.15.10) is intractable in dactylic verse (the fragments of Ennius have only the nominative and vocative). Cf. the designation of Rome's citizenry at Cat. 49.1 *disertissime Romuli nepotum.*

custos: also of Augustus at 15.17; it is particularly used of tutelary deities: 1.12.49 Jupiter; 1.28.29 Neptune; 1.36.3 *custodes Numidae deos*; 2.17.30 Faunus; 3.22.1 Diana; *S.* 2.6.15 Mercury; *Epist.* 2.1.255 Janus (after Virg. *Aen.* 7.610 *custos . . . Ianus*); *AP* 239 Silenus.

abes iam nimium diu: *abes* is most frequent in the case of letters: Aug. *Epist.* fr. 22.1–3 Malc. *aue, mi Gai, meus asellus iucundissimus, quem semper medius fidius desidero, cum a me abes*; Cic. *Att.* 2.1.4 *nimis abes diu*; six times in the *Heroides* (1.57, 66; 2.23; 14.80; 15.78; 19.70); Sen. *Phaed.* 972–7 *cur . . . hominum nimium securus abes, | non sollicitus prodesse bonis, nocuisse malis. nimium diu*, metrically intractable in the dactylic hexameter, is found in Latin poetry only here. Cf. 37–40n. on *longas.*

3–7 patrum . . . populo: the state is united in its joy, as the poem turns from the complaint of 2 to springtime for Caesar and Italy.

3–4 maturum reditum pollicitus patrum | sancto concilio, redi: a remarkable sentence, with the effects of framing noun-adjective homoeoteleuta (*-um, -um | -o, -o*) compounded by internal rhyme (*reditum | patrum*) and anaphora (*reditum . . . redi*). The effect could easily have been avoided (cf. 3.5.52 *populum reditus* [sc. *Reguli*] *morantem*). Although there are 30 instances of noun-adjective/participle homoeoteleuta in the *Odes*, the jingle created by these lines is unique, as is the doubling itself, if we exclude 3.5.55–6 (*Venafranos in agros | aut Lacedaemonium Tarentum*), where the preposition, the conjunction and the polysyllabic adjectives dilute the jingle. Two examples occur in Iullus Antonius' imagined praise of Augustus (2.35 *per sacrum cliuum*, 42 *publicum ludum*), and there are similar effects in another address to Augustus (14.43–4 *o tutela praesens | Italiae dominaeque Romae*). There are subjectivities involved in interpreting prosodic or rhythmical effects, but the fact is H. in his higher lyric mode studiously avoids juxtaposition of similarly inflected nouns and adjectives, whereas here he has striven to achieve such placement, more at home in prose than verse. Outside the *Odes*, *Epist.* 1.3.36

pascitur in uestrum reditum uotiua iuuenca is unusual, mimicking Virg. *G.* 3.219 *pascitur in magna Sila formosa iuuenca*, where it is also unusual, perhaps with an intertext from Calvus' *Io* (see Thomas *ad loc.*).

redi: imperative expressing urgency, as at Cic. *Phil.* 2.118 *redi cum re publica in gratiam.* This form is found mostly in Plautus, Terence and the tragedies of Seneca, only here in H. The apparent triple repetition *reditum . . . redi . . . reditum* strengthens the hymnic sense; see 31 *redit* and 31–2n. Cf. also 2.43 *Augusti reditu* and 7.1–2 n. on the return of spring.

5 lucem redde tuae . . . patriae: cf. 15.4 *tua . . . aetas*; conventional encomiastic language, as Cic. *Dom.* 75 *utrum me patria sic accepit ut lucem salutemque redditam sibi ac restitutam accipere debuit*; *Leg. Man.* 33 *tantamne unius hominis . . . uirtus . . . lucem afferre rei publicae; TLL* s.v. *lux* 1915.20–76. In view of 6–8, where Augustus' face shines like spring on the people, H. perhaps alludes to Ennius' creation of an actual identity between *lux* and saviour: Enn. *scaen.* 72 Ribb. *o lux Troiae, germane Hector*; Accius fr. 163a Ribb. *<tammodo He>ctor lux Dardaniae <nunc idem> in tenebris <situs>*; Virg. *Aen.* 2.281 *'o lux Dardaniae, spes o fidissima Teucrum'*; cf. *TLL* s.v. *lux* 1914.58–1915.19.

dux bone: forms a frame with 37 *dux bone*, and cf. 8.14–15 *bonis | . . . ducibus.* Dickey 2002: 313 separates uses of *bone* into two categories, one genuinely laudatory, the other ironic and indicating the speaker's superiority. Other instances in H. (bare *bone* or *o bone*) are of the second type: *S.* 2.3.31; 2.6.51; 2.6.95; *Epist.* 2.2.37. Here a somewhat understated phrase, it is used at Cic. *Off.* 3.100 of the Carthaginian hostages, whose value outweighed that of Regulus: *reddi captiuos negauit esse utile; illos enim adulescentes esse et bonos duces.* For H., as at Tib. 1.1.75 (*hic ego dux milesque bonus*) and Ov. *Ars* 3.527, it indicates capability, while at Sen. *Ben.* 4.37.2 there is an explicit ethical contrast between the good general and the good man: *non potest quisquam eodem tempore et bonum uirum et bonum ducem agere.* In the view of Tacitus, Domitian was anxious about this quality in Agricola, for obvious reasons: *Agr.* 39.2 *cetera utcumque facilius dissimulari, ducis boni imperatoriam uirtutem esse.*

6–8 'when your face like springtime has gleamed upon the people, more gladly goes the day, and suns shine better'. Fraenkel (442) notes that 'the stanza is radiant with light (*lucem, adfulsit, soles . . . nitent*) and with happiness at spring's return'. But everything about these three lines – diction, syntax and imagery – is direct and simple in the extreme, almost simplistic, not unlike *CS* 9–12 (and n.).

instar ueris . . . uultus: perhaps with focalization of the people (7 *affulsit populo*), which may help explain the jejune style, as at 2.46–7 (see n.), and cf. the plural at 38 *dicimus*, the only first person in the poem. When in higher lyric mode H., in accord with Callimachean principles, kept the *populus* at a distance: 1.1.30–32 *me gelidum nemus | Nympharumque leues cum Satyris chori | secernunt populo. instar* occurs only here in H., who has for now left the Tiburtine grove, giving rise to questions of sincerity.

gratior it dies: cf. 2.14.5 *quotquot eunt dies*. In Plautus *it dies* = 'time's flying' (*Bacch.* 1203; *Pseud.* 241; *Rud.* 1001); cf., closer in sense to H., *Cas.* 510 *nostro omine it dies*. The combination is otherwise not found before H. but is common enough in Ovid and Seneca; cf. *TLL* s.v. *dies* 1045.31–37. For a similar expression, also in the context of popular enthusiasm, cf. Cic. *Ligar.* 37, of Caesar, *si ille dies tibi gloriosissimus, populo Romano gratissimus fuit*.

9–16 A striking simile, in marked contrast in style and content to what precedes and what follows (see 17–24n.), with tenor (*patria*) and vehicle (*mater*) framing the two-stanza sentence in syntactically parallel units: *(ut) mater iuuenem | patria Caesarem*. After the opening words the entire first stanza is taken up with a relative clause that carries forward the intensity of the simile, as the verbs belonging to *mater (uocat, dimouet)* are held off till the first two line-ends of the following stanza. There is an intensity of language and of imagery, with elevated register throughout. H. has adapted Ennius' lines (*Ann.* fr. 105–9) on grief of the *patria* for the deceased Romulus, changing the relationship of the griever from child (108 '*o pater, o genitor*') to mother (see 1–16n.). The claim of Du Quesnay 1995: 159 that '[t]he image is almost certainly drawn from a lost Hellenistic classic, perhaps one describing the yearning of parted lovers', while possible, could also understimate Horatian originality.

9 iuuenem: here appropriate for the young man of the simile, since he represents Augustus of the outer narrative (16 *Caesarem*), who, though no longer such in reality, was described as *iuuenis* at 1.2.41 (with the name *Caesar*, i.e. Augustus, coming only at 52), and at *S.* 2.5.62–3 *ab | alto demissum genus Aenea*. Virgil has him as *iuuenem* at *G.* 1.500 (cf. 503 *Caesar*) and *iuuenem* without any other identification at *Ecl.* 1.42. See 4.24n. Though he was 50 by the time *C.* 4 was published, the iconography of Augustus continued long after this period to depict him as eternally youthful (Zanker 1988: 162).

9–10 inuido | flatu 'with malicious blast'; the adjective here contains no real sense of 'envy' (a sense present at 8.23–4, with n.), rather spite or malice, as at 1.11.7–8 *fugerit inuida | aetas*; *Epist.* 1.10.18 *est ubi diuellat somnos minus inuida cura*.

maris aequora: formal and elevated; cf. Tib. 1.7.19 *utque maris uastum prospectet turribus aequor*; Virg. *Aen.* 2.780 *longa tibi exsilia et uastum maris aequor arandum*; 3.495 *nullum maris aequor arandum*.

10 Carpathii trans maris aequora: the sea around Carpathos (also at 1.35.8), the island between Crete and Rhodes, and so a long way from Rome. The word order is highly poetic. Penney 1999: 263–7 gathers varied instances in Virgil (and, to observe persistence of the Virgilian pattern, Lucan) with this abbreviation: P[reposition], S[ubstantive], [Attributive] G[enitive], A[djective in agreement with the Substantive = As, or with the Genitive = Ag]. The order of H., Ag—P—G—S (*Carpathii trans maris aequora*), seems not to be represented in Virgil, but is clearly as mannered as any of Penney's examples.

11 cunctantem spatio longius annuo literally 'delaying longer than a year's stretch'. Was the *iuuenis* spending his gap year studying in Rhodes? A Roman parent might feel empathy.

13 uotis ominibusque et precibus: corresponds outside the simile to 33 *te multa prece . . . prosequitur*, again with elevation of style; cf. from Livy's preface: 1 *pr.*13 *cum bonis potius ominibus uotisque et precationibus deorum dearumque, si, ut poetis, nobis quoque mos esset, libentius inciperemus*; also Virg. *Aen.* 7.133 *precibusque uocate.*

uotis: vows presumably for a sacrifice to be carried out on the return of the son; cf. *Epist.* 1.3.36 *pascitur in uestrum reditum uotiua iuuenca*; also 4.2.53–56.

ominibus: spoken wishes or prayers, as at Ov. *Met.* 6.447–8 *dextera dextrae | iungitur et fausto committitur omine sermo*; cf. *TLL* s.v. *omen* 575.10–30.

15 desideriis icta fidelibus 'smitten with loyal longing', a powerful noun-adjective combination, which in its two parts well suits both the mother's longing and the loyalty of the *patria* towards the *pater patriae* (though he would not be given the title until 2 BCE according to *Mon. Anc.* 6.24–7, and cf. 20 *fides*; for a similar context cf. *Epist.* 1.7.2 *desideror* (and 1–4n.).

icta: cf. Lucr. 3.159–60 *anima . . . corpus propellit et icit*, 4.1050 *icimur ictu*; Virg. *Aen.* 6.180 *sonat icta securibus ilex* is in an intensely Ennian context; and cf. *TLL* s.v. *ico* 160.13–18; also *Aen.* 12.926 *incidit ictus* (where Servius needed to gloss *percussus*, as Porph. did in the present instance, *percussa*).

17–24 'There is in Horace's lyrics nothing really comparable to this long series of strictly parallel asyndetic sentences, each of them filling a line, without a single enjambement to vary the uniformity of the structure and soften the rigidity of the rhythm' (Fraenkel 443). Fraenkel notes that the effect of the whole is complex, but in these lines from his 'favourite ode' (443, n. 1), he sees the compactness, solidity, slightly archaic feel as all conspiring to support the achievements of the new régime, including the 'recently enacted *Lex Iulia de adulteriis*'. Other interpretations of this list style are available, although it is certainly the case that the details coincide with Augustan claims and propaganda. Johnson 121 puts it well: 'he lists off for three stanzas a catalogue of the *Res Romanae*, as if he is rehearsing a grocery-list outline and wants to be sure he does not leave out an item (17–28)'. The closest analogy is to be found in *Epode* 2 (see 29–32n.), which Ross 1979: 244 has shown more or less in its entirety 'consists of sequences of parallel clauses'. He connects this monotonous and balanced syntactical ordering with the surprise ending – the speaker is Alfius the moneylender, which, in view of the style, should come as no surprise: 'the almost dream-like succession of rustic delights (clichés all), strung out with such naive simplicity, was hardly intended to represent any compelling reality'. The propagandistic simplicity of 17–24 may be interpreted in line with the style of lines 3–4: the poem continues to be focalized by *patria* and *populus*, with the Horatian voice describing their point of view, its own point of view introduced only by the first-person voice of the final stanza, and there only as a symposiast. Cf. 37–40 and 15.4–16nn. Currie 1996: 79 notes the 'epigraphic' nature of the lines.

The 'hyperparataxis' (Johnson 121) is accompanied by other simplicities: repetitions whose point is not always clear (17, 18 *rura*; 20 *culpari*, 24 *culpam*; 21 *domus*, 22 *edomuit*); an abcabc rhyme from 18–20 is repeated 22–24: *-as* | *-ae* | *-es* |.

17 tutus: things were different back in the days of civil war: *Epod.* 16.10 *ferisque rursus occupabitur solum*; in between cf. *C.* 1.17, where the security now prevalent throughout the countryside was only to be found on H.'s farm (cf. 5 *tutum per nemus*).

17–18 rura perambulat, | nutrit rura: Housman disapproved: 'Horace was as sensitive to iteration as any modern; and those who choose to believe that he wrote *tutus bos etenim rura perambulat, nutrit rura Ceres,* which not even Lucan could have written, are as blind to truth as to beauty', Housman 1926: xxxiii. Shackleton Bailey 1982: 137–8, with reference to Thomas 1979: 337–8 on *errare* as an equivalent of *pasci*, sees point to the repetition: the ox grazes and so takes nourishment out of the land, while Ceres puts it back in. The style of 17–24 could also account for the repetition: the thought of each line is independent and almost hermetic (17–24n.), so the repetition is less strongly felt; cf. 21–2n. In general Housman overstated H.'s sensitivity, as Helmbold 1960 has shown. Finally the repetition may be both incompetent and deliberate (cf. 17–24n.).

perambulat: the image of a strolling cow seems slightly comic, though other instances of the verb in H. are no less striking: *Epod.* 17.42 (Canidia) *perambulabis astra sidus aureum*; *Epist.* 2.1.79–80 *recte necne crocum floresque perambulet Attae* | *fabula si dubitem*. *ambulo* is not found of animals until Sen. *Ep.* 85.41 (elephants) but is already used with an inanimate subject at Cato *Agr.* 1.3 *amnis qua naues ambulant.*

18 nutrit rura Ceres almaque Faustitas: Ceres and Auspiciousness or 'Fair Weather' (*OLD* s.v. *Faustitas*) are seen as giving nourishment to the fields (with Ceres seeding and Faustitas causing to grow). Cf. *CS* 29–32, where *Tellus* is paired with favourable weather conditions: *fertilis frugum pecorisque Tellus* | *spicea donet Cererem corona;* | *nutriant fetus et aquae salubres* | *et Iouis aurae*; also 4.25–6 of the upbringing of Tiberius and Drusus, *indoles nutrita faustis sub penetralibus*. The etymological sense of *alma* (from *alo*) works to intensify *nutrit*, as did *penetralibus* with *nutrita*, on which see 4.25–8n. *Faustitas* is only here in Latin (did H. invent a deity?), with Porph. feeling the need to explain it by analogy with *felicitas* and *iucunditas*, which suggests it did not take hold on the language. A glance at the *TLL* article s.v. *faustus* 388.23–389.49 shows a proliferation of the word in connection with Julius Caesar and Augustus. On *alma* see also *CS* 9n.

19 pacatum uolitant per mare nauitae: the claim is part of the Augustan programme: Aug. *Mon. Anc.* 4.1 *mare pacaui a praedonibus*, there referring especially to the defeat of Sextus Pompey in 36 BCE (*eo bello seruorum* . . .); it is more generalized for H., more than 20 years after the event.

20 'honour/trust fears to be faulted (and therefore avoids being faulted)'; *metuo* appears thus first at Virg. *G.* 1.246 *Arctos Oceani metuentis aequore tingi* (representing Arat. *Phaen.* 48 Ἄρκτοι κυανέου πεφυλαγμέναι; cf. *C.* 2.2.7 *pinna metuente solui*; *TLL* s.v. *metuo* 905.55–61). Related instances suggest unwillingness and aversion rather than actual avoidance: 3.11.10 *metuitque tangi*; *S.* 2.5.65 *metuentis reddere soldum*; *Epist.* 1.16.60 *labra mouet metuens audiri*; 1.18.1–2 *metues . . . scurrantis speciem praebere*; cf. *TLL* 905.45–55.

fides: notably in the *Res gestae*: *Mon. Anc.* 6.6–7 *plurimaeque aliae gentes expertae sunt p. R. fidem me principe*. The breaking of trust, *perfidia*, is among the most negative of Roman concepts, whence Livy's depiction of the quartering of Mettius Fufetius as the first and last instance of such severe punishment: 1.28.5 *cum proditione ac perfidia sociorum*, 9 *'si ipse discere posses fidem ac foedera seruare'*; also the sketch of Hannibal, 21.4.9 *perfidia plus quam Punica, nihil ueri, nihil sancti, nullus deum metus, nullum ius iurandum, nulla religio*.

21–4 Chastity, purity and family values are now the order of the day, a reversal of the situation in *C.* 3.6.21–32 (see also 25–28n.) and similar to *CS* 17–20. In a few short years, in the fiction of this checklist, morality has returned to Rome. H. surely alludes to the *Lex Iulia de adulteriis* (?*coercendis*) of 17 BCE; whether such legislation had the immediate effect these lines suggest is open to debate. The lines are moralizing clichés, ironic in effect, particularly in view of the author, but they work as a focalization of upright popular sentiment.

21–2 domus . . . edomuit: although they are not cognates, the repetition seems to suggest a connection; cf. 17–24n.

casta domus: a cliché; cf., all in moralizing contexts, Cat. 64.384 *domos . . . castas*; Virg. *G.* 2.524 *casta pudicitiam seruat domus*; Prop. 2.6.28 *casta . . . domo* (also similar in tone 3.12.37 *casta domi persederat uxor*); Tib. 3.4.60 *nec gaudet casta nupta Neaera domo*. Lucan 9.190–214 has the phrase in a string of rhetorically ordered moralizing antitheses on the greatness of Pompey: 201–2 *casta domus luxuque carens corruptaque numquam | fortuna domini* – with marked juxtaposition and contrast with *stupris*.

mos et lex: custom and law, the unwritten and written bonds of society; cf. 3.24.35–6 *quid leges sine moribus | uanae proficiunt*; *trag. inc.* fr.117 Ribb., cited by Cic. *Att.* 2.19.3 *si neque leges neque mores cogunt*; Serv. *ad Aen.* 8.316 *mos est lex quaedam uiuendi nullo uinculo adstricta, hoc est lex non scripta*.

maculosum 'stained', 'tainted'; first of an abstract phenomenon (*nefas*) here, and not otherwise so used until Tertullian; cf. *TLL* s.v. *maculosus* 30.48–57.

23–4 laudantur . . . culpam: one line for each part of the merism (rhetorical term for two or more components of a familiar phrase, i.e. 'praise and blame'). The implicit praise and blame of contrasting types of wife finds resonance at Tac. *Agr.* 6.1–2 *uixeruntque mira concordia, per mutuam caritatem et in uicem se anteponendo, nisi quod in bona uxore tanto maior laus, quanto in mala plus culpae est*.

simili prole: '[are praised] for offspring who look like the father'; causal ablative.; cf. 5.29–32.

puerperae 'women who have given birth' (*puer* + *pario* + *-a*).

Poena: the penalties for adultery (i.e. extra-marital sexual intercourse by or with a married woman) were quite severe, normally '*relegatio* (banishment) to different islands, and partial confiscation of property and dowry' (*OCD* s.v.

'adultery'). Upper case since *comes* creates a slight personification, like *deseruit* at 3.3.31–2 *raro antecedentem scelestum | deseruit pede Poena claudo*.

25–8 See 14.41–4n. for Augustus' consolidation and expansion in these areas in the years H. was engaged with *C.* 4.

quis . . . | quis: cf. 1.21n.

paueat, curet: potential subjunctives, or perhaps apodoses of future less vivid conditionals, *incolumi Caesare* being the protasis, with the uncertainties thereby implied.

gelidum: first here of the inhabitant (*Scythen*) of a cold land, and otherwise so only at Sen. *Herc. O.* 125 *gelidus Dolops*; cf. *TLL* s.v. *gelidus* 1728.74–8, which conflates two quite separate categories ('de hominibus et bestiis eorumque membris').

Germania . . . horrida: rare of a place, perhaps suggesting the shagginess of the people (*fetus*); cf. Cat. 4.8–9 *horridamque Thraciam | Propontida*, where *Thraciam* is an adjective, unless we read with Thomson (*CR* 54: 90) *Thracia* 'the Propontis bristling from the stormy wind'; if so, H.'s *horrida*, like his *frigida* is the first instance; see *TLL* s.v. *horridus* 2993.22–8 ('de barbaris'). Germany is generally uninviting from an Italian point of view: Tac. *Germ.* 2.2 *Germaniam . . . informem terris, asperam caelo, tristem cultu aspectuque*.

quos . . . parturit | fetus: H. clearly refers to the German people, but the language suggests something monstrous (*fetus* is more commonly of non-human offspring), and *TLL* s.v. *fetus* 638.73 wrongly places this instance with others in which the earth etc. actually gives birth. The oddity of expression may conceal a pun, a single Germania gives birth to *germani*.

incolumi Caesare: pointed. The absence of fear depends on Caesar's being safe and sound (see 31–2n.).

ferae | bellum . . . Hiberiae: cf. 2.12.1 *ferae bella Numantiae*, genitive in both cases. Tac. *Ann.* 1.3.7 and elsewhere has *bella ciuium* for *bella ciuilia*, on which see Goodyear *ad loc.*, with reference to Löfstedt I 122–3 on the interchangeability of genitive and adjective. N–H *ad* 2.12.1 refer to 'characteristic Horatian adaptation of the prosaic *bellum Numantinum*' (or *Hispanicum*); nevertheless the genitive is hard to define precisely.

29–36 The lines form an idyllic contrast with what precedes as tranquillity abroad brings security to the farm, with reminiscence of Virgil and of *Epode* 2 (see 17–24n.) and its rustic subject. The farmer returns from working in his hills and wedding the vine to its support tree, after which he offers a wine libation to Augustus. This sets up the poem's close, in which H. reveals his attitude: the Augustan age means more holidays, and opportunities for drinking.

29–32 condit . . . diem: Virgilian: cf. *Ecl.* 9.51–2 (Moeris has lost his land to veterans) *'saepe ego longos | cantando puerum memini me condere soles'*; *G.* 1.458 *cum [sol] referetque diem condetque relatum*. The phrase anticipates 39–40 (*mane die . . . sol Oceano subest*), with which it frames the final stanzas. Du Quesnay 1995: 173–4 sees in the reference to *Ecl.* 9 an allusion to new (non-land) settlements for veterans, proposed to the senate on Augustus' return in 13 BCE (Dio 54.25.5–6), of which H. must have been aware 'considerably in advance of those outside the most intimate circle of Augustus' friends'. Or the intertextuality could draw attention to the fact that a non-prescient H. was expressing anxiety, doubtless felt by Italian farmers, about new dispossessions to come with Caesar's return. If the biographical is to be invoked, it is notable that H. some years earlier disavowed any inside knowledge of precisely the issue of land settlements (*S.* 2.6.55–8).

collibus in suis 'in his own hills'; cf. *Epod.* 2.1–3 *beatus ille, qui . . . paterna rura bobus exercet suis*; cf. *OLD* s.v. *suus* 8.

uitem uiduas ducit ad arbores: *suauiter et uiduas arbores dixit, priusquam uites adiunctas habeant, quia cum habent maritari dicuntur a rusticis* (Porph.). The 'wedding' of the vine to its support tree (*uitis arbustiua*) is an old metaphor: Cato. *Agr.* 32.1 *susum uorsum . . . uitis facito uti ducas*, 32.2 *arbores facito ut bene maritae sint*; Cat. 62.49–50 *uidua in nudo uitis quae nascitur aruo | numquam se extollit.* H. varies the spousal situation (*uiduas . . . arbores*), as does Col. 5.6.31 *ut* [*uitis*] *uiduum ramum maritet.* The elm is the most common such tree (foliage not too abundant): *C.* 2.15.4–5 (unwed shade-tree poplar wins out over productive, useful elm) *platanusque caelebs | euincet ulmos*; *Epist.* 1.7.84 *praeparat ulmos*; 1.16.3 *amicta uitibus ulmo*; Virg. *G.* 1.2 (and Thomas *ad loc.*) *ulmisque adiungere uites*; Col. 11.2.79 *per hos dies . . . ulmi quoque uitibus recte maritantur.* An exception is *Epod.* 2.9–10 *adulta uitium propagine | altas maritat populos* (with Mankin *ad loc.*), the poplar being next best after elm according to Plin. *HN* 17.200.

31–6 The rustic pours a libation and prays to Augustus, adding the *princeps* to his household Lares. Dio 51.19 enumerates the various honours and positions accruing to Augustus in the years following Actium, ending with a provision that prayer and libation be offered to him both in public and in private (51.19.7): τούς τε ἱερέας καὶ τὰς ἱερείας ἐν ταῖς ὑπέρ τε τοῦ δήμου καὶ τῆς βουλῆς εὐχαῖς καὶ ὑπὲρ ἐκείνου ὁμοίως εὔχεσθαι (*multa prece*), καὶ ἐν τοῖς συσσίτιοις οὐχ ὅτι τοῖς κοινοῖς ἀλλὰ καὶ τοῖς ἰδίοις πάντας αὐτῶι σπένδειν (*mero | pateris defuso*) ἐκέλευσαν, 'and they decreed that the priests and priestesses in their prayers for the people and senate were to offer the same prayers for him too, and at all banquets both public and private everyone was to offer a libation to him'. H.'s lines mirror the decree referred to closely, but notably he does not involve himself in the praise and libation; rather the rustic is the subject throughout (cf. 37–40n.).

31 hinc . . . laetus: because of his work on the vine, he gets to enjoy the product. There is thus point to the progression *uitem* > *uina* and no good grounds for emending (e.g. *tecta* for *uina* Shackleton Bailey); cf. *Epod.* 2.39–48, where the Sabine or Apulian farmer's wife breaks out wine on her husband's return from work: *lassi sub aduentum uiri | . . . horna dulci uina promens dolio*; also Virg. *G.* 2.514–31, where the farmer's work (*hic . . . hinc . . . hinc*) is followed by wine-drinking and relaxation (528 *socii cratera coronant*). *laetus* corresponds to 7 *gratior.*

31–2 uina: for the nominative and accusative, with the exception of *S.* 2.2.58, 2.4.60 and *Epist.* 1.14.24, H. consistently uses the plural, the singular for the other cases (i.e. *uini, uino*); see K–H on *C.* 1.11.6 *uina liques.* For other patterns of usage and for various explanations, see Löfstedt I 48. Metre is not an issue, and the sense of collectivity is part of the reason: *OLD* s.v. *uinum* 1b '(pl.) separate lots, jars, bowls, etc., of wine'.

redit: the poem has forgotten about the return of Caesar (3–4 *reditum . . . redi*), sought by the people. The rustic's tranquil return from work depends not on that but on the safety of Caesar as he keeps foreign foes at bay – away from Rome.

alteris . . . mensis 'at the dessert course', normally *mensa secunda* (cf. *OLD* s.v. *mensa* 5), in fact the third course, following the *gustatio* or *promulsis* (eggs, dormice and other appetizers) and the *cena* itself (consisting of as many as seven dishes, *fercula*); see *OCD* s.v. 'meals'. Libations were poured at the beginning of this last dish, at which the god is invited to be present (*te . . . adhibet deum*); cf. Virg. *Aen.* 5.62–3 '*adhibete penates* | *et patrios epulis et quos colit hospes Acestes*'; also *G.* 1.42 (addressed to Augustus) *uotis iam nunc assuesce uocari.*

32–4 te . . . te . . . te tuum: hymnic style, as at 14.41–52 (see n. and Wills 361–2).

adhibet: Caesar will be present, but only in his divine capacity in the prayers and thoughts of the rustic (see 35–6n.).

33–6 mero | defuso pateris: as libations; cf. 1.31.2–3 *quid orat de patera nouum* | *fundens liquorem*; Virg. *Aen.* 7.133 *nunc pateras libate Ioui*; Val. Max. 2.6.8 *defusis Mercurio delibamentis.* For folk etymologies see Macrob. *Sat.* 5.21.4 *patera . . . , ut et ipsum nomen indicio est, planum ac patens est*; Isid. *Etym.* 20.5.2 *uel quod in ipsis potare solemus uel quod patentes sunt.*

Laribus . . . numen: presumably images of Augustus are brought out along with the Lares at the libation offering. Ov. *Fast.* 2.635–8 treats the prayer that accompanies the joining of these statues with the Lares; cf. Du Quesnay 1995: 175–6. At Petron. 60 the diners exclaim (referring to one of Augustus' successsors) '*Augusto patri patriae feliciter!*' Slaves then bring out two Lares and set them on the table: *Lares bullatos super mensam posuerunt.* According to Dio 51.20.1 after the Parthian settlement Augustus' name was to be 'written into hymns on equal terms with the gods' (ἔς τε τοὺς ὕμνους αὐτὸν ἐξ ἴσου τοῖς θεοῖς ἐσγράφεσθαι).

35–6 Three times elsewhere in H. *praesens* is applied to Augustus, with the implication, as first at Virg. *Ecl.* 1.41 (the *iuuenis* of that poem = Octavian), that he has some sort of divine status already: 3.5.2; 4.14.43 (see 41–4n.); *Epist.* 2.1.15–17 (with Brink *ad loc.* especially pp. 52–3). At 3.3.9–12 Augustus will drink nectar with Pollux and Hercules. Here the rustic, 'mindful like Greece of Castor and mighty Hercules', prays and pours a libation to Augustus; or is it 'as Greece does, which remembers C. and H.'? Either way, the lines are at odds with *Epist.* 2.1.5–17, whose whole point is that Rome gives divine honours and sets up altars to Augustus in contrast to the Greeks and earlier Romans, who waited for Romulus, Liber, Castor and Pollux and Hercules to die before so honouring them.

magni . . . Herculis: there is no particular reason to require that H. points specifically to either Hercules Magnus Custos (so Putnam 112, comparing 2 *custos* of Augustus) or Hercules Invictus, conqueror of barbarians and recipient of sacrifice at the Ara Maxima (Du Quesnay 1995: 179).

37–40 In a move familiar from his earlier lyric (2.1.37–40; 3.3.69–72), H. closes by asserting his private role within the larger celebratory goings-on. Appearing in the first person for the first time in the poem (38 *dicimus*) he situates himself as one who enjoys the purely sympotic advantages of the holidays that attend *pax Augusta* without Augustus – as at *Epist.* 1.5.9–10: *cras nato Caesare festus* | *dat ueniam somnumque dies*. The recently published Prop. 4.6 ends on a similar note: 85–6 *sic noctem patera, sic ducam carmine, donec* | *iniciat radios in mea uina dies*. DuQuesnay 1995: 180–1 sees in the reference to morning and evening an allusion to conquest east and west at 15.13–16, but the current emphasis on time rather than space, drinking rather than conquest, perhaps distinguishes the two passages.

longas: a good thing, unlike the time Augustus was away (2 *nimium diu*), with which it forms a contrastive frame.

dux bone: see 5n.

ferias: Dyson 1991: 126–9 argues plausibly that H. is anticipating additional holidays connected with the triumph he expects on the return of Augustus, while others see *ferias* as coterminous with the reign of Augustus.

Hesperiae: here of Italy, of Spain at 1.36.4; cf. 15.16 *Hesperio cubili* of the sun's western setting.

integro . . . die 'when the day is whole' (i.e. in the morning); cf. *OLD* s.v. *integer* 5b. *integro*, 'untouched' looks to the condition as does 27 *incolumi Caesare* 'Caesar unharmed'.

sicci . . . uuidi: well reflects the two parts of the poem, namely the sober public image and Augustan *res gestae* of 17–24, as opposed to the party, carried on in Augustus' absence at 29–40. The two adjectives are found together in this sense only here in Latin. For *siccus*, 'sober', see 1.18.3 *siccis omnia nam dura deus proposuit*; Cic. *Leg. agr.* 1.1 *haec per deos immortales! utrum esse uobis consilia siccorum an uinulentorum somnia . . . uidentur?*; *Luc.* 88 *uinulentorum . . . siccorum*. For *uuidus*, 'soused', 'drunk' (Porph.: *id est: poti atque madidi*), first in H., cf. 2.19.18 (of Bacchus) *tu separatis uuidus in iugis*; also 1.7.22–3 *uda Lyaeo* | *tempora*.

die . . . sol: ring composition with 7–8 *dies . . . soles*, with the year they mark in between: 11 *spatio . . . annuo*.

subest: appropriate as the last word of the poem, which comes to an end along with the day.

6

METRE

Sapphic stanza (see *CS*, 2 intro.).

INTRODUCTION

You god whose avenging power was felt by Niobe's children, Tityos and even Achilles, not your match even though he made Troy shake under his attack, for even he was felled like a tree and lay in the dust. He wouldn't have hidden away in the Horse and tricked the rejoicing Trojans, but would have openly burnt their youth, infants and even children in the womb, if Jupiter hadn't been persuaded by Venus so Aeneas could go on to better things.

Phoebus, lyre-teacher, protect the glory of the Daunian Muses. Phoebus gave me breath, art, the name of poet. You well-born boys and girls, wards of Diana, keep the Lesbian measure as you sing of Apollo and Diana and prosperity through time. After you are married you will say 'I sang the Carmen saeculare, *taught the song by the bard Horace.'*

H. moves from Drusus (4) to Augustus (5) to Apollo in this the third of his Pindaric and generally hymnic series. The ode to spring (7) will bring a close to the movement and begin the next triad. This hymn to Apollo opens with striking reference to those who felt the god's punishment, the children of Niobe, Tityos and the great Achilles, the latter a greater soldier than all other mortals, but no match for Apollo, who laid the hero low in the dust of Troy.

The poem then becomes almost a hymn to Achilles, emphatically referred to at the start of the third and fourth stanza: 9, 13 *ille . . . ille*. Like the subject matter, the metre ties it to the *Carmen saeculare*, on which the final stanzas meditate, as the poet credits the god for his art and his poetic reputation and addresses the choristers of that poem. The poem closes with the words of one of them years later, when H. imagines she will recall the performance of her youth. Fraenkel 405–6 imagines H.'s communicating the poem ('which was obviously designed to please and encourage them') to the young men and girls: 'how much must he have enjoyed conversing with those fine young people at a time when he found it often very hard to accept the melancholy fact that he was growing old!'

The poem focuses on two of Apollo's attributes in stark contrast. The first 24 lines address the archer god, capturing him at his most violent and destructive. The second part (25–44) turns rather to the god of music and to his close association with H. and his lyric art. The poem thus moves the reader out of the cycle of poems 4–6, re-establishing the familiar lyrical voice glimpsed at the end of 4.5 but not seen in full form since the end of 4.3; it will return in 4.7, the closest poem to his earlier lyrical collection and one whose only topical marker (addresses to Torquatus) also distinguishes it from the world of Augustus and his princes and colleagues in power (7.23–4n.). Some have found the transition between the two parts too harsh, but there are no grounds for seeing, as did some nineteenth-century scholars (see Fraenkel 400–1) a new poem beginning at 29. The poem is modelled on the genre of paean, the hymn directed specifically to Apollo, and K–H, Pasquali 751–5 and Fraenkel 400–1 have demonstrated that Pindar's sixth *Paean*, which can be seen as an intertext in its focus on Achilles, in its general style and various specific verses (see 3–4, 6, 7–9, 9–24, 15–16, 25–44nn.), provides a model for the abrupt transition in the second part of the poem. As H. turns from the deadly exploits of Apollo, chiefly in killing Achilles, to an address to the choristers of the *CS*, so Pind. *Pae.* 6.122–3 turns from the death of Neoptolemus to address the young men of his chorus: <ἰὴ> ἰῆτε, νῦν, μέτρα π̣αιηό- | ν]ων ἰῆτε νέοι, 'Ie, sing now, sing the measures of paeans, young men!'

Barchiesi 1995 and 1996 suggests that the 'New Simonides' (cf. 9–12n.) takes its place alongside Pindar as an important intertext, though in our current state of knowledge, the Pindaric element seems uppermost. As in *C.* 4.2, the second part of the poem also sees a receding of the Pindaric and Simonidean elements as the more Callimachean aspect comes to the fore; see 25, 29–30, 33–4nn.

1–2 Diue: cf. 5.1 *Diuis orte bonis*, also missing the name of the addressee, in both cases to be supplied from the details that follow; cf. 26 and 29–30n.; similarly 1.35.1 *O diua, gratum quae regis Antium* (Fortuna, never named in the poem). In contrast, cf. 1.10.1 *Mercuri*; 1.21.1 *Dianam tenerae dicite uirgines*; 1.30.1 *O Venus*. See Löfstedt I 94–96 on the absence of the bare address θεός in archaic Greek, compared to the relative frequency of θεά, a distinction no longer felt by H. For openings of hymns see Rutherford 2001: 74 in general, and 307 on the complete absence of Apollo from the beginning of *Paean* 6, a poem perhaps known to H. (see 3–4n.); also Dickey 2002: 321.

In fact, the poem completely loses sight of the addressee, who exists in the opening vocative and in the dative *tibi* in 5, but who is replaced by a focus on Achilles, the subject until Apollo returns at 21 (*tuis*), and by name at 26 *Phoebe*. See also 25–44n.

proles Niobea: pointedly Niobe's children, and not Niobe herself, are made to feel the vengeance in this most savage of the ἀρεταί ('exploits') of Apollo the archer, who takes vengeance on Niobe for boasting that she had more children than Leto. Although the myth, familiar from Greek epic (Hom. *Il.* 24.599–620) and tragedy (chiefly Aesch. fr. 154a–67b Radt) is common enough in Greek lyric (Lesky, *RE* s.v. 'Niobe' 647), it appears in H. only here; before Ovid's elaborate treatment (*Met.* 6.148–312), which goes to great lengths to describe and dwell on the deaths and agonies of each of the seven sons and seven daughters, it is not commonly treated in Latin literature (briefly, Prop. 2.20.7; 3.10.8). The Homeric context may flavour its appearance here.

Niobea: the use of the personal adjective for the genitive is a feature of poetry, sometimes, but not necessarily, *metri causa*. See L–H–S 60–1; Austin *ad* Virg. *Aen.* 2.543; Harrison 1991: 103.

magnae . . . linguae: i.e. *magniloquentiae*, a prose word. H.'s phrase is found only here in Latin, and cf. Soph. *Ant.* 127–8 (its only appearance in Greek, except for the literal Hipp. *Epidem.* 5.1.53 etc.) Ζεὺς γὰρ μεγάλης γλώσσης κόμπους | ὑπερεχθαίρει, 'Zeus despises the boasts of a big tongue' – perhaps it was used of Niobe in Greek tragedy. Similarly of her at Ov. *Met.* 6.213 (Latona is the speaker) '*exhibuit linguam scelerata paternam*' (i.e. Tantalus); Diod. Sic 4.74.3 ἐπὶ δὲ τῶι πλήθει τῶν τέκνων μέγα φρυαττομένη πλεονάκις ἐκαυχᾶτο καὶ τῆς Λητοῦς ἑαυτὴν εὐτεκνοτέραν ἀπεφαίνετο 'very haughty over the number of her children she often boasted and said she was more fortunate in her children than Leto'; Luc. *Salt.* 41.9 τῆς Νιόβης ἡ μεγαλαυχία 'Niobe's boastfulness'.

Tityosque raptor: a giant who made the mistake of attempting to rape Leto (Hom. *Od.* 11.576–81) and so ended up in the Underworld, with vultures eating away at his liver. He is dispatched by various gods, including Zeus and Artemis, here by Apollo, as at Ap. Rhod. *Arg.* 1.759–62, in the ecphrasis of Jason's cloak, where the young god shoots Tityos as he is dragging Leto off by her veil.

3 Troiae . . . altae: cf. the Homeric Ἰλίου αἰπεινῆς, *Il.* 9.419, 686; 13.773; 15.215, 558; 17.328 (always in the context of the city's destruction, as here for H.); similarly Eur. *Andr.* 103.

3–4 Achilles, the prize prey, closes the stanza, as Apollo (*diue*), his antagonist, had opened it. Various texts hint at or spell out the role Apollo will play in the hero's death: Hom. *Il.* 21.275–8 (Achilles challenging the veracity of Thetis' prediction that he would 'die by the arrows of Apollo') 'ὀλέεσθαι Ἀπόλλωνος βελέεσσιν'; 22.359–60 (Hector to Achilles) '. . . ἤματι τῶι ὅτε κέν σε Πάρις καὶ Φοῖβος Ἀπόλλων | ἐσθλὸν ἐόντ' ὀλέσωσιν ἐνὶ Σκαιῆισι πύλῃσιν' 'on the day when Paris and Phoebus Apollo kill you at the Scaean Gate, good as you are'; Pindar, *Pae.* 6.83–6 κυανοπλόκοιο παῖδα ποντίας | Θέτιος βιατάν, | πιστὸν ἕρκος Ἀχαι- | ῶν, θρασεῖ φόνωι πεδάσαις, 'binding in bold slaughter the trusty defence of the Achaeans, the powerful son of dark-haired Thetis, goddess of the sea'. The stately address by Aeneas to Cumaean Apollo, shows the importance of the divine exploit from the Trojan/Roman point of view (Virg. *Aen.* 6.56–8): *'Phoebe, graues Troiae semper miserate labores, | Dardana qui Paridis derexti tela manusque | corpus in Aeacidae'.*

Pthius Achilles: in spite of the Homeric appearance, Achilles is not so described in Homer, though he does refer to 'deep-soiled Phthia, nourisher of men' (Φθίηι ἐριβώλακι βωτιανείρηι) at *Il* 1.155. The formula seems to be the invention of Aeschylus: *Myrmidons*, fr. 132 Radt Φθιῶτ' Ἀχιλλεῦ; also Eur. *Tro.* 575. The Aeschylean adjective is Φθιώτης, rather than Horatian Φθῖος, perhaps because the latter *is* Homeric (*Il.* 13.685–8 and Janko *ad loc.*), but only in the plural where it designates the followers not of Achilles but of Medon and Podarces. At Ar. *Ran.* 1264 Euripides is made to use the phrase Φθιῶτ' Ἀχιλλεῦ at the beginning of a sequence parodying Aeschylus' dactylic rhythms and use of refrain – the latter notably paeanic: 1265, 1267 ἰὴ κόπον. The comic poet Strattis (*PCG* VII fr. 17) applied the address to the dithyrambic poet Cinesias. Prop. 2.13.38 calls Achilles *Pthii . . . uiri.* The inscriptional evidence (searchable at www.manfredclauss.de) here supports application of 'Schulze's Law' (in Latin if two aspirated stops are together, only the second is written with an 'h'), for which see, on *Pthius*, Schulze 1958: 50, 75.

5 ceteris maior, tibi miles impar: recalls the frequent Homeric designation of Achilles, ἄριστος Ἀχαιῶν; but with the qualification that he is no match as a soldier for Apollo, in spite of the divinity of Thetis.

6 Thetidis marinae: one of a number of places H. seems to be drawing from Pind. *Pae.* 6 (see intro.); cf. 83–4 κυανοπλόκοιο παῖδα ποντίας | Θέτιος (see 3–4 n.), also perhaps, as Barchiesi 1995: 36 notes, Simonides fr. 10.5 West κούρης εἰν]ạλίης ἀγλαόφη[με πάϊ; 'bright-famed son of the daughter of the sea'; 11.19–20 West θεᾶς ἐρικύ[δεος υἱέ | κούρης εἰν]αλίου Νηρέος, 'son of the glorious goddess daughter of sea-god Nereus' (see 9–12n.) – though *marinae* is closer to Pindaric ποντίας. This use of the Latin adjective (with a person or deity) is unusual and is found only in H. modifying a god's name: 11.15 *Veneris marinae*; 1.8.13–14 *marinae . . . Thetidis*; 3.26.5 *marinae . . . Veneris*; Cat. 64.16–17 has *marinas . . . Nymphas*. Ov. *Met.* 11.228 calls Thetis *uirginis . . . marinae*, the more Catullan construction. See *TLL* s.v. *marinus* 397.82–398.10, with, however, insufficient recognition of the uniqueness of H.'s practice, which is strongly Hellenizing. Eur. has (*Androm.* 108) ἁλίας Θέτιδος 'Thetis of the sea' and (*El.* 450) Θέτιδος εἰναλίας 'sea goddess Thetis', and it may be that here, too, H. is looking to lyric and tragedy as much as epic. In Homer Thetis is often without epithet, occasionally is called θεὰ Θέτις or θεὰ Θέτις ἀργυρόπεζα, and elsewhere is accorded a more formal naming: *Il.* 1.538, 556 ἀργυρόπεζα Θέτις θυγάτηρ ἁλίοιο γέροντος 'silver-footed Thetis, daughter of the old man of the sea'. Only there by implication and at 20.207 is she associated in her name with the sea: Θέτιδος καλλιπλοκάμου ἁλοσύδνης 'fair-tressed Thetis, daughter of the sea'.

7–9 The peripety or reversal of fortune occurs across the stanza division, with the like-suffixed adjectives corresponding to each other: *tremenda | cuspide pugnax || . . . mordaci uelut icta ferro*. The violent, Homeric *icta ferro* of the simile will become the Horatian – musical – *pollicis ictum* of 36.

9–24 Achilles is now the main subject, so replacing the divine addressee of the hymn, perhaps in imitation of Simonides' hymn to Achilles in the elegy on the Battle of Plataea (see intro, 9–12n.). The fate of Achilles (9 *ille*) is followed by contemplation (13 *ille*) of what would have happened had Apollo and Venus not persuaded Jupiter to favour the Trojan side. The replacement is effected via a counterfactual aretalogy of Achilles had he been alive at the fall of Troy: he would not have been shut up in the deceptive Trojan horse or have ambushed the celebrating Trojans, rather he would have openly taken the town, brought Greek fire to infants, even to the unborn still in their mothers' wombs. The sense of violence, transferred from Apollo to Achilles, has become very marked. The lines are an expansion of Pind. *Pae.* 6.89–91 πρὸ πόνων | δέ κε μεγάλων Δαρδανίαν | ἔπραθεν, εἰ μὴ φύλασσεν Ἀπό[λ]λ[ω]ν, 'before great labours he would have sacked the Dardan town had Apollo not been on guard'. This in turn is similar to Hom. *Il.* 16.698–701 ἔνθα κεν ὑψίπυλον Τροίην ἕλον υἷες Ἀχαιῶν | Πατρόκλου ὑπὸ χερσί, περιπρὸ γὰρ ἔγχεϊ θῦεν, | εἰ μὴ Ἀπόλλων Φοῖβος ἐϋδμήτου ἐπὶ πύργου | ἔστη τῶι ὀλοὰ φρονέων, Τρώεσσι δ' ἀρήγων, 'then the sons of the Achaeans would have taken high-gated Troy at the hands of Patroclus – for around and in front he raged with his spear – had not Phoebus Apollo taken his stand on the well-built tower intending destruction for him, while helping the Trojans'. See also 18–20n.

9, 13 ille . . . | ille: cf. 1.21n.

9–12 H. achieves high style with an aesthetically appealing stanza devoting two lines each to tenor and vehicle, each of which is shaped by an assonant doublet (*icta . . . aut impulsa | procidit . . . posuitque*). These densely intertextual lines constitute a challenge to the Virgilian art of conflation and multiple allusion. They first recall Hom. *Il.* 13.389–93, repeated at 16.482–6 (Patroclus' killing of Sarpedon, an anticipation of the death of Achilles): ἤριπε δ' ὡς ὅτε τις δρῦς ἤριπεν ἢ ἀχερωῖς | ἠὲ πίτυς βλωθρή, ... ὣς ὁ πρόσθ' ἵππων καὶ δίφρου κεῖτο τανυσθείς | βεβρυχὼς κόνιος δεδραγμένος αἱματοέσσης, 'he fell as when an oak falls, or a poplar, or a tall pine, ... so did he lie stretched out before his horses and chariot, crying out and clutching at the bloody dust'. K–H also point to *Od.* 24.39–40 (the ghost of Agamemnon addressing that of Achilles, and referring to the very same context as H.) σὺ δ' ἐν στροφάλιγγι κονίης κεῖσο μέγας μεγαλωστί, 'and you lay in the whirl of dust, mighty in your mightiness'. It is now clear, as Barchiesi 1995 has shown, that Simonides is as important a source as any, and indeed perhaps the primary one for this simile, a version of which the Greek poet produced, after the Homeric models, precisely in the context of the death of Achilles: Simonides fr. 111.1–3 West = *POxy.* 2327 fr. 5.1–3 (supplements by West, without which Horatian parallels are still valid: Barchiesi 1995: 34) σὺ δ' ἤριπες, ὡς ὅτε πεύκην | ἢ πίτυν ἐν βήσ[σαις οὔρεος οἰοπόλου | ὑλοτόμοι τάμ[νωσι, 'you fell, as when woodsmen cut a fir or a pine in the lonely mountain glens'. The presence of woodsmen (elsewhere the trees simply fall down) guarantees the presence of Simonides in H. (cf. *mordaci . . . ferro*). Finally Barchiesi 1995: 35 with Nisbet *per litteras* notes the unmistakable Catullan intertext at 64.105–9 (the fall of the Minotaur): H.'s phrasing (*ille . . . uelut . . . pinus . . . procidit late*) closely tracks that of his Latin predecessor (*uelut . . . pinum . . . illa . . . pro(na) cadit late*).

mordaci: only here of an axe, sword etc., and distinct from the examples with which it is gathered at *TLL* s.v. 1483.70–80 (with *ianua*, *pumex*, *fibula* etc.). Adjectives in *-ax* seem to have something of a colloquial tone (Cooper 1975: 109–10), often pejorative (Leumann 1977: 376).

cupressus: not part of the Homeric simile (9–12n.), and doubtless added by H. for the funereal associations of the tree, as at *Epod* 5.18 *cupressos funebres*, with Watson *ad loc.*, noting that the association may stem from the tree's belonging to the class *arbor infelix*. See also N–H on 2.14.23 *inuisas cupressos* and Horsfall on Virg. *Aen.* 3.64 *atraque cupresso*, including continuity to modern times of the presence of the cypress around graves.

13–16 A stanza of intense Virgilian recomposition, as at 21–4 (see n.), in the course of a movement that goes from Pindar and Simonides to H., from the death of Achilles and fall of Troy to Aeneas' escape and the walls of Rome; on this see Barchiesi 1996: 10–11.

inclusus equo: cf. Virg. *Aen.* 2.18–19 *huc delecta uirum sortiti corpora furtim | includunt*, 45 *inclusi . . . Achiui*, 258 *inclusos utero Danaos*.

equo Mineruae | sacra mentito 'in the horse which deceptively posed as sacred offerings to Minerva'. Cf. Virg. *Aen.* 2.31 *innuptae donum exitiale Mineruae*.

male feriatos | Troas 'Trojans (Τρῶας) who picked a bad time to celebrate'. Cf. Virg. *Aen.* 2.248–9 *nos delubra deum miseri, quibus ultimus esset | ille dies, festa uelamus fronde per urbem*.

laetam Priami choreis | . . . aulam 'Priam's palace, joyous with (?exulting in) the dance'. There is a hint of Neoptolemus, struck down by Apollo at Delphi for killing Priam at the altar of Zeus Herkeios (see Pind. *Pae.* 6.105–120) situated in Virgil inside the palace. Cf. Priam's words to Neoptolemus at *Aen.* 2.540–1 (essentially counterfactual as in 13–16) '*at non ille, satum quo te mentiris, Achilles | talis in hoste fuit Priamo*'. There is some irony in *laetam*, in that the adjective can indicate richness or abundance in the agricultural sense (*TLL* s.v. 883.79–884.79), whereas the palace of Priam, fecund with its 50 daughters and 50 daughters-in-law (Virg. *Aen.* 2.499–505), is about to be desolated.

16, 19 falleret . . . ureret: imperfects for pluperfects in the apodosis of a past counterfactual. Possibly an archaism, and certainly a feature of early Latin, but Clackson and Horrocks 2007: 213 note that 'at least until the time of Livy the imperfect subjunctive continued to be used to refer to the past in certain special circumstances, i.e. with the distinctive sense of "it was likely/going to be the case that X": e.g. *quas si occupauissent, mare totum in sua potestate haberent* (Caesar *de bello Ciuili* 3.111.4), meaning "if they had seized these (ships) [pluperfect], they were likely/destined to have the whole sea in their power [imperfect]", rather than simply "would have had"'. K–H note *S.* 1.6.79–80 *si qui uidisset . . . crederet.*

17 palam captis 'captured in the open', *palam* contrasting with 13 *inclusus.*

17–18 nefas . . . ne(scios) fari: Putnam (119–20) notes the play, including, perhaps, 14 *male feriatos.* See also ἄφαντοι (18–20n.). Cf. similar play at Virg. *G.* 1.478–9 *pecudesque locutae | (infandum).*

18–20 Adapted from Hom. *Il.* 6.57–60, where Agamemnon chides Menelaus for his (short-lived) decision to spare the life of the Trojan Adrastus: τῶν μή τις ὑπεκφύγοι αἰπὺν ὄλεθρον | χεῖράς θ' ἡμετέρας, μηδ' ὅν τινα γαστέρι μήτηρ | κοῦρον ἐόντα φέροι, μηδ' ὃς φύγοι, ἀλλ' ἅμα πάντες | Ἰλίου ἐξαπολοίατ' ἀκήδεστοι καὶ ἄφαντοι, 'Let not one of them escape utter destruction and our hands, not even the boy still carried in his mother's womb, but let them all perish together out of Troy, unmourned and unseen.' There is an irony here in that Achilles' acts (not to speak of Apollo's, he the greater soldier), had he lived, would have been more brutal, and less heroic, than those his early death kept him from participating in.

latentem | matris in aluo: a more vivid image than in the Homeric expression, with the unborn boy sentient and hiding; H. also perhaps conjures up the Trojan horse, in whose womb the Greeks hid: Virg. *Aen.* 2.18–20, 39–40, 257–9, 401 *nota conduntur in aluo.*

21–4 'had not the father of the gods, swayed by your words and those of pleasing Venus, granted to the fortunes of Aeneas walls traced with better augury'. Something of a *non sequitur*, since the survival of Achilles would not necessarily have prevented Aeneas' escape from Troy. K–H (*ad loc.*) set out the close Virgilian intertexts of this stanza, an aspect of the poem in general: *ni*, normally archaic and colloquial, and only here in the *Odes*, seems in Virgil more elevated (not in *Ecl.*), as here; *diuum pater* is likewise a stately Virgilian formula: *Aen.* 1.65; 2.648; 10.2, 743, in each case followed by the phrase *atque hominum rex*. The persuasive powers of Apollo and particularly of Venus strongly evoke contexts from *Aen.* 1 and 3: 1.250 '*nos, tua progenies, caeli quibus annuis arcem*'; and Jupiter's response to Venus: 1.258–9 '*cernes urbem et promissa Lauini | moenia*'; the phrasing *potiore ductos | alite muros* recalls Aeneas' words to Helenus at 3.497–9 '*Troiamque uidetis | quam uestrae fecere manus, melioribus, opto, | auspiciis*', while *ductos* points to 1.423 *instant ardentes Tyrii: pars ducere muros* (unusual enough of a wall that Servius felt the need to gloss: *exaedificare, hoc est construendo in longitudinem producere*; cf. *TLL* s.v. *duco* 2151.70–1) – pairing the building of Rome with that of Carthage.

21 Venerisque gratae: cf. 1.19.7 *[me Glycerae] urit grata proteruitas*. The epithet with Venus, or any deity, is unique, perhaps representing Jupiter's point of view; cf. Virg. *Aen.* 1.254–6 (immediately following Venus' persuasive words to her father) *olli subridens hominum sator atque deorum | . . . oscula libauit natae*.

23–4 potiore . . . alite: see *CS* 43–4 *daturus plura relictis*. Cf. also Juno's words on the contrasting option that Troy be rebuilt: 3.3.61–2 *Troiae renascens alite lugubri | fortuna*.

25–44 The hymn resumes but lasts only six lines, 25–30, as H. then (31–44) turns his attention to the choristers. Fraenkel 401 points to Pindar's sixth *Paean* (see 9–24, 15–16nn.), which likewise opened with an address to Pytho, but at line 121 turned to the young men of the chorus; see intro.

25–8 A suitable transition from the god of the bow to the god of the lyre, though the power of poetry has been celebrated throughout, both implicitly and, with the internal audience at 15, explicitly, from Homer to Virgil. H. bids Apollo, teacher of a Greek Muse (*Thaliae*) and in a Greek place (*Xantho*), come to the protection (*defende*) of the poet's Italian Muse (*Dauniae . . . Camenae*). Similarly of Pan/Faunus at 1.17.1–4 *uelox amoenum saepe Lucretilem | mutat Lycaeo Faunus et igneam | defendit aestatem capellis | usque meis pluuiosque uentos*.

25 doctor argutae fidicen Thaliae: K–H note Apollo's role not so much as singer, rather as χοροδιδάσκαλος. As the Callimachean Virgil invoked Thalia when he turned – on the advice of Apollo – from kings and battles to his bucolic *deductum carmen* at *Ecl.* 6.1–5, so H. brings her up here for the first and only time, as he goes through a transition from the warlike and violent Apollo to the more Callimachean, musical god (see 29–30n.).

26 Phoebe: finally named, with the same vocative found at the beginning of the *CS* and at 1.12.24.

qui Xantho lauis amne crines: cf. 3.4.61–3 *qui rore puro Castaliae lauit | crines solutos, qui Lyciae tenet | dumeta natalemque siluam, | Delius et Patareus Apollo*, including the three main cult places, Delphi, Delos and Patara (south of the town and river Xanthus, in Lycia). *Xantho* may be chosen in part to resonate with *crines*, ξανθός ('blond', 'golden') being a common epithet for hair.

27 Dauniae . . . Camenae: forms a frame with 44 *uatis Horati* – an insistently Roman poet (*uates*), in an Italian setting (the Daunii are from northern Apulia around Argyripa, Arpi), with an Italian Muse (*Camena*); cf. *CS* 62 *Phoebus acceptusque nouem Camenis.*

28 leuis Agyieu 'smooth-cheeked Agyieus'; cf. 1.21.2 *intonsum* . . . *Cynthium.* Apollo Agyieus ('god of streets') appears in Latin only here (until Macrob. 1.9.6 *idem Apollo apud illos et* ἀγυιεύς *nuncupatur, quasi uiis praepositus urbanis: illi enim uias quae intra pomeria sunt?* ἀγυιάς *appellant*) and is to be found mostly in Attic drama, appropriately since Athens was one of the cult places, and the aniconic pointed pillar that represents the god may have been part of the stage scenery. See, with further bibliography, Mastronarde on Eur. *Phoen.* 631. Since we have a terracotta image from the sanctuary of Palatine Apollo depicting a 'baitylos' (pointed stone image) decked out with lyre and quiver (Zanker 1988: 90, fig. 73), we may assume H.'s choice of Apollo Agyieus had something to do with Augustan iconography. If Apollo Agyieus is connected with homecoming, the movement of this stanza from Greek myth to H.'s native land (*Dauniae*) may reflect that fact. See also Putnam 124–8.

29–30 Phoebus . . . Phoebus: 1–2n.

spiritum / artem carminis / nomenque poetae: a terse and elegant tricolon, with H. laying claims to *ars* as well as *ingenium* (*spiritum*), a reversal of the pure Callimachean stance (e.g. 1.6.5–12), as is appropriate for the singer of the *Carmen saeculare.* For similar contexts, cf. 2.16.37–9 (still Callimachean) *mihi parua rura et* | *spiritum Graiae tenuem* (i.e. λεπτόν) *Camenae* | *Parca non mendax dedit*; *S.* 1.4.45–7 *quidam comoedia necne poema* | *esset quaesiuere, quod acer spiritus ac uis* | *nec uerbis nec rebus inest.* See also 3.24 (to Melpomene) *quod spiro et placeo, si placeo, tuum est.*

31–2 uirginum primae puerique claris | patribus orti 'foremost among maidens and boys sprung from famous fathers'. After establishing his poetic pedigree, H. turns to the young girls and boys who sang the *CS* (cf. 42 *saeculo festas referente luces*), and who identify themselves in that poem: *CS* 6 (and n.) *uirgines lectas puerosque castos*; 34–6 *audi pueros . . . audi . . . puellas*; 71 *uotis puerorum* (of both). In the pseudo-sacral context of 3.1.2–4 the pairing also figures: *carmina non prius* | *audita Musarum sacerdos* | *uirginibus puerisque canto.* See intro. for Pindar's turning from god to singers.

33 Deliae . . . deae: Diana is introduced in the context of the *CS*, where her role is equal to that of her brother. The absence of her actual name indicates the non-performative nature of the poem, as compared to the *CS* – though not every god of that poem was addressed (cf. *CS* intro., 37–72).

tutela: cf. Cat. 34.1–2 *Dianae sumus in fide* | *puellae et pueri integri.* The young singers are the 'charge' of Diana, a sense of the word (normally 'guardian' or 'guardianship') first found in H. and at Prop. 4.8.3 (*Lanuuium annosi uetus est tutela draconis*), although it is found earlier (*OLD* s.v. *tutela* 4b) as the legal term for 'ward' or 'property of a ward'. Cf. also Ov. *Ib.* 595–6 (perhaps with ironic reference to H.) *tutela Dianae* | . . . *turba canum*, of the dogs that were held to have torn Euripides to death; also Festus 343.10 M *Dianae . . . cuius tutelae sint cerui.*

33–4 fugaces | lyncas et ceruos cohibentis arcu: as K–H note, from Callim. *Hymn* 3.16–17, of Artemis at rest, ὁππότε μηκέτι λύγκας | μήτ' ἐλάφους βάλλοιμι, 'when I no longer shoot at lynxes or stags'.

35–6 'keep the Aeolic metre and the follow the beat (*ictus*) of my thumb'. The first injunction refers to getting their quantities right, following the metrical system of the Sapphic stanza (metre of 6 and of the *CS*, for which the instructions apply); on the second it is somewhat harder to be sure, and opinions may vary according to one's view of Latin *ictus*. Allen 1973: 341–9, on 'ictus' (348–9 on these lines), points to the most likely meaning: the beat of the thumb would come for the Sapphic stanza on the long first, fourth, (short) sixth (occasionally eighth) and tenth syllables of each of the three hendecasyllables (Σ̱́ Σ̮ Σ̱ Σ̱́ Σ̱ : Σ̮́ Σ̮ Σ̱ Σ̮ Σ̱́ Σ), and on the long first and fourth syllables of the adonic (Σ̱́ Σ̮ Σ̮ Σ̱́ Σ). After H. introduced the requirement that the fourth syllable of the hendecasyllable be a long (rather than anceps, as in Greek and in Catullus) and that the fifth syllable be followed by a caesura, he created a regularly occurring 'stress-peak' on the fourth and sixth syllable, matching the regularly occurring stress-peaks on the first and tenth syllables of the hendecasyllable, and on the first and fourth syllables of the adonic. Fraenkel 403–4 rightly rejects the notion that the lines refer to H.'s actually conducting the choir.

ictum: cf. 7–9 n. on *icta*.

37–40 A summary of the *CS*, distributing a line each to Apollo and Luna, with the last two lines elaborating the latter's function as regulator of the calendar. Immediately there comes the bride of 41, following references to months, growing, a torch and fertility.

rite . . . | rite: cf. 1.21n. for the repetition and *CS* 13–14n. on *rite* in the *CS*.

Latonae puerum 'Leto's son'; cf. 1.21.3–4 *Latonamque supremo | dilectam penitus Ioui*; 3.28.11–12 *tu curua recines lyra | Latonam et celeris spicula Cynthiae*; Liv. Andron. *Od.* 19 Buecheler *filius Latonas*; at 1.31.18 Apollo is addressed as *Latoe*, the first occurrence of the form; cf. also Virg. *Aen.* 12.198 *Latonaeque genus duplex*. For *puer* = *filius*, a poeticism, see *OLD* s.v. *puer* 2.

crescentem face 'increasing in its torch', 'waxing'; *face* best seen as ablative of respect, some instances of which 'may be locative, others instrumental in origin' (Woodcock 38).

Noctilucam 'Night-lighter'; cf. Varro, *Ling.* 5.68 *Luna, quod sola lucet noctu. itaque ea dicta Noctiluca in Palatio: nam ibi noctu lucet templum. hanc ut Solem Apollinem quidam Dianam uocant*; Laev. 26.3 Courtney *alma Noctiluca*. At Varro, *Sat. Men.* 292 the word means 'lantern': *noctilucam tollo, ad focum fero, inflo, anima reuiuiscit.* It appears in Latin after H. only at Avienus *Ora Marit.* 429 (iambics), perhaps in part since it is metrically intractable for dactylic verse, unlike *noctiuagus*, which is found in Virgil and Statius (and in Seneca). *Noctiluca* does have the ring of an 'affectation of archaic phraseology', as Page put it, and may have been a marked term used in ceremonial contexts. Courtney *ad* Laev. 26.3 denies the form both antiquity and any cult associations, claiming it has none in H., which may overlook the context of the *ludi saeculares* (whose *Acta* however did not include the word). It is surely notable that Varro, long before the *ludi*, associates the name with the Palatine, site of the singing of the *CS*. See further Lindner 1996: 124.

39–40 prosperam frugum 'favouring crops'. *frugum* is either a genitive of respect or an objective genitive, assuming H. subscribed to the (wrong) popular etymology of *prosperus* found at Non. p. 171.23 (*'sperem' ueteres spem dixerunt, unde et prospere dicitur, hoc est pro spe*) and implied at Livy 6.32.6 (*ut nondum satis claram uictoriam, sic prosperae spei pugnam imber . . . diremit*). The difference in quantity is no impediment to a popular etymology, as noted most recently, with further references, by Adams 2007: 53, n. 61. But see de Vaan 2008: 493 for the unproblematic correct etymology (PIE *sph_1-ro- 'thriving').

celeremque pronos | uoluere menses 'swift in rolling out the headlong months'. The phrase well catches the rapid passing of time, with Diana, through her lunar cycles, seen as causing the months to go by. *uoluere* is an epexegetical infinitive dependent on *celerem*.

41–4 H. imagines one of the *puellae innuptae* who sang the *CS* reflecting in later years on her *res gestae* as a chorister. A good instance of relative temporal value of the Latin participle: *nupta* is in the future, and prior to *dices*, while *referente* is contemporaneous with the past *reddidi*, itself however being a future utterence of the future *nupta*. Appropriately the girl 'echoes' the text of the *CS* (see 41–3, 42nn.).

41 nupta iam dices: *nupta* doubles as noun ('as a married woman') and (future) perfect participle ('after you get married'). Cf. 10.6n.

41–3 dis amicum . . . carmen: cf. *CS* 70–2 (her memory of the words of the *CS*) *Diana . . . uotis puerorum amicas | applicat aures*, 7–8 *dis . . . dicere carmen.*

dis: frame with 1 *Diue*, with both picked up by the exact centrepiece at 22 *diuum pater.*

42 saeculo festas referente luces: cf. *CS* 21–2 *certus undenos decies per annos | orbis ut cantus referatque ludos.*

43 reddidi carmen: the verb implies reciprocity, naturally inherent in a hymn. Cat. 68.149–50 *hoc tibi, quod potui, confectum carmine munus | pro multis, Alli, redditur officiis.*

docilis modorum '(I) skilled in the measures (of the bard Horace)'. The genitive with *docilis* is first in H. (cf. *S.* 2.2.52 *praui docilis Romana iuuentus*), and not much attested after him; cf. *TLL* s.v. *docilis* 1768.48–51. Lee takes *docilis* as genitive with *Horati* ('a hymn . . . by that skilled metrician | the poet Horace'), which seems most unlikely, H.'s words at 35–6 (*Lesbium seruate pedem meique | pollicis ictum*) make the referent of *docilis* quite clear, though an amphibole is always possible. Cf. *CS* 75–6 *doctus . . . | dicere*, and Barchiesi 1996: 8–9 on the alignment with the *CS.*

44 uatis Horati: the possessive attaches to *carmen* as well as to *modorum*; see Bell 1923: 293–303 for such amphibole. On *uates*, cf. *uate me* at *Epod.* 16.66, also the final line of that poem, and *C.* 1.1.35, the penultimate line, *quodsi me lyricis uatibus* *inseres*. In the present context the poem that begins with a prayer to the god of prophecy ends by identifying H. as a prophet and bard. There is none of the ambivalence associated with pre-Augustan uses of the term, e.g. N–H on 1.1.35: 'In early Latin *uates* was given a bad name . . . The word was ennobled in the Augustan period to describe the poet in his inspired aspect.' See also Newman 1967: *passim*.

Horati: the poet's name serves as a *sphragis*. It appears only here in the *Odes*, and even then only through the voice of the *nupta*, referring to the historical composer of the *CS*; it is otherwise found at *Epist.* 1.14.5 (cf. *S.* 2.6.37 *Quintus*; *Epod.* 15.12; *S.* 2.1.18 *Flaccus*). H. will presumably have admired his name in a parallel setting at the very end of the *Acta*, right before the list of *XVuiri* in attendance: 149 *carmen composuit Q. Horatius Flaccus*; see *CS* intro. Here at the end of the song that records his earlier feat, he makes sure future ages will know the singer, knowing his verse was to be more perennial than monuments, which can also go missing, as did the *Acta*.

7

METRE

A dactylic hexameter (–⏔–⏔–⏔–⏔–⏔–×) followed by a hemiepes (–⏑⏑–⏑⏑×), an epodic metre, like that of 1.4 (see below), 1.7, 1.28. The hexameters all have a third-foot strong caesura. Final monosyllables at 11 and 23 contribute to the strong enjambment that follows (as at the end of 9, punctuation after *interitura* (10)). There is no spondaic line (spondee in fifth foot), and the ratio of dactyls to spondees through the first four feet is fairly balanced (27:29). No line begins with a double spondee, evidence perhaps for the maintenance of some dactylic integrity. The metre has a truncated elegiac feel to it (half a dactylic 'pentameter' in the second line), consistent with its content and also with the Simonidean intertexts (see below), and in all but two cases (10, 14) has end-stopped second lines. No ode of comparable length (3.9 is a special case) has such consistently end-stopped quatrains.

INTRODUCTION

The snows have fled, vegetation returns and the rivers go by less swollen as the Graces return to their naked dance. The passage of time warns against the hope of immortality. Each succeeding season erases what went before, and yet the cycle of seasons brings constant renewal. Not so for us, for we are destined to be dust and shadow. Who knows how much time we have left? Use for yourself what otherwise your heir will get his hands on. Once Minos passes judgement on you, Torquatus, family, eloquence, goodness will not bring you back. Diana could not bring back Hippolytus, nor Theseus Pirithous.

1.4 AND 4.7

Housman considered it 'the most perfect poem in the Latin language' – the basis for its opening words' becoming the leitmotif of Tom Stoppard's play *The Invention of Love*. For La Penna 1969: 77 it was 'la regina delle odi oraziane'. Many critics have inevitably been led to compare it to 1.4, whose diction, themes and movements are in a close intratextual relationship. Woodman 1972: 752 notes that 'scholars seem to take a particular delight in letting us know which is their favourite', then proceeds to do so himself, finding 1.4 superior because it is in his view more unified – not itself necessarily the only criterion for an ode of H., whatever Philodemus may or may not have thought (754, n. 3).

There can be little doubt that the two poems have a strong relationship to each other, but they have quite distinct dynamics and effects. Each poem begins with winter dissolving into spring and ends with reflection on the inevitability of death. But, simply on the level of diction, there is much in common:

1.4		4.7	
1	uice	3	uices
5	choros ducit	6	ducere . . . choros
6	iunctaeque Nymphis Gratiae	5	Gratia cum Nymphis
13	pauperum	15	diues
14	regum	15	Aeneas . . . Tullus . . . Ancus
15	uitae summa	17	hodiernae . . . summae
	spem	7	speres
16	nos	14	nos
17	quo simul mearis	21	cum semel occideris
17	quo	15	quo . . . quo

Whatever the relative merits, 4.7 is the more complex and intricate poem, particularly in the way it fails to sustain the sharp separation between reflection on spring and the seasons on the one hand and the inevitability of death on the other. H.'s intratextuality aids in precisely permitting this violation of unity and normative writing, since the reader knows what is coming anyway, once the traces of 1.4 are recognized. The poem opens (1–4) with a single thought, iterated by an accumulation of detail: the snows have gone, grass appears on the plains, foliage on the trees, the earth's appearance is changed and rivers flow less rapidly. No season is mentioned, but it is spring, late spring given the last detail. Elaboration comes through the most extensive intratext with 1.4: it is warm enough for the Graces and Nymphs to dance naked (5–6 in both poems). But where 1.4.7–8 stayed with the celebratory mood, things have changed in the corresponding lines of 4.7, which rather give strong intimations of mortality, with the indirect command after *monet* that speaks of the inevitability of death preceding the basis for those intimations (*immortalia ne speres monet annus* . . .). The elaboration of that basis (the remorseless cycling of the seasons) is only revealed in the course of the next quatrain (9–12), where each season is named (*uer* . . . *aestas* . . . *autumnus* . . . *bruma*), with winter framing the whole (9 *frigora* | 12 *bruma* . . . *iners*).

Far from constituting an 'absence of convincing cohesion' (Woodman 1972: 756–7), all this is part of the poem's play with our reading of it in its own right, as well as against our prior reading of 1.4 and other texts. In the next stanza (13–16) we encounter further disruptions of unity, as *tamen* functions almost as the poem's pivot, looking back to what precedes (and yet the seasons renew themselves) but also anticipating what follows (we, however, are dust and shadow). With the words *pius Aeneas*, Virgil is once again and inevitably brought into play. The quatrain at 17–20 delicately leads into the *carpe diem* theme, with a strong marker to the most prominent poem in that subgenre (2.14; see 19–20n.). This in turn leads to another (21–24), shifting the focus to the addressee, now Torquatus rather than us (see 7n.), as H. rewrites Catullus (see 21n.) to communicate the inevitability of that man's death, for all his breeding, eloquence and *pietas* – again alluding to Virgil. The poem ends with an epigram, invoking failed catabases of myth to prove the point. Diana could not save Hippolytus, nor could Theseus rescue Pirithous.

The connection with Simonides (mentioned in the lyric catalogue at 9.7, and alluded to at 6.9–12; see n.) has long been noted (Cataudella 1927–8, though at least one fragment was already noted by K–H), particularly *Eleg.* 19–20 West[2], already connected with H. on the basis of Stob. 4.34.28 before the appearance of *POxy.* 3965 fr. 26, which has at least four different lines before the start of fr. 20. The fragments are themselves also ostentatiously intertextual:

> ἓν δὲ τὸ κάλλιστον Χῖος ἔειπεν ἀνήρ·
> 'οἵη περ φύλλων γενεή, τοίη δὲ καὶ ἀνδρῶν'·
> παῦροί μιν θνητῶν οὔασι δεξάμενοι
> στέρνοις ἐγκατέθεντο· πάρεστι γὰρ ἐλπὶς ἑκάστωι
> ἀνδρῶν, ἥ τε νέων στήθεσιν ἐμφύεται.
>
> fr. 19.1–6 West

'and this was the best thing the man of Chios ever said "As the generation of leaves, so is that of men". Few mortals having heard it with their ears have deposited it within their breasts. For hope is present with each man, hope which grows in the hearts of the young' (tr. Campbell, *Eleg.* 8.1–6).

> θνητῶν δ' ὄφρά τις ἄνθος ἔχηι πολυήρατον ἥβης,
> κοῦφον ἔχων θυμὸν πόλλ' ἀτέλεστα νοεῖ·
> οὔτε γὰρ ἐλπίδ' ἔχει γηρασέμεν οὔτε θανεῖσθαι,
> οὐδ', ὑγιὴς ὅταν ἦι, φροντίδ' ἔχει καμάτου.
> νήπιοι, οἷς ταύτηι κεῖται νόος, οὐδὲ ἴσασιν
> ὡς χρόνος ἔσθ' ἥβης καὶ βιότου ὀλίγος
> θνητοῖς. ἀλλὰ σὺ ταῦτα μαθὼν βιότου ποτὶ τέρμα
> ψυχῆι τῶν ἀγαθῶν τλῆθι χαριζόμενος.
>
> fr. 20.5–12 West

'as long as a mortal has the lovely flower of youth, he ponders with light heart many impossibles; for he neither expects to grow old or die, nor when he is healthy does he worry about illness. Fools, to think like that and not realise that mortals' time for youth and life is brief: you must take note of this, and since you are near the end of your life endure, indulging yourself with good things' (tr. Campbell, *Eleg.* 8.6–13).

Oates 1932: 76–90 has a good discussion of the connections, while Barchiesi 1996: 33–7 sees the presence of Simonides not just in this poem, but generally in 6, 8 and 9, which he sees 7 as 'interrupting'. The multiplicity of intertexts makes it difficult to isolate a single source, and Barchiesi himself discusses the presence of Homer, Mimnermus, Theocritus and others (see 17–20n.). On the Latin side, Catullus 5 is prominent, in meaningful ways rather than, as Woodman 1972: 761 and n.2 puts it, having 'the appearance of being a careless series of borrowings'. Putnam 142 sees a reference to Cat. 46.1–3 *iam uer egelidos refert tepores* etc., but this seems more remote, since the single focus on spring in that poem creates a very different mood.

Traina 1997: 402–4 explores some of the Virgilian connections (see 15, 25–6nn.). Dyer 1965 sees ideological undercutting but ultimately, as an alternative to the problematic political world, private joy that comes through a focus on the theme of *carpe diem* (1n.). The third triad of the book opens with the arrival of spring, as H. moves away from the world of Drusus, Augustus and the *Carmen saeculare*, back into the personal and private lyric world.

1–4 Receding snow (*diffugere niues*) is accompanied by the return of vegetation (*redeunt . . . gramina*). Although they are part of the same process of seasonal change, the opening verbs (*diffugere* | *redeunt*) capture and anticipate the contrasting themes of the poem, nature's eternal return and the flight of human time. The stanza moves from the specific (snow, grass, foliage) to the encapsulating general (*mutat terra uices*), then back to the specific (rivers, banks), *terra* also forming a contrast with *flumina*. Woodman 1972: 756 found fault with this orchestration, as with the stanza in general, finding *mutat terra uices* to be a cliché. *uices (-em) mutare* is not found before H. (frequently enough after; cf. *TLL* s.v. *muto* 1727.75–81); nor does Woodman's citation of Hirzel's choice of *mutauere uices* (following the *TLL*) for the clearly correct *mutauere uias* at Virg. *G.* 1.418 change that fact. The very simplicity of the words, as of the syntax, of this stanza creates a series of vivid vignettes. Each couplet mirrors the other with the opening utterances metrically equivalent and rhyming, each then followed by a more complex enjambed clause, one dealing in chiastic, the other in enclosing word order – *simplex munditiis*, one could say.

Diffugere niues: the verb, used absolutely with subjects from the physical world, is a favourite of Lucr.: 1.761, 762 *fulmina*; 1103 *moenia mundi*; 2.457–8 *fumus, nebulae, flammae*; 3.121–2 *calor*; 6.231–2 *uina*; also of mental states (as in H. at 1.18.4 *diffugiunt sollicitudines*): Lucr. 3.16 *animi terrores*; 254–5 *animai* | . . . *partes*; see *TLL* s.v.

diffugio 1106.57–68. Dyer 1965 suggests a reference to the opening at 1.2.1–2 and its larger political context (see intro.): *Iam satis terris niuis atque dirae | grandinis misit Pater*. N–H in their intro. note to 1.4 point to the relationship between *C.* 1.4 and Lucr. 5.737–40, and it is clear Lucretian intertextuality continues here.

Diffugere . . . redeunt: the antithesis is only apparent with the two verbs referring to the same thing (the arrival of spring). Perhaps a reference to the less rhetorically loaded opening of 1.4 *soluitur . . . trahuntque* – both verbs also fronted in their clauses.

redeunt: the return of spring grass and leaves recalls other returns, that of Augustus at 2.43 and particularly at the beginning of 5 (cf. 5.3–4n.). Cf. also 12 *recurrit*, 13 *reparant* of nature but 23–4 *non . . . restituet* of Torquatus, and us.

gramina campis | arboribusque comae: chiasmus. Cf. 1.39–40 *per gramina Martii | Campi*; *AP* 162 *aprici gramine Campi*, distinct in that they both refer more specifically to the Campus Martius. Virgil has *gramineum in campum* at *Aen.* 5.287. For *comae*, see 3.10–11n.

mutat terra uices 'the earth goes through changes'; cf. 1.4.1 *grata uice ueris et Fauoni*; see 1–4n. H. avoids the regular term for 'change of seasons', *temporum uices*, which occurs exclusively in prose (and will not go into the hexameter). Apul. *Mun.* 29 *sol . . . IV temporum uices mutat* looks to those usages, rather than to H.

praetereunt: a pregnant usage, in the view of Porph.: the rivers *pass by* their banks and therefore do not overflow them.

5–8 A very different stanza, with the continuation of the springtime picture interrupted at mid-point by reflection on mortality, even before the fully cyclical nature of the year, the basis for such reflection, has been revealed (in 7–12).

5 Gratia cum Nymphis geminisque sororibus: Nymphs and the Graces seem to appear together only in H.; cf. 1.4.6–7 *iunctaeque Nymphis Gratiae decentes | alterno terram quatiunt pede*; 1.30.5–6 *feruidus tecum puer et solutis | Gratiae zonis properentque Nymphae*; 3.19.16–17 *Gratia | nudis iuncta sororibus*. The Graces, daughters of Eurynome, are named by Hesiod (*Theog.* 909 Ἀγλαΐην τε καὶ Εὐφροσύνην Θαλίην τ' ἐρατεινήν) but are not much individualized thereafter, in Latin notably in Seneca, quoting Hesiod (*Ben.* 1.3.6). Θαλία is not be confused (as she is in the *OLD*) with the metrically distinct Muse Θάλεια. H.'s *Gratia* here almost has the look of an individual's name, as it will come to be in its English translation.

6 ducere . . . choros: cf. 1.4.5 *iam Cytherea choros ducit.*

nuda: goes closely with *audet*: with the weather warming they now venture to dance naked. The epithet is also consistent with the iconography, as they are naked in Hellenistic and Roman art: *LIMC* III 2 s.v. *Charis, Charites, Gratiae* 1–139 (the Greek *Charites* are clothed, albeit lightly).

7 immortalia ne speres: indirect command, emphatic in position and abrupt in the transition it brings, but not surprising once the reader recognizes the parallel with 1.4 (e.g. 15 *uitae summa breuis spem nos uetat incohare longam*), on which see intro.

immortalia functions as an abstract noun.

ne speres monet 'warns you not to hope for'. The address seems to be to the reader, who would be the subject of *speres*, as of *dederis* (20) and even *occideris* (21), but at 23 (*Torquate*) the reader must change the identification, at least for *occideris*, while for *speres* and *dederis* the ambiguity lingers. The effect is similar, but on a larger scale, to that of 1.9.1 *Vides ut alta stet niue candidum . . . ?* 5–8 *dissolue . . . o Thaliarche*; likewise 4.9.1 *Ne forte credas . . .* 30–3 *non ego te . . . silebo . . . Lolli. C.* 3.24.1–8 is a special case, unique in the *Odes*, of an unidentified addressee: *licet occupes . . . non . . . expedies*; but in that poem the speaker's voice is throughout strongly didactic and moralizing, so that the didactic addressee is generically familiar. In no other ode is there any such ambiguity, rather the identification by name or otherwise (e.g. 3.8.5 *docte sermones utriusque linguae*, i.e. 13 *Maecenas*) is always made in the sentence in which the verb occurs. The effect in the present poem is clearly to universalize and to implicate the reader in the inevitability of death, one of the powerful themes of this poem. In 1.27.1–8 (*tollite . . . prohibete . . . impium | lenite clamorem, sodales*) the plural and the obviously sympotic setting prevent confusion as to the identity. In 2.5.1 the addressee is clearly an acquaintance of the speaker: *Nondum subacta ferre iugum.*

7–8 annus . . . | hora diem: the accumulation gives a strong sense of the passage of time. Bold phrasing, with the image of the day being seized off by its constituent elements (*hora*), and with *rapit* opposed to and cancelling *almum* (*alo*).

almum: used of day with particular reference to the *light* of day and its nourishing effects, for which cf. Virg. *Ecl.* 8.17 '*nascere praeque diem ueniens age, Lucifer, almum*'; *Aen.* 5.64–5 *si nona diem mortalibus almum | Aurora extulerit.* Cf. also *CS* 9–10 *alme Sol curru nitido diem qui | promis*; 4.39–41 *pulcher fugatis | ille dies Latio tenebris | qui primus alma risit adorea.*

rapit: common in contexts of mortality and in epitaphs, where death typically 'snatches off' (see 2.21n.), but here more strikingly of the personified hour's snatching away the day, a unique expression.

9–12 See intro. on the shape of the stanza, which is both an expansion and a contraction of the opening four lines; its first three words go back to the return of spring, but now as a prelude to tracking with exquisite concision the entire cycle of the seasons. The balance of the first line iconically suggests continuity from winter through spring to summer, while *simul* and *et mox* establish parallel movements from summer to autumn then from autumn to winter respectively. The whole movement is perhaps imitated at *Laus Pisonis* 149–51 *cessat hiems, madidos et siccat uere capillos; | uer fugit aestates; aestatum terga lacessit | pomifer autumnus, niuibus cessurus et undis.*

9 A very mannered line, consisting of two autonomous parts (NVN, NVN) which at the same time interact with each other: the line is framed by the antonyms, winter's cold (*frigora*) and summer (*aestas*), while it is centred around and encloses quasi-synonyms, spring and its breezes (*Zephyris/uer*).

frigora 'the cold (conditions of winter)'; winter itself will appear at the end of the cycle (12), so framing the entire stanza.

mitescunt: originally 'become soft, juicy (and therefore "ripe", of fruits)'; whence 'soften, become mild'. Of natural forces first here and at Livy 23.19.1 *mitescente iam hieme*; see *TLL* s.v. *mitesco* 1146.14–27.

Zephyris: causal ablative. Cf. 12.1–2n.

proterit 'tramples down, treads underfoot'; a striking figurative use, picked up by *recurrit*, and variation of the equally striking metaphor at 1.4.13 *pallida Mors aequo pulsat pede* etc.

10 interitura: emphatic in placement at line-beginning and colon-end, in implied contrast to *proterit*: 'it too bound to die'. Although used of incorporeal things from Plautus on (*beneficium*, *oratio*, *salus* etc.; see *TLL* s.v. *intereo* 2187.31–56), first here of a season, which seems a more vivid use; cf. Sall. *Iug.* 106.3 *morbo interiturae uitae*.

11 pomifer: the word is not found before H., who twice uses it in a transferred sense, here modifying autumn, and similarly at 3.23.8 *pomifero . . . anno* ('when the year is in its apple-bearing phase'). Except for Prop. 4.7.81 (*ramosis Anio qua pomifer incubat aruis*) it is otherwise found only in its conventional application, of trees. Eur. *Herc.* 396 has μηλοφόρος of leaves of the fruit-bearing tree.

effuderit: like *pomifer*, the verb is found first in H. in a transferred sense. As is clear from *TLL* s.v. *effundo* 222.42–53, the usage is an extension of the language of parturition (*OLD* s.v. 10 'of female animals, only contemptuously of women') but normally it is the earth, or even a plant (*OLD* 10 b), that is the subject, rather than, as here, a season. H.'s passage is parallel in shared *iunctura* (*effundere fructus*) but distinct in view of the difference in subjects from the other instances at *TLL* s.v. *effundo* 218.3, such as Cic. *Leg. agr.* 2.89 *effusis et dissipatis fructibus*.

12 bruma: original superlative of *breuis*: 'the shortest day, winter solstice, mid-winter' (de Vaan 2008: s.v. *breuis*, with bibliography of varying explanations of how the superlative may have come to be); cf. Varro *Ling.* 6.8 *dicta bruma quod breuissimus tunc dies est*.

recurrit: cf. *Epist.* 2.1.147 *libertasque recurrentes accepta per annos*.

iners 'inactive, idle', since nothing gets done in winter; grouped with *S.* 2.6.61 *somno et inertibus horis* at *TLL* s.v. *iners* 1310.84–1311.12: for 2.9.4–6 *nec . . . stat glacies iners | menses per omnes*, referring more to the material than the temporal aspect of winter ice, see *TLL* 1311.45–7.

13–14 'And yet (even if summer dies and winter comes running back: 9–12) the lunar cycles swiftly renew heaven's losses (so spring and summer will return): but as for us . . .' Peerlkamp emended *tamen* to *etiam*, since he saw no contrast between 9–12 on the one hand and 13 on the other – both seeming to deal with the cycle of the seasons. But this is clearly mistaken, and Woodman 1972: 759–60 rightly notes that *damna . . . reparant* refers to the recovery of summer, which is then contrasted with the unrecoverability of *human* seasons; for *tamen* thus anticipating a following adversative, cf. *OLD* s.v. 4.

damna . . . caelestia: i.e. the losses that accompany the cycling of the seasons, as observable from the sky. *caelestia* sets up a contrast with *decidimus*. It is tempting to see the *damna* as exclusively the waning of the moon (as at *TLL* s.v. *damnum* 27.5–7; *OLD* s.v. 2b – significantly neither includes H., which would be the first attestation), but the sense of seasonal, rather than simply monthly, change suggests a broader set of celestial renewals, particularly of the loss associated with winter and the renewal that comes with spring and summer.

14 nos ubi: the fronting of *nos*, through postposition of *ubi*, lends emphasis, and contrast with what preceded. Cf. the allusion to Catullus 5.4–6 (intro. and 21–2n.): *soles occidere et redire possunt: | nobis, cum semel occidit breuis lux, | nox est perpetua una dormienda.* In Cat. *nobis* naturally refers to the poet and Lesbia (1–3 *uiuamus, mea Lesbia, . . . amemus . . . aestimemus*), while in H. it refers to the poet, the reader and the as yet unencountered Torquatus (see intro. and 7n.).

decidimus: like leaves from a tree (11–12), anticipating the more emphatic compound at 21 *occideris.*

15 pius Aeneas: the epithet points unavoidably to the *Aeneid*: 'when we go down to where pious Aeneas went' brings to mind the catabasis of *Aen.* 6 (see also 25–6n.), motivated as it was by the *pietas* of Aeneas towards his father; cf. 24 *pietas*, immediately before unsuccessful attempts to recue from the Underworld. But when we get to wealthy Tullus and Ancus, Aeneas becomes, like them, just a figure of history, a mortal of the past, who also went down in death, his *pietas* no more effective at evading the inevitability of death than was Tullus' wealth. The line is a pointed questioning of the myth of Julian and Augustan divinity, an effective refutation of Jupiter's promise to Venus at Virg. *Aen.* 1.259–60 *sublimemque feres ad sidera caeli | magnanimum Aenean.* Some editors prefer the reading *pater*, which works less well with *diues* (concessive, like *pius*).

Tullus et Ancus: the third and fourth kings of Rome, Tullus Hostilius and Ancus Martius, also together before they emerge from the lower to the upper world at Virg. *Aen.* 6.812–16 *cui deinde subibit | otia qui rumpet patriae residesque mouebit | Tullus in arma uiros et iam desueta triumphis | agmina. quem iuxta sequitur iactantior Ancus | nunc quoque iam nimium gaudens popularibus auris.*

diues: Tullus Hostilius was held to be from old money: Dion. Hal. 3.1 (of his grandfather, an Alban in the service of Romulus) ἀνὴρ εὐγενὴς καὶ χρήμασι δυνατὸς Ὀστίλιος ὄνομα ('a noble and wealthy man called Hostilius'). The adjective also looks to 1.4.13–14 *pauperum tabernas | regumque turres*, where the point is made more explicitly: death comes to the taverns of the poor and the castles of kings, with *regum* now specified – and politicized: Aeneas, Tullus and Ancus.

16 puluis et umbra: Page notes Soph. *El.* 1158–9 (Electra thinks Orestes is dead) ἀντὶ φιλτάτης | μορφῆς σποδόν τε καὶ σκιὰν ἀνωφελῆ 'instead of your dearest shape dust and useless shade'. These seem to be the only two instances of the expression in Greek and Latin literature and are something of an oddity in combining upper- (*puluis*) and underworld (*umbra*) concepts.

17–20 The brevity and uncertainty of life and the inevitability of death encourage spending one's wealth. For uncertainty about the morrow, cf. 1.9.13 *quid sit futurum cras fuge quaerere.* Oates 1932: 78 points to Simonides, fr. 32.1–2

Bergk (Campbell fr. 521.1–2), from the lament for the Scopadae, ἄνθρωπος ἐὼν μή ποτε φάσηις ὅ τι γίνεται αὔριον, | μηδ' ἄνδρα ἰδὼν ὄλβιον ὅσσον χρόνον ἔσσεται, 'since you are man, never say what will happen tomorrow, nor when you see a wealthy man how long he will be that way'. H. frequently expresses indignation at the prospect of an (unworthy) heir's enjoyment of his bequest; cf. 2.3.19–20 *exstructis in altum | diuitiis potietur heres*; 2.14.25–8 *absumet heres Caecuba dignior | seruata centum clauibus et mero | tinget pauimentum superbo, | pontificum potiore cenis*; 3.24.61–2 *indignoque pecuniam | heredi properet*; *S.* 2.3.122–3 *filius aut etiam haec libertus ut ebibat heres, | dis inimice senex custodis?*; *Epist.* 1.5.13–14 (also addressed to Torquatus; see 23–4n.) *parcus ob heredis curam nimiumque seuerus | assidet insano*.

Shackleton Bailey notes of the lines: 'a nonnullis sine causa suspecti'. The wording *quis scit an* otherwise occurs only at Ov. *Her.* 10.85 (*quis scit an et fuluos tellus alat ista leones*), from a couplet athetized by Bentley. Woodman 1972: 766 is strongly hostile to the stanza, which seems perfectly in the manner of H.

hodiernae crastina: an effective juxtaposition.

adiciant: although in colloquial Latin and in prose the present subjunctive may be used in place of the future in indirect questions, it is preferable particularly where there is some marker of future time, as here with *crastina* (cf. K–S II 2.180–1; Woodcock 136–7), to take this as a real present: 'who knows whether they are (now) adding tomorrow's time to today's tally?' H. may also be imitating the present tense of Simon. fr. 32 Bergk (above) ὅ τι γίνεται αὔριον 'what will happen tomorrow'. Cf. the future at 1.9.13 (above) *futurum sit*.

di superi: normally in the company of *di manes* or *inferi*: cf. *Epist.* 2.1.138 *carmine di superi placantur, carmine Manes*. The latter will come in the first couplet of the next stanza (21 *Minos*).

manus auidas: for instances after H. (depending on the dating of Livy 5.20.6 *auidas in direptiones manus*), see *TLL* s.v. *auidus* 1427.25–34. In the only instance before H., the 'greedy hands' are those of Death: Tib. 1.3.4–5 *abstineas auidas, Mors, modo, nigra, manus. | abstineas, Mors atra, precor*. By transferring the hands to the heir who will profit from the death, H. seems to allude to, and transform, Tibullus. If so, he is therefore hardly to be accused of resorting to 'weak verbal cliché' (Woodman 1972: 766).

amico | quae dederis animo: as K–H noted, the wording is close both to Simon. 20.11–12 West[2] (see intro.), and Theoc. 16.24: ἀλλὰ τὸ μὲν ψυχᾶι, τὸ δέ πού τινι δοῦναι ἀοιδῶν, 'to be generous to oneself, then perhaps to one of the poets'. *amico* = Gk. φιλῶι, i.e. *tuo*.

21–2 cum semel occideris: cf. Cat. 5.5 *cum semel occidit breuis lux* (see intro.; 14n.), also 1.4.17 *quo simul mearis*; on *occido* ('die') see 4.70–2n.

splendida . . . arbitria: the adjective is paralleled by none of the examples given in *OLD* s.v. *splendidus* 3 ('(transf., often as a general compliment) Of shining quality, splendid, brilliant'), since we want to know why the *arbitria* are *splendida* – as we would want to know why they were *bona*, had they been so designated (as opposed to *uera*, say). It does not help to cite, as K–H do, Caesar, *B. Gall.*

1.41.2 *legio . . . ei gratias fecit, quod de se optimum iudicium fecisset,* where the context explains *optimum*. The obscurity of Page ('"stately," in reference to the "state" in which the judge sits') cannot simply be ascribed to his Victorian language. De Rosaria 1997: 433 gives the reasoning of Porph. (because Minos is 'splendid' so are his judgments) and La Penna (the judgments illuminate Torquatus and hence are splendid). Minos gives out judgments to the dead at Hom. *Od.* 11.568–71 (θεμιστεύοντα νέκυσσιν . . . δίκας), and it is possible that *splendida* is transferred from the Homeric adjective that describes Minos himself: 568 Διὸς ἀγλαὸν υἱόν, 'the splendid son of Zeus'. Torquatus will have to follow the ultimate judgment passed by Minos, however good his way with words (23 *facundia*).

23–4 non, Torquate, genus, non te facundia, non te | restituet pietas: Fraenkel 420–1 well compares 1.4.18–19 [*quo simul mearis,*] | *nec regna uini sortiere talis* | *nec tenerum Lycidan mirabere*: 'One could hardly find a more significant illustration of the wide difference between the Greek παίζειν with its elaborate regulations for the συμπόσιον and its devotion to παιδικὸς ἔρως on the one hand and on the other the full *grauitas* of the *res Romana* as embodied in the traditions of the nobility.' While this is true, it is also the case that the *grauitas* in question is undermined by the death that will cancel out its attributes. The asyndeton and anaphora of *non* (and *non te*), for which see Wills 367, give a particularly emphatic ring to the couplet.

genus: i.e. the *gens Manlia* (cf. below).

pietas: cf. 15n.

Torquate: clearly the same Manlius Torquatus as in *Epist.* 1.5 (*PIR*² M162; his praenomen is nowhere recorded), since in each case we are dealing with a) orators (the likely implication of *facundia*, and cf. *Epist.* 1.5.8–9 *mitte . . . Moschi causam*), b) the theme of *carpe diem* and c) the specific injunction to consume in preference to leaving an inheritance (17–20n.). The name also resonates with that of Manlius Torquatus the executioner of his disobedient son (Livy 8.7.19) and occupant of the Virgilian Underworld (*Aen.* 6.825). The Manlii Torquati were generally anti-Caesarian, which may inform the presence of T. here (n. below). On the basis of Plin. *Epist.* 5.3.5, in a catalogue of writers of verse (*Torquatum, immo Torquatos*) Syme 1986: 395–6 suggests T. may have been a poet, but *facundia* and *causam*, the latter exclusively, point more to oratory; he could have been both orator and poet. Munzi 1998: 426–7 has argued that T. Manlius Sura Septicianus, who was honoured on a recently discovered Cypriot inscription of early imperial date, was probably a son of Septicius, the mutual friend of H. and Manlius Torquatus, adopted by the latter, whose praenomen would have been Titus. John D. Morgan will argue that this Torquatus is the now elderly quaestor of Pansa in 43 BCE, for the implications of which see 8.1–4n. Judging from the specificity, it may be assumed Porph. had access to the speech mentioned in *Epist.* 1.5.8–9 (*ad loc.*): *Moschus hic Pergamenus fuit rhetor notissimus. reus ueneficii fuit, cuius causam ex primi<s> tunc oratores egerunt, Torquatus hic, de quo nunc dicit, cuius exstat oratio, et Asinius Pollio*; cf. Mastrocinque 1996b: 921–2. Obviously distinct from the L. Manlius Torquatus (who died in 46 BCE, soon after Thapsus; cf. Cic. *Brut.* 265), son of the consul of 65 BCE, the year of H.'s birth: 3.21.1 (*o nata mecum consule Manlio*) and *Epod.* 13.6 (*tu uina Torquato moue consule pressa meo*); for whom see Mastrocinque 1996a: 789.

non . . . restituet: in view of the republicanism of the recent Manlii Torquati, and the fact that their last consulate was in 65 BCE (see Syme 1986: 395–6: 'Thus ended the Manlii.'), there may be a political meaning lurking here (*OLD* s.v. *restituo* 6). Cf. Marcus Lepidus' reinstatement of Sextus Pompey at Cic. *Phil.* 5.39 *Sex. Pompeium restituit ciuitati*; or H. of another 'Pompeius', who was reinstated years after Philippi: 2.7.3 *quis te redonauit Quiritem.*

25–8 The poem ends with a pair of mythological exempla whose doubling drives home the point: if those favoured by gods and heroes cannot be brought back, there can be little hope for Torquatus, or for the rest of us. The two couplets mirror each other, with *pudicum . . . Hippolytum* and *caro . . . Pirithoo* in the same position; likewise the opposites, *liberat* and *uincula* (cf. *uincio*). The syntax is inverted: *Hippolytum* and *uincula* are direct objects. The pairing is underscored by the fact that Hippolytus and Pirithous are both connected to Theseus, who is father of the former, comrade of the latter. Traina 1997: 402–4 has a good treatment of the lines.

25–6 infernis . . . tenebris: ablative of separation. For the noun-adjective combination, cf. Virg. *Aen.* 7.325 (of the summoning up of Allecto) *infernisque ciet tenebris.*

tenebris Diana . . . | liberat: possibly an etymological play on the name; cf. Cic. *Nat. D.* 2.69 *Diana dicta quia noctu quasi diem efficeret*; cf. *CS* 1–4n; 6.37–40n.

Diana . . . Hippolytum: Euripides' *Hippolytus* is the most extensive surviving witness for the Athenian versions of the story of Hippolytus, whose preference for Artemis, and neglect of Aphrodite (and of his stepmother Phaedra), led to his destruction at the hands of Poseidon – by bulls sent from the sea, with input from Hippolytus' father Theseus, varying according to the source. The author of the *Naupactica*, (? sixth century BCE), has Asclepius restoring Hippolytus to life (for which Zeus strikes him with a thunderbolt), and Philodemus (*Piet.* 52) says Asclepius acted 'at the request of Artemis'. For this see Barrett *ad Hipp.* 7–8. The dead Hippolytus is mainly connected with the cult of Aphrodite in Greece, but in Italy Diana assumes a greater role, one that seems to have been treated by Callimachus (fr. 190 Pf. and Pfeiffer *ad loc.*). Of chief importance for the present context is Virgil's version, which H. contradicts and 'corrects': at *Aen.* 7. 761–82, in the catalogue of Italian heroes, we find Virbius (*uir bis*), son of the restored Hippolytus (also renamed Virbius) and the nymph Aricia, settled at the precinct in the grove of Diana Nemorensis. H.'s *neque . . . liberat*, then, responds to Virg. *Aen.* 7.767–9 *ad sidera rursus | aetheria et superas caeli uenisse sub auras | Paeoniis reuocatum herbis et amore Dianae.* Porph. noted the apparent contradiction, but made a different suggestion (*ad loc.*): *sed nunc non ad illud refert, quod post distractionem illam, quam ab equis suis passus est, in uitam restitutus fertur, sed ad condicionem mortalitatis, quam non potuit perpetuo effugere per Dianae fauorem.*

pudicum: i.e. he resisted Aphrodite's and Phaedra's power. Particularly juxtaposed to *Diana*, the adjective has a concessive sense: 'although he was chaste (and therefore her favourite)', Diana could not rescue him. Since in the Virgilian version Hippolytus/Virbius had a union with Aricia, H.'s use of *pudicum* is another instance of 'correction' of Virgil (see 15n.). Servius *ad Aen.* 7.761 was troubled by the son's existence: *adeo omnia ista fabulosa sunt. nam cum castus ubique inductus sit et qui semper solus habitauerit, habuisse tamen fingitur filium.*

enim: explanatory of 21–4.

liberat Hippolytum: the verb perhaps glosses the name Hippo-lytos, 'loosened' (λύω) by his 'horses' (ἵππος). Cf. Virg. *Aen.* 7.767, where the pulled-apart word order creates an iconic effect, *turbatis distractus equis*; see O'Hara 1996, Horsfall *ad loc.*

27–8 Lethaea . . . | uincula: see Löfstedt I 109–24 on the formation and use of such adjectives in place of genitive nouns.

abrumpere . . . | uincula: at Enn. *Ann.* sed. inc. fr. 535 Skutsch (*uincla . . . abrumpit*) in a Homeric simile translating *Il.* 6.507 = 15.264, of a horse breaking its bonds, δεσμὸν ἀπορρήξας, whence Virg. *Aen.* 11.492 in the same context, *abruptis . . . uinclis*; also 9.118 *abrumpit uincula*, then sparingly in Livy, Lucan, the younger Seneca and Silius.

Pirithoo: the Lapith was a friend of Theseus, who helped him in the fight with the Centaurs and in the attempt to make off with Persephone. P. was unable to escape the Underworld in this latter exploit, to which H. here alludes. In the rationalizing account at Plut. *Thes.* 31.4, the object of the quest (which follows Theseus' kidnapping of the young Helen for himself) is Cora the daughter of Aïdoneus, king of the Molossians, and his wife Persephone, and Pirithous is killed by Cerberus, the family dog. Putnam 141 refers to the 'implicitly homosexual liaison of Theseus and Pirithous', though *caro* (27) need not imply that. Theseus failed to get Pirithous back while the latter was making a sexually motivated attempt on Persephone, for which he is punished at 3.4.79–80 (also closing the poem) *amatorem trecentae | Pirithoum cohibent catenae* – where *amatorem* refers to heterosexual transgression. Cf. Traina 1997: 402–4.

8

METRE

Lesser Asclepiadean (– – – ⏑ ⏑ – – ⏑ ⏑ – ⏑ ×), otherwise in H. only at 1.1, 3.30 – the framing poems of *C.* 1–3, as here in the central one of *C.* 4.

INTRODUCTION

I would give my companions precious art, Censorinus, if I were rich in art. But you don't need such things, rather it is song you delight in, and that we can give. Those who defeated Hannibal are not remembered through inscriptions, but rather through the poetry of Ennius. Without song

Romulus himself would be unknown today. Great poetry put Aeacus in the Isles of the Blest. For the Muse rewards with heaven, as is shown by Hercules, the Tyndaridae and Bacchus.

Harrison 1990: 35 has among recent scholars written on the Pindaric nature of this opening and of the poem in general: 'Pindar is a constant presence in the poem, more constant than scholars have thought; 4.8 is not only a covert epinician ode for Censorinus [father or son, see 1–4n.] but also makes much of the central Pindaric topic of the fame conferred on great men by poetry.' Similarly Highbarger 1935: 245 notes: 'in the eighth and ninth odes of this book Horace is strongly under the influence of Pindar's thought and style' – though 'under the influence of' is hardly the right way of putting it. Pasquali 756 quotes Pind. *Isthm.* 1.13, compares Pindar's opposing himself to the sculptor (757), points to the very Pindaric zeugma at 13–20 (758) and notes the presence of *Inuidia* (cf. *Nem.* 4.6, *Isthm.* 1.43, 5.24) and the use of Aeacus as a model of virtue, as at *Isthm.* 5.36, *Ol.* 8.31, *Isthm.* 8.23 (758–9).

But this is a curious poem, an intensely Pindaric ode that nevertheless omits a basic ingredient of Pindaric epinician, actual praise of the *laudandus*. While it often takes Pindar some time to get around to delivering the praise, he generally does so. H., on the other hand, in the first two stanzas creates an expectation of praise only to retreat further and further from the addressee to the point that the second-person verbs later in the poem are not even directed at Censorinus, who functions as a foil (20–22, 28–9nn.) for the failure to deliver. What replaces him is song, but song detached from the man who looked as if he was to receive that song, with his name hidden beneath glosses on *census* (1–4n.). This move will be repeated in the following poem (cf. 9.45n.), where encomium will become problematic in different ways (see 9 intro.). H. again engages in deflection and qualification, in short he gives a demonstration of the power of poetry to take away the praise it is supposed to bestow. Hayden Pelliccia *per litteras* notes a similarly curious strategy in Ibycus 1, fr. 282 (a) *PMG* (S 151), the Polycrates Ode. The beginning of the poem is missing, but for 45 lines Ibycus gives an anti-Homeric *recusatio* of the Trojan War themes he will not sing, including treatment of the handsome youths Cyanippus, Zeuxippus and Troilus, with Polycrates added as a coda: τοῖς μὲν πέδα κάλλεος αἰέν | καὶ σύ, Πολύκρατες, κλέος ἄφθιτον ἑξεῖς | ὡς κατ ἀοιδὰν καὶ ἐμὸν κλέος 'These have a share in beauty always: you too, Polycrates, will have undying fame as song and my fame can give it' (tr. Campbell). But at least Polycrates does receive his praise, abbreviated as it is, while Censorinus gets nothing that could go by that name.

Kovacs 2009 has argued for a lacuna, in which the actual praise would have appeared, before the final couplet, a proposition that would cut the knot and normalize what may rather always have been a strange encomium. He elicits support from the fact that the MSS are unanimous in giving us a 34-line poem, which therefore offends against Meineke's Law. August Meineke in his 1834 edition divided the poems up into quatrains, so applying to his edition his observation that, with the exception of 4.8, all of the *Odes*, stichic and strophic poems alike, consist of a total of lines divisible by four. Those who have otherwise attempted to remove this anomaly have resorted to one of two procedures: remove six lines or remove two. The task of removing two lines is a relatively straightforward one. Line 17 (see n.) is seen as doubly offensive; and line 33, while not as offensive, has been faulted on two counts (see n.). This is the recourse of K–H, Pasquali, Büchner, Klingner, Dornseiff, Bohnenkamp, Borszák and Rudd; see Harrison 1990: 32 for bibliography.

Another group take out a total of six lines (Lachmann, Jachmann, Becker, Syndikus, Shackleton Bailey), removing 15b–19a (*non celeres . . . rediit*). They also take out 33 and are compelled to find a sixth line, namely 28, which is held to mar the thought of the poem at that point (see 28–9n.). The motivation here becomes more subjective, but there is one philological argument, initially persuasive but not water-tight (see 18n.), and one interpretive argument, which Harrison 1990 has countered well (see 13–20n.). Furthermore, removal of 15b–19a should be resisted on two grounds: 1) the resultingly simpler poem is less intensely Pindaric, thus losing much of its point; 2) *Calabrae Pierides* becomes very problematic (see 20n.).

If Meineke's Law is to be ignored, its violation might be explained as a deliberate defect, along with other signs of archaism, assimilation to Ennian topics, failure to provide actual praise and the like; see nn. on 5–8 (on *artium*), 13–20 (on affinities to republican inscriptions), 17 (lack of caesura), 18 (on *eius*), 20–22 (on the conditional), 22–24 (Ennian diction), 33 (repetition of 3.25.20). There is much to link the poem with the ode to Lollius that follows, not least the fact that both artfully fail as encomia (see also 20–2, 25–7n). Quinn 313 notes 'even more than 4.9, it reads like an epistle (the metre slightly altered); much of it, indeed, reads like prose – limpid, logical, but pedestrian'. To the extent it is about the inscribing of names and deeds on stone memorials, its plodding nature may be part of its art.

This is the central poem of the book, self-consciously so, as it shares its metre only with the opening and closing poems of the earlier lyric collection (1.1, 3.30). It can thus function via its relationship to those two poems as proem and epilogue in the middle, ending with the same word that closed the *Epode* book, *exitus*. If the poem is to be printed with all 34 lines, emphatically stichic and with the 'defects' acknowledged as intentional, this central poem – the only central ode H. ever wrote – is the metapoem of the book, communicating the precarious marriage of lyric and propaganda.

1–8 A present counterfactual conditional (with 5 *diuite me* = *si diues essem*) serves as priamel and *recusatio* at the same time. The 'foil' consists of the epinician *praemia Graiorum* (*pateras . . . aera . . . tripodas*) that will not be forthcoming; the 'climax' will be the song of 11 (*carminibus; carmina*); see Race 1982: ix for the terms. The conditional is more Horatian, and part of the *recusatio*, and this type is less common in Pindar, for whom Gildersleeve 1882: 445 records only four counterfactual, or 'unreal' conditionals (*Ol.* 12.16; *Pyth.* 3.73; *Nem.* 4.13; 7.24), none of them similar to H.'s opening.

1–4 Donarem pateras . . . donarem tripodas: cf. Pind. *Isthm.* 1.19–20 (each similarly at line beginning) καὶ τριπόδεσσι . . . καὶ λεβήτεσσι 'both tripods and cauldrons'. Cf. 5.33–4 on *patera*; for the anaphora, 1.21n.

grataque commodus: catches the reciprocity of epinician, even though the counterfactual in reality sets up a *recusatio*: he would give them gladly and they would be welcome. The reciprocity and the language of financial exchange, perhaps keyed by the addressee's name (Censorinus/*census*), will continue throughout, even after C. himself has ceased to be addressed: 1, 3 *donarem*, *praemia*, 4 *munerum*, 5 *diuite*, 12 *donare et pretium dicere muneri*, 19 *lucratus*, 21 *bene feceris*, 22 *mercedem tuleris*, 24 *meritis*, 26 *uirtus et fauor et lingua potentium*, 27 *diuitibus*, 28 *dignum*, 29 *beat*, 30 *optatis*.

grataque . . . aera: bronze works of art, vases, statues etc., an indication of value; cf. *S.* 1.4.28 *stupet Albius aere*; *Epist.* 1.6.17–18 *aeraque et artis* | *suspice*. The separation of noun and epithet is quite pronounced, one of the poem's many Pindaricisms; cf. intro., 13n.

Censorine: on the question of whether this is L. Marcius Censorinus (cos. 39 BCE; *PIR*² M223) or his son, C. Marcius Censorinus (cos. 8 BCE; *PIR*² M222), Harrison 1990: 32–34 argued for the latter, with assistance available since Bowersock 1964, which, however, is in part refuted by Eilers 2004. The inscription adduced by Bowersock shows that a certain Gaius Censorinus was a *legatus Caesaris* (*AE* 1906.1 πρεσβευτὴν Καίσαρος = D. H. French, *The inscriptions of Sinope*, Bonn 2004: no. 98) at some unknown date in the area of Sinope, perhaps soon after a rebellion in the Cimmerian Bosporus, opposite Sinope on the Euxine. The rebellion was put down by Agrippa and was not insignificant according to Dio 54.24.6. Eilers, however, has suggested that this honorand was an otherwise unattested legate of the elder Caesar, who defeated Pharnaces at nearby Zela in 47 BCE. Whatever the identity of this C. Censorinus, and whenever he was honored at Sinope, John D. Morgan in a forthcoming publication (anticipated by Syme, *Anatolica* 1995: 302–7) will argue convincingly that Gaius was only *quaestorius* at the time of his legateship, and so will not have 'done deeds of such magnitude as to be celebrated in panegyric verse' (Putnam 155). Morgan may be right in finding that the elder Censorinus is therefore the likely addressee. But H. does not actually get around to celebrating much in the way of *res gestae* (see intro, 20–2, 28–9nn.), and the connection between praise and actual achievement in *C.* 4 is at times tenuous (for Drusus, Tiberius and Lollius, at any rate). As Harrison and others have noted, the younger Censorinus would be more appropriate in view of the other youthful addressees of the book: Tiberius (cos. 13 BCE), Fabius Maximus (cos. 11 BCE), Iullus Antonius (cos. 10 BCE) and Drusus (cos. 9 BCE). Other than Augustus himself, the only certainly consular addressee of the book is Lollius, whose consulship (21 BCE) puts him in age between the two Censorini. And Lollius is a special case (see 9 intro.). On the other hand, if, as Morgan argues, the Torquatus of 4.7 is an elderly man, perhaps Pansa's quaestor in 43 BCE (see 7.23–4n.), then it might be that the central triad of the book (7–9) concerns itself with older addressees.

The question is ultimately unresolved, and likely to remain so, and that may be the point, as Lizzie Mitchell will point out in a forthcoming study of *C.* 4.8. A poem that seems to have the same Scipio fighting Hannibal and destroying Carthage (16–17, with 16n.) also permits its addressee to be taken as father or son. H. may be displaying his unsuitability for this sort of thing. Virgil did the same at *Aen.* 1.286–8 *Caesar* . . . *Iulius* (whom most, but not all, take = Augustus).

praemia fortium | Graiorum: the reference is to epic as well as epinician: cf. Hom. *Il.* 23.259 νηῶν δ' ἔκφερ' ἄεθλα, λέβητάς τε τρίποδάς τε κτλ., 'and from the ships he carried out prizes, cauldrons and tripods . . .'; and see Richardson *ad loc.*, West *ad* Hes. *Op.* 657.

Graiorum: H. uses *Graius* in the *Odes* here and at 2.4.12 as substantive, while outside the *Odes Graecus* and *Graius* are used without distinction, as are adjectival forms throughout H. Virgil never uses *Graecus* (noun or adjective) and has 29 instances of *Graius*. See Austin *ad* Virg. *Aen.* 2.148.

neque tu pessima: litotes, another particularly Pindaric phenomenon: Race 1990: 78: 'instead of the positive statement "X is the greatest", Pindar resorts to the formula "no one is better than X"'. *neque tu* is a favoured combination for H.: 1.9.16; *S.* 2.3.132; *Epist.* 1.18.37; frequent in comedy, it is otherwise absent from republican and Augustan poetry until Ovid.

munerum: partitive genitive.

5–8 diuite me scilicet artium | quas 'if I were well-endowed, I mean in the skills which . . .'; ablative absolute as protasis. For the sense of *scilicet*, which adds specification to *diuite* (*me*), cf. *OLD* s.v. *scilicet* 5.

artium: a type of partitive genitive with adjectives or verbs indicating abundance (*plenus, compleo* etc.) or lack of abundance (*inops, indigeo* etc.), as at *S.* 1.2.74 *diues opis natura suae*. First in Virg. *Ecl.* 2.20 *diues pecoris* . . . *lactis abundans*; *G.* 2.468 *diues opum uariarum* etc.: see *TLL* s.v. *diues* 1589.63–79. H., and later Latin generally, prefer the instrumental ablative with such adjectives: *Epod.* 15.19 *sis pecore et multa diues tellure licebit*; *S.* 1.2.13 (= *AP* 421) *diues agris, diues positis in faenore nummis*. See L–H–S 77; Woodcock 55.

aut Parrhasius . . . aut Scopas: Parrhasius, a native of Ephesus, was an important painter active near the end of the fifth century, though Pliny (*HN* 35.60) has him more in the fourth, putting his father Evenor's *floruit* in the 90th Olympiad (420–417 BCE). According to Pliny (*HN* 35.67) he was the first to give painting proportion (*symmetria*), facial expression (*argutiae uultus*), elegance of the hair (*elegantia capilli*) and beauty of the face (*uenustas oris*); a good exemplary choice therefore for H. He was very arrogant and self-satisfied according to Plin. *HN* 35.71. Scopas of Paros was a mid-fourth-century sculptor, and architect. Pliny has high praise for him (*HN* 36.25–29) and clearly knew a number of his works, many of which found their way to Rome, among them what would become the Apollo Citharoedus in the Temple of Palatine Apollo, a work also known very well to H.

protulit 'brought before the public'; *OLD* s.v. *profero* 6a. There is a slight zeugma, again perhaps self-consciously Pindaric: *artium* in 5 means 'skills' (not 'works of art', *pace* Quinn), but it is the products of that skill that P. and S. 'brought forth', perhaps with the sense of 'put on view, show, display' (*OLD* s.v. *profero* 2b), and cf. especially Plin. *Epist.* 7.25.1 *eos . . . qui studia sua proferunt.*

7–8 A balanced couplet, referring to the separate media of Scopas (*hic saxo*) and Parrhasius (*ille coloribus*), then to their shared genius in depicting (*nunc*) human and (*nunc*) divine.

liquidis . . . coloribus: possibly 'flowing colours', as opposed to the rigidity of the sculptor's medium; cf. *TLL* s.v. *liquidus* 1484.40–5, citing Val. Flacc. 2.466–7, where marble and paint are again juxtaposed, *Pariusue notas et nomina sumit | cum lapis aut liquidi referunt miranda colores*; or perhaps just 'clear, bright', as at Plin. *NH* 37.66 *dos eorum* [sc. *smaragdorum*] *est in colore liquido*, as at *TLL* 1486.54–1487.2, where it is used of flame, stars, precious stones and the like.

sollers . . . ponere 'skilled at representing', epexegetic infinitive, with *sollers* here for the first time and perhaps a Grecism (cf. the common δεινός + infinitive = 'skilled/clever at'); also at Ov. *Am.* 2.7.17, with McKeown *ad loc.* for further examples. For *pono* 'depict' (*OLD* s.v. 19) cf. *AP* 34–5 (of artists who can get the hair and fingernails perfectly but can't see the forest for the trees) *infelix operis summa, quia ponere totum | nesciet*; first found at Virg. *Ecl.* 3.46 *Orpheaque in medio posuit*; Prop. 2.3.41–2 *si quis uult fama tabulas anteire uetustas, | hic dominam exemplo ponat in arte meam.*

nunc hominem . . . nunc deum: glossing the two classes of depiction at least in sculpture: ἀνδριαντοποιοί ('sculptors of men') and ἀγαλματοποιοί ('sculptors of gods'); the words survive at *Laterculi Alexandrini* 7.3–9 (Diels 1904: 7) and partially at *POxy.* X 1241.1.1; see *OCD* s.v. Scopas. That one skill did not imply the other is clear from Quint. 12.10.8 (on Polyclitus) *nam ut humanae formae decorem addiderit supra uerum, ita non expleuisse deorum auctoritatem uidetur.*

9–12 For the culmination of the priamel with its disavowal of sculpture (foil) and focus on song (climax), cf. Pind. *Nem.* 5.1–5 οὐκ ἀνδριαντοποιός εἰμ', ὥστ' ἐλινύσοντα ἐργάζεσθαι ἀγάλματ' ἐπ' αὐτᾶς βαθμίδος | ἑσταότ'· ἀλλ' ἐπὶ πάσας ὁλκάδος ἔν τ' ἀκάτωι, γλυκεῖ' ἀοιδά, | στεῖχ' ἀπ' Αἰγίνας διαγγέλλοισ', ὅτι | Λάμπωνος υἱὸς Πυθέας εὐρυσθενής | νίκη Νεμείοις παγκρατίου στέφανον, 'I am not a sculptor, so as to fashion stationary statues that stand on their same base. Rather, on board every ship and in every boat, sweet song, go forth from Aigina and spread the news that Lampon's mighty son Pytheas has won the crown for the pancratium in Nemea's games' (tr. Race). The dismissal of sculpture in favor of poetry engages a long-standing question as to which of the arts has most potency. Cf. 2.19–20n. for the contrast between art and poetry in the context of epinician prize.

sed non haec mihi uis 'but I don't have this on supply' (i.e. art objects); for a similar *recusatio* cf. Cat. 68.33 (in Verona without his library and therefore unable to produce learned poetry) *scriptorum non magna est copia apud me.*

nec tibi . . . egens 'and you're not concerned with such luxuries nor do you have a mind that needs them'. An example of syllepsis, with *est tibi* construed differently (though correctly: *tibi res est* and *tibi animus est*) in both clauses, *talium . . . deliciarum* going ἀπὸ κοινοῦ with *res* (cf. *OLD* s.v. *res* 10c) and *egens.*

aut animus deliciarum egens: cf. *Epist.* 1.6, where H. talks of the inevitability of death in spite of our enjoyment of art work: 17–18 *i nunc, argentum et marmor uetus aeraque et artes | suspice.* If you want to live the right life and *uirtus* is all that matters, go ahead and live accordingly, setting aside frivolities: 30–1 *fortis omissis | hoc age deliciis.*

gaudes: in contrast to *egens* – he does not need objects, but positively delights in song.

carmina possumus | donare 'we *are* able to give songs (*donare* resumes 1, 3 *donarem*) and assign a price to the gift/tell you what it's worth'. H. will proceed to do the latter (13–34), but never quite delivers the song, at least not the encomium the reader, or Censorinus, has been led to expect. Consequently the counterfactual of the poem's opening continues, and *possumus* is very different from *uolumus* or *donamus.*

13–19 non . . . marmora | non . . . fugae | . . . indicant: the pairing has bothered some, since the two do not seem quite parallel, but Pasquali 758 noted in passing 'lo zeugma è figura, se mai altra, pindarica'. Race (1 31) gives two examples at *Ol.* 1.88 and *Pyth.* 1.40. Harrison 1990: 36 makes the appealing suggestion that deeds are part of the inscription of 13, producing a kind of hendiadys, and he paraphrases 'it is not public inscriptions or their recording of routs and of the defeat of Hannibal's threats which have made Scipio famous, but the poems of Ennius'. He points as an example to *ILLRP* 319, the inscription on the *columna rostrata* found in the Roman forum and commemorating victory over the Carthaginians. For the anaphora of *non,* cf. 1.21n. See Currie 1996: 82 on the reference to 'epigraphic' preservation of fame.

13 non incisa: *non* of course goes with 19 *clarius indicant*; the style, with heavy use of litotes, is again Pindaric (cf. 1–4n.); see Race 1990: 59–84.

notis . . . publicis: *per quos titulos consecrati defuncti duces qu<a>ndam inmortalitatem consequuntur* (Porph.). *notis* is shorthand for *notis litterarum* 'lettering' (see 2.53–60), which strengthens Harrison's claim at 13–20n.; see *OLD* s.v. *nota* 6b.

14 spiritus et uita: mild hendiadys, 'breath of life': both words playing on their context, with *spiritus* more appropriate to statuary than lettering (Virg. *G.* 3.34 *spirantia signa; Aen.* 6.847–8 *spirantia . . . aera | uiuos . . . de marmore uultus*) and with the recorded *uita* (cf. Nep. *Epam.* 4.6.2; *OLD* s.v. *uita* 6b.) giving rise to the actual *uita.*

15 celeres fugae: Harrison suggests emending to *celebres* 'well-known recording of routs' (see 13–20n.), which does not quite feel right. And if they are well-known recordings there is a contradiction of 19–20. Harrison 1990: 37 addresses this difficulty claiming that this constitutes a *concessio*, a concession that sculpture achieves *some* fame, but nothing like that secured by poetry. However, *celebres* introduces more trouble than it solves, and his general point stands with *celeres*. The objections of Jachmann 1935: 333–5 and others, that 'swift' flight is unhistorical because Hannibal acted with great care and courage throughout the battle of Zama, is specious in view of the Horatian context of Scipionic encomium and also confuted by the very texts they cite (Livy 30.35.4 *elapsus Hadrumetum perfugit*, 10 *cum Hadrumetum refugisset*; Nep. *Hann.* 6.4 *in hac fuga . . . Hadrumeti reliquos e fuga collegit*).

16 Threats hurled back possibly following the Roman defeat of the Carthaginians at the Metaurus (for which see 4.38), as Quinn notes, but the sense may be less specific; cf. 3.8 *regum tumidas contuderit minas*. For *minae* specifically of war threats, cf. Virg. *Aen.* 4.43–4 *quid bella Tyro surgentia dicam | germanique minas* and *TLL* s.v. *minae* 992.42–5.

retrorsum: favoured by H. (1.34.3; *Epist.* 1.1.75, 18.88) but otherwise in poetry only once each in Lucretius, Lucan and Silius, and before H. only once each in Cicero and Varro. Virgil uses the adjective *retrorsus* once at *Aen.* 3.690.

17 A troubling line: the lack of caesura combines with the conflating of the two Scipios to encourage removal by some; K–H: 'der Vers ist von einem Ignoranten etwa des vierten Jahrhunderts interpoliert'. But see intro. The phrase *Karthaginis impiae* is a little jejune, and see 4.46–8, where, unlike here, there is a context for the epithet *impio | uastata Poenorum tumultu | fana*. Such oddities are perhaps part of the effect (see intro.).

18 eius: objective genitive with *laudes* 20; not just unpoetic, as noted by Axelson 71–2, but never in the *Odes* (3.11.18 is corrupt) or in Virgil, for instance, which is used as grounds for athetizing these lines. Büchner however argued (*Bursians Jahresberichte* 267 (1939) 142–4; see Harrison 1990: 39) that this was meant to capture the flavour of early republican Latin (it is common in all poets down to Lucretius), which seems plausible, in that the subject is precisely a third-century inscription. And again, the question of wilful unpoetic writing arises. See D. Butterfield *RhM* 151 (2008) 151–67.

domita nomen ab Africa: cf. *S.* 2.1.65–6 *qui | duxit ab oppressa meritum Carthagine nomen.* The kenning as a mode of referring to the *laudandus* Scipio Africanus is also applied to the *laudator* Ennius at 20 *Calabrae Pierides.*

18–19 nomen . . . lucratus 'acquired his name'; cf. *TLL* s.v. *lucror* 1716.15–45; a striking metaphor ('laxius respicitur quodlibet emolumentum'), of which this is the first example given – though Livy 2.59.6 (*nihil praeter tempus noxae lucrarentur*) is doubtless prior. Harrison 1990: 39–40 notes the possible reminiscence of an anecdote recorded by Val. Max. 3.7.1 to the effect that the elder Scipio Africanus responded to an imputation of corruption by saying that when he subjected Africa to Rome's control he brought nothing back for himself except the cognomen 'Africanus': '*nihil ex ea quod meum diceretur praeter cognomen rettuli*'.

19–20 clarius indicant | laudes: the proposition that song makes physical deeds more celebrated is a staple of Pindaric poetics: e.g. *Nem.* 4.6–8 (with a similarly functioning comparative) ῥῆμα δ' ἐργμάτων χρονιώτερον βιοτεύει | ὅ τι κε σὺν Χαρίτων τύχαι | γλῶσσα φρενὸς ἐξέλοι βαθείας, 'for the word lives longer than the deeds, which, with the Graces' blessing, the tongue draws from the depths of the mind' (tr. Race); also *Nem.* 7.11–12, 31–6; *Isthm.* 8.56–60; see Pitzalis 1949: 338–9 for a collection of the Pindaric intertexts.

20 Calabrae Pierides: best taken as the Muses of Ennius, author of the *Scipio* (pp. 212–14 Vahlen), with *Pierides* capturing the Greek *cor* of that poet; cf. also 9.6–8 *Pindaricae . . . Camenae*. Porph. thought H. was referring to himself: *sua uult intellegi carmina, quia in urbe Venusia natus est, quae est in Calabria atque Apulia*. This conflation of Calabria and Apulia occurs with reference to H. three times in Martial: 8.18.5 *Calabri . . . carmina Flacci*; 5.30.2 *Calabra . . . lyra*; 12.94.5 *Calabris . . . Camenis*, also in some other late texts; cf *TLL Onom.* s.v. *Calaber* 64.55–63. Martial even has Tarentum in both places: 8.28.3–4 *Apula Ledaei tibi floruit herba Phalanthi, | qua saturat Calabris culta Galaesus aquis* – with obvious reference to 2.6.9–12, where H. is considering his retirement options. Now Tarentum might be considered to border on the two, but this can hardly be said of Venusia, which is almost 100 miles to the northwest. At *S.* 1.5.77–8 his home territory begins right after they leave Beneventum (*incipit ex illo montes Apulia notos | ostentare mihi*); at *C.* 3.5.9 Apulians and Marsians are paired, the latter from central Italy, due east of Rome; at *Epod.* 2.41–2 we find Apulian and Sabine paired. And the true ambiguity about Venusia would have to do with Lucania, hardly Calabria (*S.* 2.1.34 *sequor hunc, Lucanus an Apulus anceps*). To disregard the later tradition as recorded by Martial – whose misreading of H.'s line clearly gave rise to this Calabrian tradition – it is difficult to imagine *Calabrae Pierides* referring to the Muses of H. At 6.27 H. refers to his Muse as *Daunia Camena*.

20–34 The scene is set for H.'s celebration of Censorinus, for whom he will play Scipio's Ennius. But the praise never comes as H. demonstrates by his practice that at the end of the day he is no Pindar. The poem runs itself out with reflection on the exempla of those whose fame and name, and place in heaven, are due to unspecified bards.

20–2 neque | . . . mercedem tuleris 'and if writings were to be silent about your good deeds there'd be no payout for you'. H.'s writing will in fact be silent about Censorinus' deeds, which go unmentioned. Quinn tries to avoid this conclusion by taking *sileant* and *tuleris* as representing as 'equivalent to the normal imperfect and pluperfect ("nor, if there were no mention of you in literature, would you have got your due reward of fame")' – i.e. taking them as counterfactuals; he proposes that 'Censorinus has already had his achievements celebrated in an epic poem' – for which there is absolutely no evidence, let alone material. Quinn compares *Aen.* 2.599–600 (Venus to Aeneas) '*ni mea cura resistat | iam flammae tulerint inimicus et hauserit ensis*'. Woodcock 155 gives that very example of the present (and perfect) subjunctive to 'represent a hypothetical condition more vividly by not excluding the idea of fulfilment', a type that was dying out in classical Latin.

si chartae sileant: cf. 9.30–1 *non ego te meis* | *chartis inornatum silebo. charta* is not otherwise found in the *Odes* or *Epodes* (eleven times in the hexameters). In view of the distribution in H. and beyond, it seems to be a low-register way of referring to poetry which, with the idiomatic phrase *mercedem tuleris*, contrasts with the elevated wording of 22–4 *Iliae* | *Mauortisque puer* (see n.).

feceris: best taken as future perfect.

22–4 Iliae | Mauortisque puer: a rather ample designation, though perhaps implying that the parentage of Romulus is a poetic fiction. The genitive is itself Ennian (*Ann.* 1.99 Skutsch), and of high register, otherwise before H. only once in Ciceronian verse, also of Romulus (and Remus: fr. 10.43 Courtney = *Diu.* 1.20.2 *paruos Mauortis semine natos*), and twice in Virgil (*Aen.* 6.872, of Rome at the death of Marcellus, *magnam Mauortis ad urbem*, and 8.630, the wolf on the shield with the brothers in the Lupercal, *Mauortis in antro*). Ovid broke the mould and used it of the Areopagus: *Met.* 6.70 *Mauortis in arce.*

taciturnitas | . . . inuida 'silence born of envy'; cf. 9.33–4 *liuidas* | *obliuiones.* The notion that envy suppresses speech, report (*fama*) so as to create silence and hence oblivion is a potent one. Cf. Pind. *Isthm.* 4.30 for the near-personification of *taciturnitas*: τῶν ἀπειράτων γὰρ ἄγνωτοι σιωπαί. ('non-participants reap the silence of oblivion'). K–H note that *taciturnitas* and *inuida* will find their opposites in 26 *lingua* and *fauor.*

obstaret: though a present counterfactual works ('silence would continue to obstruct'), this could be another sign of an older Latin, with the imperfect equivalent to the pluperfect subjunctive of classical Latin ('would have obstructed'); see Woodcock 197.

25–9 It is song that has saved humans from Hades and given them immortality. Pind. *Ol.* 10.91–3 puts it more negatively than H.: καὶ ὅταν καλὰ ἔρξαις ἀοιδᾶς ἄτερ, | Ἁγησίδαμ', εἰς Ἀίδα σταθμόν | ἀνὴρ ἵκηται, κενεὰ πνεύσαις ἔπορε μόχθωι βραχύ τι τερπνόν, 'so, when a man who has performed noble deeds, Hagesidamos, goes without song to Hades' dwelling, in vain has he striven and gained for his toil but brief delight' (tr. Race). The difference from H., however, is that the addressee of Pindar is exempt precisely because of the praise he *does* receive: 93–4 τὶν δ' ἁδυεπής τε λύρα | γλυκύς τ' αὐλὸς ἀναπάσσει χάριν 'upon you, however, the sweetly speaking lyre and and melodious pipe are shedding glory' (tr. Race). H. also looks to Theoc. 16.34–57, addressed to Hieron II on the subject of the fame secured by the patrons of Simonides and other early recipients of song. Theocritus, however, unlike H., after enumerating those who achieve fame, eventually returns to the name of his *laudandus*: 80–1 ἐν δ' αὐτοῖς Ἱέρων προτέροις ἴσος ἡρώεσσι | ζώννυται, 'and among them Hiero girds himself up like the heroes of old . . .' Cf. intro. and 9.26–8n.

25–7 ereptum Stygiis fluctibus: cf. Virg. *Aen.* 6.362–5 (Palinurus pleading unsuccessfully) '*nunc me fluctus habet . . . eripe me his, inuicte, malis*'; K–H refer to

Athena's digression at *Il.* 8.369 οὐκ ἂν ὑπεξέφυγε Στυγὸς ὕδατος αἰπὰ ῥέεθρα, 'he would not have escaped the steep streams of the water of the Styx'.

Aeacum: father of Peleus and Telamon and ruler of Aegina; almost one quarter of Pindar's epinicians are to victors from Aegina (*Ol.* 8; *Pyth.* 8; *Nem.* 3, 4, 5, 6, 7, 8; *Isthm.* 5, 6, 8). Aeacus is a just and popular leader of the island at *Nem.* 8.6–12 and *Isthm.* 9.1–8, and this doubtless explains H.'s choice.

uirtus et fauor et lingua: there is a transition across the triad: the virtue (*uirtus*) of the *laudandus* and the respect he commands (*fauor*) must be coupled with the goodwill (*fauor*) and powerful eloquence (*lingua*) of the bard, as at 9.26–8. The *fauor* shared by the *laudandus* and the poet shields each of them from *inuidia*, as K-H note. Pindaric χάρις ('lustre', and therefore 'goodwill') is shared by the victor and the poet celebrating the victory (cf. Slater, *Lexicon to Pindar* (Berlin, 1969) s.v. 1.a and 1.b). Lyne 1995: 212 points to 3.3.9–18, where being *iustus* and *tenax propositi* alone was a sufficient basis for the beatification of the self-same figures, Pollux, Hercules, Bacchus, Romulus (Quirinus) and there Augustus. Now their very divinity seems to be in question: 'The two poems are in collision, 4.8 pulls the rug from under 3.3, saps it, indeed denies the whole basis of its panegyric.' There is also a conflict with 7.21–4, where *genus*, *facundia* and *pietas* could not save Torquatus.

lingua: cf. 6.1–2 where the big tongue of Niobe was her downfall.

potentium | uatum: cf. K–H note Theoc. 16.44 δεινὸς ἀοιδός. Gow prints θεῖος but notes 'there is little to choose between them'; it looks as if H. (*potentium*) read δεινός – making him the earliest witness to the text.

diuitibus . . . insulis: cf. 2.13.22–3 *iudicantem . . . Aeacum | sedesque discretas piorum*; *Epod.* 16.41–2 *arua beata . . . diuites et insulas*, with Mankin *ad loc.*, of the Isles of the Blest, to which H. back then proposed his fellow citizens transport themselves. See Hes. *Op.* 166–73a and West *ad* 171 for the μακάρων νῆσοι 'Isles of the Blest', there ruled over by Cronus; also with further reference to Pind. *Ol.* 2.68–75, more to the point for H. here, though Pindar has Rhadamanthus dispensing justice and does not (now in a non-Aeginetan context) mention Aeacus.

28–9 Musa uetat mori | caelo Musa beat: 'the Muse forbids that he die and blesses with heaven' – a brilliant progression, which the 'removers of six' would destroy, since they need to remove 28 to fill out their tally (see intro.). For a very similar anaphora cf. 1.17.13–14 *di me tuentur, dis pietas mea | et musa cordi est.* Cf. Theoc. 16.58–9 (see 25–29n.) ἐκ Μοισᾶν ἀγαθὸν κλέος ἔρχεται ἀνθρώποισι 'good fame comes to men from the Muses', but H.'s language has gone beyond that, and his examples (Romulus and Aeacus, and at 30–1 Hercules and the Dioscuri) are of a scale to make Censorinus' praise recede even further, though the language continues to play on his name (29 *beat* etc.), now hidden under these glossing terms.

29–34 Without 33 the poem has an elegant closing quatrain with enjambment leading in, with one verse each for Hercules and Dionysus surrounding a couplet for the pair Castor and Pollux. See 25–7n. for the relationship with

3.3.9–18. With 33, also problematic in other ways (see n.), H. further disrupts the elegance.

29–30 sic Iouis . . . Hercules: Hercules shares in the banquets of the Jupiter, having achieved apotheosis through his Labours, allusively captured by the adjective *impiger*, which resonates with the athletic context of 3.4 *equus impiger*. His marriage in Olympus to Hebe is perhaps suggested by 30 *optatis*.

31 clarum Tyndaridae sidus: Castor and Polydeuces (Pollux), sons of Tyndareus and Leda, and brothers of Helen – though not in Homer (*Od.* 11.298–304), where Helen is daughter of Zeus. At 1.3.2 they are *fratres Helenae, lucida sidera*, and are to help watch over the ship to which Virgil is entrusted, as they do for sailors as early as *Hymn. Hom. Diosc.* 33; cf. also 1.12.25–8 (again with Hercules) *Alciden puerosque Ledae . . . quorum simul alba nautis | stella refulsit.* No star at all, the *sidus/sidera* refers to 'St. Elmo's fire', 'a dull blue glare ("point discharge" or "corona discharge") that appears on the masts and rigging of ships, and was even observed by Sir J. J. Thomson on the pinnacles of King's College Chapel' (N–H *ad* 1.3.2n.). John Henderson tells me 'The roof of King's Chapel was built of oak by Tudor carpenters who were the shipwrights that built the Royal Navy, and the design is that of an upturned galleon's hull.' The appearance of the light was considered a good omen by sailors.

For a variant of the word order that Solodow 1986: 129 calls 'inserted apposition' – predicate noun + adjective surrounding the noun of which they are the predicate – (e.g. Virg. *Ecl.* 1.57 *raucae, tua cura, palumbes*), cf. 1.1.29 *doctarum, hederae, praemia frontium*; 1.20.5 *clare/care, Maecenas, eques*; 3.24.42 *magnum, pauperies, opprobrium*. The instances in the *Odes* are somewhat restrained in having an unaccompanied noun in the enclosed space (Solodow 1986: 139–40), compared to the two other Horatian examples, *Epod.* 14.7 *inceptos olim, promissum carmen, iambos* (on which see Watson *ad loc.*); *Epist.* 2.1.234 *acceptos, regale nomisma, Philippos* (and Brink *ad loc.*). Most of the examples come from the *Eclogues*, Propertius and Ovid (and see Watson 455–6 for the neoteric context of *Epod.* 14, while Brink noted on *Epist.* 2.1.234 the rare loan word *nomisma* 'admirably fits the Hellenistic and sarcastic phrasing'), which led Skutsch (*RhM* 99 [1956] 198) to think of Gallus and audaciously dub it the *schema Cornelianum*; see also Norden on Virg. *Aen.* 6.7f.

clarum: cf. 19 *clarior*.

31–2 ab infimis | quassas eripiunt aequoribus ratis: K–H compare Theoc. 22.17 (the *Dioscuri*) ἀλλ' ἔμπης ὑμεῖς γε καὶ ἐκ βυθοῦ ἕλκετε νῆας 'and yet from the depths of the sea you rescue ships'.

32 eripiunt: the verb of 25 *ereptum*. They do to wrecked ships (and their sailors) what was done (by Pindar et al.) to Aeacus. The repetition is somewhat loosely motivated.

33 Suspiciously close to 3.25.20 (*cingentem uiridi tempora pampino*), and the fact is that H. has a great aversion to repeating himself in the *Odes* (see intro.); therefore a candidate for removal, along with 17, for those who strive for strict adherence to Meineke's Law (see intro.).

tempora: retained accusative; cf. 11.5n.

34 bonos . . . ad exitus: cf. 14.37–8 *Fortuna . . . belli secundos reddidit exitus. bonus exitus* elsewhere has the sense of a good end or death: Cic. *Nat. D.* 3.89 '*at non numquam bonos exitus habent boni*'; Sen. *Contr.* 8.1.1 '*quisquis est* [sc. *sacrilegus*], *non ipse bonum exitum faciet*'.

exitus: a good word for an ending, as at the end of *Epod.* 17 and the *Epode* book; and cf., also at the end, *Epist.* 1.16.79 *mors ultima linea rerum est.*

9

METRE

Alcaic stanza (see on 4).

INTRODUCTION

In case you think my poetry will die, the fact is that even though Homer has first place, Greek lyric still survives. Helen wasn't the only married woman to fall for a dandy, and the heroes of Troy were not the only or first ones to fight in battle; there were heroes before Agamemnon, but they are lost to fame because they lack a bard. Valour which is thus hidden is indistinguishable from cowardice once we are dead and buried. I won't be silent about you, Lollius: you have all the right qualities, prudence, justice, lack of corruption, consul not just for one year but as often as you have preferred what is right to the useful, you have rejected bribes and beaten your enemy. You wouldn't call the wealthy man happy, rather the person who can use the gifts of the gods, endure poverty, die for friends and country.

Syme 1986: 176 noted of the addressee 'the notorious M. Lollius (*cos.* 21 BC (cf. *Epist* 1.20.28 *collegam Lepidum quo dixit Lollius anno*)), singled out by H. for integrity, by Velleius for craft and corruption – and a bitter enemy of Tiberius'. The more youthful Lollius addressed in *Epist.* 1.18 is a different person. A *nouus homo*, the consular Lollius (*PIR*² L311) was among those who helped Augustus establish his principate in the 20s. He held the first propraetorship of Galatia (25–22 BCE), where Augustus sent him after annexing the kingdom of Amyntas (Eutrop. 7.10). In 19–18 BCE, after his consulship, he subjugated the Bessi in Thrace (Dio 54.20.3), was involved as a *XVuir* at the Secular Games of 17 BCE (a direct connection with H.?) and, significantly *after* serving in that capacity, in 17 or 16 BCE, went as a legate to Gaul, where he lost the eagle of *legio* V *Alaudae* ('Larks'), after the Sygambri, Usipetes and Tencteri crossed the Rhine and defeated him in an initial encounter – although it was recovered soon enough, but not before it became clear that Augustus had come to the area (Dio 54.20.4–6).

The defeat became known as the *clades Lolliana* (at least by the time of Tac. *Ann.* 1.10.3, or as T. interpreted it), and while less disastrous than the *clades Variana* of 9 CE (Suet. *Aug.* 23 *maioris ignominiae quam detrimenti*), the loss, even temporary, of a Roman eagle, was no small matter and would surely have come into play for readers of H.'s poem. According to Dio 54.21.1, Augustus spent 16–15 BCE on various arrangements in Gaul. Syme 1933: 18 followed Julius Obsequens 71 in putting the *clades* in 17 BCE, which also suits his minimizing of the defeat of Lollius (i.e. Augustus' journey to Gaul was not an emergency response to the *clades*) and notes 'he enjoyed, and perhaps deserved, the confidence of Augustus, and therefore received from the dutiful Horace a glowing testimonial of virtue and integrity' (see also Syme 1939: 449; 1986: 396–7). Syme does not include the final sentence of Obsequens: *insidiis Germanorum Romani circumuenti sub M. Lollio legato grauiter uexati*, which makes slightly more of the combat than Dio's account. See Woodman on Vell. 2.97.1 for effective argument (based on clear language at Tac. *Ann.* 1.10.4; Suet. *Aug.* 23.1; Dio 5.20.4; Obseq. 71) against Syme's assertions that the defeat was trivial. H.'s poem (anyway hardly 'glowing'; see below) cannot easily be used for evidence of Augustan policy, and in any case it would be 15 years before Lollius was heard from again, when in 1 BCE Augustus made him *comes et rector* (Suet. *Tib.* 12.2) or *uelut moderator* (Vell. 2.102.1) to Gaius Caesar, who was in the east with proconsular *imperium*. Lollius himself seems to have had no actual *imperium*, so perhaps the *clades Lolliana* continued to affect his fortunes (see 39n.). According to Tac. *Ann.* 3.48.1, he fell out of favour in 2 CE, and soon died, while still in the East. See Syme 1986: Index s.v. 'Lollius'. Wolff, *CAH* X 537, following Dio 54.20, treats the possibility that Roman policy in the Central Alps and the northern foothills of Rhaetia (not previously pursued in any systematic way) was probably motivated by a desire, following Lollius' defeat, to prevent Germans east of the Rhine from escaping towards Italy. For possible etymological play see 30–4n.

The poem addressed to this man has seemed not particularly successful, in part because of the *clades Lolliana*, but for other reasons too. Fraenkel 426 notes: 'If, nevertheless, the eulogy sounds somewhat laboured, this is clearly not the poet's fault. He did what he could, but the fact remained that to him *laudes Lollii* did not prove a congenial topic.' Similarly for Williams 1968: 80 Lollius is a friend of H., who tried his best: 'What Horace writes, grand and dignified though the sentiments are, sounds like an attempt at rehabilitation and is a little on the defensive – an awkward situation for the poet.' For Quinn 316, it is a matter of wattage: 'It is easy to read 4.9 as perfunctory praise; it is perhaps intended as a cautious rehabilitation . . . the ode is apt to strike the reader as an example of H.'s failing powers . . . Stanzas 1–8 are not without rhetorical merit, but we are disconcerted to find them used as a preamble for the vague rhetoric that follows.'

It is preferable, with Ambrose 1965, to confront the general dissatisfaction head on: encomium riddled with irony ceases to be encomium (see 17–21, 30–4, 50–2nn.). On the other hand, Ambrose seems less on the mark in imagining that H. was compelled to write the poem (and *C.* 4 in general) and reacted by writing as he did. Putnam 168–9, n. 19 allows the possibility of Ambrose's reading, but invokes Syme's view that the defeat was minor and that irony would not therefore be activated. Sage 1994 sees the poem as a warning to Lollius of what he needs to be concerned about in his own character; she further observes various ambiguities in 34–44, which conspire to push the poem away from encomium. Johnson is similarly agnostic on the syntax of 30–4 but 'agree[s] with Ambrose that the praise of the introduction is not unequivocal' (241, n. 100) and well quotes (240, n. 90) *Epist* 2.1.262–3 *discit enim citius meminitque libentius illud* | *quod quis deridet quam quod probat et ueneratur*. Were the Sygambri and the lost eagle forgotten by the time H. wrote this poem? Sage 1994: 581, n. 46 notes that the poem is replete with negative phrasing (1, 3, 5, 9, 13, 18, 19, 21, 30, 39, 45 and 51) and privatives (26 *illacrimabiles*, 27 *ignoti*, 29 *inertiae*, 31 *inornatum*, 33 *impune*, 37 *abstinens*, 42 *reiecit*). Race 1990: 59–84 treats the use of negatives in *Pyth.* 9 (cf. 80 'the ποικιλία of negative expressions'), but that does not explain away the general negativity that hangs over this ode, on which Seager 1993: 37 may put it best: 'Thus in the course of some twenty lines of "encomium" Horace succeeds in twice ramming it down the honorand's throat that he has neither been victorious in battle nor died in the attempt.' For different reasons *C.* 4.8 and 4.9 remain bizarre instances of encomium, the former never getting around to praise the *laudandus*, the latter praising for qualities and achievements that seem to be negated in the actual life of the *laudandus*.

1–8 The word order is as complex as the syntax – seven verbs or verbal parts within the main subordinate material of 1–4; nor is it simply a matter of quantity, rather the stanza gains complexity and density through the syntactical ποικιλία ('variety') and avoidance of parataxis (cf. 13.1–4 also with seven verb forms, but all in compound or simple clauses). It will be useful to recompose: *ne forte credas uerba chordis socianda quae (ego) natus ad Aufidum longe sonantem per artes non ante uulgatas loquor interitura (esse), non latent Camenae Pindaricae etc., (etiam) si Maeonius Homerus sedes priores tenet.* The amount of information in these 19 words is only decipherable at the end, and the style seems deliberately obscure: *interitura* only becomes comprehensible with *uerba*, *sonantem* with *Aufidum*, *natus* with *loquor*, *uulgatas* with *artes*.

1 Ne forte credas: a slightly casual or conversational opening, the collocation *ne forte* occurring elswhere in H. outside lyric at *S.* 2.1.80, *Epist.* 1.1.13, 13.12; 2.1.208 and *AP* 176, 406. It is found three times in Plautus and occurs over thirty times in Cicero, chiefly in the speeches and letters. Lucretius is fond of it, using it in strongly didactic contexts ('in case you think . . .'): 1.80, 466; 2.718, 731, 842; 4.37, 129; 5.78, 114, 890, 1091, while Virgil's single use is colloquial: *Ecl.* 3.29–30 *ne forte recuses,* | *bis uenit ad mulctram, binos alit ubere fetus*. Most editors place a colon after *chordis* (Borzsák has a period), thereby implying that *ne forte credas* = *noli credere*, and commentators give as a parallel 1.33.1, where *ne doleas* could be a subordinate clause or a prohibition (with alternatively a comma or period after 4 *fide*). See N–H *ad loc.*, with a preference for the latter, distinguishing 2.4.1 (which seems clearly subordinate, *pace* Shackleton Bailey, who has a semi-colon after 2 *Phoceu*), but not on substantial grounds. Brink rightly takes the *ne*-clauses of 9 and 1.33 as subordinate (*PCPS* 15 (1969) 5–6). The better parallels are at *Epist.* 1.1.13–15 *ac ne forte roges . . . , deferor*; 2.1.208–10 *ne forte putes . . . , ille . . . uidetur*; *AP* 176–8 *ne forte . . . mandentur . . . morabimur.*

interitura: anticipating the immortality of poetry: cf. 2.20.5–7 *non . . . obibo*; 3.30.6 *non omnis moriar*; cf. 52 *perire*, with *interitura* framing the poem.

2 longe sonantem: cf. Cat. 11.3–4 *litus ut longe resonante Eoa* | *tunditur unda*; Virg. *G.* 1.358–9 *resonantia longe* | *litora misceri et nemorum increbrescere murmur*; 2.163 *longe sonat unda*; *Aen.* 5.866 *longe sale saxa sonabant*; 7.701–2 *sonat amnis et Asia longe* | *pulsa palus.* Otherwise only once in Calp. *Ecl.* and twice in Sil. Ital.; cf. *TLL* s.v. *longus* 1644.40–50; unlike most of the examples before him, H. is without accompanying sonic effects, and *longe sonantem* rather looks as if it represents a Greek compound with τηλε-, for which the only candidate is τηλέθροος, which survives (given by LSJ out of alphabetical order as τηλύθροος) only in Hesychius. It may have been used in Greek lyric, but that is pure speculation. Cf. below also in programmatic context at 3.30.10 *obstrepit Aufidus.*

natus: perhaps on the same farm from which his father sent him not to the local school but to Rome: *S.* 1.6.71–2 *macro pauper agello* | *noluit in Flaui ludum me mittere*; *Epist.* 2.2.51 (loss of the farm after Philippi).

Aufidum: cf. 14.25, *S.* 1.1.58 and especially *C.* 3.30.10–14 (where, as here, the river is connected with H.'s fame) *dicar, qua uiolens obstrepit Aufidus* | . . . *princeps Aeolium carmen ad Italos* | *deduxisse modos*; the Aufidus descends from the Apennines and curls around Venusia 10–15 miles to the west and north, ending up in the Adriatic some 40 miles to that town's northeast. Cf. Virg. *Aen.* 11.405 (in an adynaton refuting Drances' claim that the Rutulians are defeated) *amnis et Hadriacas retro fugit Aufidus undas.* In its lower reaches was fought the Battle of Cannae (Livy 22.44.2–3).

3 non ante uulgatas per artes: cf. *Epist.* 1.19.32–3 *hunc ego, non alio dictum prius ore, Latinus* | *uulgaui fidicen*; also Virg. *G.* 3.4 *omnia iam uulgata* and Thomas *ad loc.* for the Callimachean intertexts, intensified by H. with the addition of *artes* = τέχνηι (*Aet.* 1 fr. 1.17 Pf.).

4 uerba . . . socianda chordis: lyrics are to be allied with musical arrangement, presumably a generic fiction, *pace* Lyons 2007; see also 3.21–4n. *uerba sociare*, well suggesting musical harmony, is striking and original and is not found elsewhere in Latin. Ov. *Met.* 11.5 has *Orphea percussis sociantem carmina neruis*; see Bömer *ad loc.* for similar expressions.

5–12 A canon of six Greek lyric poets: Pindar, Simonides, Alcaeus, Stesichorus, Anacreon and Sappho. Greek lyric survived in spite of the primacy of the Homeric poems. By analogy, H. may be hinting that the recently published *Aeneid* will not cause erasure of his new lyric enterprise. From these lines (*non . . . latent* | *nec deleuit aestas* | *spirat adhuc*) it may be assumed that a considerable amount of Greek lyric was available to the Greek-reading Roman of the Augustan period.

5–8 priores . . . tenet | sedes 'comes first'; the reference is to importance rather than temporal priority, with *sedes* figurative (as at Cic. *Sull.* 77 *in impiorum partem atque in parricidarum sedem ac numerum*, *OLD* s.v. 1c), though K–H see a reference to seating privileges (*sedes priores* = προεδρία) in the context of an athletic victor: Xenoph. fr. 2.7 Diels-Kranz καί κε προεδρίην φανερὴν ἐν ἀγῶσιν ἄροιτο 'win a prominent proedria at the games'. In a Roman context one might think of the seating of the equites in the first fourteen rows of the theatre according to the *lex Roscia*.

Pindaricae . . . Camenae: a hybrid. At 2.16.38 *Graiae . . . Camenae* is a 'paradoxical collocation' that 'underlines the fusion of elements in Horace's lyrics' (N–H *ad loc.*). Things have gone further, with the *Camenae* having extended their influence, against any real logic, back on to the Greek poets (Pindar, Simonides, Alcaeus and Stesichorus). By this stage *Camenae* may simply = 'Muses', but it is hard to avoid feeling a strongly Italian flavor, given the literary history of the word, since Ennius substituted the Greek Muses for the Livian Camenae. Cf. the inverse at 8.20 *Calabrae Pierides* – though there of Ennius, who has access to Greek Muses.

non . . . latent 'are not consigned to obscurity'.

Ceaeque: adjective, with *Camenae*; i.e. Muses of Simonides of Ceos (c. 556–467 BCE), as at 2.1.37–8 *sed ne . . . | Ceae retractes munera neniae*. Cf. 6.9–12n. Simonides wrote epinicians, dirges, dithyrambs, elegy and epigram.

Alcaei minaces: cf. *TLL* s.v. *minax* 996.57–8: 'sc. στασιωτικά', 'factious'; of the themes of Alcaeus (of Mytilene on Lesbos, born c. 625–620 BCE), as at 2.13.26–8 *te sonantem plenius aureo, | Alcaee, plectro dura nauis, | dura fugae mala, dura belli*. For a more balanced and particularly affectionate vignette of H.'s favourite Greek lyric poet, cf. 1.32.4–12, calling on his lyre, effectively a *laus Alcaei*: *barbite . . . | Lesbio primum modulate ciui, | qui ferox bello tamen inter arma, | siue iactatam religarat udo | litore nauim, | Liberum et Musas Veneremque et illi | semper haerentem puerum canebat | et Lycum nigris oculis nigroque | crine decorum* – adding the ingredients of wine, women (boys rather) and song.

graues 'serious', 'weighty'. Stesichorus (of South Italy and Himera in Sicily, *c.* 632–556 BCE) produced lyric on epic mythological themes, and often with close connection to Homer (Antip. Thessal. *Anth. Pal.* 7.75; Anon. *Anth. Pal.* 9.184.3–4), who is also assigned *grauitas* among other contrasting qualities at Quint. 10.1.46 *idem laetus ac pressus, iucundus et grauis, tum copia tum breuitate mirabilis*. For the epithet elsewhere, cf. *Epist.* 2.1.82 *quae grauis Aesopus, quae doctus Roscius egit*, with elaboration from Quint. 11.3.111 *Aesopus grauior fuit, quod . . . tragoedias egit*; *AP* 255 (substitution of spondees for iambs in the tragic trimeter) *tardior ut paulo grauiorque ueniret ad auris*. Later, with some disparagement from a Callimachean point of view, of Ennius: Ov. *Trist.* 2.423–4 *utque suo Martem cecinit grauis Ennius ore | Ennius ingenio maximus arte rudis*. The epithet serves to strengthen the contrast between the poets of this stanza and those to follow (cf. 9 *lusit*).

9–10 nec si quid olim lusit Anacreon | deleuit aetas: cf. 1.32.1–3 *si quid uacui sub umbra | lusimus tecum, quod et hunc in annum | uiuat et plures*. Anacreon of Teos was born *c.* 575–570 BCE and spent time in Samos under Polycrates, in Athens under Hipparchus. *lusit* is particularly appropriate given his reputation for erotic and sympotic verse, reflected in *Epod.* 14.9–10 *non aliter Samio dicunt arsisse Bathyllo* | *Anacreonta Teium*; also the context of *C.* 1.17.18 *fide Teia*. There is a strong contrast with the preceding stanza and especially 8 *graues*. Generally on *ludus poeticus* see Wagenvoort 1956: 30–42, and esp. 31–32 'the minor over against the major, the light over against the serious (*maiora, grauiora*)'. Hence too Anacreon, rather than Alcaeus, shares a stanza with Sappho. The commas most editors place after *nec* and *Anacreon* are removed here, since the material in between is simply an object noun clause.

10–12 Cf. 2.13.24–5 *Aeoliis fidibus querentem* | *Sappho* [acc.] *puellis de popularibus*.

spirat . . . amor | **uiuuntque . . . calores**: an increase in enthusiasm from the negative expressions that precede (*non . . . latent* | *nec deleuit*). *Aeoliae . . . puellae* is productively ambiguous, a subjective genitive with *amor* and *calores*, but also possessive with *fidibus*, with the two verbs in emphatic initial position.

calores: for the collective plural of an abstract noun see 12.13n. (*tempora*). K–H cite Plut. *Erot.* 18. 762F 'ἄξιον δὲ Σαπφοῦς παρὰ ταῖς Μούσαις μνημονεῦσαι . . . αὕτη δ' ἀληθῶς μεμιγμένα πυρὶ φθέγγεται καὶ διὰ τῶν μελῶν ἀναφέρει τὴν ἀπὸ τῆς καρδίας θερμότητα "Μουσαις εὐφώνοις ἰωμένη τὸν ἔρωτα" κατὰ Φιλόξενον' (Philox. fr. 9 *PMG*) 'since we are at the Muses' shrine it is worth mentioning Sappho . . . she too [like fire-breathing Cacus] speaks words which are truly mingled with fire, and through her songs communicates the heat in her heart: "healing love with sweet-voiced Muses", in the words of Philoxenus'. Cf. also Sapph. fr. 48.2 L-P ἔμαν φρένα καιομέναν πόθωι 'my heart which was burning with desire'.

commissi . . . fidibus 'entrusted to the strings of the lyre'; cf. Joni Mitchell, 'For the Roses': 'Remember the days when you used to sit and make up your tunes for love, | and pour your simple sorrows to the sound hole on your knee?' Perhaps H. plays on *fidei* (= 'trust') *committere* as at Ter. *Eun.* 886 *ego me tuae . . . committo fide*; Ov. *Am.* 1.12.21 *his ego commisi nostros insanus amores*; *Met.* 10.418 *officium commisso spondet amori*. Cf. *TLL* s.v. 2. *fides* 'lyre' (prob. loan from Gr. σφίδες = χορδαί) 691.70–6 for folk-etymological connection to *fides* 'trust' and Maltby s.v. *fides* (2). In this connection, cf. Lucilius as described at *S.* 2.1.30–1: *ille uelut fidis arcana sodalibus olim* | *credebat libris*.

13–26 The poem takes a new turn, treating Homeric characters and the area of their fame (κλέος). None was original in his exploits, but through poetry they gained immortality. H. stresses the lack of uniqueness or primacy (*non sola* | *primusue* |*non semel* | *non . . . solus* | *non . . . primus* | *ante*), with appealing placement at stanza-beginning (13 *non sola*, 17 *primusue*) and -ending (20 *solus*, 24 *primus*); enjambment and a general lack of line-end punctuation (except for 16; see 13–16n.) effectively counter any sense of catalogue.

13–16 non sola . . . Helene Lacaena: Helen gets a stanza to herself, adjectives and name serving as a frame, and with an artful tricolon, more or less equally weighted (*crinis* | *aurum* | *cultus et comites*). She provides a neat transition, enflamed (13 *arsit*) as was Sappho (11 *calores*). H. had made the same point, somewhat more crudely, at *S.* 1.3.107–8 *nam fuit ante Helenam cunnus taeterrima belli | causa, sed ignotis perierunt mortibus illi*; cf. 26–7 *illacrimabiles . . . ignotique.*

comptos . . . crines: Paris is notable for his hair as early as Hom. *Il.* 3.55, where Hector predicts neither lyre-playing nor gifts of Aphrodite nor the beauty of his hair (ἥ τε κόμη τό τε εἶδος) will help when he mingles with the dust at his death – in the prophecy of Nereus in H.'s version at 1.15.13–14 *nequiquam Veneris praesidio ferox | pectes caesariem*, 19–20 *tamen, heu, serus adulteros | crines puluere collines.* For similar contempt cf. Aeneas as Paris seen through the eyes of Iarbas: Virg. *Aen.* 4.216–17 (Dido for Helen) '*Maeonia mentum mitra crinemque madentem | subnexus*', and Turnus, also alluding to Hector's words: 12.97–100 (Lavinia for Helen) '*da . . . foedare in puluere crines | uibratos calido ferro murraque madentes*'. See Axelson 51 for the distribution of *capillus* : *coma* : *crinis* in various poets; Virgil, for instance, generally avoids *capillus* (2 : 28 : 30) while H. in the lyrics is indifferent (11 : 10 : 12).

arsit: according to *TLL* s.v. *ardeo* 486.74–80, with an accusative of the object of desire otherwise only at Virg. *Ecl.* 2.1 *Corydon ardebat Alexin* (Ter. *Phorm.* 82 is uncertain), then Mart. 8.63.1 (in imitation of *Ecl.* 2.1). It could be argued that *crines* and *aurum* are formally objects of *mirata* ('burns with admiration for'), even though the participle would be in a markedly delayed position.

aurum uestibus illitum 'gold smeared across his clothes', with traditional contempt for finery. *TLL* s.v. *illino* 383.39–46 has a category, created virtually for this use 'sensu latiore', glossing *aurum* (*auro*) *inducere.* But the supporting example (Plin. *HN* 33.64 *oui candido illinitur*) has to do with the use of eggwhite wash to apply gold leaf to materials that cannot be heated, such as marble and wood, so the sense of 'smear', 'bedaub' is appropriately present, as it is for H., in view of the subject; Sen. *Phaed.* 387–8 reverses H.'s syntax, *remouete, famulae, purpura atque auro illitas | uestes*, as Phaedra goes native to appease Diana: 403 *talis in siluas ferar.*

regalesque cultus et comites: Helen, an austere Spartan, was blinded by the regal eastern finery of Paris.

Helene Lacaena: cf. 3.3.25 *Lacaenae . . . adulterae*; Virg. *Aen.* 2.601 *Tyndaridis facies inuisa Lacaenae*; in the context of *Aen.* 6.511 (Deiphobus' shade relating the grisly death and defilement dealt him by the Menelaus, with help from Helen, whom Deiphobus married following the death of Paris) the epithet on its own is contemptuous: *scelus exitiale Lacaenae*; see Austin *ad loc.* and below 22–4n.

17–21 Teucer was not the first to use the Cretan bow, Troy is not the only city to have been attacked, Idomeneus and Sthenelus were not the only ones to fight battles that could be sung by the Muses.

Teucer: half-brother of Ajax and the great archer of the *Iliad*, where he shoots from behind Ajax's shield. He then went in exile to Cyprus after his father refused to allow him to return to Salamis after the suicide of Ajax. Ambrose 1965 sees a connection between Lollius, who lost his eagle, and Teucer, who was exiled for failing to bring back his brother Ajax.

tela Cydonio | direxit arcu: with an eye to the words of the lovelorn Gallus at Virg. *Ecl.* 10.59–60, where the adjective modifies arrows rather than bow, *libet Partho torquere Cydonia cornu | spicula – tamquam haec sit nostri medicina furoris.*

non semel Ilios | uexata 'more than once has Ilium been attacked in war', but only the attack of the *Iliad* is known to fame. For at least one other attack cf. 3.3.65–7 *ter si resurgat murus aeneus | auctore Phoebo, ter pereat meis | excisus Argiuis.* H. rightly assumes other attacks on the famous city. Page rejects this meaning, preferring 'Not once only has an Ilium (i.e. a city such as Ilium) been harassed in war.' His translation ('not once only') is an attempt to make *semel* mean 'only', which is hard to parallel.

pugnauit . . . proelia: the combination is very common in prose, and found in Lucr., but not otherwise in Augustan or much other poetry.

ingens | Idomeneus Sthenelusue: Greek warriors from the *Iliad*; Idomeneus was a grandson of Minos, and fought at Troy with one of the four Cretan contingents. By the time Aeneas reaches Crete, word has it that Idomeneus has returned and settled there (Virg. *Aen.* 3.121–3). Sthenelus, one of the *epigonoi* whose father fought at Thebes, was included in the Trojan horse (Virg. *Aen.* 2.261).

dicenda Musis proelia 'battles to be sung by the Muses', with *Musis* dative of agent with *dicenda*. Implies a Homeric or oral stance (*Il* 1.1 μῆνιν ἄειδε θεά, 'sing goddess of the wrath'; *Od.* 1.1 ἄνδρα μοι ἔννεπε, Μοῦσα 'tell me Muse of the man'). Cf. Virg. *G.* 4.5 (of the bees) *mores et studia et populos et proelia dicam.*

21–2 non . . . uel: *uel* (cf. 30–2 *non . . . -ue*) follows a negative in late republican prose and in poetry from the Augustan period; cf. L–H–S 499–500.

22–4 Hector . . . pro pudicis | coniugibus puerisque: as true for Hector as it is false for Deiphobus; at Hom. *Il.* 24.729–30 Andromache laments Hector, with reference to his protecting Troy's wives and children: ὅς . . . ἔχες δ' ἀλόχους κεδνὰς καὶ νήπια τέκνα 'you who kept safe its noble wives and infant children'; the phrasing comes from *Il.* 21.460 σὺν παισὶ καὶ αἰδοίῃς ἀλόχοισι 'with children and well-regarded wives'.

Deiphobus: 'oddly enough, the only wife of his we hear of is Helen whom Deiphobus married after the death of Paris' (Quinn *ad loc.*; also Putnam 163–4) – oddly enough indeed. K–H think H. cannot have imagined that the *pudica coniunx* of Deiphobus is to be identified with the adulterous Helen who appeared six lines earlier, but they do not give an alternative, and the record knows of none. H. can hardly bring up Deiphobus without implicating Virg. *Aen.* 6.494–547, Aeneas' encounter with the shade of Deiphobus, who relates his betrayal, death and mutilation at the hands of Menelaus, egged on by Helen, the '*scelus exitiale Lacaenae*' as he puts it (511). It is as if H. pretends not to catch the sarcasm of the Virgilian Deiphobus (523 *egregia . . . coniunx*). Or perhaps he is correcting the Virgilian Deiphobus' account against the Homeric one (*Od.* 4.270–89), which has Deiphobus and Helen (in the account of Menelaus) going three times around the

Trojan Horse, with Helen imitating the voices of the Greeks' wives in an attempt to get them to give themselves away. Either way, lyric rewrites epic.

graues | . . . ictus: both heroes were defiled, Hector after his death, his brother Deiphobus before, perhaps by Helen herself, to judge by his words at Virg. *Aen.* 6.512 *'illa haec monimenta reliquit'*.

25 fortes 'heroes'.

26–8 omnes . . . urgentur . . . longa nocte: cf. 1.24.5 *ergo Quintilium perpetuus sopor urget*; 1.28.15 *omnis una manet nox*; 2.3.25 *omnes eodem cogimur*, where, however, the forms of *omnis* are all-inclusive, while in the present poem those who find their bard are implicitly, tendentiously, held to be exempt from the long night. Although the sentiment is something of a commonplace, H.'s examples show the *disiecta membra* of Cat. 5.6 *nox est perpetua una dormienda*. So Prop. 2.15.24 *nox tibi longa uenit, nec reditura dies* and Ov. *Her.* 10.112 (Ariadne, so with Catullan flavour) *aut semel aeterna nocte premenda fui*. The use of *urgeo* at 1.24.6 (in a poem addressed to Virgil) may look to *Aen.* 10.745–6 *olli dura quies oculos et ferreus urget | somnus*.

illacrimabiles: perhaps a Horatian invention, after ἀδάκρυτος 'unweeping' (Hom. *Il.* 1.415; *Od.* 24.61), here with passive force 'unwept', at 2.14.5–7 active 'that cannot be moved to tears': *non si trecenis quotquot eunt dies, | amice, places illacrimabilem | Plutona tauris* (and N–H *ad loc.*); cf. 1.24.9 *multis . . . flebilis*.

carent quia uate sacro: as at 8.26–7 (*lingua*) *uatum . . . consecrat*. Cf. *OLD* s.v. *sacer* 8 'Partaking of divine nature, holy: a (of poets, their utterances, etc.)'. Here for the first time, and cf. Ov. *Ars am.* 3.403 *quid petitur sacris, nisi tantum fama, poetis?*

29–30 A slightly obscure *sententia*, though it is clear enough what is meant: if human excellence and achievement is not celebrated in song (i.e. it remains *celata*), it ends up being not much different from lack of achievement or indolence. Bentley was bothered by *sepultae*, since he felt it was *living inertia* that unrecorded virtue resembled; but *sepultae* is just proleptic: indolence, 'which ends up being consigned to oblivion' – as does *celata uirtus*; for this sense of *sepelio* cf. *OLD* s.v. 3.

sepultae distat inertiae: for the dative with *disto* = 'be different from' (cf. *dissimilis*) of things, as here, cf. *TLL* s.v. *disto* 1535.39–51, which includes the ambiguous *Epist.* 1.7.23; 2.1.72; for the dative with persons cf. *TLL* 1534.60–1, with the unique instance *Epist.* 1.18.4 *infido scurrae distabit amicus*. The verb in this sense is also found with *a* at *S.* 2.2.53 *sordidus a tenui uictu distabit* (*uictui* will not go into the hexameter). *disto* = 'be distant from' is regularly and naturally used with ablative, as at *Epist.* 1.7.48 *foro nimium distare Carinas*.

30–44 H. turns to the *laudes Lollii* – if that they be.

30–4 Ambrose 1965, who sees irony throughout, points to the true ambiguity of this sentence. The normal reading takes *inornatum* proleptically ('will not be silent about you so as to leave you unadorned'), struggles with *impune* (Wilkins 'without an effort to resist it', Bennett 'undisturbed'), and takes *liuidas obliuiones* as the subject of *carpere* (for which see, e.g. Plin. *Pan.* 55.9 *arcus enim et statuas, aras etiam templaque demolitur et obscurat obliuio, neglegit carpitque posteritas*). But Ambrose

1965: 6, followed by Sage 1994: 577–8, suggests a different reading, and one that makes the poem a monument to Lollius' incompetence: (Sage) 'I will not allow you to be unheard of, unadorned by my pages, nor will I allow your many deeds (Ambrose: 'troubles'), unpunished, Lollius, to take and enjoy envied oblivion.' While such a passive and positive sense for *liuidus* is unparalleled, the sentence seems susceptible to such a reading.

non . . . te . . . inornatum silebo: also in a hymnic context at 1.12.21–2 *neque te silebo, | Liber*, where N–H refer to *Hymn. Hom. Ap.* 1 and Xen. *Ages.* 8.1. See also 8.21 (and 8 intro.) *si chartae sileant*; cf. Cat. 68.41–2 *non possum reticere, deae, qua me Allius in re | iuuerit*; Virg. *Aen.* 10.793 *non equidem nec te, iuuenis memorande, silebo.* See Race 1990: 73–5 for Pindar's use of negatives and litotes in dealing with praise and blame. For the collocation *non ego te*, see 12.22n.

non . . . -ue: cf. 21–2 *non . . . uel* and n.

chartis: cf. 8.20–2n.

inornatum: could this be a reference to the loss of the eagle? Suet. *Claud.* 13.2 (the eagle's hangings fall off, bad omen) *neque aquila ornari neque signa conuelli mouerique potuerunt.*

tuos . . . labores: taken by Bo to mean '*res gestae*', the only other Horatian instance being 4.45, where the noun is modified (*secundis . . . laboribus*) – another possible reference to Lollius' 'troubles'.

carpere: with *obliuiones* as subject 'reduce (by taking part away), wear away' (*OLD* s.v. 7b); with *labores* as subject, 'seize', pluck' (*OLD* s.v. 2). It is hard to parallel a non-personal subject in this sense, though *labores* is at least attached to a person (*tuos*).

liuidas | obliuiones: perhaps a word play and *ad hoc* folk etymology: ob*liv*ion is the result of *liuor* getting in the way (*ob*) of memory and repute (they are in fact not cognates); for the thought cf. 8.23–4 and 8.22–4n. *taciturnitas . . . inuida.* Even with the conventional reading (see n. above) with some irony perhaps, since Lollius could only profit from a little oblivion of his exploits. The name of Lollius in proximity to *Liu(or)*, may hint at a further etymologizing through *lolligo* 'squid', also attested in the form *lollium*, though much later (*TLL* s.v. 2. *lollium* 14–16). At *S.* 1.4.93 H. denies that he should appear *liuidus et mordax* for his mild jesting about the smell of Rufillus and Gargonius, but of malicious innuendo about a supposed friend he exclaims 100–1 *hic nigrae sucus lolliginis, haec est | aerugo mera*; *liuidus* connects in colour and in metaphorical meaning to *nigrae . . . lolliginis*, with each connoting envy and spite.

34–44 The heart of the encomium, a sentence full of vague clichés and ambiguities, and with syntax that breaks down in the middle; as Bentley said, 'Locus hic perdifficilis est, et varia hominum iudicia expertus.' The problem stems from 39 *consul*, which looks as if it must be, along with 37 *uindex*, 41 *iudex* and 44 *uictor*, an adjectival or participial predicate of *animus* ('a mind which consults'), the subject of the sentence. That might just be possible were it not for the phrase *non unius anni*, which becomes impossible to construe with *consul* understood thus.

Rudd's translation finesses the syntactical problem, by translating 39–41 'the mind of one who has been consul not just for one year, but as often as, like a good and reliable judge, he has put honour before convenience, etc.' So *animus* is connected to *consul* logically but not strictly as its predicate, with anacoluthon from *est animus tibi* ('you have a mind') to *consulque* (*erat*) ('he was a consul'); in fact *uindex* and *abstinens* are already looking to Lollius the person, rather than to his *animus*. Though the sentence is difficult, if not impossible, to decipher in conventional syntactical terms, it is best to understand some sort of ellipsis of *fuit*, e.g. 'and served as consul not just of one year, but as often as, a good and faithful judge, he has put the right before expediency, has rejected bribes and carried his arms'. He will continue through his civil and military acts to seem a virtual consul.

Bentley defended *animus consul* with an impressive array of parallels: Sall. *Iug.* 64.1 (of Jugurtha) *inerat contemptor animus et superbia*; Virg. *Aen.* 9.205 *est hic, est animus lucis contemptor*; Sen. *Epist.* 24.8 *generosum illum contemptoremque omnis potentiae spiritum*; *Dial.* 6.23.3 *uictorem omnium uoluptatium animum*; 12.2.2 *animum tot miseriarum uictorem* etc. He provides examples of *animus* with *aestimator, liberator, deprecator, contemplator, admirator, carnifex, proscriptor* and so on. *OLD* s.v. *consul* 3 '(w. ref. to supposed etym. connexion w. *consulo*)' gives inter al. Varro, *Ling.* 5.80 *consul nominatus qui consuleret populum et senatum*, itself quoting Accius from the *Brutus* (fr. 39 Ribb.): *qui recte consulat, consul cluat*; and then an applied entry consisting solely of H.'s line: 'cf. *est animus tibi . . ~l . . non unius anni*'. But the verbal essence of all of Bentley's examples, most of which are agent nouns, distinguishes *consul*, which is not demonstrably/formally so. *consul* is, and feels, different, and in particular the dependent phrase *non unius anni* in effect demands the otherwise consistent sense of *consul* = 'consul' rather than 'consulting'. Stephen Harrison *per litteras* suggests inserting *es* after *anni*.

The style is reminiscent of 8.13–20 (see 8 intro.), and here as there obscure language in the context of encomium or deflected encomium produces the urge to emend; so Shackleton Bailey on 39–44: 'locus perdifficilis, ut ait Bentley; quattuor uersus post 38 excidisse suspicor'. Possibly, but it is also a possibility that in both cases the difficulty, obscurity and ambiguity are part of the encomiastic falling short.

34 est animus tibi: cf. 8.9–10 *nec tibi talium* | *res est aut animus deliciarum egens.*

35 rerumque prudens 'worldly wise', as compared to *Epist.* 1.3.33 *rerum inscitia*, 'general inexperience' (Mayer); somewhat lame for a man who lost an eagle to German tribes.

que . . . et 'both . . . and', in poetry an archaism used in higher style, as also at 14.46 *Nilusque et Hister*; L–H–S 515; see 2.41–4n.

35–6 secundis | temporibus dubiisque rectus: by now a bit of a cliché. It recalls 2.10.1 *rectius, uiues Licini*, and cf. 13 *sperat infestis, metuit secundis* and 21–2 *rebus angustis animosus atque* | *fortis*. The issue is complex, but the addressee of that poem may have been the brother of Terentia, Maecenas' wife, killed by the régime in 23 or 22 BCE for involvement in a plot to kill the *princeps*; on which see inter al. Syme 1986: 387–91 and J. S. Arkenberg, *Historia* 42 (1993) 350–1, 489–91; for the various names by which the brother went see N–H *ad* 2.10 *praef.* It may be relevant that both poems are written to controversial public figures and both contain maxims about the need to take the middle course whether times are good or bad. But behind the slight triteness of the sentiment, there is the fact that both men may have paid for their ambition with their lives – certainly so in the case of Licinius, while the fate of Lollius is unclear (Plin. *HN* 9.118 claiming suicide, Vell. 2.102 agnostic on the cause of death).

37–43 H.'s characterization of Lollius is contradicted by Velleius, who seems the more credible witness, in spite of the hostility between Tiberius and Lollius (see 45–9n.): Vell. 2.97.1 *sed dum in hac parte imperii omnia geruntur prosperrime, accepta in Germania clades sub legato M. Lollio, homine in omnia pecuniae quam recte faciendi cupidiore et inter summam uitiorum dissimulationem uitiosissimo, amissaque legionis quintae aquila uocauit ab urbe in Gallias Caesarem.*

37–8 There is no reason to think Lollius was known for possessing such qualities, rather plausible evidence for his tendency toward avarice and venality; see 37–43, 45–52 nn. Nevertheless these lines could generally apply to Lollius' judicial activities as praetor.

uindex 'punishing greedy deceit', with participial force; cf. Livy 25.3.13 *populus seuerior uindex fraudis erat*; Cic. *Cat.* 2.27 *quem* [sc. *carcerem* = the *Tullianum*, place of execution] *uindicem nefariorum ac manifestorum scelerum maiores nostri esse uoluerunt.* Since Lollius seems to have been quite content with wealth (cf. 45–9n.), and in spite of the Livian parallel, the ambiguity of *uindex* (noted by Ambrose 1965: 8) cannot be ruled out ('avenger' or 'champion'?), though the parallels at *OLD* s.v. 2 have to do with positive concepts, such as *u. libertatis, ueritatis* etc.

auarae fraudis 'monetary fraudulence'; unlike the idea, the phrasing is bold, with a slight personification of *fraudis*, and is unique (*TLL* s.v. *fraus* 1272.57–8), as distinct from the combination *fraus et auaritia* etc., which is frequent.

abstinens . . . pecuniae: *abstineo* with 'Greek' genitive (cf. ἀπέχομαι) first in H. (also 3.27.69–70 *'abstineto'* | *dixit 'irarum calidaeque rixae'*, N–R *ad loc.*, and cf. L–H–S 83) and next at Apul. *Apol.* 10; cf. *TLL* s.v. 197.23–6 and *OLD* s.v. 8, which omits the present example.

ducentis ad se cuncta pecuniae: Porph. noted an ambiguity: *utrum pecuniam pro auaritia posuit, quae merito ad se ducere cuncta dicitur, quia auari rapere omnia student, <an> ducentis ad se cuncta pecuniae ad hoc referens dixit, quia pecuniosorum gratiam omnes sequuntur?* – allowing *cuncta* to effectively mean *cunctos*. For the expression, cf. Vitr. 8.1.5, on moisture's attraction to heat, *omnis tepor ad se ducit umores*; Sen. *Epist.* 60.13, on the power of grief (*dolor*), *qui recens consolatorem inuenit et aliquos ad se adducit, inueteratus uero deridetur*; or 65.22, on the power of the soul, *animus ad se omne ius ducet.*

39 consulque non unius anni: 'consul of not just one year'; the genitive is odd, perhaps an extension of objective genitive or genitive of description. See 33–44n. for the syntax within the whole sentence. For the litotes cf. Eur. *Med.*

952 οὐχ ἓν ἀλλὰ μυρία 'not in one respect but in thousands'. He was of course consul for just one year (21 BCE), but he behaved like one year after year in legal, civil and military affairs (40–4). K–H place a colon after *anni*, which helps the reader. He was in fact never consul again, and unlikely to be from the immediate post-Sygambrian perspective, so *unius* may be a pointed projection.

41 honestum praetulit utili: the first of the situations in which Lollius has seemed most like a perpetual consul – or king: K–H and Quinn both note H.'s allusion to the Stoic maxim that only the philosopher is king, spelled out at *Epist.* 1.1.106–7 *sapiens uno minor est Ioue, diues, | liber, honoratus, pulcher, rex denique regum* – unless, that is, he has a cold. It is not clear that preference for the *honestum* over the *utile* is something that commands approbation. So Dyck (*De off.* p. 81) 'throughout Book 3 Cicero insists there can be no actual conflict between *honestum* and *utile*, since the true *utile* coincides with the *honestum*'; this is so since 'the *utilitates* of the individual and of the community coincide' (Dyck, p. 33). Cf. *De off.* 3.9 *quia numquam posset utilitas cum honestate pugnare*, and 3.11 on the Stoic agreement with Socrates that the *honestum* defines what is and is not *utile*: *cui quidem ita sunt Stoici assensi ut et quicquid honestum esset, id utile esse censerent, nec utile quicquam quod non honestum*. See Dyck *passim*.

42–3 reiecit alto dona nocentium | uoltu: sounds good, but did he really (37–43n.)? And what about the gifts (i.e. bribes) of those not actually guilty?

alto . . . uoltu: hints at arrogance or worse; cf. Petron. 5.1.4, one of the prerequisites for the artist: *nec curet alto regiam trucem uultu*.

43–4 Military exploits come last and give a bathetic effect. He had reduced Galatia in 24 BCE, but the recent *clades Lolliana* would have overshadowed that.

explicuit sua . . . arma 'deployed his troops' (*OLD* s.v. *explico* 4; s.v. *arma* 7). A poetic variant for technical terminology, with the notion of 'unfolding a legion' from *agmen* to *acies*, as e.g. at Caes. *B.Ciu.* 2.26.4 *priusquam plane legiones explicari et consistere possent*; *TLL* s.v. *explico* 1726.16–51. Sen. *Phoen.* 628 reuses the phrasing of actual weapons: *licet arma longe miles ac late explicet*.

uictor: not always the case for Lollius.

45–52 The poem ends with another string of clichés, and worse, or, as Fraenkel put it (426), 'general maxims, fine maxims indeed, but not particularly relevant to Lollius': you would not call happy the man who possesses much; that name rather goes to the person who knows how to use the gifts of the gods, endure the hardship of poverty, fears disgrace more than death, is unafraid to die for friends and country. The lines in fact seem to describe the precise opposite of M. Lollius.

45–9 non possidentem multa . . . pauperiem: as Syme put it 1933: 429, 'the charges of rapacity and avarice . . . may perhaps be held confirmed rather than refuted by this poem'. These years did not see such men, even when not so elevated as to be left at least for a while in sole occupancy of the consulship, experiencing *dura pauperies*. Even if one downplays the witness of Velleius 2.97.1 (37–43n.), whose view may be extreme (in view of the bad relationship between Lollius and the young Tiberius) but will not have been created out of thin air, the details at Plin. *HN* 9.117–18 show that poverty was not something with which Lollius or his family will have had much familiarity. He recalls seeing Lollius' granddaughter, Lollia Paullina, at a modest wedding party with 40,000,000 sesterces' worth of emeralds and pearls intertwined all over her 'head, hair, ears, neck and fingers', gifts not from emperors (she was married to Gaius Caligula for a year) but part of the wealth accumulated by her grandfather Lollius through his plundering of the provinces (117 *auitae opes, prouinciarum scilicet spoliis partae*), as he 'disgraced himself by taking gifts from kings throughout the East' (118 *infamatus regum muneribus in toto oriente*). It is clear from what follows (C. Caesar's dismissal of Lollius) that Pliny is thinking primarily of the final stage of Lollius' career, a decade after publication of *C.* 4, but there is no reason to believe his tours in the east in the 20s and early teens were any less lucrative or that he decided he could no longer live the life of poverty after publication of H.'s poem, which, if read without irony, implicitly has him living such an unencumbered life. According to Tac. *Ann* 3.48.2, Lollius fostered C. Caesar's *prauitas* and *discordiae* towards Tiberius. Woodman (*ad* Vell. *loc. cit.*) tries to have both H. and the later tradition reflect reality, suggesting 'the man had simply become corrupted in the interval'. While this is possible, an ironic reading of H., in line with his encomiastic stances and ability throughout *C.* 4, would also provide an explanation.

45 uocaueris: a 'generalizing' second person singular potential perfect subjunctive and not addressed to the *laudandus*; see Woodcock 119, with e.g. Tac. *Ann.* 4.11.1 *haec prompte refutaueris.*

46 recte . . . rectius: see Wills 232–6 for the apparently common polyptoton of positive and comparative adjectives.

47–8 deorum | muneribus: high-minded things such as the gift of poetry: 3.21 *muneris hoc tui* [sc. *Melpomenes*]; Cic. *Arch.* 18, quoting Ennius, fr. incert. 19 Vahlen *quasi deorum aliquo dono atque munere commendati nobis esse uideantur*; the Bruti as a gift to the Roman state: Cic. *Phil.* 4.7 *ad libertatem populi Romani uel constituendam uel recipiendam*; the gift of the earth's habitable zones: Virg. *G.* 1.238 *munere . . . diuum* etc.; see *TLL* s.v. *munus* 1664.35–59. Cf. 10.1 *Veneris muneribus* and Putnam 178, n. 1 on other possible links between the two poems: 9.5, 10.4 *prior*; 9.10, 10.1 *adhuc* (neither occurring elsewhere in *C.* 4).

nomen beati: genitive of definition; cf. *Epist.* 1.6.15 *insani sapiens nomen ferat, aequus iniqui.* Cf. Cic. *Tusc.* 5.85 *hoc nomen beati longe et late patet.*

49 duramque callet: with a play on *calleo* 'to be/grow hard' ~ 'to be experienced/skilful in'; cf. Plaut. *Pers.* 304–5 TO. *quae dixi ut nuntiares, | satine ea tenes?* SO. *magis calleo quam aprugnum callum callet.*

pauperiem pati: doubly a cliché, repeated from 3.2.1–3 *pauperiem pati | robustus . . . puer | condiscat.* K–H distinguish between being poor and being practised in enduring poverty.

50 peius 'to an exceeding degree'. For the adverb thus, see *OLD* s.v. *peius* 2 ('adding force to vbs. expressing repugnance or distress'), as at *Epist.* 1.17.30–1 *alter Mileti textam cane peius et angui | uitabit chlamydem* – which works against taking the present instance as an adjective 'as being worse than death'. The same usage is found with *male* to intensify verbs 'possessing an unpleasant, depreciatory, etc. sense' (*OLD* s.v. *male* 10). For examples just with *metuo, odi* etc. (including both Horatian passages), see *TLL* s.v. *malus* 244.44–56. Examples are found mostly in Old Latin, but also sparingly in Cicero, Seneca, Petronius, but not in poetry after Plautus and Terence.

flagitium: general disgrace or dishonour; the *clades Lolliana* would presumably have qualified.

50–2 Death is preferable to disgrace, and the Stoic is unafraid to die for friends and country, just like Codrus at 3.19.2 *pro patria non timidus mori.* Ambrose 1965: 10 is put in mind of Cato's death after Thapsus (cf. 1.12.35–6 *Catonis | nobile letum*). Lollius in contrast suffered disgrace rather than death for country, and Ambrose suggests 'the conclusion of the ode suggests the means of atonement' (see intro.). Cf. Cic. *Phil.* 14.32 *o fortunata mors quae naturae debita pro patria est potissimum reddita!*; *Rab. perd.* 37 *ut eum <qui> pro patria nu<llum> umquam mor<tis pe>riculum fugit <in> patria mori pati<amini>*. For a more cynical view of the merits of dying for country, cf. Cicero's characterization of L. Calpurnius Piso Caesoninus at *Sest.* 23 *eos autem qui dicerent dignitati esse seruiendum . . . adeunda pro patria pericula, . . . mortem oppetendam, uaticinari atque insanire dicebat.*

timet | non . . . timidus: an effective repetition: fears disgrace more than death, doesn't fear to die.

perire: K–S II 1.685–7 include this and 3.19.2 with infinitives which describe the sphere in which the action implied by the adjective takes place (see 12.19–20n.), but in the case of *perire* and *mori* they are better seen as extensions of the prolative infinitive with *timeo*, which occurs often in H.: 1.8.8; 3.24.56; *S.* 1.4.23; *Epist.* 1.5.2; 1.19.27; 2.1.114; *AP* 170, 197, 455; so too 3.2.21–2 *Virtus, recludens immeritis mori | caelum.*

10

METRE

Fifth Asclepiadean, consisting of stichic repetition of the 'Greater Asclepiadean', that is, a glyconic with double choriambic expansion (– – – ⏑⏑ – – ⏑⏑ – – ⏑⏑ – ⏑ ×), otherwise only for 1.11, 18.

INTRODUCTION

You who are still cruel and still potent through the gifts of Venus, when unexpected downiness comes to your arrogance, and the hair that now floats about your shoulders falls (to the barber), and the complexion that outdoes the flower of the crimson rose is changed, Ligurinus, and turned into a bristly bush, you will say 'Alas', as often as you see a different you in the mirror, 'why didn't I have the same state of mind when I was a boy as I do today, or why don't those unscathed cheeks return to join my current outlook?'

With 1.30 and 1.38 the shortest of the *Odes*. More than any other in the corpus the poem strives for a close identity with Hellenistic epigram, of which it is in part a Romanizing adaptation. The whole run of *Anth. Pal.* 12.24–41, as commentators have noted without close scrutiny, almost all in the Meleagrian *Garland*, and therefore long available to the Roman poets, deals with boys whose pederastically appealing bloom is contrasted with the mature, unappealing state in which they will soon find themselves (see Tarán 1985 for good treatment of the topic). The thrust of these poems has to do with the art of persuasion of the older *erastes*, as it would seem to for H. To that extent it is in close connection with the ending of the first poem of the book. A number treat the contrast between the smoothness of youth and the bristly state that lies ahead, when the younger *eromenos* will find the tables turned (to include only those available to H. in Meleager's anthology): Alcaeus 8 G-P (= *Anth. Pal.* 12.30) ἡ κνήμη, Νίκανδρε, δασύνεται· ἀλλὰ φύλαξαι, | μή σε καὶ ἡ πυγὴ ταὐτὸ παθοῦσα λάθηι· | καὶ γνώσηι, φιλέοντος ὅση σπάνις. ἀλλ' ἔτι καὶ νῦν | τῆς ἀμετακλήτου φρόντισον ἡλικίης, 'your leg is getting shaggy, Nicander; but watch out that the same thing doesn't sneak up on you and happen to your buttocks; then will you know what a shortage of lovers there is. But even now reflect on the irrevocability of youth' – and therefore be persuaded. Similar conceits are found in Phanias 1 G-P (= *Anth. Pal.* 12.31); Mel. 90 G–P (= *Anth. Pal.* 12.33). Variations include Mel. 94 G–P (= *Anth. Pal.* 12.41): it is time to move back to women, now that Theron and Apollodotus have become 'hairy-arsed' (3 δασυτρώγλων). In Anon. *Anth. Pal.* 12.39 – whose final words could stand as the title for all these poems – there is a closeness of tone, and the same connection between the hirsute youth and arrogance: 3–4 ἀλλὰ φρονεῖτε | μηδὲν ὑπὲρ θνητούς, ὦ νέοι· εἰσὶ τρίχες, 'don't have thoughts above mortal station, lads: there are hairs'. H.'s poem is generically as close to epigram as any of the *Odes* and is clearly intended to be read as such. Anyone who believes in the reality of Ligurinus in 1 will have difficulty attaching biographical significance to the L. of 10, 'whose artist's dummy has no closer contact with reality than fair-haired Ganymede in the talons of an eagle' (Bradshaw 1970: 152).

Critics have long been bothered with *pluma* in the second line. How, they have asked, can H. say to Ligurinus, 'When the down comes to your face' while also saying 'and turns your appearance into a bristling beard' (5 *faciem . . . hispidam*). One possibility would be to see a progression from the early feathering, which will curb L.'s pride, to the more hirsute stage when he looks in the mirror at 6. The problem has seemed more serious to many and has led to an array of emendations of *pluma*; see Asztalos 2008: 290–3 for the candidates. H. has his eye on Greek epigram, which deals in facial hair, but also with hair elsewhere on the body as signifiers of the transition; cf. again Alcaeus 8.1–2 G–P (see above); Phanias 1.3 G–P (= *Anth. Pal.* 12.31.2–3) βαιὸς ἔχει τὸν σὸν ἔρωτα χρόνος· | ἤδη γὰρ καὶ μηρὸς ὑπὸ τρίχα, καὶ γένυς ἡβᾷ 'there's little time left for your love: already your thigh gets hairy, and your cheek is pubescent'. H. is in this poem dealing with a specific intertext: *Anth. Pal.* 12.36 is attributed to an otherwise unknown Asclepiades of Adramyttium. With no great confidence that he is to be identified with the Samian poet of the same name, G–P nevertheless include him, as Asclep. 46 (see also Tarán 1985: 90–1). The epigram's theme of hairy thighs is shared by the two Philippan epigrams that precede it and the two Meleagrian that follow, and it seems particularly close to 10:

νῦν αἰτεῖς, ὅτε (*cum*) λεπτὸς ὑπὸ κροτάφοισιν ἴουλος
ἕρπει καὶ μηροῖς ὀξὺς ἔπεστι χνόος· (*ueniet pluma superbiae*)
εἶτα λέγεις· '"Ηδιον ἐμοὶ τόδε.' καὶ τίς ἂν εἴποι
κρείσσονας αὐχμηρὰς ἀσταχύων καλάμας;

'Now you come asking, when the light fluff creeps under your temples and there is bristly down on your thighs. Then you say "I think I'm better like this". Yet would anyone else say "dry stubble is better than eared corn"?'

Down and bristles together, just on different parts of the body, and the metaphor from the plant world will also be important. This *eromenos* whose youth has passed looks like a model for Ligurinus. H. could not write *ueniet pluma clunibus/cruribus* in the *Odes* (as opposed to the *Epodes*), but that is what is behind the vague *ueniet pluma superbiae*, which conflates two separate themes of models which H. could write. Cf. also the opening of Automedon 10 (= *Anth. Pal.* 11.326): πώγων καὶ λάσιαι μηρῶν τρίχες, ὡς ταχὺ πάντα | ὁ χρόνος ἀλλάσσει, 'beard and thigh-hair, how swiftly time changes everything'.

Asztalos 2008 offers a radical re-reading, with no connection to Hellenistic epigram. She sees 10.1–2 and the whole poem as consisting of self-address by H., connecting the poem to earlier programmatic passages (2.20 and 3.30), and argues that the *pluma* of 4.10.2 is to be seen as having an intratextual relationship with 2.20.12, where H. talks of the *plumae* that will overcome him when he attains poetic immortality and turns into a bird (*superne* if not *superbe*, one might add). The argument is ingenious and may find favour with readers, but I have chosen not to include a full description of it here. The absence of identifying personal pronouns and adjectives in 1–2 and 7–8 makes it hard for the reader to follow the putative switch in identities that Asztalos argues for in those lines. And coming off the older lover's address at Virg. *Ecl.* 2.6 (*o crudelis Alexi*; see 1n.), and the most recent encounter with Ligurinus at 1.40 (*dure*), it may be asking too much of the reader to see this as self-address.

1 O crudelis: as ps.-Acro noted (*ad loc.*), the *incipit* alludes to and invokes the context of Virg. *Ecl.* 2.6, the opening of the shepherd Corydon's elegy over the house-slave Alexis (*o crudelis Alexi*), also Corydon's recapitulation at 17–18; see 4–5n. The opening *o* is more characteristic of sepulchral than erotic epigram, though Thgn. 1234–1351 shows eleven instances of ὦ παῖ 'my boy', at couplet-initial position (see intro.).

Veneris muneribus potens: cf. 9.47–8 (and n.) *deorum* | *muneribus*, also 1.17–18 (there ablative of comparison) *potentior* | *largi muneribus riserit aemuli*. The thought originates in archaic Greek: Hom. *Il.* 3.54–5 (Hector to Paris on how little his charms will help in the encounter with Menelaus) οὐκ ἄν τοι χραίσμηι κίθαρις τά τε δῶρ' Ἀφροδίτης | ἥ τε κόμη τό τε εἶδος ὅτ' ἐν κονίηισι μιγείης, 'the lyre will not help you, nor the gifts of Aphrodite, or your hair and your beauty, when you mingle in the dust'; cf. 65; *Hymn. Hom. Dem.* 102; Hes. *Eoiai* fr. 76.6, 10 (= 48.31, 35 Most, the huntress's rejection of love); Thgn. 2.1293–4 (also of Atalanta, but in a pederastic, persuasive context, as for H.), 1304 Κυπρογενοῦς δῶρον 'gift of the Cyprus-born'. Cf. also Anacreon, fr. 2.3 West (in a priamel) Μουσέων τε καὶ ἀγλαὰ δῶρ' Ἀφροδίτης | συμμίσγων, 'combining the shining gifts of the Muses and of Aphrodite'; Catullus reproduced the Anacreontic pairing at 68.10 *muneraque et Musarum hinc petis et Veneris*.

potens: see 1.17n.

2 cum ueniet pluma: cf. Asclep. 46.1–2 G–P (= *Anth. Pal.* 12.36.1–2) ὅτε . . . ἔπεστι χνόος, 'when the fluff appears' (see intro.).

pluma: a striking and original way of referring to the first growth of hair (down) that marks the transition away from pederastic appeal – but with ample Greek precedent. Putnam 180–2 sees a connection with the metamorphosis of Cupavo (from Liguria) who turned into a swan (1.33–4n.). See intro. on this and on the approach of Asztalos 2008.

insperata: the signs of puberty creep up; cf. Alcaeus 8.1–2 G–P (= *Anth. Pal.* 12.30.2) μή σε καὶ ἡ πυγὴ ταὐτὸ παθοῦσα λάθηι, '(beware) that the same thing doesn't sneak up on you and happen to your buttocks' (see intro.). Given the setting of *C.* 1.5, to Pyrrha (*multa . . . in rosa*), whatever the precise meaning of that setting, there is in *insperata* a hint of the unexpected change that that would come to the *gracilis puer* of that poem: 10–11 *qui semper uacuam, semper amabilem* | *sperat*.

superbiae: 'a refusal of sexual favours could be represented as arrogance', so N–R, with further examples, on 3.10.9, to Lyce, *ingratam Veneri pone superbiam*.

3 inuolitant: cf. 1.37–40 (on *uolucrem*) and Putnam 181 for Ligurinus' ornithological associations.

deciderint: i.e has been cut and fallen, as at Lucr. 3.644–5 *id quod* | *decidit abscisum*, not 'has fallen out': again the future Ligurinus is not old, but rather mature. Cf. *TLL* s.v. *cado* 23.9–24.58 for the quasi-passive use of *cado* = *caedi*, 23.74–80 with *a* or *ab*. Long hair is a sign of youthful male beauty: cf. 2.5.23 (and N–H *ad loc.*), 3.20.14 *sparsum odoratis umerum capillis*; *Epod.* 11.28 (and Mankin *ad loc.*); cf. Serv. *ad Aen.* 1.740 *CRINITVS IOPAS: aut puerum intellege aut . . .*; also of attractive slave-boys: Sen. *Epist.* 119.14; Mart. 12.49.1. At Plut. *Ant.* 11.6 Antony and Dolabella's long hair indicate profligacy. H. again has his eye on Greek epigram, here Rufinus *Anth. Pal.* 5.28. 3–4 νῦν μοι προσπαίζεις, ὅτε τὰς τρίχας ἠφανικάς σου | τὰς ἐπὶ τοῖς σοβαροῖς αὐχέσι πλαζομένας, 'so now you flirt with me, when you've lost your long hair, that wandered (cf. *inuolitant*) on your proud (cf. *superbiae*) shoulders'. The poem is post-Horatian but is remarkably similar to ours – and Rufinus borrows in the same poem from *Anth. Pal.* 11.53.2 (see 4–5n.).

4–5 'and when, Ligurinus, your complexion now brighter than the flower of the crimson rose has changed and turned into a prickly appearance'; perhaps alludes to Virg. *Ecl.* 2.17–18 (Corydon making the same argument) *o formose puer, nimium ne crede colori: | alba ligustra cadunt, uaccinia nigra leguntur.* Alexis the indoor slave is the ideal of feminine beauty, while Ligurinus, the athlete of 1, has a ruddy complexion. But the image also shows a debt to the Meleagrian Anon. *Anth. Pal.* 12.40.3–4, where the *eromenos* asks to be looked at only with his cloak on, since he has developed body hair: γυμνὴν Ἀντιφίλου ζητῶν χάριν, ὡς ἐπ' ἀκάνθαις | εὑρήσεις ῥοδέαν φυομένην κάλυκα 'seeking out the naked beauty of Antiphilus, you will find the rose blossom growing as on thorns'. The emendation of *Ligurinum* of the MSS is highly desirable, though sense can be made of the accusative.

puniceae: cf. 13.13 and n. *purpurae*, and Lucr. 2.830 *purpura poeniceusque color clarissimus multo.*

in faciem . . . hispidam 'into a prickly appearance'. *faciem*, if retained, may connote general appearance as well as the face. Indeed *facies* on its own = 'face' is not secure before H. (*TLL* s.v. *facies* 46.11–13), who has it so at 5.14 and *S.* 1.2.94, 5.62, 6.33; 2.8.36. Examples of *in faciem* (= 'appearance') *uertere* at Ov. *Met.* 1.126–7, 160; 12.560 support *faciem* in H., but in none of these is there the ambiguity of H.'s situation ('face' or 'appearance' possible). Even though *faciem* does not offend so much given that *pluma* could refer to hair other than facial, it has seemed weak to some, and, if naturally pointing towards 'face' specifically, is concrete after the deliberate vagueness of *ueniet pluma superbiae*. On the basis of Pers. 4.41 (body-hair out of control) *non tamen ista filix ullo mansuescit aratro*, Nisbet (*Gnomon* 58 (1986) 615) suggested *filicem* ('bracken', 'fern') for *faciem*, also citing Tarán 1985 and *Anth. Pal.* 11.53 (also, significantly, appended in *Syll. S* (see G–P *ad loc.* to the Meleagrian Alcaeus 7 = *Anth. Pal.* 12.29): τὸ ῥόδον ἀκμάζει βαιὸν χρόνον· ἢν δὲ παρέλθηι | ζητῶν εὑρήσεις οὐ ῥόδον, ἀλλὰ βάτον, 'the rose blooms for a short season; if you pass by looking for it, you will find not a rose but a briar'). The idea of change is right, but this hardly supports *filicem* – what is needed is not a fern but a roseless rose-bush, a briar. I therefore propose for consideration *fruticem* 'briar'. Columella *Arb.* 1.2 begins by dividing woody plants into trees, shrubs and a third type consisting of vines: *ex surculo uel arbor procedit, ut olea, ficus, pirus, uel frutex, ut uiolae, rosae, harundines, uel tertium quiddam, quod neque arborem neque fruticem proprie dixerimus, sicuti est uitis*; for Pliny the rose grows on a *spina* rather than a *frutex*, but that is a technicality that makes it clear *spina* and *frutex* can both be used for 'briar' or 'rosebush': *NH* 21.14 *rosa nascitur spina uerius quam frutice.* Ovid twice applies the metaphor precisely to the situation in H.; at *Ars am.* 2.115–18 he treats the fleeting nature of physical beauty: *nec uiolae semper nec hiantia lilia florent, | et riget amissa spina relicta rosa. | et tibi iam uenient cani, formose, capilli* [cf. 2 *ueniet pluma*], | *iam uenient rugae, quae tibi corpus arent*; and at *Fast.* 5.353–4 Flora herself takes the metaphor from her own realm as she urges rosebud gathering: *et monet aetatis specie, dum floreat, uti;*

| *contemni spinam, cum cecidere rosae*. H.'s *puniceae . . . rosae* ~ *fruticem . . . hispidam* is in good company. Cf. 13.9–10 and n. for a similar metaphor.

uerterit: for *uerto in* as an intransitive see *OLD* s.v. *uerto* 22 (e.g. Lucr. 5.831 *omnia commutat natura et uertere cogit*; Virg. *G.* 3.365 *et totae solidam in glaciem uertere lacunae*).

6 dices: Ligurinus shares the verb, with interesting resonance, with the choir girl of 6.41, reflecting in later life on her earlier days (*nupta iam dices*), with H. in the past for each of them.

quotiens: implies obsessive frequency of L.'s looking in the mirror. For the mirror and fading looks, cf. Ov. *Medic.* 47–8 *tempus erit, quo uos speculum uidisse pigebit,* | *et ueniet rugis altera causa dolor.*

speculo: either instrumental ablative, where the image is conveyed by means of the mirror; cf. Juv. 2.99–101 *ille tenet speculum . . . quo se ille uidebat* | *armatum*; Mart. 2.66.3 *hoc facinus Lalage speculo, quo uiderat, ulta est*; or perhaps better a locatival ablative, though parallels have the preposition: Cic. *Pis.* 71 *tamquam in speculo uitam intueri*; Ov. *Her.* 9.118 *uidit et in speculo coniugis arma mei!*; *Met.* 15.232. Lucr. 4.269–70 imagines the image as being through and beyond the mirror: *nunc age, cur ultra speculum uideatur imago* | *percipe.*

alterum: predicative with *te*, with the meaning, here for the first time, 'changed', 'different'; cf. *TLL* s.v. *alter* 1736.27–48. In meaning not quite the second person of *alter ego*, which does not occur in Classical Latin – at Ov. *Am.* 1. 7.32 *alter ego!* means 'I was the second (after Diomedes) to strike a deity!'

7–8 When his bloom is lost Ligurinus will ask why his newfound sexual appetite did not exist in his boyhood, or why his boyhood could not return to that newfound appetite, an elegant inversion of the same idea.

puero: predicate noun, with possessive dative, *mihi*, understood.

incolumes . . . genae 'cheeks unsullied' by facial hair, and by the razor.

redeunt: again the theme of return, or rather now of non-return, not just for himself as in 4.1, but for the once-youthful boy of his desires. See 5.3–4, 7.1–2nn.

11

METRE

Sapphic stanza (as in 2).

INTRODUCTION

All is ready, Phyllis: a cask of nine-year-old wine, parsley and ivy for wreaths, a lamb ready for the knife, slave-boys and girls going back and forth making preparations and a fire ready to do its work. You should know the occasion: we will be celebrating Maecenas' birthday, 13 April. I know you're preoccupied with Telephus, but that is a hopeless case, since he is happily ensnared with a higher-class woman, so like Phaethon and Bellerophon you should realize your limits, not reach too high and therefore be content with – me. You'll be my last flame, I'll teach you to sing, and song will relieve care.

An invitation to Phyllis to a private party of two, it seems. *Pace* Quinn (intro.) there is no reason to assume that Maecenas will be present, and the fact that H. does not mention other guests is revealing. What begins as an invitation poem soon turns into an erotic persuasion poem, in contrast to the preceding ode in its sexual orientation. Cairns 1972: 74 notes the ad hoc nature of the invitation poem: 'The epideictic *kletikon* (speech of official invitation) has a parallel specialized "unofficial" form, the informal invitation (*uocatio*), often to a meal and so known as *uocatio ad cenam*.' N–H *ad* 1.20 (pp. 244–6) refer to it as a 'minor category of Hellenistic epigram', and this may well be so, but the 'prototype' (*Anth. Pal.* 11.44) is by Philodemus, who lived, worked and dined with Romans, and the epigram is an invitation to a Roman (L. Calpurnius Piso Caesoninus, cos. 58 BCE). There is no way of knowing whether that poem was written before or after, say, Cat. 13. Edmunds 1982 therefore seems right to suggest the form looks more to Roman social convention than to a scarcely represented Hellenistic epigram type produced in Italy. Extrapolating from a number of invitation-poems (Cat. 13, Hor. *Epist.* 1.5, Mart. 5.78, 10.48, 11.52), Edmunds identifies three components, under each of which 11 also qualifies: (A) invitation proper: 13–20 (including the date); (B) menu: 1–12; (C) entertainment: 34–6 (song, but other things too, at least in the mind of H.).

As often in H., the formal model is only the starting point. As her name suggests, Phyllis is hardly the type of person to whom Q. Horatius Flaccus would have sent any dinner invitation. The form allows him archly to develop his persuasive move and also allows a lingering on Maecenas, since dinner with Phyllis is set for his birthday. This is the sole appearance of H.'s friend in the book.

There is a close relationship between 11 and 12. Both are invitation poems, but they are inversions of each other, and in odd ways. Here Phyllis will find everything present (cask of wine, wreath-making materials, lamb for feasting), whereas in 12 Virgil will end up sharing a cask of wine with H. only if he brings along the purchase price (a jar of nard), which H. will use to buy the actual wine (12.17–19n.). Of course, given the goal of H. in 11, it is in his interests to paint as rosy a picture as possible. The poems of the triad 10–12 all treat sympotic or erotic themes, with Ligurinus (10.5), Maecenas (11.19) and Virgil (12.13) all set in the centre. Porter 1985, on the other hand, building on Fuqua (*CP* 63 (1968) 44–6) draws attention to the ways 11–13 map onto a similar cycle at 1.23–25: 1.23, 4.11: seduction/invitation poems to Chloe (χλόη, 'shoot'), Phyllis (φυλλίς 'leaf'); 1.24, 4.12: poems to Virgil; 1.25, 4.13; Lydia will be, Lyce has become, an old woman. A number of Virgilian touches in particular anticipate 4.12 (see 1–5, 2–3, 3, 4–5, 5, 15–16, 19, 21–31, 21–4, 29–31, 31–2nn.). As with 10, the cycle of the seasons and passing of time are very much in the air in both poems.

1–12 The anaphora of *est*, the asyndetic accumulation of details and the verbs of the third stanza (*festinat* | *cursitant* | *trepidant rotantes*) have an iconic effect, communicating hustle and bustle. H. gives the impression of reading from a list, with everything directed at persuading Phyllis that this is the place to be. By the center, and particularly by the end, things have changed (17–20, 35–6nn.).

1–5 Est mihi . . . est . . . est: cf. 3.29.2–5 *non ante uerso lene merum cado* | *cum flore . . . apud me est.* But in the present lines the language of pastoral self-advertisement is distinguishing, as at Theoc. 5.104–5 ἔστι δέ μοι γαυλὸς κυπαρίσσινος, ἔστι δὲ κρατήρ | ἔργον Πραξιτέλευς 'I have a pail of cypress-wood, I have a bowl, the artwork of Praxiteles'; 9.9 (of the *locus amoenus*) ἔστι δέ μοι παρ' ὕδωρ ψυχρὸν στιβάς 'I have a couch by the cool stream'. The entire opening speech of the Syrian 'hostess' in the pseudo-Virgilian *Copa* is constructed as an extravagant example of this style: 7 *sunt*, 11 *est*, 12 *est*, 13 *sunt*, 17 *sunt*, 18 *sunt*, 20 *est . . . est . . . est*, 21 *sunt*, 23 *est*. Virgil had already adapted this style for the *Eclogues*: 2.36–7 (Corydon's erotic persuasion of Alexis) *est mihi disparibus septem compacta cicutis* | *fistula*; also 3.33 (there an excuse rather than an advertisement) *est mihi namque domi pater, est iniusta nouerca*. By the time the addressee is named at 3 (*Phylli*), the reader recognizes a situation that goes back through *Ecl.* 2 to Theoc. 11, the hopeless cases of Corydon and Polyphemus and their attempts to persuade Alexis and Galatea respectively. The ageing H. will presumably be as unsuccessful in his attempt at one last fling (33–4n.).

1 nonum superantis annum: oddly specific; has it been waiting to be used since publication of *C.* 1–3 ten years before publication of *C.* 4? The play which H. pretends to have curtailed when turning to the *Epistles* (1.14.36 *nec lusisse pudet, sed non incidere ludum*) included the drinking of wine (34). He frequently designates the vintage, often in colourful terms: 1.20.2–3 (with N–H); 3.8.11–12; 3.14.18 *cadum Marsi memorem duelli*, i.e. 91–87 BCE, 'when Venusia had joined the revolt of Rome's Italian allies' (N–R *ad loc.*), the oldest wine mentioned by H.; 3.21.1–4 *O nata mecum consule Manlio* (sc. *Torquato*, i.e. 65 BCE); 3.28.8 *Bibuli consulis amphoram*; *Epod.* 13.6 (and Mankin *ad loc.* including reference to *ROL* IV 208–11) *uina Torquato . . . consule pressa meo*; *S.* 2.8.47 *uino quinquenni, uerum citra mare nato*; *Epist.* 1.5.4 *uina . . . iterum Tauro diffusa* and Mayer *ad loc.*: i.e. casked (from the *dolium*) in 26 BCE, the second consulship of T. Statilius Taurus.

2 plenus Albani cadus: in contrast to the as yet unpurchased *cadus* of 12.17.

Albani: a vintage Alban, one of the wines on offer at Nasidienus' dinner-party, where Maecenas was in attendance, at *S.* 2.8.16–17, as the host points out: '*Albanum, Maecenas, siue Falernum* | *te magis appositis delectat, habemus utrumque*'. At Plin. *HN* 14.64 it is named as the third best of Italy's wines, following *uinum Pucinum* (northern bay of the Adriatic, around the River Timavus) and Falernian.

2–3 est in horto | . . . nectendis apium coronis 'in my garden I have celery for wreathing garlands'. 'Loose attachment of the dative gerundive to a noun [to express purpose], as in legal formulae like *duumuiri sacris faciundis*, is common in early Latin, rare in Caesar, Cicero and Sallust, but fairly common in Livy and Tacitus' (Woodcock 165).

apium: probably 'celery' rather than 'parsley'. The word is used for a wide range of plants, on which see André 1956: 35, and Plin. *HN* 19.123 on the various types of celery. For the connection with garlands, cf. 1.36.15–16 (with N–H on 16) *neu desint epulis rosae | neu uiuax apium neu breue lilium*; 2.7.23–5 *quis udo |deproperare apio coronas |curatue myrto?* The Virgilian atmosphere continues, since *apium* as an ingredient for garlands appears first in *Ecl.* 6.68 *floribus atque apio crinis ornatus amaro* (with Clausen *ad loc.*) and otherwise only in H. and again at Virg. *G.* 4.120–1 (the gardens of Paestum) *quoque modo potis gauderent intiba riuis | et uirides apio ripae.* Gk. σέλινον (whence Eng. 'celery') was used to crown victors at the Nemean and Isthmian Games (Juv. 8.226) and for garlands at symposia (Anac. 65 Page σελίνων στεφανίσκους 'little garlands of celery'); cf. also Theoc. 3.22–3, where the singer, in expectation of the arrival of Amaryllis, wears a garland of ivy (see 4–5n.), rosebuds and celery. See *ThLL* s.v. *apium* 240.22–25.

3 Phylli: the invitee has interesting associations, none diminished by the fact that the name survives in inscriptions, clearly of respectable women. She seems to be generic at 2.4.14: for all one knows a blond Phyllis might turn out to have wealthy parents and so be worth marrying. In the current context H. may have borrowed her from Propertius 4.8, where that poet invites over two local ladies of easy virtue, Phyllis and a Teia, the former amorous when tipsy, the latter when drunk not to be satisfied by a single man. Nothing happens – even though they are bare-breasted by line 47 – since he cannot get his mind off Cynthia, who arrives back *in mediis rebus* from Lanuvium, where she had gone to observe the rites of Juno, as she claimed – of Venus in Propertius' imagination. H. as reader of Propertius might have reasons to be hopeful.

Perhaps even closer to home in view of the Virgilian associations of this poem and its relationship to the poem that follows, Phyllis appears several times in the *Eclogues*: 3.76, 78, 107; 5.10; 7.14, 59, 63 (*bis*); 10.37, 41. She is not Theocritean, is quite expert in the ways that matter to shepherds and is even, in the view of Menalcas, a fit 'birthday present', perhaps of interest given the birthday context of H.'s invitation: 3.76–7 M.: *Phyllida mitte mihi: meus est natalis, Iolla; | cum faciam uitula pro frugibus, ipse uenito*. Damoetas, in reply, has his own fantasies: D.: *Phyllida amo ante alias; nam me discedere fleuit | et longum 'formose, uale, uale,' inquit, 'Iolla'*. By the end of the poem Damoetas can have Phyllis for himself if he gets the answer to Damoetas' riddle (107 *et Phyllida solus habeto*). The sexual innuendo is pervasive.

4–5 hederae uis | multa 'an abundant supply of ivy', also for garlands, as at Virg. *Ecl.* 7.25 *hedera crescentem ornate poetam*, 8.12–13 *hanc sine tempora circum | inter uictrices hederam tibi serpere lauros*; also to be found in the gardens of Paestum (2–3n.) at Virg. *G.* 4.124 *pallentesque hederas*. K–H note *uis multa* avoids the prosaic *uis magna*.

5 crinis religata 'with your hair tied back'; cf. 1.5.4 *cui flauam religas comam?* Virgilian diction and syntax (*E.* 6.68 *crinis ornatus*, see 2–3n.), specifically the use of the 'retained accusative' (called by some a 'Greek' accusative of respect, by others an accusative with 'middle' verb, also Greek), a preferable way of seeing the accusative of a body part or clothing item, in which we can hypothesize an active *religat crines* (*crinem*) *sibi*. When passivization 'occurs' the possessive dative (as owner or controller of the body part or item of clothing) becomes the subject, and the accusative is 'retained' in the passive expression (as in 'I had my hair cut'); see L–H–S 36–7; K–S II 1.285–92; Courtney 2004: 425–31. Similarly in H. at 8.33 *ornatus uiridi tempora pampino*; 2.11.23–4 *in comptum Lacaenae | more comam religata nodum*. It is particularly favoured by Virgil, e.g. (just in the case of *crinis*) *Aen.* 3.365 (= 11.35) *Iliades crinem de more solutae*; 4.216–7 *mentum mitra crinemque madentem | subnexus*, 509 *crines effusa sacerdos*; 6.281 *uipereum crinem uittis innexa cruentis*; 12.605–6 *flauos Lauinia crines | et roseas laniata genas*.

6 ridet argento domus: an appealing image: the house is ready to give a silver-sparkling welcome; cf. 4.41 (*dies*) *primus alma risit adorea*. Homer uses γελάω of nature (with the sense of 'shine'; cf. Chantraine for cognates such as γλῆνος 'bauble') at *Il.* 19.362–3 γέλασσε δὲ πᾶσα περὶ χθὼν | χαλκοῦ ὑπὸ στεροπῆς 'the whole earth smiles from the gleam of bronze' (with Richardson *ad loc.* and especially West on Hes. *Theog.* 40). See N–H on 2.6.14 (13–14 *ille terrarum mihi praeter omnes | angulus ridet*) for instances from Ennius on, including the synaesthesia at Cat. 64.284 (also of *domus*) *quo permulsa domus iucundo risit odore*; also Virg. *Ecl.* 4.20 *ridenti . . . acantho*; 7.55 *omnia nunc rident*; *OLD* s.v. 3 'of things having a bright and cheerful or welcoming aspect'. H.'s *ridet* also interacts well with the immediately preceding metaphor in *fulges*.

6–8 Sound patterns and rhyme create the effect of a *carmen*, appropriately in context: *ara castis | uincta uerbenis | auet immolato | spargier agno*.

castis: the ingredients of the sacrifice, corporeal or otherwise, could all be designated thus; so Varro, *Sat. Men.* 181 *ergo tum sacrae, religiosae castaeque fuerunt res omnes*; cf. 1.12.59–60 *parum castis . . . lucis*; Virg. *Aen.* 7.71 *castis adolet dum altaria taedis*. See *TLL* s.v. *castus* 565.45–70.

uerbenis: according to Donat. *ad Andria* 726, the twigs and leaves of a variety of plants used to garland altars; cf. 1.19.13–16 (with N–H *ad* 14) *hic uiuum mihi caespitem, hic | uerbenas, pueri, ponite turaque | bimi cum patera meri: | mactata ueniet lenior hostia*. It is derived from *uerbera* 'twigs for flogging, whip, lashes' (de Vaan 2008: 664). For the use of wreaths on altars, see Horsfall on Virg. *Aen.* 3.25.

auet: the altar is seen as craving blood; cf. Cat. 68.79–80 *quam ieiuna pium desideret ara cruorem | docta est amisso Laodamia uiro*.

immolato | spargier agno: the compression verges on the grotesque, at least to modern taste; cf. Lucr. 5.1201–2 (with disapproval) *aras sanguine multo | spargere quadripedum*.

8 spargier: the archaic present passive or deponent infinitive, appropriate in this sacral setting (see 6–8n.), is otherwise absent from the *Odes* and *Epodes* and is in the *Satires* and *Epistles* (where it is found eight times) occasionally marked due to metrical convenience: *S.* 1.2.35–6 (formal) '*nolim laudarier*' *inquit | 'sic me'*, 78 (cf. Plaut *Mil.* 91 *mulieres* (subject) *sectarier*) '*desine matronas sectarier*', 103–4 '*an tibi mauis | insidias fieri pretiumque auellier*'; 2.3.24–6 (smacks of Plautus) '*hortos egregiasque domos mercarier unus | cum lucro noram; unde frequentia Mercuriale | imposuere* *mihi cognomen compita*'; 2.8.67–8 (mock elevation) '*tene, ut ego accipiar laute, torquerier omni* | *sollicitudine districtum*'; *Epist.* 2.1.94 (treating Greek literary history) *coepit et in uitium Fortuna labier aequa*; 2.2.147–8 (homely advice?) *quod quanto plura parasti,* | *tanto plura cupis, nulline faterier audes?*; 149–51 *si uolnus tibi monstrata radice uel herba* | *non fieret leuius, fugeres radice uel herba* | *proficiente nihil curarier*. See Axelson 132 and Brink III 424–6; also Skutsch on Enn. *Ann.* 574, the only instance in the *Annals*, *laudarier*.

9 cuncta festinat manus *ad multitudinem ministrorum refertur* (Porph.); a literal translation of *manus* produces a striking image.

9–10 The adverbs (*huc et illuc*), the frequentative verb (*cursitant*), the alliterative second half (*pueris puellae*), and 'ictus' (for which see Allen 1973: 341–9) + end rhyme (*-ae* | *-ae*) – everything conspires to create an appealing image, full of movement.

11–12 'the flames (of the kitchen fire) flicker as they send the dirty smoke up in a whirling spiral'; an exquisite instance of H.'s economical style, as noted by Porph.: *energos dictum est.*

13–20 The date of the party, a necessary detail for the genre (see intro.), but the motive goes well beyond giving Phyllis information: 'the topic "birthday of Maecenas" is brought into full relief by the magnificent period stretching from 13 *ut tamen noris* to 20 *ordinat annos*' (Fraenkel 417).

13 ut tamen noris 'just so you know what party you have been invited to'; the poem gets to its official business in epistolary fashion; cf. Cic. *Fam.* 15.17.2 *nos hic, ut tamen ad te scribam aliquid, P. Sullam patrem mortuum habebamus*; Ov. *Trist* 2.279–80 *ut tamen hoc fatear, ludi quoque semina praebent* | *nequitiae: tolli tota theatra iube!*

gaudiis: cf. 12.21n.

14 Idus tibi sunt agendae: Phyllis is to celebrate the Ides because they are the *dies natalis* of Maecenas. Ides, Kalends, Nones etc. are not otherwise found as the object of *ago* in this sense; cf. *TLL* s.v. *ago* 1389.77–1390.18.

15–16 13 April; Maecenas was born some time around 70 BCE. It is not clear how much celery (2–3) would be available at that time of the year, even in the warmer climate of Italy, but we are not here in any particular reality.

mensem Veneris . . . Aprilem: *Aprilis* ἀπὸ τῆς Ἀφροδίτης *dictus uidetur, nec immerito, cum in res uenerias eo tempore omnia animalia excitentur* (Porph.). Varro indicates that the etymology, appropriately, may not go back beyond the second century BCE (*Ling.* 6.33: *secundus* [*mensis*], *ut Fuluius* [Servius Fulvius Flaccus, cos. 135 BCE] *scribit et Iunius, a Venere, quod ea sit Aphrodite*). He found no evidence for this in the old writings (*antiquis litteris*) and himself prefers the obvious: *magis puto dictum, quod uer omnia aperit, Aprilem*, as does Virgil implicitly, when he describes the time for sowing: Virg. *G.* 1.217–18 *candidus auratis aperit cum cornibus annum* | *Taurus*; see O'Hara 1996: 101, 260. Ovid was to dramatize the ζήτημα ('debate'), perhaps referring to Varro and Virgil when he apostrophizes Venus (*Fast.* 4.85–6) *sunt qui tibi mensis honorem* | *eripuisse uelint, inuideantque, Venus*. He then mentions the competing claim (87 *quia uer aperit tunc omnia* . . . , 89 *Aprilem memorant ab aperto* *tempore dictum*), but ends by claiming that Venus has vigorously reclaimed it: 90 *quem Venus iniecta uindicat alma manu*). H. alone is emphatic about the single etymology in his address to Phyllis, since that plays into his designs.

marinae: bilingual gloss on the desiderated etymology, ἀφρός = 'sea foam' > *Aprilis*. For similar bilingual play, cf. Cat. 64.6 (etymology of the Argo) *cita decurrere puppis*, 9 *uolitantem* > ἀργός = 'swift' > *Argo*, with Thomas 1982b: 148–54.

findit: see 17–20n.

17–20 Lavish language describes the honour H. feels on the topic of Maecenas' birthday – it is almost more sacred than his own. It is curious that the sole reference to Maecenas in Book 4, indeed the sole reference in H. after publication of *Epist.* 1 in 20–19, should be so extravagant, although it is also notable that H. does not actually address his friend and patron. This central stanza, reflecting not only on Maecenas' birthday but also on that of H., splits the poem (as the Ides split the month, 16 *findit*) and serves as pivot for its larger movement. The light, bustle and youthful energy of the first half is succeeded in the second by an attempt to persuade – unlikely to succeed – and a conclusion that settles for a song from Phyllis.

19 Maecenas: in the middle stanza, as Virgil (*Vergilius*) will be at 12.13 (see n.). Has he become a structural prop, as he was in his four balanced appearances in the *Georgics* (1.2, 2.41, 3.41, 4.2)?

meus: elsewhere, where he receives an epithet, he is addressed as follows: *care* or *clare* (1.20.5), *dilecte* (2.20.7), *iocose* (*Epod.* 3.20), *beate* (*Epod.* 9.4), *candide* (*Epod.* 14.5), *optimus* (*S.* 1.5.27), *docte* (*Epist.* 1.19.1). He is without epithet (voc. unless otherwise indicated) at 2.12.11, 17.3; 3.8.13, 16.20, 29.3; *Epod.* 1.4; *S.* 1.1.1, 3.64, 5.31, 48 (nom.), 6.1, 47, 9.43 (nom.), 10.81 (nom.); 2.3.312 (nom.), 6.31 (acc.), 38 (nom.), 41 (nom.), 7.33 (nom.), 8.16 (addressed by Nasidienus), 22 (nom.); *Epist.* 1.1.3; 1.7.5.

affluentes: unusual, and perhaps a pun on his wealthy patron's affluence (*affluo*/*affluentia* in the English sense is quite common in Cicero, Lucretius and other republican authors). *OLD* s.v. *affluo* 4 gives the meaning 'come streaming along', adding 'poet., of years', with this the only example – nor are any of the surrounding parallels at *TLL* 1243.6–16 quite the same (the example is included with atoms, the power of love etc.). Could H.'s punning on his Maecenas' wealth be anticipating the mercantile language that will come to the fore in his addresses to Virgil (see 12.15n.)?

20 ordinat: also unusual, designated '*poet.*', at *OLD* s.v. 1d under 'arrange in chronological order'.

21–31 The persuasion intensifies: H. notes that the object of Phyllis' affections, Telephus, is socially out of her league and involved with a wealthy and wanton girl, so the cause of Phyllis is hopeless – again there is a hint of Virg. *Ecl.* 2, with the imbalance between Corydon and Alexis' master (2 *nec quid speraret habebat*). Cf. also 1.33, where H. had consoled Tibullus (or at least an Albius) with the fact that love is ever unmatched, with the further conclusion that the lover should settle for what he or she can get (see 21–4n.). So it is that H. warns Phyllis by way of two mythological exempla against the dangers of overreaching. The inevitable consequence will come at 31–2 *age iam, meorum | finis amorum*.

21–4 Telephum: 'Far-lighting' looks to 25 *Phaethon* 'Shining', with its gloss *ambustus*. N–H on 1.13 (intro.) treat this young lover of 1.13, 3.19 and the current poem. 1.13 is a variant, with H. annoyed that Lydia is in fact sexually involved with Telephus, while in 3.19.25–8 Rhode (ῥοδῆ 'rose-bush') has her sights set on the young man. See also 1.18n. for the rival of Paullus Maximus. N–H productively speculate as to why the name of a king famous for being brought on stage in rags by Euripides should turn up in such Hellenistic and erotic contexts. They note that the myth focused on the curing of Telephus with the very spear that wounded him and that this 'hair of the dog' trope may have led some Hellenistic poet to give the name to a 'love-lorn youth' (it becomes an elegiac exemplum at Prop. 2.1.63–4; also Ov. *Am.* 2.9.7–8, with McKeown *ad loc.*). The further presence of the name and its erotic application at Lucian *Nigr.* 38 and in late Greek epigram (Paul. Sil. *Anth. Pal.* 5.291.5–6; Macedonius, *Anth. Pal.* 5.225.5–6) makes this very likely. However, it is also the case that the Telephus of all three Horatian poems seems pretty much in control of things, and in no way lovelorn. However, the eroticized myth does make the name more generally suitable in contexts such as these. John D. Morgan suggests the possibility of a real person, a freedman of Livia buried in the *monumentum Liviae*: *CIL* VI 4193 *Telephus Liviae l.* | *dat* | *Fufiae Clymene et Fufiae* | *Euche sorores*, noting the *puer furens* of 1.13 could a decade later be the *iuuenis* of 4.11.

quem tu petis 'on whom you have your eye'; cf. in the same context 1.33.13; 2.5.16; 3.19.27.

non tuae sortis 'of higher station than you', modifying *iuuenem* (rather than *puella*, whose wantonness combines with her wealth to persuade Phyllis (so H. hopes) that she should forget her designs on Telephus. *diues* at 23, the exempla at 25–8 and the maxim at 29–31 support taking *sortis* as 'social position, degree, station', *OLD* s.v. *sors* 9b (rather than referring to luck: 'destined not to be yours'); this is the first example, but the second is unambiguous: Val. Max. 9.3.3 *Cn. Flauius humillimae quondam sortis praeturam adeptus erat.*

puella | diues et lasciua 'wealthy and wanton', a winning combination, and an unusual one in such contexts. At Virg. *Ecl.* 3.64 Galatea is described as *lasciua puella*, but what is clearly marked here is *diues*; that is H.'s trump card in his case that Telephus is beyond the reach of Phyllis, for which cf. *Ecl.* 2 (21–31n.). The *puella* plays the role of the wealthy rival (here see 1.18n.).

grata | compede uinctum: cf. 1.33.14 (see 21–31n.) *grata . . . compede*, where *seruitium amoris* is also hinted at, appropriately in a poem addressed to Tibullus; cf. also *Epist.* 1.3.3 (of the frozen Hebrus) *niuali compede uinctus*.

25–8 Two myths exemplify overreaching: Phaethon got too close to the sun, and Pegasus eventually threw Bellerophon when he tried to ride to Olympus. The myths are straightforward and unambiguous, their function, to create immediate persuasion and subsequent compliance.

25–6 ambustus Phaethon 'the scorching of Phaethon', the '*ab urbe condita* construction' is repeated at 27 *Pegasus . . . grauatus*, on which see 4.37–8 and n. *Hasdrubal* | *deuictus*. The story of Phaethon, absent from Homer, Hesiod and Greek lyric, is first found in Aeschylus' *Heliades* and is relatively well preserved in the remains of Euripides' *Phaethon*, the edition of which by Diggle 1970: 3–32 gives a good account of the myth. He records (7–8) the brief pre-Ovidian references in Latin literature (Cic. *Arat.* 146–8; Cat. 64.290–1; Lucr. 5.397–405; Varro Atac. fr. 11 Courtney; Virg. *Ecl.* 6.62–3; *Aen.* 10.189–93), where much of the interest is aetiological (the sisters of Phaethon become poplars on the Po) or homoerotic (the love of Cycnus for Phaethon). Ovid's extensive account (*Met.* 1.750–2.400) has a somewhat reluctant Jupiter shooting down Phaethon after a scorched Tellus sends in a request (2.304–18), but for H. Jupiter doubtless acted out of anger at Phaethon's hybris, as at Lucr. 5.399 (*at pater omnipotens ira tum percitus acri*), so the myth will have been unambiguous for him. Ovid's more apologetic version takes on Lucr.: *Met.* 2.304 *at pater omnipotens* – followed by a regretful account of Jupiter's acting as a last resort.

terret: i.e. for those who know the story.

auaras | **spes**: i.e. 'those with greedy hopes'; a fairly easy transference with *spes* = more or less *sperantes*.

26–8 The story of Bellerophon, in contrast to that of Phaethon, is old and Homeric, occurring at *Il.* 6.152–211, where Lycian Glaucus tells it to Diomedes by way of relating his own descent from Sisyphus, and from Bellerophon, Glaucus' grandfather. Pegasus is of course absent from the story in Homer, where the hero performs all three labours without any help, killing the Chimaera and defeating first the Solymi, then the Amazons. In Hes. *Theog.* 280–6 Pegasus is an offspring of Poseidon, born from Medusa's severed neck, while Pind. *Ol.* 13.63–93 more or less repeats the details of the Homeric story but adds Bellerophon's taming of Pegasus, who then helps the hero with his labours. H. probably borrows from Pind. *Isthm.* 7.44–8 not just the story of Bellerophon's attempt on Olympus, but also the fact that it served there too as an *exemplum graue*: ὅ τοι πτερόεις ἔρριψε Πάγασος | δεσπόταν ἐθέλοντ' ἐς οὐρανοῦ σταθμούς | ἐλθεῖν μεθ' ὁμάγυριν Βελλεροφόνταν | Ζηνός. τὸ δὲ πὰρ δίκαν | γλυκὺ πικροτάτα μένει τελευτά 'indeed winged Pegasus threw off his master Bellerophon when that one wanted to go into the lodgings of heaven and assembly of Zeus. A most bitter ending awaits that which is sweet without justice'. Euripides' *Bellerophon* treated the issue, but Pindar seems the more likely source for H. (see 29–31n.).

exemplum graue 'a weighty example', with obvious play on Bellerophon's fall as well as on *grauatus* in the next line, of Pegasus' feeling oppressed by his load. Is the pun intended to impress young Phyllis? There is further play and contrast between *ales* and *terrenum*.

grauatus: *grauiter ferens* (ps.-Acro). *grauo* in the mediopassive + accusative (= 'feel burdened by' and therefore 'refuse') is found once each in comedy (Plaut. *Rud.* 434–5), Cic. *Att.* 11.7.3 (*id . . . uelim ne grauere*) and Virg. *Aen.* 10.628–9 ('*si quae* *uoce grauaris*, | *mente dares*'), and after H. not till Seneca, though it then catches on; cf. *TLL* s.v. *grauo* 2314.17–49.

29–31 *difficilis phrasis* (Porph.): 'that you may always pursue what is worthy of you and avoid an ill-matched relationship, thinking it wrong to have hopes beyond what is permitted'. The ostensibly high-minded pronouncement is self-serving and aimed at getting Phyllis' mind off Telephus (*disparem*). There is perhaps a deliberately Pindaric obscurity in the gnomic phrasing (see 26–8n.).

putando: the ablative of the gerund, which is instrumental from the earliest period ('by doing something'), eventually loses its instrumental force (so, e.g., a number of times in Tacitus; see Woodcock 1939: 23) and becomes equivalent to a present participle, surviving as such in Romance languages. See also Palmer 1954: 324. Tränkle 14 cites this as the sole Horatian instance of the participial use, along with three Lucretian and twelve Virgilian occurences (*G.* 1.119; 2.36; *Aen.* 2.6, 81, 361; 3.671; 4.175, 333, 394, 413; 6.80, 539). H.'s *putando*, like some of Virgil's instances, may have weak instrumental force, however ('avoid an unequal partner by considering it wrong . . .'), and it is sometimes hard to draw a distinction. Cf. with further bibliography Austin *ad* Virg. *Aen.* 2.6 for the distinction between more participial instances, as here, and more common instrumental uses (in H. at 14.31; 1.8.2; 2.2.9, 10.2–3; 3.11.2; *Epod.* 12.9; 14.5; *S.* 1.4.106; 2.2.21, 3.64, 140; 2.5.58 *Epist.* 1.7.87, 13.16; 2.1.19).

disparem: cf. 1.33.10–12 *sic uisum Veneri, cui placet impares* | *formas atque animos sub iuga aenea* | *saeuo mittere cum ioco.*

31–6 H. gets to the point. Phyllis is to register as the last of his lovers and so learn the measure which she will render. Song will take away their cares, as in a more successful day at 1.17.17–28.

31 age iam: with 34 *condisce*; a rare locution, connoting intense urgency, or used at moments of resolution and conclusion. So in Plautus, almost at the end of *Bacchides* (1191), of *Mostellaria* (1175) and of *Stichus* (767); twice, urgently, in the same paragraph (5) of the letter to Atticus Cicero wrote after he left Formiae on the night of 18 Feb. 49 BCE, 'VIII.3 [= 153 SB] on the great question – should he follow Pompey overseas, or no?' (Shackleton Bailey IV. 455); and here in H. in the *dénouement* of his attempt to get Phyllis on board; see *TLL* s.v. *ago* 1406.18–20 (which includes Lucr. 2.333, not quite the same: *nunc age iam*, where *iam* is separate; Bailey: 'Now come, next . . .).

31–2 meorum finis amorum 'you the last of my loves'; she is the last erotic addressee of the book (attraction to Lyce, 4.13, to H. is a thing of the past). A play perhaps on the elegiac obsession: Prop. 1.12.20 *Cynthia prima fuit, Cynthia finis erit* – just as Phyllis herself may be 'borrowed' from Prop. 4.8 (see 3n.). Indeed, with emphasis on *meorum* the phrase 'last of *my* loves/*Amores*', perhaps exploits the sense of *amorum*, with the same ambiguity found at Virg. *Ecl.* 10.6, 34, 53–4 (Gallus' loves/*Amores*). Even if an edition of Ovid's *Amores* had not been published at the time of composition of 11, H. was doubtless aware of the new writer of *Amores*, who claimed to have heard recitations of what must be *C.* 1–3 (*Trist.*

4.10.49–50); see McKeown I 74–89 for the chronology. Slightly different in sense is the more commonplace elegiac thought: Prop. 2.15.29 *errat, qui finem . . . quaerit amoris*; Ov. *Am.* 3.1.15 (Tragedy speaking) *'ecquis erit' dixit 'tibi finis amandi?'*

33–4 The parenthesis is no less aimed at persuasion than the rest of the poem. Phyllis has the chance to be the last of the great laureate's passions; don't miss this opportunity, says H.

non . . . alia calebo | femina: cf. 1.4.19–20 *Lycidan . . . quo calet iuuentus | nunc omnis*; causal ablative; for *calere* + *amore, cupiditate, furore* etc. see *TLL* s.v. *caleo* 148.22–51, with ablative of the person, 52–8.

femina: in H. *femina* is the umarked word for 'woman' (cf. 1.29; 1.15.14; *Epod.* 9.12; *CS* 19), whereas *mulier* = 'woman' (neutral in comedy and in prose) is pejorative and suggestive of sexual experience or appetite (*OLD* s.v. *mulier* 2, 3), unless defined by an epithet (e.g. 1.37.32 *non humilis mulier*): *Epod.* 12.1, 24; *S.* 2.7.65, 90.

condisce modos . . . quos reddas 'thoroughly learn the measures you are to render'; relative clause of purpose. So *OLD* and *TLL* for *condisco*; or perhaps 'learn in my company', as at Apul. *Fl.* 18, an early version of 'come up and see my etchings' – and very different from the singer of the *CS* at 6.43–4 *at reddidi carmen docilis modorum | uatis Horati.*

34–5 amanda | uoce: another hint and perhaps another elegiac touch: Phyllis will become a *docta puella* it seems. Cf. Prop. 1.10.10 *tantus in alternis uocibus ardor erat*, of the poet's joy in hearing the alternating *uoces* of Gallus and his *puella* (obviously *the* Gallus, as is now recognized by most critics; cf. Cairns 2006: 116–17). For the adjectival use of *amandus* (a colloquialism?), see *TLL* s.v. *amo* 1959.59–68.

35–6 minuentur atrae | carmine curae: here song, in the next poem wine, relieves care: 12.19–20 *amaraque | curarum eluere efficax*. For this function of music see Harrison 1991: 121. The brightness and sparkle of the pre-party activities (cf. 1–12n.) are replaced by the dark realities of the ageing lover, hoping at best for his cares to be lightened by song, and that's good enough for now.

12

METRE

Third Asclepiadean, as in 5.

INTRODUCTION

Signs of spring are all around: 'Thracian' winds blow, the snows are gone, the swallow builds its nest. Shepherds sing their bucolic song on their pipes and bring delight to Pan. The season brings thirst, Vergilius. If you want to drink wine pressed at Cales, you'll have to deserve it, you client of young nobles, by bringing a little jar of spikenard, which will draw the cask from its warehouse. Come with your merchandise then; I won't be letting you drink free. Forget cares and love of money. It's sweet to be reckless on occasion.

Various readings of this poem depend on the assumed identity of the addressee Vergilius (the poet or someone else?), and the putative time of composition (before or after the death of Virgil in 19). Clay 2002: 130–1 has a good summary of critical opinion.

1) Vergilius is not the poet, just a friend of H. There is no contemporary external evidence for such a claim. The view is first found in ps.-Acro (*ad Vergilium negotiatorem scribit*), and in two Paris MSS of the 10th century, 7974 and 7971, which have the superscription 'ad Vergilium quendam unguentarium'. As Bowra 1928: 165 pointed out, *quendam* 'is a patent confession of ignorance', while *unguentarium* is a clear extrapolation from 15–17 (the invitee is to bring a free sample of his wares). The case for the *unguentarius* is most strongly put by Page ('Whoever the Vergilius was to whom this Ode is addressed, it certainly is not the poet . . . When we recollect the language used by Horace of him elsewhere . . . we shall be able to appreciate the taste of those who here consider that Horace, in a book published after his death, can speak of him as the "client of noble youths," and sneeringly hint at his meanness and fondness for money-making! Martin adopts this view which is worthy of his translation of the Ode') and Fraenkel ('It has not escaped my notice that from time to time somebody attempts once more to show that the addressee of this Ode is the author of the *Aeneid.* Even if we disregard for a moment the improbability of a much earlier poem being included in the fourth book – fancy Horace addressing the poet Virgil of all men as *iuuenum nobilium cliens* and ascribing to him *studium lucri*, and then publishing the poem after his friend's death. A minimum of common human feeling should save us from the sense of humour that turns Horace, the most tactful of poets, into a monster of callousness'). Putnam 205–6, n. 13 concurs with the Virgilian essence of the poem set out by Belmont 1980, and noted, as Putnam says, by 'numerous critics from Bowra on' (and particularly by Bowra), but in the end subscribes to the non-Virgilian addressee, though Putnam 2006: 93 accepts the identification with the poet.
2) Vergilius is the poet, and the poem was written some years before the death of Virgil in 19 BCE, either some time between 23 and 19, or else before the publication of the first three books, from which it was omitted 'because of its personal nature' (Bowra 1928: 167) or because of its low quality – not good enough for 1–3, but fine for 4!: 'in order to fill out the fourth book, still a slender collection, to something approaching acceptable dimensions' (Quinn 1963: 14). The phrases that offend Page and Fraenkel are to be understood as light-hearted banter from friend to friend or as part of the overall allusion to Cat. 13: Virgil is to drop his *studium lucri*, but H. reveals *himself* to have such an interest when he enjoins Virgil to bring expensive

spikenard to enhance the wine that H. will provide. Apart from Bowra and Quinn, a number of scholars favour some variant of this version: cf. Moritz 1969.

3) Vergilius is the poet, and the poem was written after Virgil's death. It has him fictionally still alive, or has a putative date of composition before 19, precisely because it is a contemplation of mortality. The fact that most of the Virgilian intertexts are to the *Eclogues* and *Georgics* keeps the focus on Virgil's youth and therefore underscores this central theme of the poem. This is the view of Porter 1973, which I essentially share.
4) Clay 2002 takes this further and reads the poem as an invitation to Virgil beyond the grave, to come to an imaginary party. There is a conflation of sympotic and sepulchral, not untypical of sympotic contexts. This reading has some attractions, but it does not make the poem any less strange.

Everything that follows assumes that 1) is impossible and that the addressee is indeed the poet. *C.* 4.12 is replete with Virgilian diction, style, rhetorical devices, and it seems perverse to take the addressee as being anyone but the poet Virgil, the Vergilius to whom H. refers by the same name on nine other occasions, seven before publication of *C.* 4; see Thomas 2001: 55–8, with further bibliography, particularly Minadeo 1975–76 and Belmont 1980. Just as the first collection of *Odes* opened with Maecenas–Augustus–Virgil (1.1–3), so Book 4 closes with Maecenas–Virgil–(Lyce)–Augustus–Augustus (4.11–15). Minadeo 1975–76: 163 puts it well: 'Let us therefore finally recognize the authentic problem that 4.12 presents. In order to fathom its meaning we must come to terms not only with the certainty that its Vergilius is the poet Vergil, but a Vergil represented, on the face of it, as somehow fallen from Horace's unqualified good graces – and this in an ode published years after Vergil's death'. Picking up on the observation of N–H *ad* 1.3.1 that 1.3 is a *quid pro quo* (fair winds for the safe return of Virgil), Minadeo sees an ironic relationship to 4.12, which now stipulates that Virgil, who can afford it, is to ante up if he is to share with H.. There is now a price to pay for qualifying as *animae dimidium meae* (1.3.8), a phrase which has its own ironies (Thomas 2001: 63–5).

For the financial aspects of 1.3, 1.24 and 4.12 see 15, 21–24nn. and Belmont 1980: 13. Indeed many references to Virgil in the corpus of H. are tinged with a sense of reciprocity: at *S.* 1.5.42 no one is *deuinctior* to Tucca, Varius and Virgil (the three are not distinguished) than H. The term ('obligated', 'bound over to') does not suggest warmth; at *S.* 1.6.54–5 Virgil and later Varius told Maecenas what H. amounted to (*quid essem*), and after an interview Maecenas admits H. to the group of *amici*; at *Epist.* 2.1.247–57 Virgil and Varius (but not H.) are examples of poets whose encomium results in *munera*, which fits perfectly with the *iuuenum nobilium cliens* who is to drop his *studium lucri* and bring his fair share to the symposium. As for 'tone', those who have difficulty with a bantering and playfully critical attitude from H. towards Virgil are first of all assuming too much about the friendship between the two (see Thomas 2001: 55–73) and are in addition out of tune with the *licentia* of lyric and other poetry in the second half of the first century BCE (Belmont 1980: 11–13). *C.* 2.12, addressed to Maecenas' wife Terentia (as Licymnia), shows the sort of freedom permitted in the lyric reformulations and reshaping of real social circumstances and relationships. Similarly *Epod.* 3.19–22, joking about the effects Maecenas' garlic-eating will have on his *puella.*

The poem is a conflation of two distinct genres or subgenres: the spring poem (1–12) and the invitation poem (13–28). For the former, see 7 intro., for the latter, 11 intro. Both parts are also marked by strong intertexts in two distinct poems of Catullus, namely 46 (*iam uer egelidos*) and 13 (*Cenabis bene*), separate instances of the two genres in question (see 1–2, 13–28nn.). There is a strong connection with the preceding poem, itself replete with Virgilian language, and Phyllis and 'Vergilius' thereby come into close alignment (cf. 21n.).

1–12 Spring manifests itself in the world of inanimate (*pace* 2 *animae*) nature (1–4), the animal world (5–8) and the world of man (9–12), with breath and song common to all three (*animae* | *gemens* | *dicunt*... *fistula*) – the final element particularly appropriate in a poem centred on Virgil. The three stanzas, like those of the rest of the poem, are all end-stopped. The first two stanzas allude to Virg. *G.* 4.305–7 *hoc geritur Zephyris primum impellentibus undas,* | *ante nouis rubeant quam prata coloribus, ante* | *garrula quam tignis nidum suspendat hirundo.*

1–2 Iam ueris comites: cf. Cat. 46.1 *Iam uer egelidos refert tepores.* The same poem also bids farewell to Catullus' actual *comites* at 46.9 *o dulces comitum ualete coetus.* Virgil is one of the *comites* of H. on the journey to Brundisium at *S.* 1.5.8–9 (although he has not yet joined the group at this point of the journey) *cenantes*... | *exspectans comites* (see below on *animae*). The position of the appositive phrase before the main term seems unusual and puts emphasis on the seasonal aspect of the wind, which makes *animae*... *Thraciae* (on which see n. below) somewhat surprising.

uer(is)... mar(e): Belmont 1980: 15 suggests a word play which will not convince all (Vergilius Maro); if so, perhaps an allusion to Virgil's own signature in the reverse acrostic of *G.* 1.433–29 PV–VE–MA; see Thomas *ad G.* 1.427–37n.; Katz 2008.

temperant 'moderate', of restoring balance, as of Neptune at Virg. *Aen.* 1.146 *temperat aequor*; cf. also *G.* 1.110 [*aqua*] *arentia temperat arua*; 3.336–7 *cum frigidus aëra Vesper* | *temperat*; *Epist.* 1.16.8 (of the balanced climate of H.'s farm) *temperiem laudes*, alluding to the landscapes of the *Georgics*, on which see Thomas 1982a: 11–12.

impellunt: first here of the wind pushing sails, perhaps an extension of Virg. *G.* 4.305 (also of spring) *Zephyris primum impellentibus undas* (see 1–12n.); cf. *TLL* s.v. *impello* 537.69–82.

animae... Thraciae: should be Zephyrs, i.e. the West Wind, which herald spring, as at 7.9 *frigora mitescunt Zephyris* and 1.4.1 *Soluitur acris hiems grata uice ueris et Fauoni*; cf. Virg. *G.* 1.43–4 (the first lines of the poem following the opening prayer) *uere nouo, gelidus canis cum montibus umor* | *liquitur et Zephyro putris se glaeba resoluit* etc.

So Plin. *NH* 2.122 *[ueris] in principio Fauonii hibernum molliunt caelum*. Conversely, at *Epod.* 13.3 *Threicio Aquilone* is clearly the cold north wind, as is traditional since Hes. *Op.* 553; cf. also *C.* 1.25.11–12 *Thracio bacchante magis sub inter- | lunia uento*. Mesturini 1997: 207–12 treats winds in H., with a chart that puts *Thracius uentus* with *Aquilo* but *animae Thraciae* with Zephyrus/Favonius – because the latter occurs in a spring poem! What accounts for the discrepancy? Clay 2002: 132 proposes that H. was focalizing the Homeric or Trojan situation (appropriately in a poem addressed to Virgil), which is possible but in Homer the Thracian winds, Boreas and Zephyrus, are storm winds: Zephyr at *Il.* 4.422–6, with Boreas at 9.5; and cf. *Od.* 5.295 Ζέφυρός τε δυσαής, 'stormy Zephyr'. There is one place where a Thracian wind may actually come from the west in the spring, namely Nicaea, where Catullus experienced the traditional Italian Zephyrs transplanted to Bithynia: 46.2–3 *iam caeli furor aequinoctialis | iucundis Zephyri silescit auris*.

animae: all of the prior parallels in this sense (Acc. *trag.* 11; Varro, *Men.* 224; Lucr. 5.1229; cf. *TLL* s.v. *anima* 70.48–54) are accompanied by a form of *uentus*, and *animae* clearly puns on ἄνεμος 'wind'. The closest parallel for an absolute use (cited by Porph.) is Virg. *Aen.* 8.403 *ignes animaeque*, of Vulcan's bellows. Clay 2002: 132 suggests that '*Thraciae animae* might evoke the tragic tale of Orpheus [who comes from Thrace] and Eurydice' as treated in *Georgics* 4. Belmont 1980: 15 notes that forms of *anima* are used in connection with Virgil in two other places in H.: 1.3.8 *animae dimidium meae*; *S.* 1.5.41–2 (of Plotius Tucca, Varius Rufus and Virgil) *animae quales neque candidiores | terra tulit*.

lintea: first at Cat. 4.4–5 as a pure metonymy for 'sails': *siue palmulis | opus foret uolare siue linteo* (where the metonymy for 'oar' is also a neologism); also Prop. 3.4.7 *date lintea*, 3.7.5 *tendentem lintea*; once in Virgil (who has *uela* some 20 times), in the Callimachean *Aen.* 3 (686 *certum est dare lintea retro*).

3–4 There is a strong reminiscence of the two spring poems, 1.4 and 4.7:

iam nec prata rigent: cf. 1.4.4 *nec prata canis albicant pruinis*.

nec fluuii strepunt | hiberna niue turgidi: cf. 7.3–4 *decrescentia ripas | flumina praetereunt*.

5–8 An allusive reference to the story of Procne, Philomela and Tereus, none of whom is actually named (for the Alexandrian, and Virgilian, style see also 11–12n.). At Hom. *Od.* 19.518–23, the nightingale is simply the 'daughter of Pandareus', who in bird form laments her son Itys, whom she killed thoughtlessly (δι' ἀφραδίας) with a sword. In classic form in Sophocles' lost *Tereus*: Tereus, king of Thrace, is married to Procne, daughter of Pandion, king of Athens. Tereus rapes Philomela, sister of Procne, and cuts out her tongue so she cannot tell the tale. Procne is enlightened by a tapestry into which Philomela weaves the story and so avenges her sister by serving up her and Tereus' son Itys as a meal for T. When T. pursues the sisters, he is changed into the hoopoe, while Procne becomes the nightingale, Philomela the swallow. The story is told most extensively at Ov. *Met.* 6.424–674 (and see Bömer *ad* 6.668–9).

It is often said that the Romans transposed the roles of Procne and Philomela, but this needs refining. Varro, *Ling.* 5.76 is traditional (*lusciniola* <*appellata*> *quod luctuose canere existimatur atque esse ex Attica Progne in luctu facta auis*), and at Plaut. *Rud.* 604 swallows (*hirundines*) are made to be descended from Philomela *and* Procne. For Virgil, however, Procne of *G.* 4.15 is decidedly the swallow (*manibus . . . pectus signata cruentis*, and Mynors *ad loc.* on the swallow's breast markings), while *philomela* at *G.* 4.511–12 is the nightingale, the ἀηδών of *Od.* 19.518–23 in the famous simile of Orpheus lamenting his loss: *qualis populea maerens philomela sub umbra* | *amissos queritur fetus*. Earlier, at *Ecl.* 6.78–81, Philomela seems to be the wife of Tereus 78–79 <*quid loquar*> *aut ut mutatos Terei narrauerit artus,* | *quas illi Philomela dapes, quae dona pararit . . . ?* And although the word comes to mean 'nightingale' for Virgil, this Philomela is also flying about her house (81 *sua tecta*, and Clausen *ad loc.*). For possible reasons for this confusion, see Thomas 1998b: 670–1. H.'s refusal to commit to one or the other bird (6 *infelix auis*) may be an artful reference to Virgil's treatment of the myth and to the tradition of confusion; so may that of Ovid at *Met.* 6.668–9 *quarum petit altera siluas,* | *altera tecta subit.*

5 nidum ponit: more appropriate of *Hirundo rustica*, the barn or plain swallow, which returns in the spring; cf. *Epist.* 1.7.12–13 *te, dulcis amice, reuiset* | *cum Zephyris, si concedes, et hirundine prima.* With *nidum ponit* (only here in Latin, *nidum facere* being the usual term), H. possibly alludes to the swallow's building its nest on rafters or other sheltered ledges, as does Virg. *G.* 4.306–7 (also of spring's arrival) *ante* | *garrula quam tignis nidum suspendat hirundo*; *Aen.* 12.473–4 *nigra uelut magnas domini cum diuitis aedes* | *peruolat et pinnis alta atria lustrat hirundo*; cf. Varro, *Men.* 579 *uer blandum uiget aruis* <*et*> *adest hospes hirundo*, with *hospes* implying the same nesting habit. But the nightingale cannot be ruled out since *nidum ponere* does not require an indoor nest. For Sappho the nightingale marks the arrival of spring, so the variation is old: fr. 136 L-P ἦρος ἄγγελος ἰμερόφωνος ἀήδων 'messenger of spring, lovely-voiced nightingale', given by the scholiast of Soph. *El.* 148–9 ἃ Ἴτυν, αἰὲν Ἴτυν ὀλοφύρεται | ὄρνις ἀτυζομένα, Διὸς ἄγγελος 'the bird distraught with grief, messenger of Zeus, laments Itys, always Itys'.

Ityn flebiliter gemens: cf. Cat. 65.14 *absumpti fata gemens Ityli.*

flebiliter: a rare adverb, three times in Cic. *Tusc.* 1.85; 2.39 (*non flebiliter*), 49, characterizing lines from Ennius (*Andromacha*) and Pacuvius (*Niptra*) on suffering and death in Trojan war tragedies, at Livy 1.26.2 of the sister of the Horatii grieving for her fiancé (*flebiliter nomine sponsum mortuum appellat*), twice in Val. Max. and otherwise not until late antiquity. More importantly, the adjective appears in polyptoton at 1.24.9–10, also in a Virgilian poem, *multis ille bonis flebilis occidit,* | *nulli flebilior quam tibi, Vergili* (see intro.), for which see Wills 232–6.

6 infelix auis: use of the epithet unparalleled in H. in context and tone and pointing straight to Virg., who has it 52 times in the nominative or vocative vs. seven in the accusative or genitive, particularly arresting as a molossus in line-initial position – as at *Ecl.* 6.81, of Philomela. Its root agricultural sense, 'barren, without issue', applies well to the killer of Itys/Itylus and is present, but only metaphorically, in the two other Horatian appearances (*S.* 1.1.90; *AP* 34, 'fruitless'). For similar Virgilian uses of a person or animal doomed or suffering loss of offspring: *Ecl.* 6.47, 52 (of Pasiphae) *a uirgo infelix* (reapplied from Calvus, *Io* fr. 9 Courtney); *G.* 3.498–9 *labitur infelix . . . | uictor equus*; *Aen.* 1.475 (of Troilus) *infelix puer*, 712, 749 *infelix Dido*; 2.455–6 *infelix . . . Andromache*, 772 *infelix simulacrum . . . Creusae*; 3.50 *infelix Priamus* (on death of Polydorus), 4.68, 450, 596, 6.456 *infelix Dido*; 5.328–9 *Nisus | labitur infelix*; 6.521 *infelix . . . thalamus* (the marriage chamber of Deiphobus), 618 *infelix Theseus* (kept in Underworld), 822 *infelix* (of Brutus, killing his sons for treason); 9.390 *'Euryale infelix'*, 477 *infelix* (mother of dead Euryalus); 10.325 *infelix . . . Cydon* (pederast, about to die); 10.829 *'infelix'* (Aeneas to Lausus after killing him), 849–50 *heu, nunc misero mihi demum | exitium infelix* (Mezentius after the death of Lausus); 11.53 *infelix, nati funus crudele uidebis!* (Evander after the death of Pallas), 85 *infelix . . . Acoetes* (surrogate of Evander), 175 *infelix* (self-address of Evander), 563 *infelix . . . Camilla* (anticipating her death); 12.598 *infelix* (Amata, *moritura*, supposing 'son' Turnus to be dead), 608 *infelix . . . fama* (of the news that follows), 641 *infelix . . . Vfens* (father of four of the Latins taken for human sacrifice at 10.518–19), 941 *infelix* (of Juturna as she abandons her brother's cause), 941–2 *infelix . . . | balteus* (deaths of Pallas, Turnus).

The bare epithet applied to the speaker is colloquial and frequent in comedy (*TLL* s.v. *infelix* 1361.68–82; Virg. *Aen.* 4.596 *infelix Dido* (self-address) is in unusual company), and the word is used as a substantive chiefly in prose authors (*TLL* 1361.53–61). Further see *EV* s.v. *felix/infelix*; Hardie *ad Aen.* 9.390.

6–7 Cecropiae domus | aeternum opprobrium: the unwitting cannibalism of Tereus becomes a source of shame for Athens in general, with the nightingale's spring arrival in Attica and lament for Itys an everlasting reminder of the crime.

Cecropiae domus: same metrical *sedes*, also in the sixth line, as in the propempticon to Virgil, 1.3.6 *finibus Atticae.*

7–8 'in that she committed an evil act of vengeance for the uncivilized lust of kings', i.e. of Tereus. Cannibalism trumps rape and the cutting out of Philomela's tongue, although the juxtaposition of *male* with *barbarus* creates momentary uncertainty.

barbaras: i.e. Thracian, connecting 2 *Thraciae* and in contrast to *Cecropiae*, Athenian and therefore (normally) civilized.

regum: Page suggests the plural is 'generic', suggesting that such 'vicious acts were common among kings'. Cf. 1.16.6 for a similar generalizing plural *mentem sacerdotum* – there was only a single Pythian priestess.

9–12 Pastoral spring. An intense engagement with the *Eclogues*. It is difficult to imagine a reader – as yet unaffected by the offending phrases at 15 and 25 – arriving at the name in the next line (13 *Vergili*) and successfully fending off the obvious identification that emerges from the pastoral stanza (see intro.).

9–10 dicunt . . . carmina: *carmen dicere*, may seem commonplace, but it in fact occurs first in the *Eclogues*: *Ecl.* 6.4–5 *'pastorem, Tityre, pingues | pascere oportet* *oues, deductum dicere carmen*'; 10.2–3 *pauca meo Gallo, sed quae legat ipsa Lycoris, | carmina sunt dicenda; neget quis carmina Gallo?*; also *G.* 1.350 *det motus incompositos et carmina dicat*; *Aen.* 6.644 *pars pedibus plaudunt choreas et carmina dicunt*; Prop. 1.9.9–10; Tib. 1.2.56–7; App. Verg. *Dirae* 75 *tristius hoc rursum dicit mea fistula carmen*. See also *CS* 8. The usage is distinct from Cat. 62.4 *iam dicetur hymenaeus* (also 61.39; 62.18), where the word '*Hymenaee!*' is actually said (an example of 'performative utterance'). See *TLL* s.v. *dicere* 977.65–978.3; s.v. *carmen* 469.58–64.

pinguium . . . ouium: in the context of singing and piping the phrase must allude to Apollo's Callimachean advice to Tityrus at *Ecl.* 6.4–5 (see previous n.), already adapted by H. in his prayer to Mercury upon receiving the gift of the Sabine farm: *S.* 2.6.14–15 *pingue pecus domino facias et cetera praeter | ingenium utque soles, custos mihi maximus adsis*.

10 custodes ouium: only here as a designation of shepherds; cf. Porcius Licinus fr. 7.1 Courtney *custodes ouium tenerae propaginis, agnum*, where, however, *agnum* = *agnorum*, an objective genitive with *custodes*, while *o. t. p.* is a predicate of *agnum* ('guardians of the lambs, tender offspring of the sheep'). Cic. *Phil.* 3.27 makes it clear *custodes ouium* was a commonplace, since it is presupposed by his proverbial application to Antony: *o praeclarum custodem ouium, ut aiunt, lupum!*; cf. also Servius *ad Ecl.* 10.19 *VPILIO ouium custos*. Perhaps for that reason Virgil avoids it as a term for 'shepherd', *custos* alone being applied to Damoetas (*E.* 3.5), who in the view of Menalcas is overmilking the sheep of Aegon, which he is supposed to be looking after (*hic alienus oues custos bis mulget in hora*), and to Pan in the prayer that opens the *Georgics*: 1.17, *Pan, ouium custos*. For *custos* with a variety of objective genitives (*boum, gregis, pecoris, pecudum*) see *TLL* s.v. *custos* 1572.60–70. Cf. also *Ecl.* 2.33 *Pan curat oues ouiumque magistros*, a more elevated term, since at Varro, *Rust.* 1.2.14 the *uilicus* and the *magister pecoris* are the two overseers of farm workers and of herds and herdsmen repectively; cf *TLL* s.v. *magister* 78.58–66; also 80.45–63 for *magister* = 'herdsmen' in poetic texts, including Virg. *G.* 3.445.

fistula: primary instrument of the *Eclogues*, the syrinx or 'Pan-pipes', constructed of disparate pipes joined together, as at Virg. *Ecl.* 2.36–7 *disparibus septem compacta cicutis | fistula*. Virgil could only use *fistula* in the nominative, which he does six times (2.37, 3.22, 25, 7.24, 8.33, 10.34) with alternatives in the oblique cases, as Clausen notes *ad Ecl.* 2.37: *auena* (1.2, 10.51), *calamus* (1.10, 2.34, 5.2, 48, 6.69), *cicuta* (5.85), *harundo* (6.8) and *stipula* (3.27).

The instrumental ablative, 'sing songs with the pipe' might seem odd without the precedent of the song-singing pipe of the Arcadians (cf. 12 *Arcadiae*) of Virg. *Ecl.* 10.34 '*uestra meos olim si fistula dicat amores*'.

11–12 cui pecus et nigri | colles Arcadiae placent: Pan, alluded to in oblique style (see 5–8n.). This is the only appearance of Arcadia in H., and it points directly to Virgil, to be associated with Arcadia in the mind of any Roman reader – whether or not he was the actual creator of Arcadian pastoral; on which see, *pro*, Clausen: 215–16, 289–90; *contra*, Jenkyns 1989.

nigri: a particularly Virgilian usage; cf. 4.57–8n.

13–28 The invitation is a clever inversion of Catullus 13 (see intro.), in which C., who is broke, will bring the *unguentum* his girlfriend gave him, while Fabullus is to bring dinner, a girl and wine. Here Virgil is to bring nard, which will be used to 'elicit' (i.e. procure) the wine.

13 adduxere sitim tempora 'the season has brought on thirst'. The plural may be poetic (of an abstract noun, as at 2.4 *nomina*, 9.11 *calores*; cf. K–S II 1.77–82; also Löfstedt I 34–6) or an abbreviation for *uices temporum*. The line marks the transition from spring poem to sympotic invitation poem. Coming immediately before the address to Virgil, the striking phrase inverts Virg. *G.* 3.482–3 *sed ubi ignea uenis | omnibus acta sitis miseros adduxerat artus*. For the compound-simplex shift in meaning with shift of form (*adduxere . . . ducere*) see Wills 442, n. 21, with 1.23.10–12 *persequor . . . sequi*.

tempora, Vergili: with some punning activated by the fact that the season in question, spring, is also the time of the Vergiliae, that is, of the Pleiades, which rise on 10 May according to the Julian calendar: Columella 11.2.40 *VI Id. Mai. Vergiliae totae apparent, Fauonius aut Corus, interdum et pluuiae*. Cf. Hygin. *Astr.* 2.21 *eas stellas nostri Vergilias appellauerunt, quod post uer oriuntur*. On the placement of *tempora*, see 13.14n.

Vergili: the name comes in the central stanza, as it does at 1.24.10 (along with the sepulchral subject Quintilius), a place generally reserved for important addressees, as Moritz 1968 has shown. In particular the preceding poem has Maecenas in the central stanza (11.19), as at 1.20.5; 3.8.13. At 3.16.20 Maecenas appears in the line immediately preceding the central stanza, while Licymnia, who is doubtless to be identified as his wife, is in the same position of 2.12.13. Caesar is in the first stanza and the first line of the second half of the book's final poem (15.4, 17), as he is in the last line of the first half of the Cleopatra ode (1.37.16), the last stanza of the first half of 3.4.37 and the central stanza of 3.14.16. Drusus and Tiberius (*Neronibus*) appear at 4.37, in the central stanza of that poem. Aeneas appears in the *Odes* only in Book 4, in the central stanza in consecutive poems (6.23, 7.15). It is unlikely that in such a prominent position we would find Vergilius, an otherwise unknown ointment merchant. Moritz 1968: 120–3 also noticed that Rome herself occupies such a central position in two poems, again consecutive, of *C.* 4, namely 3.13 (first line of second half) and 4.37 (along with the Neros), and in the central stanza of the *CS* (37, with Aeneas in the following stanza, 42). Juno's speech at 3.3.44 has Rome in the middle stanza while an earlier appearance of the city (38) comes at the start of the second half of the poem.

H. may have taken his lead from Virgil in all of this: in the *Georgics* Maecenas appears only four times, in elegantly balanced positions: 1.2, 2.41, 3.41, 4.2. Octavian, the unnamed young man who saved Tityrus' farm, appears at *Ecl.* 1.42 as *iuuenem*, in the middle of the middle line of the poem. He again appears in the middle of the *Georgics*, at the start of the third book, with his centrality underlined: 3.16 *in medio mihi Caesar erit templumque tenebit*. See Thomas *ad loc.* The exact middle of the *Aeneid* comes at 7.182 or 203, depending on the authenticity of the Helen episode – in either case the Trojan delegation to the *tectum augustum* in the middle of which sits Latinus on his ancestral throne: 7.169 *solio medius consedit auito*. For the middle generally in Virgil, in ecphrases and elsewhere, see Thomas 2004.

14 pressum Calibus . . . Liberum 'wine pressed at Cales', on the eastern edge of the Falernus Ager in Campania, i.e. a wine of high quality, the wine of the wealthy, as at 1.20.9, 31.9.

ducere 'drink'; 'the word implies a leisurely process' (N–H *ad* 1.17.22). H. seems oddly oblivious of the cognate in the previous line, *adduxere*, with the sense of the two quite separate, unlike the normal practice by which the simplex following the compound iterates the meaning of the former, a feature of Indo-European, for which see, with reference to contributions from Clausen, Watkins, Jocelyn and Renehan, Adams 1992: 295–8. Or perhaps H. does mean *(ad)ducere* (*OLD* s.v. *adduco* 11e 'draw up, drink').

15 iuuenum nobilium cliens: not simply a form of address, rather, coming as it does between protasis and apodosis, with causal force: 'in that you are the client of the young nobility', you will have to contribute expensive nard. The tone is playful, but the words also set in play a suggestion of mercantile interests (cf. 21–2 *tua* | . . . *merce*, 23 *immunem*, 24 *diues*, 25 *studium lucri*); see Minadeo 1975–76: 163 on the commercial aspects of 1.3 and add 1.24.11 *non ita creditum*; cf. also 11.19n.

16–17 nardo . . . nardi: the distribution across the two stanzas, with line-initial positioning, is emphatic (see 1.21n.): H. makes sure Virgil understands the deal. This is presumably the *Assyria nardus* ('Syrian nard') of 2.11.16 (see N–H *ad loc.*). It was particularly valued according to Plin. *HN* 12.45 *nardo colos, si inueterauit, nigrior meliori. in nostro orbe proxime laudatur Syriacum.*

merebere 'you will (have to) earn'.

17–19 paruus . . . largus: a good bargain, with an appealing contrast between *onyx* and *cadus*.

onyx: the material (*OLD* s.v. 1 'A much-prized kind of marble, prob. a stalagmitic limestone') stands for the object from which it is made, a jar containing the nard Virgil is to bring.

eliciet cadum, | qui nunc . . . accubat: the punch-line of the joke: at the time of writing H. does not have the *cadus* in question, which he will only acquire once Virgil brings that which will elicit it. Involved in the joke is *accubat*, whose primary sense is 'lie, recline (at a table)', *OLD* s.v. *accubo* 1. The *cadus* will need inducement to switch couches. At *Aen.* 6.605–6 a Fury keeps the sinners of myth from the feast: *Furiarum maxima iuxta* | *accubat et manibus prohibet contingere mensas.* H.'s use is the second attested instance in the figurative sense, with an inanimate subject (*OLD* s.v. 2 '(of things) to rest, be situated (by or on)'), the first being at *G.* 3.333–4 *sicubi nigrum* | *ilicibus crebris sacra nemus accubet umbra* – Virgil would have appreciated this part of the joke.

eliciet: sleight of hand is suggested: Virgil will contribute nard, sale of which will draw out the cask. Along with *accubat* there is slight personification: the perfume will wake the sleeping cask up; cf. the strong personification of the *pia testa* of *C.* 3.21.

18 Sulpiciis . . . horreis 'extensive warehouses in the district known as Praedia Galbana (*CIL* 6.30983 = *ILS* 3840) between the southwest slope of the Aventine and Monte Testaccio, possibly extending as far east as the Porta Ostiensis and as far west as the so-called Porticus Aemilia' (Richardson 193). Porph. *ad loc.* knew them as the Horrea Galbae, and they were probably part of the estate of the Sulpicii Galbae in the Republic and took on the name of the *princeps*: *hodieque autem Galbae horrea uino et oleo et similibus aliis referta sunt.* Cf. 3.28.7, where *horreum* = 'wine-store'; also *TLL* s.v. 2987.23–40.

19–20 'Generous at providing fresh hope and effective at washing away distressing fears'. An elegant couplet, with *largus* and *efficax* each controlling an epexegetical infinitive, which describes the sphere in which the action implied by the adjective takes place: K–S II 1.685–6; Horatian examples are found at 1.12.26–7 *hunc equis, illum superare pugnis | nobilem*; 1.24.17 *non lenis precibus fata recludere*, 35.2–4 *praesens uel . . . tollere . . . uel . . . uertere*, 28 *ferre iugum . . . dolosi*; 3.29.50 *ludum . . . ludere pertinax*; *S.* 1.4.8 *durus componere uersus*; 2.8.24 *ridiculus . . . absorbere placentas*; *Epist.* 1.15.30 *opprobria fingere saeuus*. For such powers attributed to wine cf. 1.7.17–21; *Epod.* 9.37–8 (with Mankin *ad loc.* for further references); it is a commonplace in Greek lyric and epigram, while for the elegiac condition wine has no such powers: Tib. 1.5.37–8 *saepe ego temptaui curas depellere uino, | at dolor in lacrimas uerterat omne merum*; also Ov. *Her.* 16.231–2. We perhaps hear an echo of Evander's fears at *Aen.* 8.579–80 *nunc, nunc o liceat crudelem abrumpere uitam | dum curae ambiguae, dum spes incerta futuri*; or those of Aeneas on the Libyan shore: *Aen.* 1.208–9 *curisque ingentibus aeger | spem uultu simulat, premit altum corde dolorem.*

amaraque | curarum 'cares' bitterness', with chiastic sound patterning (m–r–q | c–r–m). Cf. *acuta belli* at 4.76, with n. on the syntax.

eluere: perhaps with a play on λύω/Lyaeus, as at *Epod.* 9.37–8 *curam metumque . . . | dulci Lyaeo soluere* (with Mankin on 9.38).

21–4 The stanza is replete with the language of financial reciprocity (see 15n.). H. is not about to give his 'friend' Virgil anything for free.

21 gaudia 'delightful event', 'party' cf. 11.13–14 *ut tamen noris quibus aduoceris | gaudia*, where, unlike the case of Virgil, there are no conditions on Phyllis' invitation (see intro.).

21–2 cum tua | uelox merce ueni 'hurry up and come with your commodity'; bald and brusque language exposes H.'s mercenary attitude, referring specifically to the commodity (*merx*) without which there will be no party; cf. 1.27.13–14 *non alia bibam | mercede* (*merces* being more abstract, 'payment').

22 non ego te: four times in the *Odes* (9.30; 1.18.11, 23.9), and appropriately in addressing Virgil, who used it at *Ecl.* 3.17, *G.* 2.101 and *Aen.* 10.185; also 4.333–4 *ego te . . . numquam.* It appears twelve times in Plautus, frequently in the formulaic *non(ne) ego te . . .?* (thus once in Afranius 253 R. *non ego te noui tristem saeuum serium?*), and occurs in Republican Latin otherwise only once each in Catullus (64.221) and Cicero (*Quint. fr.* 1.3.1); often of a strong denial, with the juxtaposition of pronouns bringing speaker and addressee into close contact: see Adams 1994: 126–7. *ego te* alone, on the other hand, is standard and appears more than 70 times in Cicero, but only once in H., at *S.* 2.6.60.

non . . . poculis 'it's not my plan to give you a free soak with my cups'; *OLD* s.v. *tingo* 1b 'to wet, soak' isolates this usage as 'poet.', but it seems rather colloquial, even slightly vulgar: 'give you a sousing' – particularly given 2.14.25–7 *heres . . . mero | tinget pauimentum superbo*, with Virgil now in the position of the paving surface. This further adds to the poem's sense of play.

24 plena diues ut in domo: somewhat pointed ('you may be a rich man, don't think I'm going to play one to your parasite') if we are to believe the Suetonian *Vit. Verg.* 13 *possedit prope centiens sestertium* (= 10,000,000 sesterces) *ex liberalitatibus amicorum habuitque domum Romae Esquiliis iuxta hortos Maecenatianos.*

plena: an echo of Cat. 13.7–8 *nam tui Catulli | plenus sacculus est aranearum.*

25 pone moras et studium lucri: a slight syllepsis, with a strong sense of urgency, with the imperatives continuing (22 *ueni*, 27 *misce*). *pone moras* seems to be unique and is best paralleled by similarly urgent exhortations, again particularly in Virgil: 3.10.9 *pone superbiam*; Virg. *Aen.* 11.365–6 (Drances to Turnus, with similar urgency) *miserere tuorum, | pone animos et pulsus abi*; Tib. 3.10.15 *pone metum* – to become, along with *pone metus*, an Ovidian favourite. With other verbs cf. Virg. *Aen.* 8.443 *praecipitate moras*; 4.569; 9.13 *rumpe moras*. Campbell's *rerum pone moras*, accepted by Shackleton Bailey with approval of Delz (*Gnomon* 60 (1988) 497), disrupts the urgency, and is anyway unlikely in that the genitive at Cic. *Fam.* 10.22.2 (*propter tarditatem sententiarum moramque rerum*, i.e. 'suspension of business') is objective, whereas in H. it would need to be subjective: *rerum pone moras* would most naturally mean 'get down to business', the opposite of what H. is saying here.

studium lucri: see 15n. Clay 2002, who reads the poem as an invitation to Virgil to return from the dead (see intro.), sees in *lucri* a possible reference to Plutus and the Underworld.

26 nigrorumque memor . . . ignium: *memento mori*, the standard justification for a symposium. Cf. 1.24.17 (also addressed to Virgil; see intro.) *nigro . . . gregi* (of the dead).

27–8 Nothing wrong with a little silliness, at least as a temporary distraction; a comment on the poem as a whole and the fun it has had with the great, now dead poet? *stultitiam* looks to *desipere*, as *breuem* does to *in loco*, these two coming at line-end and therefore receiving emphasis. The epigram is an envoi to Virgil and the poetry of his youth, recalling the days when he and Varius introduced H. to Maecenas and the world of the powerful who populate this final book of lyric. The book itself will end with H. anticipating song that looks not to the *Eclogues* and *Georgics*, but more to the *Aeneid*, in that case in the company of *matronae*

(15.27n.). Chloe in her bloom preceded (11), Lyce grown old, with memories of the dead Cinara, will follow (13) as the shadows draw in. Time for a get-together with Virgil from the old days.

28 dulce est desipere in loco: one of the more notable Horatian epigrams. Similarly in final position, 2.7.27–8 *recepto | dulce mihi furere est amico*; not final, but obviously related, is 3.2.13 *dulce et decorum est pro patria mori.*

desipere: the register of *desipere* is deliberately colloquial, in keeping with the urging that the poet drop his seriousness for a while: while it is common in Cicero and Lucretius and appears in H. three times (outside the *Odes*: *S.* 2.3.47, 211; *Epist.* 1.20.9), it is otherwise absent from poetry (except for Juv. 6.612) and very rare in post-republican Latin.

Although *sapientia* is not specifically attested as a prime Virgilian trait until the Middle Ages (*VT* 109, 281, 290, 330, 720, 804, 870), the poet was clearly known for his knowledge and wisdom from the very beginning. Cf. Serv. *ad Aen.* 6.2, before singling out the particular prominence of *Aen.* 6 in this regard, *totus quidem Vergilius scientia plenus est*; and see *VT* 463–7 ('Virgil as philosopher and compendium of knowledge').

in loco 'at the right moment, opportunely', *OLD* s.v. *locus* 21b. In view of 25, H. may be alluding specifically to Ter. *Ad.* 216 *pecuniam in loco neglegere maxumum interdumst lucrum*, particularly since the phrase is extremely rare in this sense: otherwise only at Ter. *Haut.* 537, 827; *Ad.* 827; Cic *Verr.* 2.5.37; Tac. *Ann.* 2.4.3; cf. *TLL* s.v. *locus* 1598.80–1599.8.

13
METRE

Fourth Asclepiadean: Asclepiadean (glyconic with choriambic expansion: – – – ⏑⏑–|–⏑⏑–|⏑×) *bis* + pherecratean (– – –⏑⏑–×) + glyconic (– – –⏑⏑–⏑×).

INTRODUCTION

The gods have answered my prayer, Lyce: you've become an old woman. Still you go to the symposium, get drunk and try to be arousing, but that capacity, along with exquisite lyre-playing, now belongs to Chia. Nothing can restore you to your former beauty, to the days when, second only to Cinara, you won my heart. Cinara was short-lived, but the Fates kept you around, Lyce, so the young men could have a good laugh at you.

Greek erotodidactic poetry, particularly epigram, abounds with examples of the attempt to persuade the spurning woman or boy to submit before the ravages of old age set in (as in 4.10). Along with the attempt to persuade we also find the further stage in which the speaker wishes that old age in fact arrive, do its damage and give rise to regret for earlier resistance (Thgn. 1299–1304; Asclep. *Anth. Pal.* 5.85, 5.164; Callim. *Epigr.* 63 Pf. (suspected) = *Anth. Pal.* 5.23; Theoc. 29.25–34; see N–H on 1.25.9ff.). Catlow 1976 examines close similarities with

1.25, *Parcius iunctas quatiunt fenestras*. This topic also becomes a feature of Roman elegy: Tib. 1.1.69–74; Ov. *Ars am.* 3.57–82. Here Lyce is in fact *becoming* old and has become repulsive, a fate she deserves for her youthful resistance to H. Esler 1989: 175 sees a shift from a 'conventional triumphant scorn in the opening lines' towards 'pity and even identification with its subject'. She refers to the pathos of the questions at 17–22. Similarly Catlow 1976: 820: 'Beauty's ruin can never be a source of triumph, but is a source of tears, and Lyce's loss is his also . . . Horace realises that his victory is a hollow one.' It is true that H. turns to himself at 20 *quae me surpuerat mihi*, but that just sets up the contrast with Cinara/Cinura (see 1.3–4n.), who died along with her youthful beauty, and the finale (22–8), as brutal and inhumane as anything H. wrote, gets back on topic and removes any trace of empathy. To that extent, the overall effect is an inversion of the ending of 1.14, whose final lines (for those who see the *nauis* of that poem as metaphorical) leave the reader with a sense of empathy towards the ageing addressee.

Although repeated names do not necessarily establish narrative continuities across poems, the Lyce of 13 looks very much like her namesake of 3.10, a straightforward *paraclausithyron*, 'for the first time since Plautus' *Curculio*, a complete paraclausithyron in the form of the lament of the *exclusus amator*', Copley 1956: 62–3. Again the poem captures the passing of time, for Lyce and also for H., as he is led to reminisce about Cinara/Cinura, the phantom lover from the days of, but not to be found in the text of, *C.* 1–3. Lyce also resembles Ligurinus of 10 as H. uses similar dendrological metaphors for their ageing (see 9–10, 10.4–5) and has *color* (17, 10.4) and *genae* (8, 10.8) in both. The abusive language at times moves the poem close to the nastiest of the *Epodes* (10–12n.).

1–2 Audiuere, Lyce, di . . . di | audiuere, Lyce: the emotional repetition with variation is a 'stylistic device of popular eloquence' (Fraenkel 1961: 48), with the same reversal at Plaut. *Most.* 603 *redde faenus, faenus reddite*, and with a shift in the vocative but no reversal of the *flagitatio* at Cat. 44.11–12 *moecha putida, redde codicillos, | redde, putida moecha, codicillos*. For repetition (of *audiuere*) at line-beginning, see Wills 180–1. The repetition forms an elegant ring, with *mea uota* enclosed first by the gods (*di*), then by repeated verb + repeated vocative, their order inverted. A discovery has just occurred; cf. the similar dramatic opening of *S.* 2.6.1 (on receiving the gift of the farm) *Hoc erat in uotis*; or, less close, of *C.* 2.19.1–2 *Bacchum in remotis carmina rupibus | uidi docentem (credite posteri)*. For the anaphora, see. 1.21n.

audiuere: for the verb (= *exaudio* 'be receptive to') in addresses to gods see *TLL* s.v. *audio* 1289.83–1290.34. See also 1.2.27–8 *minus audientem | carmina Vestam*; 2.18.40 *uocatus atque non uocatus audit;* also 3.22.1–3; 3.27.50–1. The imperative of *audio* is unsurprisingly a feature of actual prayers: *CS* 34–6 *supplices audi pueros, Apollo; | siderum regina bicornis, audi, | Luna, puellas*; Livy 1.24.7 *legibus deinde recitatis, 'audi' inquit, 'Iuppiter; audi, pater patrate populi Albani; audi tu, populus Albanus'*; Virg. *Aen.* 4.612 *'nostras audite preces'*; also *Aen.* 4.22; 9.630; 10.424. At *Aen.* 10.460–5 Hercules hears the prayer of Pallas (10.461 *te precor, Alcide*) but cannot grant it: *audiit Alcides iuuenem magnumque sub imo | corde premit gemitum*; cf. also Virg. *G.* 4.6–7.

Lyce: i.e. 'she-wolf', 'whore' (cf. *lupa, lupanar*), though not so in actual Gk. The name fits here (cf. 4–6), as in 3.10, though there Lyce is resistant, and Porph. gives as heading *haec ad puellam Lycen dicuntur, asperam et intractabilem*. Serv. Dan. at Virg. *Aen.* 12.516 claims Lycia was named after a nymph, Lyce, by whom Apollo had a son, Lycadius. Lycus is a pimp in Plaut. *Poen.*

fis anus 'you're turning into an old woman'. The verb form is extremely rare: before this only at Cic. *Phil.* 2.99 of present general time: *cum tua quid interest, nulla auspicia sunt; cum tuorum, tum fis religiosus*. Otherwise once at *Epist.* 2.2.211 *lenior et melior fis accedente senecta?*, then not again until a single instance in Apuleius (*Apol.* 20.20). The present tenses of the poem (*fis, uis, ludis, bibis, excubat, transuolat, refugit, turpant, referunt, fugit*) conspire to give the impression that the change has just happened and is still underway. See Cameron 1995: 177–81 for evidence that the Romans thought of 46 or so as the onset of old age, as also suggested by Cic. *Sen.* 61, Gell. 10.28.1, though Powell (*ad* Cic. *loc. cit.*) shows this was an earlier view, not so prevalent in Cicero's own time when 60 was rather the threshold.

fis . . . uis: the rhyming monosyllables capture the conflict between reality and delusion.

3–4 uis formosa uideri: cf. Prop. 2.18.28 *mi per te poteris formosa uideri*; Ov. *Met.* 9.462 *nimiumqe cupit formosa uideri*; also Tib. 1.9.71 *non tibi sed iuueni cuidam uult bella uideri*; 3.19.5 *atque utinam posses uni mihi bella uideri*, with which cf. Cat. 8.16 *cui uideberis bella?*

ludisque et bibis impudens: cf. Cic. *Phil.* 2.104 of Antony's habits: *ab hora tertia bibebatur, ludebatur, uomebatur. ludo* is broad and ambiguous, and far from innocent, since *impudens* is to be taken ἀπὸ κοινοῦ with both verbs – and as is clear from 5–6. Such things are acceptable, but in their season; cf. *Epist* 1.14.36 (H. of his earlier days, with Cinara/Cinura and drinking at midday): *nec lusisse pudet, sed non incidere lusum.*

5–6 et . . . sollicitas 'when drunk you try to arouse with your quavering song a Cupid who is unresponsive'; cf. Prop. 1.8.20 *hostibus eueniat lenta puella meis* and *OLD* s.v. *lentus* 8. In contrast, the god takes up residence with Chia, who is youthful (*uirentis*), attractive (*pulchris*) and a skilled (*doctae*) singer – she has everything that Lyce lacks.

cantu tremulo: cf. Tib. 1.2.92–3 (an old man in the same position as Lyce; cf. 26–8n.) *senem* | . . . *sibi blanditias tremula componere uoce.*

6–8 ille [sc. Cupido] . . . pulchris excubat in genis 'keeps watch on her beautiful cheeks', (or 'eyelids' and ultimately 'eyes') – ready to snare a lover; so Porph. *de palpebris intellexisse uidetur*; and cf. *OLD s.v. gena* 2 and 3 for the area around the eyes and the eyelids, respectively. This is the first instance in Latin of *genae* as the seat of young feminine beauty (*TLL* s.v. 1765.3–19). In favour of translating as 'cheeks', the striking metaphor seems to be taken from Soph. *Ant.* 782–4 (so *TLL* s.v. *gena* 1765.4–7), from the ode on the power of Eros and Aphrodite: Ἔρως . . . | ὃς ἐν μαλακαῖς παρειαῖς | νεάνιδος ἐννυχεύεις 'Love . . . you who spend the night on the soft cheeks of a girl'; and παρειά does not have the flexibility granted to *gena*. In the antistrophe of the same ode the eyes have it, so in a sense H.'s line takes in both Sophoclean passages: 795–7 νικᾶι δ' ἐναργὴς βλεφάρων | ἵμερος εὐλέκτρου | νύμφας, Griffith *ad loc.*: 'The primary sense may be (roughly) "victorious is the allure shining in the eyes of the ready young bride". But the associations are multiple, suggesting the mutually irresistible radiance of *both* lovers (implicitly Ant. and Haimon).'

uirentis: in contrast to 12 *niues*.

doctae psallere: epexegetical infinitive; a little like Sallust's Sempronia: *Cat.* 25.1 *litteris Graecis Latinis docta, psallere saltare elegantius quam necesse est probae.*

Chiae: such names ('the girl from Chios') are unusual for H., though the name is well attested in inscriptions; cf. *TLL Onom.* s.v. *Chius* 398.81–399.12; also in Gk., esp. in Magna Graecia, according to *LPGN*. The substantivized *Chia* (sc. *ficus*) was used for a fig, of the smaller and more desirable type (than the *marisca*, for instance), and thence (we cannot know when) came to be used for the desirable male *culus* in pederastic situations: Petr. 63.3 '*nam a puero uitam Chiam gessi*'; Mart. 12.96.9–10 (addressed to a wife who should not be worried about her husband's preferences in this area since he does not have affairs with women) *non eadem res est: Chiam uolo, nolo mariscam: | ne dubites quae sit Chia, marisca tua est.* Adams 113 sees the metaphor as Martial's own and finds no evidence for the regular use of *ficus* = *culus* in Martial's time. Still, the names are worth thinking about, since Adams also notes (114 and n. 1) that Italian *fica* = *pudendum muliebre* is taken as a 'late calque' on σῦκον in that sense, e.g. at Ar. *Pax* 1354; cf. on Cinara/Cinura at 1.3–4n., Ligurinus at 1.33–4n.

9–10 'for he is unaccommodating and so he flies past your dried-out oaks and flees from you'. Again, a striking metaphor, here from the plant world, involving a dead and dried-out oak – oddly looking ahead to the famous simile of Pompey as a dying oak at Luc. 1.136–43. The implicit infertility of old age will contrast with Lyce's former state (21 *felix*), and the dead oak will soon be ash (see 28 and n.). Cf. also the agricultural metaphor (soil exhaustion) in Turnus' taunt to Calybe–Allecto at Virg. *Aen.* 7.440 (and Horsfall *ad loc.*) *uicta situ uerique effeta senectus*. If 10.5 *fruticem* is what H. wrote (see n.), the metaphors are similar (and cf. 17, 10.4 *color*).

10–12 Yellowing teeth, wrinkling and white hair, an ugly (*turpant*) combination. White hair and wrinkles are the standard expression for old age, not necessarily in pejorative terms: cf. 2.14.2–4 *nec pietas moram | rugis et instanti senectae | afferet indomitaeque morti*; Tib. 2.2.19–20 (a long and happy marriage to Cornutus) *uincula quae maneant semper, dum tarda senectus | inducat rugas inficiatque comas.* The prayer that grey hair may come, or has already come, to the spurning woman develops into something of a commonplace (Callim. *Epigr.* 63 Pf. = *Anth. Pal.* 5.23, Rufinus, *Anth. Pal.* 5.21, 92, 103). Here it has actually happened, much to H.'s delight, and takes the reader back to the world of *Epod.* 8.3–6 *cum sit tibi dens ater et rugis uetus | frontem senectus exaret | hietque turpis inter aridas nates | podex uelut crudae bouis*, the end of which (19–20 *quod ut superbo prouoces ab inguine, | ore allaborandum est*) may spell out the meaning beneath 6 *lentum* in the present poem.

capitis niues: a unique expression for white hair. Quintilian thought the metaphor went too far, lumping it in with a line of Furius Bibaculus: 8.6.17 *sed copia quoque modum egressa uitiosa est, praecipue in eadem specie. sunt et durae, id est a longinqua similitudine ductae, ut 'capitis niues' et 'Iuppiter hibernas cana niue conspuit Alpes'.* H. had himself had some fun with that other line (*S.* 2.5.41 *Furius hibernas cana niue conspuet Alpis*), and must have judged his own metaphor to have been within the bounds of taste. Nor is it clear that Quintilian's judgement is valid here; the snow of Lyce's hair is a fitting match for the green bloom of Chia (6 *uirentis*); cf. also *C.* 1.9.17–18 *donec uirenti canities abest | morosa*, with *uirentis* at 13.6. Does snow-peaked Mt. Soracte of that poem come to mind?

13, 14: nec . . . | nec: cf. 1.21n.

13–14 Coae . . . purpurae: Coan purple will be no substitute for the purple tint (cf. 17 *quoue color?*) of youth (cf. 10.4 *color . . . puniceae flore prior rosae*). Coan silk left little to the imagination: *S.* 1.2.101–2 *Cois tibi paene uidere est | ut nudam.* It suggests *coitus* as is clear from Caelius Rufus' joke about Clodia: fr. 26 Malcovati *in triclinio coam, in cubiculo nolam* (with *Nolam* reduced to *nolam* – unwillingness in the bedroom). The material was favoured by the ladies of Roman elegy and formed part of their sexual appeal: Prop. 1.2.1–2 (= 4.5.55–6) – here, though, Cynthia has no need of such adornment – *quid iuuat . . . | tenuis Coa ueste mouere sinus*; also 2.1.5–6; 4.2.23, 5.23, [56], 57; Tib. 2.3.53 (and Maltby *ad loc.*); Ov. *Am.* 1.5.13–14 (and McKeown *ad loc.*); *Ars am.* 2.298. Ovid has Tyrian or purple also as a mark of erotic luxury, but distinct from Coan silk, as at Ov. *Ars am.* 2.297–8 *siue erit in Tyriis, Tyrios laudabis amictus | siue erit in Cois, Coa decere puta* – with the last two words implying that such attire may not suit decorum. H. conflates the two, in the process giving us what looks like a hybrid, a sign of his distance from the topoi of elegy?

cari lapides: like Coan silk, also part of the uniform of the elegiac *puella*: Prop. 1.2.13; 1.15.7.

tempora: see *OLD* s.v. *tempus* 4b for the plural = 'period, time (in the life of a person, etc.)'; cf. 24–6 *temporibus*. Time is on his mind: cf. 12.13 *tempora*, also the central stanza of a seven-stanza poem.

14–16 '(cannot bring back) the span of your life, which once and for all the fleeting day has stored away and entered into the public record book'. These fictional *fasti*, modelled on consular or triumphal *fasti*, are records of Lyce's precise age and also perhaps of her *res gestae* over the years, there for all to see. This sets up a pointed contrast with the real thing, coming up at 14.4 (to Augustus) *memoresque fastos* (see n.), all the more pointed since H. seems to be the first to apply *fasti* to such frivolous catalogues; see *TLL* s.v. *fastus* 328.57–70; and cf. 3.17.4 *per memores . . . fastus*, with N–R *ad loc.*; *S.* 1.3.112; *Epist.* 2.1.48.

condita 'stored away, closed out', in the same sense as in the sacral formula *lustrum condere*; cf. *TLL* s.v. *condo* 152.19–26 (general), 26–43 (of *lustrum*).

uolucris dies for which cf. 3.28.6 (Lyde hesitates to drink) *ueluti stet uolucris dies*, seems like a cliché, but otherwise only at Sen. *HF* 178 (in a Horatian context) *uolucrique die rota praecipitis uertitur anni.*

17–22 A remarkable stanza, with three brief questions marked by anaphora of *quo* (see 1.21n.), followed by a distinct fourth question (*quid*) and two subordinate relative clauses (*quae . . . quae*), whose predicate and the narrative it contains are enjambed into the next stanza. The structuring repetitions are striking: *quo–quo–quo/illius–illius/quae–quae.* The tone changes as the fleeting nature of time leads H. to reflect now with some empathy on the past, on his time with Lyce and before that his time with the mysterious ideal lover, always of the past, Cinara/Cinura (see 1.3–4n.). The regret and the focus on lost vigour and lost capacity, including H.'s, is also found at *Epist.* 1.7.25–8, which similarly ends with a focus on Cinara/Cinura. In the present poem H. will recover his disdain for the final stanza (see intro., 26–8n.).

quo fugit uenus, heu, quoue . . . ?: for a similar surprise at the new turn of thought that creeps up cf. 1.33 *sed cur, heu, Ligurine, cur . . .?*

uenus . . . color . . . decens | . . . motus: sexuality, complexion, proper carriage (including dancing?). *decens motus*, in combination with *uenus*, may refer to a different sort of movement, as in Prop. 1.4.13–14 *ingenuus color et motis decor artubus et quae | gaudia sub tacita discere ueste licet.* See Gibson on *Ars am.* 3.299ff. for treatment of carriage and gait; cf. also Cic. *Off* 1.131. For Quintilian (1.10.26) *decens motus* is a feature of the orator's training, Gk. εὐρυθμία.

color: her complexion has changed, like that of Ligurinus at 10.4–5, and n.

quid habes: stark language; Lyce is unrecognizable.

illius, illius: unique in this inflection, one antecedent for each relative pronoun (*quae . . . quae*), with the doubling highly emphatic; cf. Axelson 73. For the repetition of demonstratives see Wills 76–9.

quae . . . facies: *pace* K–H '*illius* sc. *Lyces*, nicht *faciei* – sonst würde der Leser bis zum letzten Wort des Satzes getäuscht'. On the contrary, that seems quite Horatian.

spirabat amores: internal accusative; cf. Cic. *Att.* 15.11.1 *oculis Cassius (Martem spirare diceres) se in Siciliam non iturum*; Prop. 1.3.7–8 *talis uisa mihi mollem spirare quietem | Cynthia*, and Fedeli *ad loc.* with reference to Theoc. 17.51–2 (of Berenice, focalized by Ptolemy) μαλακοὺς μὲν ἔρωτας | προσπνείει 'breathes soft loves'. Cf. 9.10 (of Sappho's love poetry) *spirat adhuc amor.*

me surpuerat mihi 'stole me away from myself', dative of disadvantage. The contraction *surpo* (*surpuerat* = *surripuerat*), doubtless colloquial (and a morphological 'stealing away'?) also occurs at *S.* 2.3.283 and in Plautus, Lucretius and Martial; cf. *OLD* s.v. *subripio*, *init.* There is a reminiscence of (the Sapphic) Cat. 51.5–6, also of the first flush, *misero quod omnes | eripit sensus mihi.*

21–2 felix post Cinaram: Lyce was a 'blessing', i.e. for H., following the death of Cinara/Cinura (cf. 1.3–4n.); *felix* may also indicate amorous success (*TLL* s.v. *felix* 442.63–84); cf. *Epod.* 12.25–6 *o ego non felix, quam tu fugis ut pauet acres | agna lupos capreaeque leones!*; Cat. 100.8 *sis felix, Caeli, sis in amore potens.* For a collection and subdivision of instances of *felix* in Roman elegy (but not including H.), see Pichon 1902: s.v. *felix*. Some take *post* to denote preference ('runner up to Cinara'), but temporal succession seems more likely with *felix* (compared, say, to *pulchra*); and see n. below.

Cinaram . . . Cinarae: closing the first and second choriambs of successive lines, with appealing rhythmical effect. Cinara/Cinura intrudes into the relationship, with *post* clarified after it is revealed that C. was dead when H. moved on to Lyce. For those enamoured of a flesh and blood C. (see 1.3–4n.) the question arises as to when the relationship occurred. C. is not mentioned before *Epist.* 1, already retrospectively by then. Her absence from *C.* 1–3 (although that should be the world *sub regno Cinarae*) means that C. reigned and died, while Lyce rose and fell in H.'s books (and in physical appeal) with astonishing rapidity. *C.* 4 began with C., already a thing of the past, and with her and Lyce its private and lyric world is here closing down.

notaque et artium | gratarum facies 'a beauty also well known for her delightful skills'. Her *artes* presumably filled the whole range, since she was a familiar (*nota*) figure; cf. 1.15 (of Paullus) *centum puer artium.*

22–8 A brilliant sentence focused on the happy past with Cinara/Cinura and Lyce's contrasting treatment by the fates: a brief life for C., a long one for L. so that her burnt-out looks might be mocked by young lovers. The details of the latter's fate shed positive light on C.'s brief life, who stays forever young and is always depicted in a positive light in H.

22–3 breues | annos 'a few brief years', i.e. *paucos*. Porph. felt the need to explain: *ad* 1.36.16 *quod breuis temporis est, hoc est cito deflorescit*; *ad* 2.14.24 *id est: breuis uitae*. For this elliptical use, alluding to the transience of flowers, cf. 1.36.16 *breue lilium*; 2.3.13–14 *nimium breues | flores*; *Epist.* 1.19.26 *ne me foliis . . . breuioribus ornes*; and *TLL* s.v. *breuis* 2176.18–21; of humans 2.14.24 *breuem dominum* and *TLL* s.v. *breuis* 2176.22–8. There is a sepulchral feel to all of these instances, and the usage seems to be a Horatian invention which did not particularly catch on.

23 fata dederunt: a common combination; cf. *TLL* s.v. *fatum* 361.72–80.

24–6 seruatura diu . . . Lycen . . . ut: the fates act maliciously so as to make a spectacle of Lyce, in accordance with the prayer whose success is announced at the beginning of the poem.

parem | cornicis uetulae temporibus 'equal in years to the ageing crow' (literally, to the seasons [as with 14 and n. *tempora*] of the crow). Cf. 3.17.13 *annosa cornix*, and with references to the bird's proverbial age, N–R *ad loc.*, including Hes. fr. 304 M-W: the crow lives nine generations of men.

uetulae: of the crow, but very much humanized, with reminiscence of a related poem to the ageing wife of Ibycus: 3.15.13–16 *te . . . non citharae decent | nec flos . . . nec poti uetulam.* The other instance in H. stands between the human and animal world: *Epist.* 1.10.5–7 *uetuli notique columbi | tu nidum seruas, ego laudo ruris amoeni riuos.*

26–8 'so the lusty young men can have a good laugh when they take a look at this torch burnt down to ashes'. A brutal close to the poem, devoid of empathy, as Lyce has become an object of amusement and mockery, her appeal completely gone. This is the first laughter since 1.18, where Paullus laughted at the gifts of the rival. The language is hard to reconcile with Quinn's claim (*ad* 22–8) that 'H. is taken aback on seeing Lyce again, not vindictive; their quarrel is too much a thing of the past for vindictiveness.' At *Epod.* 5.57 the perfumed *senex adulter* has a similar effect: *quod omnes rideant.* Cf. also Tib. 1.2. 91–8, where the poet warns that those who mock the unrequited love (here in a paraclausithyron) of the young may find themselves mocked by the next generation when they themselves grow old: *hunc* [sc. *senem amantem*] *puer, hunc iuuenis turba circumterit arta* | *despuit in molles et sibi quisque sinus* (see 2–6n.). The Tibullan intertext activates the irony that Lyce has become what H. was at the end of 4.1, chasing after Ligurinus.

27 multo non sine risu: the fronting of the adjective with *non sine* happens first in Augustan poetry but only in H. and the elegists (not Ovid) and not in Latin thereafter: 2.4.29 *albo non sine Coo*; *S.* 1.5.80 *lacrimoso non sine fumo*; 2.8.87 *multo non sine farre*; Tib. 1.8.6 *multis non sine uerberibus*; Prop. 2.9.50 *Thebani media non sine matre duces*; similarly Prop. 4.8.20 *famae non sine labe meae*. The combination *non sine* itself is favoured most by H., with 16 instances vs. three in Catullus, none in Virgil, three in Ovid, one in Lucan, two each in Statius and Silius. Prose authors, beginning with Cicero (83 times, taken from Gk. οὐκ ἀνεῦ?), account for the remainder of the 400 appearances.

28 dilapsam in cineres facem: Porph.: ἐνφατικῶς *illam ut Amoris facem dilapsam ait in cinerem et consumptam refrixisse* 'he forcefully says that she has fallen into ash like the torch of Love, and is spent and gone cold'. The dried-out oak of 9 has become a burnt-out torch, *dilapsam in cineres*, in stark contrast to the sexual heat of the young men (*feruidi*). K–H *ad loc.* well refer to Meleager 94 G–P = *Anth. Pal.* 12.41, where M. gives up pederastic love and turns to women, since the *eromenos* Apollodotus has similarly lost his fire, though naturally at a younger age than did Lyce, νῦν δ' ἤδη δαλὸς Ἀπολλόδοτος. | στέργω θῆλυν ἔρωτα. 'Apollodotus is now turned to ash. I look to love of women.' Cinara/Cinura has become real ashes, but the living *cineres* into which Lyce turns are much worse, at least in the world of erotic lyric. Better the memory of C., even when she is *cineres* – with obvious verbal play.

14

METRE

Alcaic stanza, as in the closely related 4.

INTRODUCTION

How are the senate and people, Augustus, to immortalize you sufficiently, you whose power the Vindelici recently learned to its cost? For with your soldiers Drusus threw down the Genauni and Breuni, while Tiberius then routed the Raetians. As the South Wind whips up the seas, so he attacked the enemy. As the Aufidus rolls along and floods the crops, so Claudius mowed down his foes, with soldiers supplied by you. Fifteen years after Alexandria opened its harbour to you, Fortune again has given a successful outcome, adding to other successes. It is to you that the Cantabrian, Mede, Indian, Scythian, to you the Nile, Danube, Tigris and Ocean, to you the land of Gaul and Spain, all listen. Now the Sygambri lay down their arms and venerate you.

How to praise Augustus? Fraenkel 432 put it so: 'By writing the epinikion for Drusus in his grandest style [4] Horace had made it exceedingly difficult for himself to produce a poem to match this ode when he was soon afterwards called upon to celebrate the victories won by Tiberius in the course of the same campaign in which his younger brother had distinguished himself.' In his proem to this ode Orelli notes the contrast between the lavish praise of Augustus and the rather half-hearted attitude towards Drusus and Tiberius. And for the view that the achievement itself was overstated, see van Berchem 1968.

The poem is clearly related to 4 in fundamental ways (see 4 intro.), but it has separate dynamics and should be judged independently. The first half (1–34) is devoted, although not addressed, to Drusus and Tiberius, whose Alpine campaigns are the topic at hand, with a transition via the ablative absolute of 33–4 to an effusive aretalogy of Augustus (34–52), to whom the entire poem is also addressed (3). Drusus and Tiberius are both structurally and thematically something of a side-issue. Some see this as a muted attitude towards Tiberius in particular, and it is true Drusus gets more attention (4 and part of 14) and is named more intimately (10 *Drusus*) than Tiberius (14 *maior Neronum*; 29 *Claudius*).

1–24 The mode is again very much Pindaric (Norden 1913: 152–3). Cf. Fraenkel 432: 'Like iv.4, iv.14 opens with one long unbroken period; this time it consists not of seven but of six stanzas.' This fact is not apparent from editions since K–H, which place a question mark (ambiguous as to whether it marks a syntactical break as well as a query) after 6 *principum*, a full-stop after 9 *posses* and in some cases a semi-colon after 13 *simplici*. This edition retains the question mark in 6, which is intended syntactically to represent a comma, follows K–H in placing a colon in 9 (see 9n. on *nam*) and assumes asyndeton between 13–14. The periodic integrity of the lines, although under stress at these points, is so preserved. The main clause of the period (1–5) is quite overloaded, with an instrumental ablative and two prepositional phrases qualifying *aeternet*; *auxesis* for Augustus, as encomiastic excess and Pindaric syntactical ποικιλία ('variety') are in the air (see 34–52n.).

1–5 Quae cura . . . tuas . . . uirtutes . . . aeternet 'what attentive action is to immortalize your virtues'; a deliberative rather than a potential subjunctive.

Quae . . . quaeue: the interrogative opening is Pindaric, as was noted by Norden (1913) 152: *Ol.* 2.1–2; *Isthm.* 7.1–15; *Hymnoi* fr. 29; *Pros.* fr. 89a Maehler; see also Fraenkel 432, n. 2. H. begins a number of the odes thus: 1.5, 12 (after *Ol.* 2.1–2), 24, 31; 3.7, 21.

cura patrum: *cura* taken with both genitives (i.e. poetic for *cura senatus populique Romani*), with which it creates a double *figura etymologica* or at least pun: 1) with *patrum*, cf. Varro *ap*. Non. p. 57M *CVRIAM a cura dictam Varro designat de Vita Populi Romani lib. II 'itaque propter curam locus quoque, quo suam quisque domo senator confert, curia appellatur'*; *Ling*. 5.155 *curiae duorum generum: nam et ubi curarent sacerdotes res diuinas . . . et ubi senatus humanas*; 2) with *Quiritium*, cf. Varro, *Ling*. 6.68 *Quirites a Curensibus*. For *cura* = 'attention (resulting in action)', cf. Cic. *Mur*. 34 *neque tanta cura senatus et populus Romanus suscipiendum putasset*; Sall. *Iug*. 26.1 *de ceteris senatui curae fore*; *OLD* s.v. *cura* 2.

plenis honorum muneribus 'abundant granting of honours/offices', deliberately vague and presumably including any number of honours and offices to be found throughout the *Res gestae* and elsewhere. K–H list past instances that will have served as exempla for H. and his readers: conferring of the name 'Augustus', renaming the month of *Sextilis*, founding of the *Ara Fortunae reducis* in 19 BCE and so on. Future honours would include the *Ara pacis Augustae* (decreed 13 BCE, dedicated 9 BCE), though *pax* is not yet an issue in this poem. But given the republican sense of *honor*, H. also includes consulships, lifetime tribunician power etc.

3 Auguste: the vocative is only here in H. and rare in Augustan poetry generally, perhaps indicating elevation, sincere or otherwise: Prop. 2.10.15 (the elegist turns to *laus Caesaris*); 4.6.38 (Apollo, anachronistically or prophetically in addressing the future *princeps* at Actium); and twice in Ovid: *Met*. 1.204; *Trist*. 2.1. See 15.4n.

uirtutes: the aretalogy of the second part will elaborate, in the military sphere (34–52n.).

3–5 in aeuum . . . aeternet 'immortalize for ever and ever', emphatic to the point of redundancy; cf. Varro *Ling*. 6.11 *aeuum ab aetate omnium annorum (hinc aeuiternum, quod factum est aeternum)*. The play is emphasized by the novelty of the verb (see below 5n.); for this type of *figura etymologica* see Wills 245. There is a similar play at Ov. *Met*. 1.662–3 *praeclusaque ianua leti | aeternum nostros luctus extendit in aeuum*. *in aeuum* without adjective is rare, first at Prop. 3.4.19–20 (also of Augustus) *ipsa tuam serua prolem, Venus: hoc sit in aeuum, | cernis ab Aenea quod superesse caput*. In light of the beginning of the next poem (15.4 *tua, Caesar, aetas*), H.'s play with time and age (and the Age of Augustus), evident throughout the book, is moving into new territory.

4 titulos memoresque fastos 'inscriptions and public records' (Rudd); *tituli* would include inscriptions, any monumental writing, labels on images etc. As for *fasti*, H. may imply a contrast with the records of Lyce's 'career' at 13.14–16 (see n.), and here he probably means the historical record in general, preserved in any number of ways, which suits H.'s usage elsewhere (3.17.4; *S*. 1.3.112; *TLL* s.v. *fastus* 328.57–72); ps.-Acro suggests this broader sense: *annales, qui ad commemorationem honorum uel rerum gestarum inuenti sunt, ipsi enim fasti dicuntur*. There is a slight personification in *memores*.

fastos: there is somewhat better support for *fastus* (from *fasti, -orum*, not *fastus, -us*), but there is no clear-cut consensus here or at 3.17.3–4 *nepotum | per memores genus omne fastus* (cf. N–R *ad loc.*); *S.* 1.3.112; *Epist.* 2.1.48, on which Brink (who there prints *fastos*): 'Either form is possible, and Horace may have used different forms in different places.' Shackleton Bailey regularizes to *fastos* in all four places, but the evidence suggests a more complex situation; cf. *TLL* s.v. *fastus* 326.47–51. Luc. 10.187 *fastibus* shows that *fastus* is possible in H., and cf. Priscian *GL* II 256 on 3.17.4: *apud Horatium duplicem inuenio scripturam et 'fastos' et 'fastus' in III carminum: 'per memores genus omne fastos'* (3.17.4).

5 aeternet: very rare, but not to the extent of Porph.'s comment: *fictum uerbum est 'aeternet'*. Otherwise securely attested only at Varro *ap.* Non. p. 75M '*AETERNARE. Varro Rerum humanarum lib. II* [fr. 19 Mirsch] *"litterisque ac laudibus aeternare"*'. This may cause suspicion of the supplement of Bormann at *Acta lud. saec. sept.* 1.12 *diligenti<ssime aet>ernata est*, for which see *TLL* s.v. *aeterno* 1141.75–81.

5–6 o: cf. 2.46 (also to Augustus) *o laudande*. The exclamatory particle is rather left hanging, not completed till 6 *maxime principum*, and parallels (*TLL* s.v. *o* 10.72–84) seem less audacious, e.g. Plaut. *Capt.* 835–6 *o mihi, | quantum est hominum optumorum, optume*; and many are with exclamatory accusative, rather than vocative, which is distinct: e.g. Cic. *Att.* 10.16.3 *o, si id fuerit, turpem Catonem!*

qua . . . oras: i.e. an empire on which the sun never set; indebted to Virg. *Aen.* 7.99–101 (with Horsfall *ad loc.* for later parallels) *'quorumque a stirpe nepotes | omnia sub pedibus, qua sol utrumque recurrens | aspicit Oceanum, uertique regique uidebunt'*; Tib. 2.5.58–60 (the Sibyl) *'Roma, tuum nomen terris fatale regendis | qua sua de caelo prospicit arua Ceres, | quaque patent ortus et qua fluitantibus undis | Solis anhelantes abluit amnis equos'*. Something of a cliché; cf. *CS* 9–12.

sol . . . | illustrat: the verb is somewhat rare, and otherwise only in prose with its literal meaning: cf. Cic. *Verr.* 2.4.71; Varro *Rust.* 1.12.3; *TLL* s.v. *illustro* 398.26–38.

habitabiles: cf. ἡ οἰκουμένη 'the world' (Orelli); cf. Virg. *G.* 1.237–8 (of the habitable zones) *duae mortalibus agris | munere concessae diuum*, from Eratosth. *Hermes* 16.18–19 Powell (of the same two zones) ἐν δέ μιν ἄνδρες | ἀντίποδες ναίουσι 'in it live men with feet opposite'.

maxime principum: *princeps* is used of republican leaders (*TLL* s.v. 1283.17–39), of those connected to Augustus, including Drusus and Tiberius (1284.40–54) and of the younger members of his household vaguely marked out for succession (1285.44–58). In such a context *maxime* may be seen as appropriate here, but *maxime principum* seems to be reaching for something unavailable in the republican lexicon (as in 'Generalissimo'), since *princeps* alone is felt as a superlative (cf. e.g. Cic. *Planc.* 32 *postea princeps inter suos, plurimarum rerum sanctissimus et iustissimus iudex, maximarum societatum auctor, plurimarum magister*). The combination reveals its new force (= 'greatest of the emperors') at Mela 3.49, on Claudius' invasion of Britain: *tamdiu clausam aperit ecce principum maximus*.

7–9 quem . . . didicere . . . quid Marte posses 'whom they learned what you are capable of in war'; a somewhat tortuous example (see 1–24n.) of the 'proleptic accusative' construction (*te scio qui sis*), on which see Adams 2005: 90: 'the construction had been common in early Latin, particularly comedy, but is rare in the late Republic. It was not dropped from the language as a whole, but from the high literary language' (see also Laughton 1960: 6). Its presence here contributes to the archaic and Pindaric flavour. Here *quem* is treated as a true relative, not resumptive, designed to keep the sentence going.

legis expertes Latinae: cf. Dio 54.22.2 (of the Raetians just before the campaign) τοῖς οὐκ ἐνσπόνδοις 'not under treaty'; after 15 BCE Raetia was first under the control of a prefect and only became a province, *Raetia et Vindelicia et uallis Poenina*, in the time of Tiberius or Caligula, when it was under the command of a *procurator Augusti et pro legato*; see Dietz 1995: 69–73. The cultural implication was perhaps picked up by Tacitus at *Germ.* 19.5 *plusque ibi boni mores ualent quam alibi bonae leges.* Justice in the absence of laws is an aspect in depictions of golden age or primitive, including Roman, societies: cf. Sall. *Cat.* 9.1 (early Romans) *ius bonumque apud eos non legibus magis quam natura ualebat*; Virg. *Aen.* 7.2–3 (the old Latins) *neue ignorate Latinos | Saturni gentem haud uinclo nec legibus aequam*. Cf. N–R *ad* 3.24.35–6 (again on the virtues of the primitive) *quid leges sine moribus | uanae proficiunt?*; cf. Ovid's golden age, *Met.* 1.90 *sponte sua, sine lege fidem rectumque colebat*; see Gatz 1967: *passim*, 231 (Index). Cf. 17–19n. on other positive aspects of the Raetians.

Vindelici didicere: parallel in all respects (morphological, syntactical, positional and thematic) to 4.17–18 *uidere . . . Vindelici*, 22–5 *cateruae . . . sensere*; see 4 intro.

nuper: perhaps suggests a date of composition in late 15 BCE, early 14 BCE at the latest.

9–13 The language is elevated and epic in flavour so as to magnify the achievement; H. shows he can rise to the high style if he wishes. K–H note the parallels between H.'s treatment of the campaign and that found at Vell. 2.95.2 *quippe uterque, diuisis partibus, Raetos Vindelicosque aggressi, multis urbium et castellorum* [11–12 *arces | Alpibus impositas*] *oppugnationibus nec non derecta quoque acie* [14 *graue proelium*] *feliciter functi gentes locis tutissimas, aditu difficillimas, numero frequentes, feritate truces* [10 *implacidum genus*, 15 *immanisque*] *maiore cum periculo quam damno Romani exercitus* [32 *sine clade*], *plurimo cum earum sanguine* [19 *quantis fatigaret ruinis*] *perdomuerunt*. It may be that both authors are reflecting some inflated dispatches, doubtless aiming to promote the status of the Neros.

milite . . . tuo: forms a frame with 33–4 *te copias . . . praebente*; presumably *legio XXI Rapax*, raised by Augustus some time before 27 BCE; see 4.50–5n. For the use of the collective singular of such nouns (*miles, eques, pedes* etc.) cf. 1.15.6 *multo . . . milite* and K–S II 1.67. The possessive adjective (*tuo*) shows the new realities of the Roman army: Augustus has the auspices and is the official commander.

nam: here as a causal conjunction, 'because'; cf. *OLD* s.v. *nam* 3.

Genaunos . . . Breunosque: the *Genaunes* (H. seems to have just mistaken their declension) and *Breuni* come sixth and seventh respectively on the *Tropaeum Alpium* (*CIL* V 7817; see 4 intro.); they are situated in eastern Raetia, towards Noricum.

implacidum genus: the adjective is rare, first here and at Prop. 4.9.14 *implacidas diruit ira fores* [sc. *Caci*], in epic contexts by ostensibly un-epic poets; not in epic itself till Statius. The 29 instances of *placidus* in Virgil suggest the negative may have been coined by H. or Prop., though that seems hard to imagine, and none of the Virgilian instances is negativized. For the style more generally cf. also Virg. *Aen.* 1.339 *genus intractabile bello*; 4.40 *genus insuperabile bello*.

ueloces: ethnographical flavouring, but presumably quite true of mountain people, particularly from the perspective of the Roman legionnaire; cf. Livy 22.18.3 *ea* [*cohors*] *assuetior montibus et ad concursandum inter saxa rupesque aptior ac leuior cum uelocitate corporum tum armorum habitu.*

arces | Alpibus impositas tremendis | deiecit: reminiscent of Virgilian language; e.g. *G.* 1.281–3 *ter sunt conati imponere Pelio Ossam . . . ter pater extructos disiecit fulmine montes*; 3.474–5 *aërias Alpes et Norica . . . | castella*. Not surprisingly, since this is precisely the sort of thing H. would say he could not do, while Virgil and Varius could: *Epist.* 2.1.250–3 *nec sermones ego mallem | repentes per humum quam . . . dicere, et arces | montibus impositas et barbara regna.*

tremendis 'awe-inspiring'.

deiecit: a mild syllepsis with the tribal names (*OLD* s.v. 8a 'to drive out from a position') and *arces* (*OLD* s.v. 6a 'to overthrow a structure'). The verb implies violent overthrow and is a favourite of Virgil, at emphatic line-initial position in the imperative (*G.* 3.422), present (*G.* 1.333; *Aen.* 8.428; 10.753; 11.642, 665) or perfect (*Aen.* 3.320; 8.226; 10.319), an effect replicated by H.'s enjambment into the stanza following the rest of the predicate.

acer plus uice simplici 'fierce in inflicting more than a mere reprisal'; for *uices* as the discharging of a debt, cf. 1.28.33 and N–H *ad loc.*, citing Serv. *ad* Virg. *Aen.* 2.433 *legimus etiam poenas 'uices' dici.* Behind the litotes is the reality that the campaign seems to have been one of choice (see 4.4 intro.). Dio 45.22.4–5 reports the overwhelming defeat and subsequent deportation of most of the male population.

14–32 Tiberius' turn. Before the death of Agrippa in 12 BCE, and even until that of his younger brother Drusus in 9 BCE, Tiberius was just one of those acting in the interests of Augustus, not yet the most important: he gets more space than Drusus, because the latter was the subject of 4, which only included Tiberius with the designation *pueros . . . Nerones* (28).

14–24 The sentence continues, with asyndeton from 13, and culminating in the first of Tiberius' two similes.

14 maior Neronum: sc. *natu* (though cf. 5–6n. on *maxime* [*principum*]), by just over three years. Before his adoption, Tiberius Claudius Nero (cf. 29 *Claudius*), after adoption by Augustus (along with Agrippa Postumus), on 26/7 June 4 CE, he was called Ti. (Iulius) Caesar and after his adoptive father's death Ti. Caesar Augustus (*PIR*² C941). As a youth he was dubbed 'Biberius Caldius Mero' because of his taste for wine: Suet. *Tib.* 42.1. He was born 16 Nov. 42 BCE, died 16 March 37 CE.

mox: soon after Drusus' engagement, i.e.; see 4 intro.

graue proelium: cf. 9–13n. and Vell. 2.95.2 *nec non derecta quoque acie.*

immanesque: a strongly negative word, embracing *malus, improbus, crudelis, ingens* etc.; negative of *manus* = *bonus*: cf. Varro, *Ling.* 6.2.4 *bonum antiqui dicebant manum*; cf. Caes. *B. Gall.* 4.1.9 (with 6.16.4 his only use of the word) on the Suebi, most warlike of the Germans, whose diet (milk, meat, with much time devoted to hunting) makes them physically formidable: [*hoc genus cibi*] *et uires alit et immani corporum magnitudine homines efficit.*

auspiciis . . . secundis 'under favourable auspices'; i.e. 'with good fortune'; *OLD* s.v. *auspicium* 5b '(poet.) fortune, luck'; cf. Virg. *Aen.* 3.497–9 *effigiem Xanthi Troiamque uidetis | quam uestrae fecere manus melioribus, opto, | auspiciis.* The actual *auspicia* would have been taken by Augustus, as is clear from 33–4 (and n.).

17–19 spectandus . . . quantis fatigaret ruinis 'worthy of spectacle in the enormity of the destruction with which he assaulted . . .' *quantis . . . ruinis* is an instrumental ablative introducing the indirect question.

17 certamine Martio: cf. Virg. *Aen.* 12.73 *duri certamina Martis*, 790 *certamina Martis anheli*; [Tib.] 3.7.98 *audacis . . . certamina Martis*; five times in Silius. H.'s usage (as an adjective) is less usual, and otherwise only at Val. Max. 1.1.2 *Martio certamini.* See Harrison 1991: 103 for the adjective preferred to the genitive of the noun in general. The lack of a caesura before the choriamb is unusual, indeed, hard to parallel securely; another instance of deliberate mediocre writing?

18 deuota morti pectora liberae: resistance to the Roman yoke is put in terms reminiscent of Roman republican military courage, with an implication that the Raetians fight on terms of a *deuotio*; cf. Gellius 9.2.10 (on the Athenian taboo on naming slaves after Harmodius and Aristogeiton) *quoniam nefas ducerent nomina libertati patriae deuota seruili contagio pollui*; Serv. *ad Aen.* 1.712 *'deuota' uero de oratione Augusti translata locutio, quam habuit in laudatione funeris Marcelli, cum diceret, illum immaturae morti deuotum fuisse.* Cf. 9.50–1 *non . . . patria timidus perire.* As with the Cleopatra ode and the victory of Augustus, so here commentators claim H. praises the enemy so as to make the victory of Tiberius seem more impressive, but there is more to it than that in both cases, since the suggestion of Roman values creates empathy.

20–4 Tiberius' first simile, with two-and-a-half lines each for the simile and the predicate clause that takes the reader back to Tiberius. The simile of Tiberius as the South Wind moving across the water is particularly apt since that is the direction from which T. advanced, according to Dio 54.22.4 even proceeding by ship up Lake Garda (Benacus). Cf. Virg. *Aen.* 6.335–6 *quos . . . | obruit Auster, aqua inuoluens nauemque uirosque.* Porph. was unhappy with what he thought was an anacoluthon involved in *qualis* responding to 22 *impiger*; however *impiger . . . ignes* is part of the predicate, dependent on 15–16 *commisit...pepulit*, with the simile sandwiched within the tenor or narrative.

prope quales 'almost as': *prope* has an apologetic touch to it; is the Matine bee somewhat uncomfortable with such similes and such elevation, or is T. not quite worthy of an unqualified simile such as this? *quales* mirrors 4.1, 13 (similes for Drusus) *qualem... qualemue*.

indomitas... undas | exercet 'the South Wind stirs up the waves and makes them wild'; *indomitas* is proleptic and highly poetic, also quite rare of natural forces (e.g. Cat. 64.107 *turbo*; Tib. 2.3.45 *claudit et indomitum moles mare*); *TLL* s.v. *indomitus* 1225.33–8. *indomitas* creates something of a paradox with *exerceo*, given the latter's implication of control and even taming. There is much to be said for *indomitus* (*Auster*) in the codd. deteriores, put forward by Bentley and printed by Shackleton Bailey, accepted by Delz, *Gnomon* 60 (1988) 497; the word then applies more to Tiberius than the Raetians. Cf. Ovid *Her.* 15.9–10 (of the East Wind) *uror, ut, indomitis ignem exercentibus Euris, | fertilis accensis messibus ardet ager.*

Auster: Tiberius riding (22–4 *impiger... mittere equum*) like the South Wind recalls Hannibal as East Wind, in parallel position at 4.43–4 *ceu flamma per taedas uel Eurus | per Siculas equitauit undas.*

Pleiadum choro | scindente nubis 'when the band of Pleiades splits the clouds', i.e. when the wind breaks open the clouds to reveal the Pleiades, who therefore seem to do the splitting; cf. Lucr. 6.137–8 *fit quoque ut interdum ualidi uis incita uenti | perscindat nubem perfringens impete recto*; also 6.283 (of a thunderbolt) *perscindit subito nubem.* With *choro* H. opts for the tradition making the Pleiades the daughters of Atlas and Pleione; cf. Prop. 3.5.36 *Pleiadum spisso cur coit imbre chorus.* The Pleiades (along with the Hyades, in Taurus), also *Vergiliae* for the Romans (perhaps from *uergo*, 'slope', 'sink'), had their morning rising (just far enough ahead of sunrise to be visible) in May and morning setting (just far enough ahead of sunrise to be visible) in November, and so were very useful in marking the beginning and ending of the seafaring and farming seasons; see Kidd on Arat. *Phaen.* 265, with reference to Peck's Loeb edn. of Aristot. *HA* II: Appendix A.

22–4 impiger... uexare... et... mittere 'relentless at harrying... and... sending'; epexegetical infinitives. The lines are very generic and have a clichéd feel to them, again suggesting the uneasiness of the celebrant?

frementem... equum: cf. *Epod.* 9.17 *frementes... equos*; Virg. *G.* 1.12–13 *frementem |... equum*; *Aen.* 12.82 *equos...frementes*; also Lucr. 5.1074–6 *equus...fremitum... edit*; *Aen.* 11.493–6 *equus...fremit*; 599–600 *fremit... sonipes*; 607 *fremitus... equorum.* Cf. *TLL* s.v. *fremitus* 1279.13–20; *fremo* 1282.28–37; by now a somewhat tired Homeric trope (*Il.* 16.506 ἵππους φυσιόωντας, also 4.226–7).

medios per ignes: cf. Virg. *Aen.* 7.296–7, Juno's grudging concession, *medias acies mediosque per ignes | inuenere uiam*, where the anaphora and gender switch (cf. Horsfall *ad loc.*) makes for a more varied expression. *medios* will find its partners at 31 *primosque et extremos.*

25–34 Tiberius' second simile compares him to the Aufidus in flood, then gives another stanza of achievements before effecting a transition to Augustus. The main model is Hom. *Il.* 5.87–92, where the destructive power of Diomedes is compared to an all-destructive river in flood, which broke through a garden wall and before which (92) 'many fair works of vigorous men fell into ruin' (πολλὰ δ' ὑπ' αὐτοῦ ἔργα κατήριπε κάλ' αἰζηῶν). This is particularly appropriate since the simile at 25–8 is of the River Aufidus (modern *Ofanto*), which comes from the Apennines down into northern Apulia, past the town of Canusium, traditionally founded by the same Diomedes (*S.* 1.5.91–2 *nam* [*panis*] *Canusi lapidosus aquae non ditior urna* | *qui locus a forti Diomede est conditus olim*); see 25–6, 27–8nn. It is presumably a coincidence that Suet. *Tib.* 21.6, an extract from a letter of Augustus on his longing for Tiberius, quotes the actual words of Diomedes from *Il.* 10.246–7 (the hero's wish for partnership with Odysseus). Could it be that Tiberius, a literary man, somehow projected himself as a new Diomedes? It is also a slight curiosity that the river of 4.38 (in parallel position), the Metaurus, is associated with a poem on Drusus and his victorious ancestor, while Tiberius is here associated with the Aufidus, on whose banks Hannibal handed the Romans a crushing defeat at the Battle of Cannae. Saint-Denis 1942 saw a further allusion to Hom. *Il.* 4.446–56, a simile with two mountain torrents crashing down and meeting where two valleys join; those rivers, however, cause no damage to crops, unlike the one at *Il.* 5.87–92, matching 27–8 in H.'s simile. In conflating two Homeric similes, H. demonstrates he can be quite Virgilian in his intertextuality.

25–9 sic . . . ut: *sic* introduces the simile, which is the wrong way around, and seems to put Tiberius into the simile; cf. *OLD* s.v. *sic* 7b 'resuming after a simile'. The inversion is unique; for normal practice see 5.9–16; 1.7.15–21; *Epod.* 5.77–82; *S.* 1.3.43–4; *Epist.* 1.1.20–6; 1.2.51–3; 1.8.17; 1.13.11–15; 1.18.10–14; *AP* 136, 357, 374–8 (*ut* + vehicle, *sic* + tenor); Cat. 62.39–45, 49–58 (*ut* + vehicle, *sic* + tenor); 64.269–77 (*qualis* + vehicle, *sic* + tenor); Virg. *Ecl.* 5.79–80 (*ut* + vehicle, *sic* + tenor); *Aen.* 6.205–9; 10.565–70 (*qualis* + vehicle, *sic* + tenor); *Aen.* 12.365–70, 684–92, 908–14 (*ac uelut*(*i*) + vehicle, *sic* + tenor); Ov. *Ars am.* 1.93–8, 117–20; 2.439–44; *Rem. am.* 731–4; *Her.* 4.23–6; 11.77–80; 14.41; *Met.* 1.533–9; 2.716–21; 3.487–90, 704–7; 5.164–9, 604–6; 9.659–65; 10.190–5; *Fast.* 2.231–4, 775–8; 4.459–62; *Trist.* 1.6.9–14; 3.11.11–14; 4.1.79–82; *Pont.* 1.1.69–74; 4.1.29–36 (*ut* + vehicle, *sic* + tenor), *Fast.* 2.219–24 (*uelut* + vehicle, *sic* + tenor).

25–6 tauriformis: only here in Latin (it is not usable in the dactylic hexameter, which is where it would otherwise turn up). Porph.: *omnium fluminum genii taurino uultu, etiam cum cornibus, pinguntur propter impetus et fremitus ipsarum aquarum.* At Eur. *Ion* 1261 the River Cephisus has a 'bull-shaped face' (ταυρόμορφον ὄμμα), but rivers are figured as bulls as early as Homer: so the Scamander at *Il.* 21.237 μεμυκὼς ἠύτε ταῦρος 'bellowing like a bull', with Richardson *ad loc.*, referring to Easterling on Soph. *Trach.* 10–14; also S. Dalley, *Myths from Mesopotamia*, Oxford 1989, 31, *Atrahasis* (17th century BCE): 'The flood roared like a bull.'

Aufidus, | qui regna Dauni praefluit Apuli: cf. 3.30.10–11 *qua uiolens obstrepit Aufidus | et qua pauper aquae Daunus agrestium | regnauit populorum*. Daunus was the mythical father-in-law of Diomedes, who married the local king's daughter Euippe (see 25–34n.). It is somewhat odd that H. thus associates his own homeland so strongly with Tiberius; there are plenty of other rivers he could have used. See below 47–8 on *obstrepit*: H. has reasons for putting the Aufidus into play.

praefluit 'flows past'; cf. 3.10 *quae Tibur aquae fertile praefluunt*; 7.4 *praetereunt*.

27–8 Tiberius as river in spate rages and plans terrible deluge for the cultivated fields. The lines are reminiscent of the end of *Georgics* 1, with *saeuit* perhaps suggesting 511 *saeuit toto Mars impius orbe*, and with the Aufidus' destructive intentions recalling the destructive power of the Po in response to the death of Caesar: 481–3 *proluit insano contorquens uertice siluas | fluuiorum rex Eridanus camposque per omnes | cum stabulis armenta tulit*; also the Tiber flooding Rome in vengeance for the death of Ilia at *C.* 1.2.13–15 *uidimus flauum Tiberim . . . | ire deiectum monumenta regis*.

horrendamque cultis | diluuiem meditatur agris: Tiberius as river is plotting a deluge against cultivated fields, which seems at odds with the detail of the lines to follow, destruction of the barbarian bands; the cultural situation is turned upside down (see Putnam 245). Agriculture recurs in 31–2, where Tiberius carries out metaphorical reaping (*metendo*), again with Homeric overtones (see 31–2n.).

diluuiem: otherwise at 3.29–40, also in a simile and in a highly Pindaric setting (and cf. 2.5–8); N–R speak of 'the archaic *diluuies* (instead of the more normal *diluuium*)', but both are rare, with the former otherwise appearing twice in Lucr. and once in Pliny, while *diluuium* is found twice in Virgil (*Aen.* 7.228; 12.205), thus ensuring that it was disseminated, though not very widely: twice in Pomponius Mela, once in Ovid (*Met.* 1.434), then in the younger Seneca, once in Val. Flacc. etc.

meditatur: involves active planning; cf. Cic. *Phil.* 11.3 (Antony's plans for Cicero et al.) *maiora tamen in nos quam in hostem supplicia meditatur*; Virg. *G.* 3.153 (Juno's plans for Io – the gadfly) *Inachiae Iuno pestem meditata iuuencae*; and, closer to home, Prop. 3.4.1 *arma deus Caesar dites meditatur ad Indos*.

29–30 Claudius: cf. 14n.

agmina | ferrata 'iron-clad columns'; *ferratus* here first of people; cf. *TLL* s.v. *ferratus* 572.71–82. It is notable that Julius Caesar instituted the *Legio VI Ferrata* in 52 BCE (Keppie 1984: 179).

uasto . . . impetu: suggests an inordinate and wild attack; cf. *OLD* s.v. *uastus* 1, 3: 'lacking signs of civilization', 'desolate', 'awe-inspiring' etc. Cf. Ov. *Met.* 10.551 *impetus est fuluis et uasta leonibus ira*.

31–2 primosque . . . humum 'mowing down the first ranks to the last he strewed the ground (with corpses)'. The agricultural language embeds vehicle into tenor, in a sentence that has already upset the order of such things. Tiberius as reaper looks most immediately to Aeneas, on a rampage after the death of Pallas at *Aen.* 10.513 (with other wording that resonates with H.) *proxima quaeque metit gladio* *latumque per agmen* | *ardens limitem agit ferro*. Lyne 1989: 154–5 notes the violence of this first extant use of *meto* of a human harvest, clearly influenced by Gk. ἀμάω and in particular Ap. Rhod. *Arg.* 3.1380–95 (Jason mowing down the Earthborn, 1380–5, with a simile of actual reapers, 1386–95); see *TLL* s.v. *meto* 890.35–53; Brink on *Epist.* 2.2.178–9 (the Grim Reaper himself) *si metit Orcus* | *grandia cum paruis*. The Homeric intertextual mood continues, with important modifications via Catullus on the savagery of Achilles, as noted by Quinn, and by Lyne 1989: 155–6: *Il.* 11.67–71, warriors as reapers, working the cornfields from both sides, 'across from each other' (67 ἐναντίοι ἀλλήλοισιν), perhaps represented by H.'s *primosque et extremos*; Cat. 64.353–5 *namque uelut densas praecerpens messor aristas* | *sole sub ardenti flauentia demetit arua,* | *Troiugenum infesto prosternet corpora ferro*. Through these intertexts Tiberius takes on a degree of savagery.

metendo: perhaps for *metens*; for the instrumental use cf. 11.29–31n.

sine clade: without casualties, presumably an exaggeration but by implication in line with Vell. 2.95.2 *maiore cum periculo quam damno Romani exercitus plurimo cum earum* [sc. *gentium*] *sanguine*; this was a reality or an advertised claim for Tiberius in general, at least in Velleius: 2.97.4 *peragratusque uictor omnes partes Germaniae sine ullo detrimento commissi exercitus*; 2.107.3 (now in 4 CE) *incolumi inuiolatoque et semel tantummodo magna cum clade hostium fraude eorum temptato exercitu*; see Woodman *ad loc.* for Tiberius and the title *Inuictus*, grandiloquently used in H. by Trebatius of Octavian at *S.* 2.1.10–11 *'aude* | *Caesaris inuicti res dicere'*.

33–4 te . . . te . . . tuos . . . praebente: an artful transition to the second part of the poem: the forces, counsel and gods (i.e. *auspicia*) of Augustus are what produces military success. Even before the sentence with which his simile began has ended, Tiberius has been left behind. What looks secondary on the level of syntax (*te . . . praebente*) is, in fact, primary, as H. inserts an oblique kletic pattern familiar from hymnic odes. The triadic second-person markers will have a more formal responsion at the onset of each of the final three verses of the aretalogy with which the poem plays itself out (see 41–52n.).

34–40 The successful campaign is happily concluded on 1 August 15 BCE, the fifteenth anniversary of the fall of Alexandria in 30 BCE, eleven months after Actium: cf. Pelling, *CAH* X 63 'On 1 August Octavian attacked, and Alexandria fell. First came a naval fiasco in the harbour: Antony's whole fleet deserted to Octavian. Then came an infantry exchange, which Octavian once again won decisively. Antony returned to the palace, and he died.' Cf. Dio 51.19.6 for the importance of the date: τήν τε ἡμέραν ἐν ἧι ἡ Ἀλεξάνδρεια ἑάλω ἀγαθήν τε εἶναι καὶ ἐς τὰ ἔπειτα ἔτη ἀρχὴν τῆς ἀπαριθμήσεως αὐτῶν νομίζεσθαι, 'the day on which Alexandria had been captured they declared a lucky day, and directed that in future years it should be taken by the inhabitants of that city as the starting-point in their reckoning of time' (tr. Cary). See McLean 2002: 170–6 for the dating of eras from events 'such as victories in battle, the liberation of cities, or the year of the creation of a Roman province' (170–1) – as Mussolini did following the March on Rome on 28 October 1922.

quo die . . . lustro . . . tertio on *lustrum* cf. 1.6; *CS* 67 nn.

supplex . . . patefecit: well focalizing Augustan propaganda and revisionism of the victors.

uacuam . . . aulam: cf. 2.10.7–8 *inuidenda . . . aula.* Empty at least once Antony killed himself, followed by Cleopatra some days later. The absence of either name suggests that H., and more importantly Augustus, had moved beyond those events, indeed wished them laid to rest. Apart from Prop. 3.13.39 (of the ram king before shepherds existed) *uacuam pastoris in aulam*, the phrase is otherwise found before H. at Virg. *G.* 4.90 (cited by Putnam 249–50), where Virgil advises killing the *ductor deterior* of the two bee kings, thus allowing the better one to rule alone; [*deteriorem*] *dede neci; melior uacua sine regnet in aula.* Whether or not Virgil meant some sort of allegory for civil war with possible reference to Octavian and Antony (see Thomas on *G.* 4.88–102), Seneca certainly took it so (*Apoc.* 3.2), and H.'s wording maps well onto such a reading, supported by the *absence* of reference to Antony and the dead queen; similarly Statius on Eteocles' power-grab: *Theb.* 1.165–7 *quis tunc tibi, saeue, | quis fuit ille dies, uacua cum solus in aula | respiceres ius omne tuum.*

37–40 Marked and formal language: Fortuna, which has proved favourable, has rendered positive outcomes in response to prayers and devotion and has added this desired praise and glory (i.e. the Raetian success) to (that coming from) commands already brought to perfection (and enumerated in the lines that follow).

Fortuna: here presumably with specific reference to the cult of *Fortuna Redux*, an altar to whom was erected outside the *porta Capena* by Augustus after his return from Syria in 19 BCE (consecrated 12 Oct.), as noted in the *Res gest.*: *Mon. Anc.* 2.29–33 *aram Fortunae Reducis ante aedes Honoris et Virtutis ad portam Capenam pro reditu meo senatus consecrauit*; see Coarelli, *LTUR* II 275.

prospera 'propitious', perhaps with the flavour claimed at Nonius p. 171M 'SPEREM ueteres spem dixerunt; unde et *prospere* dicitur, hoc est *pro spe*'; works well thus with *reddidit*, 'rendered'.

tertio | . . . secundos: a play with numbers.

secundos . . . exitus: if the gods are propitious they render good outcomes; cf. 8.34 *Liber uota bonos ducit ad exitus.*

peractis | imperiis: refers to commands Augustus has held, including the Raetian ones Drusus and Tiberius carried out under the emperor's auspices.

arrogauit 'assigned', 'attributed' to Augustus, and not to Drusus and Tiberius. There may be some play here: *arrogatio* is the process of adoption, occurring through the *comitia*, which are asked (*rogatio*) to assent to the adoption, vs. *adoptatio*, which is done through the praetor. The *laus* and *decus* of Tiberius and Drusus, rather than their persons, undergo the *arrogatio.*

41–52 Aretalogy of Augustus the conqueror. Corresponds to Hannibal's recognition of Rome's greatness beginning at 4.37, also in final position if the last stanza – through 76 – is included in his speech. Unambiguously and hyperbolically encomiastic, and intensely hymnic in style, the lines do what H. elsewhere (1.6, *Epist.* 2.1, etc.) said he could not manage. He does so in part through the comparative treatment of Augustus, *maxime principum*, in relation to the princes, the *maior* and *minor Neronum*. At 4.15 H. will pull back somewhat and allow the focus to shift to the end of lyric (see 15 intro.).

te . . . te etc.: also at 5.32–3, and cf. 3.21.13–24, where the hymnic addressee (in that case *pia testa*, the trusty wine-jar) is similarly positioned at the start of the last three verses, with enumeration of the virtues and qualities of the wine-jar. Cf. also 1.10.5, 9, 17 and N–H on 1.10.9; Norden 1913: 143–63; cf. 152–3; Wills 361–2. Lucr. 1.1–40 (hymn to Venus) has some nineteen instances of *tu/tuus*. H. here positions *te* at the beginning of the second half of stanzas two and three (47, 51), and in the same strong metrical position (choriambic onset) in the second lines of stanzas one and two (42, 46); see 1.21n. All seven instances of *te* are syntactically identical (not the case in 1.10, 1.35 or 3.21), objects of *miratur*, *audit* and *uenerantur*. It may be that *tutela* plays on this clustering.

41–4 The world had changed since publication of *C.* 1–3 (see below), chiefly with consolidation in Spain, Gaul and Germany (Sygambri), Raetia, Pannonia, Dalmatia and Illyricum; see 4.5.25–8.

Cantaber non ante domabilis: the Spaniards of the northwest had proven resistant to Roman subjugation; cf. 2.6.2 *Cantabrum indoctum iuga ferre nostra*; 2.11.1 *bellicosus Cantaber*; 3.8.22 *Cantaber sera domitus catena*; cf. Dio 54.11.3 (of the legions of Agrippa in 19 BCE) τούς τε Καντάβρους ὡς καὶ δυσπολεμήτους δεδιότες 'fearing the Cantabrians as being hard to fight against'. H. in his first lyric collection well reflects the reality that the Spanish victory of 26/25 BCE (for which Augustus was present), in spite of pronouncements of success along with the closing of the Temple of Janus, was incomplete. Already in 24, and again in 22 BCE, the Cantabrians, and the Asturians to their west, caused further trouble. For all of this see Syme, *Roman papers* II 846–9. H. would not be emphatic until Agrippa in 19 BCE defeated the Cantabri, wiped out the men of military age and relocated the rest away from their mountains and into the plains (Dio 54.11.5): *Epist* 1.12.25–7 *ne tamen ignores, quo sit Romana loco res: | Cantaber Agrippae, Claudi uirtute Neronis | Armenius cecidit.*

Medusque et Indus: central and western Asia, south of the Caspian Sea; the reference is vague but doubtless includes the installation of Tigranes on the throne of Armenia after the assassination of the unpopular Artaxias and the diplomatic recovery of the standards lost by Crassus at Carrhae in 53 BCE, both effected while Augustus was in the area in 20 BCE; see *CAH* X 158–60. *Medus* often stands for *Parthus* (1.2.51–2, 29.4–5; 2.9.21–2; 3.3.43–4; *CS* 53–4). Both were treated as great victories back in Rome, but H.'s language does not quite participate in the triumphal fictions (*miratur*); the same goes for the language of *Epist.* 1.12.57 *Claudi uirtute Neronis | Armenius cecidit.* Cf. 4.25–8 and n., *Epist.* 1.29.2–5 (to Iccius) *acrem militiam paras | non ante deuictis Sabaeae | regibus, horribilique Medo | nectis catenas?*

For Suetonius things will be more settled: *Aug.* 21.3 *qua uirtutis moderationisque fama Indos etiam ac Scythas auditu modo cognitos pellexit ad amicitiam suam populique Romani ultro per legatos petendam.*

te profugus Scythes: cf. 1.35.9 (prayer to Venus) *te profugi Scythae* (*metuunt*), referring to the strategy of simply running away from a superior force, given they are essentially nomadic anyway: 3.24.9–10 (and N–R *ad loc.* for further references) *campestres melius Scythae, | quorum plaustra uagas rite trahunt domos.* Sall. *Iug.* 56.6 has the Numidians behaving similarly: *sed milites Iugurthini paulisper ab rege sustentati, postquam maiore ui hostes urgent, paucis amissis profugi discedunt.*

miratur: Augustus is a *thauma* to distant peoples, a nice reversal of the usual situation, where features of distant lands are a source of wonder to Greek and Roman ethnographers.

o tutela praesens: fulfils the prediction of 3.5.2–4 *praesens diuus habebitur | Augustus adiectis Britannis | imperio grauibusque Persis*; *Epist.* 2.1.15 (to Augustus, with Brink *ad loc.*) *praesenti tibi maturos largimur honores.* Although *tutela* is used of humans (*OLD* s.v. 2a), with *praesens* it strongly suggests the epiphany of a deity, although the primary meaning, as Bo notes, is *uiuens, superstes*, while still living and before actual deification; cf. *TLL* s.v. *praesens* 843.64–844.9; cf. 1.35.1–2 (Venus) *o diua, gratum quae regis Antium, | praesens uel imo tollere de gradu | mortale corpus, uel* . . . ; Virg. *Aen.* 9.404 *tu, dea, tu praesens nostro succurre labori.*

Italiae dominaeque Romae: sc. *orbis terrarum* with *dominae*; cf. 3.13 *Romae principis urbium*; Cic. *Phil.* 6.12 *populi Romani uictoris dominique omnium gentium*; Virg. *Aen.* 1.282, a favourite quote of Augustus, preceded by '*en*', (*ap.* Suet. *Aug.* 40.5 = *Dicta et apophthegmata* 35 Malcovati) *Romanos, rerum dominos gentemque togatam.* For the homoeoteleuton cf. 5.3–4n.

45–52 -que . . . et . . . -que: see 2.41–4n.

45–8 Rivers stand in for the conquered territories through which they flow, as on Aeneas' shield at *Aen.* 8.726–8 (Euphrates, Rhine, Araxes); also see 45–6n. H.'s three rivers (Nile, Danube, Tigris) represent victories (real or for public consumption) against Antony and Cleopatra, the Vindelici and other German tribes, Pannonia, Armenia and Parthia. Cf. Virg. *Aen.* 6.798–800 (Anchises' prediction of Augustus' far-flung conquests) *huius in aduentum iam nunc et Caspia regna | responsis horrent diuum et Maeotia tellus, | et septemgemini turbant trepida ostia Nili.*

45–6 fontium . . . Nilus: cf. Virg. *Aen.* 8.711–13, where the Nile is depicted as grieving for Cleopatra and calling the defeated Egyptians to its lap and into its 'hidden rivers' (*latebrosaque flumina*). The source of the Nile is an old puzzle going back to the Pharaonic period and only solved in relatively modern times. Its two main source-rivers are the White Nile (the more distant, flowing from Lake Victoria in Uganda, identified in 1862 by John Speke) and the Blue Nile (the more abundant, flowing from Lake Tana in Ethiopia, fed by the waters of the Ethiopian central highlands and identified in 1770 by James Bruce). The two rivers unite at Khartoum in Sudan. Herodotus treats the issue at 2.28–34, and the obscurity of the origin is thereafter a *topos* among Greek and Roman writers. Plin.

HN 5.51–8 has an extensive discussion of the Nile, beginning with the question of its sources.

Nilusque et Hister: for *-que . . . et* see 9.35n.

Hister: in concluding his discussion of the Nile, Herodotus brings up (2.33–4) the question of the source of the Danube (*Hister*, Ἴστρος), which rises in the Black Forest and eventually issues into the Black Sea. It figures as the site of an uprising at Virg. *G.* 2.497 *aut coniurato descendens Dacus ab Histro*. Citing Sall. *Hist.* fr. 79 M., P. Knox (forthcoming on Ov. *Pont.* 1.8.11) notes that the Romans did not connect the Danuvius, first mentioned by Caesar at *B. Gall.* 6.25, with the Hister until Octavian's Illyrian campaign in 35 BCE.

rapidus Tigris: the Tigris flows so quickly it 'seizes' (*rapio*) everything in its path. The Tigris rises in the western Taurus Range and flows through Southern Armenia (Turkey) down into Media and Assyria (Iraq). There is play with the speed of the tiger (Varro, *Ling.* 5.100, Maltby s.v. *tigris*), well brought out by Lucan, who first uses the adjective of the river (3.256–7 *quaque caput rapido tollit cum Tigride magnus Euphrates*), then glosses the animal in a simile on Caesar (5.405–8 *inde rapit cursus et . . . ocior et caeli flammis et tigride feta | transcurrit*).

47–8 H. had urged conquest of Britain (along with Parthia and the East, in part as an antidote to civil war) at 1.21.13–16; 1.35.29–32; 3.5.2–4 (see 41–4n. on *praesens*); *Epod.* 7.3–10. Although Augustus planned expeditions against Britain on three separate occasions, 34 BCE (Dio 49.38.2), 27 BCE (Dio 53.22.5) and 26 BCE (Dio 53.25.2), he never actually went. Embassies, along with offerings on the Capitol and pledges of Roman protection (Strabo 4.5.3) allowed Augustus to make claims about his achievements in Britain; cf. *Mon. Anc.* 5.54–6.2 *ad me confugerunt reges . . . Britannorum Dumnobellaunus et Tincommius*. Hence the understated language: the Ocean, as close as reality permits H. to get to British rivers, 'listens to' Augustus.

beluosus 'full of sea-monsters'; a nice *hapax legomenon* (though twice in Avienus). Cf. Tac. *Germ.* 17.2 (on the Germans' use of seal-skin clothing) *eligunt feras et detracta uelamina spargunt maculis pellibusque beluarum, quas exterior Oceanus atque ignotum mare gignit*.

remotis: a justification of cancelled invasion plans? Cf. Cat. 11.11–12 *ulti- | mosque Britannos*.

obstrepit: cf. 3.30.10 *dicar, qua uiolens obstrepit Aufidus . . .* in the context of H.'s fame, a contrast to Ocean and the reach of Augustus (above 25–6n.): Horace::Aufidus::*obstrepit*/*obstrepit*::Ocean::Augustus. The verb forms an odd but appealing contrast with 50 *audit*. The Ocean 'makes a din against' the Britons while it 'listens to' the *princeps*. H. cannot quite make the Briton the subject of *audit*, which may account for the oddity. Cf. 2.18.20 (of sea dinning against those who build out into it) *marisque Bais obstrepentis*.

Oceanus Britannis: the pairing connects rivers that precede (45–6) and lands that follow (49–50).

49–52 Gaul, Spain (separate from the Cantabri) and back to Germany and the Sygambri, each coming at line-end to give the impression of a list, a miniature of documents such as the *Tropaeum Alpium*. Augustus was in Gaul, Germany and Spain for much of the time H. was writing *C.* 4 and was succeeded by Drusus when Augustus returned to Rome in 13 BCE (Dio 54.25.1). This is therefore a fitting end and fitting introduction to the final poem and its exploration of *pax Augusta*.

49–50 non pauentis funera: cf. Luc. 1.452–62 on the Druidic belief in the soul's continued existence after death and especially 459–60 *quos ille timorum | maximus haud urguet leti metus*.

duraeque . . . Hiberiae: i.e. a land of hardy inhabitants, *patientia* being a frequent ethnographical designation; cf. Luc. 2.629 *nec licet ad duros Martem conuertere Hiberos*; 6.258 *durus Hiber*; Tac. *Ann.* 6.34.2 *nam Hiberi Albanique saltuosos locos incolentes duritiae patientiaeque magis insueuere*.

audit 'listens to', 'follows advice, orders, etc.'; cf. *OLD* s.v. *audio* 11; an improvement over earlier days: 2.1.30–1 *auditumque Medis | Hesperiae sonitum ruinae*.

51–2 The poem ends with the Sygambri, the German tribe whose uprising and initial success against Lollius (see 9 intro., 2.34–6) is in part the reason or pretext for the activities of Tiberius and Drusus in the Alps.

caede gaudentes: a dire condition; cf. Tac. *Ann.* 1.44.3 *gaudebat caedibus miles*, also Lucr. 3.71–2 (the condition of civil war) *caedem caede accumulantes, | crudeles gaudent in tristi funere fratris*.

compositis . . . armis: Porph.: *id est: pacati*; an upbeat ending.

uenerantur: Drusus continued from 13 to 11/10 BCE to make further incursions across the Rhine, and garrisons were established, but the picture is hardly this rosy, and, as Gruen notes (*CAH* X 182), 'even Velleius, who would hardly minimize Tiberius' subsequent accomplishment [after the death of Drusus, when the need to be upbeat would only have increased], speaks only of reducing Germany "almost to the form of a tributary province"'. Cf. 15.32, also middle of the last line, *Veneris*.

15

METRE

Alcaic stanza, as for 4, 14.

INTRODUCTION

Apollo stopped me when I wanted to sing of battles and conquered cities. Your age, Caesar, has restored abundance to the fields, retaken captured standards, ended war and brought back the arts by which Italy became great from west to east. With Caesar in charge civil discord is ended, and external enemies behave themselves. On feast days and work days, with wives and children, we will sing of heroes of the past, of Troy, Anchises and the son of Venus.

As 4 (Drusus) led to 5 (Augustus), so 14 (Drusus and Tiberius, but more, Augustus) leads to the finale, the arrival of *pax Augusta*. Putnam 264 treats the structure of the poem, which falls into two four-stanza halves, with Augustus named (4 *Caesar*, 17 *Caesare*) in the opening stanza of each. Past tenses predominate in the first half as Augustus' *res gestae* are enumerated; the second half deals consistently with verbs in the future, as the poem and the book end with the promise of further song (32 *canemus*). Having delivered its message of propaganda and cliché (see 4–16n.), the lyric voice retreats into one of future celebration, never actually realized in the poem. There is a broad range of reactions to the apparent capitulation: at one extreme Lowrie 1997: 351 'My flesh crawls whenever I read *Odes* 4.15'; perhaps at another Griffin 2002: 330–2 sees no great distinction from the *Res gestae*, *Carmen saeculare*, or Ara Pacis Augustae. He is more comfortable with the coming together of public and private, with H. asserting (331) 'the possibility that the two can be one, that public events can be the subject of human emotions, and that the artist does not inevitably lose his independence when he makes himself the spokesman of those emotions'.

The poem, the book and the Horatian lyric voice in fact end with a *future* song (*canemus*), never to be realized, following the enumeration, in a voice and style remote from the typical lyric register, of Augustan *res gestae* (see 4–16n.). The silence that follows, and lyric encomium deferred, are the final act of the lyric voice. Oliensis 1998: 153 puts it well: 'Perhaps the silence that follows *Odes* 4.15 marks the poet's disappearance from, rather than into, the choral plural of *canemus*'.

1–4 The complexities of the opening three-and-a-half lines are exquisite, and emblematic of the book whose final poem they introduce. At first sight they have the appearance of the standard *recusatio* but introduce a new twist to the by now well-worn trope (see Wimmel 1960: 271–6 for connections to other Augustan texts). In 1.6.5–12 there was no question of the lyric poet's incompetence, since *pudor*, the Muse and a deficiency of *ingenium* kept him slender (*tenues*) and preoccupied with erotic battles exclusively (17 *proelia uirginum*), and not those of Agrippa. Likewise in 2.12 it was up to Maecenas to do a prose account of such themes (9–10 *tuque pedestribus* | *dices historiis proelia Caesaris*), since the Muse had other plans for H. (14 *me uoluit dicere*), namely singing of the attractions of Licymnia. And more recently, in *Epist.* 2.1.245–59, he had talked of the inability of his reduced poetic mode (257–8 *paruum* | *carmen*) to respond to the greatness (258 *maiestas*; *maior*, *magnus*) of Augustus, with *pudor* again restraining him from encomium, which was to be left to the likes of Virgil and Varius.

Here at the beginning of 15 H. has become a willing encomiast, now wanting (1 *uolentem loqui*) what the Muse of 2.12 did not want, a song of battles and captured cities, and at the end of a book of lyric that has engaged with Pindaric and other praise profoundly but often in ways that lead to an aesthetic questioning of the validity of praise. Apollo, the original Callimachean agent of *recusatio*, familiar from Virg. *Ecl.* 6.3–5 and Prop. 3.3.13–15, intervenes, and, without any causal marker, the response to intervention is an elaboration of the age of Augustus. After the intervention the reader expects a display and performance of the genre at hand – as with Virgilian pastoral, Propertian elegy or the erotic and sympotic lyric of H. That is what *recusatio* is about; it is a way into the heart of the matter. What follows here is an unambiguous celebration of *pax Augusta*, a retraction of the protestations of the Matine bee of 2.27–32, as Callimacheanism itself is implicitly redefined as emperor celebration, with the Augustan Phoebus Apollo effecting the redefinition and H. singing along with Roman matrons and children.

But the opening of the poem that seals up the book also seals up what immediately preceded, the praise of battles and captured cities at 14.33–52, H.'s *laus Caesaris*, his most intensive actual, delivered song of the glorious war and conquest of Augustus. Porph. notes on 4.15 *quidam separant hanc ᾠδήν a superiore, sed potest illi iungi, quoniam et hic laudes dicuntur Augusti.* If ps.-Acro is right in taking *lyra* with *loqui*, rather than with *increpuit* (see 1–4n. for the amphibole), the opening of 4.15 is also the close of 4.14, with affinities to the end of 2.1 and 3.3. At the conclusion of the former, having sung of the wars Pollio was to write up, H. stopped his Muse and called for a lighter theme and plectrum (40 *quaere modos leuiore plectro*), while at 3.3.69–72 he similarly appended a distancing *sphragis* to the epic speech of Juno, again with a generic correction regarding the lyre (69 *non hoc iocosae conuenient lyrae*), and with an order to the Muse (70–2 *desine* . . . | *magna modis tenuare modis*). In the present setting Apollo does the ordering, and he is the old Apollo of *Ecl.* 6, the Apollo of *C.* 4.6.25–44, as he here puts an end to the preceding song and leaves H. with only one theme, *tua, Caesar, aetas.*

1–2 Phoebus . . . lyra: cf. Prop. 3.3.13–14 *Phoebus . . . nixus . . . lyra.*

uolentem: temporal, 'when I wanted to', or concessive, 'even though I was (finally) willing to' – as just evidenced in 4.14?

loqui: cf. 2.45 (preceding H.'s shouting in *uersus quadratus*) *si quid loquar audiendum*; 9.4 *uerba loquor socianda chordis*. With *proelia* a curious echo of 4.68 *proelia coniugibus loquenda*, the only other instance in Latin of *proelia loqui* together.

proelia . . . | uictas et urbes: H.'s variant for the *reges et proelia* of the Virgilian *recusatio* of *Ecl.* 6.3; also the *topoi* of historiography and epic, treated most immediately, and euphemistically, at 14.34–6 (the capture of Alexandria).

me . . . increpuit lyra: a possible amphibole. Either 'protested against me with his lyre' (Rudd, 'banged on the lyre'), for which cf., though with a different syntactical construction, Ov. *Am.* 2.11.32; *Her.* 3.118 *digitis increpuisse lyram*; also *Fast.* 6.812 (the final words of the *Fasti*) *increpuitque lyram*; or, following ps.-Acro, *non lyra increpuit, sed uolentem me proelia lyra loqui, quod est lyrico carmine, Phoebus increpuit* (similarly Porph.). The position of *lyra* makes this difficult, but not impossible on the evidence of at least two native Latin speakers, and Apollo's objection would thus be based on generic inappropriateness (*proelia . . . loqui . . . lyra*). This ultimately seems the preferable reading. See intro. for the implications of this reading in connection to the preceding poem.

3–4 ne parua Tyrrhenum per aequor | uela darem: cf. Virg. *G.* 2.41 *pelagoque uolans da uela patenti*, an expansive utterance that is immediately reined in and replaced by the more Callimachean lines, 42–5; viz. 44 *ades et primi lege litoris oram*. H. conflates these lines with the opening of *Ecl.* 6. The Callimachus Romanus also picks up on the Virgilian language and serves as a model for H.: Prop. 3.3.23–4 *alter remus aquas alter tibi radat harenas, | tutus eris: medio maxima turba mari est*; 3.9.3–4 *quid me scribendi tam uastum mittis in aequor? | non sunt apta meae grandia uela rati*.

Tyrrhenum aequor is Virgilian (*Aen.* 1.67), as noted by Putnam 270; Apollo effectively stops H. from pursuing a constructed Virgilianism, as with *proelia . . . uictas | et urbes*. The phrase also perhaps adds a political dimension to the poetic one. In *Epod.* 16, in the years following his participation on the republican side at Philippi, H., in part responding to the fourth *Eclogue* (as is likely, rather than the other way around), directed a harangue against his fellow Romans. The only solution to the troubles was emigration to the Utopia of the Isles of the Blest, in the Atlantic: 40 *Etrusca praeter et uolate litora*. No more escape from Rome now; rather Apollo wants him to do as he immediately does, sing a song of the world at peace.

4–16 The *res gestae* of Augustus are enumerated in a style about as far from the lyric register as H. could get; for such lists, see Wills 408, n. 40. The *aetas Augusta* is subject of six perfect indicatives (cf. the six instances of *non* at 17–24, and n.), each preceded by a conjunction (*et* five times and *-que* once); the only subordination comes through three parallel adjectival clauses (*derepta . . . uacuum . . . euaganti*) and through the closing relative clause, whose accumulation (four subjects of *creuere*, with *et* twice and *-que* once, and one adjectival clause, *porrecta*) reprise the linearity of the main clause. Finally, there is an unpoetic accumulation of compounds indicating removal, restoration or institution: 5 *re-*, 6 *re-*, 7 *de-*, 10 *e-*, 11 *in-*, *e-*, 12 *re-*. The effect of the whole is one of formulaic cliché, as at *CS* 49–60 and n. (and like the list at *Epist.* 1.12.25–9).

Putnam 274–80 notes the Virgilian diction and themes of the lines: for 6–8 cf. *Aen.* 8.720–2; for 8–11 cf. *Aen.* 1.293–6; for 12–16 cf. *Aen.* 6.851–3, 1.278–9, 286–8 and 6.777–84. Breed 2004: 246 well notes that, while the *Aeneid* holds itself back from unmediated praise of Augustus and his age, H. not only enters deeply into straightforward and unfiltered encomium, but also implicates Virgil in such encomium; cf. O'Hara 1990: *passim*, for ample demonstration that the primary narrative of Virgil is frequently in ambiguous relation with prophecy. Putting this together we can see that H. significantly advances what in Virgil is only a possibility and so transforms and subtly corrects the Virgilian outlook from an Augustan point of view, all the while parading his Virgilian intertexts. A similar move occurs at *CS* 49–52 (see n.). In this connection Harrison 2007a: 204–6 focuses on the poem's appropriation of epic and specifically Virgilian themes to Horatian lyric.

4 tua . . . aetas: Breed 2004: 245–6 notes this as the first reference to an 'age' of Augustus; the word implies a discrete period, coterminous with the lifetime of the *princeps*; he also notes the anticipation of the senatorial proposal following the death of Augustus, as reported at Suet. *Aug.* 100 *alius [censuit] ut omne tempus a primo die natali ad exitum eius saeculum Augustum appellaretur*. While the *Aeneid* filters the *aurea saecula* through the figures of Julian mythology, *tua . . . aetas* and its pile of present perfect verbs disambiguates.

Caesar: in H. the vocative is only here, at 1.2.52 *te duce, Caesar* and, unsurprisingly, in the Letter to Augustus, *Epist.* 2.1.4; see 14.3n. (*Auguste*).

5 fruges et agris rettulit uberes: cf. 5.18 *nutrit rura Ceres almaque Faustitas*. The combination *fruges uberes* is less common than one might think (cf. Cic. *Brut.* 16 *ager, qui cum multos annos quieuit, uberiores efferre fruges solet*) though the adjective is quite common with *fructus*, for instance in Columella. The restoration of agricultural productivity, after the disruptions of civil war, is an essential part of the régime's propaganda; cf. *CS* 59–60 *apparetque beata pleno | Copia cornu*; *Epist.* 1.12.28–9 *aurea fruges | Italiae pleno defudit Copia cornu*. All three passages are illuminated by Dio 54.1, an account of the severe famine of 22 BCE and of popular attribution of it to Augustus' failure to serve as consul that year; the people attempted to make him dictator in response to the hardship.

6–8 Particularly with *derepta* H. overstates the fate of the standards lost by Crassus at Carrhae in 53 BCE (see 14.41–4n.), and recovered by diplomatic means in 20 BCE. For the official line cf. *Mon. Anc.* 5.40 *Parthos trium exercituum Romanorum spolia et signa re[ddere] mihi supplicesque amicitiam populi Romani petere coegi*. The fiction is noted by Dio (54.8.2) and is also accepted at *Epist.* 1.12.27–8 *ius imperium Phraates | accepit genibus minor*; less dramatically at *Epist.* 1.18.56 *sub duce qui templis Parthorum signa refigit*. The propaganda must have preceded Augustus' Eastern activities (22–19 BCE), to judge from a number of passages in the mid- to late-twenties: 1.12.53–4, 35.30–2; 3.2.3–4; Prop. 3.4.6 *assuescent Latio Partha tropaea Ioui*, 9 *Crassos clademque piate!*; 3.5.48 *Crassi signa referte domum*.

nostro . . . Ioui: following Prop. 3.4.6 *Latio . . . Ioui*, with the adjectives emphatic and indicating, as K–H note, a transferral of the standards from the temple of the Parthian 'Jupiter' (Ahura-Mazda) to the Roman one. The standards would eventually end up in the Temple of Mars Ultor (consecrated 2 BCE; cf. *Mon. Anc.* 5.42 *ea autem si[gn]a in penetrali quod e[s]t in templo Martis Ultoris reposui*) but for the time being seem to have been put in the Temple of Jupiter Capitolinus, though Dio 54.8 notes that the standards were to be placed in the Temple of Mars Ultor, which he dedicated for this function 'in imitation of the Temple of Jupiter Feretrius', in which such objects were previously placed.

derepta: used also by Regulus at 3.5.18–21 in his outraged speech on arms snatched from Roman soldiers without a struggle and affixed to Punic temples.

superbis | postibus: Putnam 275 notes the Virgilian intertext at *Aen.* 8.721–2, of the gift-laden doors of Augustus' house (also *superbis | postibus*) – a reference made strange by similarity to the doors of Cacus' lair (*foribusque . . . superbis*), those decked out with the rotting human faces. In transferring the epithet from the dwelling of Augustus to the temples of the Parthians H. may be seen as 'correcting' an ambiguity of the *Aeneid*; cf. *CS* 49–52n.

8–9 The closing of the doors of the Temple of Janus Quirinus or Janus Quirini (Janus Geminus), at the forum entrance where the Argiletum comes in, indicates the cessation of war throughout the Roman world, on which H. quotes Ennius (*S.* 1.4.60–1 = *Ann.* 225–6 Skutsch *postquam Discordia taetra | belli ferratos postes portasque refregit*). The attribution, obvious anyway from H.'s context, is made by Servius, *ad Aen.* 7.622 (Virgil's adaptation of the Ennian lines, of Juno's bringing war to Latium) *Belli ferratos rumpit Saturnia postes.* The closing of the gates occurs in the future tense in Jupiter's prophecy at *Aen.* 1.293–4 *dirae ferro et compagibus artis | claudentur Belli portae*, a reality of the present for H. Tradition ascribes to Numa the institution of keeping the gate open unless there were no wars anywhere; cf. Varro, *Ling.* 5.165 (referring to Calpurnius Piso, fr. 9 Peter) and Livy 1.19.1–4, for both of whom it seems to have been open from the time of Numa down to the closing that occurred in 241 BCE, at the end of the First Punic War – or possibly in 235 BCE (see Ogilvie *ad loc.*). Skutsch *ad Ann.* 225–6 notes 'obviously what did not occur between the time of Numa and the end of the First Punic War cannot have been a custom' and puts it rather in terms of when belief in the custom arose, in his view before Ennius, since Calpurnius knew of – but did not invent – it (*contra* K. Latte). It is typical that Augustus seized upon the custom, closing the temple in 29 BCE, after his return from the East, and again in 25 or 24 BCE, following the Spanish campaigns. Syme 1978: 25, 170–1 argues that the third closing, dated by some on the basis of H. to 13 BCE, probably occurred in 8 or 7 BCE. Cf. *Mon. Anc.* 2.42–5 *Ianum Quirin[um, quem cl]aussum ess[e maiores nostri uoluer]unt [cum p]er totum i[mperium po]puli Roma[ni terra marique es]set parta uic[torii]s pax, cum priu[s qua]m nascerer a condita urbe bis omnino clausum [f]uisse prodatur m[emori]ae, ter me princi[pe senat]us claudendum esse censui[t]*. H. includes the event among the standard themes of his meta-encomium at *Epist.* 2.1.253–5 [sc. *mallem componere* . . .] *tuisque | auspiciis totum confecta duella per orbem | claustraque custodem pacis cohibentia Ianum.*

uacuum duellis: free from wars, with *uacuum* having a spatial sense appropriate to the temple, to which it is also transferred: the temple is shut when the world is devoid of wars. *duellum* is an archaism, appropriate here and at *Epist.* 2.1.254 in the context of an old republican custom. With similar effect at 3.5.38, in the speech of Regulus, *pacem duello miscuit*, at 3.14.18, of a vintage wine, *cadum Marsi memorem duelli*, at *Epist.* 1.2.7, of the Trojan War, *Graecia barbariae lento collisa duello*; otherwise at *Epist.* 2.2.98, of a gladiatorial duel.

9–12 Although the language is vague, H. implies the legislation of 18 BCE, the *Lex Iulia de maritandis ordinibus* and the *Lex Iulia de adulteriis*. See Syme 1939: 440–58 for a somewhat sardonic view of this legislation and the policy behind it, a view which H., even though no longer *sub regno Cinarae*, might well have shared.

ordinem . . . iniecit 'and has applied reins to that unruliness that strays from correct course', possibly with reference to the charioteer out of control at Virg. *G.* 1.511–14. But the metaphor is also Horatian; the fulfilment of 3.24.25–30, where the political saviour's task (implicitly but not openly Augustus) is set in these terms: *o quisquis uolet impias | caedes et rabiem tollere ciuicam, | si quaeret pater urbium | subscribi statuis, indomitam audeat | refrenare licentiam*. The reference is to legislation; cf. Val. Max. 2.9.5 (Duronius, tribune in ?97 BCE, attempts to revoke a law) '*freni sunt iniecti uobis, Quirites, nullo modo perpetiendi*'.

licentiae: a debasement of political freedom, particularly from the senatorial point of view: cf. Cic. *Rep.* 1.68.2 *ex hac nimia licentia, quam illi solam libertatem putant* (cited by Tacitus' Maternus at *Dial.* 40.2 *licentiae, quam stulti libertatem uocant*); *Flacc.* 16 (on the decline of Greek democracy) *libertate immoderata ac licentia contionum*; *Dom.* 131 *simulacrum non libertatis publicae, sed licentiae collocasti*. Possibly also a reference to Augustus' recent moral legislation.

11 culpas 'offenses', 'wrongdoings', as at 3.11.29 *fata quae manent culpas etiam sub Orco*; cf. *OLD* s.v. *culpa* 3a. Cicero speaks of the *culpa*, as opposed to *scelus*, of those like himself who supported Pompey: *Marcell.* 13 *omnes enim qui ad illa arma fato sumus nescio quo rei publicae misero funestoque compulsi, etsi aliqua culpa tenemur erroris humani, ab scelere certe liberati sumus*.

12 ueteres reuocauit artes 'has brought back the old-fashioned arts'; the expression is vague and unparalleled.

13–16 By putting a comma after *uires*, Shackleton Bailey and others imply *est* with *porrecta*, which is then on the same syntactical level as *creuere*. Either interpretation is possible, but I have preferred to see *creuere* as having four subjects, with further participial subordination at 15–16. The movement from Latium, to Italy, to the whole world from west to east, along with the accumulation of nouns (*nomen* > *uires* > *fama* > *imperi maiestas*), gives a strong, Kiplingesque sense of imperial expansion. For similar reflection cf. Virg. *G.* 2.533–4 (following the description of the farmer and his virtuous life of toil) *sic fortis Etruria creuit | scilicet et rerum facta est pulcherrima Roma*.

15–16 ad . . . ab: the eastward direction, rather than following the course of the sun from east to west, perhaps looks to the major post-Actian Augustan expansion and consolidation, in Egypt and the East.

Hesperio cubili: *cubile* first here of the sun's resting-place without elaboration, an elliptical extension of Virg. *G.* 1.447 (= *Aen.* 4.585; 9.460) *Tithoni croceum linquens Aurora cubile* (cf. Hom. *Il.* 11.1–2 = *Od.* 5.1–2 Ἠὼς δ' ἐκ λεχέων παρ' ἀγαυοῦ Τιθωνοῖο | ὄρνυθ' 'Dawn rose from her bed, from the side of noble Tithonus'), a 'correction' of Fur. Bibac. fr. 7 Courtney *interea Oceani linquens Aurora cubile*, as is *Aen.* 4.129 (no *cubile*) *Oceanum interea surgens Aurora reliquit*; cf. *TLL* s.v. *cubile* 1270.15–28.

17–24 The second half, with future verbs taking over from past, devotes one stanza to civil tranquillity, another to external pacification, with everything put in negative terms: *non* occurs six times, balancing the six verbs that give shape to the second and third stanzas. The word *pax* is absent from *C.* 4 in general but is here represented by 18 *otium*.

17–20 The end of civil discord is characterized by the absence of *furor*, *uis* and *ira*, qualities present in H.'s earliest treatment of internecine strife: *Epod.* 7.13–14: *furorne caecus an rapit uis acrior | an culpa?*; also 1.16.17–19 *irae . . . altis urbibus ultimae*

| *stetere causae cur perirent*; 3.14.14–16 (on the return of Augustus from Spain in 24 BCE) *ego nec tumultum | nec mori per uim metuam tenente | Caesare terras*. It is notable that *furor* and *ira* are qualities still in play at the end of the *Aeneid*, a fact that further intensifies H.'s rewriting of that poem; see *CS* 57–60n.

custode rerum Caesare: Augustus is also *custos* at 5.2 (see n.). See Griffin 2002: 326–7 on *custos* as a useful 'essentially unofficial' term, 'sometimes used quasi-officially: a loyal decree of the decurions of Pisa in AD 4 described Augustus as *custos imperi Romani* and protector of the whole world' (*ILS* 140.7–9 *Augusti patris patriae pontif. maxsumi custodis imperi Romani totiusque orbis terrarum praesi[dis]*). The ablative absolute is provisional, going closely with the future verbs: 'as long as . . .' For *rerum* = 'the affairs of state' see *OLD* s.v. *res* 16.

uis 'violence' generally, but perhaps also the sort of civil discord dealt with under the *Lex Plautia de ui* (to be dated between 70 and 63 BCE), which treated violence, threats of violence and the like that involved some element of action *contra rem publicam*; cf. Riggsby 1999: 79–84 and (on the data) 206 n.6.

quae procudit enses: a feature of Virgil's civil war at *G.* 1.508 *curuae rigidum falces conflantur in ensem*; and at the beginning of the Italian War at *Aen.* 7.635–6 *uomeris huc et falcis honos, huc omnis aratri | cessit amor; recoquunt patrios fornacibus enses*; cf. also *G.* 2.539–40 (of the age of Saturn) *necdum [audierant] impositos duris crepitare incudibus enses*.

inimicat 'makes hostile (to each other)'; the transitive is first here and rare, next at Stat. *Theb.* 2.418–19 *ceu . . . hostiles inimicent classica turmas*; *TLL* s.v. *inimico* 1622.58–64. Intransitive instances ('behave with hostility') are also rare, late (generally Christian, and not to be found in *OLD*) and, with few exceptions, deponent; *TLL* ibid. 1622.65–1623.18.

21–4 The age of Augustus will find no disobedience from inhabitants of the distant north and east. The lines are hyperbolic and reminiscent of 1.12.53–6 *ille, seu Parthos Latio imminentes | egerit iusto domitos triumpho | siue subiectos Orientis orae | Seras et Indos* and 3.29.25–8 (from H.'s sympotic point of view, Maecenas' concern about the threat from such places is misguided) *tu . . . urbi sollicitus times | quid Seres et regnata Cyro | Bactra parent Tanaisque discors*. To judge from parallels in the *Res gestae* (*Mon. Anc.* 5.9–6.12), H. here reflects Augustan propaganda, as does the connection with *CS* 53–6, which has foreign nations fearful (54 *timet*) and petitioning (55 *responsa petunt*).

21 profundum Danuuium bibunt: the artless sound of the line (*fun-dum . . . nu-uium . . . bunt*) contributes to an image of the uncivilized Dacians drinking (deep) of the deep Danube.

Danuuium: The Danube, regarded as the northeastern Roman boundary, is also known as the Ister/Hister in its lower reaches in Dacia and Moesia, though the latter name is also used of the entire river and is more poetic than *Danuuius*, which is first found here in poetry; see 14.45–8n.

bibunt: cf. *OLD* s.v. *bibo* 4 'To drink of (rivers, etc.), i.e. to live in or visit their neighbourhood'; cf. 3.10.1 *extremum Tanain si biberes, Lyce*; *Epist.* 1.18.104–5 (with epic elevation) *gelidus Digentia riuus | quem Mandela bibit*; cf. also *C.* 2.20.20 *discet Hiber Rhodanique potor* and N–H *ad loc.* for the (rare) instances in Greek, again in high register, e.g. Hom. *Il.* 2.825 ('a delightful description which finds no exact counterpart in Homer', Kirk *ad loc.*) πίνοντες ὕδωρ μέλαν Αἰσήποιο 'those who drink the dark water of Aesepus'; also Callim. *Hymn* 1.40–1; Crinag. *Anth. Pal.* 9.430.2. First in Latin, in stylized contexts, in the adynaton at Virg. *Ecl.* 1.61–2 *ante*... *Ararim Parthus bibet aut Germania Tigrim*; also 10.65–6 *nec si*... *Hebrumque bibamus | Sithoniasque niues*... *subeamus*; *Aen.* 7.715 (antiquarian lines on the Sabines) *qui Tiberim Fabarimque bibunt*; *TLL* s.v. *bibo* 1964.39–66.

22 edicta... Iulia: Roman proclamations and Augustan proclamations have become one and the same. In republican terms *edicta* are proclamations by magistrates, particularly praetors, but Wickham is surely right to see a general sense here and also a more poetic phrasing of the Augustan legislation, namely the various *leges Iuliae*, some passed under Julius Caesar, on which see *OCD* s.v. 'lex', p. 851, with further bibilography. Griffin 2002: 328 sees a specific reference to the *Lex Iulia de maritandis ordinibus* of 18 BCE and an 'implication, too *outré* to be fully spelled out, that as we cluster our wives and children about us (line 27), so the barbarians, too, will all live model bourgeois lives'.

Getae: Thracian tribe on the lower Danube, in Romania and Bulgaria; Ovid has much to say about them in the exile poems, claims to have learned their language and even talks of a Getic *laus Caesaris* he wrote!

23 Seres: a trochee, preserving the prosody of the Greek (Σῆρες), as at 1.12.56 (*Seras*) and 3.29.27. The Seres are generally considered to be in the Far East, though obviously the Chinese themselves did not adhere to Augustus' edicts, of which they will have been unaware. The Parthians were situated on the Silk Road, and the Seres are perceived as being east of them. *serica*, silk, is first attested at *Epod.* 8.15 (see Watson *ad loc.*), and Virg. *G.* 1.121 is a reference to silk-gathering: *uelleraque ut foliis depectant tenuia Seres*.

infidique: cf. *Epist.* 2.1.112 *inuenior Parthis mendacior*; as Brink *ad loc.* notes, 'the Carthaginians and Greeks had suffered the same accusation from the Romans'.

Tanain prope flumen orti: i.e. Scythians to the north, Sarmatians to the south of the Tanais (Don), which enters the Black Sea at its northeastern extremity.

25–32 The poem ends with H. conflating his private lyric and his public encomiastic personae in a disconcerting union. The future song of celebration will occur in sympotic or convivial settings, on any day of the year, in the company of spouses and children like the idealized rustic of *Epod.* 2.39–40, 65–6 – a scenario surely anathema to the symposium of the Greek lyric, or Horatian, tradition. At the end of 4.5, parallel in its address to Augustus, as in its relationship to the preceding poem (4.4 Drusus; 4.14 Tiberius), there is celebration, but there of a more conventional sympotic nature. Here on the other hand, apart from the mixed and more sober company, prayer to the gods will be followed by the hymning of heroes of old, Troy and the line of Venus and Anchises, that is, what looks like a version of the *Aeneid*. For evidence of heroic song at Roman banquet, cf. Cato *ap.* Cic. *Tusc.* 4.2.3 (= fr. 118 Peter) *grauissimus auctor in Originibus dixit Cato morem apud maiores hunc epularum fuisse, ut deinceps qui accubarent canerent ad tibiam clarorum uirorum laudes atque uirtutes*; so too, on the authority of Cato, Cic. *Brut.* 75 *carmina . . . in epulis esse cantata a singulis conuiuis de clarorum uirorum laudibus.* On this tradition with reference to H., see Murray 1985: 40–1, although he mistakenly believes this poem originally stood at the beginning of *C.* 4.

25 profestis lucibus 'in place of holidays', i.e. 'working days'. Normally the symposium is associated just with *dies festi* (3.9–12; 14.13–14). Cf. *S.* 2.2.116–17 for moderate eating on working days; 2.3.142–4 for the miser Opimius' distinct, but overly frugal, drinking on both working days and holidays: *'qui Veientanum festis potare diebus | Campana solitus trulla uappamque profestis'*. H.'s lack of discrimination between the two is noteworthy in the light of Gell. 2.24.14, of an undated sumptuary law from the principate of Augustus, setting limits in three classes of 200 (*profesti*), 300 (Kalends, Nones, Ides and some other *festi*) and 1,000 sesterces (weddings and wedding dinners).

26 inter iocosi munera Liberi: also of Bacchus at 3.21.15, of the wine-jar 14–16 *tu sapientium | curas et arcanum iocoso | consilium retegis Lyaeo*; also of the lyric genre, 3.3.69, in drawing back precisely from Trojan and national themes *non hoc iocosae conueniet lyrae*, with Porph. *ad loc.*: *lyrico carmine, cui iocosa conueniant.*

27 cum prole matronisque nostris: improbable Horatian company, and there is a tension in the setting, which might have been expected to call rather for flute girls (26, 30). Griffin 2002: 323 sees the contradiction with 3.8, where the bachelor H. notes the oddity of being in sympotic mode on the day of the Matronalia (which is not, in fact, what he turns out to be celebrating): 3.8.1 *Martiis caelebs quid agam Kalendis?* Likewise at 3.14.17–28 the safe return of Augustus from Spain calls for sympotic plans and an invitation to Neaera.

29–32 uirtute functos more patrum duces: either 'our generals who have played the hero's part as their fathers did before them', with Williams 1960 (also Syndikus *ad loc.*), or, as has traditionally been done, taking *more patrum* with *canemus*: so Putnam 263, 'sing of heroes as was our fathers' wont' and Rudd, 'sing in our fathers' fashion'. Williams 1960 removes the need for seeing such a hyperbaton of *more patrum* (not paralleled by the instance given by Putnam 271, n. 13, namely 3.15.13–16 *te . . . uetulam*, where there is no ambiguity) by arguing that *functos uirtute* need not mean 'the heroic dead' (*uita functus* and *functus* = rather 'those who have fulfilled the part of valour [whether living or dead]', as in Cic. *Tusc.* 1.109 *uirtutis munere fungi*). Williams' reasoning is tempting: 'why should we think that Horace, whose word order in the *Odes* is everywhere most deliberately organized, has here and here only used between a participle and its noun an adverbial phrase which is suitable in meaning for the participle but not intended to go with it?' On the other hand, formulating rules about Horatian lyric word order is hazardous, even in a strong case such as this. More importantly, Cato's claim (see 25–32n.) and particularly the wording *morem apud maiores . . . fuisse,* *ut . . . canerent* (the passage is not invoked by Putnam), leads towards assigning the phrase to *canemus*, where it also carries more meaning than in Williams' reading.

duces | . . . Troiamque et Anchisen et almae | progeniem Veneris: recalling the *Aeneid*, but also H.'s own response to the *Aeneid*, written for and of a later progeny of Venus: *CS* 50 *clarus Anchisae Venerisque sanguis* (cf. 41–2 *Troiam | . . . Aeneas*). The theme of the great Roman epic, converted to lyric in the secular hymn, stays there in the unfulfilled future of H.'s ending.

Lydis remixto carmine tibiis 'in song mingled with Lydian flutes', recalling the music (but *not* song) of 1.22–4, there lyre, flutes and pipe: *lyraeque et Berecyntiae | delectabere tibiae | mixtis carminibus non sine fistula*, and in less staid company: 25–6 *pueri . . . | . . . cum teneris uirginibus*. On whether *Lydis . . . tibiis* is to be taken as dative or ablative, Brink *ad AP* 151 *sic ueris falsa remixta* states 'the few instances of the rare compound are in fact indistinct'. At *Epod.* 9.5, H. asks when Maecenas will be able to celebrate Octavian's victory at Actium, to the sound of Dorian lyre and 'barbarous' flutes: *sonante mixtum tibiis carmen lyra, | hac Dorium, illis barbarum.* Plato, *Rep.* 398e characterizes the Lydian and other eastern modes as μαλακαί τε καὶ συμποτικαί ('soft and sympotic') and as χαλαραί ('effeminate'). In *Epod.* 9 'the two modes specified by Horace are thus appropriate respectively to the occasion of the celebration and to the relaxed convivial setting' (Watson *ad loc.*). At the end of *C.* 4.15 the Lydian mode on its own is appropriate to the symposium but less so to the Virgilian themes of Rome's foundation, and so lyric thereby wins out in the end. For the technical aspects of the Dorian, Phrygian and Lydian modes, about which H. may well have been ignorant, see West 1992: 179–82.

progeniem: a high-register word, as elsewhere in H.: 3.6.48; 3.29.1; and with mock elevation at *S.* 2.3.243 *Quinti progenies Arri, par nobile fratrum.* It is here particularly Virgilian, used by Venus in address to Jupiter at *Aen.* 1.250; 10.30 *tua progenies* (and Harrison *ad loc.*).

Veneris: fittingly in the middle of the book's last line, as of its first: 1.1 *intermissa, Venus, diu*, though she has been transformed from the Sapphic Aphrodite of the book's opening to the head of the Augustan dynasty by its end. The centrally placed *uenerantur* in the last line of 14, figuring the defeated Sygambri's worship for Augustus, hints at the source of his power. In view of the subject matter (Troy, Anchises and the offspring of Venus) and the framing function of Venus, the envoi of the *Homeric Hymn to Aphrodite* is worth noting: 293 σέο δ' ἐγὼ ἀρξάμενος μεταβήσομαι ἄλλον ἐς ὕμνον 'after beginning from you, I will pass over to another song' (cf. *canemus*).

canemus: song will get the last word, but still song deferred. Putnam notes the strong invocation of the last lines and last word at Virg. *Ecl.* 9.66–7, the close of present troubled song and hope of better future song, *desine plura, puer, et quod nunc instat agamus; | carmina tum melius, cum uenerit ipse, canemus.* For Putnam H., the new Menalcas, brings closure and recuperation: through this final ode H. 'can assure a future for his song and through it for those of whom he sings, including the savior'.

But H. never came to sing of Troy, Anchises and Aeneas, as Menalcas never arrived to sing at the end of *Eclogue* 9. H. once had to sing such a song, and in such company, but the days of the *Carmen saeculare* are now behind him. H.'s song remains in the future, as the end's disingenuous *canemus* brings forward the *Aeneid*'s beginning *cano*. H.'s prospective *Aeneid* with its choral anti-lyric ensemble (32 *cum prole matronisque nostris*), perhaps regathered from their secular hymning of a few years before, will never come together, as his promise of song is followed by silence, the ultimate *recusatio*.

APPENDIX 1
THE SECULAR GAMES

The Secular Games, celebrated in 17 BCE, came to be perceived as marking the *saeculum*, approximating to a 100-year period, the longest possible span of a human life (Varro, *Ling.* 6.11, with the popular etymology from *senex*: *seclum spatium annorum centum uocarunt dictum a sene, quod longissimum spatium senescendorum hominum id putarunt*), the idea being that no one who was alive at the opening of the *saeculum* could still be so at its close (which presumably makes the lack of regularity in intervals ritually acceptable). The association has to do as much with ringing out the old as ringing in the new, though the Augustan reinvention would look very much to the latter. The first celebration for which there is certain evidence was in 249 BCE, during the First Punic War, with the next occurring in 146 BCE. There were no games in 49 or 46 BCE, understandably in view of the turmoil of those years. The games assigned to 349 BCE are generally considered fictional (see Pighi 4–7 and esp. 6, n. 2 for the dates; also Davis 2001: 114), in part because the *gens Valeria* is associated with the founding and the aetiology may be connected with M. Valerius Corvinus, cos. 348. It is also the case that the games of 17 BCE were exclusively *ludi scaenici*, while the oldest Roman *ludi* were *circenses*, a fact that has been used to argue for a late origin (Taylor 1934: 107).

The original location for the games was at the Tarentum, or Terentum, with its altar of Dis and Proserpina, by the Tiber at the western extremity of the Campus Martius (Festus 440.17–18 *in extremo Campo Martio*), at the Tiber end of the modern Corso Vittorio Emanuele II. Varro treated the institution of the games in the first book of his *De scaenicis originibus* (*ap.* Censorinus *De die natali Liber* 17.8, 11; cf. also Livy 49, fr. 13; Mart. 4.1.8; Stat. *Silu.* 1.4.18; 4.1.38 with Coleman *ad loc.*). They were perceived as arising after the *Xuiri* consulted the Sibylline oracles (on whose instructions we do not know, perhaps the consuls on behalf of the senate?) in response to an omen that occurred during the First Punic War, a lightning strike on the city wall and a tower between the Colline and Esquiline Gates. The original games therefore have little to do with the notion of the *saeculum* but seem, rather, propitiatory in nature. There is no evidence that the elaborate sacrifice of the Augustan and subsequent versions had any precedent in the earlier celebrations; nor is there any trace of sacrifice to gods other than Dis and Proserpina. Indeed ps-Acro (*ad CS* 8) reports a full and precise summary from Verrius Flaccus, which mentions no other gods and clearly describes the pre-Augustan version.

The two major sources on the origins are Valerius Maximus 2.4.5 and Zosimus 2.1–4, and their accounts suggest self-promotion by the *gens Valeria*, not necessarily an obstacle to ancient origins. There are variations, but the essentials of the story in Valerius Maximus involve a Sabine from Eretum by the name of Valesius, who is told by the gods that his ailing children will be cured if he goes to Tarentum and refreshes them with waters from the altar of Dis Pater and Proserpina. He therefore heads down the Tiber, intending to make the daunting voyage from Ostia to the instep of Italy. He happens to stop for water and fire at the bend in the Tiber (i.e. the Tarentum or Terentum), where, following various narrative details, he discovers and sacrifices at an altar of Dis Pater and Proserpina. He then holds games lasting three nights for each of the three nights his children were sick. Notably there is no daytime ceremony in these versions of the aetion. Nilsson 1920: 1699–1702 gives tables of the presumably fictitious repetitions of the *ludi Tarentini* preceding the historical event of 249 BCE; consular Valerii feature heavily: 509 BCE (P. Valerius Poplicola I), 504 BCE (P. Valerius Poplicola IV), 449 BCE (L. Valerius Poplicola), 348 BCE (M. Valerius Corvinus). It has been assumed that Valerius Antias had a part in this reconstruction, carried out for the greater glory of the *gens Valeria*, for skepticism on which see Cornell (*OCD* s.v. 'Valerius Antias'). Versnel has a full discussion of the role of the Valerii at *Gymn.* 89 (1982) 193–235.

It is, however, not possible to rule out its being an old custom, rooted in the sixth century. An inscription in archaic Latin from southern Latium (*Lapis Satricanus*, sixth to fifth century BCE) shows that the *gens Valeria* had prominence from very early in the Republic: *.]ei steterai Popliosio Valesiosio | suodales Mamartei* ('.]ei dedicated this to Mars as companions of Publius Valerius'). It is usually assumed that the *ludi* are Greek in origin, in part because the name of the underworld deity *Dis* is a calque on the Greek god Plutus, in part because in 17 BCE Augustus sacrificed *Achiuo ritu*. Neither of these facts is decisive, since the deities and general details at the Augustan event themselves show such marked flexibility and change. Coarelli 1993 argues that the *ludi* go back to 509 or 504 BCE, mainly on the basis of the wording *utique semper Latinus obtemperassit* ('that the Latins be forever obedient') – wording only evidenced after 1931 when the correct reading for the Augustan *Acta* was restored from the Severan iteration (line 51: cf. Pighi 163). This wording is appropriate to the fourth century, or even before, but the detail may also be a piece of Augustan archaizing, aimed at lending an aura of antiquity, as is the case in the older material included in the last two lines of the Sibylline oracle (see below, and *CS* 69–72n.).

More convincingly Watkins 1991: 138 has noted that the form 'Proserpina' 'is an earlier borrowing via Etruscan: Περσεφόνα: *Φersipnai, -nei* → Etr.-Lat *Proserpina*'. Following Vetter, he convincingly shows that Tarentum, site of the *ludi saeculares* in the Campus Martius, probably has nothing to do with the city in Southern Italy, but rather has the meaning 'tomb'. The basis is a corrupt passage at Varro *Ling.* 6.23, treating the *Larentalia*, supposedly named for Acca Larentia, 'a former prostitute and benefactress of the Roman state in the time of king Ancus Martius by one account, the nurse and fostermother of Romulus and Remus by another, doubtless later' (Watkins 1991: 135). The sacrifice for this festival occurred in the Velabrum, *ad sepulcrum Accae* (*Ling.* 6.24), as stated in a sentence immediately following the phrase *tarentum Accas Larentinas* (as emended by Vetter 1957), of which *sepulcrum Accas* is a gloss.

Watkins 1991: 142–3 proposes an etymology for *tarentum* = 'tomb' that derives it from a verb meaning 'pass over, cross, overcome', with attestation elsewhere, as in the possible etymology for Gr. νέκ–ταρ 'overcoming death'. If so, the connection with south Italian Tarentum disappears, and the strong early connection with Dis and Proserpina becomes more comprehensible: a 'passing over' from one *saeculum* to the next, from life to the afterlife, a place of darkness and light. On a more prosaic level, Tarentum is one of the natural places for 'crossing' the Tiber, right by the Pons Neronianus. The Sibylline oracle specifies sacrifice in the Campus by the Tiber, where its waters are narrowest: 6 ὅππῃ στεινότατον. Without the need to factor in the city of Tarentum (which would point to a third-century origin for the story) an earlier origin becomes possible – though the homophony with the South Italian city was doubtless what germinated the Valesius aetiology.

Lipka 2009: 152–3 convincingly argues that Capito designated the Tarentum for sacrifice to the Greek gods, reserving spaces within the *pomerium* for Roman deities: Jupiter and Juno on the Capitoline, Apollo and Diana on the Palatine, with the *CS* sung on each – though, as he admits, Apollo is among the most Greek of the Roman gods. So Augustus and Agrippa performed animal sacrifices there, *Achiuo ritu*, to the Moerae, not the Parcae; to Ilithyia, not Mater Matuta, who, as Lipka observes, (142) 'apart from her functional similarity, had her own temple very close by, in the Forum Boarium (i.e. inside the *pomerium*!)'; and to Terra Mater, who corresponds to Greek *Gē Mēter*, rather than to Tellus. Juno Regina, as Lipka notes, is to be associated with the cult that arrived from Veii and was situated in the temple on the Aventine, again outside the *pomerium*, but she is brought within for the sacrifice. Similarly, Diana is included with Apollo, with whom she receives offerings not at her temple on the Aventine, but rather at his on the Palatine. Lipka well notes that this distribution has been obscured precisely by H.'s substituting Roman deities, Parcae (*CS* 25–8), Diana or Juno (13–16) and Tellus (29–32). If Lipka is right, the poet clearly had considerable licence to depart from Capito's careful choreography.

APPENDIX 2
ACTA OF THE AUGUSTAN SECULAR GAMES OF 17 BCE (LINES 90–168)

CIL VI 32323.90–152 = *ILS* 5050 = Pighi 107–19 = Schnegg-Köhler 34–44 (for text below):

90 *Nocte insequenti in campo ad Tib[erim deis Moeris imp(erator) Caesar Augustus immolauit agnas feminas IX]*

91 *prodigiuas Achiuo ritu eodemq[ue ritu capras feminas IX prodigiuas, precatusque est hoc modo:* (uacat)*]*

92 *Moerae uti uobis in illeis libr[eis scriptum est quarumque rerum ergo quodque melius siet p(opulo) R(omano) Quiritibus uobis IX]*

93 *agnis feminis et IX capris femi[nis propriis sacrum fiat; uos quaeso precorque uti imperium maiestatemque p(opuli) R(omani)]*

94 *Quiritium duelli domique au[xitis utique semper Latinus obtemperassit, – – – sempiter-]*

95 *nam uictoriam ualetudine[m p(opulo) R(omano) Quiritibus duitis faueatisque p(opulo) R(omano) Quiritium legionibusque p(opuli) R(omani)]*

96 *Quiritium, remque p(ublicam) p(opuli) R(omani)[Quiritium saluam seruetis maioremque faxitis, uti sitis]uolentes pr[opitiae (populo) R(omano)]*

97 *Quiritibus XV uir(or)um collegi[o mihi domo familiaeque, uti huius] sacrifici acceptrices sitis VIIII agnarum*

98 *feminarum et VIIII capraru[m feminarum propri]arum immolandarum; harum rerum ergo macte hac agna femina*

99 *inmolanda estote, fitote u[olentes]propitiae p(opulo) R(omano) Quiritibus, XV uir(or)um collegio mihi domo familiae.*

100 *Ludique noctu, sacrificio[co]nfecto sunt commissi in scaena quoi theatrum adiectum non fuit nullis positis*

101 *sedilibus centumque et X [ma]tronae quibus denuntiatum erat XV uirorum uerbis sellisternia habuerunt,*

102 *Iunoni et Dianae duab[us] sellis positis.* (uacat)

103 *K(alendis) Iun(iis) in Capitolio bouem m[a]rem Ioui optimo maximo proprium immolauit imperator Caesar Augustus ibidem*

104 *alterum M. Agrippa; p[re]cati autem sunt ita:* (uacat)

105 *Iuppiter optime maxime! ut[i t]ibi in illeis libreis scriptum est, quarumque rerum [ergo] quodque melius siet populo R(omano)*

106 *Quiritibus, tibi hoc bou[e] mare pulchro sacrum fiat; te quaeso precorque. ceter[a u]ti supra.* (uacat)

107 *Ad atallam fuerunt C[ae]sar, Agrippa, Scaeuola, Sentius, Lollius, Asiniu[s G]allus, Rebilus.* (uacat)

108 *Deinde ludi Latini in th[ea]tro ligneo quod erat constitutum in Campo s[ecu]ndum Tiberim sunt commissi.*

109 *Eodemque modo sellist[er]nia matres familiae habuerunt neque sunt l[udi i]ntermissi iei qui noctu coepti erant*

110 *fieri et edictum proposi[t]um:* (uacat) *XV uir(i) s(acris) f(aciundis) dic(unt):* (uacat)

111 *Cum bono more et proind[e c]elebrato frequentibus exemplis quando cumq[ue i]usta laetitiae publicae causa fuit*

112 *minui luctus matrona[r]um placuerit idque tam sollemnium sacror[um l]udorumque tempore referri*

113 *diligenterque obserua[r]i pertinere uideatur et ad honorem deorum et ad [m]emoriam cultus eorum: statuimus*

114 *offici nostri esse per ed[ic]tum denuntiare feminis uti luctum minuant.* (uacat)

115 *Noctu autem ad Tiberim s[a]crificium fecit deis <I>lithyis libeis VIIII popan[is] VIIII pthoibus VIIII imp(erator) Caesar*

116 *Augustus; precatus est [h]oc modo:* (uacat)

117 *Ilythia uti tibei in ille[is] libreis scriptum est, quarumque rerum e[rgo quodque melius si]et p(opulo) R(omano) Quiritibus*

118 *tibi VIIII popanis et VI[III] libeis et VIIII pthoibus sacrum fiat; te quae[so precorque; cetera uti supra.* (uacat)*]*

119 *<A(nte) d(iem)> IV nonas Iun(ias) in Capitol[io i]nmolauit Iunoni Reginae bouem femin[am propriam Achiuo ritu* – – –]*

120 *M. Agrippa et precatus es[t] hoc modo:* (uacat)

121 *Iuno regina uti tibi in illi[s l]ibris scriptum est, quarumque rerum [ergo quodque melius siet p(opulo) R(omano) Quiritibus,]*

122 *tibi boue femina pulchra s[a]crum fiat; te quaeso precorqu[e; cetera uti supra.* (uacat 25)*]*

123 *Deinde CX matribus famil[ia]s nuptis quibus denu[ntiatum erat – – – M. Agrippa]*

124 *praeit in haec uerba:* (uacat)

125 *Iuno regina ast quid est qu[o]d meli[us siet p(opulo) R(omano) Quiritibus – – – matres familias CX p(opulo) R(omano) Quiritium*

126 *nuptae genibus nixae te [– – – precamur oramus obsecramusque uti tu imperium]*

127 *maiestatemque p(opuli) R(omani) Quiriti[um duelli domique auxis utique semper Latinus obtemperassit – – –]*

128 *sempiternam uictoriam [ualetudinem p(opulo) R(omano) Quiritibus duis, faueasque p(opulo) R(omano) Quiritibus legionibusque p(opuli) R(omani)]*

129 *Quiritium remque publi[cam p(opuli) R(omani) Quiritium saluam serues, maioremque faxis, uti sies uolens propitia p(opulo) R(omano)]*

130 *Quiritibus XV uir(is) s(acris) f(aciundis) no[bis domibus familiis – – – matres familias CX p(opuli) R(omani)]*

131 *Quiritium nuptae geni[bus nixae, precamur, oramus, obsecramusque.* (uacat)*]*

132 *Ad atallam fuerunt M. A[grippa – – –* (uacat?)*]*

133 *Ludi ut pridie facti sunt [– – –* (uacat?)*]*

134 *Noctu autem ad Tiberim [suem plenam prodigiuam Terrae Matri Achiuo ritu immolauit imp(erator)]*

135 *Caesar Augustus; precat[us est hoc modo:* (uacat)*]*

136 *Terra mater uti tibi in ill[is libris scriptum est, quarumque rerum ergo quodque melius siet p(opulo) R(omano) Quiritibus,]*

137 *uti tibi sue plena propri[a sacrum fiat; te quaeso precorque c]etera [uti supra.* (uacat)*]*

138 *Matronae sellisternia h[abuerunt – – –]runt.* (uacat)

139 *A(nte) d(iem) III non(as) Iun(ias) in Palatio [Apollini et Dianae] sacrificium fecerunt imp(erator) Caesar Augustus M. A[grippa libeis VIIII]*

140 *popanis VIIII pthoibus VII[II; preca]tique sunt ita:* (uacat)

141 *Apollo uti tibi in illis libr[is sc]riptum est, quarumque rerum ergo quodque melius siet p(opulo) R(omano) Quir[itibus]*

142 *uti tibi VIIII popanis et V[IIII] libis et VIIII pthoibus sacrum fiat; te quaeso precorque; cetera uti s[up]ra.* (uacat)

143 *Apollo uti te popanis dat[i]s bona prece precatus sum eiusdem rei ergo macte heis libis libandis esto*

144 *fito uolens propitius.* (uacat)

145 *Idem in pthoibus.* (uacat)

146 *Eisdem uerbis Dianam.* (uacat)

147 *Sacrificioque perfecto pueri [X]XVII quibus denuntiatum erat patrimi et matrimi et puellae totidem*

148 *carmen cecinerunt. Eo[de]mque modo in Capitolio.* (uacat)

149 *Carmen composuit Q. Hor[at]ius Flaccus.* (uacat)

150 *XV uir(i) adfuerunt imp(erator) Cae[s]ar, M. Agrippa, Q. Lepidus, Potitus Messalla, C. Stolo, C. Scaeuola, C. Sosius*

151 *C. Norbanus, M. Cocceius, [M]. Lollius, C. Sentius, M. Strigo, L. Arruntius, C. Asinius, M. Marcellus, D. Laelius,*

152 *Q. Tubero, C. Rebilus, M[es]salla Messallinus.* (uacat)

*Lipka 2009: 152, n. 16 is probably right to reject the supplement *Achiuo ritu* of the sacrifice to Juno Regina (on the Capitoline); see above, Appendix 1.

The actual prayer to Apollo can be reconstructed to have been as follows (*Acta* 141–45, based on *Acta* 92–9):

Apollo! uti tibi in illis libris scriptum, quarumque rerum ergo quodque melius siet p(opulo) R(omano) Quiritibus uti tibi VIIII popanis et VIIII libis et VIIII pthoibus sacrum fiat: te quaeso precorque uti imperium maiestatemque p(opuli) R(omani) Quiritium duelli domique auxis utique semper Latinus obtemperassit, sempiternam uictoriam ualetudinem populo Romano Quiritibus duis, faueasque p(opuli) R(omani) Quiritium legionibusque p(opuli) R(omani) Quiritium, remque p(ublicam) populi R(omani) Quiritium saluam serues maioremque faxis, uti sis uolens propitius populo Romano Quiritibus, XV uir(or)um collegio, mihi, domo, familiae. Apollo! uti te popanis datis bona prece precatus sum, eiusdem rei ergo macte his libis libandis esto, fito uolens propitius p(opulo) R(omano) Quiritibus, XV uir(or)um collegio, mihi, domo, familiae. Apollo! uti te pthoibus datis bona prece precatus sum, eiusdem rei ergo macte his libis libandis esto, fito uolens propitius p(opulo) R(omano) Quiritibus, XV uir(or)um collegio, mihi, domo, familiae.

APPENDIX 3
THE SIBYLLINE ORACLE FOR THE SECULAR GAMES OF 17 BCE

Phlegon of Tralles, *Macr.* 4 Keller = *FGrH* 257 F 37.132–69 (also in Zos. 2.6.1, with variants):

Ἀλλ’ ὁπότ’ ἂν μήκιστος ἴηι χρόνος ἀνθρώποισιν
ζωῆς, εἰς ἐτέων ἑκατὸν δέκα κύκλον ὁδεύσας,
μεμνῆσθαι, Ῥωμαῖε, καὶ εἰ μάλα λήσει ἑαυτόν,
μεμνῆσθαι τάδε πάντα, θεοῖσι μὲν ἀθανάτοισι
ῥέζειν ἐν πεδίωι παρὰ Θύβριδος ἄπλετον ὕδωρ,
ὅππηι στεινότατον, νὺξ ἡνίκα γαῖαν ἐπέλθηι,
ἠελίου κρύψαντος ἑὸν φάος· ἔνθα σὺ ῥέζειν
ἱερὰ παντογόνοις Μοίραις ἄρνας τε καὶ αἶγας
κυανέας, ἐπὶ ταῖς δ’ Εἰλειθυίας ἀρέσασθαι
παιδοτόκους θυέεσσιν, ὅπηι θέμις· αὖθι δὲ Γαίηι
πληθομένη χοίροις ὗς ἱρεύοιτο μέλαινα.
πάνλευκοι ταῦροι δὲ Διὸς παρὰ βωμὸν ἀγέσθων
ἤματι μηδ’ ἐπὶ νυκτί· θεοῖσι γὰρ Οὐρανίδηισιν
ἡμέριος πέλεται θυέων τρόπος· ὣς δὲ καὶ αὐτὸς
ἱρεύειν. δαμάλης τε βοὸς δέμας ἀγλαὸν Ἥρης
δεξάσθω νηὸς παρὰ σεῦ. καὶ Φοῖβος Ἀπόλλων,
ὅστε καὶ Ἠέλιος κικλήσκεται, ἶσα δεδέχθω
θύματα Λητοΐδης. καὶ ἀειδόμενοί τε Λατῖνοι
παιᾶνες κούροισι κόρησί τε νηὸν ἔχοιεν
ἀθανάτων. χωρὶς δὲ κόραι χορὸν αὐταὶ ἔχοιεν
καὶ χωρὶς παίδων ἄρσην στάχυς, ἀλλὰ γονήων
πάντες ζωόντων, οἷς ἀμφιθαλὴς ἔτι φύτλη.
αἱ δὲ γάμου ζεύγλαις δεδμημέναι ἤματι κείνωι
γνὺξ Ἥρης παρὰ βωμὸν ἀοίδιμον ἑδριόωσαι
δαίμονα λισσέσθωσαν. ἅπασι δὲ λύματα δοῦναι
ἀνδράσιν ἠδὲ γυναιξί, μάλιστα δὲ θηλυτέρησιν.
πάντες δ’ ἐξ οἴκοιο φερέσθων, ὅσσα κομίζειν
ἔστι θέμις θνητοῖσιν ἀπαρχομένοις βιότοιο,
δαίμοσι μειλιχίοισιν ἱλάσματα καὶ μακάρεσσιν
Οὐρανίδαις. τὰ δὲ πάντα τεθησαυρισμένα κείσθω,
ὄφρα τέλη θυμέλησι ***
** <θηλυτέρησι> καὶ ἀνδράσιν ἑδριόωσιν
ἔνθεν πορσύνηις μεμνημένος. ἤμασι δ’ ἔστω
νυξί τ’ ἐπασσυτέρησι θεοπρέπτους κατὰ θώκους
παμπληθὴς ἄγυρις· σπουδὴ δὲ γέλωτι μεμίχθω.

ταῦτά τοι ἐν φρεσὶν ἧισιν ἀεὶ μεμνημένος εἶναι,
καί σοι πᾶσα χθὼν Ἰταλὴ καὶ πᾶσα Λατίνων
αἰὲν ὑπὸ σκήπτροισιν ἐπαυχένιον ζυγὸν ἕξει.

When the longest span of life for humans passes,
Having journeyed its cycle of a hundred and ten years,
Remember, Roman, even if it escapes your notice,
Remember all these things: to sacrifice
To the immortal gods on the field along the boundless waters of the Tiber
At its narrowest point, when night comes upon earth
And the sun has hidden its own light. Perform a sacrifice
Of dark sheep and goats to the all-generating Moirai
And also appease childbirth-promoting Eileithyiai
With offerings in the proper way. In that place
Let a black sow swollen with piglets be sacrificed to Gaia,
And let all-white bulls be led to the altar of Zeus
By day, not by night, for to the Ouranian gods
Sacrifices are performed in daylight. So must you yourself
Sacrifice. Let Hera's shining temple
Receive a young steer from you, and let Phoibos Apollo,
Who is also called Helios, receive equal victims,
Leto's son. Let Latin paeans
Sung by youths and maidens occupy the temple
Of the immortals. Let the maidens have a dancing place apart,
And let the boys, male progeny, likewise be apart, but
All must have living parents, the stock flourishing on both sides.
Let women tamed by the yoke of marriage sit bent-kneed
Alongside Hera's celebrated altar that day
And beseech the goddess. Give lustral agents
To all the men and women, especially to the females.
Let everyone carry from his house all that it is proper
For mortals to convey, who are offering first fruits of their sustenance,
Propitiations for the gracious spirits and blessed
Ouranian gods, and let all things lie in store
Until the offerings . . . sacrificial hearths . . .
. . . for women and men as they sit . . .
Whence remember to make them ready. During the following days
And nights let there be a teeming gathering
At seats fit for gods, and let solemnity mix with laughter.
Remember to keep these injunctions always in mind, and
All Italian earth and all the earth of the Latins
Will always bear the yoke on its neck under your rule.

(trans. Hansen 1996: 56–7)

BIBLIOGRAPHY

Adams, J. N. 2007. *The regional diversification of Latin 200 BC – AD 600*, Cambridge

2005. 'The *Bellum Africum*', *Proc. Brit. Acad.* 129: 73–96

1994. 'Wackernagel's law and the position of unstressed personal pronouns in Classical Latin', *TPhS* 92: 103–78

1992. 'Iteration of compound verb with simplex in Latin prose', *Eikasmos* 3: 295–8

1972. 'The language of the later books of Tacitus' *Annals*', *CQ* 22: 350–73

Allen, W. S. 1973, *Accent and rhythm. Prosodic features of Latin and Greek: a study of theory and reconstruction*, Cambridge

Ambrose, J. W. 1965. 'The ironic meaning of the Lollius Ode', *TAPA* 96: 1–10

André, J. 1956. *Lexique des termes de botanique en latin*, Paris

1949. *Étude sur les termes de couleur dans la langue latine*, Paris

Asztalos, M. 2008. 'The poet's mirror. Horace *Carmen* 4.10', *HSCP* 104: 289–302

Barchiesi, A. 2002. 'The uniqueness of the *Carmen saeculare* and its tradition', in T. Woodman and D. Feeney, eds. *Traditions and context in the poetry of Horace* (Cambridge) 107–23

2000. 'Rituals in ink: Horace on the Greek lyric tadition', in M. Depew and D. Obbink, eds. *Matrices of genre* (Cambridge, MA) 167–82

1996. 'Poetry, praise, and patronage: Simonides in book 4 of Horace's *Odes*', *CA* 15: 5–47

1995. 'Simonide e Orazio sulla morte di Achille', *ZPE* 107: 33–8 (= 'Simonides and Horace on the death of Achilles' in D. Bodeker and D. Sider, eds. *The new Simonides. Contexts of praise and desire* (Oxford, 2001) 255–60

Barker, D. 1996. '"The golden age is proclaimed"? The *Carmen saeculare* and the renascence of the golden race', *CQ* 46: 434–46

Bell, A. J. 1923. *The Latin dual and poetic diction*, London and Toronto

Belmont, D. E. 1980. 'The Vergilius of Horace, *Ode* 4.12', *TAPA* 110: 1–20

Bowditch, P. L. 2001. *Horace and the gift economy of patronage*, Berkeley, Los Angeles and London

Bowersock, G. W. 1964. 'C. Marcius Censorinus, legatus Caesaris', *HSCP* 68: 207–10

Bowra, C. M. 1928. 'Horace, *Odes* IV.12', *CR* 42: 165–7

Bradshaw, A. T. v. S. 1970. 'Horace, *Odes* 4.1', *CQ* 20: 142–53

Breed, B. W. 2004. '*Tua, Caesar, aetas*: Horace *Ode* 4.15 and the Augustan age', *AJP* 125: 245–53

Büchner, K. 1962. *Horaz*, Wiesbaden

Cairns, F. 2006. *Propertius. The Augustan elegist*, Cambridge

1972. *Generic composition in Greek and Roman poetry*, Edinburgh

Cameron, A. 1995. *Callimachus and his critics*, Princeton

Casali, S. 1995. *Heroidum Epistula IX. Deianira Herculi*, Florence

Cataudella, Q. 1927–8. 'L'elegia di Semonide e l'ode di Orazio IV 7', *Boll. di filol. class.* 34: 229–32

Catlow, L. W. 1976. 'Horace, *Odes* I, 25 and IV, 13: a reinterpretation', *Latomus* 85: 813–21

Charlesworth, M. P. 1923. 'Tiberius and the death of Augustus', *AJP* 44: 145–57

Christ, W. von 1868. 'Über die Verskunst des Horaz im Lichte der alten Überlieferung', *Sitzungsberichte der Bayerischen Akademie der Wissenschaften* (Munich) 1–44

Clackson, J. and Horrocks, G. 2007. *The Blackwell history of the Latin language*, Malden, MA, Oxford and Carlton, Victoria

Clausen, W. V. 1987. *Virgil's Aeneid and the tradition of Hellenistic poetry*, Berkeley, Los Angeles and London

Clay, J. S. 2002. 'Sweet folly: Horace, *Odes* 4.12 and the evocation of Virgil', in Paschalis 2002: 129–40

Coarelli, F. 1993. 'Noti sui ludi saeculares', in *Spectacles sportifs et scéniques dans le monde étrusco-italique* (Rome) 211–45

Coleman, K. M. 1988. *Statius Silvae IV*, Oxford

Coleman, R. 1975. 'Greek influence on Latin syntax', *TPhS* 74: 101–56

Coletti, M. L 1996. 'Cinara', *EO* I: 689–90

Commager, S. 1980. 'Some Horatian vagaries', *SO* 55: 59–70

Cooper, F. T. 1975. *Word formation in the Roman sermo plebeius*, 2nd edn, New York

Copley, F. O. 1956. *Exclusus amator. A study in Latin love poetry*, APA Monographs 17, Madison, WI

Courtney, E. 2004. 'The "Greek" accusative', *CJ* 99: 425–31

Currie, H. M. 1996. 'Horace's "epigraphic poetry": some comments on *Odes* IV', *Latomus* 55: 78–86

Davis, G. 1991. *Polyhymnia. The rhetoric of Horatian lyric discourse*, Berkeley, Los Angeles and London

Davis, P. J. 2001. 'The fabrication of tradition: Horace, Augustus and the secular games', *Ramus* 30: 111–27

Delamarre, X. 2003. *Dictionnaire de la langue gauloise: une approche linguistique du vieux-celtique continental.* 2nd edn., Paris

De Rosaria, A. 1997. 'Minosse', *EO* II: 433

Dettmer, H. 1983. *Horace: A study in structure*, Hildesheim, Zurich, New York

de Vaan, M. 2008. *Etymological dictionary of Latin and other Italic languages*, Leiden

Dickey, E. 2002. *Latin forms of address from Plautus to Apuleius*, Oxford

Diels, H. 1904. 'Laterculi Alexandrini aus einem Papyrus ptolemäischer Zeit', *Abhandlungen der königlichen preussischen Akademie der Wissenschaften*, 1904, Abh. 2: 1–16

1890. *Sibyllinische Blätter*, Berlin

Dietz, K. 1995. 'Okkupation und Frühzeit', in W. Czysz, et al. eds. *Die Römer in Bayern* (Stuttgart) 18–99

Diggle, J. 1970, ed. and comm. Euripides, *Phaethon*, Cambridge

Du Quesnay, I. M. Le M. 1995. 'Horace, *Odes* 4.5: *Pro reditu imperatoris Caesaris diui filii Augusti*', in S. J. Harrison, ed. *Homage to Horace: a bimillenary celebration* (Oxford) 128–87

1976. 'Vergil's Fourth *Eclogue*', *PLLS* 1: 25–99

Dutoit, E. 1936. *Le Thème de l' adynaton dans la poésie antique*, Paris

Dyck, A. R. 2008, ed. and comm. Cicero, *Catilinarians*, Cambridge

Dyer, R. R. 1965. '*Diffugere nives*: Horace and the Augustan spring', *G&R* 12: 79–84

Dyson, M. 1991. 'Horace *Carmina* 4.5.36–7', *CP* 86: 126–9

Edmunds, L. 1982. 'The Latin invitation-poem: What is it? Where did it come from?', *AJP* 103: 184–8

Eich, A. 2000. *Politische Literatur in der römischen Gesellschaft. Studien zum Verhältnis von politischer und literarischer Öffentlichkeit in der späten Republik und frühen Kaiserzeit*, Cologne, Weimar, Vienna

Eilers, C. 2004. 'The date of Augustus' edict on the Jews (Jos. *AJ* 16.162–165) and the career of C. Marcius Censorinus', *Phoenix* 58: 86–95

Esler, C. C. 1989. 'Horace's old girls: evolution of a topos', in T. M. Faulkner, ed. *Old age in Latin literature* (Albany, NY) 172–82

Estévez, V. A. 1982. '*Quem tu, Melpomene*: The poet's lowered voice', *Emerita* 50: 279–300

Feeney, D. 1998. *Literature and religion at Rome*, Cambridge

1993. 'Horace and the Greek lyric poets', in N. Rudd, ed. *Horace 2000: a celebration* (London) 41–63

Fraenkel, E. 2007. *Plautine elements in Plautus (Plautinisches im Plautus*, Berlin 1922), trans. T. Drevikovsky and F. Muecke. Oxford

1961. 'Two poems of Catullus', *JRS* 51: 46–53

1932–3. *Das Pindargedicht des Horaz*. Sitzungsberichte der Heidelberger Akademie der Wissenschaften. Philosophische-historische Klasse 2, Heidelberg

Freis, R. 1983. 'The catalogue of Pindaric genres in Horace *Ode* 4.2', *CA* 2: 27–36

Galinsky, K. 1996. *Augustan culture*, Princeton

Gatz, B. 1967. *Weltalter, goldene Zeit und sinnverwandte Vorstellungen*. Spudasmata 16, Hildesheim

Gianotti, G. F. 1997. 'Priamel', *EO* II: 726–7

Gildersleeve, B. 1899. *Pindar. The Olympian and Pythian Odes*, New York

1882. 'Studies in Pindaric syntax. I. The conditional sentence in Pindar', *AJP* 3: 434–55

Griffin, J. 2002. 'Look your last on lyric: Horace, *Odes* 4.15' in T. P. Wiseman, ed. *Classics in progress. Essays on ancient Greece and Rome* (Oxford and New York) 311–32

1994. 'The long Latin line', *New York Review of Books* 41.16: 42–4 (Review of G. B. Conte, *Latin Literature. A history*, Baltimore 1994)

Habinek, T. 2005. *The world of Roman song. From ritualized speech to social order*, Baltimore and London

1986. 'The marriageability of Maximus: Horace, *Ode* 4.1.13–20', *AJP* 107: 407–16
Hansen, W. 1996. *Phlegon of Tralles' book of marvels*, Exeter
Hardie, P. 2002. 'Another look at Virgil's Ganymede' in T. P. Wiseman, ed. *Classics in progress. Essays on ancient Greece and Rome* (London) 333–61
1986. *Virgil's Aeneid: cosmos and imperium.* Oxford
Harrison, S. J. 2007a *Generic enrichment in Vergil and Horace*, Oxford
2007b *The Cambridge companion to Horace*, Cambridge
2001. 'Simonides and Horace', in D. Bodeker and D. Sider, eds. *The new Simonides, Contexts of praise and desire* (Oxford) 261–71
1996. 'Hereditary eloquence among the Torquati', *AJP* 117: 285–7
1995. 'Horace, Pindar, Iullus Antonius, and Augustus: *Odes* 4.2', in S. J. Harrison, ed. *Homage to Horace: a bimillenary celebration* (Oxford) 108–27
1991. *Vergil, Aeneid 10*, Oxford
1990. 'The praise singer: Horace, Censorinus and Odes 4.8', *JRS* 80: 31–43
Helmbold, W. C. 1960. 'Word repetition in Horace's *Odes*', *CP* 55: 173–4
Henderson, J. 1998. *A Roman life. Rutilius Gallicus on paper and in stone*, Exeter
Heyworth, S. J. 2007. *Cynthia. A companion to the text of Propertius*, Oxford
Highbarger, E. L. 1935. 'The Pindaric style of Horace', *TAPA* 66: 222–55
Holland, L. A. 1953. 'Septimontium or saeptimontium?', *TAPA* 84: 16–34
Housman, A. E. 1926. *M. Annaei Lucani Belli civilis libri decem*, Oxford
Hummel, P. 1993. *La syntaxe de Pindare*, Paris
Hunter, R. 2007. 'Sappho and Latin poetry', in G. Bastianini and A. Casanova, eds. *I papiri di Saffo e di Alceo* (Florence) 213–25
Hutchinson, G. O. 2002. 'The publication and individuality of Horace's *Odes* books 1– 3', *CQ* 52: 517–37
Jachmann, G. 1935. 'Calabrae Pierides', *Philologus* 90: 331–51
Jacobson, H. 1996. 'Two conjectures in Horace, *Odes*', *CQ* 46: 582–3
Jenkyns, R. 1989. 'Virgil and Arcadia', *JRS* 79: 26–39
Kambylis, A. 1965. *Die Dichterweihe und ihre Symbolik. Untersuchungen zu Hesiodos, Kallimachos, Properz und Ennius*, Heidelberg
Katz, J. 2008. 'Vergil translates Aratus: *Phaenomena* 1–2 and *Georgics* 1.1–2', *MD* 60: 105–23
Keppie, L. J. F. 1984. *The making of the Roman army*, London
Knox, P. E. 2009. 'Texts and topography', *CQ* 59: 658–64
Kovacs, D. 2009. 'Horace, Pindar and the Censorini in *Odes* 4.8', *JRS* 99: 23–35
La Penna, A. 1969. *Orazio e la morale mondana europea*, Florence
1963. *Orazio e l'ideologia del principato*, Turin
Lapidge, M. 2005. 'Poeticism in pre-conquest Anglo-Latin prose', in T. Reinhardt, M. Lapidge and J. N. Adams, eds. *Aspects of the language of Latin prose, Proceedings of the British Academy* 129: 321–37
Laughton, E. 1964. *The participle in Cicero*, Oxford
1960. 'Observations on the style of Varro', *CQ* 10: 1–28

Lazenby, J. F. 1978. *Hannibal's war*, Warminster

Lebek, W. D. 1970. *Verba prisca. Die Anfänge des Archaisierens in der lateinischen Beredsamkeit und Geschichtsschreibung*, Göttingen

Lee, G. 1998. trans. *Horace, Odes and Carmen saeculare*, Leeds

Lee, M. O. 1970. 'Everything is full of gods: a discussion of Horace's imagery', *Arion* 9: 246–63

Lefèvre, E. 1968. '*Rursus bella moves?* Die literarische Form von Horaz, c. 4, 1', *RhM* 111: 166–89

Leumann, M. 1977. *Lateinische Laut- und Formenlehre*, 6th edn., Munich

Lindner, T. 1996. *Lateinische Komposita: ein Glossar vornehmlich zum Wortschatz der Dichtersprache*, Innsbruck

Lipka, M. 2009. *Roman gods. A conceptual approach*, Leiden and Boston

Lowrie, M. 1997. *Horace's narrative Odes*, Oxford

Lugli, G. 1914. 'Le antiche ville dei colli albani prima della occupazione domizianea', *BCAR* 42: 251–316

Lyne, R. O. A. M. 2007. *Collected papers on Latin poetry*, Oxford

1995. *Horace. Behind the public poetry*, New Haven and London

1989. *Words and the poet. Characteristic techniques of style in Vergil's Aeneid*, Oxford

Lyons, S. 2007. *Horace's Odes and the mystery of do-re-mi*, Warminster

Martin, R. H. and Woodman, A. J. 1989. *Tacitus. Annals Book IV*, Cambridge

Mastrocinque, A. 1996a. 'Manlio Torquato', *EO* 1: 789

1996b. 'Torquato' *EO* 1: 921–2

Macleod, C. W. 1977. 'The poet, the critic, and the moralist: Horace, *Epistles* 1.19', *CQ* 28: 359–76 (= *Collected essays* Oxford 1983: 262–79)

McGann, M. J. 1969. *Studies in Horace's first book of Epistles*, Brussels

McLean, B. H. 2002, *An introduction to Greek epigraphy of the Hellenistic and Roman periods from Alexander the Great down to the reign of Constantine (323 B.C.–A.D. 337)*, Ann Arbor

Meiggs, R. 1982. *Trees and timber in the ancient mediterranean world*, Oxford

Menozzi, E. 1905. 'La composizione strofica del *Carmen saeculare*', *SIFC* 13: 67–73

Mesturini, A. M. 1997. 'Meteorologia e venti' *EO* II: 199–212

Minadeo, R. 1975–76. 'Vergil in Horace's *Odes* 4.12', *CJ* 71: 161–64

Mitchell, E. 2009. *Time for an emperor: old age and the future of the empire in Horace Odes 4*. MPhil. thesis. Cambridge

Moretti, L. 1982. 'Frammenti vecchi e nuovi del commentario dei ludi secolari di 17 A. C.', *Rendiconti della pontificia accademia Romana di archeologia* 55: 361–79

Morgan, L. 2002. 'Victory Songs', *TLS* 18 October, 27 (Review of Putnam 2001)

Moritz, L.A. 1969. 'Horace's Virgil', *GR* 16: 174–93

1968. 'Some "central" thoughts on Horace's *Odes*', *CQ* 18: 116–31

Munzi, M. 1998. 'T. Manlius Sura Septicianus', *Parola del passato* 53: 419–29

Murray, O. 1985. 'Symposium and genre in the poetry of Horace', *JRS* 75: 39–50

Nagy, G. 1994. 'Copies and models in Horace *Odes* 4.1 and 4.2', *CW* 87: 415–26

Neville, K. P. R. 1901. *The case-construction after the comparative in Latin*, Cornell Studies in Classical Philology 15, Ithaca, NY

Newman, J. K. 1967. *The concept of vates in Augustan poetry*. Collection Latomus 88, Brussels

Nilsson, M. P. 1920. 'Saeculares ludi', *RE* 1A: 1696–1720

Nisbet R. G. M. 2007. 'Horace: life and chronology', in Harrison 2007b: 7–21

1986. 'A rival Teubner Horace', *CR* 36: 227–34 (Review of Shackleton Bailey)

Norden, E. 1957. *P. Vergilius Maro Aeneis Buch VI*, 4th edn., Stuttgart

1913. *Agnostos theos. Untersuchungen zur Formengeschichte religiöser Rede*, Berlin (repr. Darmstadt 1974)

Oates, W. H. 1932. *The influence of Simonides of Ceos upon Horace*, Princeton

Ogilvie, R. M. 1965. *A commentary on Livy books 1–5*, Oxford

O'Hara, J. J. 1996. *True names. Vergil and the Alexandrian tradition of etymological wordplay*, Ann Arbor

1990. *Death and the optimistic prophecy in Vergil's Aeneid*, Princeton

Oliensis, E. 1998. *Horace and the rhetoric of authority*, Cambridge

Oniga, R. 1985. 'Il canticum di Sosia: forme stilistiche e modelli culturali', *MD* 14: 113–208

Palmer, L. R. 1954. *The Latin language*, London

Paschalis, M. 2002. ed. *Horace and Greek lyric poetry*, Rethymnon Classical Studies 1. Rethymnon

Pasquali, G. 1952. *Storia della tradizione e critica del testo*, 2nd edn., Florence

Penney, J. H. W. 1999. 'Archaism and innovation in Latin poetic syntax', in J. N. Adams and R. G. Mayer, eds., *Aspects of the language of Latin poetry* (Oxford) 249–68

Pichon, R. 1902. *De sermone amatorio apud latinos elegiarum scriptores*, Paris (repr. as *Index verborum amatoriorum*. Hildesheim 1966)

Pickard-Cambridge, A. 1962. *Dithyramb, tragedy and comedy*. 2nd edn., rev. by T. B. L. Webster, Oxford

Pitzalis, L. 1949. 'Il motivo ispiratore di Horat. Carm. IV 8', *GIF* 2: 329–40

Porter, D. H. 1985. 'Chloe and Phyllis: Horace *Carmina* 1.23 and 4.11', *CP* 80: 137–9

1975. 'The recurrent motifs of Horace, *Carmina* IV', *HSCP* 79: 189–228

1973. 'The motif of spring in Horace, *Carmina* 4.7 and 4.12', *CB* 49: 57–61

1972. 'Horace, *Carmina*, IV, 12', *Latomus* 31: 71–87

Pulleyn, S. 1997. *Prayer in Greek religion*, Oxford

1994. 'The power of names in classical Greek religion', *CQ* 44: 17–25

Putnam, M. C. J. 2006. *Poetic interplay: Catullus and Horace*, Princeton

2001. *Horace's Carmen saeculare. Ritual magic and the poet's art*, New Haven

1990. 'Horace *Carm.* 2.9: Augustus and the ambiguities of encomium', in K. A. Raaflaub and M. Toher, eds. *Between republic and empire. Interpretations of Augustus and his empire* (Berkeley, Los Angeles and London) 212–38

Quinn, K. 1963. *Latin explorations: critical studies in Roman literature*, London
Race, W. H. 1990. *Style and rhetoric in Pindar's Odes*, Atlanta, GA
1982 *The classical priamel from Homer to Boethius. Mnemosyne* Suppl. 74. Leiden
Reckford, K. J. 1960–1. 'The eagle and the tree (Horace, *Odes* 4.4)', *CJ* 56: 23–8
Riggsby, A. M. 1999. *Crime and community in Ciceronian Rome*. Austin
Ross, D. O. 1979. 'Ancient logs and old saws (Horace, *Epode* 2.43)', *AJP* 100: 241–4
1975. *Backgrounds to Augustan poetry*, Cambridge
Rotsch, L. 1957. 'Zur Form der drei Horaz-Oden im Asclepiadeus maior', *Gymn.* 64: 89–98
Russi, A. 1996. 'Apulia', *EO* 1: 389–406
Rutherford, I. 2001. *Pindar's Paeans. A reading of the fragments with a survey of the genre*, Oxford
Sage, P. W. 1994. 'Vatic admonition in Horace *Odes* 4.9', *AJP* 115: 565–86
Saint-Denis, E. de. 1942. 'Un comparaison homérique dans Horace (*Od.*, 4.14.25–32)', *Les Études Classiques* 11: 152–6
Salmon, E. T. 1946–7. 'The political views of Horace', *Phoenix* 1.2: 7–14
Schoonhoven, H. 1978. 'Purple swans and purple snow (Hor. *C.* IV 1, 10 and *Eleg. in Maec.* 62)', *Mnemosyne* 31: 200–03
Schulze, W. 1958. *Orthographica et Graeca Latina*, ed. E. Fraenkel (orig. Marburg 1894) Rome
Seager, R. 1993. 'Horace and Augustus: poetry and policy', in Rudd, N., ed. *Horace 2000: A celebration. Essays for the bimillennium* (Ann Arbor) 23–40
Shackleton Bailey, D. R. 1990. 'Horatian aftermath', *Philologus* 34: 213–28
1982. *Profile of Horace*, Cambridge, MA
Smith, K. F. 1913, ed. and comm. *The Elegies of Albius Tibullus, The Corpus Tibullianum*, New York, Cincinnati
Smith, W. S., Jr. 1984. 'Horace directs a carouse: *Epistle* 1.19', *TAPA* 114: 255–71
Solodow, J. B. 1986. '*Raucae, tu cura, palumbes*: study of a poetic word order', *HSCP* 90: 129–53
Sutherland, C. H. V. 1987. *Roman history and coinage 44* BC–AD *69. Fifty points of relation from Julius Caesar to Vespasian*, Oxford
Syme, R. 1986. *The Augustan aristocracy*, Oxford
1978. *History in Ovid*, Oxford
1958. *Tacitus*, Oxford
1939. *The Roman revolution*, Oxford
1933. 'Some notes on the legions under Augustus', *JRS* 23: 14–33
Tarán, S. L. 1985. 'ΕΙΣΙ ΤΡΙΧΕΣ: an erotic motif in the Greek Anthology', *JRS* 105: 90–107
Tarrant, R. J. 1995. '*Da capo* structure in some odes of Horace', in S. J. Harrison, ed. *Homage to Horace: a bimillenary celebration*, (Oxford) 32–49
Taylor, L. R. 1934. 'New light on the history of the secular games', *AJP* 55: 101–20

Thomas, R. F. 2004. '"Stuck in the middle with you": Virgilian middles', in S. Kyriakidis and F. De Martino, eds. *Middles in Latin poetry* (Bari) 123–50

2001. *Virgil and the Augustan reception*, Cambridge

1998a. 'The isolation of Turnus', in H.-P Stahl., (ed.), *Vergil's Aeneid. Augustan epic and political context* (London) 271–302

1998b. 'Voice, poetics, and Virgil's sixth *Eclogue*', in J. Jasanoff, H. C. Melchert and L. Oliver, eds. *Mír Curad: Studies in honor of Calvert Watkins* (Innsbruck) 669–76

1996 'Premessa generale' [of 'Località e popolazioni'], *EO* I: 375–8

1983. 'Callimachus, the *Victoria Berenices*, and Roman poetry', *CQ* 33: 92–113

1982a. *Lands and peoples in Roman poetry. The ethnographical tradition*, *PCPS* Supp. 7

1982b. 'Catullus and the polemics of poetic reference (64.1–18)', *AJP* 103: 144–64

1979. 'Theocritus, Calvus, and *Eclogue* 6', *CP* 74: 337–9

1978. 'Ovid's attempt at tragedy (*Amores* 3.1.63–64)', *AJP* 99: 175–8

Tosi, C. F. 1997. 'Fonostilistica', *EO* II: 841–50

Traina, A. 1997. 'Ippolito', *EO* II: 402–4

Trevelyan, G. O. 1978. *The life and letters of Lord Macaulay*. Oxford (Revised from 1878 edn.)

Vahlen, J. 1907–8. *Opuscula Academica*, 2 vols., Leipzig

van Berchem, D. 1968. 'La conquête de la Rhétie', *RhM* 25: 1–10

Vetter, E. 1957. 'Zum sechsten Buch Varros De lingua Latina', *Vjesnik za Arheologiju i Historiju Delmatinsku (Mélanges Abrami)*, 56–9: 76–80

Wagenvoort, H. 1956. 'Ludus poeticus', in H. Wagenvoort, *Studies in Roman literature, culture and religion* (Leiden) 30–42 (= (Dutch version) *Les Études classiques* 4 (1935): 108–20)

Watkins, C. 1995. *How to kill a dragon. Aspects of Indo-European poetics*, Oxford

1991. 'Latin *tarentum Accas*, the *ludi saeculares*, and Indo-European eschatology', in W. P. Lehmann and H.-J. Jakusz Hewitt, eds. *Language typology 1988: typological models in reconstruction* (Amsterdam) 135–47

1966. 'An Indo-European construction in Greek and Latin', *HSCP* 71: 115–19

Wells, C. M. 1972. *The German policy of Augustus*, Oxford

West, M. L. 2007. *Indo-European poetry and myth*, Oxford

1992. *Ancient Greek music*, Oxford

White, P. 1993. *Promised verse. Poets in the society of Augustan Rome*, Cambridge, MA

Wilamowitz-Moellendorff, U. von 1924. *Hellenistische Dichtung*, 2 vols., Berlin

Williams, G. 1990. 'Did Maecenas "fall from favor"? Augustan literary patronage', in K. A. Raaflaub and M. Toher, eds. *Between republic and empire. Interpretations of Augustus and his empire* (Berkeley, Los Angeles and London) 212–38

1972. *Horace*. Greece and Rome New Surveys in the Classics No. 6, Oxford

1968. *Tradition and originality in Roman poetry*, Oxford

Williams, R. D. 1968. 'Virgil *Aen.* 9.25–32', *CP* 63: 148

1960. 'Horace, *Odes* iv.15.29', *CR* 10: 6–7

Wimmel W. 1965. 'Recusatio-Form und Pindarode', *Philologus* 109: 83–103

1960. *Kallimachos in Rom. Die Nachfolge seines apologetischen Dichtens in der Augusteerzeit.* Hermes Einzelschriften 16, Wiesbaden

Wölfflin, E. 1881. 'Über die alliterierenden Verbindungen der lateinischen Sprache', *Sitzungsberichte der Bayerischen Akademie der Wissenschaft* II: 1–94 (= *Ausgewählte Schriften*, Leipzig 1933: 225–84)

Woodcock, E. C. 1939. *The Annals of Tacitus Book XIV*, London

Woodman, A. J. 1972. 'Horace's odes *Diffugere niues* and *Soluitur acris hiems*', *Latomus* 31: 752–78

Zanker, P. 1988. *The power of images in the age of Augustus*, Ann Arbor

INDEXES

1. LATIN WORDS

2. GENERAL